California Maritime Academy Library (CSU)
WITHDRAWN
3 0060 77701361 4

D0712612

WITHDRAWN

NAVIGATION FOR MASTERS

By the same author, D. J. House

Anchor Practice – A Guide for Industry, (1st Edition) 2001 Witherby, ISBN 1 856092127.

Cargo Work (7th Edition) Revised, 2005 Butterworth/Heinemann, ISBN 0750665556

Dry-Docking and Shipboard Maintenance, (1st Edition) 2003 Witherby ISBN 1856092453

Heavy Lift and Rigging 2005, (1st Edition) Brown Son and Ferguson, ISBN 0851747205

Helicopter Operations at Sea – A Guide for Industry, (1st Edition) 1998 Witherby, ISBN 185609168 6

Marine Ferry Transports – An Operators Guide, (1st Edition) 2002 Witherby, ISBN 1856092313

Marine Survival and Rescue Systems (2nd Edition) 1997 Witherby ISBN 1 856091279

The Seamanship Examiner, 2005, (1st Edition) Elsevier Ltd., ISBN 075066701X

Seamanship Techniques (3rd Edition) 2004, Elsevier Ltd., ISBN 0750663154

Seamanship Techniques Volume III 'The Command Companion' (1st Edition) 2000, Elsevier Ltd., ISBN 0750644435

British Library Cataloguing in Publication Data

House, D. J.
Navigation for masters. – 3rd ed.
1. Navigation 2. Seamanship
I. Title
623.8'9

ISBN-10: 1856092712

[5841]

NAVIGATION FOR MASTERS

by

DAVID J. HOUSE

LONDON
WITHERBY & CO LTD
32-36 Aylesbury Street
London EC1R 0ET

First Published 1995

Second Edition 1998

Third Edition 2006

ISBN 13: 978 1 85609 271 5
ISBN 10: 1 85609 271 2

Published and Printed by
Witherby & Co Ltd
32-36 Aylesbury Street
London EC1R 0ET
Tel No: 020 7251 5341   Fax No: 020 7251 1296
International Tel No: +44 (0)20 7251 5341
International Fax No: +44 (0)20 7251 1296
E-mail: books@witherbys.co.uk
www: witherbys.com

FOREWORD

This text, now in its third edition, has been compiled to address the age old practice of seamanship and the safe navigation of ships. It will bring the reader up-to-date with the modern technical aspects of the profession, that are now so much a part of a seafarers current way of life, including the topics of satellite navigation, GMDSS communications, helicopter operations, AIS recognition and traffic reporting systems, while at the same time not losing the essential basics of keeping an effective lookout or maintaining primary and secondary position monitoring.

Books, written by the practitioners of any science, add to the wider knowledge of even the most experienced professional. They allow the newcomer to look for early guidance, while at the same time promoting high standards within an industry that demands the most stringent safe practice.

Maritime accidents generally occur with errors in navigation, often involving human error. The author acknowledges that accidents will not be eliminated, because of the numerous external factors affecting the eventual outcome, not least, the weather. However, the human input can be trained to analyse situations in greater depth, think ahead that much sooner and avoid the catastrophic pitfalls within a passage plan.

The text illustrates the needs of Pilotage, efficient watch keeping practice, the need for standing orders and dangers from ice or tropical storms. It highlights navigational problems in offshore areas, the practice of Search and Rescue operations and at the same time draws on the essential use of radar and electronic systems.

The general public and the professional mariner alike, are both aware that the knowledge to prevent is available. We should not need to cure a problem that is preventable in the first place. This book should go some way in providing the knowledge to establish such preventative procedures, to become standard practice.

Alan Witherby
Publisher
2006

PREFACE TO THIRD EDITION

Since the first edition of Navigation for Masters, in 1995 it would be an understatement to say that communications have passed through a development explosion. No more so than with the GMDSS requirements of 1999, and the approval of the fully operational ECDIS coming on line.

All aspects of navigation have experienced technological change. While the sextant is still discussed in historical content, it is the GPS (U.S. Military Controlled) that has dominated the future of position fixing. Satellite systems are here to stay and GPS has shown itself to be the most successful of Satellite Navigation Systems. It must be anticipated that the civilian controlled European System, "Galileo" which received the official go-ahead in 2002 will be operational by 2008/2009.

The advances of modern systems, for which the navigator must become familiar, can still be enhanced by the reliability, accuracy and continued availability of such stalwarts as: Radar, Echo Sounder and of course the Three Point Visual Bearing. Position fixing in its many forms remains in the forefront of safe navigational practice and methods employed must still provide both a primary and secondary system. Ideally, position monitoring operations need to take account of both clear and poor visibility conditions and to this end good instrument usage forms an essential element for any visibility condition.

Watch keeping practice has also been considerably influenced with the STCW '95 requirements, but the fundamentals of maintaining an effective lookout, while the vessel is at sea, have not changed. The Collision Regulations, incorporating the latest amendments of 2003, continue to affect all ships on the 'High Seas', inclusive of 'High Speed Craft'.

The 'integrated bridge' together with the bridge team, forms an infrastructure of safe navigation practice within the ship and continues to remain the essential backbone of today's maritime industry. The men and women who make up the team, need enhanced training to stay ahead in such a rapidly expanding industry. Their needs are proving paramount to ensure that human error is reduced and safe navigation practice is retained.

Good sailing,

David J. House 2006.

CONTENTS

ABOUT THE AUTHOR

With this current edition of Navigation for Masters the Author, David House, has drawn extensively on the modernisation that is affecting the marine industry and in particular the movement towards the advances in electronic systems such as GPS and ECDIS.

He continues to lecture in the Navigation and Seamanship disciplines within the Nautical Education environment where the research for this and other publications has been drawn.

Navigation for Masters is one of fourteen technical publications written by David House for the maritime industry. His more recent works have been concentrated on specified topics, such as; Marine Ferry Transports, Dry-Docking and Anchor Work Practice which have all followed in the footsteps of Helicopter Operations at Sea.

His works continue to be widely read in all the maritime nations of the world. He now has over twenty-five years of teaching experience to Officer Candidates, of all ranks, of the Mercantile Marine, covering most aspects of Maritime Training. His works and research continue to provide well illustrated and topical marine texts, that are easy to read and attract the respect of the professional mariner, world-wide.

ACKNOWLEDGEMENTS

The author would like to express his appreciation to the following companies and representatives for their welcome additions and presentations which have been included in this publication:

The Royal Fleet Auxiliary Service.

The Fleet Air Arm of the Royal Navy, and Ministry of Defence.

The permission of the Hydrographer of the Navy:
Crown Copyright reproduced from British Admiralty Chart 5058, and for extracts from Admiralty Tide Tables, Mariners Handbook, Weekly Notices to Mariners, Ocean Passages of the World and Sailing Directions.

The Meteorological Office, Bracknell.

The Blackpool and the Fylde College, Fleetwood Nautical Campus.

Jotron Ltd.

RFD Limited,

Avon Inflatables.

A/S Nordisk Gummibaadsfabrik Denmark.

Westland plc Westland Helicopters Ltd.,
& E.H. Industries Ltd.

Butterworth Heinemann Ltd: Extracts from:
Marine Technology Reference Book.
Authors – Minoo H. Patel & Geoffrey J. Lyons

Ministry of Defence: Naval Aviation
FONA HQ Yeovilton, Yeovil Somerset.
819 Naval Air Squadron.

The Scottish Vocational Council.

Lilley & Gillie. Nautical Instrument Makers & Admiralty Chart Agents. North Shields, Tyne & Wear.

Shell Tankers (UK) Ltd., London.

International Maritime Organization, London.

The Maritime and Coastguard Agency for use of "M' Notices. Reproduced by permission of the Controller of Her Majesty's Stationery Office.

INMARSAT – International Maritime Satellite Organization.

United States Coast Guard.

Kelvin Hughes Limited, The Naval and Marine Division of Smiths Industries Aerospace.

Furuno Electric Co. Ltd.

Trimble Navigation Ltd., Marine Products.

C. Plath Navigation & Automation.

Elliott Turbomachinery Ltd.

Lokata Ltd.

Raytheon Marine Company.

Philips Navigation A/S.

Additional Photography:

Mr J. Wardle. Extra Master, Lecturer in Nautical Studies.

Mr. G. Edwards, Marine Engineer (Rtd).

Mr. N. Lovick 2nd Officer MN.

Mr. P. Brooks CH/OFF MN.

Mr. P. Simpson CH/OFF MN.

Mr. Z. Anderson CH/OFF MN.

BIBLIOGRAPHY

The reader may find the additional references beneficial when seeking further information on related subjects:

Anchor Practice, D. J. House, 1st Ed. 2002 Witherby & Co. Ltd.

The Annual Summary of Notices to Mariners. Crown Copyright Hydrographic Department. Ministry of Defence, Taunton.

Bridge Procedures Guide (ICS) 3rd Ed. 1998
Witherby & Co. Ltd.

Collision Cases: Judgements and Diagrams H. M. C. Holders and F. J. Buzec 2nd Ed. 1991

Dictionary of Shipping International Business Trade Terms and Abbreviations, Alan E. Branch 5th Ed. 2004 Witherby & Co. Ltd.

Drift Characteristics of 50,000 to 70,000 DWT Tankers (OCIMF) 1982 Witherby & Co. Ltd.

Guidelines and Recommendations for the Safe Mooring of Large Ships at Piers and Sea islands (OCIMF) 2nd Ed Witherby & Co. Ltd.

Guide to Helicopter/Ship Operations (ICS) 3rd Ed. 1989
Witherby & Co. Ltd.

A Guide to the Planning and Conduct of Sea Passages (HMSO)

Guide to Port Entry 2002-2003 (2 vols) Ed. Colin Pielow, Shipping Guides Ltd.

Guide to the Collision Avoidance Rules – A Cockcroft and J. N. F. Lemeijer

Helicopter Operations at Sea D. J. House 1st Ed. 1999
Witherby & Co. Ltd.

Law of Harbours and Pilotage 4th Ed.
G. K. Green and R. P. A. Douglas

Marine Technology Reference Book
Edited by Nina Morgan Butterworths

Maritime Weather and Climate.
Burroughs and Lynagh 1st Ed. 1999 Witherby & Co. Ltd.

The Mariners Handbook (N. P. 100) 8th Ed.
Hydrographic Department. Ministry of Defence, Taunton.

Modern Shipping Disasters 1963-87 Norman Hooke 1989

Marine Survival and Rescue Systems. D. J. House
2nd Ed. 1998 Witherby & Co. Ltd.

Mooring Equipment Guidelines (OCIMF)
2nd Ed. 1998 Witherby & Co. Ltd.

Ocean Passages of the World (N. P. 136) 4th Ed.
Hydrographic Department. Ministry of Defence, Taunton.

Oil Rig Moorings Handbook J. Vendress 2nd Ed. 1985

Passage Planning Guidelines. Salmon 1st Ed. 1993
Witherby & Co. Ltd.

Peril at Sea and Salvage: A Guide for Masters (ICS/OCIMF)
5th Ed. 1998 Witherby & Co. Ltd.

Piracy at Sea. Edited by Eric Ellen. Witherby & Co. Ltd.

Prediction of Wind and Current Loads on VLCCs (OCIMF)
2nd Ed. 1994 Witherby & Co. Ltd.

Radar Observer's Handbook for Merchant Navy Officers.
W. Burger

Recommendations for Equipment Employed in the Mooring of Ships at Single Point Moorings (OCIMF) 1st Ed. 1993
Witherby & Co. Ltd.

Recommendations on Equipment for the Towing of Disabled Tankers (OCIMF) 1981 Witherby & Co. Ltd.

Routing in UK Waters for Ships Carrying Oil or Other Hazardous Cargoes in Bulk. Chamber of Shipping.

Shipboard Operations. H. I. Lavery 2nd Ed. 1990

Ship Manoeuvring Principles and Practice for Pilots.
P. Williamson 1st Ed. Witherby & Co. Ltd.

Steering Gear: Test Routines and Check-List Card (ICS) 1987
Witherby & Co. Ltd.

Straits of Malacca and Singapore: A Guide to Planned Transits by Deep Draught Vessels (ICS/OCIMF) Witherby & Co. Ltd.

Supply Ship Operations. Vic Gibson

Tanker Safety Guide (Liquefied Gas) (ICS) Witherby & Co. Ltd.

Tugs and Towing. M. J. Caston

ABBREVIATIONS AND DEFINITIONS

A.B.S.	American Bureau of Shipping
AC	Alternating Current
ACSC	Australian Coastal Surveillance Centre
ACV	Air Cushion Vehicle
ADN	European Provisions concerning the International Carriage of Dangerous Goods by Inland Waterways.
ADR	European Agreement concerning the international Carriage of Dangerous Goods by Road.
ADT	Admiralty Distance Tables
AIS	Automatic Identification Systems
ALL	Admiralty List of Lights
ALRS	Admiralty List of Radio Signals
AMD	Advanced Multi-Hull Design
AMVER	Automated Mutual - Assistance Vessel Rescue
ANTS	Automatic Navigation and Track keeping System (The name adopted by the Furuno Electric Company to describe its navigation system for use with integrated bridge design)
AR	Arrival report
ARCS	Admiralty Raster Chart Service
ARPA	Automatic Radar Plotting Aid
ASW	Anti-Submarine Warfare
ATT	Admiralty Tide Tables
AUSREP	Australian Ship Reporting System
Aux	Auxiliary
BBS	Bulletin Board System - A computer based information source operated for the general public by the United States Coast Guard Navigation Information Service.
BHC	British Hovercraft Corporation (now called GKN Westland Aerospace)
BSF	British Shipping Federation
BST	British Summer Time

B.V.	Bureau Veritas
C_b	Centre of Buoyancy
CCTV	Close Circuit Television
CD	Compact Disc
CES	Coast Earth Station
Ch	Channel
Changerep	Change Report
CMG	Course Made Good
CNIS	Channel Navigation Information Service
Co	Course
CoG	Course over Ground
COLREGS	International Regulations for the Prevention of Collision at Sea
Comp	Complement
CPA	Closest Point of Approach (a term used extensively with radar plotting)
CPP	Controllable Pitch Propeller
CRS	Coast Radio Station
CSH	Continuous Survey Hull
CSM	Continuous Survey Machinery
CSS (code)	IMO Code of Safe Practice for Cargo Stowage and Securing
CW	Continuous Wave
DBL	Dunlop Beaufort Canada
DC	Direct Current
DEFREP	Defect Report
Dep	Departure
DETR	Department of Environment, Transport and the Regions
DF	Direction Finder
DGPS	Differential Global Positioning System
Dist	Distance
D.Lat	Difference in Latitude
D.Long	Difference in Longitude

DMA	Defence Mapping Agency (U.S.) – An American organisation which is responsible for broadcasting specialised and selective navigation information.
DMP	Difference in Meridional Parts
DNV	Det Norske Veritas
DNV-W1	One Man Operation (DNV requirements)
DOC	Document of Compliance
DoD	Department of Defence (U.S.)
DP	Dynamic Positioning – A position reference system employed to maintain station holding and heading.
D.R.	Dead Reckoning
DSC	Dynamically Supported Craft
DSC (2)	Digital Selective Calling
DSV	Diving Support Vessel
EBM (EBI)	Electronic Bearing Marker (as employed with marine radar)
EC	European Community
ECDIS	Electronic Chart Display and Information System
E.C.R.	Eastern Counties Railway (merged with Great Eastern Railway Company 1862)
ECR	Engine Control Room
ECS	Electronic Chart System
ECTAB	Electronic Chart Table
EGC	Enhanced Group Calling
EITZ	English Inshore Traffic Zone
EMS	Emergency Schedule
ENC	Electronic Navigation Chart
E.P.	Estimated position
EPIRB	Emergency Position Indicating Radio Beacon
ETA	Estimated Time of Arrival
ETD	Estimated Time of Departure
ETV	Emergency Towing Vessel

Fin. Co.	Final Course
FLIR	Forward Looking InfraRed
FMEA	Failure mode and effects analysis
FP	Fixed Pitch (propeller)
FRC	Fast Rescue Craft
FSM	Free Surface Moment
Galileo	Name given to a commercial GPS operational system due to become operational 2008/2009
GC	Great Circle
GE	General Electric
G.E.R.C.	Great Eastern Railway Company (merged into L.N.E.R. in 1923)
GHA	Greenwich Hour Angle
GHz	Gig hertz
GM	Metacentric Height
GMDSS	Global Maritime Distress and Safety System
GMP	Garbage Management Plan
GMT	Greenwich Mean Time
GPS	Global Positioning System
GRP	Glass Reinforced Plastic
grt	Gross registered tonnage
GT	Gas Turbine
g.t. (GT)	Gross tons
GZ	Ships righting lever
Hav	Haversine
HDOP	Horizontal Dilution of Precision - an expression that reflects the continual movement of satellites and the effect on the crossing angles of the range circles of the GPS navigation system.
HLO	Helicopter Landing Officer
HMCG	Her Majesty's Coast Guard
HMSO	Her Majesty's Stationery Office
HP (i)	High Pressure
h.p. (ii)	Horse Power

HRN	House Recovery Net
HRU	Hydrostatic Release Unit
HSC	High Speed Craft (code)
HSS	High Speed Sea-Service
HSSC	Harmonised System of Survey and Certification
HW	High Water
IACS	International Association of Classification Societies
IAMSAR	International and Aeronautical Maritime Search and Rescue (manual)
ICR	Intercooled and Recuperated
ICS	International Chamber of Shipping
IEC	International Electro Technical Committee
IFR	Instrument Flying Rating
IHO	International Hydrographic Office
ILO	International Labour Organisation
IMDG	International Maritime Dangerous Goods (code)
IMO	International Marine Organization
IMTA	International Maritime Transit Association (now renamed Interferry)
INS	Integrated Navigation System
INSPIRES	The Indian Ship Position and Information Reporting System
INT. CO.	Initial Course
IOPP	International Oil Pollution Prevention (certificate)
IPMS	Integrated Platform Management System
IPS	Integrated Power System (Controllable 'Podded' Propulsion)
IRU	International Road Transport Union
ISM	International Safety Management
ISO	International Organization for Standardization
ISPS	International Ship and Port Facility Security (code)
ITU	International Telecommunications Union
ITU	Intermodal Transport Unit

KG	Measured distance from the ships Keel to the ships Centre of Gravity
kHz	Kilo Hertz
KM	Measured distance from the ships Keel to the ships Metecentre
Kts	Knots
kW	Kilowatt
L.A.T.	Lowest Astronomical Tide
Lat	Latitude
LCD	Liquid Crystal Display
LCG	Longitudinal Centre of Gravity
LHA	Local Hour Angle
L.N.E.R.	London & North Eastern Railway (fore runner to British Rail 1948)
LNG	Liquid Natural Gas
LOA	Length Overall
Lo-Lo	Load On - Load Off
Long	Longitude
LOP	Line of position
LP	Low Pressure
LPH	Landing Platform Helicopters
LUT	Local user terminal
L.R.	Lloyd's Register
LSA	Lifesaving Appliances
LW	Low Water
MAIB	Marine Accident Investigation Branch
MAREP	Marine Reporting System
MCA	Maritime & Coastguard Agency
MEC	Marine Evacuation Chute
Medivac	Medical Evacuation
MEPC	Marine Environment Protection Committee
MES	Marine Evacuation System
MFAG	Medical First Aid Guide. (for use with accidents involving Dangerous Goods)

MGN	Marine Guidance Notice
MHHW	Mean High High Water
MHLW	Mean High Low Water
MHW	Mean High Water
MHWI	Mean High Water Interval
MHz	Mega Hertz
MIN	Marine Information Notice
MLLW	Mean Low Low Water
MLW	Mean Low Water
MMSI	Maritime Mobile Service Identity Number
'M' Notices	Merchant Shipping Notices
MN	Merchant Navy
MNTB	Merchant Navy Training Board
MOB	Man Overboard
M.P's	Meridional Parts
MPCU	Marine Pollution Control Unit
m.rads	metre radians
MRCC	Marine Rescue Co-ordination Centre
MSC	Maritime Safety Committee (of IMO)
MSN	Merchant Shipping Notice
MSR	Mean Spring Range
M.V.	Motor Vessel
MW	Mega Watt
Nat	Natural Logarithm
NFD	Non-Federated
NGS	National Geodetic Survey - a branch of the US National Ocean Service Administration. It is responsible for the supply of GPS orbit data via the NIS Bulletin Board
NINUS	An integrated navigation system developed by Kelvin Hughes for Nucleus Integrated Navigation System. Nucleus being a trade name for a sophisticated radar set.
NIS	Navigation Information Service
NUC	Not Under Command

NVE	Night Vision Equipment
NVQ	National Vocational Qualification
OCIMF	Oil Companies International Maritime Forum
OMBO	One Man Bridge Operation
OOW	Officer of the Watch
Ops/Rg	Operational Range
O/S	Offshore
OSC	On Scene Co-ordinator
OSP	Own Ship Pilotage
P/A	Public Address System
PCC	Pure Car Carrier
PCTC	Pure Car, Truck Carrier
PEC	Pilotage Exemption Certificate
ppm	Parts per million.
PR	Position report
PRS (i)	Position Reference System - (a term used in Dynamic Positioning Operations)
PRS (ii)	Polish Register of Shipping
RAF	Royal Airforce
RCC	Rescue Co-ordination Centre
RCDS	Raster Chart Display System
RGSS	Register General of Shipping and Seaman
RINA	Registro Italiano Navale (Classification Society - Italy)
RN	Royal Navy
RNCs	Raster Navigational Charts
RoPax	Roll On/Roll Off + Passengers
Ro-Ro	Roll On-Roll Off
RoT	Rate of Turn
rpm	revolutions per minute
R/T	Radio Telephone
Rx	Receiver

SA	Selective Availability – This is the option of the US Department of Defence to scramble GPS signals and alter positional accuracy of the GPS operation.
SAR	Search and Rescue
SART	Search and Rescue Radar Transponder
SCBA	Self Contained Breathing Apparatus
SECU	StoraEnso Cargo Units
SES (i)	Ship Earth Station
SES (ii)	Surface Effect Ships
SFP	Structural Fire Protection
s.g.	Specific Gravity
s.h.p.	Shaft Horse Power
S.I.	Statutory Instrument
sin	Sine
SMC (i)	Safety Management Certificate
SMC (ii)	SAR Mission Co-ordination
SMG	Speed Made Good
SMS	Seaworthy Management System
SNCM	Société Nationale Maritime Corse-Mediterraneé
SoG	Speed over Ground
SOLAS	International Convention for the Safety of Life at Sea.
SOPEP	Ships Oil Pollution Emergency Plan
SP (i)	Sailing Plan
SP (ii)	Special Performance
SRR's	Search and Rescue Region's
ST	Super Transport
STCW	Standards of Training, Certification and Watch-keeping (1995 code for seafarers)
STOL	Short Take Off and Land
SWATH	Small Waterplane Area Twin Hull
Tan	Tangent
TBT	Tributyltin
TCPA	Time of Closest Point of Approach
TMC	Transmitting Magnetic Compass

TRC	Type Rating Certificate
TRS	Tropical Revolving Storm
TSS	Traffic Separation Scheme
Ts & Ps	Temporary and Preliminary Notices to Mariners
Tx/Rx	Transmit /Receive
U.K.	United Kingdom
U.K.C.	Under Keel Clearance
UKHO	United Kingdom Hydrographic Office
UMS	Unmanned Machinery Space
UN ECE	United Nations Economic Commission for Europe
UN No.,	United Nations Number
UPS	Uninterrupted Power Supply
U.S.A.	United States of America
USCG	United States Coast Guard
UTC	Universal Co-ordinated Time
UV	Ultraviolet
VCG	Vertical Centre of Gravity
VDR	Voyage Data Recorder
VDU	Visual Display Unit
VHF	Very High Frequency
VMS	Voyage Management System
VRM	Variable Range Marker
VTMS	Vessel Traffic Management Systems
VTS	Vessel Traffic Services/ System
WAT	Wing assisted Tri-Maran
WGS	World Geodetic System, a datum reference
WiG	Wing in Ground, effect
WPC	Wave Piercing Catamaran
WPT	Way Point – a term used when passage planning and laying off charted course tracks.
ZT	Zone Time

LIST OF ILLUSTRATIONS

Chapter One

BRIDGE PROCEDURES

1.1 The Navigational Watch

It is in the interests of all persons at sea that the officer of the watch is accepted as the Master's representative and as such should carry the confidence of that Master to carry out relevant duties. It should be equally understood by that officer that the final responsibility of command rests with the Master and he should therefore not hesitate to call his superior in the event of any of the following:

1.2 Calling the Master (by the OOW, Officer of the Watch)

1. If restricted visibility is encountered or expected.
2. If traffic conditions or the movements of other ships are causing concern.
3. If difficulty is experienced in maintaining a course.
4. On failure to sight land, a navigation mark, or to obtain soundings by the expected time.
5. If unexpectedly, land or a navigational mark is sighted or a change in soundings occur.
6. On the breakdown of engines, steering gear or any essential navigational equipment.
7. If heavy weather is encountered, or if in doubt about the possibility of weather damage being expected.
8. If the ship meets any hazard to navigation such as ice, derelict or in receipt of a distress signal.
9. In any other emergency or situation in which he/she is in doubt.

1.3 Standing Orders

Many companies operate their ships under a comprehensive set of 'standing orders' or 'company instructions'. These tend to define and expand on the duties of individuals such as chief officers responsibilities, or the general duties of junior officers.

The Master's standing orders are specifically for the well being of the ship to cover any eventuality to maintain the safety of the vessel. The standing orders should cover periods when the Master might be temporarily indisposed allowing such time for the Master to gain the 'con' of the vessel.

Standing orders are not designed to impose limitations on the duty officer, rather to increase responsibility and provide positive direction in the Master's absence. They should be clearly understood by the officer of the watch (OOW) and the Master is obliged to satisfy himself that all his officers are aware of the content of the same. (Usually by OOW's reading and signing).

1.4 Principles for Compiling Masters Standing Orders

The purpose of the ship's Master writing and issuing 'Standing Orders' and respective 'Night Orders' is to provide the Watch Officers with clear and precise procedures regarding the safe management of the ships bridge and the navigation of the vessel. Such stipulated orders, once compiled should suit the geography of the ship's current and future positions and not stand the vessel into danger.

1. Standing Orders - should be pertinent to the following concerns:-

a) the maintenance of a proper lookout throughout the watch period.
b) the position monitoring of the vessel by primary and secondary methods.
c) the monitoring of the ships under keel clearance during the vessels progress.

2. Standing and Night Orders – should account for any or all of the relevant topics:

a) safe passing distances off hazards;
b) bridge manning at all stages of the voyage;
c) correct use and application of navigational instruments;

d) relevant use of reference material inclusive of charts and publications;
e) the following of and adherence to, the Passage Plan;
f) the need and relevance to calling the Master.

3. Specific advice in Standing and Night Orders – should apply when:

a) the ship is engaged on passage.
b) when the ship is in Port.
c) when the ship is at anchor.
d) as and when the ship is under Pilotage.
e) the vessel experiences poor visbility.

1.5 Standing Orders Examples

1. For a vessel passing through/entering an area of expected 'ice concentration'.

   NB. It is a SOLAS requirement for ships entering known ice areas that they must alter course away from dangerous ice concentrations and proceed at a moderate speed at night.

   In the event that 'dangerous ice is sighted' this fact needs to be reported and reference to the 'Mariners Handbook' would reflect the content of such a report.

The Masters standing orders should therefore reflect these requirements:

(a) call the Master as per company 'standing orders' or if in any doubt or other emergency situation.
(b) a continuous lookout is to be maintained by the OOW and two lookout personnel from:
    (i) The forecastle head.
    (ii) Crows nest (or other appropriate high point). 'Monkey Island'.
(c) radar should be continually monitored at peak performance (Radar alone should not be solely relied upon).
(d) weather conditions should be monitored throughout watches.
(e) call the Master in the event of restricted visibility below 3 miles, and place the engines on stand-by.
(f) call the Master if any ice fragments or ice concentrations are sighted.

(g) on sighting ice the vessels course should be altered to pass well clear of any danger zone.
(h) a description and position of any sighting should be noted and the Master informed, immediately.

It should be realised that ships entering ice limits, would be expected to operate with a bridge team in place with the Master on continuous call. Depending on the circumstances it must be considered as not being unusual for the vessel to 'stop' during the hours of darkness, when in ice infested waters.

Additionally:
The position of the vessel should be monitored closely, if this is possible.

Watchkeeping staff should be increased in numbers when a continuous radar watch or specific duties require the need of double watchkeepers.

2. For a vessel navigating under pilots advice.
   (a) the Officer of the Watch is and will remain the Masters representative throughout any period of pilotage.
   (b) the OOW should call the Master if any doubt or if he requires verification on any aspect of the vessels safe navigation.
   (c) the OOW will at no time leave the bridge while under pilotage conditions unless relieved by the Master or his designated representative.
   (d) the Master should be kept informed of all communication check points and reporting stations.
   (e) manual steering will be maintained throughout all pilotage periods.
   (f) an effective lookout will be maintained throughout the pilotage.
   (g) the vessel should be allowed to proceed at a safe speed throughout pilotage waters.
   (h) the OOW will monitor the vessel's position, communications, underkeel clearance and the weather conditions throughout and not stand the vessel into danger.

3. For fixing the vessels position.
   (a) the OOW will obtain a morning twilight, a noon and an evening twilight position and enter the same into the deck log book;

(b) when on the coast the OOW will obtain a position at fifteen (15) minute intervals, or less, as deemed necessary by the geographic conditions; (Company policy may vary)

(c) all visual fixes should employ a minimum of three position lines;

(d) a 'primary and secondary', position fixing system, should be employed at all times;

(e) buoys and floating marks should not be used for position fixing unless the position of the mark has first been ascertained. Even then, any position so obtained, should not be considered as reliable and an alternative confirmation should be obtained as soon as possible;

(f) where a position is considered doubtful or unreliable, for whatever reason, the Master should be informed;

(g) if the OOW cannot obtain the vessels position for any reason, the Master should be informed;

(h) when transferring the ships position from one chart to another, the transferred position must be checked against Latitude and Longitude as well as by 'Bearing and Distance' from a fixed datum;
(Not applicable when working on Electronic Navigation Charts);

(i) all coastal positions should be corroborated by soundings as and where appropriate;

(j) should positions show a deviation from the designated tracks of the passage plan, the Master should be informed.

4. For Navigation in Restricted Visibility

(a) place the engines on 'Stand -By' and reduce the vessels speed in accordance with the Regulations for the Prevention of Collision at Sea and appropriate to the prevailing conditions (Reference Regulation 6);

(b) radar(s) should be operational and systematic plotting of all targets commenced;

(c) the Master should be informed of the state of visibility as soon as deterioration is expected or as soon as possible after reduced visibility is encountered;

(d) the prescribed fog signals will be sounded in accord with the regulations;

(e) manual steering should be engaged;

(f) engine room must be informed as to the state of visibility and a safe manoeuvring speed maintained until conditions have improved;

(g) VHF, listening watch maintained;
(h) lookouts will be posted in addition to the normal watch;.
(i) navigation lights will be switched on throughout any period of impaired visibility;
(j) water tight doors should be closed;.
(k) a contingency plan should be considered where appropriate, e.g. Anchoring;
(l) echo sounder should be employed where appropriate.

1.6 Summary

All standing orders must be concerned with the safe operation of the vessel at all times, whether at sea, or in port. When at sea, Masters and Company standing orders must stipulate conditions of Traffic Observation and take account of collision avoidance in the light of the "Regulations for the Prevention of Collision at Sea". Night time conditions or adverse weather, may make additional requirements necessary, over and above good weather/daylight procedures. Such conditions must take account of specifics, as in ice conditions, passing through offshore development areas, or when engaged in special operations like Search and Rescue duties.

1.7 Bridge Procedures

Duties of the Officer of the Watch

He is primarily the Master's representative and as such is directly concerned with the safe navigation of the vessel. He should subsequently maintain an effective and efficient look-out from the bridge position, and ensure that the vessel complies with the "Regulations for the Prevention of Collision at Sea".

The Officer of the Watch will continue to be responsible for the ships well being, despite the presence of the Master on the bridge, unless the Master specifically accepts the 'con' of the vessel. During the continuation of his duties the OOW will have the authority to use all navigation equipment including sound signal equipment, whenever he deems necessary, so as not to stand the vessel into danger. In a similar manner he will also be required to adjust the ships speed as and when this is required. Main engine status will be at the direct order of the OOW and he should be aware of any condition of readiness required by engine room personnel. He should also ensure that he is familiar with the stopping distance of the vessel, at various speeds, and the manoeuvring characteristics.

The Officer of the Watch should be positive in his decisions and not hesitate to employ any of the above mentioned features. Neither should he hesitate to call additional watch keeping personnel, or his superiors should the need arise, at any time during day or night time periods.

Watch Change Over

The relieving Officer of the Watch should ensure that:

1. The members of the watch are fully capable of performing their duties, and not be impaired by, drugs, alcohol, or sickness.
2. His vision has adjusted to the prevailing conditions.
3. He is satisfied with any 'standing orders' or specific, "night orders' left by the ship's Master.
4. The position of the vessel, the course and speed and where appropriate, the draught of the ship are correct.
5. He is familiar with predicted tides and currents, weather reports, visibility state and their subsequent effect on navigation.
6. The navigational situation regarding the performance of gyroscopic and magnetic compasses together with any errors is in order.
7. All essential navigation equipment is performing in the correct manner.
8. Respective traffic and other vessels movements will not endanger the vessel.
9. Clarity in advance of any navigational hazards that might be anticipated are duly noted.
10. The effects of heel, trim or squat will not affect the under-water keel clearance of the vessel.

1.9 Officer of the Watch – Being Relieved

Many ships Masters and shipping companies are quite specific regarding instructions and guidance towards the duties of ships officers. However, one area is often overlooked and this involves a watch Officer who is being relieved. As with any change over of watch personnel, this is a critical period not only for the officer taking up the watch, but also for the officer who is duly handing on the responsibility.

Relief of the watch should not be carried out while an ongoing manoeuvre is being exercised or where detailed navigational operations are being activated. Any relief of the watch which coincides with a bridge operation should be deferred until the activity is complete.

The watch Officer should not attempt to hand the watch over, if he has reason to believe that an Officer taking the watch has a disability, for what ever reason. If the watch Officer is in any doubt as to the capabilities of his relief he should always inform the Master and remain on station until relieved by the Master, or his designated representative. The correct details and timings of relief should be noted in the log book.

Once so relieved, the Officer leaving the bridge station should complete log books and administration duties after his watch period is complete. Many shipping companies would also expect that Officer to carry out 'ship's rounds' on departure from the bridge to ensure that no potential hazards such as fire or security breach are present onboard the vessel.

1.10 Bridge Procedure: Anchoring and Anchor Watch

1. The Officer of the Watch should advise the Master of the probable anchoring time together with an ETA for that time when engine status will go to 'stand-by'.
2. The engine room should be advised well in advance of the potential time of 'stand-by'.
3. An anchor plan should be prepared.
4. Speed should be reduced in plenty of time prior to the approach to the anchorage site.
5. Anchors should be made ready for letting go or walking back, together with the respective day or night anchor signals.
6. Account should be taken of the strength and direction of: wind, tide and currents.
7. Account should be made for adequate sea room, especially if other vessels are anchored at the same anchorage.
8. Anchor party should be standing by in ample time prior to the use of anchors and cables.
9. Anchor watches should be set to provide security.
10. The anchored position for the vessel should be ascertained by visual anchor bearings and verified by alternative means at regular intervals.
11. The position of the anchor should be recorded together with the amount of cable paid out.
12. A radio VHF listening watch should be maintained.

13. The weather should be monitored closely, and any changes communicated to the Master.
14. Engine room should be informed of the status of the vessel. (Main engines should not be rung-off when the vessel is at anchor, status should be one of immediate readiness and to this end the telegraph should be left at 'stop' engines, not 'finished with engines')
15. A deck watch should be maintained to ensure ships' security, especially in certain regions where anchored vessels are considered, 'soft targets' for pirates.

1.11 Anchor Plan Details and Content

The anchor plan should be comprehensive and include a detailed chart assessment with relevant reference to appropriate publications, i.e. Sailing Directions.

Specific content of the plan should include:

- identification of position of the anchor, when 'letting go'.
- the nature of the holding ground at the anchorage site. (Mud or clay preferred as good holding grounds)
- the rise and fall of any tidal condition.
- which anchor is designated for use.
- the amount of cable expected to be used. (This would be influenced by the type and holding power of the anchor as well as the weather conditions, holding ground, length of stay, swinging room available etc.,)
- the option of using two anchors, to moor the vessel.
- the ships course of approach towards the anchorage, relevant to the direction of tidal stream.
- the position of change over from auto-pilot to manual steering is identified in ample time.
- adequate Underkeel Clearance (UKC) exists between the last way point and the anchorage site and that the echo sounder is in operation.
- the position at which the engines should be placed on Stand-By.
- the speed of approach towards the anchorage site.
- checking that no underwater obstructions are present inside the anchorage.
- ensure that adequate swinging room for the vessel is available.
- suitable position fixing and monitoring facilities are available.
- the local weather report is obtained prior to entry into the anchorage.

- the approach is monitored by primary and secondary position fixing methods.
- compass headings should be calculated in addition to Gyro and True headings. (Contingency planning in the event of the loss of the gyro compass)
- assessment that the anchorage is sheltered and clear of through traffic.
- the maximum rate and direction of the prevailing current, at the time of anchoring and throughout the anchored period.
- the times and heights of High and Low Water levels.
- the bridge manning requirement for the bridge team operation.
- the manning requirement for the anchor party and the time of 'stand by' for relevant personnel.
- VHF communication channels identified for contact with Port or Harbour Authorities, if appropriate.

Navigation Officers should be aware that Masters would expect to see the relevant points of the anchor plan incorporated into the Passage Plan in order to satisfy the 'Berth to Berth' criteria. Prior to the time of anchoring, the Ship's Master, would carry out a risk assessment to ensure that the personnel, so engaged, have relevant experience to reflect the tasks in hand. The risk assessment should also take account of the complexity and associated dangers of equipment to be used in relation to the prevailing weather and associated general conditions affecting the anchor operation.

1.12 Bridge Emergencies – OOW Actions

Main Engine Failure

In the event of a main engine failure emergency services will be activated, although a short delay must be anticipated in the majority of ships before these become operational. The Master should be informed at the earliest possible time of the reason and kept up-to-date with regard to the state of repairs.

With regard to the ship handling possibilities following loss of power, immediate actions by the Officer of the Watch could be extremely beneficial, depending on the ships position, geography and of course the prevailing weather at the time. It may be possible to maximise the use of 'Headreach' that the vessel will carry prior to the ship stopping in the water. Alternatively the use of anchors, if navigating in appropriate depths, may also be a prudent action. Deep water anchoring may become a viable option to prevent drift towards a lee shore for instance.

In any event 'not under command' signals/lights should be displayed and depending on circumstances an 'emergency signal' may also be a necessity. Without doubt the Master will call for an assessment of the situation regarding state of repairs and future actions will depend greatly on what can and cannot be carried out by way of repairs. The use of a 'tug' may become a consideration.

A position should be placed on the chart and the rate of drift established. This may not be an easy task for watch officers who could well be left without instruments and out of sight of visual targets.

Steering Gear Failure

If steering gear fails, the OOW should immediately engage alternative emergency steering gear. The engine room should be informed and the Master informed of the situation. The watch officer should exhibit 'Not Under Command' signals/lights and if appropriate sound signals "D" or "U" to warn other shipping of the vessels predicament.

In the event of emergency and auxiliary steering systems being lost, the vessel would most certainly be stopped. In this situation a navigation warning and/or report may become necessary, depending on ships position, e.g. TSS, English Channel.

Compass Failure

If the ship's gyroscopic compass became unreliable this would normally be noticed instantly by the 'off course alarm' being activated. The Officer of the Watch would then engage manual steering and adopt steering by use of the magnetic compass.

The Master would be informed and an inspection of the gyro compass by either the navigation officer or the electrical officer would be an expected line of action.

The loss of the gyroscopic compass could well have a detrimental effect on other navigational instruments, such as radars which may be 'gyro-stabilised' and automatic steering, off course alarms etc.

Associated Shipboard Emergencies – Bridge Reactions

Bridge Informed of Fire

The Officer of the Watch will immediately raise the fire alarm and expect emergency stations to be manned. The engine room would be placed on 'stand-by' status and the Master would be informed of all known details including the location of the fire.

The OOW would be expected to carry out specific duties, dependent on the type of vessel involved:

1. Automatic closure of all fire doors. This can often be activated from the bridge and if this can be done it should be.
2. Ventilation and/or cargo fans are also sometimes controlled from the bridge or from a localised station. These should be shut down as soon as possible.
3. In all cases the course of the ship should be altered in conjunction with the wind, assuming adequate sea room to reduce forced draft within the confines of the vessel. (Unless the draft is required to clear smoke).
4. The ship's position should be plotted and made available to the communications officer prior to transmission of an 'urgency signal'.
5. The bridge watch and the monitoring of other traffic should be continued throughout and if appropriate, 'deck lighting' may be switched on.
6. N.U.C. lights/shapes would be displayed.

Bridge Informed of Flooding

Although unusual in its own right, the possibility of underwater damage and subsequent flooding is always present in the marine environment. However, it is more common following a collision incident. In many cases the emergency alarm may have already been sounded for an associated incident, but in the event no alarm has been activated, watch officers should immediately activate the 'general alarm signal'.

Additional actions will include:

1. Closing of all watertight doors.
2. Inform the Master and give update on the situation.
3. Engine room informed and respective pumps activated.
4. Position of vessel charted and made available for radio dispatch by the communications officer.

5. Following damage assessment an 'urgency' or 'distress' signal may become necessary.
6 N.U.C. signals may be appropriate.

Man Overboard

In any incident where a man is overside the immediate tendency is for the ship to return to the datum position by one of the several manoeuvres considered appropriate, i.e. Williamson turn, single delayed turn, elliptical turn or short round. Usually initiated when the man is seen to fall and the subsequent alarm raised simultaneously.

With any situation where the vessel is turned through 180° whilst at full sea speed, there is bound to be a subsequent decrease in the overall speed. In some cases the watch officer could expect a reduction of up to around 30% depending on sea state and weather conditions. The time factor to complete the turn will vary but it could be assumed that the OOW, would place main engines on a stand-by status and subsequently reduce approach speed to suit rescue boat launch and/or recovery, during the interim period.

In the event that the casualty is not found the IAMSAR manual recommends that a sector search pattern is employed. However, the time factor for the man in the water is critical and any search pattern should reflect a small track space "leg length'. If the speed of the vessel is also considered while the search is ongoing (probably about 3 knots) then the reason for short leg lengths is directly related to the wellbeing of the casualty. When conducting a sector search, Masters may well consider track space in time as opposed to distance, e.g. 10 minutes away from datum at any one time. (*Refer Chapter 9 for "Sector Search"*).

Bridge Procedure

From the onset of the incident Masters should ensure that the bridge is placed on an alert operational status and the following actions take place:

Assuming the alarm has been sounded, the helm has been applied to clear the propeller from the casualty, that the engine room has been placed on stand-by and the bridge wing lifebuoy has been released.

1. Con of ship to be maintained and manoeuvre completed.
2. Manual steering to be engaged.
3. Datum position plotted and relevant search pattern laid on the chart.
4. Ship's position to be monitored continually.
5. Lookouts strategically posted high and forward.
6. Communications established with coast radio station. Urgency message and/or distress, if required.
7. Local signals made to inform other shipping in the area: 'O' flag displayed and sounded on whistle.
8. Rescue boat turned out and made ready for immediate launch.
9. Hospital made ready to treat for shock and hypothermia.
10. Obtain updated weather report.

1.14 Navigation in Fog

Every mariner is ever wary of reduced visibility conditions and the associated dangers of 'fog'. Obviously certain geographic areas are well known for poor visibility in certain seasons and these are well publicised in Climatic Chartlets. However, the realisation that fog could be and is, encountered virtually anywhere world wide, is of concern to all at sea.

There are several different types of fog which may be encountered within the marine environment:

1.14.1 fog and mist

Fog is of greater intensity than mist. Although both contain visible quantities of water vapour, fog most certainly impedes navigation. Usual occurrence is when winds are light, temperature low and the barometer high.

Fog exists when visibility is less than 1000 yds (914 metres).

1.14.2 sea fog

This is normally formed by a warm wind passing over relatively cold water. This causes moisture in the air to be condensed and turn to visible water vapour. It is often low lying and would obscure most targets to the naked eye. Large, high freeboard vessels may have masts and upper superstructure projecting above the fog bank.

Alternatively, a cold wind which passes over warmer water, may cause the relatively warm moisture rising from the surface to be chilled, and a fog bank of considerable height could be formed. Sea fog may also be encountered where warm and cold ocean currents join.

1.14.3 coast fog

Often caused by cold air moving into an area after a period of warm weather. Alternatively, a warm air current after a cold spell.

1.14.4 haze

Numerous dry particles suspended in the atmosphere. Particles are invisible to the naked eye but when encountered they may collectively reduce visibility up to about 1 kilometre.

Visible detection of vessels at night will be influenced by the prevailing conditions. Navigation lights will suffer from some dispersion effects from fog. White lights may appear with a reddish effect in fog. Red rays have greater penetration than green rays and hence red lights could expect to be seen before green lights. Clear glass will absorb less light than a red glass and consequently a white light will be seen further than a red light. (By the same reasoning a red light will be seen further than a green light).

The quality of air can also be expected to influence the detection ranges of 'ships' lights. If the atmosphere is heavy in moisture content and/or dust particles their presence will cause light rays to be:

- reflected and scattered by dust particles
- refracted by moisture particles

1.15 Navigation Precautions

Proximity of Heavy Weather/Storm Conditions

Every Master on receiving a heavy weather report will attempt to re-route and avoid the storm vicinity, if at all possible. On the basis that avoidance is not possible then early deck preparations, by way of securing, would be in the interests of good seamanship.

With regard to the navigation of the vessel, all departments should be informed of impending heavy weather, and in particular the engine room should be advised of a time to go to 'stand-by' status. The communications officer should obtain updates on current weather reports while the navigator would be expected to plot and project the storms position and track.

It is prudent action to reduce speed in plenty of time to avoid structural stress on the vessel. Heavy rolling can be relieved by an alteration of course while the adjustment of speed will reduce pounding effects. If progress is affected to such an extent that the vessel would sustain damage to either the hull or the cargo, the only remaining options would be to either 'heave to' or turn and run before the wind for the lee of any available land mass.

The option of 'heaving to' will delay the vessel for an indefinite period. However, the vessel is less likely to sustain damage to herself or cargo. The ship's head should be set to a heading relative to the wind at which experience will show the vessel to ride easy. As the wind backs or veers the heading would need to be adjusted. Reduce revolutions in order to maintain steerage while the ship is in this position.

The alternative option of seeking the 'lee of the land' is widely used in coastal regions and of course is not readily available to vessels in open sea conditions. Where high cliff shorelines or coastal mountain ranges are present Masters would be well advised to run for the 'lee of the land'. Fuel consumption could be increased and the time factor may effect sensitive cargoes. These would have to be judged against possible ship/cargo damage.

The mariner should be aware of all the above as being viable options if directly involved with heavy weather. Far better though, is not to get involved in the first place. The obvious options prior to departure should involve seeking out the most detailed weather information and if appropriate taking advantage of Shore Routing Systems (*Ref. Chapter 5*).

N.B. Nautical literature expands the possibility of going to anchor in bad weather, as being an alternative. The Author agrees with this only when combined with the 'lee of the land' option, as mentioned above. It is clear that the depth of water or the geography, will not always suit the use of anchors.

The dangers of a wind change, with anchors down, and being caught on a lee shore, is an experience that Masters could well do without. In general the Author would suggest that most mariners would prefer open sea conditions to being handicapped by several tonnes of anchors and cables limiting a vessel's movement.

1.16 Keeping a Proper Lookout

Regulation 5, of the Regulations for the Prevention of Collision at Sea, is concerned with the keeping of a 'Proper Lookout'.

Watch keepers are advised on this essential element of Bridge Procedures and Masters should not let any duty interfere with what must be considered a prime directive for any bridge watch keeping schedule.

Pic. 1: Wide aspect bridge windows of the modern vessel, actively engaged in a sea going situation. The OOW monitors Radar while an additional duty lookout is engaged as additional support for the well being of the ship.

The first and foremost duty of the OOW is to maintain an effective look out by all available means inclusive of audible, visual and radar detection of possible threatening targets. This function should not be impeded by imposed duties which are detrimental to the well being of the ships safe progress.

It should be noted that under the STCW '95 standards, watch-keeping personnel are required to have ten (10) hours rest between periods of duty, of which 6 hours must be continuous. Such standards have been established to avoid the possibility of key personnel becoming affected by fatigue and the efficiency of the watch being detrimentally affected.

The OOW should consider himself/herself as the prime lookout and crew members are engaged as additional lookout personnel as and where required by the Master and/or the OOW. Although a bridge team, inclusive of lookout(s) is common practice, the lookout function of the OOW is not diminished in any way.

APPENDIX

EXTRACT FROM SCHEDULE 1 TO THE MERCHANT SHIPPING (CERTIFICATION AND WATCHKEEPING) REGULATIONS 1982

6. **Look-out**

In addition to maintaining a proper look-out for the purpose of fully appraising the situation and the risk of collision, stranding and other dangers to navigation, the duties of the look-out shall include the detection of ships or aircraft in distress, shipwrecked persons, wrecks and debris. In maintaining look-out the following shall be observed:

(a) the look-out must be able to give full attention to the keeping of a proper look-out and no other duties shall be undertaken or assigned which could interfere with that task;

(b) the duties of the look-out and helmsman are separate and the helmsman shall not be considered to be the look-out while steering, except in small ships where an unobstructed all round view is provided at the steering position and there is no impairment of night vision or other impediment to the keeping of a proper look-out. The officer in charge of the watch may be the sole look-out in daylight provided that on each such occasion:

(i) the situation has been carefully assessed and it has been established without doubt that it is safe to do so;

(ii) full account has been taken of all relevant factors including, but not limited to:

state of weather
visibility
traffic density
proximity of danger to navigation
the attention necessary when navigating in or near traffic separation schemes;

(iii) assistance is immediately available to be summoned to the bridge when any change in the situation so requires.

1.17 Watchkeeping and Special Traffic

Specialist Craft to be Given a Wide Berth

(Ref: to the Regulations for the Prevention of Collision at Sea)

Masters and watch Officers are advised that certain types of vessels and marine activities warrant being given a wide berth. Recognition of these specialist activities is generally not a major problem for the experienced watchkeeper, however, depending on the circumstances, the action taken to avoid them is often observed to be inadequate and could also involve the vessel in either another close quarters situation or bring the vessel into areas of additional navigational hazards.

Special attention should be given to the following types of craft and their associated activities:

Surveying Ships

As defined by Rule 3(g) ii, will exhibit restricted in ability to manoeuvre lights and shapes described in Rule 27(b). These vessels may also show the signal 'IR' signifying that they are engaged in submarine survey work or other underwater operations. Vessels are advised to keep clear at slow speed.

The clearance on these vessels is established by the direction in Rule 16, however, the nature of the activity could well involve the towing of instruments at an undefined distance astern. An example of this may be experienced with vessels engaged in seismic surveys where cables up to 4 miles long may be being towed. These cables could very well be submerged with the end being marked by a tail buoy and/or radar reflector.

Navigational warnings normally accompany such operations, especially in areas of heavy traffic or in known shipping lanes. Use of VHF may also be restricted by these survey craft which tend to make acceptable communications difficult. Use of international code and light communication can therefore be considered as viable alternatives.

Pic. 2: Pipe Layer seen in the offshore waters near Stavanger, Norway. Such vessels would operate under Restricted in Ability to Manoeuvre signals and would expect to be given a wide berth.

The actual operation that the vessel is engaged in, could well dictate the level of manoeuvrability, stopping distance, and turning capability that is available to the craft. Action by the give way vessel should therefore take these facts into consideration when taking avoiding action. These vessels by the very nature of their employment could well be encountered in any region, often with no previous warning. Early action, which must be substantial, is strongly recommended in order to pass an absolute minimum of 2 miles clear of the operational craft.

Additionally, some activities may involve the use of 'air' or 'gas' explosions in the proximity of operations and small launch or boat activity may be featured. Watch Officers should maintain an effective and all round lookout and brief lookouts accordingly.

Mine Clearance Vessels

As defined by Rule 3(g)v, is classed as being within the category of being restricted in ability to manoeuvre. the day signal and night signal being as specified in Rule 27(f). If these vessels are encountered then the Master should always be informed of their presence. Vessels are recommended not to pass any closer than 1000 metres of the mine clearance vessel, and should also establish cleared water areas where navigation is considered safe.

With the hostilities of the Falklands (1982) and the Gulf Wars (1991/2003) these types of vessels may well be engaged in actual operations of clearing live mines. In which case communications with the minehunter to obtain known limits of danger zones and the current situation regarding navigable waters is essential.

Whether the vessel is engaged in exercise or in actual mine clearance will not alter the recommended clearance of 1000 metres. The circumstances and conditions could well dictate that the vessels who encounter these warships may have to alter their intended tracks considerably, in the light of hazards known to be in the area.

The activities of mine clearance operations can be varied depending on the types of mines being cleared. Small boats could well be within the operational area and in the general vicinity and watch officers are advised to maintain effective and all round lookout by all available means. Boats may display flag 'A' or a rigid replica of the same and speed of through vessels should be adjusted to take account of the use of divers below the surface. If at night morse 'A' may be flashed to approaching vessels.

Mine clearance vessels are often constructed in wood or Glass-Reinforced Plastic (GRP). It is unlikely that they would not be detected by radar, but the echo return, depending on the aspect of the vessel, could very well be diminished. Overall size of the target is approximately 50 metres in length, of about 400 tonnes displacement. Speeds average 15 knots when not actively engaged.

As with many warships, they may not be working alone. Joint operations or working with escorts is not unusual. Helicopter activity may also be present in and around the area of operation.

Pic. 3: Para-vane surface floats racked on the deck of a mine clearance vessel, employed for trailing sweeping cutting equipment.

Mine Clearance – Situation

Day signal : Three black balls in place of three all round green lights.

Night signal : All round green lights displayed in a triangle in addition to the lights of a power driven vessel.

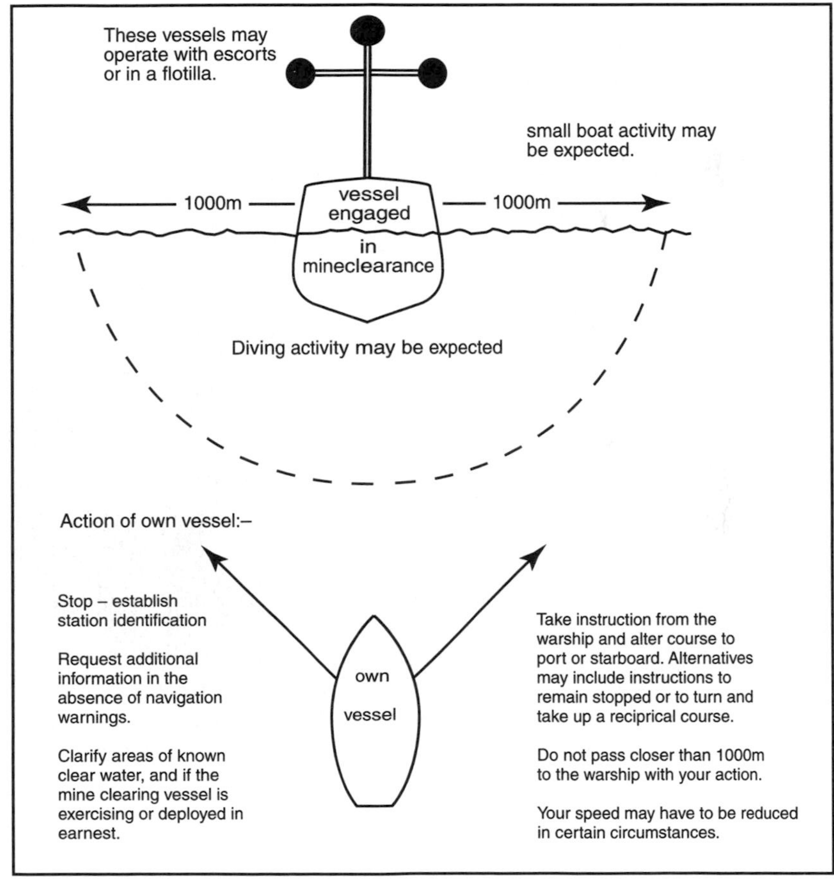

Diagram 1.1: Mine clearing operations

Vessels Undergoing Trials

New tonnage or vessels which have received structural alterations may be encountered undergoing trials for 'turning circles' or 'speed' capabilities. In many cases they will be in a 'light' condition of loading, which can render them high out of the water. This overall condition could effect the disposition of navigation lights visible to an approaching vessel. Also they may make abrupt sharp angled turns, 180° or more, for no apparent reason. A wide berth to these vessels is recommended so as not to interfere with their course runs or impede their trials.

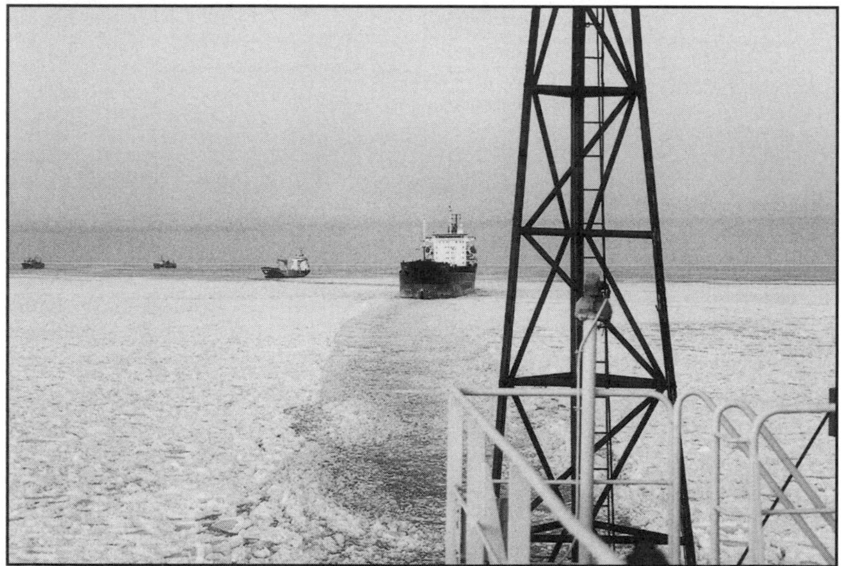

Pic. 4: Ships proceeding in convoy along the St Lawrence River, Canada. The optimum distance between vessels can vary to suit the conditions but the ideal position is determined as that distance which will gain most benefit from the evolved channel while at the same time allowing the vessel to stop without involving collision.

Pic. 5: The new EH-101 'Merlin' ASW helicopter engages with HMS 'Norfolk'

Vessels so engaged are normally encountered in open waters clear of navigational obstructions, or in waters which are in close proximity to shipbuilding centres, e.g. Belfast/Harland & Wolf – Irish Sea region. These vessels may show the international code signal 'SM'.

Vessels in Formation or Convoy

The dangers of a single ship approaching a convoy of either merchant ships or warships should be noted and early action taken to avoid close quarter encounters. General advice to single ships is for them to keep well clear of convoy formations and avoid passing ahead or through the formation. This advice does not however give the convoy the right to proceed without regard to the movement of approaching vessels.

Convoy formations if encountered are proceeding at a limited speed, usually relative to the slowest vessel in the formation or because of overall conditions, i.e. heavy ice concentration. The risk of collision within and between the vessels in the convoy is always present and would not be helped by close navigation of another single vessel approaching the formation.

Vessels in convoy may also be impaired by being deep draughted, encumbered by ice, poor visibility or other conditions which place additional burdens on their navigational capabilities. Early measures and good seamanlike practice in collision avoidance should be adopted if encountering ships in convoy.

Vessels Engaged in the Launching or Recovery of Aircraft

As defined by the regulations, Rule 3(g)iv, this class of vessel has in the past been predominantly warships. However, with the extensive offshore developments worldwide and greater personal wealth, many types of the larger private yachts as well as offshore workboats are being fitted with helicopter facilities.

The increased use of the helicopter for pilotage transfer, or as an ambulance service within the marine environment, continues to grow and will subsequently bring more types of vessels into this category. The courses set by these vessels when engaged with aircraft are often predetermined by the direction of the wind. Rotary, as well as fixed winged aircraft always take account of wind force and direction when engaging in marine activities.

The vessels should display the lights or shapes to indicate that they are restricted in their ability to manoeuvre but may additionally show extensive deck lighting at night during landing or take off periods. Some commercial vessels especially the deep draughted tanker or the larger passenger liner, by the fact of their size, may require more sea room compared with a smaller, shallow draught inshore craft.

Conventional aircraft carriers and those with angled flight decks are well known to have their navigation lights sometimes offset from the fore and aft centreline of the ship. Other designated carriers are now fitted with through decks to facilitate Short-Take-Off-and-Land (STOL) or the 'ski jump' launching ramp. These carriers could well be engaged with vertical take off aircraft e.g. Harriers, and the continuous sighting of navigation lights may be impaired.

Large capital ships like aircraft carriers are usually escorted by one or more smaller faster moving ships, which are meant to provide a protective shield around the carrier. Helicopter and submarine activity could also be prominent in the area of the carrier and support vessels may also be in attendance.

Ships meeting vessels engaged in aircraft operations should provide a wide berth to them and take substantial and early action so as not to encroach on their activities. Commercial vessels navigating too closely to warships can expect to be monitored by either surface escorts or helicopters and may be challenged.

Pic. 6: HMS 'Ocean'. Helicopter/Commando carrier.

Hovercraft, Hydrofoils and Wig Craft

High speed, 'air cushion craft or hydrofoil' craft have increased their numbers considerably in many areas of the globe and can be expected to be encountered at any time by ocean going commercial vessels. Although operating at high speeds, sometimes up to 120 knots, they are extremely vulnerable to wind effects. The leeway that they experience may sometimes present a misleading picture to watch officers, giving a false indication of the actual direction of travel.

These vessels all comply with the Regulations for the Prevention of Collision at Sea, whether they are operating in the air cushion mode or only partly airborne or fully waterborne. they are also required to exhibit a yellow flashing light in addition to the normal lights shown by a power driven vessel. This light will operate at 120 or more flashes per minute. (It should not be confused with similar lights exhibited by some submarines).

Other vessels meeting these types of craft should be aware that their operation is accompanied by considerable noise levels and as a result sound signals made by either vessel may not be readily heard. Also, because of their construction, the disposition of navigation lights may not always be as specified by the regulations. The positioning of lights should be, as near as practical to what the regulations specify.

Popular areas of navigable waters where these vessels are regularly known to operate are as follows:

English Channel British/French Ports, Florida Coast/Bahamas, Malta/Gozo Islands, Mediterranean Sea, Thames Estuary/European Continent.

NB. WiG craft (Wing in Ground – multi-modal craft) which have recently been defined by amendments to the Regulations (November, 2003) will exhibit a high intensity Red Flashing Light, in addition to the lights exhibited by a power driven vessel, when taking off, landing and in flight near the surface.

Such craft are directed by Regulation 18, to keep well clear of all other vessels, and avoid impeding their navigation when taking off, landing or in flight near the surface.

WiG craft operating on the surface are also directed to comply with the Rules as a power driven vessel.

WiG Craft Design

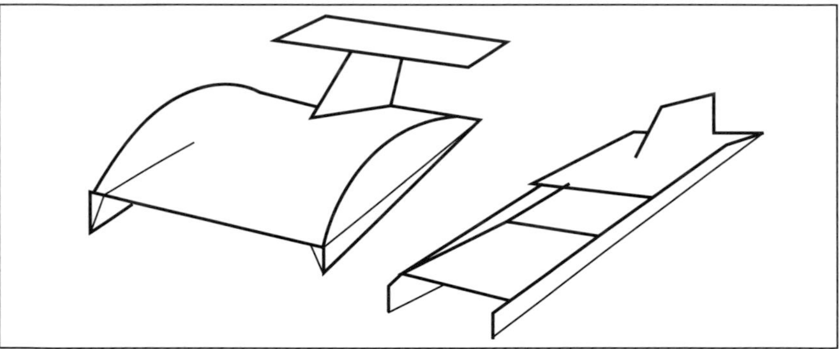

Diagram 1.2: WiG craft only when taking off, landing and in flight near the surface shall, in addition to the lights prescribed in paragraph (a) of Rule 23, exhibit a high intensity all round flashing red light.

Ships Engaged in Replenishment at Sea

As defined by Rule 3(g) iii, vessels engaged in replenishment are usually warships being re-supplied by auxiliaries. The vessels will all show the lights and shapes as for vessels restricted in their ability to manoeuvre.

By the very nature of the operation the ships will be in close proximity to each other and will be interconnected by jackstays and possibly hoses. They may appear as a single target on radar screens, depending on the aspect. Visually, one vessel may obscure the other and the two targets may not be easily discernible.

All other vessels that encounter this operation should be aware that high levels of ship handling and station holding are required by the participants. In any 'pacing' or that of a similar nature or operation, the dangers of interaction are ever present. Consequently other traffic should keep well clear in accordance with Rule 18. Early action to avoid close quarters would reduce any possibility of causing disruption to such operations.

Submarines

Submarine activity may not always be readily apparent but on occasions can be noted by escorting vessel's showing the International Code signal 'NE 2'. All ships sighting this signal are advised to keep a sharp lookout and provide a wide berth to them. If submarines are sighted on the surface the navigation lights are placed well forward and low over the water and may present themselves in an unusual configuration. Stern lights of submarines are exceptionally low and may often be obscured by sea surface conditions, or spray. Additionally, some submarines are fitted with a 'yellow flashing light' flashing at the rate of 90 flashes per minute (not to be confused with yellow lights on hovercraft). Certain submarines of various navy's may carry similar distinctive lights:

Royal Navy Submarines ...... Yellow flashing light 90-150 per min.
Danish Submarines ...... Blue flashing light 105 fl. per min.

These additional lights are meant to indicate to approaching vessels the need for extra caution.

Submarines may have cause or reason to use smoke candles or similar pyrotechnics as described in the Annual Summary of Admiralty Notices to Mariners. (N.P. 247).

(NB: Special instructions effect mariners who encounter submarines in difficulty beneath the surface).

Pic. 7: Royal Fleet Auxiliary Tanker engages in replenishment at sea

Pic. 8: A Royal Navy 'Sea King' lifts off from the well ordered heli-deck of the RFA 'Fort Austin'.

Vessels Constrained by Their Draught

(in relation to the available depth and width of navigable water)

As defined by Rule 3(h) of the regulations a vessel will display the lights or shapes as described in Rule 23 and Rule 28. The attention of mariners is drawn to recent amendments to the regulations which directly affect the action by vessels meeting a ship which is constrained in this manner. Amendments which came into force in November 1989/2003 concern Rule 8(a) and 8(f) which directs vessels in their actions, when required, not to impede the passage or safe passage of another vessel.

Night signal: 3 red lights in a vertical line.
Day signal: a black cylinder where it can best be seen.

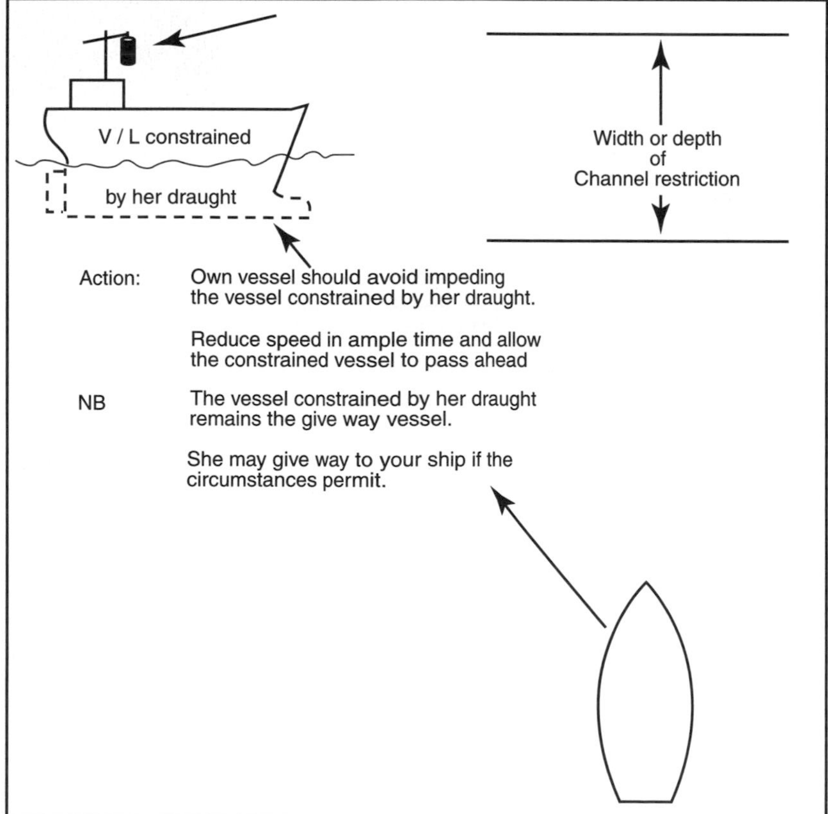

Diagram 1.3: Suggested action by own vessel which meets a vessel constrained by her draught. Crossing from port to starboard ahead of own ship.

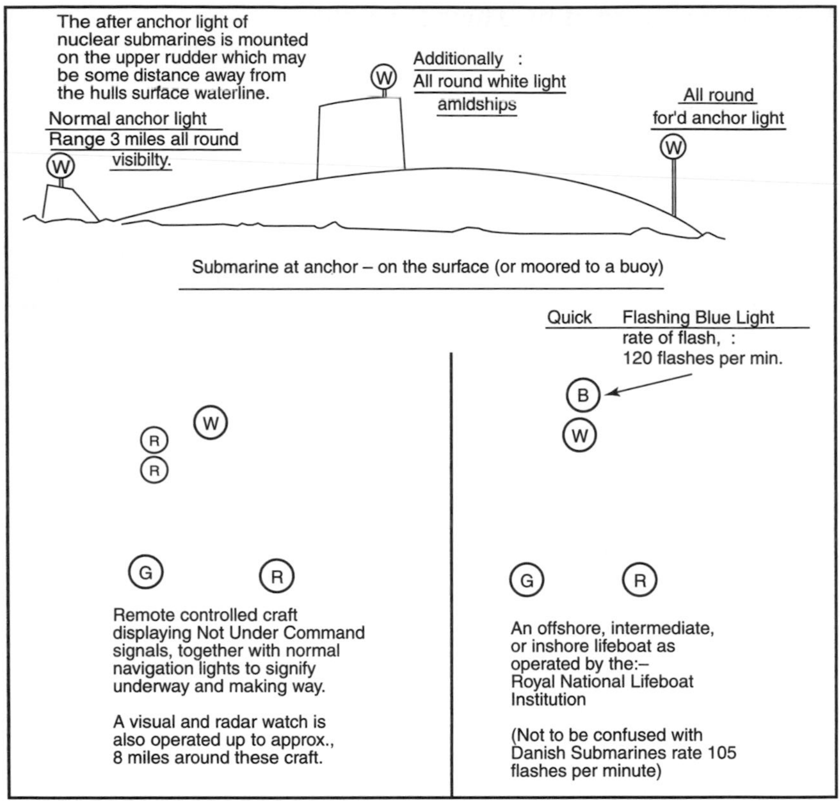

The after anchor light of
nuclear submarines is mounted
on the upper rudder which may
be some distance away from
the hulls surface waterline.
Normal anchor light
Range 3 miles all round
visibilty.
W
Additionally :
All round white light
amldships
W
All round
for'd anchor light
W
Submarine at anchor – on the surface (or moored to a buoy)
W
R
R
G
R
Remote controlled craft
displaying Not Under Command
signals, together with normal
navigation lights to signify
underway and making way.
A visual and radar watch is
also operated up to approx.,
8 miles around these craft.
Quick Flashing Blue Light
rate of flash, :
120 flashes per min.
B
W
G
R
An offshore, intermediate,
or inshore lifeboat as
operated by the:–
Royal National Lifeboat
Institution
(Not to be confused with
Danish Submarines rate 105
flashes per minute)

Diagram 1.4: Special Navigation Light – Configurations

Chapter Two

NAVIGATION IN PORT

2.1 Navigation in and Around Small Craft

There are numerous occasions when commercial deep sea vessels can expect to encounter small craft. Pilot launches, harbour craft, tugs, cargo barges to mention but a few. Apart from the dangers of interaction Masters and bridge Officers should be aware of some basic bridge procedures and precautionary actions prior to engagement with smaller craft, in close proximity.

2.1.1 approach plan

Any engagement with small vessels should be planned and well thought out prior to commencement of the operation. Full consideration should be given to the geography of the area of intended operation. It should preferably be clear of navigational hazards and in clear water, to allow a suitable course setting to present a favourable aspect to prevailing weather.

The under keel clearance should be noted for all stages of the engagement and any areas of limiting water depth should be clearly marked on the chart. Areas where the under keel clearance may give cause for concern should be identified in relation to the early use of echo sounder and with relevant position fixing methods.

The plan should incorporate early timings for standard operations such as: Manual steering change from automatic steering, engine room status prior to reduction of speed, preparation of anchors. Masters requirement on the bridge, lookouts posted etc.

2.1.2 charting the plan

All tracks and courses should be clearly identified on the chart with both the gyro and compass headings noted. Position monitoring points together with projected ETA's should also be chartered.

The use of clearing bearings, transits and sector lights can be particularly useful during small boat engagement and can provide simple checks for monitoring the safe navigation of the vessel. Radar conspicuous targets should be highlighted before the vessel enters the area of engagement.

Special attention being given to racon's and buoys carrying radar reflectors. Course alteration points with wheel over points should be identified and charted in accordance with recommendations of relevant speeds. Special attention should be given to areas where course alterations or speed changes may be adversely effected by strong currents, etc. (e.g. eddies).

2.1.3 shipboard preparations

All flags and/or navigational day/night signals should be clearly indicated prior to the approach. It should be normal practice for early communications to be established by VHF either channel 16 or if known, the most suitable working channel.

Pic. 9: Modern type pilot cutter, high speed, engages in pilotage transfers in most harbours and ports around the world.

Pic. 10: Mooring boat engages in securing ship's lines to mooring buoys inside a harbour complex.

A listening watch on the working channel would then be maintained with relevant ETA's being passed to the target vessel.

Information regarding new navigational dangers in the area, together with weather updates should be sought from the approaching craft as appropriate. In the case of pilots, ladders should be rigged in ample time and in a position to suit the weather and the needs of pilot launches.

Instrument checks should be made and a safe speed established prior to engagement. Radars adjusted to a practical working range for the circumstances. Ships progress and all relevant operations should be noted in the log book especially the monitoring of the ships position at appropriate stages of the approach.

2.1.4 operations

An early sighting of the target is always beneficial, but it should always be borne in mind that the most direct route to the rendezvous is not always the safest or most prudent. Echo sounder should be running and the position monitored as often as the situation demands. A sharp lookout should be maintained for other traffic while at the same time maintaining visual contact with the target vessel once this has been established.

The direction of the wind should be ascertained immediately prior to engagement, with the view to adjusting the vessels head so as to provide a 'lee' for the smaller craft. Speed should be continually adjusted to allow the two vessels to close and maintain station on each other.

Officers of the watch and/or Masters should ensure that reductions of speed do not result in the vessel losing steerage way. Clear instructions to the bridge team, especially to the helmsman and lookouts to report anything untoward, should be clearly expressed.

Internal and external communications, will without doubt play a major role in any operation of this nature. If precise records are maintained in the form of old log books, they can form a valuable directive for future operations and help to inform in similar activities at a later date.

2.2 Navigation and Manoeuvring with Tugs

The employment of tugs is always generally accepted as being a welcome addition by the majority of Masters/Pilots when engaged in manoeuvring. However, this welcome addition will only remain so while the tug and the Tug Master continue to respond to the navigational needs of the parent vessel. It is not unusual to see six or more tugs engaged in the berthing or undocking of a large ULCC or VLCC. Provided each tug responds as part of an overall team then full control of the operation becomes the accepted norm. To this end a clear and understandable communication system must be known and practised by all Tug Masters and the bridge team of the parent vessel. Clear and identified VHF channels together with recognised whistle signals must be familiar to all operators.

2.2.1 approaching tugs/rendezvous

Early communication with Tug Masters to ascertain position of rendezvous and projected ETA must be considered essential information. Prudent Masters would also obtain such practical details as to whether the ships towing springs are to be used or the tugs lines. The relative position that the tug will secure to the vessel and how the lines are to be secured. (Some tugs will secure by employing the eye only, others will require the wires figure '8' on the bitts. Other tugs may be engaged to push as opposed to securing). When approaching tugs a continuous lookout should be maintained and the operation of securing tugs should not be allowed to distract from essential watchkeeping duties. The vessel should be in manual steering and all flags and/or respective navigation signals displayed.

The Master/Navigator should make an early chart assessment of the area of rendezvous. It should be clear of obstructions and without heavy traffic density. The prevailing direction of anticipated weather could be usefully displayed on the chart to provide indication for ships head and visually present the overall ship handling scenario to the bridge team. Current and tide conditions must be considered prior to engagement of tugs.

2.2.2 tug engagement

Deck preparation by way of crew at deck stations, heaving lines and towing springs (if ship's lines) flaked and made ready to pass to tugs, should all be ready by the time the parent vessel makes visual contact with tugs. The engines should be on 'Stand By' and the vessel at manoeuvring speed.

One of the main areas of danger when securing tugs is through interaction. To this end the speed of the parent vessel must be adjusted well in advance to remove excessive risk of interaction between the two vessels as they close.

It is normal, for a tug's line to have a rope tail attached to the eye of the towing wire. This aids control of the wire when heaving up to secure and also when letting go. Once brought on board the parent vessel the rope should be kept clear of bitts when belaying the towing wire or placing the eye.

NB: The eye should not, under normal circumstances be placed over bitts as a means of securing. In the event of an emergency if it is required to let go the wire, this cannot be achieved unless the tug eases back on the weight of the towing spring. Therefore, temporarily, control is in the hands of the tug, not the Master of the parent vessel. A most undesirable situation in any towing operation.

In the event that the tug is to be engaged in a pushing capacity, the tugs bow should be well fended to provide a spread of the load and avoid potential hull damage. Many tugs when pushing will use a bow steadying line to hold itself against the parent ship, but not in every case.

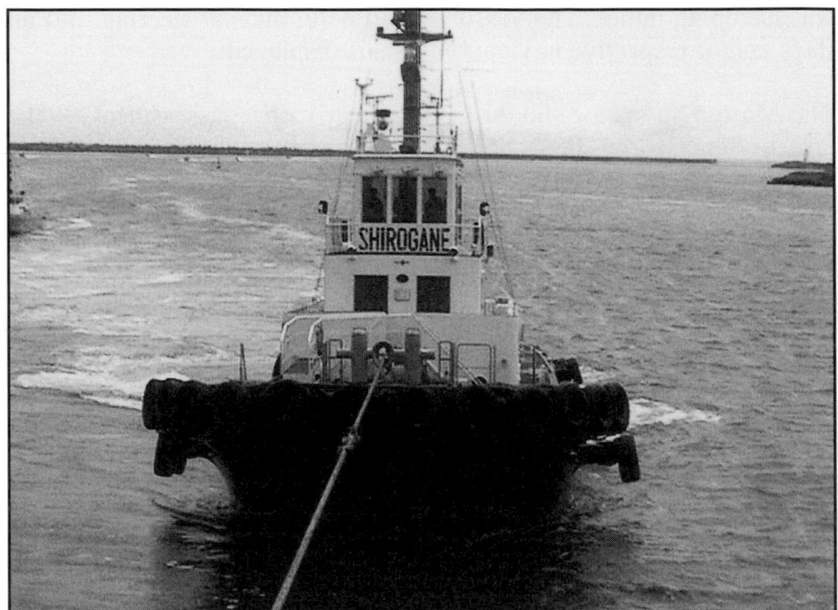

Pic. 11: The Japanese tug 'Shirogane' seen secured by a towline through its centre stag horn lead.

Pic. 12: Alternative use of 'Gob Rope'.
Winch wire with heavy duty shackle to the 'towing line'

Tugs and Towing Features

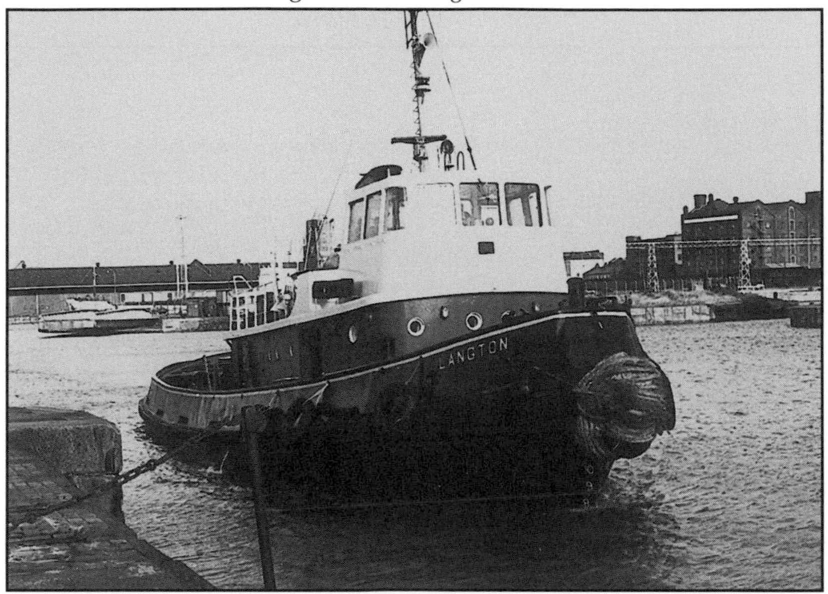

Pic. 13: Docking Tug – Liverpool.
Note pudding fender over the bow specifically for pushing

Pic. 14: Tugs after deck with towline secured and 'Gob Rope' employed.

CLOSE QUARTERS – Areas of Interaction and Potential Hazard.

Pic. 15: Ferry activity in the port of Dover. Vehicle parking area in the foreground of the terminals. P&OSL *'Dover'* Passenger Vehicle Ferry, alongside at Pier 3. The P&OSL *'Canterbury'* lying portside to, is engaged in loading trailer units, while the P&OSL *'Provence'* manoeuvres to turn, prior to berthing starboard side to, at Pier 2, opposite the *'Dover'*.

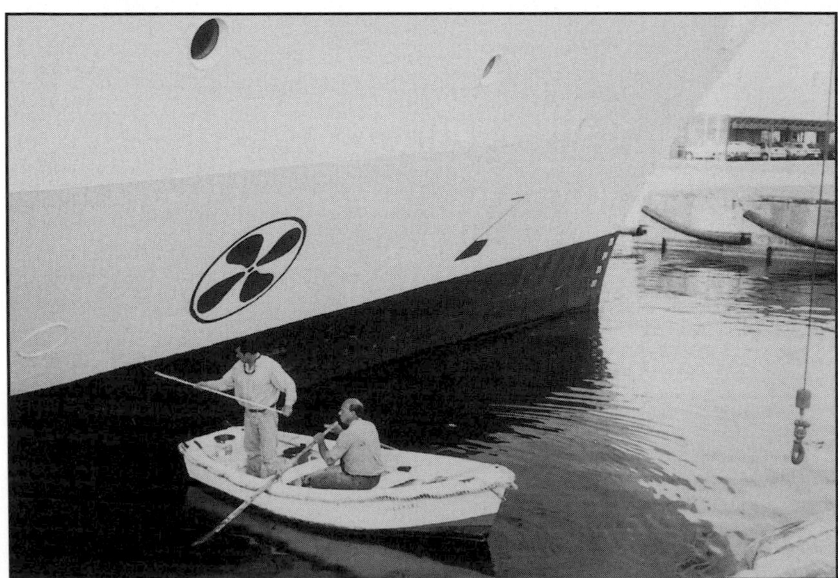

Pic. 16: Dangers of interaction inside harbour limits with small craft engaged in overside painting.

Interaction Examples and Inshore Congestion

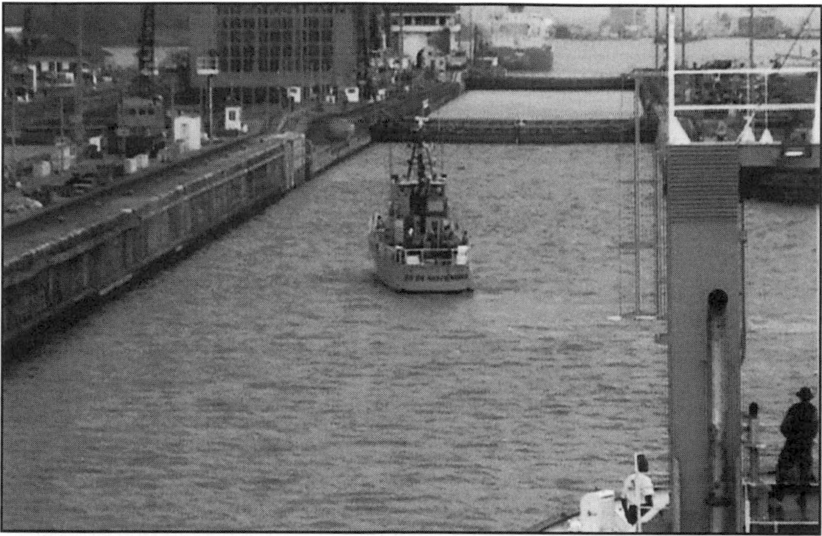

Pic. 17: Vessels navigate in close proximity at focal points like the Panama Canal and are exposed to the forces of interaction through the proximity of the canal banks and/or other vessels.

Pic. 18: Hydrofoil operating at high speed. High speed craft tend to generate powerful 'wash' effects when operating at high speed and may generate interaction between any craft in close proximity.

2.2.3 deployment and use of tugs

The number of tugs employed and the designated function of each tug will depend on several factors:

1. The type of vessel (or rig) being towed or pushed.
2. The weight of the towed vessel/craft.
3. The handling capability of the towed craft.
4. Relevant direction of currents/eddies.
5. Prevailing weather conditions.
6. Manned or unmanned tows could well reflect whether the tow is self-propelled or being moved in a 'cold' condition.
7. Anchor availability for stopping or emergency actions could well dictate the need for one or more tugs to be deployed for slowing or stopping the operation (usually astern).
8. The time of the towing operation. Length and duration must lie within the endurance and capabilities of tugs.

2.3 The Dangers of Interaction

Stand by vessels hold station in close proximity to offshore oil/gas installations. While support vessels have to move within the radius of crane jibs to allow cargoes to be discharged. The more modern vessels are fitted with 'dynamic positioning' also, the majority have rotable thrusters or bow/stern thrusters to assist ship handling. However, the risk of contact and landing with the installation is a real one and watch officers need to be aware in all weathers, in this station holding capacity. Prudent use and deployment of fenders on working boats can be beneficial in avoiding minor contact damage.

2.4 Restricted in Ability to Manoeuvre – Navigation Proximity

Obvious dangers exist when vessels navigating in and around craft which, by the very nature of their work, restrict their manoeuvrability. Not only is the task of interaction often present with the target vessel but also interaction could occur with overside gear or with the activity in which the restricted craft is engaged.

Examples of potential hazards could be experienced with close quarter situations with the following types of vessels:

1. Dredgers, especially suction pipe dredgers, where interaction could cause the pipe to break.
2. Towing operations where risk of collision may exist with the vessel being towed. While at the same time having no risk of collision with the towing vessel.

3. Survey vessels engaged in underwater operations where extending cables may obstruct channels or other navigable waters.
4. Mine clearance (sweeping operations) or fishing activity where the risk of fouling outlying gear is possible.
5. Rig supply tenders in close proximity to installations, whether engaged in load/discharge operations or not, could be extremely hampered by the geography of the rig and or interaction from another source, i.e. another vessel navigating too close.

The need for extreme caution at reduced speed by associated traffic cannot be over emphasised when circumstances cause such situations to be encountered.

2.5 Moored Vessels and Associated Hazards

A vessel is said to be moored, when on mooring buoys or at anchor with two anchors deployed. Types of moorings employing both anchors include: the running moor, standing moor, open moor and Mediterranean moor (for details of these operations, readers should refer to the Author's sister publications, '*Anchor Practice*' or '*Seamanship Techniques*').

The use of two anchors usually implies greater holding power is achieved and/or reduced swinging room is established. Reducing swinging room being a particular feature of rivers or canals where a limited area is restrictive. A second anchor is also often employed underfoot when an additional holding facility is required, or to prevent excessive 'Yaw' of the vessel, from side to side.

In all cases of mooring, the danger of fouling the cables, known as the 'foul hawse' or fouling another ships anchor, becomes a real hazard. This is especially so in the cases of running or standing moors, where a change in the direction of wind could cause the vessel to turn against the direction of the deployed anchors, causing the cables to intertwine themselves.

NB. The ebb and flood tides would tend to generate an anticipated direction of turning when in tidal waters. However, a change in the wind direction is unpredictable and could cause an alternative direction of swing to take place, which is more likely to foul cables.

In the case of a Mediterranean moor, because ships moor up in close proximity, the anchors themselves could be compromised by incorrect position keeping of the ship, when at the point of 'letting go anchors'.

Mooring and Anchor Use

Pic. 19: Supply vessel and rig proximity.

Pic. 20: Three Roll On-Roll Off, passenger/vehicle ferries seen in the aspect of Mediterranean Moors at the Greek Island of Rhodes. Two anchors deployed from each ship and the vessels' sterns are secured to the quayside by mooring ropes.

2.6 PILOTS AND PILOTAGE

2.6.1 introduction

With few exceptions the presence of a Pilot on board never relieves the Master or members of his crew of their duties and obligations regarding the safe navigation of the vessel. The 'bridge team' principle, where all relevant parties are inter-linked within a communication loop must include the marine pilot as a key member. Full exchange of information from the onset of picking up the pilot and a continuous flow of positive assistance between and towards all bridge team contributors, should be the order of the day.

Pic. 21: Close passing traffic inside the Kiel Canal.

2.7 Master/Pilot Relationship

With the arrival of the marine pilot aboard a vessel, the Master would normally be expected to receive documentation reflecting the Pilots licence and/or the pilotage authority. The recognition and acceptance of the Pilots credentials and the respect and reputation of the pilotage authority is assessed initially at this time. On regular liner trades, where Pilots are often known personally to the Master the task of Pilot assessment is obviously made with increased peace of mind.

As with any relationship, mutual respect is two ways. The Pilot will require an equal level of respect from the Master as well as the ship's criteria (see panel). In the majority of cases the Pilot is a professional mariner and his competency is attested to by the pilotage authority that issues the licence to practice. In the case of the Master his competency lies within the possession of his masters certificate, so both meet on equal terms.

Open and frank discussion between Master/Pilot regarding manoeuvres of berthing or other navigational aspects would be expected. There is however, a danger of excessive fraternisation and it must be remembered fully that final decisions and the necessary 'power of command' remain with the Master. In the past shipping companies retained 'Company Pilots' but this practice is not as prevalent as it used to be. This Master/Company Pilot relationship was one that could, if allowed to, easily develop to a point of distraction for the pilot and the Master, away from the task in hand.

Masters who are engaged on world wide trades can expect to experience varying degrees of competence in the Pilots who board their vessels. It must therefore be assumed that at some time in the future Masters will encounter a Pilot that they may consider inadequate for maintaining the safety of the vessel. In this case the level of competence may well not be revealed until the pilotage is underway. The options at this stage for the Master would appear to be as follows:

1. Master relieves the Pilot and takes on the pilotage duty.
2. Master relieves the Pilot and requests another Pilot.
3. Master relieves the Pilot and holds the ship's position, either stopped or at anchor, until a relief Pilot is available.

Should this unlikely situation develop a statement should be entered into the ship's log book and evidence and witness statements obtained where relevant.

2.8 Navigational Procedure – Embarking/Disembarking Marine Pilots

In any operation which involves the embarkation or the disembarkation of a 'Marine Pilot', it is essential that early and effective communications are established from the onset. If the inbound vessel requires the services of a Marine Pilot ample notice should be given to the pilotage station/authority, by the ship's agents or direct from the

Master of the vessel. Relevant call signs and frequencies being found for respective stations in the Admiralty List of Radio Signals.

A provisional ETA, once passed to the pilot station, can always be revised up or down as the ships progress can more accurately be projected with the closing range. Once contact is established by radio, additional information will be sought by the Pilot stations, to enable the planning of an appropriate coastal route.

Such information could include:

1. Draught of vessel when at Pilot roads.
2. Manoeuvring speed of vessel.
3. Size of vessel, with respect to:
   (a) length overall (for berthing)
   (b) mast height (for bridges)
   (c) beam width (for locks)
   (d) navigation equipment
   (e) manoeuvring aids.
4. Requirements for tugs, linesmen, docking Pilot, mooring boats, etc.
5. Nature of cargo.

2.9 Master's Requirements

Initially the Master will be concerned with accepting the 'con' of the vessel and creating a safe environment for the ship and in so doing provide the Pilot with a safe embarkation scenario. When Pilots join vessels, either from Pilot launches or from helicopters, the Masters main concern must always be for the overall safety of the vessel, by way of operational sea room, clearance from other traffic and the nearness of associated navigational dangers. Duty officers can all too easily be concerned for the safe embarkation of the Pilot, which is essential and in doing so, lose sight of other priority navigational duties.

The Master would normally gain information local to his needs from communication prior to approaching the station. This information would include a local weather situation, so that the ship can be steered to create a lee for a boat, or a heading for a helicopter delivery. Working details would also include which side the pilot would require the boarding ladder and at what height fixed above the waterline, in the case of a surface craft engagement.

2.10 Shore-to-Ship Pilot/Master Exchange and Communications

Prior to approaching a Pilotage Station it would be normal procedure to request pilotage details. These would expect to include the Name of the Pilotage Authority, a contact name, together with an operational VHF communication channel. (Often obtainable from Sailing Directions).

On establishing communications 'Pilot Boarding Instructions', including the Rendezvous Position, time and method of boarding should be clarified. The pilot himself may provide relevant information regarding the use of anchors, tugs, moorings, gangways etc. failing this, such information can usually be obtained from the harbour authority via the VHF.

Inspection of the Passage Plan would be of mutual concern to both Pilot and Master. It is also pointed out that many authorities now engage pilots who board with computer lap top facilities bearing an authority approved passage plan for use with the particular vessel at its specific draught. Masters are however, advised that such facilities do not render the ships charted Passage Plan, obsolete. Clearly in the event of malfunction of the pilot's equipment or a power loss, the ships plan becomes only too relevant.

Bearing in mind that Passage Plans are devised berth to berth and that many pilotage regions are enhanced by VTS operations, all communication positions would be considered a formal element of the plan during execution. As such, these positions should be clearly identified on charted or computerised passage plans.

NB. It is highly unlikely that a Pilot's lap top computerised plan will contain the same contingency elements as the ships own charted plan. Hence, a further reason that Masters would be ill advised to reduce the value placed on ships own charted plans.

2.11 Master/Pilot – Questionnaire

Once the pilot has boarded and the Master accepts his advice an exchange of information would normally be made between the two men. The purpose of the exchange is to make the Pilot familiar with the manoeuvring characteristics of the ship and to update the Master with any relevant or new dangers and clarify the ships movements. Typical questions that might be asked by the Master of the Pilot are as follows:

1. Are there any navigational warnings, affecting the ship's proposed track/route?
2. With the ship's present draught and the Pilots local knowledge, where are the particular areas of shallow water that the vessel might encounter with a reduced underkeel clearance?
3. What tide or current features could be expected to affect the vessels ETA?
4. Have any changes in port regulations occurred regarding communications or navigational operations?
5. Will the present or projected weather conditions cause problems on route or in berthing?
6. Will'tugs' be employed on route or for docking operations and if so, at what positions are tugs to be made fast?
7. Which berth is to be used and which side to?
8. Is there any specialised traffic known to be engaged on route towards the berth e.g. dredging operations?
9. Will the pilot change or will a 'docking Pilot' be used?
10. Assuming no traffic congestion, at what points on route are speed reductions planned and what would subsequently be the vessels ETA at destination?

With all ship handling operations there are bound to be specific needs required for individual ships and specified operations. An example of this would be if a vessel is to take tugs. Would ship's lines be employed or the tugs lines used. If tugs are being employed will they be secured or employed for pushing. If secured at what respective points and how will they be secured etc. Some operations may or may not make use of anchors and some ships may require a stern discharge as opposed to a port/starboard, load/discharge, so each situation must be judged on its own merits.

The above questions are meant as a general guideline which could well affect the majority of vessels when engaging a marine pilot on boarding a vessel for the first time.

It is normal practice to have such information on permanent display on the bridge.

GENERAL SPECIFICATIONS S.S./M.V...

International Call Sign ....
Built (yard) .... at ....
In service
Construction number ....
Official number (where stamped ....)
Registration number (where stamped ....)
Place of registration .... 19.........
Power .... ship at .... r.p.m.
Service speed .... ship at .... r.p.m.
Classification ....
Equipment number..

DIMENSIONS

	Feet	Inches	Metres
Length – overall			
– between perpendiculars			
Breadth – overall			
– moulded breadth			
Depth – moulded depth			

TONNAGES

Mark	Freeboard	Draft	Deadweight	Displacement
TF				
F				
T				
S				
W				

Displacement light ship = ... when draft forward = ...
aft = ...

TPI light ship .... laden ship = ...
Freeboard allowance = ...

CAPACITY ACCORDING TO TONNAGE CERTIFICATE

Tonnage Certificate	Gross Register Tons	m^3	Net Register Tons	m^3	Date of Issue
International					
Suez Canal					
Panama Canal					

DISTANCES

	Feet	Metres
Bridge – bow		
Bridge – stern		
Manifold – bow		
Manifold – stern		
Manifold – railing		
Manifold – side		

TOTAL HEIGHT FROM KEEL

	Feet	Metres
Fore mast		
Main mast		
Radar mast		
Aerial mast		
Funnel		

GROUND TACKLE

Anchor weight – Port = ... tons.
– Starboard = ... tons.
– Spare = ... tons.

Chain weight – per length = ... tons.
– 22 lengths = ... tons.

Chain diameter = ...

Total weight 2 anchors plus 22 chain lengths = ... tons.

2.12 Dangers when Embarking/Disembarking Pilots

Danger	*Action*
High freeboard vessels.	Combine use of pilot ladder with accommodation ladder. *Or* Use pilot hoist.
Rough sea conditions.	Create a lee for pilot transfer and adjust vessels speed. *Or* Anchor and wait for improved conditions.
A sudden change in the wind direction.	Alter the vessels course to meet and account for change.
Twisting ladder when engaged in pilot transfer.	Stand by personnel to correct and rig man ropes to provide additional support. *Or* Ladder rigged with anti-twist battens (spreaders).
Incorrect ladder rigging.	Rigging inspected by a responsible officer. Lifebuoy, lights, rescue line, adequate manpower available. Safe access to deck provided.
Restricted waters with additional traffic.	Gain sea room and adjust ETA.
Fast operations. (Sometimes necessary).	Plan approach in detail, reduce speed early and brief crew.
Interaction/pilot boat capsize or man overboard.	Vigilance at all times. Parent vessel prepared. Pilot boat itself provides best means of rescue boat. Alternatively use ships rescue boat.
Visible contact lost during manoeuvre under freeboard or around stern. Poor visibility.	Post lookouts and brief them. Maximise use of bridge wings.

2.13 Air to Surface – Transfer of Marine Pilots

With the ever growing use of helicopters in the marine environment, transfer of marine pilots to ships by rotary winged aircraft is becoming a regular occurrence. Masters should observe the recommendations enumerated by the ICS *Guide to Helicopter Operations*.

It should also be noted that when vessels engage with aircraft the following navigational aspects should be observed.

1. Display correct signals for vessel engaged with aircraft: red/white/red all round lights by night or black ball, diamond ball, by day.
2. Steer towards a recognised rendezvous point to conserve aircraft fuel.
3. Display a wind indicator to show relative wind direction.
4. Ensure that the position of engagement is clear of navigational hazards and sea room is adequate.
5. Brief 'bridge team' inclusive of lookouts and helmsman, regarding safety of operations.
6. Ensure main engines are on stand-by and vessel can readily manoeuvre.
7. Display identify signal flags to aid recognition.
8. Transmit homing signal if requested by the helicopter Pilot.
9. Establish early communications with aircraft.
10. Alter course to pilots request, to suit position of engagement. *Ref. Annual Summary* suggests that the ships course should be such as to present the wind on the port bow, when hoist operations are scheduled for the port side. Alternative courses respective of the wind direction are suggested if the operation is to take place in the after part of the vessel, e.g. Starboard quarter.
11. Maintain an efficient bridge watch while on route and while engagement takes place.
12. Do not transmit on radio during hoist operations.
13. Enter statements of activity into log books.

2.14 Relevant Seamanship Aspects

Ensure that all decks are clean and clear of loose objects. High rigging such as aerials or stays should be clear for the helicopters approach and all fire-fighting/safety precautions observed.

Pic 23: A tanker manoeuvres to secure to an SBM, the dangers of interaction with terminal mooring launches, buoys and the floating hose, expose the need for the maine pilots skill.

Chapter Three

PASSAGE PLANNING

3.1 Introduction

The safe navigation of the vessel has historically always been the responsibility of the Master. However, it is customary for the Master to delegate navigational duties to his officers and in particular to identify an individual who acts as the 'navigation officer'. The principle of passage planning generally falls into his/her expected duties whether for ocean passage or coastal passage.

The expected standards of 'Passage Planning' are not new but the procedures have become more formalised over recent years and must conform to principles published in *SOLAS Chapter 'V' (2002) Safety of Navigation*. These principles expand on four essential areas of activity required to achieve a safe passage between ports:

Namely
1. Appraisal
2. Planning
3. Execution
4. Monitoring

By necessity these individual operations must follow on from each other to achieve the objective.

Once completed, the plan is for use by the 'bridge team', and to this end it should be presented as a complete product, to the Master, by the navigation officer. This is not to say that the plan is rigid in its guidelines. On the contrary, any passage plan must retain operational flexibility to take account of the unexpected. The plan in its entirety must therefore cover the period from when the vessel departs her berth to her arrival at her new berth. The saying 'berth to berth' is appropriate, but contingency plans, where applicable should be included.

The practical construction of a passage plan becomes the personal composition of the navigator and can be effectively achieved by alternative methods. The Department of Trade's Guide contains a recommended check-list and any method employed should incorporate all these features. Many navigators complete the objective by means of:

1. Use of a data notebook.
2. Tabular presentation.
3. Chart – passage plan – check-list.

The following is offered as a possible approach to ensure that the four principles of passage planning are comprehensively covered.

1. The Navigators Data Notebook

No one can pre-empt passage conditions or anticipate ETA's prior to the event. Certain aspects must, by the nature of the beast, be carried out en route or when an arrival time is realised.

Such items that might usefully be employed towards the plan which the navigator could be expected to hold are:

- times of sunset/sunrise at landfall positions, fairways or harbours;
- tidal data for rivers, harbours, locks etc;
- rising and dipping ranges of navigational lights, prominent to the plan;
- port signals for destination;
- frequencies for radio beacons intended for use on route;
- call signs/VHF channels for respective coast radio stations on passage;
- departure draughts and expected arrival draughts of the vessel;
- detail of clocks advancing or being turned back as longitude is changed;
- special hazards and prominent features of the overall plan;
- details on contingency plans for unusual occurrences, such as (a) no pilot available, (b) poor visibility in congested areas, (c) engine or steering gear failure in areas of reduced sea room;

2. The Tabular Presentation

The use of a 'table' related directly to the 'passage plan' can be the ideal check for the navigator. It can provide a running update on the distance and subsequently deliver a continually revised ETA. The basic table entries would be comparable with the 'charted legs' of the passage and this in itself ensures an additional check against the measured distance.

Table presentations can be as detailed as the conditions of the passage dictate but should include the following example entries:

all 'alter course', positions, with the specified courses and distances between them. Courses being in degrees 'true'.

distances 'to go' and the respective steaming time for each 'leg' of the passage is useful in providing an update to the ETA as the passage proceeds.

Additionally, some presentations may show 'primary' and 'secondary' position fixing methods and frequency of their use. Engine status may also be shown for appropriate periods in the passage together with under keel clearances when necessary.

Examples of a basic table with a more detailed alternative are shown overleaf.

LIVERPOOL TO HALIFAX (Canada) *Route North about Ireland (Great Circle)*

Name *From*	*To*	*Bearing x Distance*	*Tr. Course*	*Steam Time at 15.0kts*	*Distance*	*Dist to Go*
Berth (Pilotage)	Bar Pilot Stat'n	–	Various to Masters Orders	0.5 hrs	6.5	2436
Bar Station	Chicken Rk.Lt.	054° x 5.0'	295°	4.3 hrs	64.0	2372
Chicken Rk.Lt.	Mew Island Lt.	256° x 4.5'	341°	3.0 hrs	45.0	2327
Mew Island Lt.	Altacarry Hd.Lt.	225° x 8.8'	333°	3.0 hrs	45.0	2282
Altacarry Hd.Lt.	Inishtrahull Lt.	180° x 4.0'	277°	2.9 hrs	44.0	2238
Inishtrahull Lt.	Cape Race	000° x 12.0'	269° Int. Co.	118.6 hrs	1780.0	458
Cape Race	Egg Island	000° x 9.4'	254°	28.7 hrs	430.0	28
Egg Island	Chebucto Hd.	270° x 3.0'	270°	1.8 hrs	27.0	1
Chebucto Hd.	Pilot Station	–	315°	0.1 hrs	1.0	0
Pilots Station	Berth* (To be advised)	–	Various to Masters Orders	1.0 hrs	*	
Total Distance					2442.5'	
Steaming Time		(excluding Halifax Pilot)		162.8 hrs = 6 days 18.8 hrs		
				Provisional ETA = XXXXXX		

Clocks to be retarded 4 hours from BST.

3. Passage Plan – Chart – Check-list

Without doubt the completed chart, which illustrates the proposed route, is the most central and the most essential visual presentation of the 'passage plan'. It is required to carry all items that could effect the safe navigation of the vessel, without obscuring relevant detail. The plan should reflect continuity which will allow all watch officers to take over the navigational duties and to this end will be required to indicate the following items:

1. Course tracks and distances with respective margins of safety.
2. Radar conspicuous targets should be prominent.
3. Projected ETA's at alter course positions.
4. Tidal streams with indicated maximum/minimum rates and directions.
5. Visible landmarks, transits or clearing bearings.
6. VHF calling/communication points.
7. Where expected use of the echo sounder would be anticipated.
8. Next chart indication to allow positional transfer.
9. Crossing traffic or known areas of heavy traffic density.
10. Traffic separation schemes and relevant references.
11. Those positions on route where extra personnel may be required.
12. Station call points for advising the Master, engine room, pilot stations etc.
13. Positions where anchors should be prepared.
14. Advance warning of potential hazards or dangers.
15. Raising/dipping ranges of lights that would aid position fixing methods.
16. Alternative position fixing methods for night or day passage.
17. Those positions where manual steering must be engaged.
18. Navigational warnings which might be currently effecting the chart.
19. Navigational radio aids and their accuracy within charted area.
20. Highlight 'NO GO AREAS'.

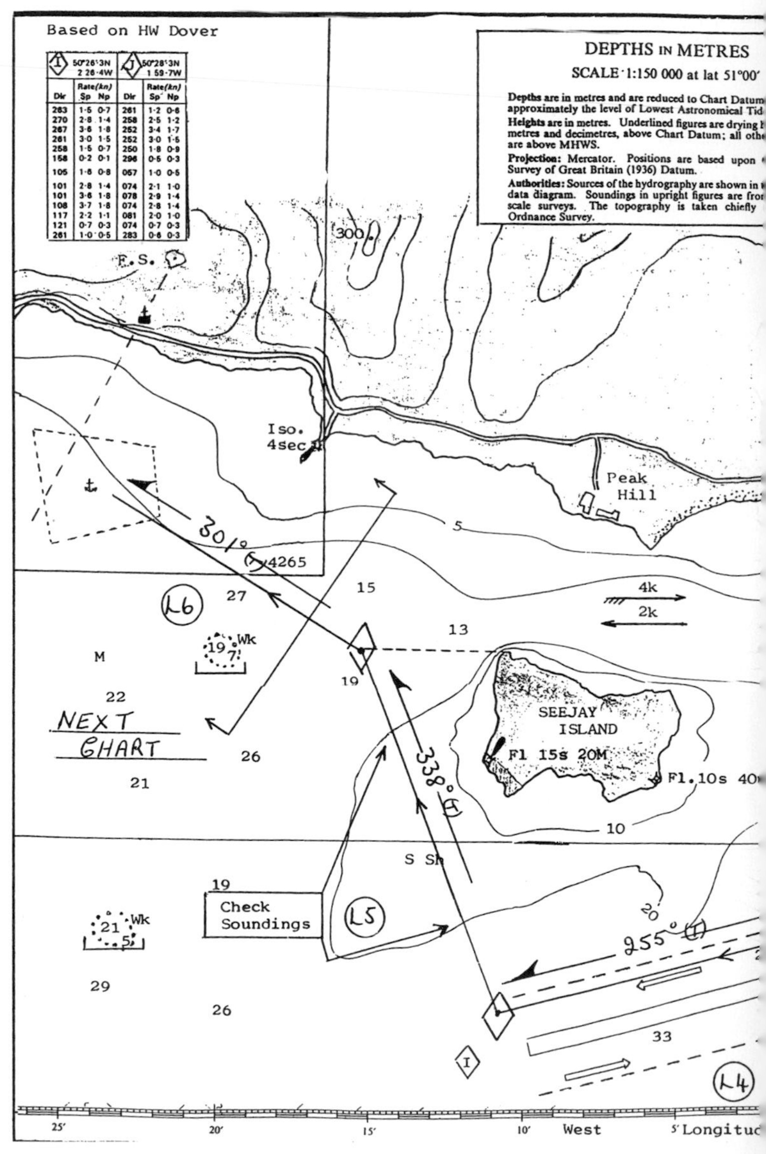

I 50°26'·3N 2 26·4W			J 50°28'·3N 1 59·7W		
Dir	Rate(kn) Sp	Np	Dir	Rate(kn) Sp	Np
283	1·5	0·7	261	1·2	0·6
270	2·8	1·4	258	2·5	1·2
267	3·6	1·8	252	3·4	1·7
261	3·0	1·5	252	3·0	1·5
258	1·5	0·7	250	1·8	0·9
158	0·2	0·1	296	0·5	0·3
105	1·6	0·8	067	1·0	0·5
101	2·8	1·4	074	2·1	1·0
101	3·6	1·8	078	2·9	1·4
108	3·7	1·8	074	2·8	1·4
117	2·2	1·1	081	2·0	1·0
121	0·7	0·3	074	0·7	0·3
261	1·0	0·5	283	0·6	0·3

Diagram 3.1:P

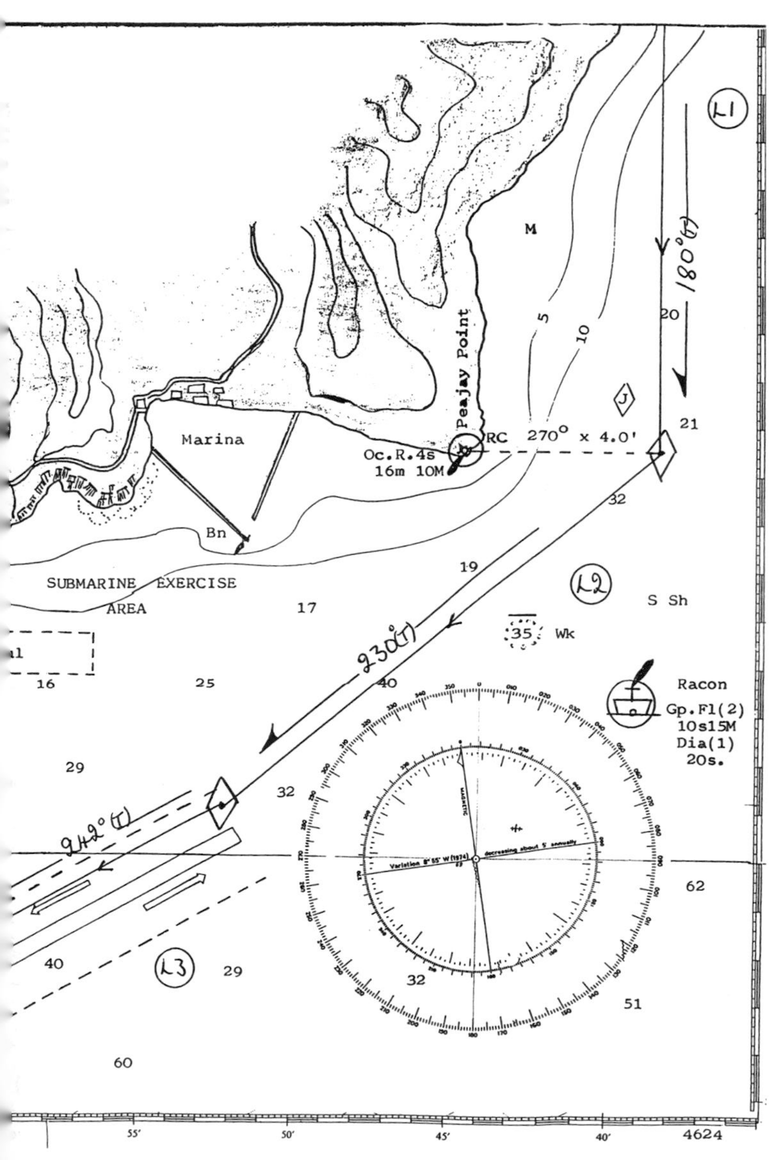

nning example

PASSAGE PLANNING FORMAT   Arrive/Depart/Transit ________   Date ________   Sheet No. ________

Bridge Manning

	1.	2.	3.	4.	5.	6.
Master			√	√	√	√
Pilot						
OOW (1)	√	√	√	√	√	√
OOW (2)						√
Helmsman		√	√	√	√	√
Lookout	√	√	√	√	√	√
Legs	1.	2.	3.	4.	5.	6.

VHF Channels

Port Control	12
Pilots	–
Tugs	–
Berth	–
CRS. (1)	16

High Waters

Place	Dover
Time	1320
Place	–
Time	–
Springs/Neaps	

Critical Depths

Anchorage approach

Draught	*7.0m*
Sunrise	*0605*
Sunset	*1956*

Arr/Dep Weather

Wind	W x 5
Sea	mod.
Vis.	good
Precip	nil
Outlook	fair

Remarks

Arrival Anchorage

Pass Leg Ref.	Positions	ETA/ Track Time	Track (T)	Tr/offset Tide/L'way	Course Gyro Mag/Comp	Distance	Engine Status	Ground Speed	U.K.C.	Pos'n Fix mthds	Remarks
L1.	Peajay Pt. 270° x 4.0'	1hr 12'	180°	nil	180° G.	12+	Full	10 kts	OK	Rad. Lt/ves.	Tide J
L2.	Lat. 50° 1' .2N Lg. 01° 52.3W	1hr 11'	230°	nil	230° G.	11.7	Full	10 kts	OK	Visuals Lt/ves. Peajay/ Pt.	–
L3.	Seejay Isle East Lt. 315° x 4.6'	0hr 36'	242°	nil	242° G.	6.2	Full	10 kts	OK	Vis/Rad Seejay Isle.	
L4.	Lat. 49° 56' .6N Lg. 02° 10' .8W	0hr 40'	255°	nil	255° G.	6.7	Full	10 kts	OK	Vis/Rad Seejay lights.	
L5.	Lat. 58° 04' N Lg. 02° 15.4W	0hr 48'	338°	L'way 3° W'ly wind	335° G.	8.0	SBE Man/Spd	10 kts	OK	Visuals Seejay- Nth. Hd. W. Ltd.	Echo Sound.
L6.	Anchorage	Est. 1hr 00'	301°	nil	301° G.	6.1	½ Ahd. Slow. Dd. Slow	5 kts	3m	Visual Transit	6 shackles cable

3.1.1 passage plan – appraisal

The operation is that carried out by the navigation officer which gathers together all relevant information that will benefit the future stages of the passage plan. Obviously certain items of information will require regular updating as the plan develops and becomes operational, e.g. weather reports or navigational warnings.

Much of the navigators information can be short and obtained from the official publications (see list, page 100). However, other items may be contained within the ships internal papers, as with manoeuvring information. While ships equipment may also be another valuable source of additional information, i.e. Navtex transmissions and the prognostic charts obtained from facsimile equipment.

Local knowledge of Pilots, harbour control and other experienced officers should be welcome whenever available in compiling the completed plan. However, local information should be cross checked against a second source and its reliability confirmed prior to its use within the plan.

Many navigators, in order to avoid oversight, often employ a 'check-list' for appraisal and if this is a method being used it should contain such topical investigation on:

Currents, tides and the relevant draught of the ship with the Under Keel Clearance (UKC) in mind. The navigational use of lights, beacons etc, and comparison of Admiralty List of Lights (ALL) and Admiralty List of Radio Signals (ALRS). Particular attention should be given to 'routing schemes' and the use of Traffic Separation Schemes (TSS).

The weekly notice to mariners is a valuable source of navigational information and includes the Temporary and Preliminary (T & P's) Notices that, if ignored, could be detrimental to the safety of any ship. A chart inspection would reveal the required charts and their availability. Navigators should check the correctness and ensure the Ps and Ts are entered if appropriate.

3.2 Use of Sequential Charts

The essential element of the plan will employ the navigator's greatest aid, the chart. During the appraisal period, sequential charts for the passage must be extracted from the relevant folios. This activity would, in the first instance, make full use of the Chart Catalogue.

The proposed route being related to the respective geographical areas of the catalogue and relevant chart numbers applicable to the proposed route can be identified. These chart numbers once listed from the catalogue will be in route order and as such in a general sequential order for the voyage, with the possible exception for port entry charts.

Individual charts to be employed would need to be checked for the latest corrections and also for being the most relevant chart, with the largest scale. These would subsequently be known as the working charts. Should any be missing, these must be ordered before sailing and sighted on board prior to the commencement of the voyage.

Summary

Navigation officers are advised that in planning a passage, especially into unfamiliar waters, that they will benefit considerably by asking questions. Nobody, especially a prudent Master, expects everyone to know all the answers, all of the time. Where questions and/or problems arise do not avoid the issue. People are, more often as not, pleased to be asked to assist with problems.

3.3 Passage Plan–Main Points for Masters Appraisal

When considering a navigators passage plan for approval the Master should take note of the following areas of concern:

1. That the largest scale charts have been employed.
2. That all charts used are corrected up to date
3. Ensure that all navigation warnings have been received and where applicable applied to the plan.
4. Ensure that relevant publications are on board and correct for the forthcoming voyage.
5. Estimated draughts are correct for different stages of the passage and that adequate under keel clearance is available throughout the passage.
6. That the chosen route has taken account of the climatological information for the areas associated weather patterns.
7. Consider the route for traffic flow and the volume of traffic that can expect to be encountered.
8. Ensure adequate coverage of position fixing methods, including the range and viable use of radio aids.

9. Take note of all pilotage positions or positions of high interest with regard to potential marine hazards.
10. Compare recommended route with sailing directions and routes advised by *Ocean Passages for the World*.
11. Assess with care all landfall positions for shallows, currents and other possible dangers.
12. Compare the qualities and capabilities of the vessel to ensure that manoeuvring characteristics, bunker capacity and speed capability will allow safe completion of the voyage.
13. The loadline regulations are not infringed.

When making up a plan for a voyage, some navigators will lack experience, especially if it is their first attempt. Both Masters and navigators are advised that the prime concern is for the safety of the vessel, 'throughout' the voyage. With this in mind navigators should not hesitate to seek advice even when an individual has ample experience. Neither should Masters seek to chastise a young officer for an obvious error of judgment in recommending a chosen route.

3.4 Passage Plan – Planning

The operation of actually constructing the 'plan' must include, 'pilotage water' and cover the total period, from 'berth-to-berth. One of the main functions of the plan is to highlight where the ship should NOT GO and in the construction and build up, this objective should not be lost by the Master or his navigation officer. To this end the charts employed should be of the largest scale available and should show:

1. The intended tracks, with margins for error. Be clearly identified with their respective three figure, numerical notation in a 'true heading'. Tracks should be clear of 'hazards' and laid-off at a safe distance and advance warning of all dangers should be readily visible to another watch keeper. When charting the intended track for the vessel, due regard should be made to the possibility of engine failure or steering gear malfunction.
2. Radar conspicuous targets – such as RAMARKS or RACONS, or buoys carrying radar reflectors, which could be gainfully employed in position fixing, should be well indicated.
3. Maximum use of 'transit marks' and clearing bearings should be included in the plan. Where radar is employed, clearing ranges may be used to distinct advantage.
4. Key elements of the plan – must take into account:
   (a) a safe speed throughout the passage, bearing in mind the

ships draught and the possibility of 'squat' and reduction in under keel clearance.
(b) critical areas where minimum under keel clearance can be maintained taking into account the state of tide.
(c) those alteration points where because of the ships turning circle, a wheel over position must be planned to be appropriate to the ships speed and to any tidal effects present.
(d) the reliability and necessity for accurate position fixing methods, both of a primary and secondary nature.
(e) planned contingency action in the event of deviation from the plan becoming necessary.

Summary

The plan should flow easily between way points and highlight hazards and dangers on route. It should not be over complicated with irrelevant material but reflect the essential detail for junior watch officers, Pilots and the Master to allow them clear understanding and visible continuity.

3.5 Passage Plan – Execution

The execution of any passage plan is the formulation of the tactics which are intended to carry the plan through. Consideration should therefore be given to the following specific topics:

- the reliability of ship's equipment, specifically the navigation equipment. Its condition and limitations together with its degree of accuracy. Account should also be given to the level of expertise of ships officers and whether they are familiar with that ship's type of equipment.

- the projection of ETA's towards critical points to allow a more detailed assessment of tide heights and flow. Under Keel Clearance (UKC) being a main consideration for the plans execution. By advancing the ETA, while on passage, the possibility of anticipating difficulties can often resolve problems before they arrive.

- meteorological conditions will be continually changing while the vessel is on passage. In order to maintain optimum passage time heavy seas and areas of reduced visibility need to be avoided, if at all possible. Historically and at certain seasons, specific areas are prone to 'fog' or 'bad-weather' conditions. If transit of these areas can be avoided or co-ordinated to coincide with daylight or similar suitable time, the overall safety aspects of the passage can be raised.

- day-time or night-time passage, especially when negotiating dangers or narrows, can often be achieved at a favourable time by early realisation and making an appropriate speed adjustment. Speed adjustments can of course be an increase in speed as well as a decrease in speed. However, if an increase in speed is employed, then the conditions should be appropriate and the contents of *Rule 6*, of the *Regulations for the Prevention of Collision at Sea*, noted.

- it should also be borne in mind that position fixing methods during the day and the night may well differ, e.g. the use of unlit headlands for visible bearings is not possible at night.

- traffic conditions, notably at navigational focal points like traffic separation schemes, or prominent geographic points, should also be considered in light of the projected ETA of the vessel. Speed adjustment can again be a prudent action to arrive at focal points at an appropriate time.

Summary

It has already been stated that no plan is rigid and by its nature, it must be flexible to suit changing conditions. The inclusion of contingency alternatives in many cases will prove to be that item which is not used. However, the plan that doesn't contain the contingency option is very often the one that turns out to need it most. In anticipation of navigational problems where additional personnel may be required to back up routine watch keeping duties, Masters should have suitable manpower routines available to handle all emergencies.

Passage Plan – Monitoring

The construction of the finished Passage Plan and the instigation of the plan in the execution phase are commendable in their own right. However, the Master of any vessel is posed with the question, "How does he know that the plan is being complied with, accurately"? The answer to the question is revealed by the progress of the vessel being monitored and visual confirmation that the plan is being drawn to a conclusion.

The monitoring of the vessels movements must therefore be 'close and continuous'. If and when problems are foreseen, or anticipated, the Master of the vessel should be informed to allow flexibility in the plan to accommodate possible deviations safely. Monitoring of shipboard equipment is common to monitoring the safe movement of the vessel and therefore to ensure continuity of safe navigational practice, recommended checks on navigation equipment should be made at the following times:

1. Prior to sailing and departure from the berth.
2. Prior to entering known hazardous areas or areas of specific dangers.
3. At regular and frequent intervals during passage time.

Reference is made to navigators and watchkeepers to consult the '*Bridge Procedures Guide*'.

3.7 Position fixing:

All the navigational equipment of a vessel is at the disposal of watchkeepers and should be used to maximum advantage whenever possible. However, the principles of efficient watchkeeping should not be lost in the hi-tech world of satellite systems. Visual bearings are still considered the most accurate and reliable means of fixing the ships position, provided fixes are based on three position lines. Bear in mind that the use of GPS, Radar, Loran or other instrument systems are liable to instrument or operator error. This is not to say that they should not be used. On the contrary, instruments may be the only method of position fixing available, as with a vessel in poor visibility.

Navigators, should use alternate position fixing methods to avoid a possible continuous operator/observer error. Full use should also be made of the echo sounder when practical, to provide corresponding data checks on obtained fixes.

The frequency of fixing the vessels position will depend on the geography and the circumstances prevailing. Obviously certain areas of navigation for the vessel will require more position checks than others and the frequency of charting fixes will be dictated by the prevailing conditions.

Buoys should not be used for fixing the vessels position but may be found to be useful as checks when fixed objects are not available. Transits and clearing bearings can also be gainfully employed in providing margins of safety for the vessel. The use of parallel indexing has grown over the years and has proved itself to be a reliable and effective method of monitoring the ships progress.

Summary

To complete the principles of passage planning, monitoring is the essential action which illustrates the safe progress of the vessel. Regular, alternative primary and secondary position fixing methods, must be the order of the day.

3.8 Errors in Position Fixing

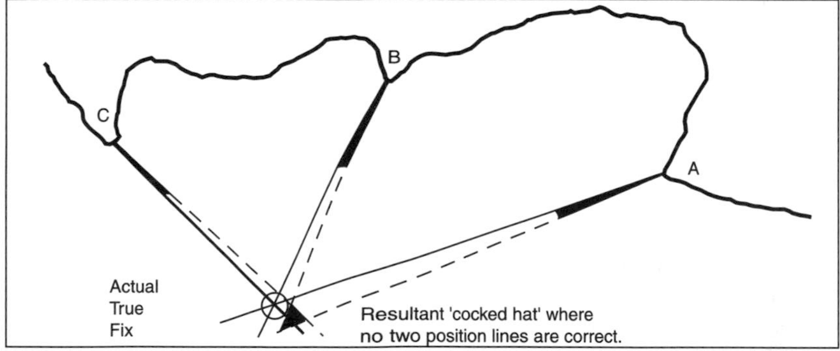

Example 1. Diagram 3.2: Fixed error on compass or regular observer error:

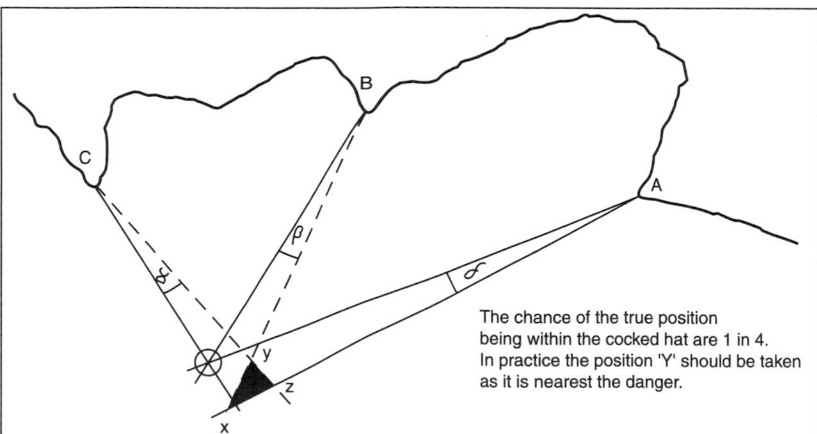

Example 2. Diagram 3.3: Variable errors in bearings:

(NB: If the variable error on bearing 'A' passed through 'Z' then an incorrect but perfect plot is obtained. Random/variable errors because of:)

1. Observational error.
2. Changes in compass error for different bearings (i.e. compass card not steady).

Distance off by Vertical Angle

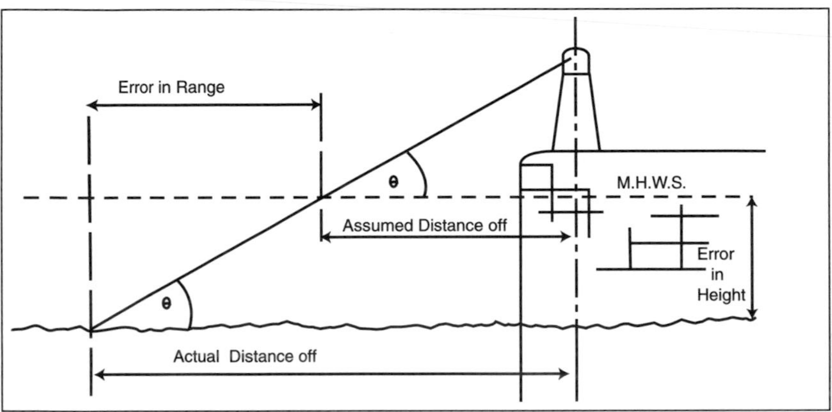

Example 3. Diagram 3.4: Error in distance by vertical angle

Inaccuracy in this method of fixing is due to:

1. Errors in the measured angle **θ**.
2. Errors in the height above sea level being employed.
3. Plotting and computing the error.

Example figures illustrate error in range. (Use of distance by vertical angle tables employed, found in *Norrie's Nautical Tables*).

Assume a vessel observes a lighthouse 13 metres high and obtains a vertical angle of 0° 24' when at the time of high water. If the range of tide is 10 metres and the same vertical angle is observed at low water time, what would the two ranges be?

HW (Assumed MHWS)		*LW* (Tide 10m)	
Object	13.0m.	Object	23.0m.
Vert. Sex't Angle	0° 24'	Vert. Sex't Angle	0° 24'
Range by table	1.0 n.mile	Range by table	1.75 n.mile

If the state of the tide is not taken into account the error in this example would therefore fall anywhere between 1.0 nautical mile and 1.75 nautical miles.

Range of error 0.75 n.mile

Height above sea level, caused by draught or trim of the vessel could also effect the result in a similar manner.

Postion Line Errors

1. Errors arising from an incorrect course being used. Incorrect course used because of wind effects or unknown currents, compass fault etc.

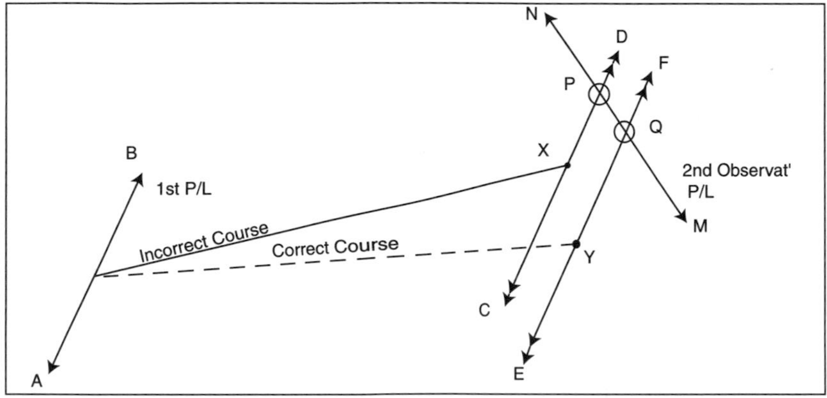

Example 4. Diagram 3.5: Errors in the use of transferred position lines.

Transferred P/L incorrectly drawn through position 'X'. If correct course is used, transferred P/L should pass through 'Y'. Error in the fix is 'PQ' where position 'Q' is correct fix.

2. Errors arising from incorrect distance being employed between 1st/2nd P/L's.

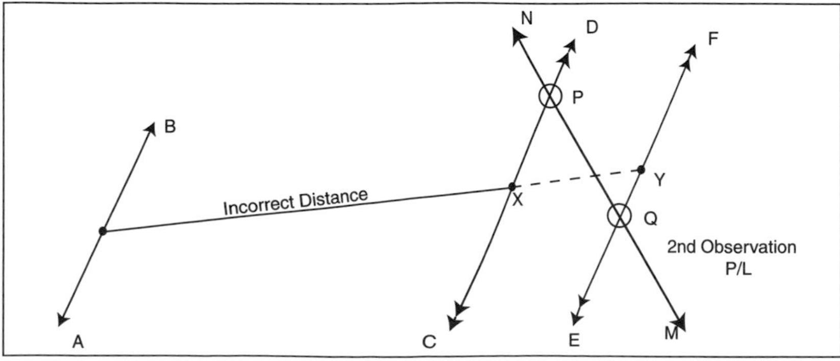

Example 4. Diagram 3.6: Errors in the use of transferred position lines.

3.9 The Use of Horizontal Sextant Angles

The impossible fix – when the three objects and the ship, all lie on the same position circle, (con-cyclic). Both constructed position circles would be coincident.

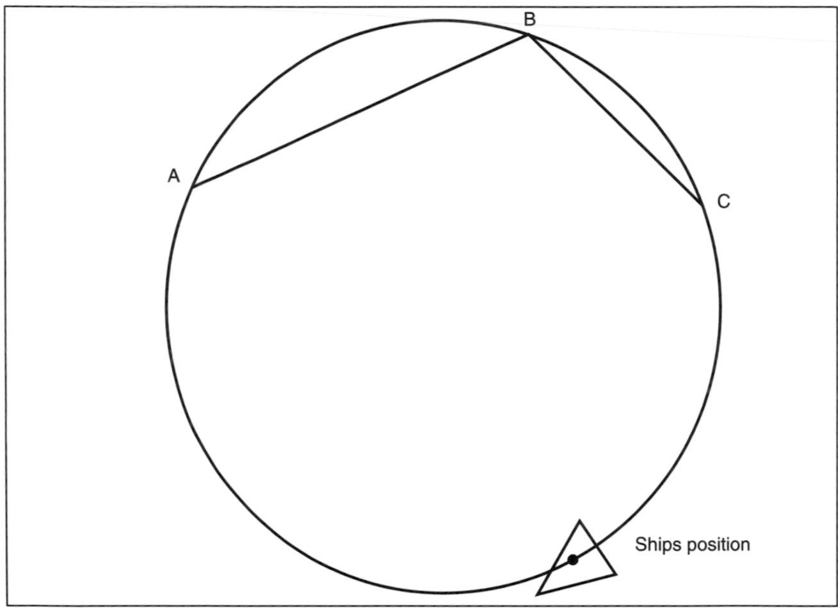

Example 5. Diagram 3.7: The impossible fix.

Notable errors when employing horizontal sextant angles:

1. Errors in angular measurement from instrument.
2. Plotting errors, (especially when angles exceed 90º).
3. Errors due to the three objects not being in the same plane.

Unsatisfactory fixes:

1. When the distance to the middle object is large, (from the ship).
2. When the angle of cut of the position circles is small.
3. Using the compass for obtaining difference in bearings when the ship is rolling heavily and the compass is unsteady.

Errors in astronomical position lines

1. An error in GMT at time of observation:

   An error in the GMT will cause an error in the GHA value. e.g. A four second error in GMT causes 1' error in GHA, therefore in Longitude.

Longitude = LHA – GHA

This would result in an error of 1 mile in the intercept, when

(a) The observed body is on the 'prime vertical' and the position line is N/S.

(b) When the ship is on the Equator and D. Long = departure.

If the vessel is not on the Equator but the position line is still north/south the intercept error can be expected to reduce in the same way as departure is reduced for a given D. Long.

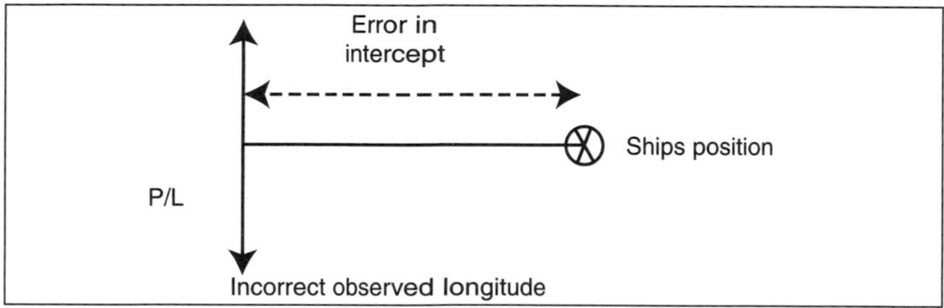

Example 6 Diagram 3.8a: Intercept error from use of incorrect longitude.

For the same error in GMT the intercept error would be further reduced when the position line it not north/south.

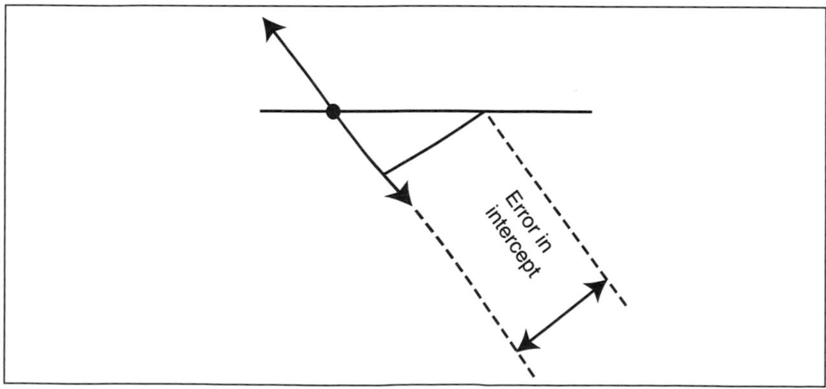

Example 6 Diagram 3.8b: Intercept error from use of incorrect GMT.

2. In working a sight the chronometer error was taken as 20 seconds slow instead of 20 seconds fast, when in DR position latitude 35° 00' N longitude 70° 00' W. The bearing of the body was 140°T and the obtained intercept was 1.8' away. What was the correct intercept?

Scale 1 cm = 1'

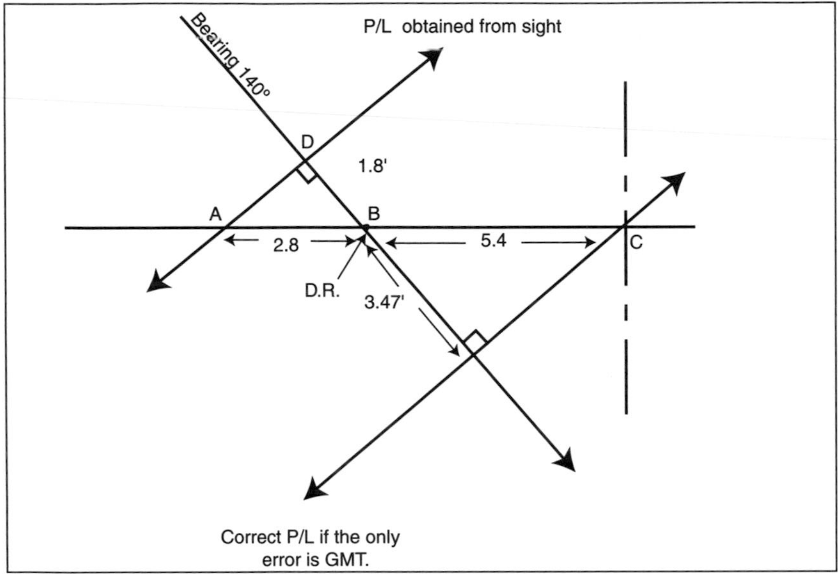

Example 6 Diagram 3.9: An example of an intercept.

Long (W) = GHA – LHA

Error is 40 seconds fast

Therefore GHA is 10' to large.

Therefore observed longitude is 10' too large.

By traverse tables or right angled trigonometry in lat. 35°N:

D. Long. 10'; Departure = 8.2'

In Triangle ABD, Angle 'D' is a right angle.

Angle A = Course 40°, DB = 1.8', AB = 2.8'

Therefore BC = 5.4'

Correct intercept = 3.47' towards

Position fixing – errors and reliability

In all passage plans the action of monitoring the plan is essential and the use of navigational instruments play a major part. It is especially so when visual fixes are not possible, either because of poor visibility or extreme range of targets. The use of instruments as an aid has become normal practice but navigators should be aware of human error and the overall standards of accuracy when they are employed.

Many instruments operate in conjunction with the ships speed and this must be an accepted variable depending on the conditions. Higher standards of accuracy are also desired at different stages of the voyage:

i.e. Harbour entrances and approaches as compared to open deep waters.

If mid-ocean navigation is compared to the ships navigation when making a landfall, then the availability of any system, together with its accuracy should, be considered.

Example 7. Astronomical navigation compared to Loran 'C' and satellite navigation in mid ocean.

Astronomical Navigation — Restricted and will vary with weather conditions. Clarity of the horizon and the availability of the celestial body will determine the possibility of a fix. Cloud cover and density could well obscure the sun, planets and stars when most needed.

Loran 'C' not available in large areas of ocean.

Satellite Navigational System — Position fixing may not always be available due to satellite or system faults. Otherwise availability of GPS is considered good for all areas.

The accuracy of these systems will vary but in general the following figures may be considered reasonable:

Astronomical navigation, in good conditions, should deliver a fix within +/–5 nautical miles. Considered adequate for mid-ocean passage but cannot be relied upon for landfall position fixing, at a specific time.

Satellite navigation system should provide fixes to +/–20 metres. This accuracy is obtainable in all areas irrespective of position.

Loran 'C' is not a world wide operation but where it is active good fixes can be obtained up to 1200 miles (ground wave) from station. Sky wave fixes are also possible. A degree of skill is required by the observer to gain improved accuracy. Accuracy of ¼ – 1 nautical mile is usually achievable with groundwave reception; this accuracy falls dramatically when only skywave transmissions are received.

Example 8. Eurofix

This is an integrated radio navigation and communication system. It combines defined satellite broadcast signals that are used for ranging and data transmission. The ranging being determined by use of a GPS receiver to measure the distance from the user to the satellite. (i.e. the propagation time between the satellite and the receiver). Positional accuracy has been improved with differential navigational techniques reducing position estimates to between 1 to 5 metres, depending on the area of operation.

Loran 'C', with a number of station broadcasts, high power (250 - 2500 kW) pulses in the 100 kHz band. Accuracy of this signal is (100 to 300 metres) depending on the geometry of the stations and the position of the user. The 'Eurofix' system employs the Loran 'C' signals as the carrier and provides the user with virtual DGPS positional accuracy. In the event of either GPS or Loran failure within the system, the level of accuracy of about 100 to 300 metres is still retained.

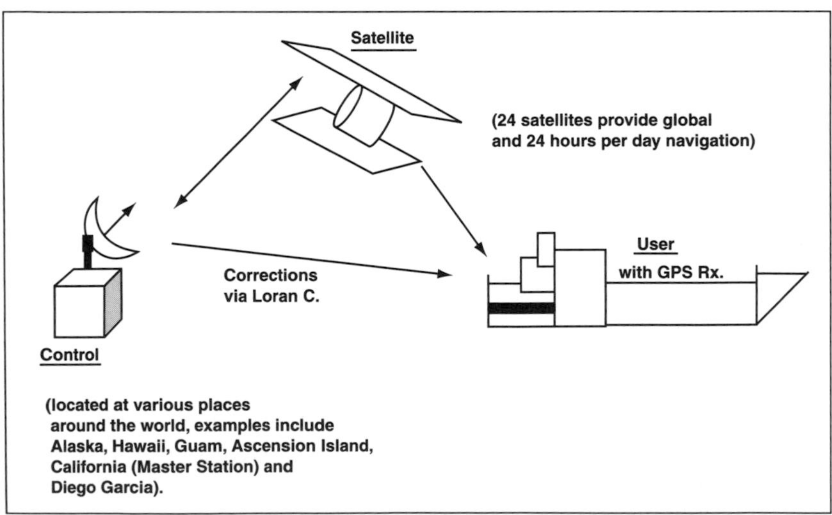

Diagram 3.10: Functional elements of eurofix.

3.10 Landfall Hazards and Coastal Navigation Practice

Nowhere is it more important to have accurate position monitoring than when making a landfall after an ocean passage. It would not be unusual for the Master to leave clear, unequivocal 'Standing Orders' for watch officers regarding procedures for making a landfall. These tend to emphasise the importance placed on tight position monitoring to ensure that associated hazards are not encountered unexpectedly. Navigation officers should be aware that when early approach to a landfall is being made, all available means, including celestial observations, should be employed to accurately fix the ships position, at regular intervals.

When on direct approach to the landfall the following is advised:

1. Use the largest scale chart available for the approach period.
2. Inspect the chart for adequate under keel clearance on the intended track.
3. Employ primary and secondary position fixing systems at regular intervals.
4. Have the echo sounder operational and monitor the actual under keel clearance.
5. Avoid use of low lying islands and employ prominent Radar Conspicuous targets.
6. Check nautical/geographic publications for recognition features.
7. Avoid the use of floating marks (i.e. Lamby's) if possible.
8. Avoid the focal traffic points or high density shipping areas if possible.
9. Employ a rising distance if and when approaching a lighthouse feature.
10. Avoid strong current affected areas where possible, if not possible, take account of set and drift elements.
11. Beware of the effects of haze, low cloud or ice formations.
12. Avoid areas with a reputation of poor visibility.
13. To approach so as not to make a landfall on a potential 'Lee shore'.
14. Standing orders to specify calling the Master in the event of:
    a) making the landfall unexpectedly
    b) not making the landfall as scheduled.
15. Include contingency within the passage plan for incorrect landfall in all states of weather conditions, or day/night periods of encounter.

3.11 Coastal Navigation and Communication Practice

3.11.1 objectives and procedures of a VTS operation
(VTS – Vessel Traffic Service/System)

The prime objective of any VTS operation is to improve safety and efficiency of marine traffic movement and protect the environment within the area of the authority. In order to carry out a service to vessels engaged within the area, the authority would require the following elements:

a) the organisational infrastructure to be in place.
b) a suitably skilled and trained work force to execute VTS operations.
c) effective communications through to all elements.
d) compliance by participating vessels and associated organisations.

3.11.2 the function of the VTS

Through communications the function of any VTS operation is to:

1. Collect data from all relevant parties including ships within the system and such allied services as pilotage or emergency participants.
2. Evaluate any data collected through ship reports or from allied services.
3. Provide an information service to all participating units.
4. Provide a navigational assistance programme to vessels engaged within the operational area.
5. Engage with and provide a traffic organisational service. (e.g.sailing schedules)
6. Support associated/allied parties, namely; pollution control, pilotage services, Port Authorities, rescue and emergency services, etc.

NB. Any VTS message directed towards a vessel must make it clear that the message is containing either:

Information, advice or an instruction.

Many areas of the globe operate acceptable traffic control systems and effective examples can be found around: Vancouver, St. Lawrence River towards Montreal, English Channel, Malacca Straits, Panama Canal etc.,

Additional Reference should be made to the IMO Resolution A.578 (14) *'Guidelines for Vessel Traffic Services'*.
Also to *MGN 239 & 240 & 242 (M & F)*

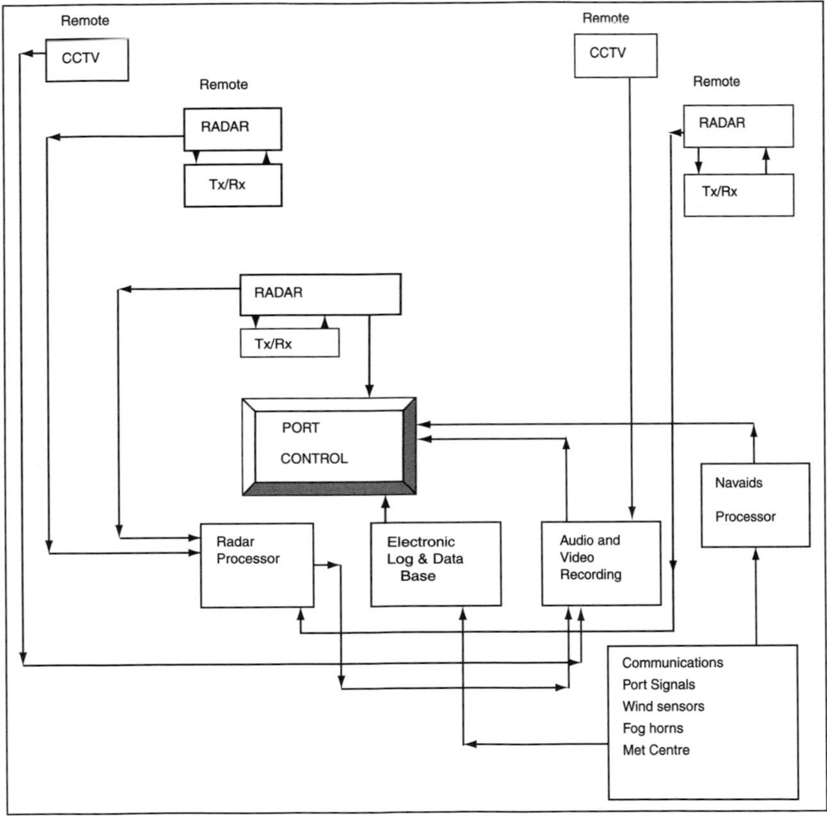

Diagram 3.11: VTS Co-ordination and Control Elements.

3.12 Navigation Through the English Channel and Dover Straits

Introduction

The English Channel and the approaches to the Dover Straits is probably the busiest waterway in the world. General advice on navigation practice is detailed in the two channel sailing directions and a further volume is concerned directly with the area of the Dover Straits themselves. Relevant information is also found in *Ocean Passages for the World (NP136)* and relevant 'M' notices also apply.

The need for extreme caution when either inbound or outbound to UK or continental ports is obvious when one considers the sheer volume of traffic. Therefore there is a need to carry out detailed navigation in accord with the Regulations for the Prevention of Collision at Sea, and monitor the ships progress continually during transit. Special reference being made to Admiralty Chart No. 5500. (Passage Plan – Advice).

The attention of mariners, is particularly drawn to the many traffic separation schemes operating inside the confines of the English Channel. Especially those which lead into and pass through the Dover Straits. Radar surveillance is in operation in this area and vessels contravening traffic control directions can expect to be monitored. Masters and ship's officer of through traffic are further advised by charted warnings that:

"While vessels using the traffic lanes must in particular comply with Rule 10, of the International Collision Regulations (COLREGS), they are not thereby given any right of way over crossing vessels. The other steering and sailing rules still apply in all respects, particularly if risk of collision exists".

The reality of navigation in this area is one which can be somewhat daunting to even the most experienced mariner and potential hazards are highlighted in the following text. The need for flexible and comprehensive passage planning to cope with established dangers and to cater for changing 'natural conditions' is essential.

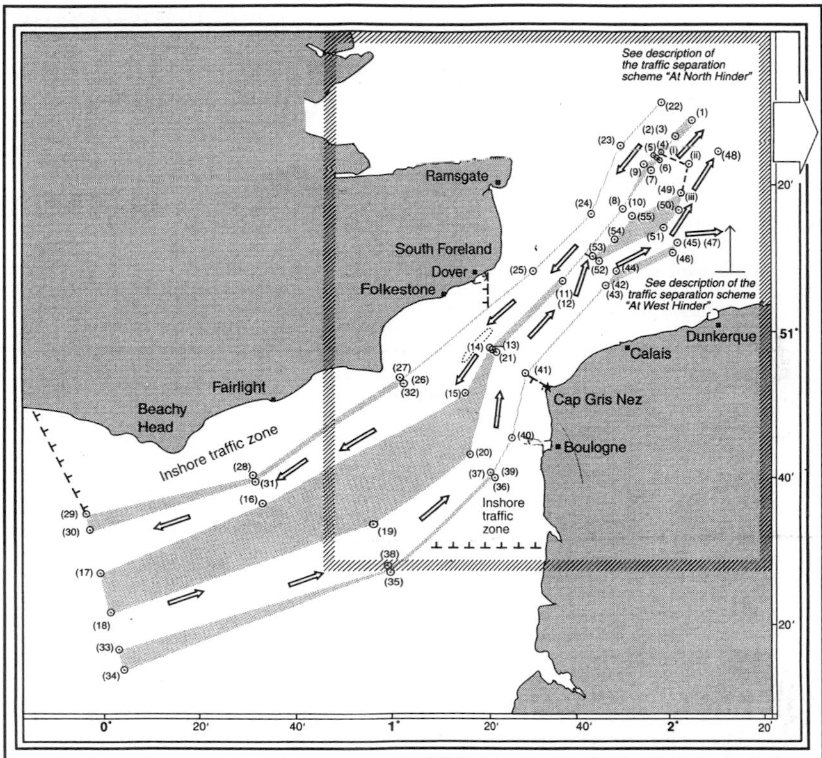

Diagram 3.12: Traffic flow and movement through the Dover Straits.

The above excerpt from the IMO publication Ship's Routing has been reproduced with the kind permission of the International Maritime Organization (IMO) London.

MARINE GUIDANCE NOTE

MGN 200 (M+F)

Observance of Traffic Separation Schemes

Note to Shipowners, Masters and all concerned with the Navigation of Seagoing Vessels

This note supersedes Marine Guidance Notice 28

Summary

The International Regulations for Preventing Collisions at Sea 1972 as amended, govern the conduct of all vessels in and near Traffic Separation Schemes (TSSs) which have been adopted by the IMO.

1. Rule 10 of the International Regulations for Preventing Collisions at Sea 1972 as amended, governs the conduct of all vessels in and near Traffic Separation Schemes which have been adopted by the International Maritime Organization (IMO). The Regulations are to be found in Merchant Shipping Notice No. M.1642/COLREG 1.

Application

2. Rule 10(a). It is important to note that this Rule only applies to schemes which have been adopted by IMO. In other schemes local regulations may apply, and these may modify not only Rule 10 but also, in some cases, other Steering and Sailing Rules. Admiralty charts show schemes established by competent national authorities but do not differentiate between IMO-adopted schemes and unadopted ones. The charts carry a note to this effect, advising mariners to refer to Annual Notice to Mariners No. 17 which lists all charted schemes and indicates which are IMO-adopted. Changes to ANM No. 17 are promulgated in the weekly editions of Admiralty Notices to Mariners. The charts also have notes referring to the existence of special provisions associated with certain schemes which may govern their use by certain classes of vessel. Sailing Directions should be consulted for these special provisions. Masters of deep-draught vessels should note that the existence of a scheme does not imply that the traffic lanes have been adequately surveyed. Charted depths and source data diagrams (if available) should be studied when planning a passage where depths are critical (Schemes introduced or amended after April 1989 are only adopted once the IMO is satisfied with the adequacy of hydrographic surveys). Traffic Separation Schemes are usually sited where there is a heavy concentration of shipping. Mariners are therefore reminded of the particular importance of strictly adhering to Rules 5-8 which refer to Look-out, Safe Speed, Risk of Collision, and Action to Avoid Collision. Mariners are also reminded that except where there are special local rules to the contrary, the other Steering and Sailing Rules – those of Section II when vessels are in sight of one another and that of Section III in restricted visibility – apply within a scheme as they do elsewhere at sea.

By virtue of using the traffic lane through vessels do not have any priority over crossing or joining traffic.

Procedure within a Traffic Lane

3. Rule 10(b) and (c). All vessels using a traffic lane must conform to the essential principles of routeing. If they are following the lane they must proceed in the general direction of traffic flow and if they are crossing it they must do so on a heading as nearly as practicable at

right angles to that direction. Vessels should normally join or leave a traffic lane at its termination, however they may join or leave from either side of a lane provided they do so at as small an angle as possible to the general direction of traffic flow. The same procedure with certain exemptions, as stated in Rule 10(k) and (l), applies to vessels which are within a lane for purposes other than for passage through or across it, such as vessels engaged in fishing, if they are making way; it is appreciated that such vessels cannot always maintain a steady course and speed but their general direction of movement must be in accordance with this principle. Any substantial departure from this direction by any vessel is only allowed if it is required by overriding circumstances, such as the need to comply with other Steering and Sailing Rules or because of extreme weather conditions. Particular attention is drawn to the requirement that vessels which must cross a traffic lane shall do so on a heading as nearly as practical at right angles to the direction of traffic flow. Steering at right angles keeps the time a crossing vessel is in the lane to a minimum irrespective of the tidal stream, and leads to a clear encounter situation with through vessels.

Inshore Zones

4. Rule 10(d). Vessels other than those of less than 20 metres in length, sailing vessels, vessels engaged in fishing, and vessels en route to or from a destination within an Inshore Traffic Zone, should if it is safe to do so use the appropriate adjacent traffic lane. It does not preclude traffic under stress of weather from seeking protection of a weather shore within such a zone nor does it impose any specific behaviour on vessels within an inshore zone and traffic heading in any direction may be encountered. Within the context of this Rule it is the view of the MCA that the density of traffic in a lane is not sufficient reason by itself to justify the use of an inshore zone, nor will the apparent absence of traffic in the inshore zone qualify as a reason for not complying with this Rule.

Anchoring within a Separation Zone

5. Rule 10 (e) and (g). The question has arisen as to whether a vessel which needs to anchor because, for example, of an engine breakdown or bad visibility, may do so in a separation zone. In the view of the MCA this would be a seaman like manoeuvre and is allowed for under paragraph (e) (i).

Vessels not using a Scheme

6. Rule 10 (h). The existence of a Scheme does not mean that it is obligatory to use it, if its use appears unsafe due to prevailing conditions or the size or state of the vessel. In these circumstances the Master should consider an alternative route and avoid the Scheme by as wide a margin as is practicable.

Fishing Vessels

7. Rule 10(b), (c), (e) and (i). Vessels fishing within a Scheme are considered to be using the Scheme and must therefore, when working in a traffic lane, conform to the essential principles laid down in Rules 10(b) and (c) as discussed above. When fishing in a separation zone they may follow any course. The requirement that vessels fishing must not impede through traffic means that they must not operate in such a manner that they, or their gear, seriously restrict the sea room available to other vessels within a lane. Rule 8(f) places further obligations upon fishing vessels with regard to their responsibility not to impede vessels following a traffic lane and this obligation remains in a developing situation where risk of collision is involved. When taking any action they must however take account of the possible manoeuvres of the vessel which is not to be impeded.

Sailing Vessels and Small Craft

8. Rule 10(j). Vessels of less than 20 metres in length and sailing vessels shall not impede traffic following a traffic lane and the same obligations as are set out for fishing vessels in paragraph 7 similarly to apply to them. No specific mention is made in the Rule of a sailing vessel having an auxiliary engine, but it is the view of the MCA that if such a vessel cannot follow the routeing procedures under sail because of light or adverse winds, then she should make use of her engines in order to do so.

Vessels engaged in Safety of Navigation Operations

9. Rule 10(k). Vessels engaged in operations for the safety of navigation of the Scheme e.g.

buoy laying, wreck removing, or hydrographic surveying if restricted in their ability to manoeuvre, are exempt from the provisions of Rule 10 to the extent necessary to carry out the operation. This exemption does not extend to vessels engaged in other survey activities in a Scheme.

Cable Laying Operations

10. Rule 10(l). Vessels engaged in cable operations, if restricted in their ability to manoeuvre, are exempt from the provisions of Rule 10 to the extent necessary to carry out the operation.

Precautionary Areas

11. Many Schemes have precautionary areas associated with them where traffic lanes cross or converge so that proper separation of traffic is not possible. Precautionary areas are not part of a traffic separation scheme and Rule 10 is not generally applicable. Ships should navigate with particular caution within such areas. Precautionary areas should be avoided, if practicable, by ships not making use of the associated Schemes or deep-water routes.

Signal – YG

12. It is important that any vessel observed in a Scheme which appears to be navigating otherwise than in accordance with the established principles of such Schemes is advised of the fact at the time. A special signal exists for this purpose: the two letter signal YG meaning "you appear not to be complying with the traffic separation scheme".

13. The master of any vessel receiving this signal by whatever means should take immediate action to check his course and position and take any further steps which appear to him appropriate in the circumstances.

14. Marine Guidance Note MGN 128 (Navigation in the Dover Strait) is complementary to this note.

Communication and Innovation Branch
Maritime & Coastguard Agency
Spring Place
105 Commercial Road
Southampton
SO15 1EG

Tel 02380 329394
Fax 02380 329204
www.mcga.gov.uk

April 2002

Ref: MNA 5/50/294

Safer Lives, Safer Ships, Cleaner Seas

An executive agency of the Department for Transport, Local Government and the Regions

3.13 Use of Traffic Separation Schemes (TSS)

The IMO published routing guide, "Ships Routing", details adopted schemes around the worlds marine coastlines. Such routing operations are often monitored by 'Radar Surveillance' operated by various Coastguard Organisations. It should be realised that heavy penalties exist for traffic observed to be in contravention of these operations. As such, Masters should ensure that their respective Passage Plans comply with the TSS recommendations and that the movement of the vessel conforms to Regulation 10, of the Anti-Collision Regulations.

In areas where the TSS forms an essential element of a traffic focal point, like the English Channel and in particular the Dover Strait or Malacca Straits, the importance of adequate watchkeeping facilities must be in place, alongside any passage through the scheme. Passage plans should provide positive indication where manual steering, double lookouts, speed changes, Masters presence required, contingencies etc. are likely to form a critical factor of the vessels continued safe movement.

Not all Traffic Schemes have been adopted by IMO and local schemes (Non-adopted) are often established by competent national authorities to suit the specific geographic locations. Masters should note that British Admiralty Charts do not differentiate between adopted and non-adopted schemes. Notice No. 17 of the Annual Summary of Notices to Mariners lists the traffic schemes shown on Admiralty Charts. The adopted schemes being identified by an asterisk (*) mark in the margin of the Notice. Charts containing TSS operations would also carry a reference to the listing in Notice No. 17.

Other publications like the respective Sailing Directions, Mariners Handbook, and special passage plan/route charts (5500) carry specific guidance to correct use of the schemes. From time to time the schemes themselves are amended in the interests of Navigation Safety and such amendments are advised through the 'Weekly Notices to Mariners' Additional information is also obtainable from the Navigation and Information Branch of the Maritime and Coastguard Agency (MCA) at Southampton, U.K.

3.14 Amended Traffic Separation Scheme (around 'Ouessant')

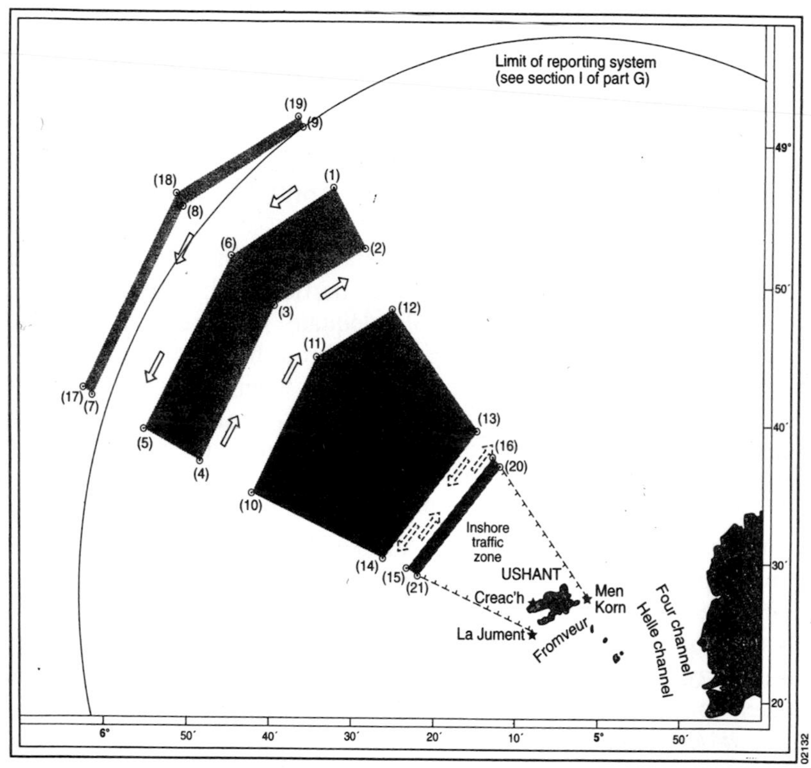

Diagram 3.13: Revised TSS arrangement about 'Ushant' entering and leaving the English Channel.

The above system was set up in 1977 and was amended in 1978 and 1979. The 28 mile range, off the coastline, (1979 amendment) was originally included for vessels carrying hydrocarbons and toxic chemicals. The new scheme will employ two main lanes, each 9 kilometres wide. One southbound at 34 miles and the other Northbound at 24 miles off the coastline. A third bi-directional lane (10 miles off) will operate exclusively for 'Coastal Traffic'.

Masters of Deep Draught vessels are also advised by the Annual Summary, that the existence of a Traffic Separation Scheme does not imply that the traffic lanes have been adequately surveyed and charted depths, where critical, should be confirmed by cross reference to other sources when planning their passage. (Source Data diagrams on the chart may prove re-assuring in this matter.)

The existence of a separation scheme does not mean there is an obligation to use it. Regulation 10, (h) of the anti-collision regulations advises that a vessel not using a TSS shall avoid the scheme by as wide a margin as is practicable. In such cases Masters should consider alternative routes that may provide a safer passage, bearing in mind the circumstances and conditions of individual cases.

NB. With the advent of Automatic Ship Identification and reporting System (AIS), mariners are advised that it is anticipated that this new system may eventually replace VHF manual reporting and influence VTS operations. Although the whole of the United Kingdom is provided with this reporting system, at the time of writing, the operation has not yet been adopted. Additional reference should be made to Notice No.,17A, of the Annual Summary of Notices to Mariners).

3.15 IMO Routing Objectives

The routing of ships, from any point of view, must reflect the safe operation of traffic guidance around the globe. As such all systems are expected to conform to the IMO Objectives. These objectives are found in the Routing Manual and are applicable to Ocean Voyage Planning as well as the VTS operations around coast lines:

1. The separation of opposing streams of traffic to reduce 'head on' incidence.
2. Reduce the dangers of Collision between crossing traffic in established shipping lanes.
3. Simplify the patterns of flow in converging areas.
4. Organise safe traffic flow in areas of 'Offshore Exploration'.
5. Organisation of traffic flow around areas where navigation by all ships or classes of certain ships is dangerous and undesirable. (e.g. Class 7T, A1 Ice Class, Deep Draught).
6. Organisation of safe traffic flow in or clear of environmentally sensitive areas.
7. Reduce the risk of grounding where depths are critical.
8. Guidance of traffic clear of fishing grounds or through fishing grounds.

NB. Safe routes are those that reduce the risk of casualties, inclusive of TSS, two way routes, inshore routes, deep water routes, roundabouts and recommended tracks.

3.16 Position Fixing Methods

There is generally no shortage of navigational landmarks for the purpose of position fixing throughout the length of the channel. The use of visual bearings, provided the state of visibility permits, remains adequate on both the French and English sides, especially when vessels are operating within the Inshore Traffic zones.

IMO also recommends that all ships of 300 grt and over which use the English Channel/Dover Straits should be fitted with electronic position fixing equipment.

Extensive use of radar conspicuous targets is made by all vessels which take passage through the English Channel. Many buoys carry Racons and/or fitted with radar reflectors to assist radar use. Radar surveillance combined with VHF can also be employed to provide position fixing assistance but extreme caution should be used in the use of VHF to ensure that correct station identification takes place.

GPS coverage is also readily available in this area. (Navigators should note prevailing charted errors).

Watch Officers are further advised that full use of the ships echo sounder should be used, with alternative position fixing methods being employed, in order to provide additional checks on fixes.

Traffic separation schemes are generally well charted and marked clearly by the IALA 'A' buoyage scheme. Masters and navigators should, however, note that vessels inbound to the Thames/London area can expect to encounter both local and general directions of buoyage.

Prevailing weather conditions may make the use of Dead Reckoning (D.R.) necessary. The reliability of the use of D.R. must be questionable because of the variable current flow either side of high water time. This is not to say that D.R. cannot be employed with other position fixing methods. It should also be realised that current stream values are predictions in both inshore areas and mid-channel areas. The exactness of such predictions can expect to fluctuate with changing conditions of the day.

Use of the Admiralty Tidal Stream Atlas for the English Channel is recommended to navigators engaged on passage planning or projecting ETA's.

BUOYAGE – Approaches to London, Thames Estuary

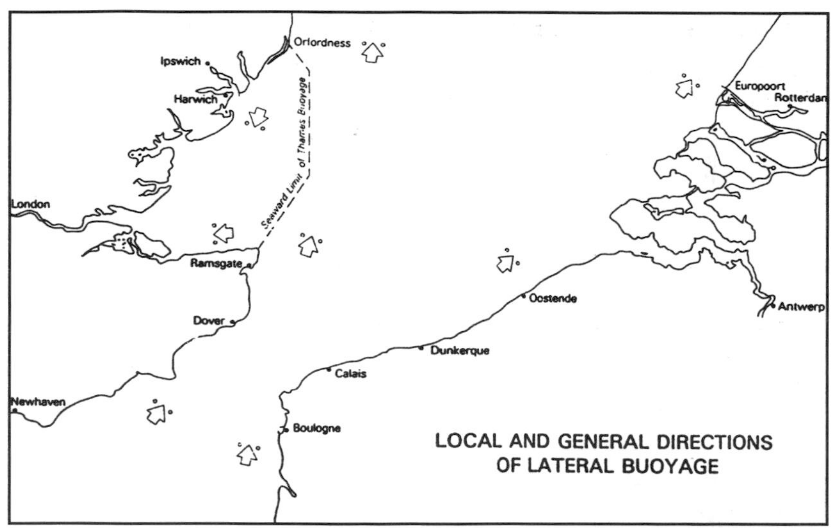

Diagram 3.14: Local and general direction of buoyage

3.17 Communications

Extensive communications exist for the benefit of marine traffic in transit through or towards ports in the English Channel. A ship reporting system is in operation known as MAREP and is a compulsory system for vessels using the Traffic Separation Schemes around Ouessant, Casquets, Dover Strait and Inshore Traffic Zones. It is applicable to all vessels but in particular to the following vessels:

1. Laden tankers and vessels carrying dangerous cargoes in bulk, as specified by the International Convention for the Prevention of Pollution from ships (MARPOL '73)
2. Any vessel that finds herself in a 'not under command' situation where she has to anchor in a TSS or inshore traffic zone.
3. Any vessel that is defined as being 'restricted in ability' to manoeuvre.
4. Any vessel with defective navigational aids/equipment.

French regulations that all tankers defined in (1) report via CROSSMA Cape Gris-Nez, when navigating north eastward through the Dover

Strait or when using the inshore traffic zone. Tankers are also required to maintain continuous VHF listening watch when in French territorial waters.

Ref. Cht 5500, ALRS Vol. 6., and Channel Sailing Directions.

3.18 Channel Navigation Information Service (CNIS)

The information service provides scheduled broadcasts together with additional information on request in an area from the Greenwich Meridian up to the West Hinder Lightship (Lat 51° 23' N Long 2° 26' E). Ref. ALRS Vol. 6.

The contents of broadcasts includes navigational and traffic information. Cross channel ferry activity is not normally mentioned.

Sources of the information are varied but may include aircraft reports concerning vessels navigating in contravention of the traffic separation schemes.

The CNIS also provides a storm/tide warning service when tidal levels are expected to be one metre or more below the astronomically predicted levels, applicable to Thames Estuary, Southern North Sea and the Dover Strait areas.

Navtex also covers these broadcasts and details of this and other services can be found in ALRS Vol. 3.

In addition to the CALDOVREP and the CNIS operations normal VHF communications are ongoing between ship to shore stations, and ship-to-ship where appropriate. i.e. Pilotage communications.

Additional communications from marine organisations such as the Coastguard (HMCG) on Channel 67, Coast Radio Stations, Port and Harbour control authorities and Marinecall. Any involvement in SAR activity could also involve Royal National Lifeboats Institution (RNLI) as well as military air and surface contacts.

Important navigational warnings may be transmitted at any time with a prefix "SECURITE" (SAY-CUAE-E-TAY) R/T.

3.19 Channel Passage and Associated Hazards

A passage through the English Channel is not always doom and gloom and the fact remains that good seamanship practice, if that can be interpreted, does tend to prevail. One might suggest that it is an area where the Masters role is extensive and the need for 'bridge teamwork' comes to the fore.

A typical transit could expect to encounter a variety of potential hazards. However, prudent planning and effective communications, coupled with common sense will usually result in an incident free passage and safe docking.

An awareness of the ship, especially its draught, and its manoeuvring capabilities, would be considered a necessity. This information is particularly important for deep draught vessels, when specific advice from publications warns of:

(a) charted depths in offshore areas may be compiled from scanty information and as such errors of unknown magnitude possibly as much as one metre may prevail.

(b) storm surges in the area due to abnormal meteorological conditions could cause water levels to rise up to 3m or fall to 2m below predicted heights, in the southern part of the North Sea.

(c) controlling depths are known to exist in traffic lanes.

Example: TSS off WEST HINDER – East going traffic lane 16.5m Lies between Kwinte Bank and the Akkaert Bank. (See Admiralty Chart 125)
also, 11.2m (1980) was charted 4 cables off the north end of the Kwinte Bank. (Lat 51° 21' N Long 2° 43' E)

(d) shoal depths may occur over wrecks that could have been disturbed by strong tidal streams, or which have become recently uncovered in newly formed channels.

(e) the dangers of ships "Squat" should not be minimised and its relationship to ships speed should be taken into account when considering the recommended underkeel clearance as being not less than 4.0m in the Dover Strait. (IMO recommended 1982).

3.20 English Channel – Collision Risks

cross channel ferries

The number of through movements via the Dover Straits is a large variable when compared with other regions of the world. The fact that this through traffic must expect to encounter extensive crossing traffic is a matter of record. Numerous cross channel ferries route across the straits, (Dover-Calais, Dover-Boulogne and vice versa). Other routes from Portsmouth-Caen, Portsmouth-Cherbourg/Le Havre, and vice versa are but a few of the well plied alternatives. Neither are all the cross ferries the norm. Many routes are used by hovercraft or high speed hydrofoils and catamarans.

leisure craft

The region is also well used by the yachting fraternity and many similar leisure craft. A notable increase in small craft can be expected during the summer months and commercial vessels are advised to keep a diligent lookout, bearing in mind that small wooden or fibre glass hulls make very poor radar targets. These craft must be expected to appear in any area, without exception, inside the confines of the English Channel.

warships

Warships are another specific group of ships which are regularly encountered in the area. Military exercises, inclusive of submarine activity, are not uncommon and evasive action to avoid close quarters situations must be considered prudent. Submarine exercise areas are charted and all Admiralty Charts so effected carry relevant warnings to mariners.

Main ports of military activity include: Portsmouth, Plymouth, and around Portland Bill.

fishing vessels

Many fishing vessels of differing nationalities are also regular users of the English Channel. These may include factory ships which may carry bold deck lighting. Watch officers may subsequently have difficulty in discerning navigation lights and they should exercise extreme caution and avoid close quarters situations.

deep draught vessels

Many routes towards continental ports employ deep water approaches. These approaches may cause certain vessels to cross traffic lanes to gain access to the deep water channels and an obvious danger could materialise for other traffic navigating within the lane.

Consideration for other traffic and the prudent use of a vessels speed could be an effective way of relieving a potentially hazardous situation. (Ref. to Regulation 10, of the Regulations for the Prevention of Collision at Sea is recommended).

3.21 English Channel Navigation

Contingency situations may make it a requirement for a vessel to go to anchor, either for adverse weather, traffic or docking delays. In this event a careful chart inspection should be made prior to anchoring the vessel. Many areas carry restrictions on the use of anchors due to wrecks, cable areas or other obstructions.

A recommended anchorage for deep draught vessels lies in position lat 52° 03' N long 03° 04' E on routes for Eurogeul. Special attention is drawn to vessels navigating in this area that liquid cargo transfer occasionally takes place in the SW part of this anchorage. Deep draughted vessels proceeding towards Deutsche Bank (Ref. North Sea (East) sailing directions) should also note that 'two way-deep water routes' are employed in this area. Careful chart inspection is recommended.

pilotage operations

Advance communications of up to 48 hours in some cases is required by pilotage agencies in the United Kingdom or European countries. Deep sea pilots may be obtained prior to entering the traffic separation schemes of Dover and the southern part of the North Sea, from several ports inclusive of:

Brixham, Cherbourg, Le Havre, Boulogne, Folkestone, Calais and Dunkerque.

The option of helicopter transfer of the marine pilot is also available through pilotage agents.

Information regarding communications between vessels and pilot stations can be found in ALRS Vol. 6.

When planning a vessels approach to a pilot station the Navigation should take full account of Regulation 10 of the Anti-Collision Regulations.

Additional reading of (IMO), *Ships Routing*, 4th edition, and the

Annual Summary of *Admiralty Notices to Mariners* is further recommended.

natural conditions

The prevailing weather conditions in the Channel have a reputation of poor visibility at virtually any time of the year. This may be caused by light rain conditions or showers as well as fog which is common to the area. Gales are frequent during the winter months and the prevailing direction is from the west or north west. The shipping forecast as issued by the BBC provides weather information daily at approximately six hourly intervals. BBC Radio 4, 198 kHz, 1515m Long Wave at:

0033, 0555, 1355 and 1750 hrs.

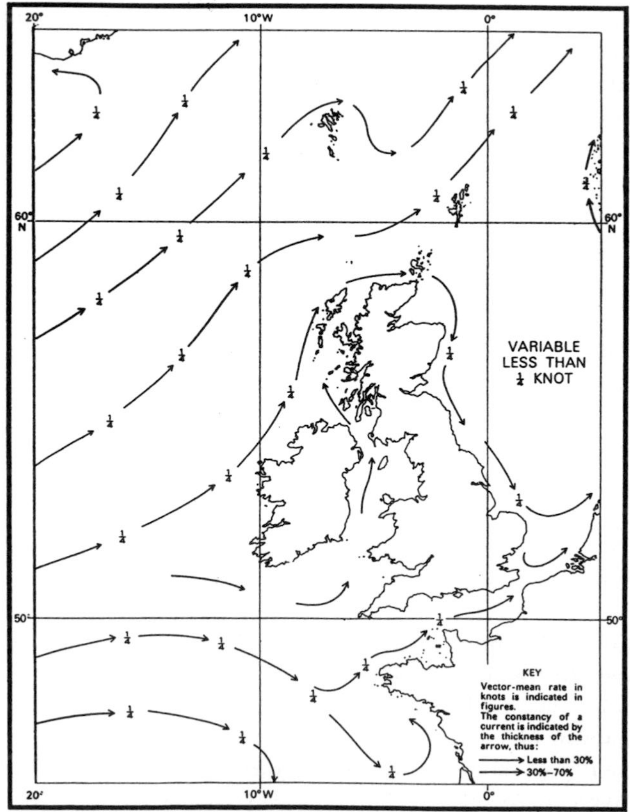

Diagram 3.15: Average surface currents throughout the year

navigation of English Channel (chart 5500)

In order to enhance navigation within the Channel, a special chart, number 5500, has been devised to assist officers planning a passage into or through this highly active region. The chart is concerned with the safe transit of vessels and informs Masters and navigators of the following points of concern:

1. Passage planning – How the principles of effective passage planning should be employed to ensure a safe passage through the Channel. Advice is given on the aspects of: appraisal, planning, execution and monitoring of the vessels progress. Particular attention is drawn to the use of a 'sea pilot' and the special requirements that some vessels may require, e.g. deep draught ships.
   Mariners are also advised that a ship movement reporting system is in operation and vessels are expected to participate.
2. Routing, general recommendations – With the extensive traffic separation scheme in operation through the Dover Straits and at prominent focal points, Masters are advised of their legal obligations under the COLREGS, in section (2) of the chart.
3. Routing, specific regulations – Any special regulations which might apply to traffic separation schemes are summarised within the passage plan charts. Recommendations for vessels of 300 GRT are such that electronic position fixing equipment should be fitted on board to improve navigation methods.
4. Passage planning (special classes of vessel) – Specific reference is made for 'deep draught vessels' and those bound for Europort. Instructions for tankers and other ships carrying dangerous cargoes are required to adhere to French regulations after rounding 'Ouessant'. Particular attention to mariners is drawn to the need for adequate under keel clearance and additional references for ships 'constrained by their draught', is also featured in this section of the charted notes.
5. Oil and dangerous cargoes – This section of the notes contains a list of oils and noxious substances that require to be reported under EC regulations. Compulsory reporting within the recommendations is necessary for any tanker over 1600 GRT which is carrying chemicals, gas or oil, where tanks are not free of vapours from these cargoes.
6. Radio reporting systems (through traffic) – Detailed information is given regarding reporting ship movement and reporting methods adopted in the Channel, a compulsory communication system which effects such areas as:

Ushant, Casquets and the Dover Strait is designed to monitor traffic movements within the Channel.

The type of reports required, namely:

POSREP – For vessels with no defects.
DEFREP – For NUC vessels or with defects to navigational aids.
CHANGEREP – For vessels amending proposed plans.

A compulsory reporting system is in operation for all vessels carrying oils or hydrocarbons, which intend to enter French territorial waters.

Additional detail on specific communications is included in this section of the Notes.

7. Radio reporting procedures to a port of destination – Advance communications and in particular projected ETA for all tankers, together with relevant ship details appropriate to cargo and the vessels navigation capabilities.
8. Maritime radio services – Details of stations/frequencies and the times of transmission of specific messages including: navigational warnings, weather reports and storm warnings.
   Details of the NAVTEX services is also included.
9. Radio beacon service – Includes an illustration of radio beacons and their groupings, together with frequency and station identification. The beacons effective range and service which is being offered is also included.
10. Tidal information and services – Offshore tidal data with an illustration/example of the use of co-tidal, co-range lines. Maximum tidal stream rates in relation to HW Dover are included in this section.
11. Pilotage service – Details of requests for deep-sea pilots for respective ports and the relevant communications required. Rendezvous points for helicopter/pilot transfer and procedural actions.

Additionally, mariners are advised that respective MGN/MSN's are in force for vessels navigating in or through the English Channel and these should be brought to the attention of all Watch Officers.

MARINE GUIDANCE NOTE

MGN 128 (M+F)

Navigation in the Dover Strait

Note to Shipowners, Masters and all concerned with the Navigation of Seagoing Vessels

This note supersedes MGN 29 (M + F)

Summary

This notice draws attention to mariners on the new mandatory reporting regime and the problems associated with navigating through and across the Dover Strait

Introduction

1. The Dover Strait and its approaches are among the busiest shipping lanes in the world and pose serious problems for the safety of navigation. The traffic separation scheme, its associated inshore traffic zones, the Channel Navigation Information Service (CNIS) and the mandatory reporting system (referred to as CALDOVREP) have been designed to assist seafarers to navigate these waters in safety. There is therefore a need for careful navigation in this area in accordance with the International Regulations for Preventing Collisions at Sea 1972 (as amended) and for use to be made of the CNIS and the CALDOVREP scheme. MGN 28 contains guidance on the observance of traffic separation schemes in general. Details of the CALDOVREP scheme and CNIS are contained in the Admiralty List of Radio Signals Vol. 6 Part 1 and the Mariner's Routeing Guide for the English Channel and Southern North Sea (BA Chart No.5500).The International Regulations for Preventing Collisions at Sea are to be found in Merchant Shipping Notice No. M1642/COLREG 1.

2. The number of collisions in the Dover Strait and its approaches has declined since the introduction of the traffic separation scheme and its mandatory application for all ships in 1977. Nevertheless the risk of collision is ever present and heightened if vessels do not comply with the requirements of the scheme, and Rule 10 in particular.

3. **MANDATORY REPORTING SYSTEM**

On 1 July 1999, a mandatory reporting system CALDOVREP was introduced, which replaced the existing system MAREP/POSREP.

All vessels over 300gt must report as follows:

(i) NE-bound traffic to Gris Nez Traffic via VHF Ch 13 when abeam the Bassurelle lightbuoy (50°33'N;000°58'E).

(ii) SW-bound traffic to Dover Coastguard via VHF Ch 11 not later than crossing a line drawn from North Foreland Light (51°23'N;001°27'E) to the Belgian and French borders (51°05'N;002°33'E).

(iii) Vessels which are not under command, anchored in the traffic separation scheme, restricted in their ability to manoeuvre or with defective navaids are also required to report.

Inshore Traffic Zones

4. The French Inshore traffic zone extends from Cap Gris Nez in the north to a line drawn due west near Le Touquet in the South. The English Inshore Traffic Zone (EITZ) extends from a line drawn from the western end of the scheme to include Shoreham to a line drawn due South from South Foreland.

5. A vessel of less than 20 metres in length, a sailing vessel and vessels engaged in fishing may, under all circumstances, use the English and the

French inshore traffic zones. With respect to the application of Rule 10(d) to **other** vessels, it is the view of the MCA that, where such a vessel commences its voyage from a location beyond one limit of either zone and proceeds to a location beyond the further limit of that zone, it should use the appropriate lane. Exceptions to this are when a vessel is calling at a port, pilot station or destination or sheltered waters within that zone. In all other cases, vessels should use the appropriate lane of the traffic separation scheme if it is safe to do so, unless some abnormal circumstances exist in that lane. In this context reduced visibility in this area is not considered by the MCA as an abnormal circumstance warranting the use of the zone.

6. Traffic surveys in the area show that, in general, the interest of safety are best served by excluding from the EITZ as many vessels, other than those with a clear need or right to use it, as possible. Accordingly, the MCA will consider legal action against vessels using the EITZ when they can safely use the appropriate traffic separation lane, (other than those exempted by Rule 10(d). NE-bound vessels voyaging to the Thames or East Coast ports are required to use the NE-bound lane of the scheme where they can safely do so. A ruling on whether in any particular case a Master of a NE-bound vessel is justified on safety grounds in choosing to use the EITZ rather than the NE-bound lane is for the Courts to decide in the light of individual circumstances.

It should be noted that neither CNIS, or HM Coastguard has authority to interpret the Collision Regulations or grant permission for vessels to use the EITZ in contravention of Rule 10(d). Masters deciding that circumstances warrant their use of the EITZ should report their decision to CNIS.

Passage Planning/Crossing Traffic Lanes

7. Radar surveillance surveys show that many vessels proceeding from the NE Lane towards the Thames and East Coast ports use the MPC buoy as a turning point irrespective of the traffic present in the SW lane. Masters are reminded that crossing the lane in compliance with Rule 10(c) can be made anywhere approximately 5 miles to the NE or SW of the MPC Buoy. In selecting the crossing point regard should be given to traffic in the SW Lane and the need to avoid the development of risk of collision situations with such traffic. Surveillance surveys also indicate that risk of collision increases if cross channel traffic, leaving Dover or the Calais approach channel, shape courses without due regard to the traffic situation in the adjacent lane. Vessels proceeding along the traffic lanes, in meeting their obligations under Rules 15 and 16, are often observed making substantial course alterations and their actions are frequently complicated when traffic converges within a particular lane. Attention is therefore drawn to the need for cross channel traffic to take into account this possible situation arising when passage planning. Consideration should also be given to where the lane is to be crossed so that the collision risk situations can be anticipated and are not allowed to develop.

Regulations for Prevention of Collisions - General

8. Use of the scheme in accordance with Rule 10 does not in any way alter the over-riding requirement for vessels to comply with the other Rules. **In particular, vessels, other than those referred to in Rule 10(k) and Rule 10(l), do not by virtue of using the traffic lanes in accordance with Rule 10 enjoy any privilege or right of way that they would not have elsewhere.** In addition, vessels using the traffic separation scheme are not relieved of the requirement to keep a proper look-out and of the requirement to proceed at a safe speed, especially in conditions of restricted visibility, or to make course and/or speed alterations in accordance with Rule 8.

Crossing Traffic

9. Mariners are reminded that there is a concentration of crossing ferry traffic, including high speed craft, in the Strait. These vessels may make course alterations outside the lanes in order to cross them at right angles.

Rules 10(b)(ii) and 10(b)(iii)

10. The MCA also wishes to draw attention to Rule 10(b)(iii) which requires vessels normally to join and leave a traffic lane at the termination of the lane. This rule does not preclude a vessel from joining a lane from the side at a small angle to the general direction of traffic flow. Consequently, vessels bound SW from location in the EITZ are advised to join the SW lane as soon as it is safe and practicable to do so.

All vessels are advised to keep clear of boundary separation lines or zones in accordance with Rule

10(b)(ii). Failure to observe this rule has resulted in repeated damage to the CS4 buoy. This buoy is protected by a charted "area to be avoided" (ABTA) by all vessels.

MSPP2D
Maritime and Coastguard Agency
Spring Place
105 Commercial Road
Southampton
SO15 1EG

Tel: 02380 329341
Fax: 02380 329204

December 1999

[MCA File Ref: MNA 5/50/294]

An executive agency of the Department of the Environment, Transport and the Regions

3.22 Carriage of Nautical Publications

For effective passage planning to take place aboard the vessel the navigator will require the use of navigational publications. Reference should be made to the Annual Summary of Notices to Mariners (Not. 18) which recommends the following publications to be carried by U.K. registered ships (exception vessels being less than 12 metres in length and fishing vessels).

International Code of Signals – Merchant Shipping Notices ('M') Notices – The Mariners' Handbook (NP100) – Weekly Notices to Mariners – Nautical Almanac – Nautical (Navigational) Tables – Admiralty List of Radio Signals – Admiralty List of Lights – Sailing Directions – Tide Tables – Tidal Stream Atlases – Operating and Maintenance instructions for navigational aids carried.

Additionally: A full set of navigational charts for the relevant areas of navigation of the vessel.
A well found ship will also carry, in addition to those stated above, any or all of the following:
A copy of the *Regulations for the Prevention of Collision at Sea*. (Copy of the same contained inside the *Mariners' Handbook*).

A copy of chart abbreviations (No 5011) – *International Aeronautical and Marine Search and Rescue Manual* (IAMSAR) – *Ships Routing* (IMO) – *Ocean Passages of the World* (NP 136) – Chart Catalogue – Relevant Statutory Instruments – *Sight Reduction Tables* (NP 401) – *Distance Tables* (NP 350) (3 volumes) – *Guide to Port Entry* – Routing Charts – Ocean Current Charts – *Star Finder and Identifier* (NP 323) – *Echo Sounder Correction Tables* (NP 139 – Chart No. 5500 English Channel Information, *Guide to Helicopter/Ship Operations* (ICS).

Supplements and updates for nautical publications are issued by the Hydrographer of the Navy at suitable intervals, e.g. Admiralty Sailing Directions (one and a half to two years interval), supplements being cumulative so that each successive supplement supersedes the previous one.

Chapter Four

OCEAN PASSAGE PLANNING

4.1 Introduction

Since the early voyages of discovery, ocean passages have been determined by economics. With today's fuel costs, the most economical route remains a high priority with shipowners.

One may be excused for thinking that the shortest route is always the most economical. Great circle sailing, for example, is the shortest distance between two points on the earth's surface, but the passage may involve high risk and damage to ship or cargo, so when comparisons are made the shortest distance route may not be the most economical.

When planning any passage due consideration must be made to the economics, but in these more informed times, the safety aspects of a voyage must expect to influence the route adopted.

The time of year and the anticipated weather conditions are assessed with potential hazards such as 'ice' or 'storm frequency' before a final route is set.

The distance by 'rhumb line' is often to be compared with the great circle or composite great circle tracks and these distance figures will be a major consideration but not limited to their influence alone.

4.2 Great Circle Sailing

A great circle is defined as a circle on the earth's surface whose plane passes through the centre of the earth.

For navigation purposes:

1. The shortest distance between two places on the earth's surface is a great circle track.
2. Great circles appear as straight lines on gnomonic charts.
3. Every great circle has two vertices (vertex), one in the northern hemisphere, the other in the southern hemisphere.
4. The course of the great circles, at the vertex, is due EAST/WEST (090 degrees/270 degrees). This provides a 90 degree angle for use with Napier's Rules.
5. The vertex of a great circle is that point nearest the pole.
6. The meridian that passes through the vertex is at right angles to the great circle.

4.3 Use of Gnomonic Charts

Once a ship's Master has orders to plan a voyage he is under obligation to investigate not only the most economical but also the safest route. In any event the distance of each and every possible track needs to be investigated. The great circle distance, being the shortest distance, will therefore be a high priority. The following is an example of how the gnomonic chart is used in conjunction with the mercator chart.

Example:

On the gnomonic chart of the North Atlantic plot the Great Circle track from:

Lat. 52° 00' N Long. 55° 00' W
to: Lat. 56° 30' N Long. 15° 00' W

Transfer this track to the Mercator Chart of the North Atlantic showing positions for every 10 degrees of longitude from the initial position.

Compare the great circle distance with the rhumb line (direct) distance.

Compare also the rhumb line distance on the four short legs (rhumb lines) which comprise the staged great circle track.

Method

1. Plot the initial position (A) and the final position (E) on the gnomonic chart.
2. Join positions (A) to (E) with a straight line, (Straight lines on a gnomonic chart are great circles).

3. Identify and mark off on the G.C. track at intervals of 10 degrees of Longitude, the intermediate positions (B), (C) and (D). (Other suitable intervals can be used).
4. Take off and note the latitude and longitude of all the positions (A) to (E) inclusive.
5. Plot all these respective positions onto the mercator chart of the North Atlantic.
6. Join up the short rhumb lines between positions: (A to B), (B to C), (C to D), and (D to E).

NB: In this example the interval of 10 degrees of longitude has been employed but in practice a more convenient interval may be used which could better suit the ships' speed or daily run.

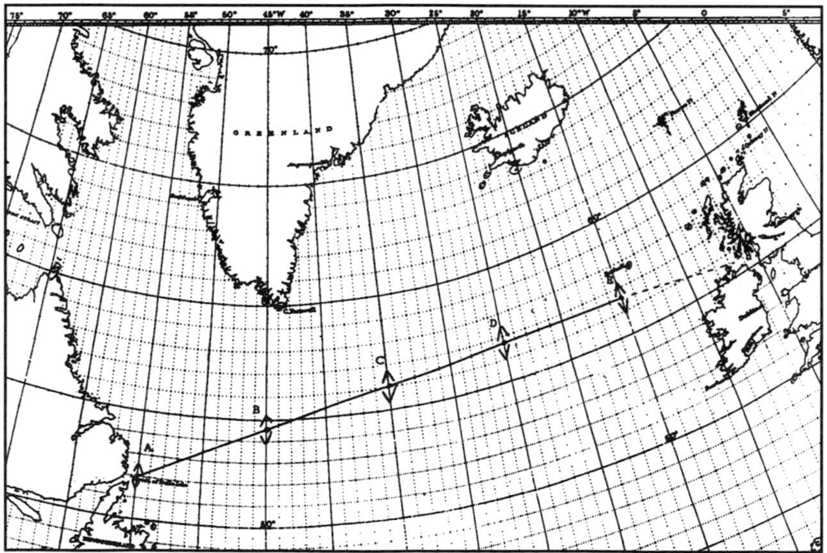

Diagram 4.1: North Atlantic (Gnomonic Chart)

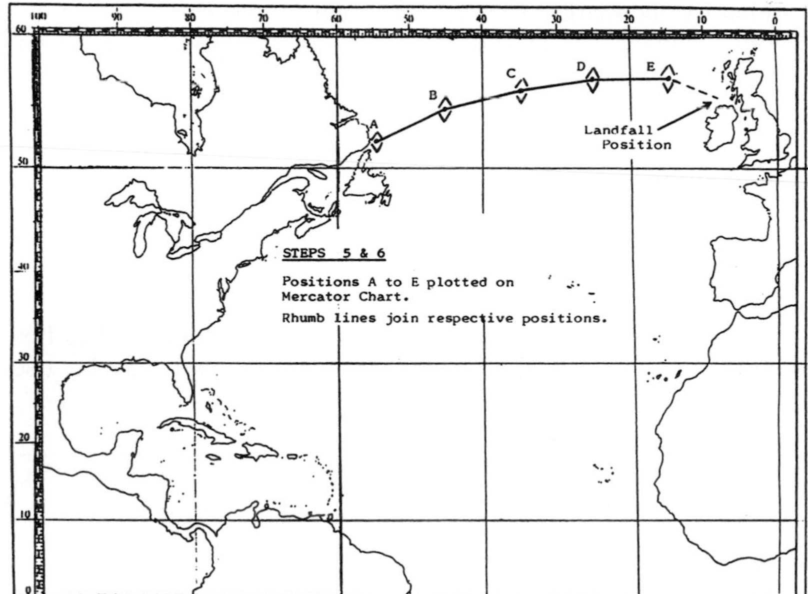

Diagram 4.2: Mercator Chartlet North Atlantic

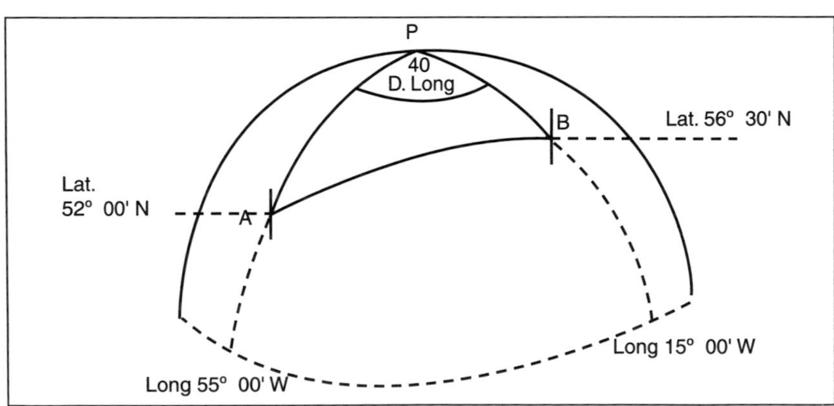

Diagram 4.3: Great Circle Distance – Example Calculation

Basic Formula: $\text{Hav AB} = \text{hav}(PA \sim PB) + \text{hav}\,\hat{P} \sin PA \sin PB.$

Example Formula: $\text{Hav AE} = \text{hav}(PA \sim PE) + \text{hav}\,\hat{P} \sin PA \sin PB.$

$= \text{hav}(PA \sim PE) + \text{hav}\,\hat{P} \sin PA \sin PB.$
sin 33° 30'

Hav $\hat{P}$	= 40° 00'	L.Hav	9.06810
sin PA	= 38° 00'	L.sin	9.78934
sin PE	= 33° 30'	L.sin	9.74189
		L.Hav	8.59933
	Nat.Hav 0.03975		
(PA ~ PE)	= 4° 30'	Nat.Hav	0.00154
Great Circle Dist	= 23° 27'	Nat.Hav	0.04129
	= 1407 nautical miles		

Rhumb Line Summary and Direct Rhumb Line Comparison

1st Leg (A – B)	Distance = 391.73'
2nd Leg (B – C)	Distance = 351.9'
3rd Leg (C – D)	Distance = 335.6'
4th Leg (D – E)	Distance = 331.3'

Total Distance = 1410.5' nautical miles

Direct Rhumb Line Distance

Lat A. 52° 00' N	MPs 3646.74	Long 55° 00' W
Lat E. 56° 30' N	MPs 4108.37	Long 15° 00' W
Lat A. 4° 30' N	DMP 461.63	.Long 40° 00' E
= 270'		= 2400'

$$\text{Tan Co.} = \frac{\text{D.Long}}{\text{DMP}} = \frac{2400}{461.63} = \text{N}79°\ 6.8'\ \text{E}$$

Distance = D.Lat. x Sec Co.
= 270' x Sec 79° 6.8'
= 1429.6' Nautical Miles

Comparisons:–

Great Circle Distance	= 1407 nautical miles
Direct Rhumb Line Distance	= 1429.6 nautical miles
Composite Rhumb Line Distance	= 1410.5 nautical miles

Great Circle Sailing –

Worked Example to find: Initial and final courses and the GC distance

Qu. Find the initial and final courses and the great circle distance between position 'A' (Lat. 38° 00' N. Long. 124° 00' W) and position 'B' (Lat. 56° 00' N. Long. 101° 00' W)

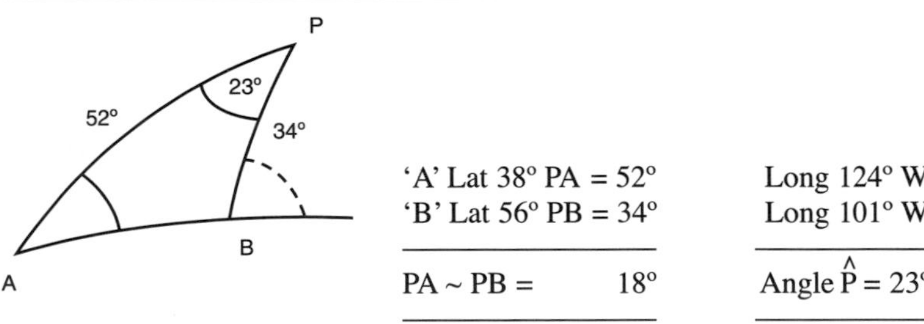

'A' Lat 38° PA = 52°
'B' Lat 56° PB = 34°

PA ~ PB = 18°

Long 124° W
Long 101° W

Angle $\hat{P}$ = 23°

To find the GC Distance

$$\text{Hav AB} = (\text{hav } \hat{P} \sin PA \sin PB) + \text{hav } (PA \sim PB)$$
$$= (\text{hav } 23^\circ \sin 52^\circ \sin 34^\circ) + \text{hav } 18^\circ$$

Nos	Logs
Log Hav 23°	8.59931
L.sin 52°	9.89653
L.sin 34°	9.74756
	8.24340
Nat Hav	0.01751
Nat Hav 18°	0.02447
hav AB	0.04198

AB = 23° 38.9'
x 60

Dist = 1418.9 n/miles

PA = 52° 00'
AB = 23° 38.9'

PA ~ PB = 28° 21.1'

PB = 34° 00'
AB = 23° 38.9'

PB ~ A B = 10° 21.1'

To find the Initial Course

$$\text{Hav}\,\hat{A} = \text{hav PB} - \text{hav (PA} \sim \text{PB) cosec PA cosec AB}$$
$$= (\text{hav } 34^\circ - \text{hav } 28^\circ\, 21.1') \text{ cosec } 52^\circ \text{ cosec } 23^\circ\, 38.9'$$

Nos	Logs
Nat Hav 34° 00'	0.08548
Nat Hav 28° 21.1'	0.05998
Nat Hav	0.02550
Log Hav	8.40650
L.cosec 52°	0.10347
L.cosec 23° 38.9'	0.39673
Hav $\hat{A}$	8.90670

Angle $\hat{A}$ = 33° 00.1'

Initial Course = N 33° 00.1' E

Check by ABC
A = 1.84 S
B = 3.79 N
C = 1.95 N
= 32.9

To find the final Course

$$\text{Hav}\,\hat{B} = \text{hav PA} - \text{hav (PB} \sim \text{AB) cosec PB cosec AB}$$
$$= (\text{hav } 52^\circ - \text{hav } 10^\circ\, 21.1') \text{ cosec } 34^\circ \text{ cosec } 23^\circ\, 38.9'$$

Nos	Logs
Nat Hav 52° 00'	0.19217
Nat Hav 10° 21.1'	0.00814
Nat Hav	0.18403
Log Hav	9.26489
L.cosec 34° 00'	0.25244
L.cosec 23° 38.9'	0.39673
Hav $\hat{B}$	9.91406

Angle $\hat{B}$ = 129° 51.6'

Final Course = N 50° 08.4' E

Check by ABC
A = 3.49 S
B = 2.00 N
C = 1.49 N
= 50.4

EXAMPLE *Use of A, B & C Tables in Great Circle Sailing*

Find the initial course and final courses and the great circle distance from 'A' 38° 00' N 124° 00' W to 'B' 44° 00' N 164° 00' E, by use of A, B, C, Tables.

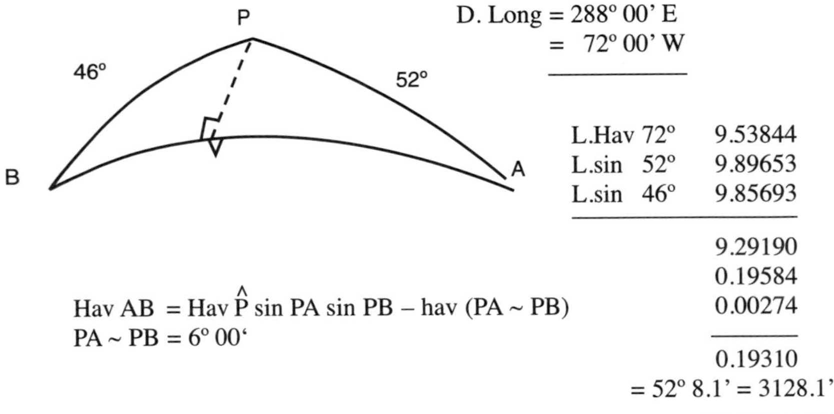

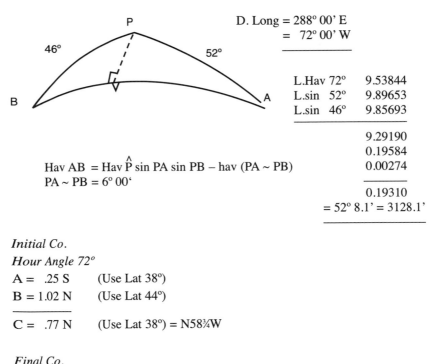

D. Long = 288° 00' E
= 72° 00' W

L.Hav 72°	9.53844
L.sin 52°	9.89653
L.sin 46°	9.85693
	9.29190
	0.19584
	0.00274
	0.19310

= 52° 8.1' = 3128.1'

$\text{Hav } AB = \text{Hav } \hat{P} \sin PA \sin PB - \text{hav } (PA \sim PB)$

$PA \sim PB = 6° 00'$

Initial Co.

Hour Angle 72°

A = .25 S (Use Lat 38°)

B = 1.02 N (Use Lat 44°)

C = .77 N (Use Lat 38°) = N58¾W

Final Co.

A = .31 S (Use Lat 44°)

B = .82 N (Use Lat 38°)

C = .51 N (Use Lat 44°) = N69.9E

Final Co = S69.9W = 249.9 = 250° (T)

EXAMPLE *Great Circle Sailing & Use or A, B & C Tables*

Calculate the distance by Great Circle from Lat. 20° 52' S Long. 57° 37' E to Lat. 32° 12' S Long. 115° 09' E and find the initial & final course by ABC Tables.

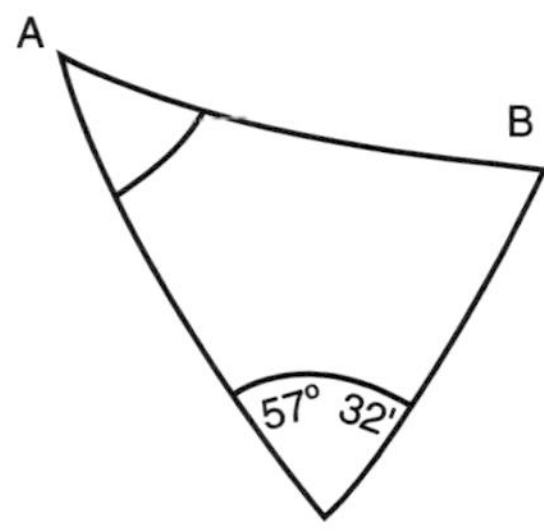

Dep. Long. – 57° 37'
Arr. Long. – 115° 09'

D. Long. 57° 32'

$$\text{Hav } AB = \text{Hav } \hat{P} \cos 20° 52' \cos 32° 12' + \text{hav } 11° 20'$$

Initial Co.

A = .243 N
B = .747 S

C = .504 S = S64¾E

= 115¼° (T)

L.Hav 57° 32'	9.36473
L.cos 20° 52'	9.97054
L.cos 32° 12'	9.92747
	9.26274
	.18312
(N. hav 11° 20')	.00975
	.19287 = 52° 06'

Distance = 3126'

Final Co.

A = .401 N
B = .450 S

C = .049 S = N87.7E 087¾° (T)

EXAMPLE *Great Circle Sailing* *(Obtaining Vertex Position)*

Find the distance, initial course and the position of the vertex on the Great Circle:–

from 'A'	Lat 51° 23' N	Lat 46° 00' N
	Long 9° 36' W	Long 49° 00' W

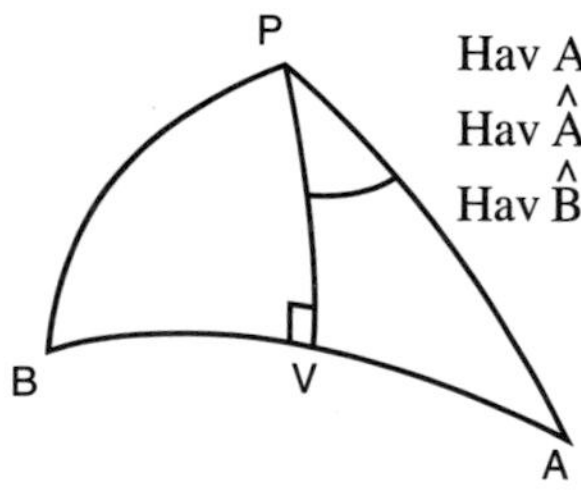

Hav AB $= \text{Hav}\,\hat{P}$ sin PA sin PB + Hav (PA ~ PB)

Hav $\hat{A}$ = Hav PB – Hav (AB ~ AP) Cosec AB Cosec AP

Hav $\hat{B}$ = Hav PA – Hav (AB ~ BP) Cosec AB Cosec BP

From $\triangle$PVA where V = 90°

Cos Lat V = Sin $\hat{A}$ Sin AP

Cot APV = Tan $\hat{A}$ Cos AP

to find:– AB	$\hat{A}$	$\hat{B}$
(PA ~ PB) = 5° 23' Hav $\hat{P}$ = 9.05551 Sin PA = 9.79526 Sin PB = 9.84177	(AB ~ AP) = 12° 23.5' Hav PB = 0.14033 Hav (AB ~ AP) = 0.01165	(AB ~ BP) = 17° 46.5' Hav AP = 0.10933 Hav (AB ~ BP) = 0.02386
8.69254 0.04926 Hav (PA ~ PB) 0.00221	0.12868 9.10948 Cosec AB = 0.35468 Cosec AP = 0.12868	0.08547 8.93182 Cosec AB = 0.35468 Cosec BP = 0.15823
0.05147 AB = 26° 13.5' Dist = 1573.5 nm.	9.66890 $\hat{A}$ = 86° 10' Int. Co. 273° 50'	9.44473 $\hat{B}$ = 63° 41.8' Fin Co. 243° 41.8'

to find Lat of V

Sin AP = 9.79526
Sin VAP = 9.99903

9.79429
Lat of V = 51° 29' N

to find $\widehat{APV}$

Cos AP = 9.89284
Tan $\hat{A}$ = 1.17390

1.06674
D.Long A to V
= 4° 54' W

Position of vertex Lat 51° 29' N
Long 14° 30' W

EXAMPLE *Great Circle Sailing – Crossing the Equator*

Find the great circle distance, the position of the vertex and the course of the vessel as it crosses the equator on the G.C. track from:–

position 'A' Latitude 05° 50' N. Longitude 81° 10' W.
position 'B' Latitude 41° 50' S. Longitude 175° 40' E.

NB: Construct the spherical triangle APB, in the usual manner and show the pole 'P' in the hemisphere of the greater latitude. e.g. Lat. 41° 50' south hemisphere.

Mariners should also note that the co-lat of the vertex is equal to the course at the equator.

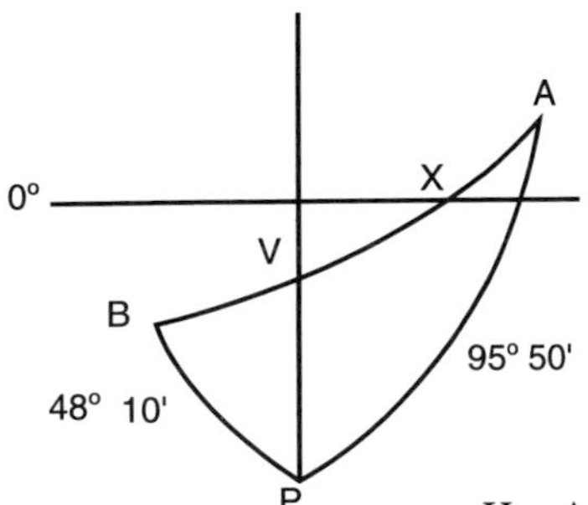

PA = 95° 50'
PB = 48° 10'
PA ~ PB = 47° 40'
$\hat{P}$ = 360° – (81° 10' + 175° 40')
= 103° 10'

To find distance AB:–

Hav AB = Hav $\hat{P}$ sin PA sin PB + hav (PA ~ PB)

Hav AB = Hav 103° 10' sin 95° 50' sin 48° 10' + hav (47° 40')

Nos	Logs
Nat Hav 103° 10'	9.78809
Log sin 95° 50'	9.99775
Log sin 48° 10'	9.87221
Log hav.	9.65805
Nat hav.	0.45504
Nat hav. (47° 40')	0.16328
Nat hav. AB =	0.61832
AB =	103° 41.3'
Dist =	6221.3 miles

To find the Initial Course $\hat{A}$:–

$$\text{Hav } \hat{A} = \frac{\text{hav PB} - \text{hav (PA} \sim \text{PB)}}{\text{sin PA sin AB}}$$

= hav 48° 10' – hav 7° 51.3' x cosec 95° 50' cosec 103° 41.3'

Nos	Logs
Nat Hav 48° 10'	0.16652
Nat hav 7° 51.3'	0.00469 (PA ~ PB)
Nat hav	0.16183
Log Hav	9.20906
Nat cosec 95° 50'	10.00226
Nat cosec 103° 41.3'	10.01251
Log Hav A	9.22383

$\hat{A}$ = S48° 18.4' W

> In order to use Napier Rules to resolve ΔPVA it is necessary to obtain more information.
>
> i.e. Initial Course A
>
> Though not specifically asked for in the question.

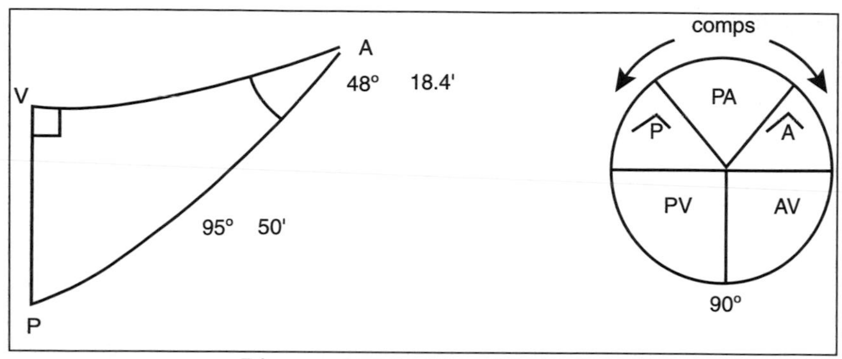

Diagram 4.4: Position of the Vertex

To find PV (Co-Lat of vertex):–
Sin PV = cos comp PA x cos comp $\hat{A}$
Sin PV = sin 95° 50 x sin 48° 18.4

Log sin 95° 50'	= 9.99775
Log sin 48° 18.4'	= 9.87316
Log sin PV	= 9.87091
PV	= 47° 58.6 = *NB: Course at the equator*
Therefore lat/vertex	= 42° 1.4' S.

To find angle $\widehat{APV}$ (Longitude of V from A):–

Sin comp PA = tan comp $\hat{P}$ x tan comp $\hat{A}$

Cot $\hat{P}$ = cos 95° 50' x tan 48° 18.4'

Log cos 95° 50'	9.00704
Log tan 48° 18.4'	10.05024
Log cot $\hat{P}$	– 9.05728

$\hat{P}$ = 83° 29.5'
(2nd quadrant) P = 96° 30.5'
Long. of 'A' = 81° 10.0' W

Long. of vertex = 177° 40.5'

Position of vertex — Latitude 42° 1.4' S
Longitude 177° 40.5 W

Course at Equator S 47° 58.5' W (228°)

EXAMPLE *Great Circle Sailing* *(Use of Natural Logarithms)*

NB: The use of natural logarithms to resolve great circle calculations is not uncommon and has become popular with navigators who regularly use a calculator as opposed to employing nautical tables.

Example

Find the great circle distance, the initial course and the final course from:–

Position 'A' Latitude 34° 00' S Longitude 18° 00' E.
to,
Position 'B' Latitude 36° 00' S Longitude 56° 00' W.

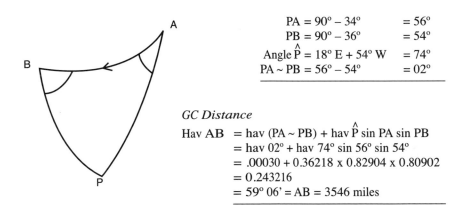

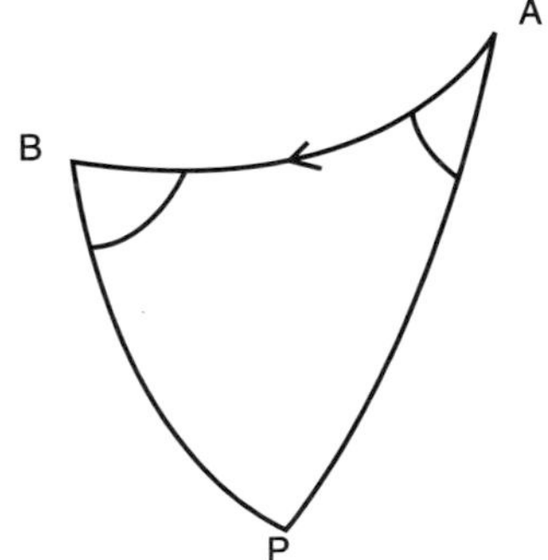

$PA = 90° – 34° = 56°$
$PB = 90° – 36° = 54°$
$\text{Angle } \hat{P} = 18° E + 54° W = 74°$
$PA \sim PB = 56° – 54° = 02°$

GC Distance

$\text{Hav } AB = \text{hav } (PA \sim PB) + \text{hav } \hat{P} \sin PA \sin PB$
$= \text{hav } 02° + \text{hav } 74° \sin 56° \sin 54°$
$= .00030 + 0.36218 \times 0.82904 \times 0.80902$
$= 0.243216$
$= 59° 06' = AB = 3546 \text{ miles}$

Initial Course

$\text{Hav } \hat{A} = [\text{hav } PB – \text{hav } (PA \sim PB)] \quad \text{cosec } PA \text{ cosec } AB$
$= [\text{hav } 54° – \text{hav } 03° 06'] \quad \text{cosec } 56° \text{ cosec } 59° 06'$
$= [0.20611 – 0.00073] \times 1.40574$
$= 0.288711 = \hat{A} = S65.2° W$
Initial course = 245.2° (T)

Final Course

$\text{Hav } \hat{B} = [\text{hav } PA – \text{hav } (PB \sim AB)] \quad \text{cosec } PB \text{ cosec } AB$
$= [\text{hav } 56° – \text{hav } 05° 06'] \quad \text{cosec } 54° \text{ cosec } 59° 06'$
$= [0.22040 - 0.00198] \times 1.44053$
$= 0.314641$
$= 68° 14.4' = \hat{B} = N68° 14.4' W$
Final course = 291° 45.6' (T)

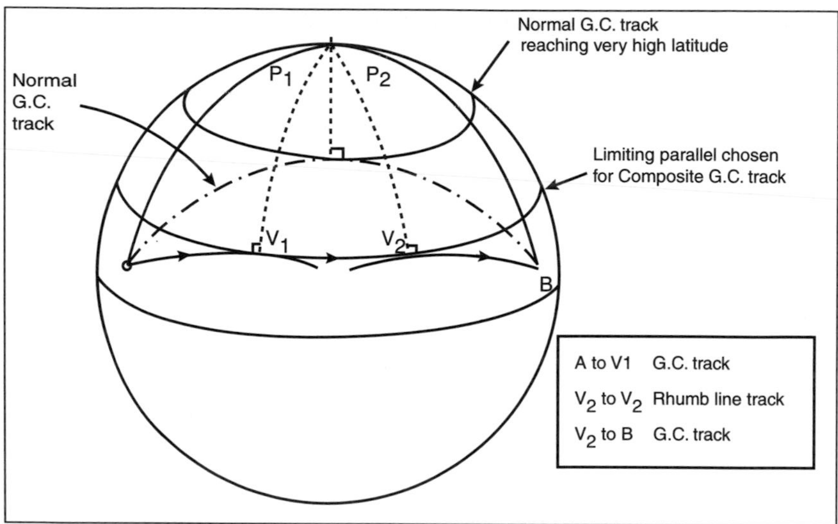

Diagram 4.5: A composite great circle track

The objective of the composite great circle is for a vessel to travel the maximum distance on a great circle between the places concerned, without passing poleward of a given latitude.

The problem can be easier to resolve than an ordinary great circle track because of the use of Napiers Rules only.

where 'A' is the initial position.
'B' is the final position.

& V_1 & V_2 are the vertices, each on the limiting latitude.

Method to resolve the problem is achieved by:–

Solve the spherical triangles PAV_1 and PBV_2 where PA, PB and PV are all known.

The longitudes of each vertex can then be found.

The total distance can then be resolved by:
$AV_1 + V_1V_2$ (parallel sailing) $+ V_2B$.

---

determination of composite great circle track

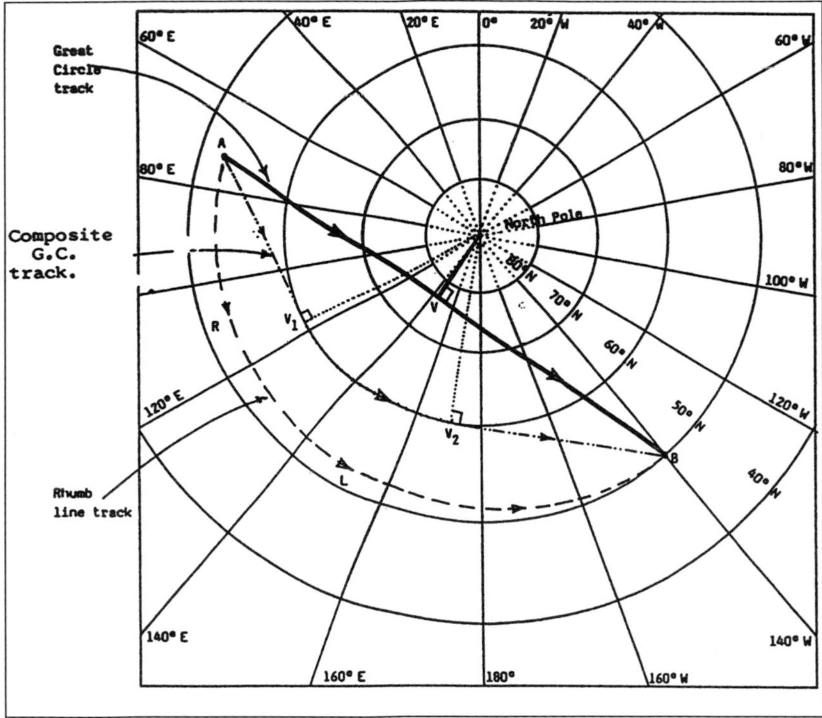

Diagram 4.6 Polar Gnomonic Chart

Limiting latitude = 60° N	First great circle log = Av_1
Initial position = A[52° N, 73° E]	Parallel sailing log = V_1V_2
Final position = B[50° N, 140° W]	Final great circle log = V_2B
Straight line AVB = true great circle track	TANGENTS to 60° N arc AV_1 and V_2B
Vertex of great circle track = V = [77° N, 144° E]	Approximate Rhumb line track = ARLB
AV_1V_2B = composite great circle track	

4.4 The Composite Great Circle Resolution Method

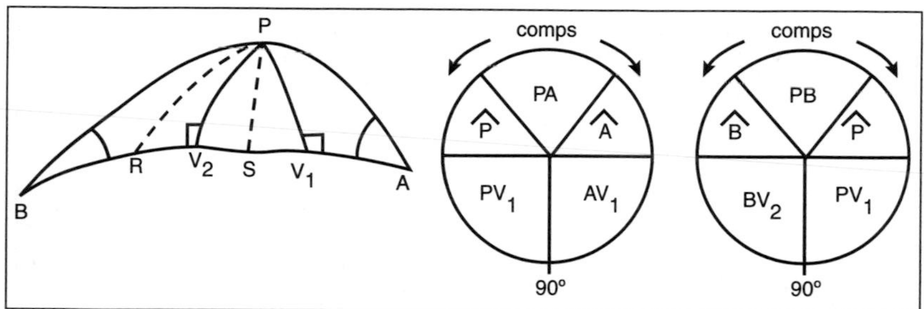

Diagram 4.7 Great Circle Resolution Method

Resolution by Napiers Rules:

(i) Sin mid part = tan adjacent x tan adjacent

(ii) Sin mid part = cos opposite x cos opposite

In $\triangle PAV_1$		In $\triangle PBV_2$	
Find $\hat{A}$	= Initial course	Find $\hat{B}$	= Final course
Find AV_1	= Distance	Find BV_2	= Distance
Find $\hat{P}$	= D. Long from A.	Find $\hat{P}$	= D. Long from B.

To find distance V_1V_2 – Use "parallel sailing formula"

Departure = D. Long. x Cos. Latitude ('V' limiting lat.)

To find 'Total Distance'

$$= AV_1 + BV_2 + V_1V_2$$

To find latitude where great circle meets a given longitude:–

Work as for great circle sailing employing Napiers Rules.

If for example the longitude of 'R' is given, between B & V_2 use the D. Long from V_2 and $\triangle PV_2R$
Latitude being obtained from (90° – PR)

If given a longitude of 'S' which lies between V_1 & V_2 then the limiting latitude is already known.

EXAMPLE *Composite Great Circle* *N. Hemisphere*

Calculate the total distance along the composite great circle track from 48° 13' N 5° 07' W to 47° 40' N 52° 26' W, given a limited latitude of 50° N. Also calculate the initial course by A, B, C tables

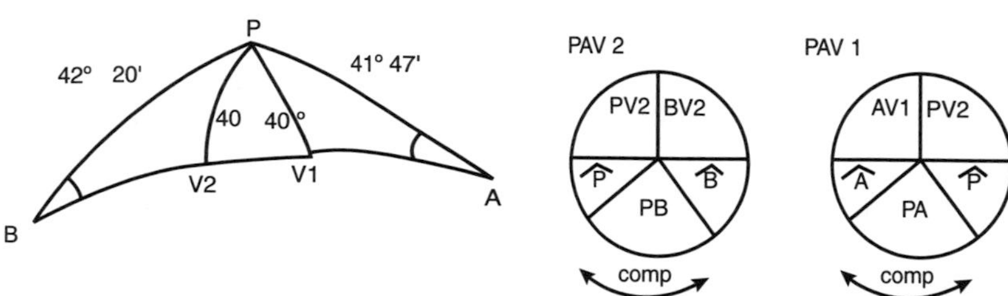

To find BPV2

Sin comp $\hat{P}$ = Tan comp 42° 20' x tan 40°

cos $\hat{P}$ = cot 42° 20' x tan 40°

cot 42° 20' = 0.04048
tan 40° = 9.92381

L.cos $\hat{P}$ = 9.96429
BPV2 = 22° 55'

To find APV1:–

sin comp $\hat{P}$ = tan comp 41° 47' x tan 40°

cos $\hat{P}$ = cot 41° 47' x tan 40°

L.cot 41° 47' = 0.04887
L.tan 40° = 9.92381

L.cos P =9.972680
L.APV1 = 20° 6.7'

D. Long between V1 & V2

APV1 20° 6.7'
BPV2 22° 55.0'

43° 1.7'

Long of B 52° 26' W
Long of A 05° 07' W

D.Long 47° 19'
43° 1.7'

D.Long V1V2 04° 17.3' = 257.3

D. Long 257.3'
M. Lat 50°

Dep. = 165.4
(by Tr/tables)

To find AV1

Sin Cp 41° 47' = Cos 40° x cos AV1
Cos AV1 = Cos 41° 47' x Sec 40°

L.Cos 41° 47' 9.87255
L.Sec 40° 0.11575

L.Cos AVI = 9.98830
AV1 = 13° 14.5'
AV1 = 794.5'

To find V2B

Sin Cp 42° 20' = Cos 40° x cos V2B
cos V2B = Cos 42° 20' x Sec 40°

L.Cos 42° 20' = 9.86879
L.Sec 40° = 0.11575

L. Cos V2B = 9.98454
V2B = 15° 12.0'
V2B = 912'

Total Dist = 794.5 + 912.0 + 165.4 = 1871.9 nm.

Initial course: A = 3.08 S
B = 3.48N

C = 0.40 N

A = 75° .1 = N75.1 W = 284.9 (T).

By Napiers Rules Int Co. = 74° 44'
= N74° 44' W.

EXAMPLE *Composite Great Circle* *Southern Hemisphere*

A vessel is expected to depart from Port Elizabeth (South Africa) to arrive at Melbourne (Australia). The Master intends to follow a composite great circle track with a limiting latitude of 42° S. from:–

Departure position	–	Latitude 34° 05’ S	Longitude 26° 00’ E
Landfall position	–	Latitude 39° 00’ S	Longitude 143° 50’ E.

The pilotage distance from Port Elizabeth to departure point is 45 miles, and from landfall to berth Melbourne is 84 miles. Calculate the total distance of the voyage.

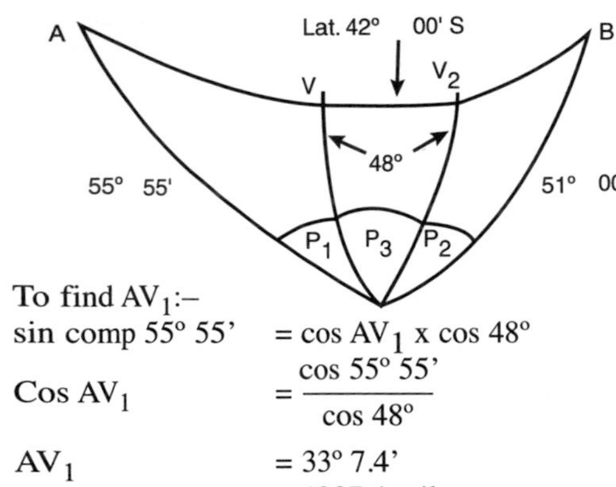

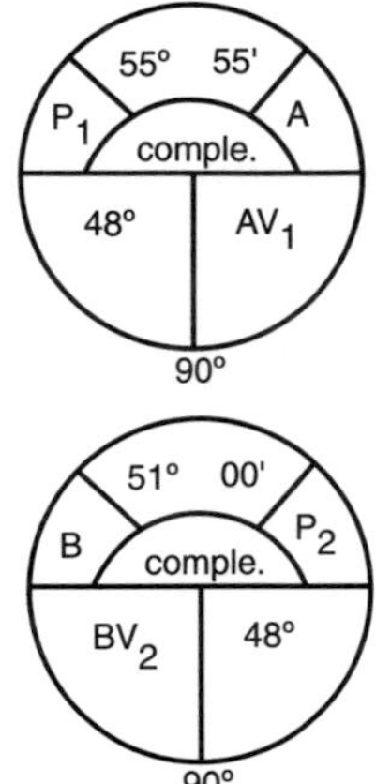

To find AV_1:–

sin comp 55° 55’ $= \cos AV_1 \times \cos 48°$

$\cos AV_1 = \dfrac{\cos 55° 55'}{\cos 48°}$

$AV_1 = 33° 7.4'$

$= 1987.4$ miles

To find BV_2:–

sin comp 51° $= \cos 48° \times \cos BV_2$

$\cos BV_2 = \dfrac{\cos 51°}{\cos 48°}$

$BV_2 = 19° 51.8'$

$= 1191.8$ miles

To find P_1:–

Sin comp P_1 = Tan comp 55° 55’ x Tan 48°

$\cos P_1 = \dfrac{\tan 48°}{\tan 55° 55'}$

$\hat{P}_1 = 41.282°$

To find P_2:–

Sin comp P_2 = Tan comp 51° x Tan 48°

$\cos P_1 = \dfrac{\tan 48°}{\tan 51°}$

$\hat{P}_2 = 25.926°$

Tot D.Long = 117° 50’

$\hat{P}_1 + \hat{P}_2 = 67° 12'$

$\hat{P}_3 = 50° 38'$

D.Long = 3038’

Dep = 3038 x cos 42°

$V_1V_2 = 2257$ miles

Tot. Dist $AV_1 = 1987.4$

$V_1V_2 = 2257$

$BV_2 = 1191.8$

Pilotage = 45’

Pilotage = 84’

Total Dist. = 5565.2’

Resolution of Great Circle Sailings
(With use of calculator)

Since the 'calculator' is a product of todays world it is only natural that its employment within the marine industry is recognised. With their origins in Napiers Rules, the following formula may be of interest to navigators generally and would I expect be useful to marine students under examination against the clock.

For distances:
$$\text{Cos A } V_1 = \frac{\text{Sin Lat A}}{\text{Sin limiting latitude}}$$

$$\text{Cos B } V_2 = \frac{\text{Sin Lat B}}{\text{Sin limiting latitude}}$$

For finding the Initial Course:
$$\text{Sin A} = \frac{\text{Cos limiting latitude}}{\text{Cos Lat A}}$$

$$\text{Sin B} = \frac{\text{Cos limiting latitude}}{\text{Cos Lat B}}$$

For finding the Final Course:
$$= \frac{\text{Cos PA} - \text{Cos PB x Cos AB}}{\text{Sin PA x Sin AB}}$$

For finding the Angle at the Pole:
$$\text{Cos } P_1 = \frac{\text{Tan Lat A}}{\text{Tan lat. of vertex}}$$

Angle at the Pole:
$$\text{Cos } P_2 = \frac{\text{Tan Lat B}}{\text{Tan lat. of vertex}}$$

For use with 'Great Circle' tracks where the latitude is required at a position where the track crosses a designated longitude and for finding the distance of a danger while crossing the meridian of the danger.

$$\text{Tan. Lat. of Hazard} = \frac{\text{Tan Lat A x Sin PB +/- Tan Lat B x Sin PA}}{\text{Sin Angle P}}$$

(Latitudes same name, use + plus)
(Latitudes different name use minus -)

Where PA = Longitude of A – Longitude of Hazard
PB = Longitude of B – Longitude of Hazard

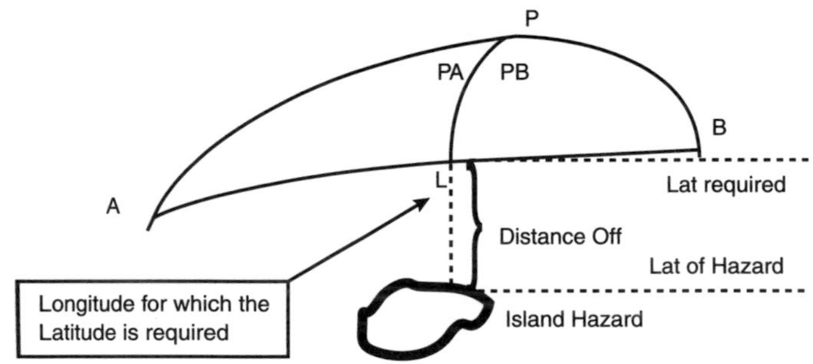

(NB. The formula is derived from the spherical cosine formula in order to solve the two triangles APL and BPL with the common latitude of PL).

Additional Navigational Formula (suitable for use with secondary navigational calculations)

Departure (Dep) = D.Long x Cos Lat
or
Departure (Dep) = Distance x Sin. Course

$$\text{Tan. Course} = \frac{\text{D.Long}}{\text{DMP}}$$

or

$$\text{Tan. Course} = \frac{\text{Departure}}{\text{D.Lat}}$$

Distance $= \dfrac{\text{D.Lat}}{\text{Cosine Course}}$

Sin. Amplitude $= \dfrac{\text{Sin. Declination}}{\text{Cosine Latitude}}$

Sin. Amplitude (alt.,) = Sin. Declination x Secant Latitude

Latitude (from Polaris) = True Altitude of Polaris – 1° 00' $+ a_0 + a_1 + a_2$

Great Circle Formula

CosAB = Cos P x Sin PA x Sin PB + Cos PA x Cos PB
or
Cos Dist = Cos D.Long x Cos Lat A x Cos Lat B +/– Sin Lat A x Sin Lat B

Cos A $= \dfrac{\text{(Cos PB – Cos AP x Cos AB)}}{\text{(Sin AP x Sin AB)}}$

Where A = Tan Lat A + Tan D.Long

B = Tan Lat B + Sin D.Long

Tan A = 1 + (C x Cos Lat A)

Tan Lat L $= \dfrac{\text{Tan Lat A x Sin D.Long +/– Tan Lat B x Sin D.Long A}}{\text{Sin D.Long AB}}$

NB – where 'L' represents the latitude of the great circle as it passes a given latitude. If latitudes A & B are the same, use plus (+), if latitudes A & B differ, use minus (–).
Where the answer is a+ the latitudes are in the same hemisphere.
Where the answer is a– the latitudes are in opposite hemispheres.

Napiers Rules

	Sin Mid Part	=	Cos Opposite x Cos Opposite
	Sin Mid Part	=	Tan adjacent x Tan adjacent
Cos Lat V		=	Cos Lat A x Sin Initial Course
Tan D.Long to V		=	1 ÷ (Sin Lat A x Tan Initial Course)
Distance	Cos VA	=	Sin Lat A ÷ Sin Lat V
D.Long to Vertex	Cos P	=	Tan Lat A ÷ Tan Lat V
Distance	Sin A	=	Cos Lat V ÷ Cos Lat A
Distance		=	D.Long ($V_1 \sim V_2$) x Cos Limiting Latitude

Using of the above formula is considerably faster than the use of tables, but the marine student is warned that careful manipulation of the calculator is essential to acquire a correct result. Once so obtained results should always be re-checked, to ensure accuracy.

Use of the above formula on the examples within the text would prove a useful exercise to marine students.

NB. Minor discrepancies may occur between the use of logs/formula.

Chapter Five

OCEAN ROUTING

5.1 The Shipowner's Preference

The Shipowner will very often provide guidelines to Masters as an aid to establishing the most suitable route and in line with company policy. The Master should therefore include these considerations in his choice of suitable route. The shipping company's preference would probably include:

1. *Speed of passage* – Short passage time is usually a major consideration especially for regular trades.
2. *Economy* – Fuel costs are high and engines should be operated at their most cost effective speed.
3. *Safety of vessel* – Preferred good weather to avoid damage to ship and cargo.
4. *Comfort* – Comfort of passengers and/or deck cargoes on routes to avoid heavy weather.
5. *Dependability* – A record of reliability, coupled with speed and safety when operating a regular service.
6. *Design of vessel* – Is the vessel suitable for the route in question i.e. Ice strengthened for transit through ice regions, or sufficient power to outrun TRS.

Maintenance of the vessel may also be a company consideration, if it is expected that ship's crew will be engaged on deck painting activity. Alternatives would be for the regular dry-docking of the ship and shore side maintenance being planned and carried out to suit vessels requirements.

5.1.1 geographic constraints and fixed parameters

There could well be constraints on the choice of route over which there is no control and these may take the form of any or all of the following:

1. The draught of the vessel could well restrict some shallow water routes and deeper water passages would need to be adopted. There could also be constraints regarding transit through winter loadline zones if the vessel is loaded to her summer draught.
2. Ice limits could well deter ships from entering specific regions during the ice season. Vessels would require ice strengthened classification prior to voyages into ice restricted waters.
3. Ocean currents which generally do not vary much could influence the choice of route. East and west bound passages between the same ports are unlikely to suit a reciprocal course because of prevailing winds. Subsequently Masters may opt for north or south alternatives when planning outward and homeward voyages.

5.1.2 variable parameters

Flexibility must always be built into any planned ocean route. It is a necessary requirement to take account of any influencing factors and of course the experienced mariner would interpret the main factor as being that of the current weather.

1. Wind direction and force will most certainly affect the vessels speed and overall performance. Violent and dangerous motions on the vessel should clearly be avoided if possible for the sake of passengers, cargo and safety. Alternatives to avoid adverse winds should be employed whenever practical.
2. Historical records of heavy seas and swell conditions should be investigated when deciding on the proposed route. For similar reasons, as stated, improved sea state conditions should be sought out and used where appropriate.
3. Sea and air temperatures could also influence routing choice when a vessel is in transit with critical temperature controlled cargoes.

5.1.3 selection of an optimum route

In addition to climatic considerations, Masters will need to consider a number of factors when selecting an ocean passage route. Not only operational and safety considerations, but also commercial influence will need to become essential elements of the chosen route.

Combined climatic/operational considerations could include all of the following:

1. Recommendations obtained from references to the publication '*Ocean Passages of the World*'.
2. The type of vessel, its draught and state of loading, to be suitable to provide adequate underkeel clearance through all stages of the voyage.
3. The time of year and any expected seasonal hazards.(Weather/sea related conditions, e.g. gales, TRS).
4. The likelihood of encountering dangerous ice formations, (with or without fog conditions) making it necessary to deviate or cause delays.
5. Recommendations made by shore side routing organisations.
6. The classification of the vessel and whether it is ice strengthened for passage through areas inside known ice limits.
7. Strength and direction of prevailing currents and whether such currents are favourable or adverse.
8. The expected wind patterns, with their anticipated strength and direction.
9. The endurance of the vessel and the need to take on bunkers.
10. The need to carry out deck maintenance operations during the voyage and the requirement for a good weather route.
11. Cargo related routes to reflect the needs of specific cargoes: e.g. Coal cargoes require surface ventilation. Timber cargoes should not be exposed to breaking seas (affected by absorption factor, reducing the positive stability). Container deck stacks should not be exposed to ice accretion.
12. Masters preferences and experience.
13. Distance differences between comparative routes.
    NB. Shortest distance is not necessarily the safest distance.
14. Size of vessel and physical restrictions caused by bridge heights or canal widths.
15. Consultation and reference to informed sources, such as Marine Superintendents, Routing Charts, Sailing Directions, and old log books if appropriate.

5.1.4 commercial influences on choice of route

These could include any or all of the following items :

1. The terms as specified by the Charter Party.
2. Owners or Charterers direct instructions/preferences.
3. A route that will not infringe Load Line Zones and affect the acceptance or rejection of extra cargo.

4. The distance of alternative routes considered against fuel burn and time.
5. The costs of bunkers and the endurance of the vessel.
6. Costs of engaging shore side routing services.(Charter Party may specify)
7. Incurred costs of canal transits.
   e.g. Panama, Suez Canals.
8. Insurance costs reduced on specified 'low' hazardous routes.
9. Charter Party may specify constant speed route, or limiting latitude restrictions.
10. Special needs of the ship or trade. e.g. Deep Water or Ice Free routes.

5.1.5 route choice

The final decision on the choice of route will ultimately rest with the Master. However, the choice must reflect the safest option available at the time, taking into account the respective navigation hazards that could be expected to be encountered on each option.

Clearly the aspects of choice will undoubtedly conflict on one or more points. The chosen option cannot hope to find everything in favour of any one single choice of route. But Masters should consol themselves, that the passage plan is meant to be flexible, and as such, the initial choice may be legitimately amended in the light of new information and/or a safer alternative presenting itself.

5.1.6 shipboard routing

This cannot be as detailed as a 'shore routing service' because it will lack the most up-to-date information that a shore side facility will provide. Although considerable information sources are available to the mariner aboard his own vessel it is unlikely that he will have the back-up computer facilities of shore based operators. The ship will most certainly not have access to the many informative contacts, or all of the required communication equipment necessary, to complete a comprehensive routing plan. However, an experienced mariner would be expected to produce a reasonable ocean passage plan from limited sources.

5.1.7 shorebased routing

Shore routing tends to be comprehensive, but it is expensive. Some benefits will be achieved in fuel economy and possible reductions in heavy weather damage will be visible. Masters will need to advise the service of ships particulars and also of company's preferences. The Master gains voyage planning from the start of a passage and receives regular weather and routing advice while on passage.

5.1.8 shore based routing organisations

Commercial companies now operate routing services for ocean going vessels, the most widely used, probably being 'Ocean Routes' of the United States. However, it should be appreciated that this is not a free service and Masters who avail themselves of it, will be charged to reflect the complexity of the route plan.

Some Charter Parties specify that vessels will route in accordance with advice supplied by the Shore Based organisation as a condition of the charter. While some shipping companies may have a policy to engage shore based routing operations.

5.1.9 advantages of shore based routing

Masters and ship owners who employ a 'shore based' system can expect to obtain some advantage over vessels which operate their own ship routing schedule, greatest delays have been found, by experience, to be caused by Masters changing their course to avoid bad weather. Distinct benefits can be gained by the use of a well tried and tested routing organisation. Additional advantages will be in the form of:

1. Savings in fuel and time. (Possibly 10-15 hours N. Atlantic, westbound).
2. Reductions in ship and cargo damage, with reduced wear on main engine propulsion systems.
3. Passengers could be expected to experience greater comfort.
4. Maintenance at sea is usually possible in better weather.
5. Possibility of reduced insurance premiums.
6. Navigation hazards avoided, e.g. like TRS or ice.
7. Reference to shore routing may be necessary to be compliant with Charter Party.
8. Better weather/satellite coverage and interpretation of data is available to the ship.
9. Post voyage information can be made available if required.
10. Continuous monitoring of the vessels progress is noted by a secondary body.

5.1.10 types of route available

In order to advise on a route one of the principle objectives must be met, that is to provide a route by which the vessel will attain her destination by the most economical passage avoiding ship and cargo damage. To this end the climatic routes east/west will probably be devised under the following types:

1. Least time.
2. Least time with least damage.
3. Least damage.
4. Constant speed.

These would be associated with additional criteria for vessels which require:

1. Ice free routes because of no ice classification.
2. Deep water routes for vessels which are compromised by deep draught.
3. An all weather route for special cargoes or passengers.

Least time	The objective being to reduce time on passage and is usually applicable to 'tanker' vessels. This type of vessel is less likely to sustain hull damage and will not suffer the possibility of cargo damage.
Least time with least damage	The objective with this option is to reduce and minimise damage costs. This option is probably the most widely used by vessels engaging in weather routing service.
Least damage	The objective being to sustain absolutely minimum damage, an option for vessels with particularly sensitive cargoes e.g. livestock, vehicles etc.
Constant speed	A requirement often stipulated by 'Charter Parties' is that the vessel maintains a given speed through out the period of passage. Failure to achieve this speed could incur financial penalties.
Fuel saving option	With today's cost of living increased fuel costs have become significant to ship owners when choosing the optimum route. Prudent weather routing can become an important consideration regarding the economics of a voyage.

5.1.11 ship examples employing 'shore based' routing

'Shore Based' Routing is suitable for all ships, but especially appropriate for the following types of vessels which may encounter typical problems:

1. Container, car carriers, high sided ferries – all of which can be expected to experience considerable windage and subsequent leeway effects.
2. Passenger or roll on/roll off vessels, all weather routes in order to reduce excessive rolling.
3. Tankers, OBO's, vessels constrained by deep draughts requiring deep water routes.
4. All vessels without Ice classification, which carry no ice strengthening or only part ice strengthening which would require an ice free route.

5.1.12 procedure for 'shore based' routing

A request for routing advice and recommendations should be made not less than 48 hours prior to departure. Communication being by means of telephone, telex, cable or fax, and should include the following items of information:

- name of ship and call sign.
- port of departure and Estimated Time of Departure (ETD).
- destination.
- estimated voyage speed.
- summer deadweight, whether loaded or in ballast. Nature of cargo.
- weather and sea conditions to be avoided if possible.
- whether maintenance is being carried out en route which requires a fair-weather passage.
- name and telephone number, fax and/or telex of local agent.

prior to sailing

Following a request for a shore side routing organisation to advise on a recommended route. A provisional route would be despatched to the Master, prior to sailing. The recommended route can then be accepted or amended to meet the needs of the ship.

Once the route has been accepted by the Master, this would be confirmed to the 'Routing Organisation'.

on sailing

The Ship's Master would advise the Routing Authority of the departure time, GMT/LMT and confirm coastal particulars to the departure 'Way Point' together with the Sailing Plan.

The Routing (Advisor) Authority would forward the latest weather reports for the immediate passage area. Such weather reports would be updated (usually at 48 hour intervals) or more frequently in the event of severe weather conditions.

on passage

Position reports of the vessel would be passed at regular intervals to the Routing Officer ashore. These would normally be accompanied by the weather details that the vessel is experiencing at the time of the report.

In return, the Routing Officer would provide continued advance weather reports at 48 hour intervals or more frequently, in the event of adverse conditions prevailing in the geographic area of the ships passage.

5.2 Shore Side Routing – for the first time

In order to provide a satisfactory service, shore based Routing Organisations would require essential information about the vessel seeking an advisory route; i.e. details of ship, its size, draught, service speed, owners address etc. This information would be computer stored for future reference employed with relevant passage information when the routing service is engaged on subsequent occasions.

Current 'Passage Information' would include the place of departure together with the intended destination, via any essential ports of call. The nature of the cargo, date and time of the intended voyage and any special requirements and preferences of either Master, Owners, or Charter Party. The endurance of the vessel, classification and special features would normally be kept in the computer data base, relevant information being used to compile a recommended voyage plan.

5.2.1 use of ship's performance data

Information gained from ships performance data can be beneficial to either a shore based or ship based routing officer. Following trials of the ship when new, various aspects of performance criteria can be graphically displayed in ship performance curves. These can be employed, bearing in mind the ships state of loading, stability, draughts etc. to establish how the vessel would be expected to perform in various sea conditions.

If relevant information could be obtained, i.e. from a facsimile machine, namely wave heights, pressure charts etc. these could be used to estimate the expected speed of the vessel over certain periods of the voyage. Equally, the source of information could well justify a deviation of the ships course in order to avoid excessive seas and resultant reduced performance by the vessel.

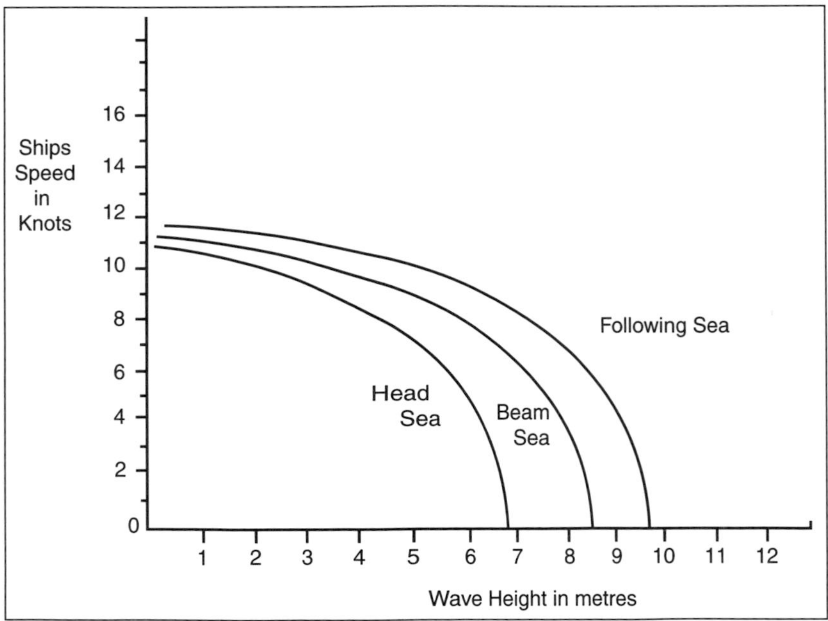

Diagram 5.1: Ships performance curves employed to determine how far the vessel will travel during the next 12 or 24hours, used in conjunction with surface analysis and prognostic charts relevant at the time of the voyage.

Any such figures derived from the use of performance curves are estimates and should be used with obvious caution.

5.2.2 radio facsimile transmissions

Many meteorological services world-wide, provide daily radio-facsimile transmissions of weather charts. Examples of some maritime navigation transmissions are included and the following break-down provides a brief insight into what they may contain:

a) SURFACE WEATHER ANALYSIS – These show weather patterns based on synoptic surface observations. They are normally made a few hours before transmission.

b) SURFACE WEATHER PROGNOSIS – These indicate future weather patterns for either a 24 hour or 36 hour outlook for specific regions.

c) EXTENDED SURFACE PROGNOSIS – These indicate forecast positions of fronts and pressure systems at the surface for a projected period of 2 to 5 days.

d) WAVE ANALYSIS – These show characteristics of 'sea waves.' They are based on synoptic wave observations made shortly before transmission, or based on calculations derived from wind and wave patterns.
Lines connect points of equal wave heights and direction of movements.

e) WAVE PROGNOSIS – These charts provide a forecast of the provisions of wave systems, normally over a 24 hour period.

f) SEA TEMPERATURE – These reflect surface temperatures and forecast contours for a given period. Normally over 1 week, ten days or monthly periods. They are based on mean values for a given period. They may also include anomalies in sea temperatures.

g) SEA ICE CHARTS – Snow and sea ice areas are depicted together with known positions of icebergs.

h) SATELLITE WEATHER PICTURES – Show cloud cover, tropical cyclones, and the positions of any disturbance in weather patterns.

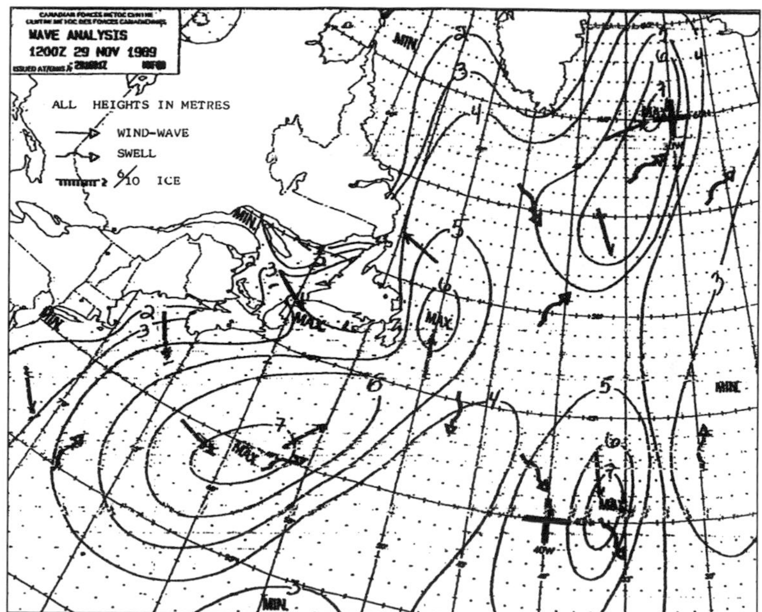

Diagram 5.2a: Facsimile example issued by the Canadian Forces Metoc Centre wave analysis for 1200z 29th November, 1989

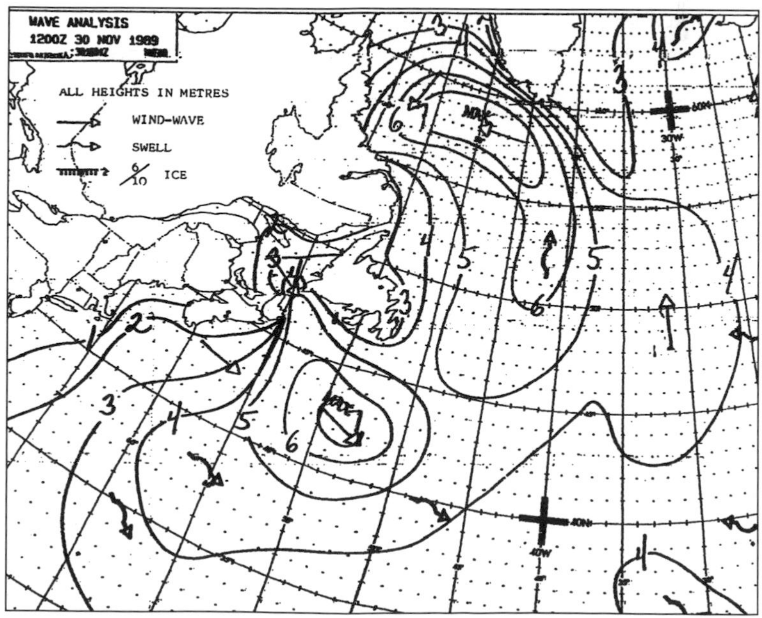

Diagram 5.2b: Facsimile example issued by the Canadian Forces Metoc Centre wave analysis for 1200z 30th November, 1989

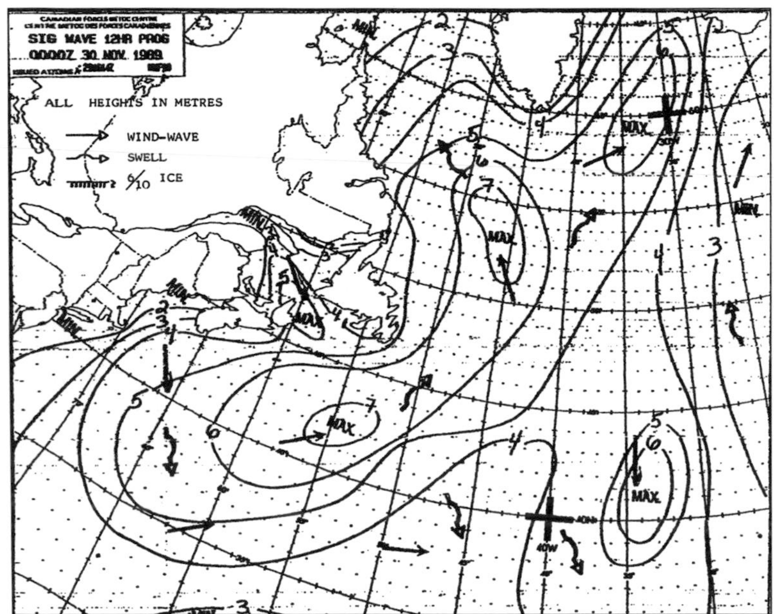

Diagram 5.2c: Facsimile example issued by the Canadian Forces Metoc Centre Prognostic wave condition for 30th November, 1989

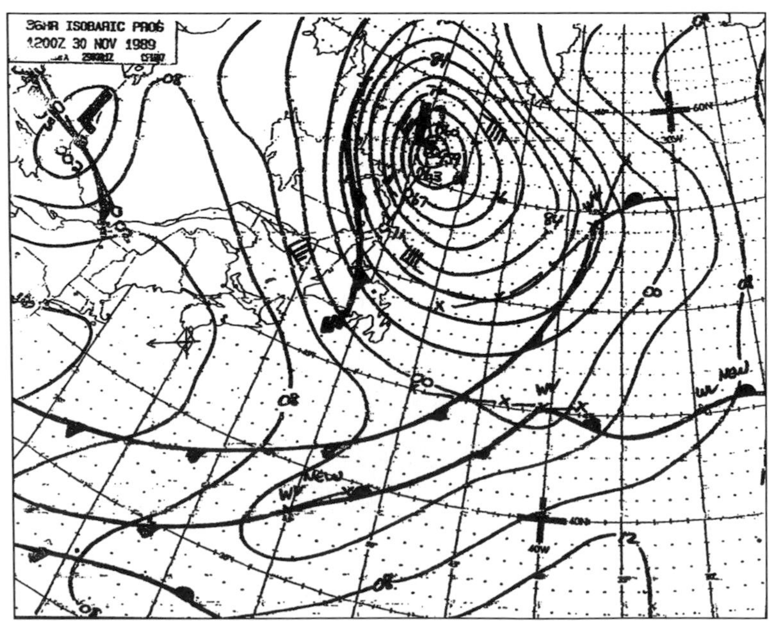

Diagram 5.2d: Facsimile example issued by the Canadian Forces Metoc Centre Prognostic isobaric chart for 1200z 30th November, 1989 Comparison of this example for 36 hrs as opposed to the 24 hour projection.

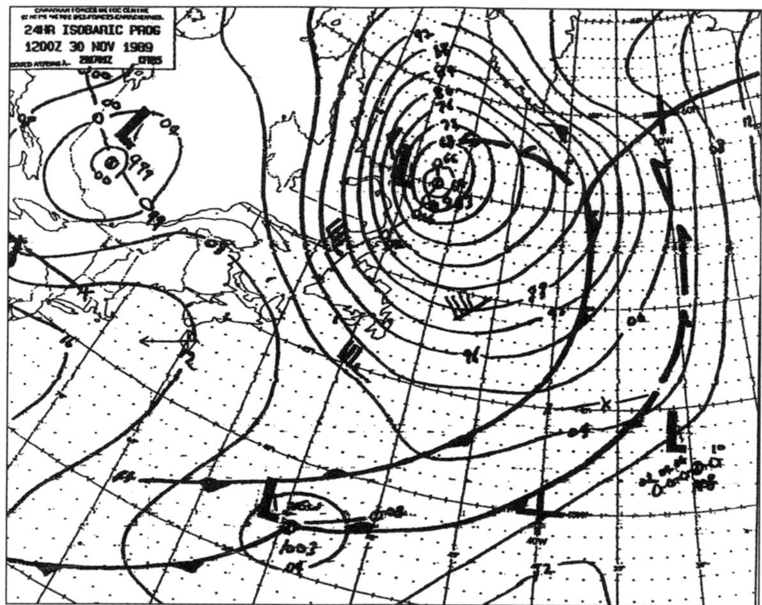

Diagram 5.2e: Facsimile example issued by the Canadian Forces Metoc Centre Prognostic isobaric chart for 1200z 30th November, 1989

NB. Position of vessel inserted on the chart to allow interpretation of the expected weather that the vessel can be expected to encounter. vessel westbound, in a position south of Nova Scotia. 1200z 30/11/89.

5.3 Routing Charts – Relevant Information and Usage

Any navigator, when planning a passage either coastal or ocean, should avail himself with the available data relevant to the specific area of the passage. A major source of information which could well effect the planned route could be located on respective routing charts. Mariners should therefore be aware of the contents and detail contained on a typical routing chart:

1. The title of the chart reflects the area that the chart covers i.e. South Atlantic Ocean.
   The specific monthly period that the chart refers to is stated underneath the title, together with the scale for a given latitude, which the chart portrays.
2. The date and number with the monthly consecutive number, and the last corrections are found in the lower border.

3. Main shipping routes between principal ports are indicated as green track lines. Mileage shown is in sea miles between ports or the ends of great circle routes.

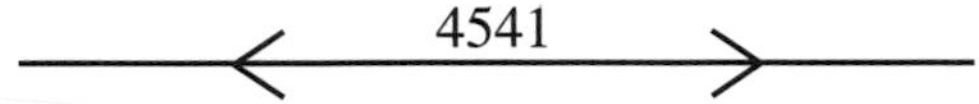

4. Limits of load line zones are indicated with the effective date and specified latitudes. These are presented in pastel colours:

Tropical zone	....	Light green
Summer zone	....	Light pink
Winter zone	....	Light blue

5. The mean maximum iceberg limit is presented by a broken line in a pale blue colour:

   Maximum limits of pack ice are also shown in the same colour but with a distinctive broken line pattern:

6. Ocean currents are presented in 'dark blue' and reflect the predominant direction of sea-surface currents for the quarter year from the monthly date of the chart.
   Constancy being indicated by presentation of lines:

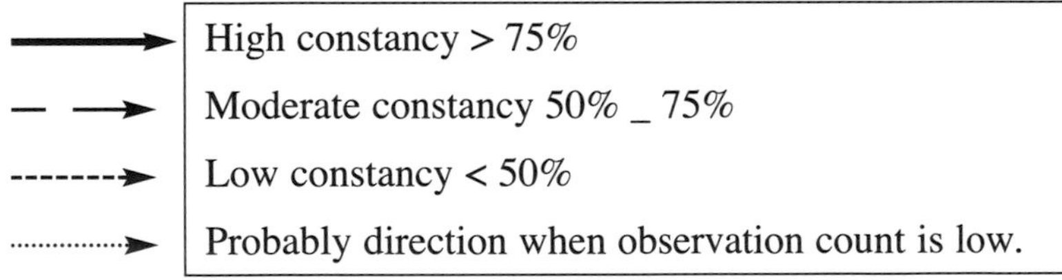

7. Wind roses are shown in a pale red colour and will be shown over the majority of sea areas.
   Arrows fly with the wind and their length indicates percentage frequency on a given scale (0% to 50%).
   The frequency scale is 2 inches (5cm) to 100%. From the arrow head to the circle is 5% and provides a ready means of estimating the percentage frequency.
   The upper figure inside the circle represents the number of observations, the percentage frequency of variable winds is represented by the middle figure, while the number of observed calms are indicated by the lower figure of each rose.

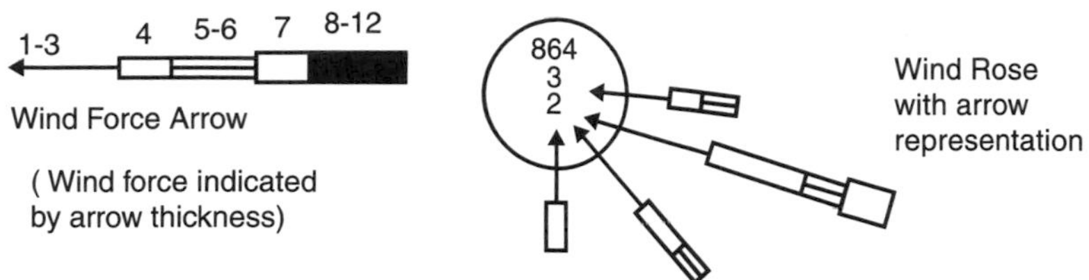

8. Meteorological information is also presented by a number of smaller insets into the chart and include information on:
   (a) percentage frequency of winds, beaufort force '7' and higher.
   (b) mean air temperature °C and mean air pressure in millibars.
   (c) mean sea temperature °C and dew point temperature °C.
   (d) percentage frequency of low visibility of less than 5 miles and percentage frequency of fog, where visibility is less than 5.0 statute miles.
9. In addition to the above stated items, prominent geographic places and landmarks are indicated with sea passages and respective course alteration points.

5.4 Climatic Routing

Climatic Routing is a routing method which gainfully employs the use of the prevailing currents and winds. It would take advantage of seasonal changes and influences caused during the monsoon periods, although the final route may be somewhat longer in distance. It is anticipated that the method would allow an overall better speed performance to be made by the vessel throughout the voyage.

Climatic routes are shown on 'Routing Charts' and are considered in the publication '*Ocean Passages of the World*'.

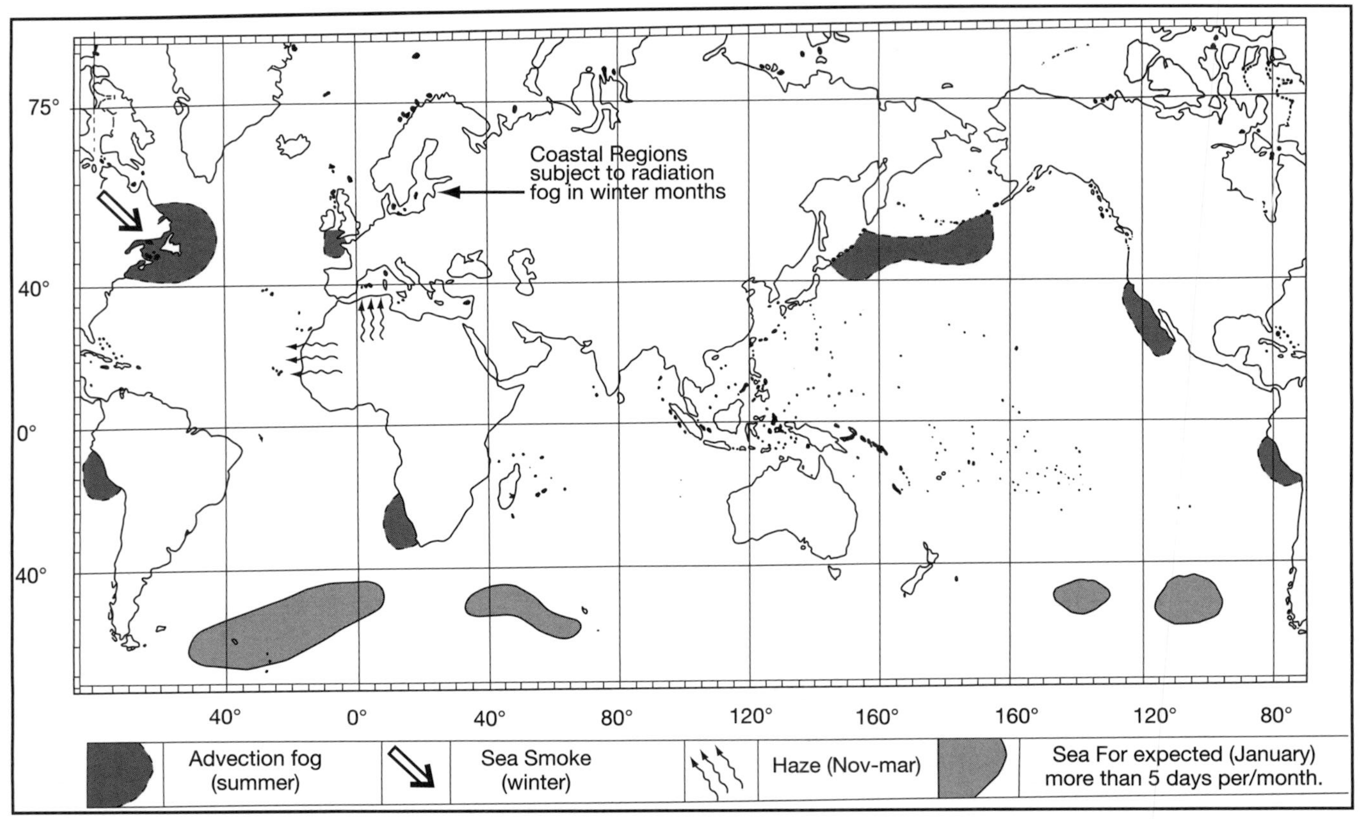

Diagram 5.3: THE WORLD (Areas of impaired visibility)

5.4.1 North Atlantic

Some of the busiest shipping routes of the world are found in the North Atlantic waters. They are also some of the most dangerous routes with problems of fog and ice hazards on approaches to North American Ports. Main routes from North European ports to the eastern seaboard of the United States of America and to the Gulf of Saint Lawrence, (via Cabot Strait) pass close to the Grand Banks. Fog is prevalent for this area during late spring and early summer. It is also notorious for ice conditions which tend to exist from January to May, extending furthest south during the months of March and April. On occasions pack ice may be experienced just south of the end of the Banks but it is more usual for floes to break up before reaching latitude 45° north.

Icebergs

An average of about 70 icebergs a year drift south with the Labrador current towards the Grand Banks region and into the main shipping lanes. The worst season is experienced between March and July with the greatest frequency occurring in April, May and June. Icebergs are not usually encountered south of latitude 40° N or east of longitude 40°W. However, mariners should note that these limits must be considered flexible with occasional bergs encountered beyond the 40° guidelines.

Grand Banks – Summary

An extensive fishing community exists in and around the shores of Newfoundland and Nova Scotia. As a consequence vessels in transit via this region can expect to encounter numerous fishing vessels. These combined with the climatic ice and fog conditions which prevail during certain seasons make this area one which requires extreme caution for navigators.

Masters should consider reduction of speed and/or stopping if encountering ice conditions which could endanger the vessel.

The use of double watchkeepers may also be a prudent action in certain circumstances.

Belle Isle Straits

Due to prevailing ice conditions the Belle Isle Straits are generally not navigable from late December until June. Visibility in this area is often impaired and vessels intending to pass via the straits may find use of the echo sounder invaluable if the position is questionable when approaching from the east.

Cabot Straits

With pack ice as far south as Cape Race by the end of January, navigation is usually limited to between April and February. Heavy ice concentrations would normally be expected in the early part of the year from January to April.

Trans-Ocean Routes (North Atlantic)

Recommended westbound routes between Europe and the east coast of the United States of America is by great circle via Cape Race, or via the way position latitude 42½° N, longitude 50°W, during the ice season. Great circles are also recommended to and from the Belle Isle Straits (when Belle Isle is navigable), and to St. John's Newfoundland from Norway, British Isles, Bay of Biscay and west coast of Portugal and Spain.

Westbound routes to the Gulf of Mexico from Europe are recommended via the NE Providence Channel. The east bound routes are recommended via the Florida Straits. This east bound route takes advantage of the gulf stream and the North Atlantic drift as well as the predominantly following winds. Routes to Panama from the European continent are great circles towards the Mona Passage, Turks Island Passage, or the Sombrero Passage.

Additional Area Information – North Atlantic

Western Approaches to the English Channel – Traffic separation schemes are in operation for vessels on passage through the English Channel. Use of Chart 5500 Mariners Routing Guide should be consulted. A high incidence of 'fog' in the vicinity of Ile de d'Ouessant can be expected and the use of soundings is recommended when making landfalls in this area.

Gibraltar Straits

A traffic separation scheme exists between the Straits of Gibraltar. Variable eddies and currents persist in the area of Cape St Vincent towards the straits. While inside the straits a strong westerly wind could result in a tidal stream of up to 6 knots.
(Distance Ile de d'Ouessant to Gibraltar Straits – 930 miles).

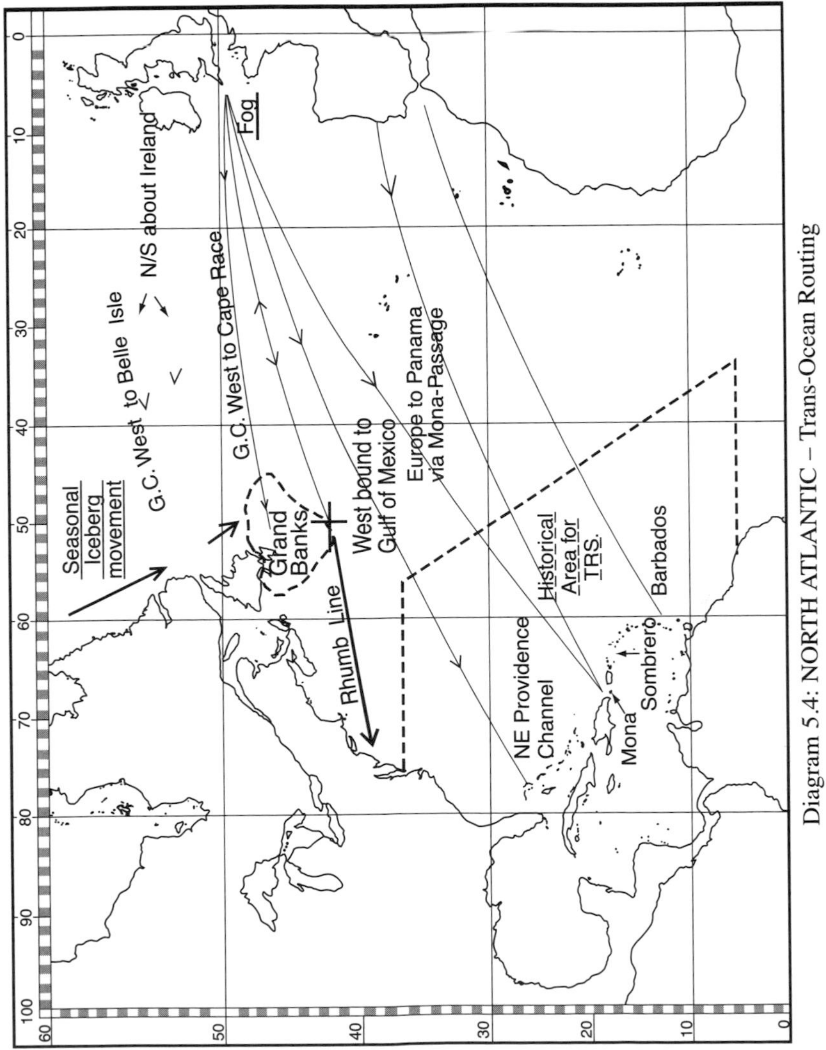

Diagram 5.4: NORTH ATLANTIC – Trans-Ocean Routing

Norwegian Coast Ports

Main ports on the west coast of Norway are not restricted by ice. Howevcr, the closure of Oslo, may occur on rare occasions.

Denmark Strait

An area which is generally navigable throughout the year, with the eastern side usually free of ice, although icebergs may be encountered on either side of the straits at any time. Occasionally the straits may be closed due to ice conditions extending from Greenland, as occurred in spring 1968.

Florida Straits

This region is effected by strong currents of up to 4 knots, and vessels should be aware that some charts are based on old surveys; these two facts combined make this a region that requires tight watchkeeping procedures with primary and secondary position monitoring in place. Traffic can expect to be heavy with considerable cruise ship activity in the area, moving inward and outward from Miami and Fort Lauderdale towards the Caribbean and the Gulf of Mexico.

Gulf of Mexico

Through traffic to Houston/ Galveston, New Orleans the Panama Canal (Colon) region and Central American Ports must expect to encounter extensive offshore activity. Many installations dominate the Gulf of Mexico and as such have the associated hazards of considerable oil field traffic. Navigation is by fairways both East/West and North/South. Use of anchors in the region can only be advised in recommended anchorages because of many under surface wells and sea bottom pipeline/manifold obstructions.

Hurricanes

These occur in the western part of the ocean and effect the Caribbean Sea, Gulf of Mexico, Bahamas and the Bermuda Islands. Their greatest frequency is during the months of August to October. However, they have been experienced from May to December (see tropical revolving storms).

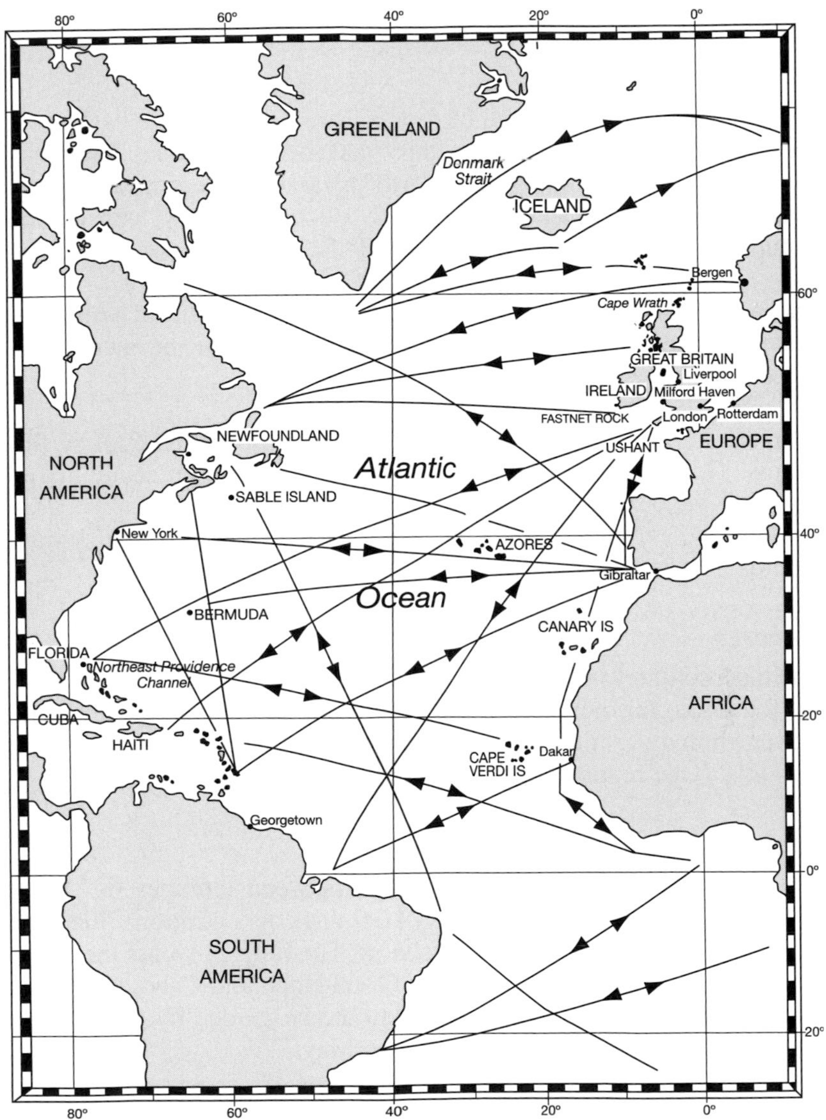

Diagram 5.5: NORTH/SOUTH ATLANTIC Example Routes

5.4.2 South Atlantic

Climatic Information

With the continuous passage of depressions from west to east strong winds and high seas dominate this vast ocean expanse. The wind pattern, although similar to the North Atlantic, differs in a way that circulation is anti-clockwise, with the oceanic anti-cyclone centred about latitude 20° S to about latitude 28° S.

The worst conditions which are likely to be experienced will occur between 40° S and 50° S. While a heavy swell may also be encountered especially up to latitude 60° S.

Tropical storms do not form in this area because of the cool surface waters. This condition is one that does not generate an accumulation of water vapour necessary for the formation of a TRS. Gales are frequent and common, south of latitude 40° S, even during the summer months. Fog is also a feature of the summer months.

Icebergs

The most southerly shipping routes are affected by icebergs which can be found as far north as latitude 31° S. Occasionally, abnormal movement may result in icebergs being experienced even further north than this. (One reported at latitude 26° S).

Pack Ice

The limit of pack ice tends to average between latitudes 60° S and 54° S, but the position of the edge (4/10 this concentration) fluctuates depending on the severity of the season. The limit prevents the use of great circle sailing between Cape of Good Hope and Cabo de Hornos, at certain times of the year Masters should be guided by seasonal ice reports except during March through to May.

Trans Ocean Routes (South Atlantic)

Westbound routes are usually by rhumb line sailing. The main reason for this is that the adverse effects from head winds and currents are reduced, while eastbound tracks usually combine great circle and rhumb line when south of latitude 25° S.

Example Routes

1. Great circle sailing in both directions is recommended between Rio de la Plata (River Plate) and ports on the African coast north of lat. 25° S.
2. Rio de la Plata towards Cape Town/Indian Ocean is recommended by great circle, but parts of the track lie within the extreme iceberg limits.
   Cape Town towards Rio de la Plata is a recommended rhumb line to position, lat. 35° S, long. 40° W, then a second rhumb line towards destination.
3. Cape Town to the Falkland Islands or Straits of Magellan.
   Routes are by rhumb line to lat. 35° S, long. 40° W then on by rhumb line to destination.
   Distance reference:
   Cape Town to Port Stanley (Falklands) 4170 miles
   Cape Town to Magellan Straits 4510 miles
   Low powered vessels: Alternative routing for low powered vessels is recommended via lat. 27° S, long. 20° W, then by a second rhumb line to the way point for the Falklands and Magellan Straits.
   This route takes full advantage of lighter winds and favour-able currents, although the distance is slightly longer by about 150 miles. (Low-powered vessels – which cannot maintain 15 kts).
   NB: When on passage via the Straits of Magellan, low powered vessels are warned that they may experience strong cross tidal streams and may subsequently be at a disadvantage when careful manoeuvrability is required.
   Violent and unpredictable squalls are also common to this area. Masters should therefore consider their passage plan with care if intending to pass through this region which has the usual hazards of a narrow waterway coupled with a reputation for bad weather.
4. Cape Town to Panama Canal (via Galleons Passage).
   Recommended routes are by great circle to a position North of Recife (lat. 4° 40' S, long 34° 35' W) then coastal towards Colon via 'Galleons Passage'.

5.4.3 Indian Ocean – Entering

Mariners have a choice of keeping inshore from Cape Agulhas and thus keeping inshore of the Agulhas current or passing to the south of the current via a position some 145' south of the Cape of Good Hope.

Indian Ocean – Leaving

Masters should obtain a position which favours the Agulhas Current and one which avoids the abnormal waves and dangerous seas that are common to the area.

North Indian Ocean

The weather patterns of the North Indian Ocean are influenced by the seasonal monsoon winds which result from the heating and cooling of the Asiatic land mass.

South West Monsoon

From June to September a low pressure area is established over the north west part of india, because of the rising temperature over the land at this time. This results in a south westerly wind being experienced. The origins of this are derived from the south west trade winds being drawn over the Equator and then deflected by the rotation of the earth. The winds then join up with the cyclonic circulation about the low pressure area to become what is known as the south west monsoon. This subsequently affects not only the North Indian Ocean but also the Bay of Bengal and the Arabian Sea.

Variable Wind Strengths

The south west monsoon has been observed to be strongest in an area approximately 250 miles east of Suqutra during the month of July. Wind speeds being noted up to force 7 or more, at this time. It is also recorded as being strong in the western part of the Arabian Sea, with average forces of 6 to 7 being the norm at the height of the monsoon season.

In the Bay of Bengal the average wind force is about 4 to 5 but may reach 7 during the months of July and August.

In the north eastern area, Karachi/Bombay, the weather is generally better with wind speeds averaging about force 4.

From the Equator to about 5° north latitude and east of longitude 60° east, average wind speeds are about force 3, though their direction is more variable.

General Weather

Over most of the North Indian Ocean the weather outlook remains cloudy and unsettled with considerable rainfall during the south west monsoon season, the west coast of India and Burma experiencing particular heavy rainfall at this time.

Normally visibility is quite good except when impaired by heavy rain. Exception to this may be found in the northern and western parts of the Arabian Sea where surface visibility may be reduced during July and August, because of dust haze.

Malacca Straits

An area which is well known to many seafarers experiences usually light winds that vary in both direction and force. The straits often being influenced by land and sea breezes with occasional strong winds reaching gale force. Squalls are also a feature of this area, notably at night and usually from the west.

Malacca Strait

This is probably the main seaway used by vessels on route from Europe, or India towards Malaysian ports, Japanese ports and onwards. In addition to what has already been stated about this very busy shipping channel the following may be found useful when navigating through the area:

Depths in the channel are liable to change and the least depth in the fairway is about 25 metres. Deep draught vessels should take special note of the most recent reports regarding the least depths in and around the fairway. Vessels which exceed a draught of 19.8 metres should not use the channel.

Distances up to about 600 nautical miles require particular vigilance by watchkeeping officers. The area is well used by fishing vessels and strong tidal streams must be anticipated. The width of the Straits varies from 8.4 nautical miles in the south to about 140 miles in the north. Although larger vessels will have to negotiate a narrow channel of around 2 miles in width. (One Fathom Bank).

Traffic density is heavy and large vessels need to proceed with extreme caution. About 140 vessels daily pass through the Straits, the alternative passage towards Japan would be via the Lombok Strait, which adds about 1200 n/miles to the journey.

Hazards – small islands are situated at the most southern end of the Straits, some with reefs and sandwaves. Uncharted wrecks and unmarked shoals are not uncommon.

Incidence of pirates boarding vessels in this area continue to be reported (2004) especially noted in the southerly traffic lane passing through Indonesian waters of the Singapore Strait.

Weather patterns are influenced by the north east monsoon (northern winter) and the south east monsoon (northern summer). Winds are generally light and variable in direction but squalls often reaching gale force are common to the area. Rainfall is heavy in the region, and may impair visibility.

Publications for use when passage planning through the Malacca Strait should include:

Admiralty Lists of Lights (Vols., F & K), Chart Catalogue, Admiralty Navigational Charts, Routing Charts, Ocean Passages of the World, Admiralty List of Radio Signals, Sailing Directions Volume 44, (Malacca Strait Pilot), Chart 5502 (Mariners Routing Guide – Malacca and Singapore Straits).

PASSAGE PLANNING FOR TRANSITING MALACCA/SINGAPORE STRAITS

WAY POINT	ONE FATHOM RACON "M"	SW TAKONG RACON "D"	BUFFALO ROCK	HORSBURGH L'T HOUSE	EASTERN BANK
MAX DRAFT	20.23	20.23	20.23	20.23	20.23
U.K.A. REQUIRED	3.50	3.50	3.50	3.50	4.00
CONTROL DEPTH	23.00	24.50	22.70	45.00	23.50
REQUIRED TIDAL HEIGHT	0.73	–0.77	1.03	–21.27	0.73
CO-TIDAL FACTOR	1.00	0.96	0.98	1.00	0.99
STANDARD POINT	O.F.B.	RAFFLES L'T HOUSE	RAFFLES L'T HOUSE	HORSBURGH L'T HOUSE	HORSBGH L'T HOUSE
REQ. TIDAL HT AT STANDARD POINT	0.73	–0.80	1.05	–21.27	0.74
TIDAL WINDOW		0000–2359	0920–1650	0000–2359	19109–0200
TARGET TIME	12/07/02 11:17	27/04/02 02:40	27/04/02 03:45	2002/4/272 06:47	27.04/02 08:31
DISTANCE	*****	200	12	38	19
ESTIMATED SP'D	*****	13.00	11.00	12.50	11.00
PROP HOURS	*****	15.38	1.09	3.04	1.73
E.T.P.	12/07/02 11:17	13/07/02 02:40	13/07/02 03:45	13/07/02 06:47	13/07/02 08:31
ACTUAL PASSED	27/04/02 00:07	27/04/02 14:05	27/04/02 15:05	27/04/02 17:53	27/04/02 19:22
ACTUAL SP'D	*****	14.32	12.00	13.57	12.81

REMARKS: PASSED SINGAPORE: 1530 ST 27TH/APRIL

F: 19.78m, A: 20.40m

Master: ____________________

SAFETY MANAGEMENT SYSTEM

SAFE DRAUGHT CALCULATION PRO FORMA

MALACCA / SINGAPORE STARITS TRANSIT SAFE DRAUGHT CALCULATION	EASTBOUND TRANSIT* ONE FATHOM BANK ETA : 7/12/02 11:17		~~WESTBOUND TRANSIT* RAFFLES LIGHTHOUSE ETA:~~		
	CONTROLLING DEPTH AREAS				
FROM (PORT) DAS ISLAND	ONE FATHOM BANK	Tidal interval 18 to 18 1/2 hours	BATU BERHANTI* ~~RAFFLES LIGHTHOUSE*~~	Passage time 4 hours at 12 knots	EASTERN BANK
Standard Port	Pelabuhan Kelang		Singapore / Keppel Harbour		Horsburgh Lighthouse
Lowest tide for data range	HW 4.16 m		HW 2.48 m		HW 1.86 m / LW 1.49 m
Co-tidal Factor	x 0.83		x 0.93		x 1.0 / x 1.0
Controlling Area Tidal Height	3.45 m		2.31 m		1.86 m / 1.49 m
Assumed Datum Depth	+ 23.00 m		+ 21.00 m		+ 23.50 m / + 23.50 m
Depth Water available	26.45 m		23.31 m		25.36 m / 24.99 m
Underkeel Allowance Requested	- 3.50 m		- 3.50 m		- 4.0 m / - 4.0 m
Controlling Draught	22.95 m		19.81 m		21.36 m / 20.99 m

Maximum Safe Transit Draught (Least HW Controlling Draught)	20.23 m
Voyage Consumption	+ 0.05 m
LOADING PORT MEAN SW DRAUGHT	20.28 m

*Delete as required

If the Eastern Bank LW controlling draught is less than the maximum safe transit draught staging may be necessary to ensure crossing this area at a suitable rise of tide

Co-tidal Factor One Fathom Bank	
	0.90 if HW above 4.3 m
	0.86 if HW is 4.3 m
	0.83 if HW below 4.3 m

Co-tidal Factor	
	0.93 for Batu Berhanti
	1.00 for Raffles Lighthouse

SAFETY FIRST

Diagram 5.6a: Safe Draught Calculation Pro Forma

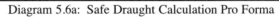

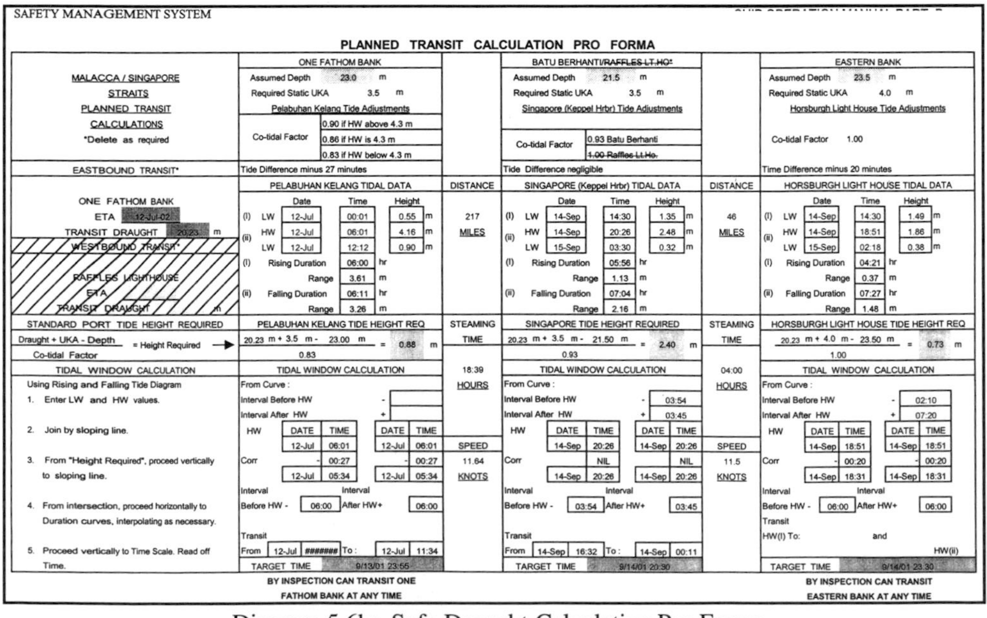

SAFETY MANAGEMENT SYSTEM

PLANNED TRANSIT CALCULATION PRO FORMA

MALACCA / SINGAPORE STRAITS PLANNED TRANSIT CALCULATIONS
*Delete as required

EASTBOUND TRANSIT*
ONE FATHOM BANK
ETA 12-Jul-02
TRANSIT DRAUGHT 20.23 m
~~WESTBOUND TRANSIT*~~
~~RAFFLES LIGHTHOUSE~~
~~ETA~~
~~TRANSIT DRAUGHT m~~

	ONE FATHOM BANK		BATU BERHANTI/~~RAFFLES LT.HO*~~		EASTERN BANK
Assumed Depth	23.0 m		21.5 m		23.5 m
Required Static UKA	3.5 m		3.5 m		4.0 m
	Pelabuhan Kelang Tide Adjustments		Singapore (Keppel Hrbr) Tide Adjustments		Horsburgh Light House Tide Adjustments
Co-tidal Factor	0.90 if HW above 4.3 m; 0.86 if HW is 4.3 m; 0.83 if HW below 4.3 m		0.93 Batu Berhanti; ~~1.00 Raffles Lt.Ho.~~		1.00
	Tide Difference minus 27 minutes		Tide Difference negligible		Time Difference minus 20 minutes

	PELABUHAN KELANG TIDAL DATA	DISTANCE	SINGAPORE (Keppel Hrbr) TIDAL DATA	DISTANCE	HORSBURGH LIGHT HOUSE TIDAL DATA
	Date / Time / Height	217 MILES	Date / Time / Height	46 MILES	Date / Time / Height
(I) LW	12-Jul / 00:01 / 0.55 m		14-Sep / 14:30 / 1.35 m		14-Sep / 14:30 / 1.49 m
(ii) HW	12-Jul / 06:01 / 4.16 m		14-Sep / 20:26 / 2.48 m		14-Sep / 18:51 / 1.86 m
LW	12-Jul / 12:12 / 0.90 m		15-Sep / 03:30 / 0.32 m		15-Sep / 02:18 / 0.38 m
(I) Rising Duration	06:00 hr		05:56 hr		04:21 hr
Range	3.61 m		1.13 m		0.37 m
(ii) Falling Duration	06:11 hr		07:04 hr		07:27 hr
Range	3.26 m		2.16 m		1.48 m

STANDARD PORT TIDE HEIGHT REQUIRED	PELABUHAN KELANG TIDE HEIGHT REQ	STEAMING TIME	SINGAPORE TIDE HEIGHT REQUIRED	STEAMING TIME	HORSBURGH LIGHT HOUSE TIDE HEIGHT REQ
(Draught + UKA - Depth) / Co-tidal Factor = Height Required →	(20.23 m + 3.5 m - 23.00 m) / 0.83 = 0.88 m	18:39 HOURS	(20.23 m + 3.5 m - 21.50 m) / 0.93 = 2.40 m	04:00 HOURS	(20.23 m + 4.0 m - 23.50 m) / 1.00 = 0.73 m

TIDAL WINDOW CALCULATION	TIDAL WINDOW CALCULATION		TIDAL WINDOW CALCULATION		TIDAL WINDOW CALCULATION
Using Rising and Falling Tide Diagram	From Curve :		From Curve :		From Curve :
1. Enter LW and HW values.	Interval Before HW -		Interval Before HW - 03:54		Interval Before HW - 02:10
	Interval After HW +		Interval After HW + 03:45		Interval After HW + 07:20
2. Join by sloping line.	HW DATE TIME 12-Jul 06:01 / DATE TIME 12-Jul 06:01	SPEED	HW DATE TIME 14-Sep 20:26 / DATE TIME 14-Sep 20:26	SPEED	HW DATE TIME 14-Sep 18:51 / DATE TIME 14-Sep 18:51
3. From "Height Required", proceed vertically to sloping line.	Corr - 00:27 / - 00:27; 12-Jul 05:34 / 12-Jul 05:34	11.64 KNOTS	Corr NIL / NIL; 14-Sep 20:26 / 14-Sep 20:26	11.5 KNOTS	Corr - 00:20 / - 00:20; 14-Sep 18:31 / 14-Sep 18:31
4. From intersection, proceed horizontally to Duration curves, interpolating as necessary.	Interval Before HW - 06:00 Interval After HW+ 06:00		Interval Before HW - 03:54 Interval After HW+ 03:45		Interval Before HW - 06:00 Interval After HW+ 06:00
5. Proceed vertically to Time Scale. Read off Time.	Transit From 12-Jul ####### To : 12-Jul 11:34		Transit From 14-Sep 16:32 To : 14-Sep 00:11		Transit HW(I) To: and HW(ii)
	TARGET TIME 9/13/01 23:55		TARGET TIME 9/14/01 20:30		TARGET TIME 9/14/01 23:30

BY INSPECTION CAN TRANSIT ONE FATHOM BANK AT ANY TIME

BY INSPECTION CAN TRANSIT EASTERN BANK AT ANY TIME

Diagram 5.6b: Safe Draught Calculation Pro Forma

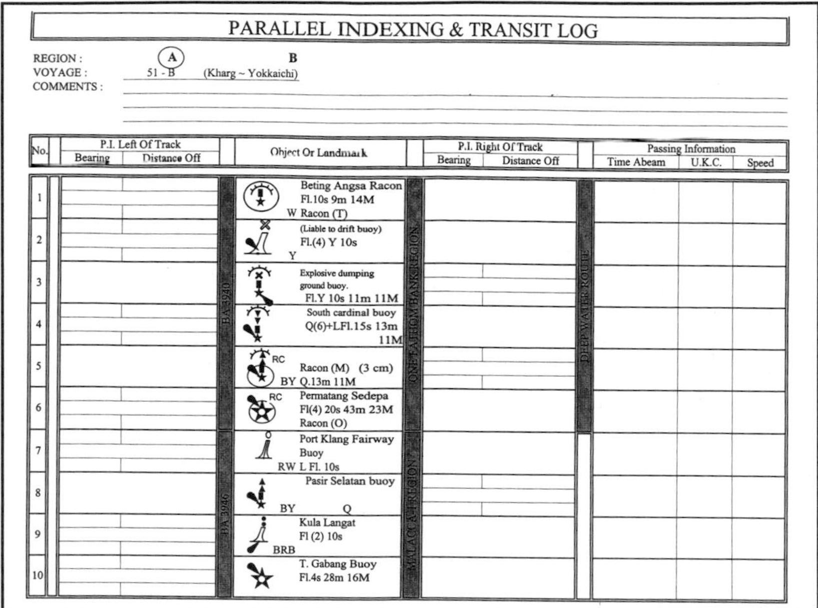

PARALLEL INDEXING & TRANSIT LOG

REGION : (A) B
VOYAGE : 51 - B (Kharg ~ Yokkaichi)
COMMENTS :

No.	P.I. Left Of Track: Bearing	P.I. Left Of Track: Distance Off	Object Or Landmark	P.I. Right Of Track: Bearing	P.I. Right Of Track: Distance Off	Passing Information: Time Abeam	Passing Information: U.K.C.	Passing Information: Speed
1			Beting Angsa Racon Fl.10s 9m 14M W Racon (T)					
2			(Liable to drift buoy) Fl.(4) Y 10s Y					
3			Explosive dumping ground buoy. Fl.Y 10s 11m 11M					
4			South cardinal buoy Q(6)+LFl.15s 13m 11M					
5			RC Racon (M) (3 cm) BY Q.13m 11M					
6			RC Permatang Sedepa Fl(4) 20s 43m 23M Racon (O)					
7			Port Klang Fairway Buoy RW L Fl. 10s					
8			Pasir Selatan buoy BY Q					
9			Kula Langat Fl (2) 10s BRB					
10			T. Gabang Buoy Fl.4s 28m 16M					

Diagram 5.7: Parallel Indexing and Transit Log

Piracy

The threat from piracy attacks on ships continues to increase on a world-wide scale with more incidents reported in 2002/2003 than ever before. The notable areas being the South China Sea and the Philippines, Far East regions, Indonesia, and in particular the Malacca Straits. Other areas such as Bangladesh, the Red Sea and around the Horn of Africa, have all recorded incidents of attacks when the ship is underway.

Locations like Nigeria, the Ivory Coast, Brazil and Central America have recorded attacks on stationary vessels while alongside or at anchor.

Such incidents are usually conducted by armed terrorists or pirates and must be considered as a risk to safe navigation. The introduction of the International Ship and Port Facility Security Code (ISPS code) adopted in December, 2002 has gone some way to raising the profile of security throughout all aspects of the maritime industry. The objectives of the code are:

1. To establish an international framework involving co-operation between Contracting Governments, Government Agencies, Local

Administrations and the shipping and port industries to detect security threats and take preventive measures against security incidents affecting ships or port facilities used in international trade.

2. To establish the respective roles and responsibilities of the Contracting Governments, Agencies , Local Administrations and the shipping and Port Industries at national and international levels for ensuring maritime security.
3. To ensure the early and efficient collection and exchange of security related information.
4. To provide a methodology for security assessments so as to have in place plans and procedures to react to changing security levels.
5. To ensure confidence that adequate and proportionate maritime security measures are in place.

The ISPS code is a positive start to combating illegal activity. However, it is realised that no single country would have the ability or resources to act as a world police authority. But collectively, it is not beyond reason that an international deterrent force could be established, staffed and resourced, to make the seas a safer place.

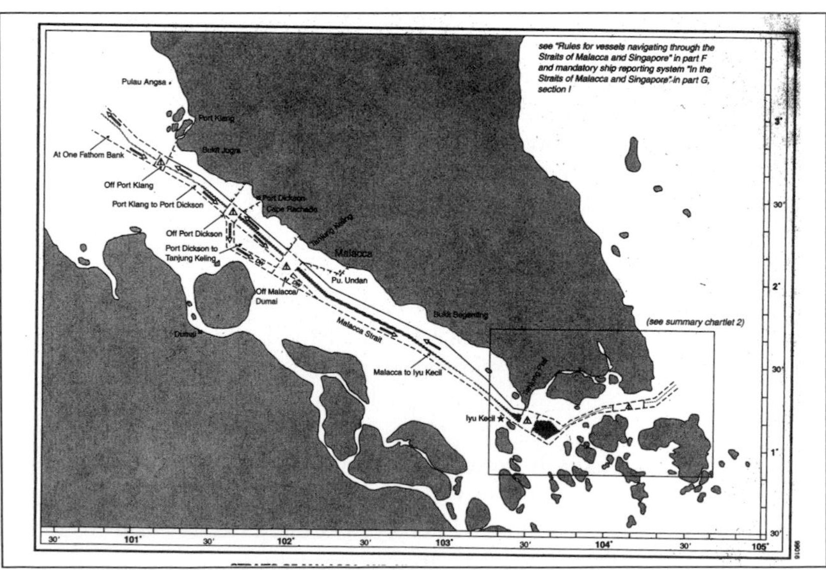

Diagram 5.8: Malacca Singapore Straits

North East Monsoon

From November to March the areas of the Arabian Sea, the Bay of Bengal and the Northern Indian ocean will experience a north easterly wind, (NE monsoon).

The average wind strengths over the greater part of the area are about force 3 to 4 and these are generally accompanied by fine weather with little or no rain. On rare occasions the wind force may reach force 7. However, during the months of December/January considerable rainfall can be expected in the Bay of Bengal, south of latitude 5° north.

Visibility during this season is usually very good with the exceptions being in the north and eastern regions of the Arabian Sea which may be effected by dust haze. The northern regions of the Bay of Bengal may also experience some reduced visibility from the prevailing northerly winds bringing smoke haze and land mists seaward.

Inter-Monsoon Seasons

These occur in the period April, May and October. Weather varies considerably with winds over open sea areas reaching force 7, only occasionally. It is often cloudy with squally conditions, accompanied by heavy showers and thunderstorms. Fine weather periods are equally just as common.

Visibility is generally quite good except in heavy rain conditions or when impaired by dust haze on the northern and eastern shores of the Arabian Sea, (April/May). The Malacca Strait has occasional squalls (Sumatras) during these periods.

Tropical Storms (Cyclones)

These occur in the Arabian Sea during the inter monsoon periods mainly during May/June, and October/November. The greatest frequency occurring in the months of June and November.

In the Bay of Bengal most storms occur from May to November, with the greatest frequency in the months of May, June, October and November.

NB: Tropical cyclones are rare in the Gulf of Aden, only 3 or 4 being recorded over the last 50 years.

The Gulf of Oman suffers dust storms and sandstorms throughout all seasons but they are noted as being more frequent during the months of June and July. Visibility is effected and can be reduced to as little as 500 metres.

Routes – North Indian Ocean, Bay of Bengal and Arabian Sea

The prevailing monsoon conditions influence routes across the Bay of Bengal and the Arabian Sea. The directional flow of currents which is reversed due to seasonal changes, must be considered by Masters when carrying out the planning and execution of their passage plan.

Navigation via Suqutra (SW Monsoon Period)

Vessels eastbound, from the Gulf of Aden are advised to route north of Suqutra and then through the 'Eight Degree Channel' (Ref. latitude 7° 30' N longitude 72° 45' E) because of rough sea conditions which exist in this vicinity during the SW monsoon.

Vessels westbound from 'Dondra Head' (Sri Lanka) towards Aden via the Eight Degree Channel have an option of either north or south about Suqutra and then on past Raas Caseyr into the Gulf of Aden. The more southern route is generally preferred as vessels are less likely to meet the need to reduce speed for bad weather.

(NE Monsoon Period)

Routes from Aden to the Eight Degree Channel pass south of Suqutra during the NE monsoon period. Whilst westbound vessels have options to the north or south of Suqutra.

Seasonal *Routes*

Vessels on voyages from South African ports, Cape Town, Durban etc. for Bombay, Karachi, Bay of Bengal or Colombo may consider routing via the Mozambique Channel. However, Masters should note that navigational hazards in the form of shoals and islands are present in the north approaches to this channel. These may impose movement restrictions especially if tropical storms (TRS) are encountered.

Mozambique Channel – Currents

The Mozambique Current sets SSW and follows the coastline to what is thought to be some 50 miles off during most of the year. This current effect extends to about 100 miles offshore during the months of June to August. The strongest rate is experienced from October to February when rates of 4 knots are attained. Some inshore counter currents may also be encountered and the boundaries and rates stated cannot be relied upon.

Routes to Aden via the Mozambique Channel

These are normally made coast wise in both directions.

NB: The east African Current flows northward continually and gives way to the Somali current in about 2° S latitude.

The Somali Current sets SW from December to February at rates up to 4 knots. From May to September a NE current is established which may have rates as much as 7 knots.

South Indian Ocean

The weather patterns of the South Indian Ocean are influenced by the movement of the NE monsoon during December and January, and the SW monsoon during May and August.

NW Monsoon

Experienced between December to March when a north to north westerly wind meets the South East Trades in about latitude 10° S. (An area known as the Equatorial Winds) are generally light and variable in direction becoming more north easterly towards the African coastline.

Squalls are common, often in association with tropical storms but wind force 7 or above is only recorded occasionally. Frequent showers and unsettled weather is the norm. Visibility is generally good except in heavy rain.

Mozambique Channel

Experiences a northerly wind between 15° S and 17° S latitudes known as the Northern Monsoon (November to March). Southern Monsoon occurs the length of the channel (April to September) when the wind blows south to south easterly.

General Weather

The oceanic high pressure area is situated about 35° S latitude in summer and around 30° S in the winter.

The Trade Winds, strongest in spring, suffer little variation in direction throughout the year, average strength in summer being 3 to 4 and in the winter being 4 to 5. Over open ocean areas the weather is mostly fair to fine with half covered skies. Some showers may be encountered.

Gales are frequent south of latitude 40° S in the summer period and south of 35° S in the winter period.

Abnormal Waves

Mariners navigating off the South African coast, especially those vessels on a south westerly heading, may encounter abnormal waves. They are thought to be generated in the southern ocean and combine with other distant wave patterns and waves from local storms. They meet the Agulhas Current head-on and are steepened or shortened as a swell might be.

Such waves may be preceded by an exceptionally deep 'trough'. Although rare, ships could flounder into this 'hole in the sea', with the following freak wave crashing down onto the ship. The danger for watch officers, is that the condition is only detected when a ship is on the brink of such a trough prior to the vessel plunging downwards. Evasive action should therefore be considered on sighting the much higher and distinctive wave crests well ahead of the ships movement.

Recent research has shown that 'freak' or 'rogue' waves can be experienced in many areas of the of the worlds oceans. However, ship reports and "*Ocean Passages of the World*" draws attention to 'abnormal waves' regularly effecting the area off South Africa, where the Agulhas, south moving current meets the Southern Ocean Drift.

Serious damage and ship losses have been recorded as being due to 'freak waves' that have been frequently associated with this region. More recently satellite imagery has shown that this is not the only region subject to this phenomena. An offshore installation in the North Sea was severely damaged, and a vessel in the Antarctic region had its bridge demolished when making such an encounter.

These experiences are of particular concern to the exceptionally long vessel, e.g. the large ore carrier or VLCC. The dangers to the ship, being faced with such a 'hole' in the ocean, preceding a freak wave, cannot be expressed too strongly. The sheer weight of water crashing onto the foredeck of a ship or a vessel being 'pooped' by such an experience is an incident that Masters and crews could well do without.

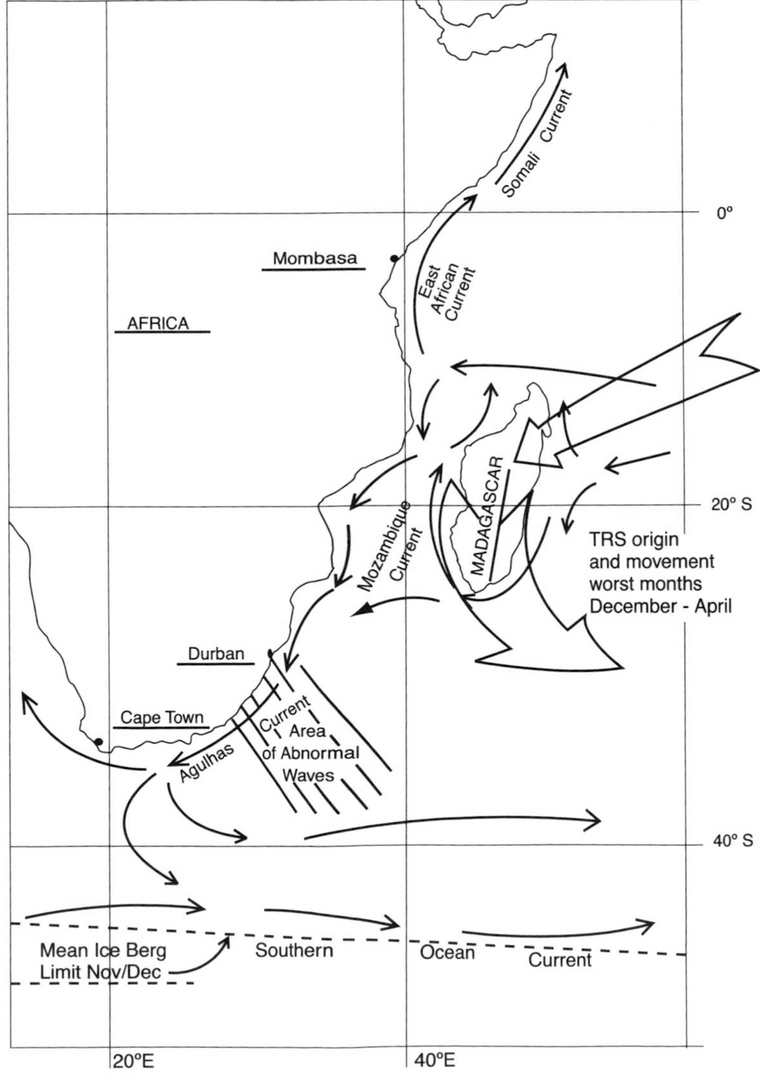

Diagram 5.9: Currents and Weather Phenomena Around Cape Aqulhus

Ice Conditions of the South Indian Ocean

The extension of pack ice (4/10 this concentration) is at its furthest during the months of August to September, reaching up to about latitude 58° S in way of longitude 50° east.

Icebergs of the 'Tabular Type' – The mean limits for icebergs during the worst months of November and December should be considered from about latitude 44° S longitude 20° E to 48° S latitude at about 120° E longitude, then passing south of Tasmania.

NB. Mariners should note that ice limits must be considered extremely flexible and are known to differ year by year depending on the severity of the season.

Trans-Ocean Routes

Great circle routes between Australian and South African ports are not normally followed. The reasoning for this is that a greater part of the passage could expect to experience areas of extreme bad weather and the additional risk of encountering pack ice is also present. Westbound routes could also expect considerable delays due to strong adverse currents i.e. southern ocean drift, setting eastward.

Vessels usually take advantage of an area of light and variable winds which lie between the South East Trades and the Roaring Forties when planning an ocean passage. The axis of this zone lies at about 33° S latitude in Southern Hemisphere summer and about 30° S in Southern Hemisphere winter.

Eastbound routes to the South and West Australian coastlines often employ a composite route with a limiting latitude to suit the season, namely latitude 40° S (S/summer) or latitude 35½° S (S/winter).

Westbound routes generally keep well north and so avoid headwinds and adverse currents.

Route North or South of Australia

The choice of whether to go north or south about Australia will depend on comparable distance and the season. The climatic conditions for either alternative would also influence the Masters choice.

Northern routes are normally set via the Torres Strait and southern routes by the Bass Strait.

5.4.4 North Pacific Ocean

Regional Routing Information

Trans-ocean routes in the North Pacific often employ a high-latitude alternative and provide a distinct saving on distance. However, some disadvantage may be experienced from weather and currents.

Westbound (Recommended) San Francisco to Yokohama

A seasonal option recommends a great circle during the summer months whereas in the winter, a rhumb line to latitude 35° N, longitude 140° W and then on to Yokohama is recommended.

Eastbound (Recommended) Yokohama to San Francisco

A great circle route, both in winter and summer, direct is recommended.

Alternatives – Westbound vessels may prefer a route north of the Aleutian Islands. The reason for such preference being that many storms pass south of the Aleutians and vessels in the Bering Sea would experience following winds and seas. Currents are generally weak north of this group of islands and fog is less likely, neither is 'ice' normally encountered in the vicinity of the islands.

The main northern route suggested is via a 'great circle' to the 'Unimak Pass' then through the 'Bering Sea' passing out north of 'Attu Island' and finally resuming the great circle track to 'Nojima Saki'.

Distance Comparison

Direct great circle route .... 4475 miles
Direct rhumb line .... 4735 miles (excess 260 miles)
Northern route (N Aleutians) .... 4540 miles (excess 65 miles)

Climatic Considerations – North Pacific

The area between latitude 32° N and 48° N would appear to average the worst weather from the point of view of westbound traffic. South of this area, there is generally a notable improvement in weather and sea conditions, but adverse currents remain a concerning factor.

A high percentage frequency of encountering waves in excess of 3½ metres on the great circle route and the rhumb line route should be of major consideration to mariners planning an ocean route in this region; while the northern route, through the Bering Sea, indicated a decreasing probability of encountering seas in excess of 3½ metres. In addition, favourable surface currents exist for virtually the total passage. Wind generated seas and swell effects are appreciably reduced by the island chain when wind direction is from the south or south west.

NB. The Aleutian Island chain, provides a 'fetch' limiting effect experienced by vessels on passage through the Bering Sea, resulting in more favourable sea conditions than ships would expect to encounter, South of the Aleutian Islands.

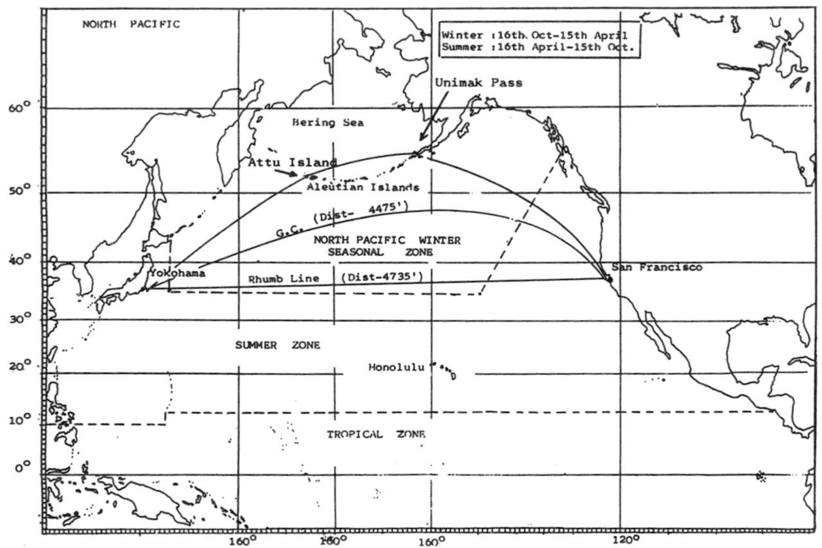

Diagram 5.10: Comparison ocean routes North Pacific

5.4.5 South Pacific Ocean

Trans-Ocean routes in the more southerly regions of the South Pacific tend not to employ great circle tracks on either east or westbound passages. The reason for this is that the extreme limit of icebergs extends to approximately latitude 40° S at all times of the year, and adverse weather can also be expected with continued regularity.

Westbound Passages

Vessels tend to track following the parallel of 30° S latitude between longitudes 120° to 150° W.

Example tracks from Panama, and South American ports via way points on latitude 30° S and then on to Australia or New Zealand ports.

Eastbound Passages

Vessels tracking towards Cape de Hornos and beyond, must expect to encounter icebergs in all seasons when taking the southern route from ports in Australia and New Zealand. Mid-Pacific routed (eastbound) may find the central route advantageous especially for vessels bound for Panama. This route being joined at suitable positions from various departure ports and makes use of the Equatorial Countercurrent (approximately 5° N latitude).

Example Routes/Distances

Wellington to Panama Great Circle .... 6490 miles
Torres Strait to Panama via Apia .... 8540 miles
Sidney to Cape Horn via Cook Str .... 5850 miles Southern Route
Hobart to Panama via Snares Islands .... 7640 miles (GC from Snares)
Torres Strait to Valparaiso .... 7800 miles GC Alternative

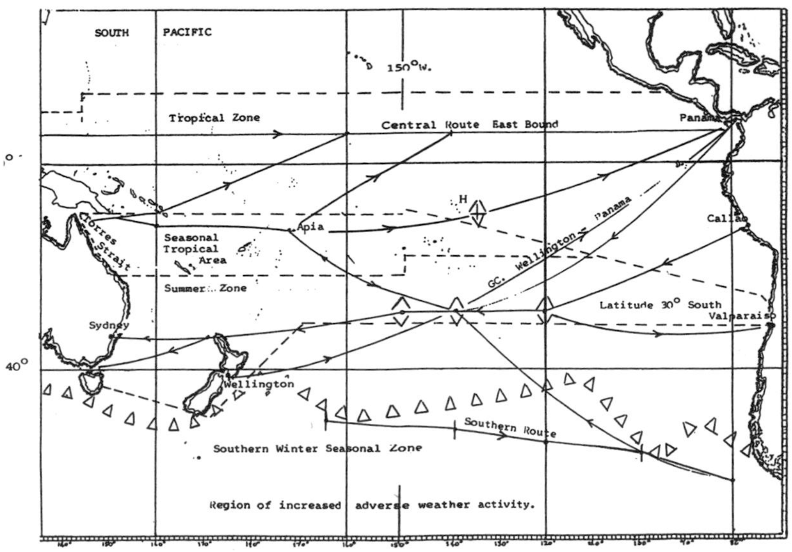

Diagram 5.11: 'H' = Lat 10° 45'S Long 136° 35'W
Extreme Limit of Iceberg sightings (at all times of the year)

Climatic Considerations – South Pacific

Pack ice limits are advanced in July and up to 5/10ths could be experienced between latitudes 60° S and 65° S (worst scenario). Icebergs can be sighted up to latitude 40° S just east of New Zealand but may be experienced on the southern route in all seasons.
Gale frequency on the most southern routes is greater than 10 days per month and in January fog may also be cause for concern. Fog is also a notable feature of the Peruvian coast between the months of March/April. There is less likelihood of fog in October in this region.

NB: When employing own ship routing methods, detailed reference to *Ocean Passages of the World* and to respective routing charts, is essential for this region. Careful study of Admiralty Sailing Directions is also highly recommended.

Meteorological Routing Information

Sources of Information:

1. **Surface Synoptic Analysis Chart** – this provides a picture of the existing conditions at the proceeding synoptic hour and shows the position of isobars and other synoptic detail such as fronts and troughs etc. It may also include ship and land reports.
2. **Surface Prognostic Charts** – These charts provide a projection of synoptic conditions ahead in time and cover periods of 12, 18, 36 and 72 hours.
3. **Change of Pressure Charts** – Charts which show 'isobaric lines', i.e. Lines joining places of equal pressure.
4. **Wave Charts** – Present sea analysis and isopleuths of constant wave height together with the direction of wave groups indicated by arrows. Prognosis charts can be produced from this information.
5. **Ice Charts** – Show the amount and the boundaries of icebergs, pack ice and leads for selected areas, e.g. NW Atlantic, Gulf of St Lawrence.
6. **Upper Air Charts** – Not intended for use by mariners but are in use by shore based meteorologists. They are employed to obtain information on the movement of depressions and other expected weather conditions. They include factual charts of:
   (a) constant pressure providing analysis and prognostic detail e.g. at 700 mb, 500 mb.
   (b) cloud thickness charts.
   (c) wind force and direction for upper levels.

7. **Nephanalysis Charts** – Satellite information charts providing information on cloud pattern and cloud thickness. They assist in the identification of meteorological features e.g. tropical revolving storms.
8. **The World Chart; General Surface Current Distribution** No. 5310.
9. **Monthly Routing Charts** for the respective area and period.
10. **World Climatic Charts** (previously included with Mariners Handbook) 5301/5302.

Named Winds – World-wide

Ref., No.,	Named Wind (Local Name)	Prevailing Direction	Location & General Remarks
1.	Mistral	NW	Gulf of Lyons
2.	Gregale	NE Gale	Malta region
3.	Sirocco	SE	Mediterranean
4.	Levanter	E	Hot – Gibraltar area
5.	Shamal	NW	Arabian Gulf
6.	Hoboob	varies	Red Sea associated with 'Dust Storms'
7.	Southerly Buster	SW	Australian South East coast
8.	Roaring Forties	W	Gale force winds of the South Atlantic.
9.	Harmattan	W	Dry wind from the African desert, laden with sand
10.	Pamperos	SW	South America
11.	Chinook	varies	A warm dry wind of North America, experienced down off mountain ranges
12.	Trades	NE & SE	Atlantic , Pacific and Indian Oceans.
13.	Bora	NE	Adriatic.
14.	Brickfielder	N	Hot wind on the Australian coast
15.	Khamsin	N	Gulf of Aden
16.	Williwaws	Squalls	Straits of Magellan
17.	Vendevale	SW	West Mediterranean
18.	Etesian	N	Aegean Sea
19.	Khamsin	S	Egypt
20.	Simood	S	Arabia
21.	Kaus	SE	Arabian Gulf
22.	Elephanta	S/SE	Malabar Coast
23.	Norther	N	Panama/Gulf of Mexico
24.	Föhn	S	Alps

THE WORLD

NORTHERN WINTER

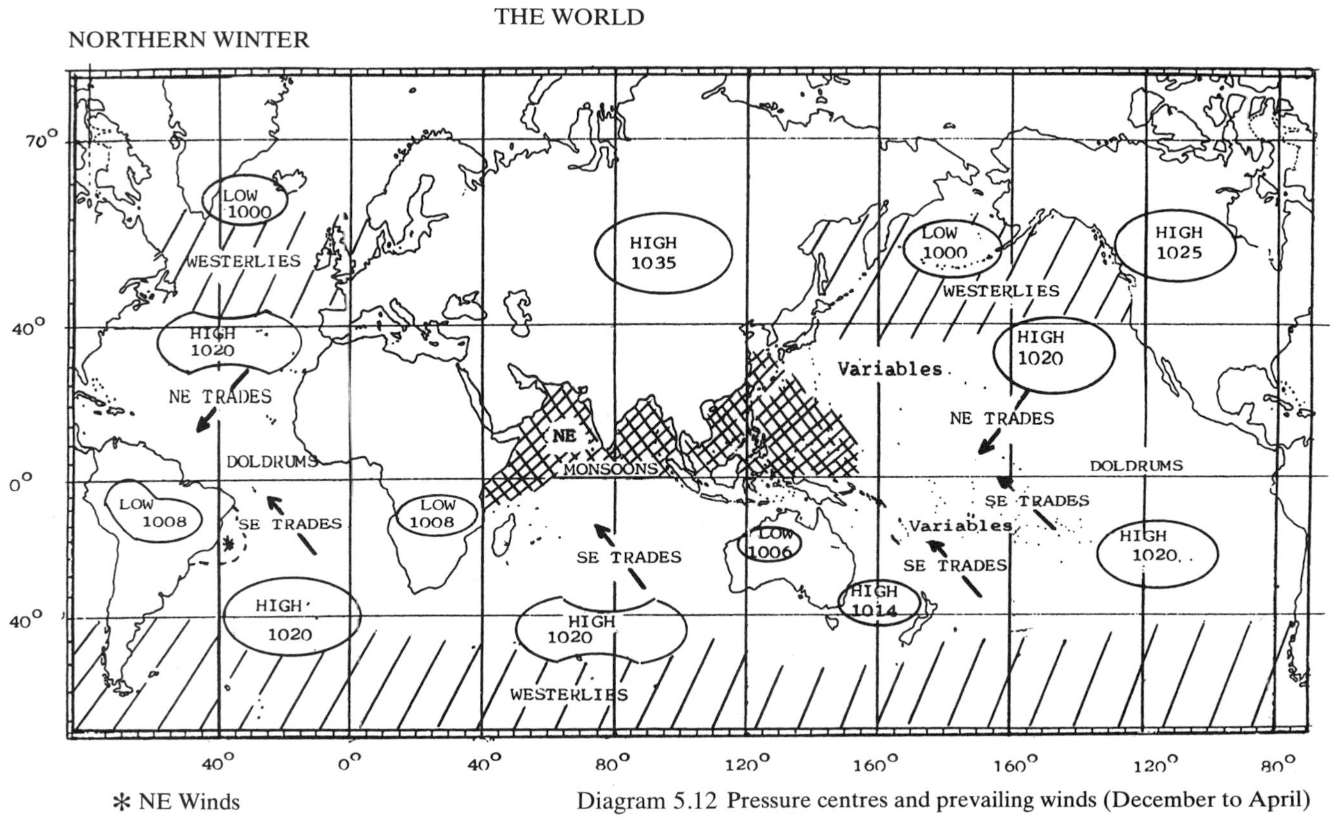

* NE Winds

Diagram 5.12 Pressure centres and prevailing winds (December to April)

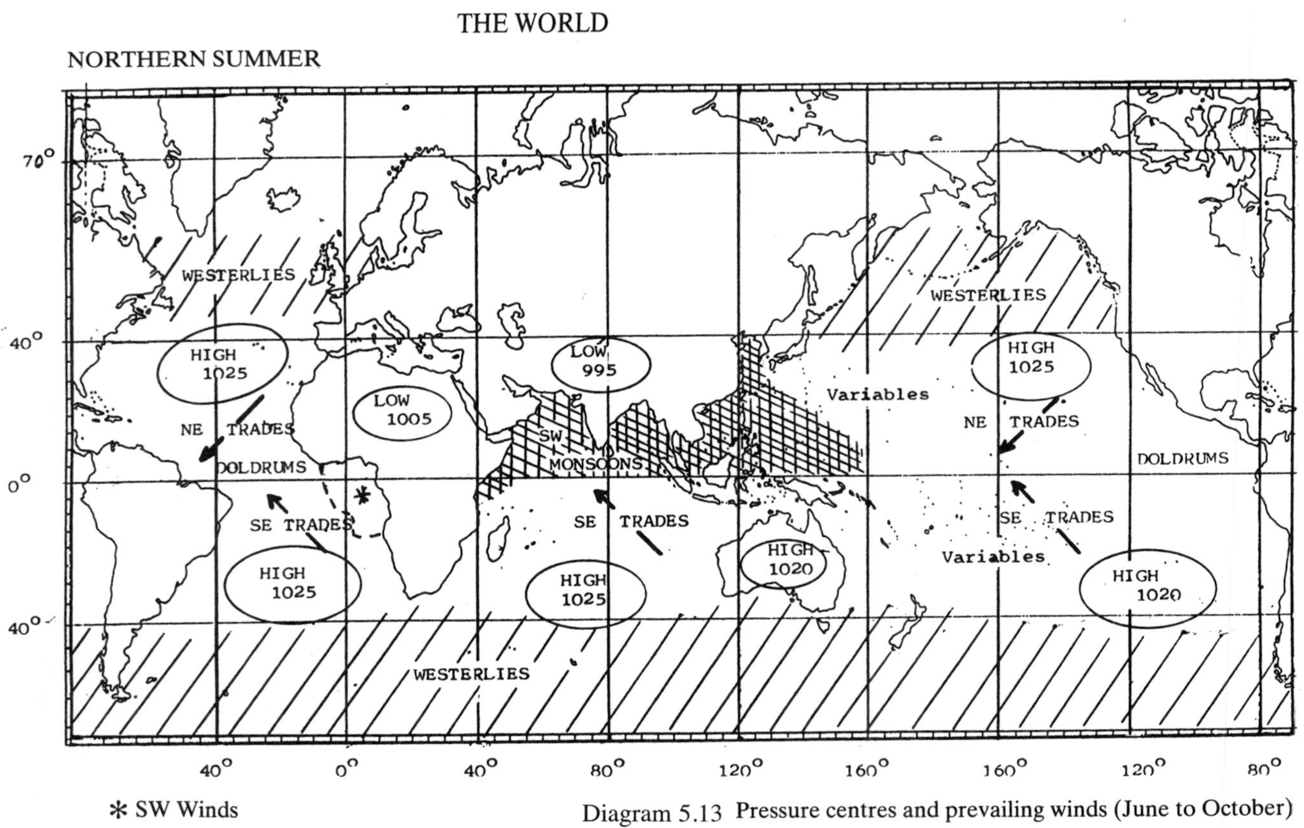

Diagram 5.13 Pressure centres and prevailing winds (June to October)

Chapter Six

OCEAN CURRENTS

6.1 Introduction

The generation of ocean currents is caused by several factors including: the prevailing winds, heavy rainfall, temperature differences, density differences, excessive evaporation, melting ice/snow and probably pressure differences changing surface levels. General circulation of water about the earths surface is right-handed (clockwise) in the northern oceans and left-handed (anti-clockwise) in the southern oceans. This is similar to the circulation of the atmosphere and hence currents are frequently observed to accelerate in the general direction of the prevailing winds common to that of currents.

6.2 Drift Current

A surface current set up by the wind.

Due to the trailing friction of the wind passing over the surface of the sea. Wind continually blowing in one direction for a prolonged period develops a thick layer of surface water.

Examples: Those due to trade winds, monsoons and westerlies on the polar side of 40° latitude.

6.3 Stream Current

(a) a continuation of a drift current, which has changed its direction by meeting an obstruction in its path such as a land mass or another current,

(b) a counter-current which acts to replace water displaced by other currents

(c) a current flow due to unequal pressures brought about by differences of density, temperature or water level.

Examples: The Gulf Stream, the Guinea current, the Kuro Shio, Agulhas and Equatorial counters.

The Gulf Stream being the most striking example, described as 'A river in an ocean'.

Example: Current caused by difference in density:

Straits of Gibraltar – East moving surface water, warmer and lighter flow along the surface from the Atlantic, while heavier layers flow out from the Mediterranean at a lower level.

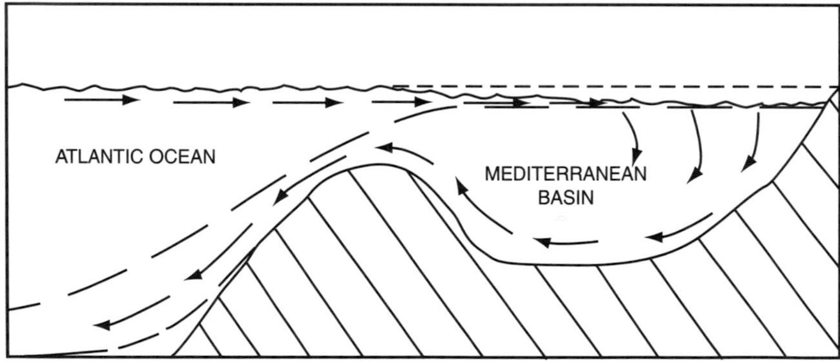

Diagram 6.1: Convergent Current

6.4 Convergent Current

A current established between basins that contain water of different densities. A surface current will flow into the sea with the higher density, while the lower bottom current will flow in the opposite direction.

An example of this can be observed with the easterly flow of surface currents from the Atlantic Ocean into the Mediterranean Sea, via the Gibraltar Straits.

6.5 Upwelling Current

The term given to the movement of cold seawater from the lower depths of the ocean rising upwards to replace warmer surface water adjacent to the shoreline which is blown seaward.

Example: Peru or Humboldt Current.

They are a feature of the middle latitudes and are encountered when the thermocline shallows (10 to 20 fathoms). Sea life is usually greatly increased because an upwelling current provides important nutrients at surface levels. Mariners can therefore expect to meet increased traffic by way of fishing boats, factory ships and the like.

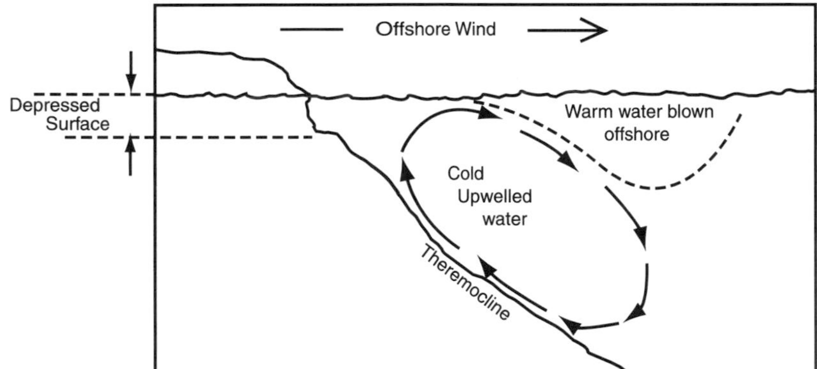

Diagram 6.2: Action of Upwelling Current

6.6 Ocean Current References

Current Rose Charts

These current roses show the variability of the ocean current in the region that it covers. The information contained in the rose is derived from all available observations which are noted as being ½ knot or more. They are meant to be a representation of the current distribution over the total area.

In order to process the data, the compass is divided into 16 equal sectors (sub-division or amalgamation may occur in certain areas). The number of observed current settings, within the limits of each sector, is noted. This number is then expressed as a percentage frequency of the total number of observations. the obtained value is then used to determine the length of the 'arrow' which is constructed in the middle of the sector.

Each arrow is sub-divided to express the percentage frequency of occurrence, and certain ranges of speed, in that direction.

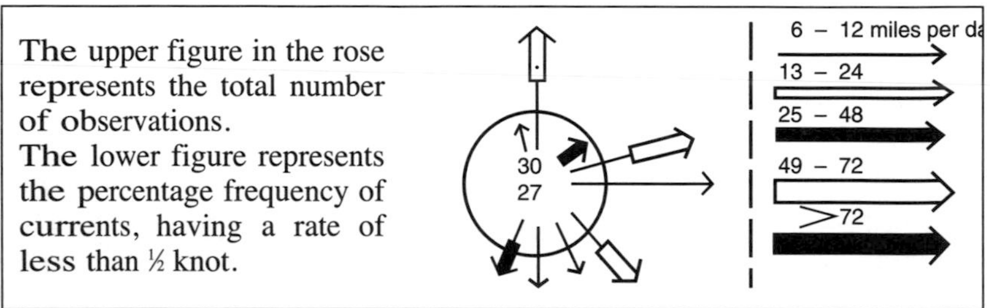
The upper figure in the rose represents the total number of observations.
The lower figure represents the percentage frequency of currents, having a rate of less than ½ knot.
30
27
6 - 12 miles per d
13 - 24
25 - 48
49 - 72
>72

Diagram 6.3: Total observation and frequency of currents

Vector Current Charts

These charts portray the overall water movement and what has become known as the general circulation. The long term displacement of water being indicated by an arrow pointing in the appropriate direction and being of variable thickness to represent a range of speeds. The figure beneath the arrow shows the number of observations employed in determining the vector mean current.

The vector mean current being the resultant value of all observations considered for that area. That is to say the derived vector mean for each basic area is found from the difference in totals of the north-south components and the difference in totals of the east-west components.

The Vector Current Chart is used to calculate the drift of objects over long periods e.g. icebergs, derelicts, etc. The longer the period, the more likely the drift will approximate to the vector mean drift, charts being devised for 3 month periods. Should periods of drift exceed this, then a combination of charts for the subsequent quarter would need to be employed.

Predominant Current Charts

Probably the chart of greatest value to the navigator as it shows the current which is most likely to be experienced in the area of consideration.
Arrows point in the appropriate direction which represents the direction of flow, the rate (an average figure) is sometimes indicated at the tail of the arrow. Arrow presentations will vary in thickness and the thickness indicates the constancy. The value of constancy being obtained by comparing the number of observations in the predominant

sector against the total number of observations and expressed as a percentage. 24

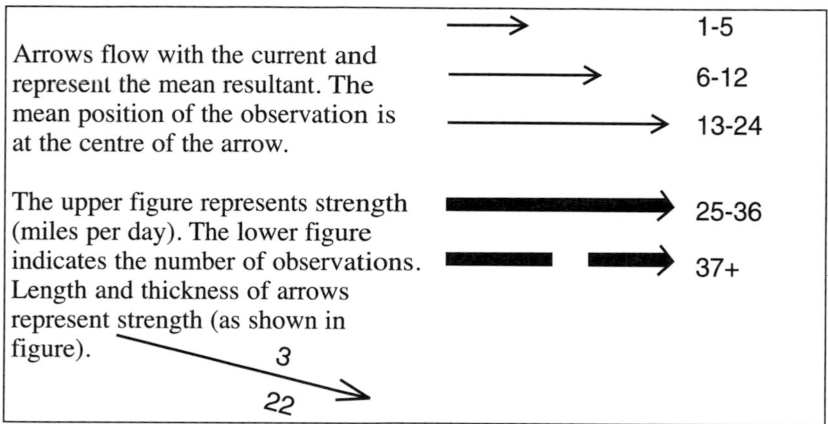

Diagram 6.4: The mean position, observation and strength

Example:

High constancy when the percentage of observations is greater than, say 75%. Low constancy, less than 50% would imply variable rated and variability in direction.

The predominant direction is determined by examination of a 90° sector over the compass (e.g. 000° – 090°). All data concerning currents is obtained within that sector together with the number of occasions that the current sets within the sector. The sector is then rotated 15° with new set limits of 015° – 105°, and the number of observations within the sector is noted again. The process is continued to provide 24 sectors in all and the mean direction of the sector containing the greatest number of observations is the direction of the charted predominant current.

6.7 North Atlantic Currents

North Atlantic Drift

Sets in an ENE, direction from latitude 40° N, longitude 40° W, and has a general flow towards the United Kingdom and then on towards Norway. Some cold water from the East Greenland Current is divided off Cape Farewell into the North Atlantic Drift. Other water is carried around the Cape into the West Greenland Current north through Baffin Bay and then sets south in the Labrador Current.

Gulf Stream

The warm waters of the Gulf Stream meet the cold waters of the Labrador Current and cause a mix which continues a general westward flow as the Atlantic Drift. A southerly set on the east side of the Atlantic takes water down the Portuguese Coast and on into the Canary Drift current. This sets SSW from Cape St Vincent to Cape Blanco. Some water is then divided into the West African Coast Drift, while other water is carried into the North Equatorial Current.

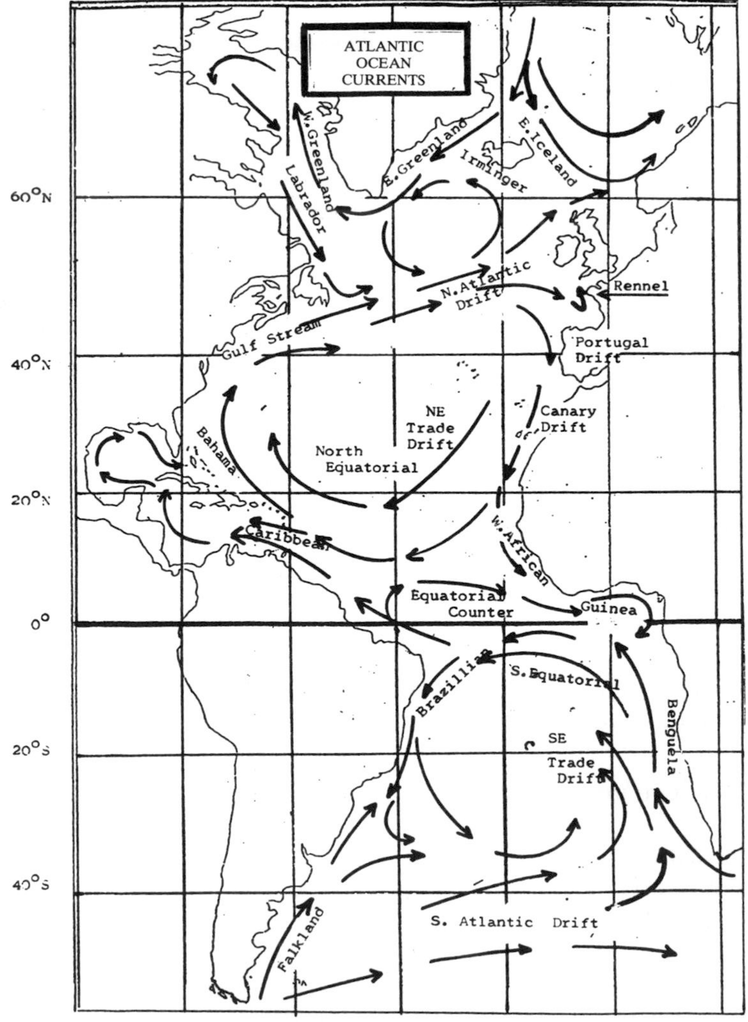

Diagram 6.5: Atlantic Ocean Currents

West African and Guinea Currents

Water from the Canary Drift flows past Cape Verde (West Africa) and continues as the West African Coast Drift to join up with the Guinea Current. The Guinea Stream sets eastward throughout the year into the Gulf of Guinea. Additional water from an Equatorial Counter Stream (sets east in about 5° N Latitude) also influences the Guinea Current.

North Equatorial Drift

This current sets in a westward direction about latitude 10° N. The Equatorial Drift is supplied by the NE Trade Drift (between latitudes 10° N and 30° N) and water from the Canary Current. It eventually joins with the South Equatorial (part) which carries it into the Caribbean Sea. The remaining water flows WNW as the Bahama Drift and carries on north past the Florida coast to join the waters of the Gulf Stream.

Caribbean Sea Drift

The considerable amount of water flowing into the Caribbean Sea from the North and South Equatorial currents follows the coastline around the Gulf of Mexico. It then exits the Caribbean via the western end of Cuba/Florida Straits and joins the Bahama current into the Gulf Stream.

Additional Currents of Interest – North Atlantic

The Irminger Current is a terminal branch of the Gulf Stream and flows west off the south coast of Iceland and into the East Greenland flow. A branch of the East Greenland current passes north of Iceland into the North Atlantic Drift and is known as the East Iceland Current.

A branch of the Atlantic Drift turns inwards to the Bay of Biscay. Westerly winds bank up the water in this region and result in a variable NW offshoot known as the Rennel Current, which flows across the southerly entrance of the English Channel.

The general circulation of the North Atlantic is of a right-hand flow (clockwise). The direction of the currents is virtually the same all year round although the strength experienced will vary with the time of year. As would be expected, the current directions bear a striking resemblance to the wind patterns from which general circulation is partly derived.

6.8 South Atlantic Currents

South Equatorial Drift

The equatorial current sets in a westerly direction and divides north/south off the coast of Brazil. The southerly divide flows down the coast of Brazil known as the Brazilian Stream at a rate of about 20 miles per day. The set is about South-West down as far as the River Plate, where it then curves east to join with the South Atlantic Drift.

The northerly divide sets WNW along the northern coast of South America towards the Caribbean Sea. Some water is known to deflect in the region of the 'Doldrums' (between 5° N and 9° N latitudes) and flows into the Guinea Current (ref: N Atlantic currents) as the Equatorial Counter Current.

6.8.1 current movement (Atlantic and Pacific)

South American Continent

The Brazil Current

This current is a weak South Atlantic flow originating from water of a southern branch of the South Equatorial Current. It runs generally in a South-Westerly direction along the Brazil coastline towards Uruguay, during the period of February to September at a rate of between 0.5 to 1.0 knot, though up to 2 knots have occasionally been recorded. It meets the northbound flow of the cold Falkland Current at about Latitude 35° S, with the general movement of water going on towards the South Atlantic Drift.

Brazil Inshore Counter Current

This current may be considered as a seasonal extension of the Falkland Current.

During the winter months of the southern hemisphere, the Brazilian Current moves away from the coastline and allows a northerly flow to set between the coastline and the waters of the Brazil Current. This movement commences at about April and extends to Latitude 24° S by May/June. By August/September the northerly limit has receded back to about Latitude 30° S and by December back further still, to 35° South latitude. The average rate of the current is 0.75 knots but may occasionally reach up to 2 knots. During the months between December to March the current is in abeyance.

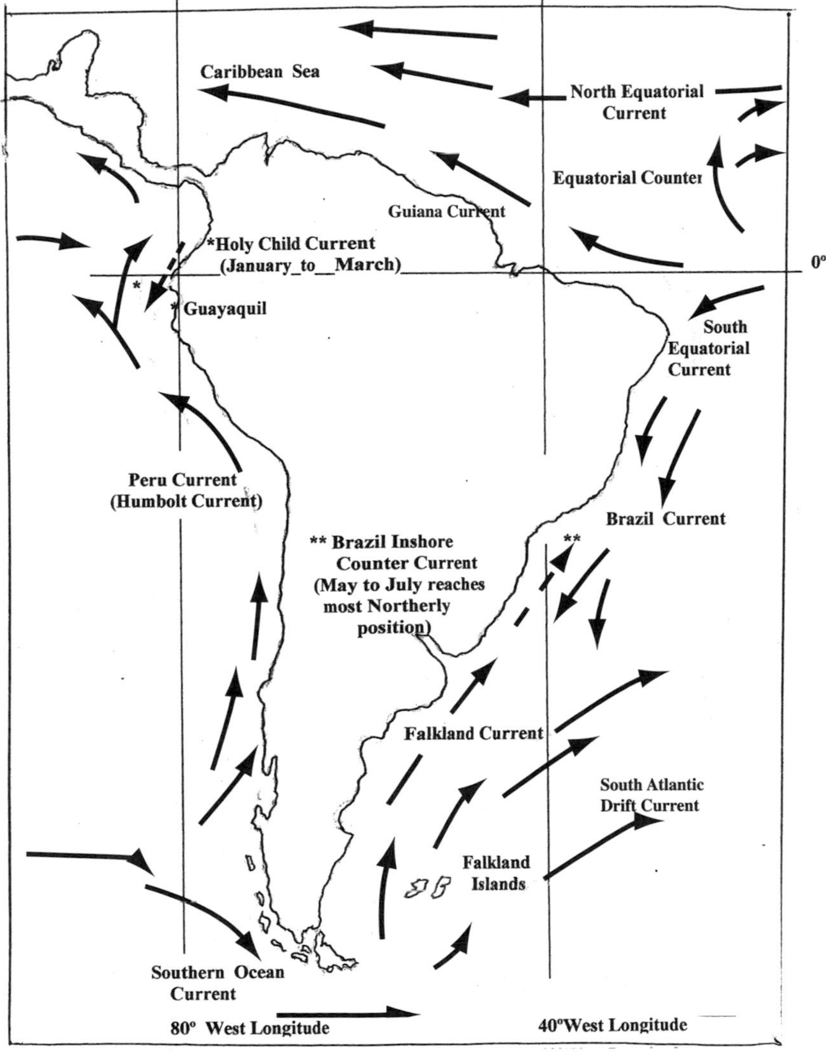

Diagram 6.6: Current movement about the South American Continent

South Atlantic Drift

Sets in a general ENE direction from Cape Horn towards the Cape of Good Hope. A branch turns northward, with water from the Agulhas current, to set NNW as the Benguela Current, but the main flow is into the Southern Indian Ocean and beyond.

Falkland Island Stream

Water for the South Atlantic Drift rounds Cape Horn and some sets NNE along the South American coast up to the River Plate area where it joins with waters of the Brazilian current. Other water has a tendency to set south of the Falkland Islands and turns east as the South Atlantic Drift.

South East Trade Drift

The eastward set across the South Atlantic provides water for the Benguela current and is also a source of water for the West African coast. This is assisted by the South East Trade Drift which eventually flows into the South Equatorial Current.

Comment – the general circulation of the South Atlantic is left-handed (anti-clockwise movement) throughout the year, although rate and intensity of currents can vary at certain periods.

6.9 North Pacific Currents

North Equatorial Current

Sets to the west and the latitude to which it extends varies with the seasons. Main source of water is from the Californian Current. It is deflected to the NW, and then northward on reaching the Philippine Islands, into the Kuro Shio Current.

Kuro Shio

This is a warm current which flows generally NE, close to the Japanese coast. The rate is between 2 to 4 knots, but this is influenced by the monsoons. At about latitude 35° N, the current flows eastward and feeds into the North Pacific Drift.

California Current

Sets south, at some distance off the United States west coast, from about 48° N to 23° N latitudes. It is a cold current which turns SW then west as it flows with the equatorial current.

NB: It is upwelling during spring and early summer.

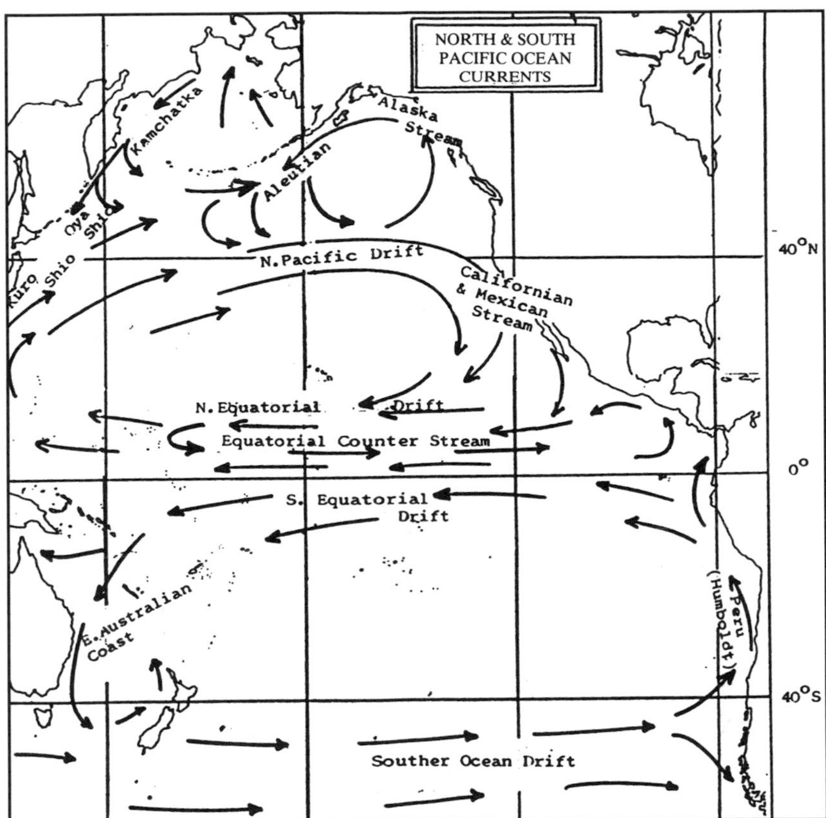

Diagram 6.7: North and South Pacific Ocean Currents

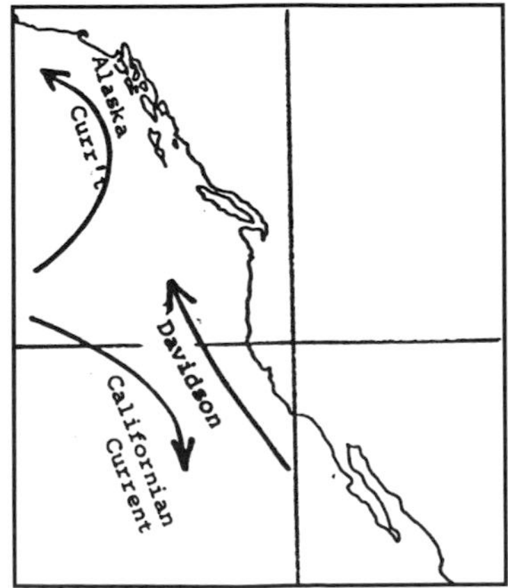

Diagram 6.8: Davidson Current (Nov-Feb)

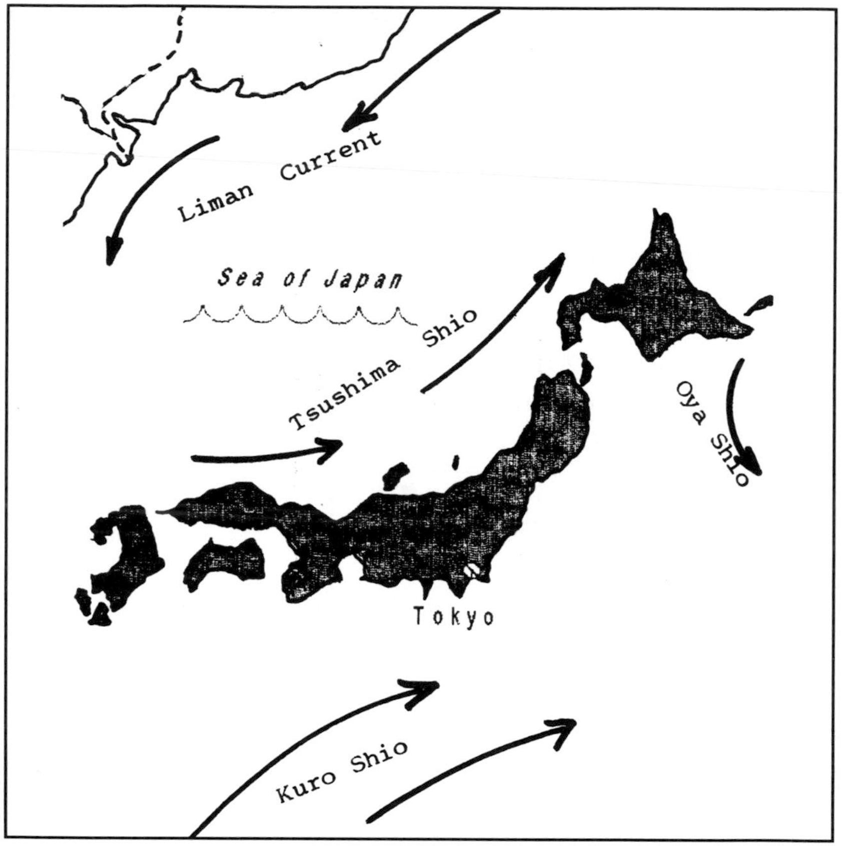

Diagram 6.9: Currents in and around the Japanese Sea

Davidson Current

An inshore relatively cool counter current which sets inside the flow of the California current between November to February and reaches up to 48° N latitude.

Alaska Coast Stream

The northerly branch of the North Pacific Drift which turns anti-clockwise round the coast of Alaska. Some water is carried on past the Aleutian Islands from the Alaskan Current and is known as the Aleutian Current.

This is known to change direction depending on the season and in July some water is deflected north through the Aleutian Islands to join with the Kamchatca Current.

The Alaskan Current is reinforced by the Davidson Current and feeds water into the Aleutian Current and the Bering Sea.

Kamchatka Current

A cold current which sets south along the Kamchatka Peninsula. The most southern part of this current is known as the Oya Shio Stream which extends to about 40° N. This current then sets eastward flowing nearly parallel to the North Pacific Drift becoming the east setting Aleutian Current.

Tsushima Shio and Liman Current

The flow of the Kuro Shio current is NE along the coasts of Taiwan and Japan until the main stream turns eastward. Some water from this source is deflected into the Sea of Japan and continues on a NE flow as the Tsushima Current along the north coast of Japan.

In the same area, a flow SW along the mainland coastline of what was previously the USSR is known as the Liman Current. The flow from these 2 currents produces an anti-clockwise flow around the Sea of Japan.

6.10 South Pacific Currents

South Equatorial Drift

The flow of this current sets either side of the equator, extending between 1° N to 5° N at various longitudes. It sets in a westerly direction from these northern limits to as far south as 25° S Latitude. Although after Latitude 6° S it becomes much weaker and more variable in direction.

The latitude limits will vary with the seasons across the ocean. The current divides as it approaches the Australian coast with some water being turned SW into the East Australian Current and the remaining water turning NW to flow past New Guinea (July).

Holy Child Current

This current is found close inshore, off the coast of Ecuador, during the period of January to March, though not equally defined in all years. In exceptional years it may be experienced to flow as far southward, to a position beyond Callao, Peru, running in a counter direction to the Humboldt (Peru) Current, next to the land.

Humboldt (Peru) Current

A cold, up-welling current which sets northward along the coastline of Chile and Peru from waters diverted from the Southern Ocean Current which divides about Cape Horn. As an up-welling current, considerable plankton is generated near the surface which encourages large numbers of fish to the area. This in turn causes increased numbers of fishing boats to be active off this coastline.

The current strength is generally consistent throughout the year at about 0.5 to 1.0 knot, except for the NE branch that passes Columbia, which has been noted to be weaker during December to April. The prevailing winds of the Pacific are experienced from the West and as such a component of the current tends to set towards the land south of Latitude 35° 40'S.

6.10.1 current movement about the South American Continent

East Australian Current

Sets southward off the east coast of Australia. It shows a marked strength between Latitudes 20° S to 25° S while it is notably weaker and of a broader flow after 32° S. It circles to the east, with some water moving northward past the west coast of New Zealand and the remaining water turning into the Southern Ocean Drift.

Southern Ocean Drift

Sets to the east in the direction of the prevailing winds and is centred on latitude 50° S. The flow extends up to the South American coast where it divides into two stream currents, (i) around Cape Horn and into the South Atlantic Drift, (ii) northward along the coast to Peru, known as the 'Humboldt' or Peru Current. This water then joins with the westerly set of the Equatorial Current, with a branch being deflected into the Panama canal region.

6.11 Indian Ocean Currents

The "Equatorial Current" has a westward flow between the latitude parallels 5° and 20° S. It divides at Madagascar with part water flow around the north of the island and down through the Mozambique Channel to join up with the alternative flow down the eastern side of the island. The current then flows around the Cape and is known as the "Agulhas Current" and varies in strength from about 1 to 4 knots.

Some deflection takes place as it meets the east flowing waters of the South Atlantic and some water joins the eastern set of the "Southern Ocean Drift". Other water from the Agulhas turns into the South Atlantic and is carried north by the "Benguela Current".

The West Australian Current sets northward off the west coast of Australia and eventually joins with the South Equatorial Current, which in turn streams to the Mozambique/Madagascar Currents. The Mozambique Current retains this name up to Delagoa Bay in latitude 26° S from where it becomes the Agulhas Stream towards the Cape of Good Hope.

6.12 Bay of Bengal and Arabian Sea

December/January (only) NE Monsoon Period

The East African Current sets down from approximately 10° N latitude to round 5° S latitude, from where it curves and sets eastward into the Equatorial Counter Stream. The strength of the current is greatly influenced by the prevailing monsoon. In the case of the NE monsoon the prevailing wind acts to retard the flow and it is subsequently not as strong as would be expected as with the SW monsoon.

The monsoon drift sets to the west from the Malacca Strait towards Sri-Lanka giving an anti-clockwise circulation in the Bay of Bengal and the Arabian Sea.

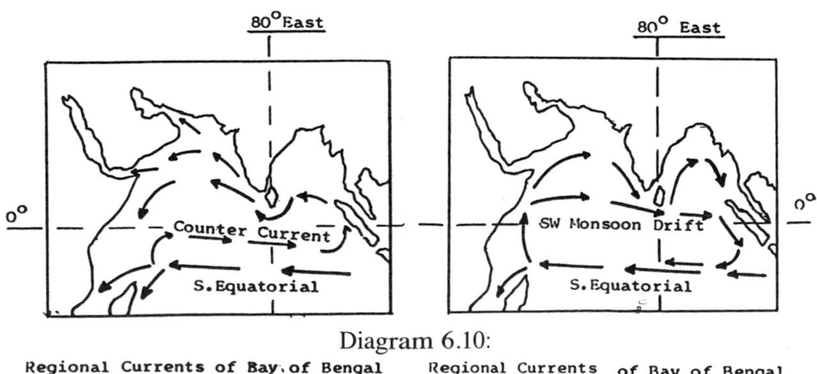

Diagram 6.10:

Regional Currents of Bay of Bengal during NE Monsoon period.

Regional Currents of Bay of Bengal during the SW Monsoon period.

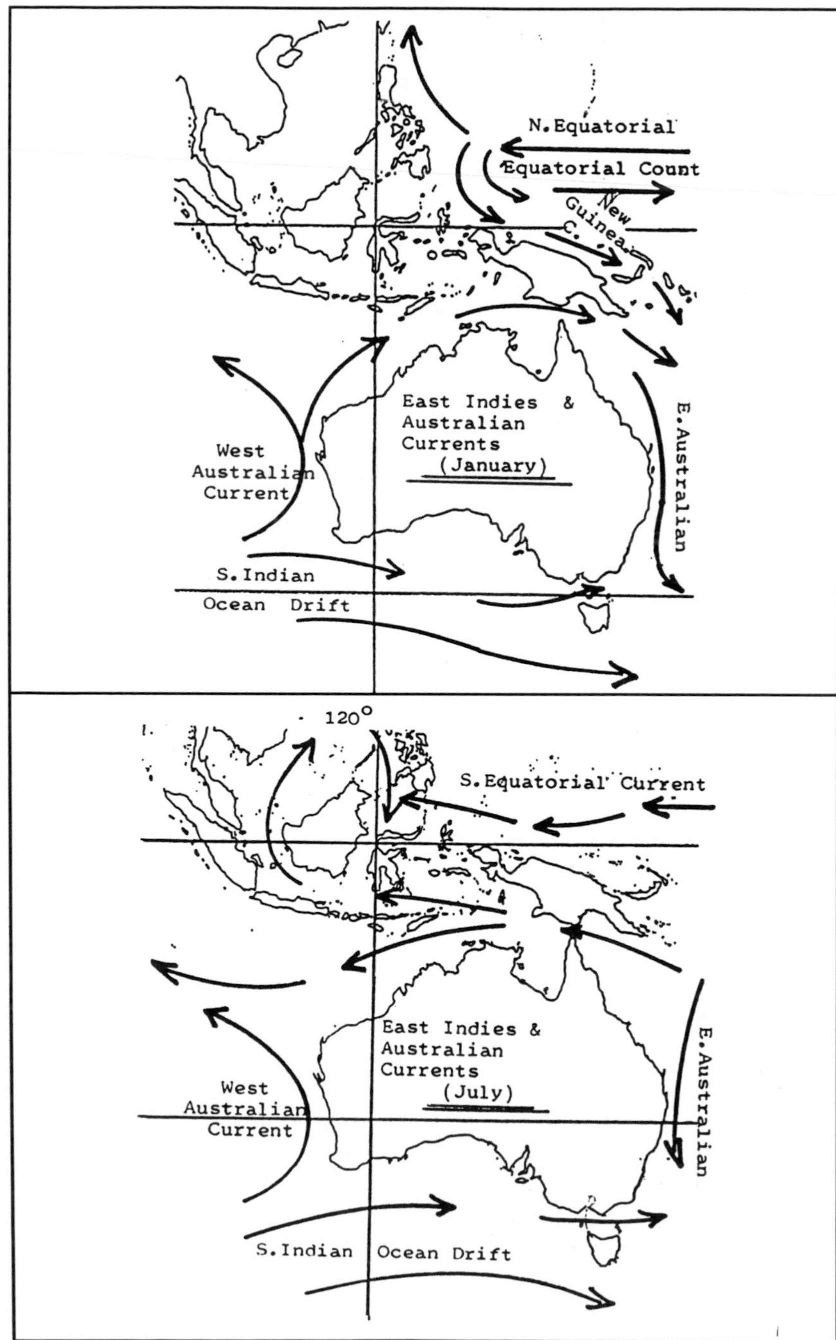

Diagram 6.11: Seasonal changes of ocean currents around Australasia

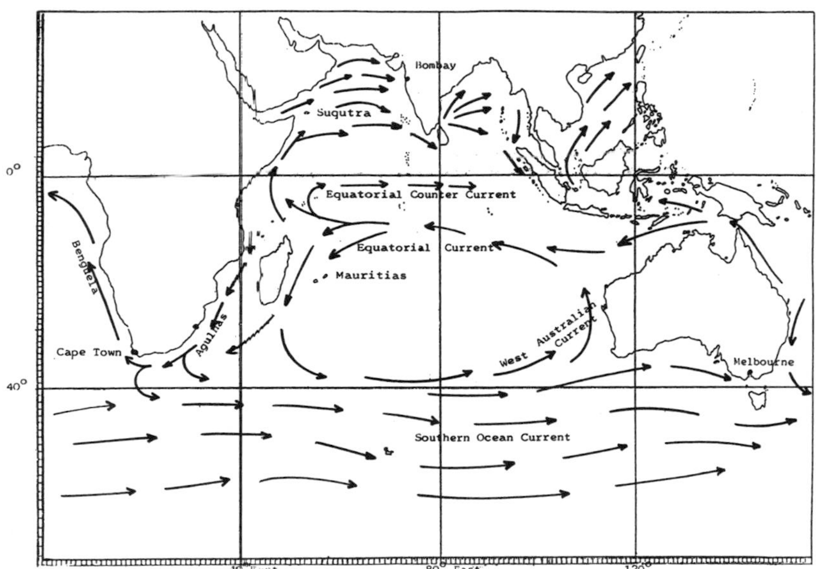

Diagram 6.12: INDIAN OCEAN (JULY) regional currents

July SW Monsoon period

The East African Current sets in a NNE direction following the coastline from 11° S latitude. The main flow curves at about 7° N and sets eastward as the "SW Monsoon Drift" sometimes referred to as the Counter Current. The strength of this current is influenced by the south west wind and can be experienced up to about 7 knots south of Suqutra. Vessels will encounter this SW Monsoon Drift between the latitude of Sri-Lanka and the Equator and also as a clockwise circulation in the areas of the Bay of Bengal and the Arabian Sea.

Chapter Seven

ICE NAVIGATION

7.1 Introduction

Most mariners, at some time in their career can expect to encounter ice in one form or another. In order to navigate through an ice region it would seem prudent therefore to have some knowledge of what might become an unexpected hazard. A glossary of ice terms is available in the Mariners' Handbook, but by way of introduction to this chapter the following, most widely used terms are expanded.

Navigators will gain experience from each passage where ice is present. They will gain confidence in the ship and respect the dangers that ice can present. It should however be remembered that with the modern aids to navigation it is all too easy to become complacent. Masters should be ever vigilant and aware that modern day aids bring modern day problems.

7.2 Ice Examples – Encountered at Sea

Sea Ice

Sea Ice is originally formed by the sea water freezing, the salt content of the water lowering the freezing point. As the water freezes its density increases and it begins to sink, while warmer water from below rises and effectively a convection process is established. (The heat loss being mainly from the water to the air).

When fresh water is cooled (Baltic waters) to a temperature of 3° C it will attain a point of maximum density and the convection process will cease. It is at this point that the surface of the water begins to cool rapidly and freezing quickly occurs. In the case of seawater, that point of maximum density will occur at a much lower temperature than 4° C because of the salinity content.

Once freezing takes place, the early ice so formed is pure and contains little or no salt. Growth takes place downwards from the surface, and ice crystals and saltwater pockets are formed. Snow and freezing temperatures cover the ice at surface level and cause an upward thickening growth. This will later become more compact and eventually turn to ice.

New Ice

First indications of ice forming appears at surface level as small plates about 2.5 cms x 2.5 cms, often referred to as 'spicules'. It is slushy and has a soup-like consistency. Subsequent stages are known as 'frazil ice', and if freezing continues will coagulate and become known as 'grease ice'. Later stages following further freezing would cause sheets of 'ice rind' or 'nilas' to form. Nilas, are ice layers formed in water of high salinity, up to about 10 cms thick and act like an elastic crust. It very often forms a base for the growth of sea ice.

Early Formation of Sea Ice

First appearance as such may be several centimetres thick. Once frozen, sea ice could grow up to 10 cms in the first twenty four hour period, and between 15 – 18 cms in the following twenty four hours. Growth is essentially noticeable in shallow waters, especially where currents are weak or non existent, as in sheltered bays. Growth would also be expected to be encountered attached to and extending outward from an existing 'ice front'.

'First year ice' is normally less than 1.5 metres thick after the first winter. Wind and wave action can cause some break-up and deterioration turning some into 'brash ice'. Brash ice being defined as a floating accumulation of ice fragments, is taken offshore with prevailing winds. However, it can cause a damping effect on wave action and this in itself encourages the growth of additional ice forms. If larger ice concentrations are in the area it is quite likely that 'bergy bits' or 'growlers' could well be obscured within floating accumulations. Should poor visibility prevail at the same time, Radar may not prove as effective in discerning targets as well as the mariner might desire.

Pack Ice – Concentration

Found in open water and when under seven-tenths concentration often termed as 'drift ice'. One-tenth to three-tenths concentration is sometimes known as 'sailing ice', more commonly referred to as 'very open pack ice'.

NB: The measure of tenths employed is a comparison which reflects the amount of ice coverage against the predominant amount of open water visible by the observer, i.e. the ice concentration.

By definition 'pack ice' is defined by coverage, and the following table should provide the mariner with reasonable awareness of the type of ice his vessel is experiencing:

1/10th – 3/10ths	Very open pack ice
4/10ths – 6/10ths	Open pack ice
Up to 7/10ths	Pack ice (still remains navigable)
7/10ths – 8/10ths	Close ice
Up to 9/10ths but less than 10/10ths	Very close pack ice
10/10ths	Consolidated pack ice (No open water visible and floes frozen together)

Ice Shelf

A floating ice sheet which is visible from 2m to 50m above sea level. The seaward edge being known as the 'ice front'. The shelf can extend for many miles to seaward and frequently contains the ends of many 'glaciers' and becomes the source of 'tabular bergs'.

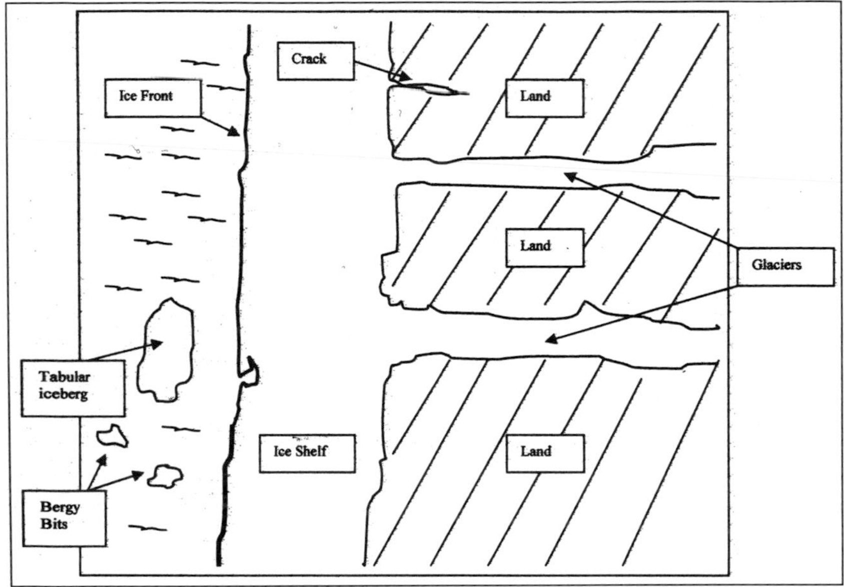

Diagram 7.1: Ice Features

Ice Tongue

Often the end of a 'glacier' (seaward end) and hence the source of 'glaciated bergs'. A projection of the ice front, which may extend several miles to seaward.

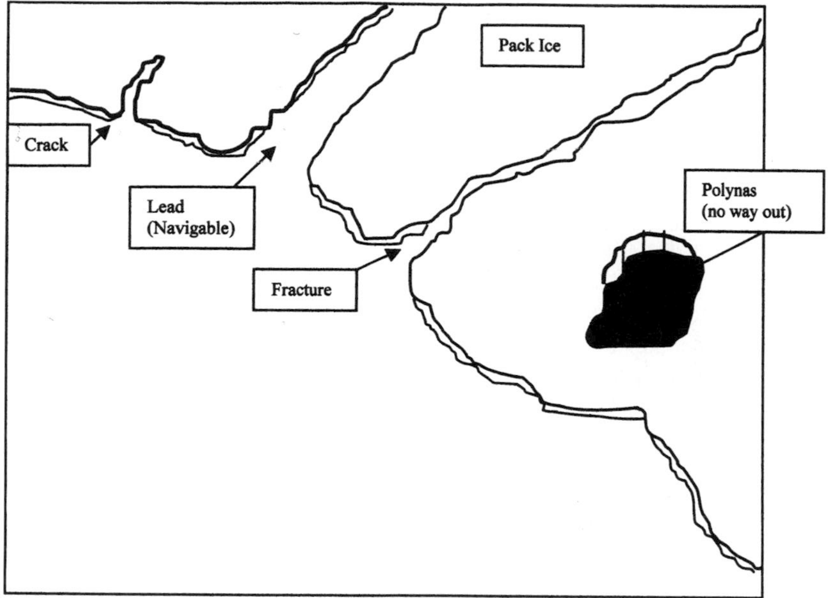

Diagram 7.2: Ice Terms, Plan View

Crack
Fracture in fast ice, measures up to 1m in size. Not considered navigable but may indicate a weak point within the ice front.

Fracture
A large fracture could be more than 500 metres in width in various forms of pack ice concentrations. Fractures can extend from a few metres in length to several kilometres. 'brash ice' or 'young ice' is often encountered on the surface inside fractures.

Lead
Any fracture in sea ice that permits navigation by surface vessels.

Polynas
An enclosed area in the ice from which there is no visible way out. The water surface may be covered by 'brash ice' or other forms of 'new ice'.

Cracks
Fractures and leads are generally formed when the pressure around the ice form relaxes. They can all be early signs of the deformation of the ice.

Iceberg Formation Life Cycles

There are two main types of ice encountered at sea, namely 'sea ice,' previously discussed and 'icebergs'. These are defined as an enormous piece of ice of varying shape which is visible more than 5.0 metres above sea level. The volume of the submerged section is about 90% of the total volume.

Icebergs can be divided by geography, in that they are either 'arctic bergs' or 'antarctic icebergs'. It is worth noting that there is approximately seven times more ice in Antarctica than in the Greenland Icecap and therefore many more icebergs are produced in the Southern Hemisphere. (No icebergs in the Baltic Sea).

Arctic Icebergs

Most icebergs of the Northern Hemisphere are carved from either a glacier and will have an irregular shape, or from an ice shelf, in which case they may be 'Tabular' or encountered as an 'Ice Island'.

Many icebergs are from the glaciers of the east coast of Greenland. They are carried south by the East Greenland Current, either round Cape Farewell and into Baffin Bay by the West Greenland Current or they drift south and melt in the lower latitudes. They have been known to extend up to 400 miles SE of Cape Farewell, during the month of April. Although the two tracks for icebergs from this region have been mentioned it is pointed out that in actual fact, very few icebergs are carried round into Baffin Bay.

Icebergs in Baffin Bay are frozen into the pack ice during the winter months and there may be as many as 40,000 in this area at any one time. As the pack ice melts during spring some icebergs drift south and either ground or break up in Baffin Bay itself. Others are carried by the cold Labrador Current towards the region of the Grand Banks.

Iceberg season: Mariners are advised that the season for encountering icebergs off the Grand Banks and the Canadian Coast is from February to August, most being encountered in April, May and June. An average figure for the worst month of April would be about 70 icebergs.

Iceberg limits will fluctuate slightly but in the region of the Grand Banks, latitude 48° N in February and 42° N in May, can be expected. Once icebergs continue south off the Banks, they meet the warmer water of the Gulf Stream and melt. Icebergs are not encountered from October through to the end of January.

Pic. 23: Small iceberg sighted in the North Atlantic in 1984 by a container vessel bound from UK to Montreal, via Cape Race, Newfoundland. The berg seen is low lying and would not make a good radar target. Such conditions would lend to 'Growlers' and 'Bergy Bits' being in the same vicinity. Sea conditions 3/4 on the Beaufort Scale.

Only on rare occasions would icebergs be encountered south of latitude 40° N, or east of longitude 40° W.

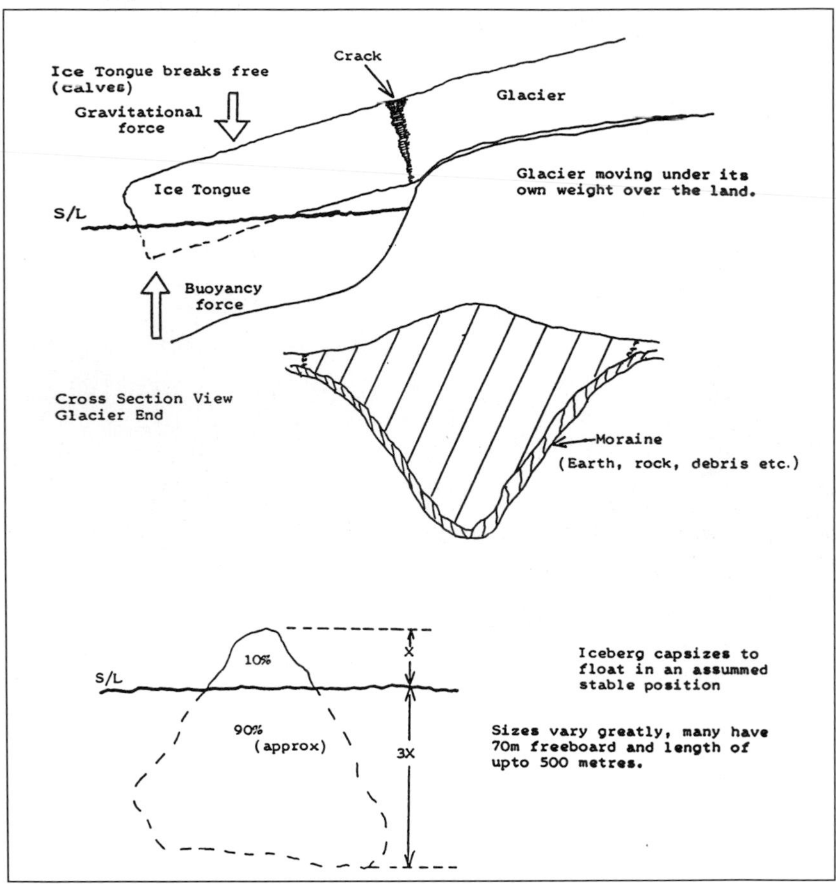

Diagram 7.3: *Glacier Iceberg – Formation* (example Greenland Iceberg)

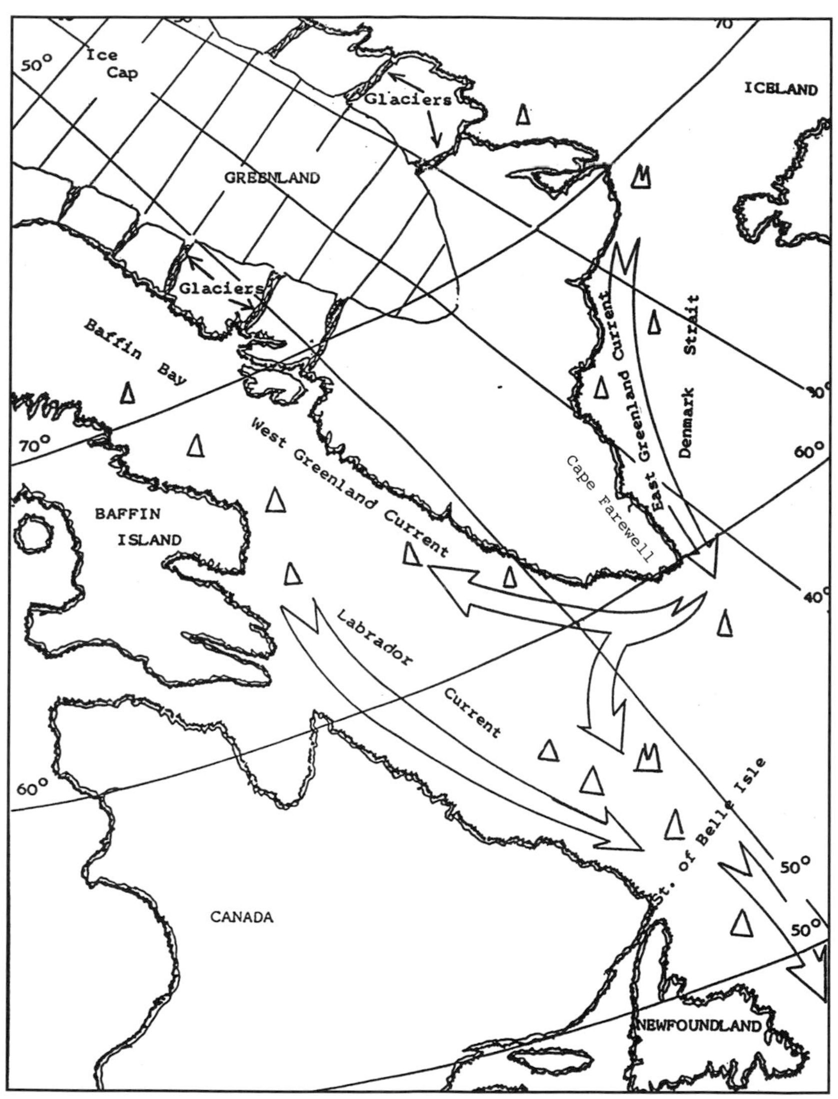

Diagram 7.4: *General Drift and Iceberg Movement – North Atlantic*

Northern Hemisphere – Navigator's Geographic Information

Winter Detail

The most southerly advance of pack ice in the northern hemisphere is dependent on the movement of the ocean currents. The East Greenland and the Labrador currents both bring cold water southwards and subsequently extend the 'ice edge'. Whereas, the ice edge, off the Norwegian west coast and in the 'Barents Sea' is restricted by the warm North Atlantic Drift Current and warm south westerly winds.

Affected Areas:

Baffin Bay Ice – Extends to Newfoundland.

Baltic Sea – The northern part freezes over. In some years the whole sea area my be affected by pack ice.

Barents Sea – Coastlines to the east of longitude 40° are affected.

Belle Isle Strait – Frozen over and usually closed to navigation between December and June.

Black Sea – Northern part may be affected by freezing.

Denmark Strait – This may be totally closed to surface navigation.

Greenland – Ice extends to engulf Jan Mayen Island.

Hudson Bay – (Davis/Hudson Straits) This area freezes over completely. Seek information from the Ice Advisory Service operated by the Canadian Coast Guard.

North Sea – (January to March) The south coast of Norway, together with some Danish, German and Dutch ports may be affected.

St. Lawrence – Considerable ice formation is expected between December to April which may close areas to surface navigation. Ice breakers operate throughout this period and information should be sought from the Ice Advisory Service of the Canadian Coast Guard.

North Pacific – The Bering Strait and the Asian Coastline north of Latitude 45° N are affected.

However, ice is not normally encountered in the vicinity of the Aleutian Islands.

The White Sea – This area is normally closed for navigation from December to May.

Ice Free Areas – These normally include the Gulf of Alaska and the west coast of Norway.

NB: The above areas are considered in winter for 'pack ice' it should be borne in mind that drifting icebergs can expect to be encountered in associated areas.

Pic. 24: 10/10ths pack ice seen in the Gulf of St Lawrence in 1987. Ships with 'Ice Breaker Bows' and full ice strengthening can still make headway when the thickness of the ice is not too heavy. Ice damage to the vessel in these conditions must however be anticipated, especially in the bow and waterline regions of the hull.

Pic. 25: *Star Princess* under way in Glacial Bay, West Coast Canada. floating Ice formations are to be expected in the immediate area where Glaciers meet the ocean. The growth in the cruise liner activity to such specialist areas as Alaska and Antarctica Regions is bound to bring ships into close proximity with various ice formations.

Iceberg Deformation

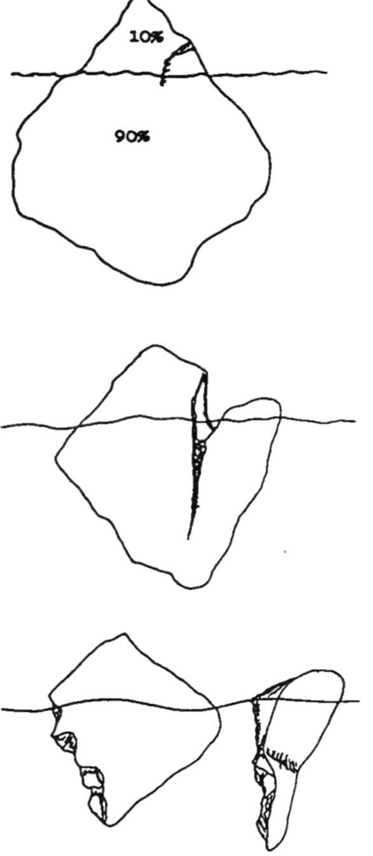

An iceberg after calving from a glacier is affected by:

- Weather (wind and rain);
- Melting on sunward facing side;
- Erosion by wave action;
- Underwater melting from warm currents.

Cracks develop for one or more of the above reasons and cause a piece to break away often making the iceberg unstable.

Cracking of the ice may not only be audible to an observer onboard ship, but may cause the iceberg to visibly topple and assume a new surface position.

As the iceberg assumes a new stable position the broken piece termed, as a 'bergy bit' drifts from the main berg.

The 'bergy bit' is defined as a large piece of floating glacier ice which has less than 5 metres visible height above sea level.

'Bergy bits' are affected by wave action and become known as 'growlers', where the height of ice above sea level does not exceed 1 metre.

Icebergs and 'bergy bits' generally present themselves as good radar targets, but 'growlers' should be considered as extremely dangerous and very poor radar targets.

An iceberg may also ground at any point where it encounters shallows. From this time onward it can be expected to break up rapidly.

Complete disintegration occurs into 'bergy bits', 'growlers' and small ice pieces.

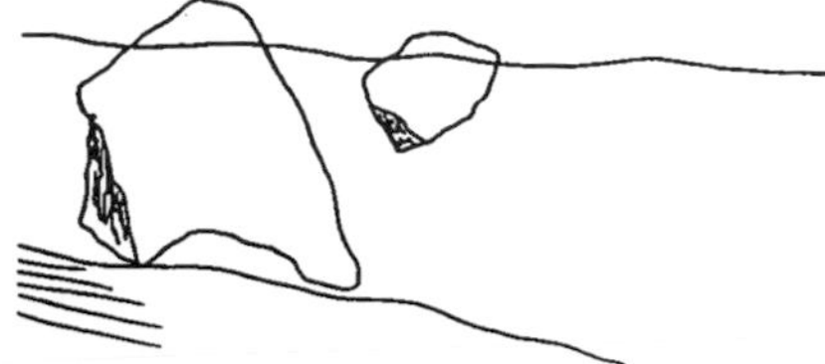

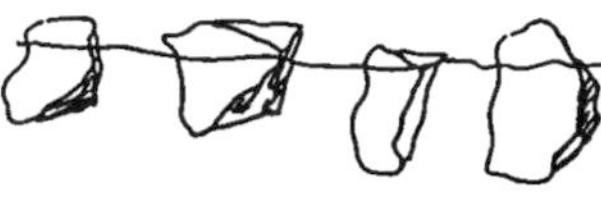

7.3 Antarctic Icebergs

Of the many icebergs encountered in the southern hemisphere, the main type is a tabular shape. These are defined as large flat-topped icebergs, which have usually calved from an ice shelf. They will vary considerably in size up to 30 miles in length and having an average height above sea level of 40-50 metres. In general, the appearance of Antarctic icebergs is white providing the observer with a 'plaster of Paris' effect, given off by the white bubbly ice, common to this region's icebergs. Occasionally icebergs will be sighted and described as 'black' or of a 'greenish-black' appearance. The composition of these is often in a banded form or distinctive layers. Masters should note any distinctive features of icebergs as these should be incorporated in respective future ice-reports. Black and white icebergs, together with weathered icebergs, are often encountered in the Weddell Sea.

The general drift of Antarctic icebergs is in a west-north-west direction. They tend to move northerly below latitude 63° S, where they are influenced by the eastward set of the Southern Ocean Current. One of the main dangers to shipping being in the areas around the tip of South America, with occasional bergs being sighted off the Cape of Good Hope and the southern coasts of Tasmania and New Zealand. Most southern hemisphere icebergs suffer erosion by weather and water of the drift current and are prevented from going into the lower latitudes, as such the main shipping routes are generally clear of icebergs.

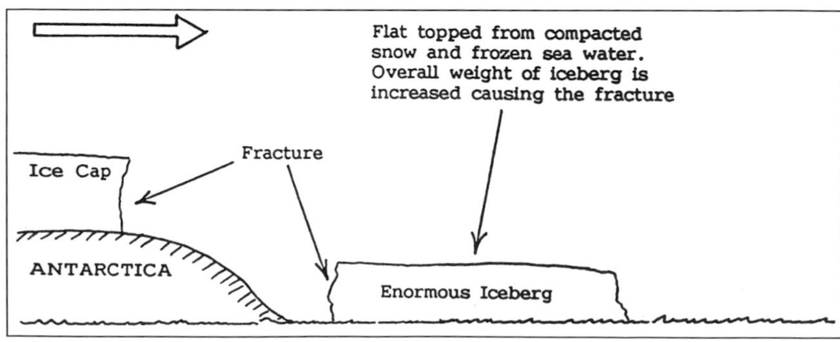

Diagram 7.5: Permanent ice cap grows outward

Tabular icebergs are characteristic of this type of formation. Sizes vary tremendously, hundreds are over 1 mile in length, scores are up to 25 miles long.

One of the largest on record measured 90 miles in length with a 35 metre freeboard.

7.4 Ice in the Southern Hemisphere

7.4.1 ice limits

The outer limits of pack ice will vary from year to year and a difference of 300 miles of the ice edge in 'good' and 'bad' seasons can be expected.

Winter Ice – new ice can be expected to form from mid-March onwards to October. This can extend as far as latitude 56° S in the Indian Ocean and latitude 60° S in the Pacific Ocean.

Summer Ice – melting occurs extensively at the outer edges of the pack ice. Deformation is accelerated by offshore winds and the general increase in temperatures of the open sea waters. Erosion and melting occur during the months of November and December and is particularly pronounced at its most northern and southern boundaries.

In comparison with Arctic ice, the ice of the southern hemisphere usually carries a heavier snow layer. This tends to resist 'puddling' (deterioration of the ice from water puddles absorbing the sun's rays and causing weakening of the ice mass). The major factors causing deformation to take place being swell action and the contact with warm ocean currents.

Pic. 26: The *S.A. Agulhas* moored ahead of a second Antarctic survey vessel against an ice wall in Antarctica. An impression of the length of the ice formation can be perceived with the two ships moored in line.

7.4.2 navigator's information

Although greater detail from satellites is now more readily available, the limits of ice should be treated with extreme caution, great circle sailing will be restricted at seasonal times on the following routes:

Cape of Good Hope to Cape Horn	South Atlantic Ocean
Australian/New Zealand ports to the southern ports of South America	South Pacific Ocean
Southern ports of South Africa to the coasts of Australia	South Indian Ocean

7.4.3 signs of the proximity of ice

In clear visibility

An 'ice blink' may appear over the ice pack, particularly on a clear day. It will be sighted as a yellowish haze usually well before the ice itself is detected. If the weather itself is overcast an 'ice blink' will tend to have a white glare reflecting with the cloud formation.

The sea surface temperature is a distinctive indication of ice proximity. If the recorded temperature is 1° C then ice can be assumed to be within 150 nautical miles. If the temperature is –0.5° ice is within 50 miles. Ice fragments would also be a distinctive feature, indicating the proximity of pack ice.

If navigating in ice regions, mariners should note that the ice edge is often accompanied by a thick band of fog. Prior to actually sighting ice or fog bands, it is more likely that observation of wildlife will provide indication of ice.

Examples of wildlife which indicate ice presence:

Walrus, seals and different species of birds far from land.

In the case of Antarctica, the sight of the 'Antarctic Petrel' or the 'Snow Petrel' indicates the presence of ice.

In poor visibility

A distinct change in sea state, where an abrupt smoothing of the sea and a reduction in swell indicates that ice could well be to windward.

Also white patches or discolouration in the fog, may well indicate ice at a short distance and close to visible range.

Proximity of icebergs

Reliable indication of icebergs is extremely difficult to establish. A cold iceberg bearing current and the sea temperature of the same, provides indication that icebergs may be in close proximity. A more positive indication is the sighting of 'growlers' or 'bergy bits'. This coupled with wildlife away from land provides circumstantial evidence. Effective use of radar and the plotting of a virtually stationary target will of course enhance any visual sightings.

Pic. 27: An enormous iceberg sighted in Antarctic waters (2002). A target of this size would provide positive radar contact and be highly visible at good range. An observer could expect to see signs of wildlife and other smaller ice configurations in the same proximity of such an iceberg.

Visibility of icebergs

From a high bridge or masthead 16 to 18 miles on a clear day. From an average bridge height 12-15 miles could be expected under the same conditions. If the day is cloudy detection by the naked eye would be reduced by approximately 2 miles.

Where conditions are obscured, i.e. by haze, only the tops of icebergs would be sighted at a range of about 11 miles.

In the case of 'mist' or 'drizzle' conditions 2 to 3 miles should be the expected maximum range of visual contact.

If navigating in 'dense fog' it is unlikely that detection range will be more than 100 metres and then the wash will probably be detected first. In conditions where no sun is experienced a dark mass may become the first indication of the iceberg. If navigating in fog, when sunshine is present, then a sunny-luminous mass is usually detectable.

Detection of icebergs at night

When no moon is present, the naked eye may detect an iceberg at approximately 0.25 miles. If binoculars are used then this range may extend to about 1.0 mile. In conditions where a moon is prominent, and it is a clear night, an iceberg could well be detected up to 5.0 miles range. However, it is pointed out that if the moon is situated in a position behind the observer then the detection range can be expected to be quite good. Should the moon be in a position in front of the observer, it may prove to be more of a hindrance than an asset.

Poor visibility and iceberg detection

An iceberg may indicate its position by radiating a white patch around its volume. Observation of such a 'white patch' would signify that the observer is at close quarters with the iceberg. A more reliable indication would be the sound of breakers within close proximity of the ice or loud cracking sounds heard on the occasions when 'bergy bits' break away from the icebergs.

A point worth noting is the absence of vigorous sea conditions in strong breezy weather. This would indicate either pack ice or a large iceberg to windward. This is particularly the case in Antarctic regions and in the proximity of large 'tabular bergs'.

7.4.4 ice detection by radar

The use of radar is invaluable when navigating through ice affected regions, but mariners should be aware of the limitations and constraints that may be imposed by use of the equipment. Abnormal weather conditions could well affect and reduce detection ranges and overall performance of the equipment in use, possibly from ice accretion.

If calm seas are considered – ice formations of all types should be detected and the following is a general guide to types and detection ranges:

Large icebergs	15-20 miles
Small Growlers	2 miles
Bergy bits (3 metres exposed)	3 miles maximum

If in rough seas, where the sea clutter extends more than 1.0 mile, it should be considered unsafe to rely on radar alone.

Strength of Radar Echo

A radar return from an ice formation will be greatly influenced by:

1. Range of target from the vessel.
2. The size of target above the water surface.
3. The inclination of the targets reflecting surface.

Observers should note that icebergs generally provide a strong echo which is regular and visible on the PPI. However, 'growlers' are more often than not extremely poor targets and frequently do not show on the PPI.

Ice Features and Radar Detection

Ice Field – An ice field of concentrated pack ice, hummocked ice, would normally be detected in all sea conditions at a range of about 3.0 miles.

Leads – A lead through static ice will not show unless it is at least 0.25 miles wide.

Small Islands/Large Icebergs – Often difficult to segregate and identify. Extreme caution is advised when position fixing.

River Mouths – These are very often frozen over and become difficult to distinguish. The coastline is subsequently presented as a continuous feature on the PPI.

Ice Targets – These are often obscured by the shadow from islands or large icebergs. Pack ice and large icebergs create a shadowy area over a wide arc of the screen. Hence a field of icebergs always appears less dense than it really is.

Close inshore navigation for position fixing should be resisted at all times.

7.4.5 position fixing and radar limitations (inside ice regions)

The limitations in the use of radar have been previously stated, but the use of radar in position fixing presents the observer with particular problems. With these in mind Masters should ensure that watch officers employ alternative position fixing methods when using radar and not rely on radar alone.

Ice features are continually changing due to movement, growth and deformation. It should not be assumed that they will present themselves in the same manner or aspect to an observer on an outward bound vessel later, when homeward bound.

Coastlines

Prominent points of a coastline, such as headlands and inlets, are regularly employed in position fixing. The observer should be wary in the event that headlands may be extended due to 'fast ice' or icebergs which may have grounded in shallows in close proximity to a headland; the obvious mistake being made by the observer in assuming that the headland is longer than it actually is and a distorted range of bearing being plotted on the chart.

Frozen Bays/River Mouths

These provide a continuous radar feature which would otherwise be discernible for use of bearings or range identification. Compacted snow on frozen areas, including coastlines, often distort the visual aspects when making comparisons with radar features.

Small/Large Icebergs

These will be detected at ranges commensurate with their size but it will rarely be possible to distinguish them from small islands of equivalent size. The identification of the target is essential, and bearings and/or ranges from islands should be double checked prior to plotting on the chart.

Icebergs with 'Pack Ice'

This type of ice feature effectively creates shadow areas over a wide sector of the screen. As a consequence a field of icebergs always looks less dense than it really is. Masters should resist the temptation to navigate their vessels in too close for the purpose of more detailed position fixing data.

It should be expected in this day and age that instruments will experience reduction in performance and limitations in effectiveness in such hostile areas of ice infested waters. Position fixing by GPS, however, is as effective in these regions as anywhere else. Visual fixing, assuming that prominent landmarks are available, is also reliable, in clear visibility. Though Masters are reminded that magnetic compasses may suffer in high latitudes and make D.R. and E.P. methods questionable.

Ice Sighting – Radar Use and Immediate Action

As officer of the watch on sighting ice (visually).

On first sighting, advise the Master of the vessel of the following:

1. Type of ice.
2. Position of ice.
3. Relative position of ice to the ship's track/position.

Radar Activity

1. Reduce the working range of radar to 6 miles or less, appropriate to the prevailing weather conditions.
2. Carry out regular long range scan checks for associated ice targets.
3. Instigate continuous radar watch (by second watchkeeper).

In addition to the above the officer of the watch should enter a statement into the log book, obtain the most up to date ice report possible and ensure that ice limits are entered on the navigational chart. Occasional icebergs should also be plotted.

Master's Duties on Meeting Dangerous Ice

Obligatory reports are required from Masters of ships which encounter dangerous ice on route.

The ice report should contain the following information:

1. The type of ice observed.
2. The position of the observed ice.
3. The GMT and the date of observation.

Shipping reports should additionally include the size and shape of ice formations as this will aid iceberg identification. Such facts as the thickness of ice, the sea temperature and the concentration of ice (in 10ths) would all be considered relevant.

NB: It is not unusual to stop the vessel at night when navigating inside ice limits. This would most certainly be prudent action if ships' radars were considered unreliable for any reason. Attention is drawn to Solas Chapter 5, Regulation 7:

When ice is reported on or near his course the Master of every ship at night is bound to proceed at a moderate speed or to alter his course so as to go well clear of the danger zone.

7.4.6 operational navigation in ice regions

Open Pack Ice

Alternative routing should be a priority option for any Master who finds concentrations of pack ice either close to or on his intended track. However, where avoidance is impossible and the vessel has no option but to proceed then the Master should organise and brief his bridge team prior to entry into the ice.

Ice operations dictate that the Master would take the 'con' when entering ice. Entry should take place at slow speed, reduced to take account of ice thickness and relevant dangers. Main propulsion systems should be retained on immediate notice and at a status that could provide immediate and continuous manoeuvring of the vessel.

Lookouts

Bridge lookouts should be advised by the officer of the watch to report all traffic and navigation marks. Ice leads and/or dangerous ice formations should also be reported. Officers in charge of watches should be aware of extreme cold conditions which may affect the efficiency and awareness of lookouts. Regular rotation to overcome fatigue or discomfort should be considered an acceptable management decision by the officer.

Helmsman

Manual steering should be the order of the day, from, prior to entry until the vessel is clear of ice regions. It would not be unreasonable to expect steerage to be lost if the vessel is navigating under heavy ice conditions. Any such loss of steerage should be reported to the Officer of the Watch by the helmsman. Regular checks on steering gear by engineers must be considered essential when navigating in such conditions.

Communication Officer

The Communication Officer aboard the vessel should ensure that essential communications are continually monitored. In particular, such items as, ice reports, navigational warnings, general weather reports, ship-to-ship or ship- to-shore transmissions, together with Ice Breaker communications where appropriate.

Navtex, and special reports should all be passed to the Master and considered as priority communications directly affecting the well being of the vessel and the safe progress of the voyage.

7.4.7 The Officer of the Watch (OOW)

The relationship between the Master and the Officer of the Watch is unique at any time but in the transit of ice it becomes clear that each relies on the other to function at peak efficiency. The OOW should not hesitate to use engines or any navigational equipment as he thinks necessary to ensure the safety of the vessel. He should at all times maintain the freedom of movement of the vessel and not allow the ship to become 'beset' in ice. To this end, Masters are expected to brief their watch officers, especially those officers with little or no ice experience. Officers should be made aware that excessive speed in ice leads to ice damage and cautionary speeds are more appropriate.

Watch Structure Arrangement in the Vicinity of Ice

The watch personnel provide the cutting edge of the vessels progress through known ice regions. The dangers from ice being well recognised by the ship's Master it must be anticipated that the watch structure will be enhanced to reflect a high profile. Normal watchkeeping personnel could expect to be supported by a continuous, additional lookout during the hours of daylight as well as during the hours of darkness. This could be given further support by doubling the Officer of the Watch position to reflect the need for a continuous 'Radar Watch'.

During the hours of darkness, the Master, even when equipped with efficient radars, may still decide to stop the vessel and take "all way off", until daylight. In any event the change to 'Manual Steering' and taking the vessel off Auto-Pilot must be considered earlier rather than late.

On entering ice limits the Master would be expected to provide an increased profile and support all elements of the Bridge Team, while at the same time remain available to take the 'con' if required.

It is normal practice to have main engines on stand-by and ready to manoeuvre while in transit through ice infested waters. As such the duty engineer officer and associated manpower, must consider themselves as Bridge Team Members and be prepared to respond as and when the need arises.

Under Pilotage – In Ice

Where a vessel finds herself in ice conditions and simultaneously under pilotage, just as at any other time, the Pilot himself must be considered as an additional pair of eyes on the Bridge. The 'Pilot' will generally never be in total charge of the vessel but would be conducting the navigation of the vessel to the Masters orders and Pilots (his/her) advice.

It should be remembered that ice conditions are continuously changing and every situation, every pilotage, will be different. No Pilot or Master can avoid learning from each experience, and neither party, will know all the answers, all of the time. Clearly, some regions, which are continuously affected by ice will produce Pilots with exceptional 'Ice Experience'. When this is known, it can be extremely beneficial to the ships progress, but it can also be associated with the danger of complacency effecting members of the Bridge Team.

Sadly, complacency has no respect for rank and the ship's Master should be vigilant of not only himself but also on behalf of his operational staff.

Use of Topographical Features in Ice

The experienced mariner will be well aware that navigational information, topographical features and soundings are extremely scarce in ice regions. Polar regions, where the use of polar charts is a requirement, are based on air photography, which tends to make geographic features unreliable. This, coupled with extreme adverse weather conditions, tends to either reduce or eliminate position fixing options to a minimum.

The following problems may be encountered when navigating in and around ice regions:

1. Headlands, especially where icebergs have grounded, may present themselves as being longer and more greatly extended than they

actually are. Notable when position fixing with visual bearings or by radar observation.

2. Special care should also be exercised if using clearing lines/bearings off such headlands.

3. The pack ice limit, especially when snow covered, may be mistakenly compared with coastline features portrayed in the sailing directions. The reliability and use of such features should be treated with extreme caution and should never be taken as the sole indicator when position fixing.

4. Beacons and navigational marks may be partially or totally hidden by a build-up of snow. Buoys and surface markers could also be 'under' ice formations or destroyed by previous ice movement, and no longer visible for navigational purpose.

5. The general maintenance on such beacons in extreme weather regions must by the very nature of the difficulties involved, be considered as limited and irregular.

6. Survey details of high latitude areas, especially soundings, cannot be considered reliable, depending on date of survey. Navigation in areas of a low underkeel clearance should be undertaken only with adequate margins of safety. Deep draught vessels are especially prone to experience related problems in this field.

7. If sights are being taken to fix the vessel's position when in the vicinity of 'pack ice', errors of up to 4.0' may be inherent within observations and calculations. The horizon often being difficult to discern, and a subsequent 'clean cut' difficult to obtain.

7.4.8 navigation in high latitudes

Although navigation in high latitudes is generally considered as a rarity rather than the norm, the professional mariner would be expected to adopt safe working practices. The following points are discussed to provide insight into potential problems and expand on suggested main navigational points.

1. In 'high latitudes' the use of meridians and parallels as references becomes impracticable. An observer will see the ship's position changing and moving very fast.

2. All 'zone times' meet and local time has little significance. Sunset/sunrise and periods of night and daylight become quite different if compared to the average day within middle latitudes.
3. Navigational practice will involve 'polar charts', based on air photography which does not normally have adequate control of 'triangulation'. Consequently, unreliable geographic positions and features may appear.
4. Soundings and topographical features, together with navigational information, is scarce in the accessible parts of the polar regions.
5. Celestial observations cannot be relied upon. When in the navigational season, i.e. when ice conditions permit, clouds tend to hide the sun during periods of long days and short nights.
6. Fog, low cloud and ice conditions generally pose continual navigational problems.
7. Sights, when only the sun is available, tend to be used with a method of 'transferred position line'. Accuracy is questionable in the upper latitudes.
8. The use of the magnetic compass near the magnetic poles is of little value. However, it is pointed out that if the ship is 'swung' to suit navigation of that region then its use can be gainfully employed.
9. Gyroscopic compasses tend to lose all directive force at the geographic poles and are subject to errors. Appropriate settings and corrections should be applied and regular checks of celestial bodies by Azimuth should be made to ensure continued accuracy.
10. Celestial observations, less than 10° of altitude, may have to be used. Corrections to these altitudes may have to come from tables employed for specific low altitudes, found in the Nautical Almanac and should also include allowances for temperature and pressure where appropriate. Margins of error on celestial observations in pack ice should incorporate up to 4.0' observer error.
11. Radio aids, radar, satellite and inertia navigation systems are as effective as in other parts of the world, but they do have limitations in use and good seamanship practice should not be disregarded.
12. The use, as necessary, of the echo sounder should be encouraged. However, it should be remembered that soundings can change abruptly and its reliability in high latitude regions becomes questionable.
13. A lack of tidal information prevents accurate use of dead reckoning and use of estimated position techniques. This is made more difficult because speed relative to ice is difficult.

14. A large scale, running plot should be established, where all alteration of course points can be checked and changes in speed can be clearly noted.
15. Overall weather conditions can change very quickly and when presented, position fixing opportunities should be taken.

7.4.9 errors in the use of sectored lights

Navigational accuracy in high latitudes and in the associated extreme cold climates tend to generate their own set of problems for the Navigator. It has already been stated that navigation marks and beacons are scarce but the use of marks that are available are not always what they seem.

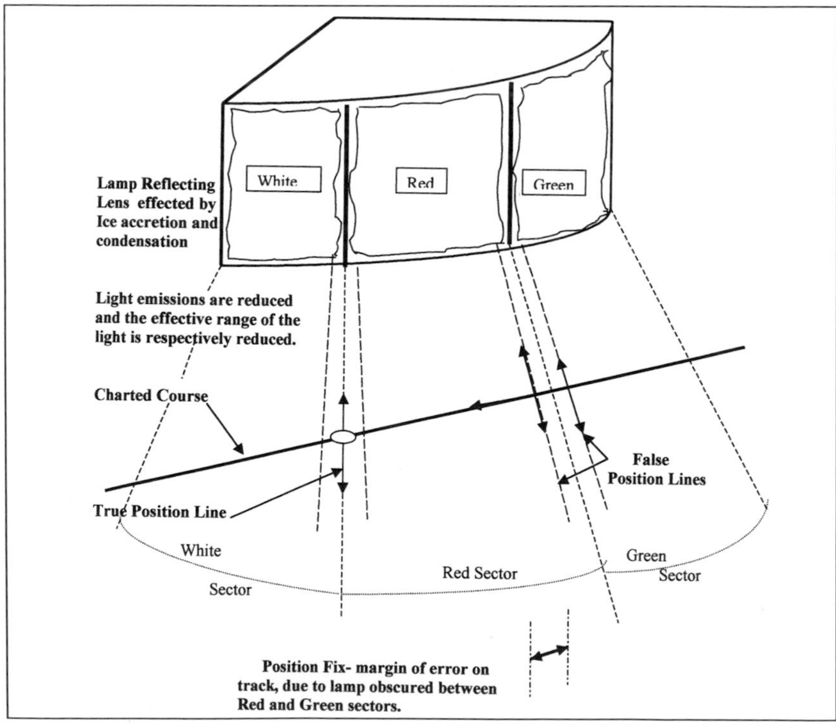

Diagram 7.6: Sector lights effected by ice and snow distorting designated sectors and light ranges making reference unreliable.

7.4.10 ice convoys – instructions for operations

Ice convoys, where several ships are being escorted by an Icebreaker, tend to assume formation at a focal point like a harbour entrance or off a prominent land mark. The Master of the icebreaker will act as Convoy Commander and participating ships would be expected to pass all communications through him.

Prior to formation, the Commander will require relevant details of the vessels in the convoy and these could include:

1. Length of the vessel
2. Turning radius of the vessel
3. Loaded tonnage
4. Sailing draught
5. Horsepower and effective maximum speed

Each participating vessel will have a designated position within the convoy, in relation to the lead commanding icebreaker vessel. This position and the distance required between other ships, must be maintained. Vigilance by watch officers for irregular movement, including stopping or astern motions of ahead vessels, should be continuous.

The actual distance between vessels, on station in convoy, is expected to vary, depending on prevailing conditions. Seemingly the optimum benefit received from an icebreaker will be about 150 metres astern. However, Masters of vessels in convoy should establish a safe distance, which must be adequate to allow his own vessel to stop without involving collision. Whatever "distance off" is adopted, Masters should invariably be prepared for changes of instructions either from the Convoy Commander or relayed from the vessel ahead. Engine movements by vessels in convoy must be anticipated and Masters of following vessels should note and respond to appropriate signals and actions made by accompanying vessels.

The adjustment of speed while engaged in convoy should be at the discretion of the Officer of the Watch or that person who has the 'con' when adjustment is required. Orders may be received at any time to operate astern propulsion, and such orders should be immediately responded to. Signals made by icebreakers and escorted vessels, should be clearly understood by "bridge personnel". These signals could well relate directly to speed or course changes required by the command vessels. The use of the 'International Code' could also be expected to be employed during such operations.

All vessels should be aware that towing operations by the Icebreaker may become a necessity. If such an event occurs, mariners are advised that icebreakers carry towing wires and winches. These towing wires will be hauled aboard and secured aboard the escorted ship. Personnel should be kept well clear once towing commences.

Single/Double Letter Signals between Ice-Breaker and Assisted Vessels

The following signals, when made between an ice-breaker and assisted vessels, have only the specifications given in this table and are only to be made by sound, visual or radio-telephony signals.

WM Ice-breaker support is now commencing. Use special ice-breaker support signals and keep continuous watch for sound, visual or radiotelephony signals.

WO Ice-breaker support as finished. Proceed to your destination.

Code letters or figures	Ice-breaker	Assisted vessel(s)
A · –	Go ahead (proceed along the ice channel	I am going ahead (I am proceeding along the ice channel
G – – ·	I am going ahead; follow me	I am going ahead; I am following you
J · – – –	Do not follow me (proceed along the ice channel	I will not follow you (I will proceed along the ice channel)
P · – – ·	Slow down	I am slowing down
N – ·	Stop your engines	I am stopping my engines
H · · · ·	Reverse your engines	I am reversing my engines
L · – · ·	You should stop your vessel instantly	I am stopping my vessel
4 · · · · –	Stop. I am ice-bound	Stop. I am ice-bound
Q – – · –	Shorten the distance between vessels	I am shortening the distance
B – · · ·	Increase the distance between vessels	I am increasing the distance
5 · · · · ·	Attention	Attention
Y – · – –	Be ready to take (cast off) the tow line	I am ready to take (or cast-off) the tow line

Pic. 28: An ice breaker leads a coastal vessel through new pack ice in the Baltic during the severe winter of 2003

7.5 Navigation in Cold Climates

In any area where air/sea temperatures are consistently cold and remain below freezing, possibly for several days in succession, related problems must be anticipated. Various steps can be taken prior to entering cold climates, in order to reduce future damage by the cold weather.

7.5.1 ballast

Air pipes and sounding pipes are often found to freeze up and anticipation of the problem, especially if soundings change for no apparent reason, could well highlight the problems developing within the tank. Any vessel which is approaching cold water climates from warm weather areas should consider taking on fresh ballast, i.e. from the Gulf Stream.

It should be borne in mind that any tanks above the water line will be more likely to freeze than those tanks below the water line. The reason behind this is the fact that tanks in a high position are exposed to the chill factor of the winds.

In any event it is always prudent action to pump out a few tonnes from each tank. This ensures that the air pipes are clear of water. However, the effect on free surface needs to be calculated, especially for high positioned tanks. Do not forget lifeboat water tanks or these may end up cracked and empty when reaching warmer latitudes. If free surface is of concern, consideration should be given to pumping tanks empty though this is not compatible with the idea of obtaining a deep draught when navigating in ice regions.

The Canadian Coast Guard recommend that, where possible, 'ballast should be recirculated' where freezing conditions persist. Alternatively, the addition of salt or anti-freeze to ballast may be considered as a viable option. Salt additions are cheaper but usually more corrosive than anti-freeze and it would be a matter of experience and the length of stay within the region, that influences the choice of what to use to prevent damaged tanks.

To reduce the problems of freezing conditions any of the following steps are to be recommended:

1. Change the Ballast Water in open ocean for the warmest salt water possible. (E.g. warm waters are found with the "Gulf Stream").
2. Take the 'head' off all tanks, to keep air pipes clear of water content. (Adjusting topside tanks could cause an increased free surface effect and care should be taken to check that the vessel retains adequate positive stability).
3. Operationally, it is a general requirement to retain the ship at its deepest possible draught when in ice infested waters. However, if the ship has adequate draught it may be possible to de-ballast upper tanks completely, so removing the possible risk of freezing waters.
4. Prudent use of Anti-Freeze liquid into ballast tanks may also be an option.
5. The alternative to anti-freeze is to introduce additional salt into the water ballast.
   NB. Salt solutions are more corrosive. Though salt is easy to obtain and cheaper than anti-freeze solutions.
6. Circulation of Ballast waters may be possible on some ships. This has the effect of not allowing time for waters to freeze.
7. Whenever working ballast lines ensure that they are completely drained after use. Operation of 'Drain Cocks' should be checked regularly.
8. Maintain a tight monitoring programme of all tank soundings when inside cold climates.

NB. Ballast Management, including the positions of taking on and emptying out tanks must be recorded by vessels in their Ballast Management Log Book, (similar to the Garbage Record Book) in conjunction with the vessels Water Ballast Management Plan (Ref. IMO Ballast Water Guidelines – Resolution A.868(20)).

7.5.2 machinery spaces

Heat circulation on the main engine in extremely cold conditions is not unusual and boiler conditions should be closely monitored. Specific areas are prone to damage, namely the 'steering gear compartment' and could well require the use of a continuous heater to prevent cracking of packing in and around the stuffing box, about the rudder stock.

Additionally, the use of a steam hose into any fresh water tank set against the ship's side could well prove useful and prevent long term damage.

7.5.3 deck machinery

All water carrying pipelines should be drained prior to entering cold climates. If this is not possible then continuous circulation should be considered. Steam pipes for such items as a 'steam windlass' or 'cargo winches' should be kept turning over at slow speed throughout passage and especially overnight when not in use.

Derricks, cranes or cargo grabs, where sheaves are likely to freeze, should be topped, slewed and used at periodic intervals. While hydraulic pumps for hatches etc. should be kept operational under continuous running. Oil reservoir tanks could also benefit from the use of a portable heater overnight.

7.5.4 navigation and personnel problems

Extreme cold will bring about the freezing and frosting of bridge windows together with any window washing arrangements. A high internal wheelhouse temperature will go some way to keeping windows clear but the use of window heaters in today's modernised ships perform the task with a lot more efficiency. These should be checked prior to entering the cold weather. The use of fan heaters directed towards windows and onto 'clear view' motors could also prevent icing up.

Navigation lights may also accumulate snow and ice on the outer glass. These may require some positive cleaning with a spirit. Spare bulbs and fuses should be readily available to remedy simple faults due to cold or moisture.

Watchkeeping personnel should not be over-exposed to extreme cold. Long periods on bridge wings or in an exposed look out post will lend to fatigue and loss of attention. Look-outs need to be rotated at shorter intervals in order to maintain efficiency. They need to be adequately clothed and protected against the cold and if possible maintained in a warm environment. Contingency actions for adverse weather should be put into operation before the temperature falls when working becomes difficult. Rigging of lifelines to assist in providing full and complete access to all parts of the vessel, should be rigged as standard. Rock salt needs to be stored in an accessible place to be used on steel decks which can be expected to become slippery. Pipe lagging should be checked and replaced where appropriate and insulation positioned on or around sensitive equipment.

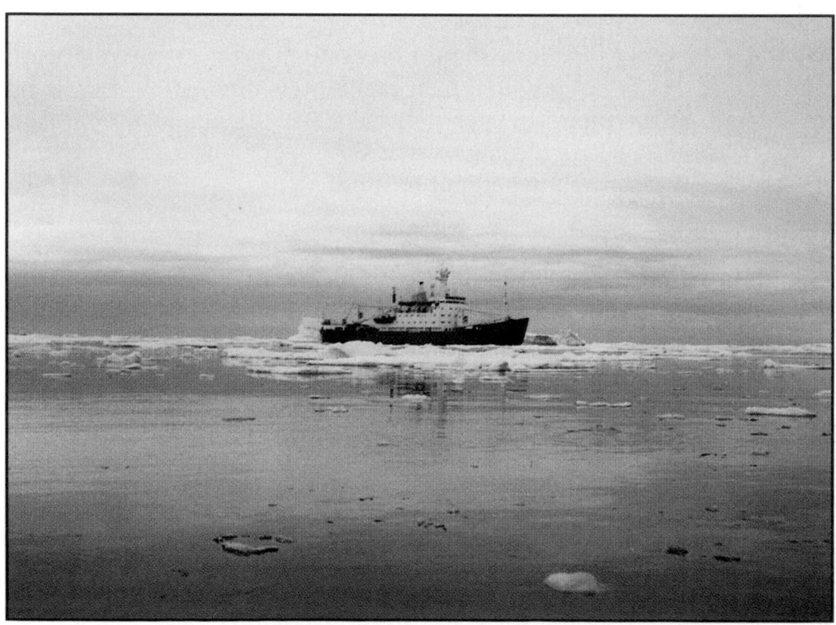

Pic. 29: The Ice research vessel *Bransfield* seen underway and making way through an area of open pack ice in Antarctic waters. Occasional large ice formations such as bergy bits, growlers, large ice floes as well as Ice Bergs are in the immediate vicinity.

When a vessel is known to be undertaking a passage through Ice regions it would be desirable to take on relevant stores to compensate for the extremely cold climate and for respective ice associated problems. It is normal practice for the ship's Chief Officer to order stores prior to commencing any voyage, but where passage through cold climates is anticipated the following stores may prove useful additions:

Stores Check-list

(Quantities will be dependant on ship's size and respective crew numbers)
Anti-freeze (Liquid in 60ltr. drums)
Rock Salt (25kg Bags)
Axes and spare handles
Shovels and deck brushes
Steam Hose with fittings (2)
Insulation/pipe lagging
Paraffin (additional quantity)
Fan heaters (4)
Spare deck light fittings
Spare Mooring Ropes
Working Gloves (cold weather working seals)
Thermal clothing: overshoes, boiler suits and waterproof jackets

Engine Room Spares

Auxiliary Boiler spares
Electric Heater Lamps
Masking Tape
Windlass and Deck winch spares
Gas Oil

7.5.5 navigation – ice accretion risk

The possibility of a vessel being effected by ice accretion is always present in cold climates of the high latitudes. Certain ships are more prone than others to the effects. i.e. Container vessels, fishing boats, high sided car carriers and ships with deck cargoes.

The increased weight, high up on a container stack or in upper rigging can and will add considerable weight to the vessel in a position above the vessels Centre of Gravity 'G'. Such added weight will effectively cause 'G' to rise twoards the Metacentre 'M', so reducing the ships 'GM'. The risk of 'G' rising above 'M' causing a possible unstable condition for the ship, becomes a real threat to the positive stability of the vessel.

The Master must consider re-routing the vessel if possible, to warmer latitudes. He/She, should also reduce speed while in a cold environment to reduce the chill factor generating a cause for ice accretion. Clearly it is not always practical to alter course away from cold climates and it may become necessary to order crew members to remove ice formations from the ship. This is a highly dangerous task and must be exercised with extreme caution.

The alternative being to compensate for the added weight of ice by adding ballast to lower tanks. This of course, is only possible where lower tanks are available for filling and the action, depending on circumstancs could also generate detrimental free surface effects.

7.6 North Atlantic – Latest Ice Information Sources

Canadian Ice Service – Ottawa
International Ice Patrol Reports
Outward bound Shipping
Ice Breaker vessels (Operational)
U.S. Ocean Routes, organisation
Navtex transmissions
Pilotage and Harbour Authorities
Ice Information Officer (Sydney)

Marine Radio Stations:	Twice daily, during the ice season, from St. John's, Halifax N.S. Camperdown, Comfort Cove, Seven Islands, Twillin-gate, Grindstone, St.Anthony, Sydney, Yarmouth.
Also from:	Cape Race, Fox River and Quebec.

The Canadian Broadcasting Corporation, Maritime Network, daily reports in winter. Facsimile Ice Charts transmitted at scheduled broadcast times from Port Authorities. Facsimile Water Surface Temperature chartlets.

St. Lawrence Seaway

Ice Advisory Service through the ice information officer at Sydney. Inbound vessels should report 36 hours prior to entering the 'Cabot Strait'.

Average Navigation Season, between Montreal and Lake Ontario is from April to December.

Great Lakes – Canada

Radio Station:– Thunder Bay for the Hudson Bay Routes (by Navtex)
– Prescott for Canadian Coast Guard ice reports
– Canadian Ice Service – Ottawa

Greenland

Ice Centre Narssarssuaq, for Southern Greenland ice information, (free information from Coast Radio Stations Ammassalik and Qaqortoq).

Ice information also by facsimile

Reykjavik, Radio Station – Greenland ice reports.

Baltic Sea Regions

Ice Breaker service vessels – various.

Radio Stations: R/T reports

Deutschlandfunk (Germany), Lyngby (Denmark), Gdynia (Poland), Tallinn (Estonia), Ijmuiden (Netherlands), Svalbard and Vardo (Norway), and Stockholm (Sweden).

Finnish Institute of Marine Research (Finland) Simplified Ice Chart every two weeks.

North Pacific

National Ice Centre and the National Weather Service Forecast Office, Anchorage. Republic Radio Station, for Alaskan Coastal waters.

Antarctica

Antarctic Research Vessels

Graham Island – Meteorological Centre (Argentina) Ice reports.

Graham Island (Palmer Radio Station) Ice Reports between 60°W and 20°E.

South Shetlands (Base Prat – Chile) and (Greenwich Island – U.K.) reports for Antarctic Peninsular.

South Shetlands (U.K.) ice reports for Southern Ocean.

Selective Web Sites

Chapter Eight

TROPICAL REVOLVING STORMS AND ABNORMAL WEATHER PHENOMENA

8.1 Navigation and Tropical Storms

In order to avoid the 'Tropical Revolving Storm' (TRS), Masters should be familiar with what it is and what they are likely to do. Any action taken will depend on numerous variables, but will also depend on the circumstances the ship finds herself in, e.g. at anchor, moored to buoys, alongside or at sea.

Some vessels which are better founded than others may take one option, whereas an alternative vessel may choose a different option to suit, i.e. Motor vessels, compared with a sailing vessel. Whatever action is taken the Master's decision should be made in the light of all available data and with regard to the safety of his vessel.

In this day and age it is highly unlikely that a tropical storm would materialise without some positive indication, say by radio, navtex, or satellite information. However, recognition of the evidence that may present itself to the mariner should be readily understood. More detailed information will no doubt become available as the storm develops following its formation,. The fact that action might need to be taken by a ships Master, who meets the storm early, following its immediate generation, would not be outside the realms of possibility.

The tropical storm

An intense depression which generates in tropical latitudes in all oceans except the South Atlantic. Tropical storms are accompanied by very high winds and extremely heavy seas. Depending on position they tend to have alternative names:

North Atlantic, West Indies areas
North East Pacific
South Pacific
New Zealand (North Island) .... 'Hurricanes'

Arabian Sea, Bay of Bengal,
South Indian Ocean (West of 80° E)
North Indian Ocean,
NW Australia[1] .... 'Cyclones'

North East Pacific, China Sea .... 'Typhoons'

[1]NB: North, north west and west coasts of Australia often use the term "Willy Willies".

Tropical Revolving Storms (TRS) are a circular feature with an average diameter of 500 nautical miles. They are known to cause excessive damage at sea or on land as they cross the shoreline, because of the associated violent winds that accompany their progress from generation to deterioration.

The Tropical Storm Feature

Circular feature of average 400/500 miles diameter.
Centre eye diameter 15/30 miles.
Steep pressure gradient with high wind speeds.

The eye wall which is approximately 15 miles wide has an area of dense cloud associated with heavy rainfall and high winds.

Tropical Revolving Storms – Definitions

PATH – The direction in which the storm is moving.

TRACK – That area that the storm centre has already moved over.

STORM FIELD – That horizontal area covered by the cyclonic condition of the storm.

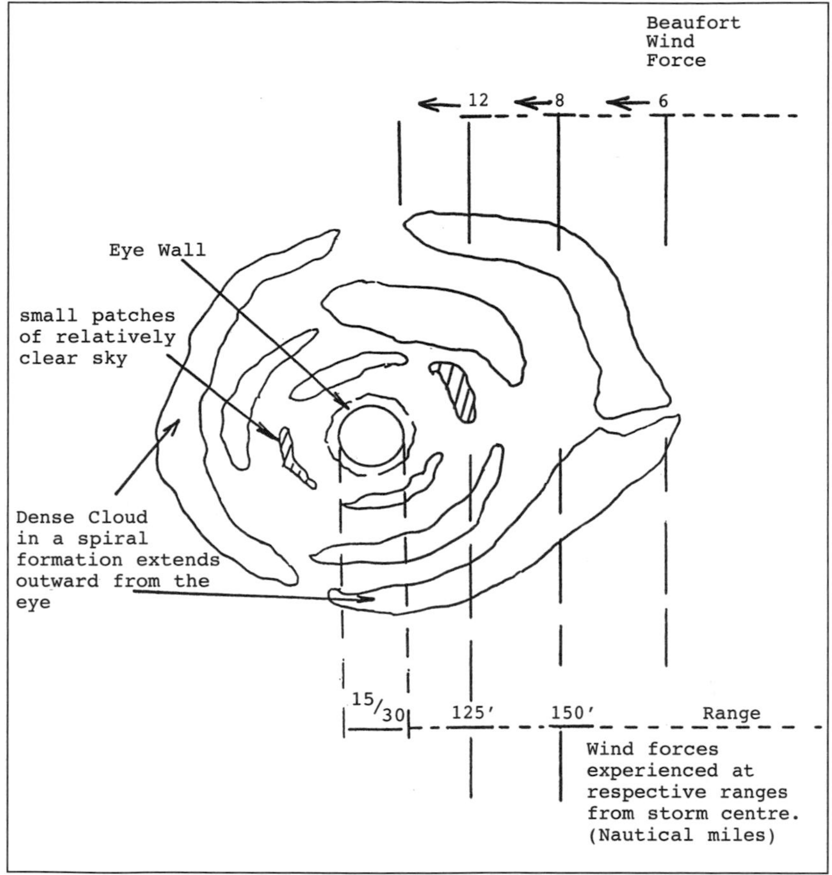

Diagram 8.1: The circular feature of a tropical revolving storm showing expected wind force and expected ranges fro mthe eye.

SOURCE REGION	– That region where the storm first forms.
VERTEX (or COD)	– The furthest westerly point reached by the storm centre.
EYE of STORM	– The centre of the storm.
BAR of the STORM	– The advancing edge of the storm field.
VORTEX	– The central calm of the storm.
ANGLE of IN-DRAUGHT	– That angle that the wind makes with the isobars.

DANGEROUS SEMI-CIRCLE	–	That half of the storm which lies to the right of the path in the northern hemisphere, and to the left of the path in the southern hemisphere.
NAVIGABLE SEMI-CIRCLE	–	That half of the storm which lies to the left of the path in the northern hemisphere, and to the right of the path in the southern hemisphere.
DANGEROUS QUADRANT	–	The leading portion of the dangerous semi-circle, where the winds blow towards the path.
TROUGH	–	The line of lowest barometer reading, which passes through the storm centre, nearly at right angles to the path.

8.1.1. general particulars TRS

The tropical revolving storm is known to generate between latitudes 5° to 10° north or south of the equator. They never occur on the equator itself. Their size will vary from 50-800 miles in distance but they generally average a diameter size of 400/500 miles.

They are associated with violent winds and over 130 knots may be experienced inside the storm field. High seas, often confused, will be predominant within 75 miles of the storm centre. Torrential rainfall around the 'eye wall' (but not in the centre), will restrict visibility in this vicinity to about zero.

Movement of the storm, after formation will be in a generally westward direction, and relatively slow moving, about 10 knots. The speed of travel will increase slightly with increased latitude but will probably not go above 15 knots before the direction changes at the point of recurve, (vertex). As the storm reaches the vertex it can be expected to slow down as it turns eastward from where an increase in movement to between 20-25 knots could be anticipated. Speeds of over 40 knots, following recurve have been experienced in the past.

The pattern of storm movement will vary in each case but once the storm moves to the higher latitudes, around the 35° north/south, it can be expected to decay. Deterioration could also be expected to occur if the storm moved erratically, making a loop on its own track, but in this case the speed of movement is usually less than 10 knots.

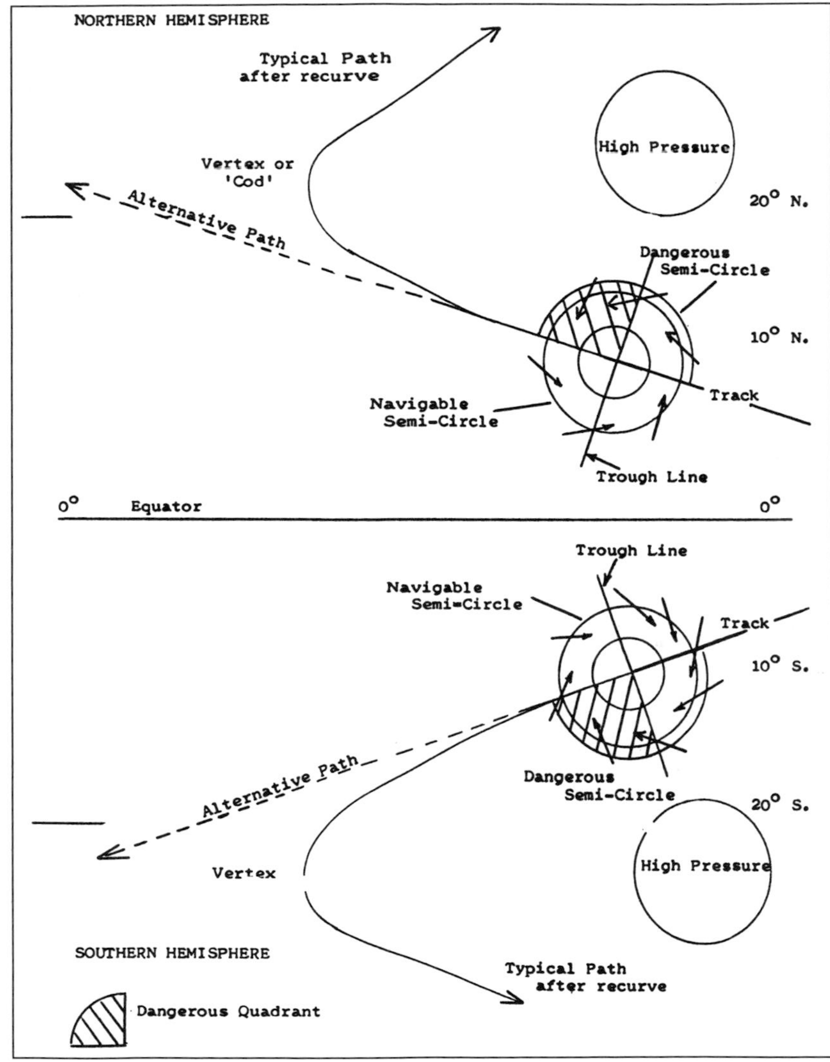

Diagram 8.2: Tropical Storm – Predicted and Alternative Movement

In the northern hemisphere, the season for tropical storms, is known to be between June and November, with the worst months being August and September. In the southern hemisphere, the season is from December to May, with the worst months being February and March. The exception being the Arabian Sea area where tropical storms normally occur with the change of the monsoons, i.e. May, June, October and November.

Mariners should of course bear in mind that storms could be encountered at any time, and although seasonal months are given as being times of maximum frequency, this is not to say that other periods are always safe and free from TRS.

8.1.2 dangerous semi-circle – so called

The dangerous semi-circle of the Tropical Revolving Storm is so called for three main reasons:

Wind circulation around the Tropical Revolving Storm is such that vessels inside the 'Dangerous Semi-Circle' would experience winds blowing the vessel towards the centre of the storm and towards more violent weather patterns. This is opposite to what a vessel in the 'Navigable Semi-Circle' would experience where the wind direction would have a tendency to blow the vessel away from the storm centre.

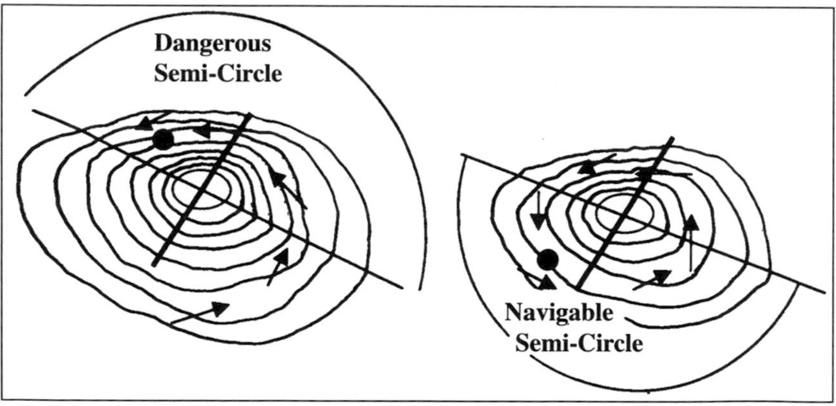

Diagram 8.3: Northern Hemisphere Storm Example

Secondly, the isobars on the Polar Side of the storm, from its conception to its vertex, are bunched together closer than in any other position in the storms pattern. Close isobars generate very strong winds and vessels in the dangerous quadrant (advance quadrant of the dangerous semi-circle), must expect to experience violent winds with high risk of associated shipboard damage.

Thirdly, the action of a TRS is often to recurve at about 20° to 25° North/South Latitude. Should a vessel find herself in the dangerous semi-circle, with the storm recurved, as they are known to do, the ship may find that the storm is turning towards her position. This can be better appreciated by realising that if a vessel was known to be in the navigable semi-circle and the storm curved, it would notably move further away from the ships position.

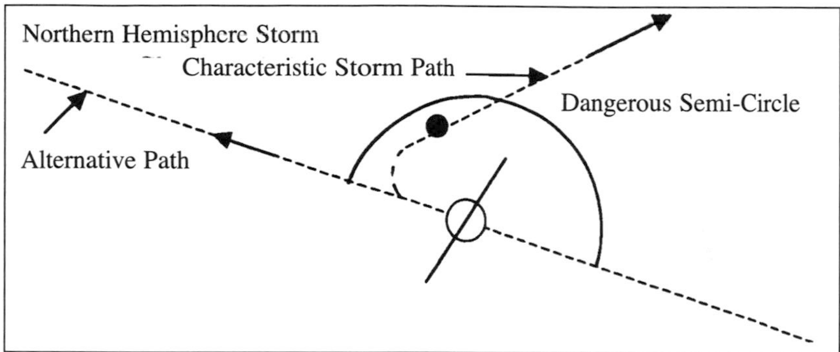

Diagram 8.4: Northern Hemisphere Storm Example

TRS Weather Sequence – Features

Pressure

On the outside of the storm the pressure slowly decreases and the pressure fall becomes much more rapid as the eye of the storm approaches. Minimum pressure will be within the eye of the storm. Behind the eye, the pressure will rapidly increase and this will be followed by a slow increase as the eye moves away.

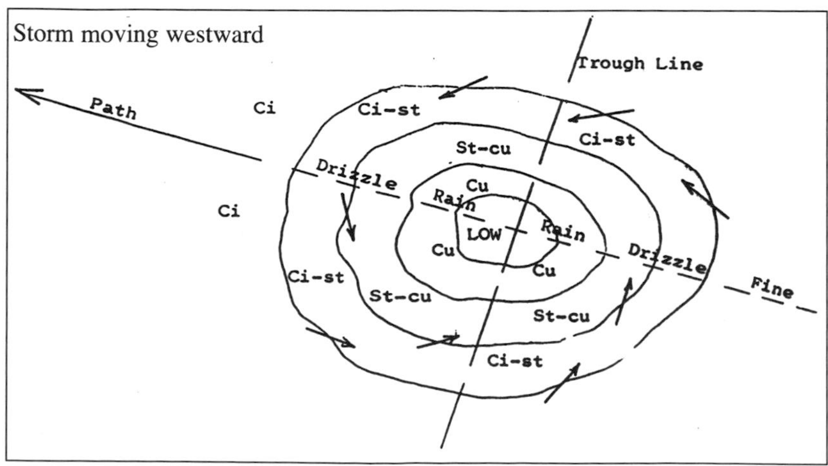

Diagram 8.5: Tropical Storm – Weather Pattern and Cloud Sequence

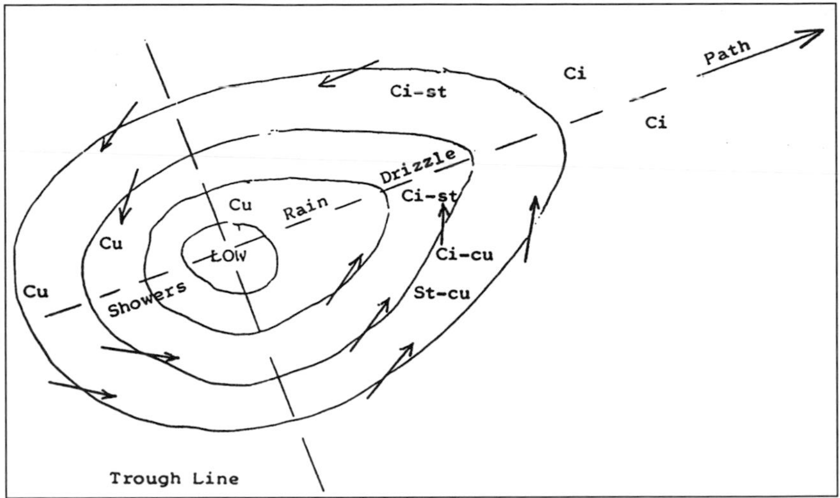

Diagram 8.6: Storm moving eastward (after recurve)

Cloud

In the outer regions there will be broken coverage of the long spiral cloud banks converging on the inner central cloud mass, where the cloud cover is mainly continuous. Around the eye is a dense mass of cloud extending to great vertical heights. This is known as the 'eye wall' and forms an annulus some 15 nautical miles wide. Within the eye the clouds break and the skies are much clearer.

Wind

On the outer edge of the storm approximately 250 miles from the centre the winds are light and are associated with the prevailing weather system, e.g. trade winds etc.

The wind speed will gradually increase as the storm approaches, and the wind direction will become that associated with the storm itself. At around 200 miles from the centre the wind force will be typically 5/6 reaching force 8 at about 125 nautical miles from the centre, and hurricane force 12 at about 75 nautical miles from centre. Maximum wind speed will be reached near the inner margins of the eye wall. Low wind speeds or calm may well exist within the eye. Behind the eye again, very high wind speeds but from the opposite direction.

Weather

In the outer regions intermittent spells of heavy rain associated with the spiral feeder banks of cloud. The rain becomes more intense and widespread in the inner regions, reaching a maximum in the eye wall where visibility is reduced to fog levels in torrential rain.

Within the eye, rain ceases and visibility improves. Very high seas exist in the inner regions and also within the eye itself. After the eye has passed, the sky again becomes overcast, the torrential rain returns and the visibility drops, conditions gradually improve after the second crossing of the eye wall although heavy spells of intermittent rain are likely to continue.

8.1.3 evidence of the Tropical Revolving Storm

Masters should be aware that even in this day of the weather satellite, little warning of the formation and development of an intense storm of small diameter can be anticipated. To this end the mariner must depend a great deal on his own observations.

The following list should provide the observer with detailed evidence for determining the presence of a storm:

1. Geographic conditions and ship's position should lie between the latitudes where storms are experienced. i.e. latitudes 5°-35°.
2. The location and season are compatible with the ship's position.
   NB N. Hemisphere June – November.
   S. Hemisphere December – May.
   Should not be taken to the exclusion of all other periods.
3. A heavy swell develops, usually from the direction of the storm and may be experienced up to 1000 miles from the storm's centre.
4. An unsteady barometer or a cessation in the diurnal range.

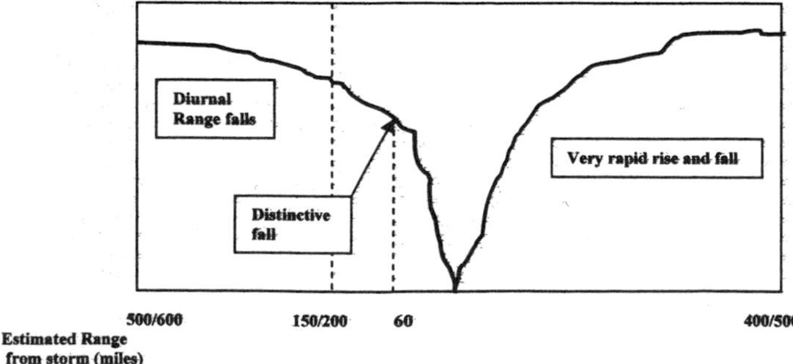

Diagram 8.7: A Barometer Reading

5. Increased wind velocity or a change in the trade wind, becoming violent.
6. Open ocean, high sea temperature over 27° C.
7. A growth of Cumulus (Cu) and/or Cumulonimbus (Cb) cloud will develop with bands of showers.
8. A changing appearance of the sky, cirriform cloud with cirrus bands, converge towards the centre. These are followed by cirrostratus, cirrocumulus, alto-cumulus and nimbostratus (black cloud).
9. Thunderstorms may occur within 100 miles radius of the storm centre.
10. Oppressive atmosphere, with squally and heavy rainfall in the vicinity of the storm.

8.1.4 Masters action following TRS evidence

Ascertain own ship details in relation to storm position:

1. Bearing of storm centre, (by Buys Ballots Law).
2. Semi-circle in which the vessel is situated.
3. Path of storm.

Ship Security

Order the following:

1. Additional lashings to cargo.
2. Reduction in free surface in all tanks.
3. Improve stability as much as possible.
4. Report position to owners/agents.
5. Obtain updated weather reports.

Legal Requirements

1. Report the storm position and movement if not already receiving warnings of same.
2. Log any deviations of course for charter party purpose.

Ship Handling

1. Heave to, while ascertaining storm details. (Plot storm position).
2. Avoid passing within 75 miles of storm centre.
3. Preferably to remain outside a radius of 200 nautical miles.
4. Adopt a course that takes the vessel away from storm centre.
5. Make frequent checks to ensure that any action taken is having the desired effect.

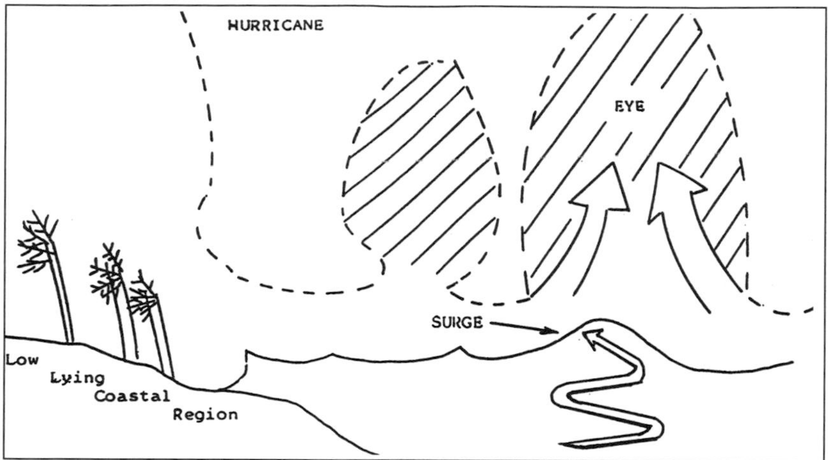

Diagram 8.8: Storm Surge – Generation Inside TRS

Considerable damage is often experienced, especially in low coastal areas, outlying islands and the like, by storm surge, increased water levels 2-4 metres is not unusual (Hurricane Andrew – North Atlantic, August 1992), can cause severe flooding and many fatalities through drowning.

The surge occurs because of an acute drop in pressure within the 'eye' of the storm. This has a plunger effect on the sea surface that generates high walls of water moving outwards, similar to ripples from a stone thrown into a calm lake. Obvious dangers to the mariner, and especially to the smaller coastal traffic are clear. Moorings will tension and may break or vessels could find themselves beached after the surge recedes. Dock areas are often flooded and associated damage to moored ships could well be the outcome from weakened harbour structures. e.g. cranes, pre-fabricated buildings etc.

For vessels secured alongside, with the passing of a tropical storm, Masters should be aware of the main areas of destruction arising from the wind and flood producing rain, however, the most lethal is 'storm surge'. Consideration for persons going ashore, and the cancellation of such shore leave should be considered necessary, not only for the individuals safety but also as 'stand-by' for the safety of the ship.

8.1.5 TRS – avoiding action in special circumstances

Following indication of an approaching storm:

Vessel Secured Alongside

Batten down and secure all hatches, lower all derricks and/or cranes. If the vessel cannot make the open sea, stretch extra moorings fore and aft, rig fenders, and lay out anchors if possible.

Place engine room on stand-by and maintain the vessel on an alert status for the passing of the storm.

Vessel at Anchor

Have both anchors down at maximum scope of cable, as an alternative to heaving up and riding the storm out in open sea conditions.

If remaining at anchor, engines should be employed to ease the weight on cables.

Vessel at Open Roadstead

Probably far better to run for open sea conditions to provide more sea room for manoeuvre. There is also less chance of a 'lee shore' situation developing. Decision to run for open water should be made early.

In all the above cases the vessel should be made as 'stable' as possible, with no free surface, slack tanks etc. Additional securing should be added to movable deck objects and to specific parcels of cargo. e.g. Heavy lifts, hazardous chemicals/ fluids etc. continue to plot and monitor the storms progress.

Vessel in Open Sea Conditions

Any action taken by the Master will depend on the ships position relative to the storms movements and general circumstances pertinent to the ship involved. The options of outrunning the storm if the vessel has sufficient power/speed, or to 'heave to' and then let the storm pass by, to open distance between the storm and the vessels position.

8.1.6 plotting the Tropical Revolving Storm

One of the early actions of any ships Master is to identify and plot the position of a TRS. Information may be received by radio, radar, satellite, navtex or from ships own observations. The pattern of the storm can then be related to the movement of the ship prior to any decision being taken regarding course alteration.

Method of Plotting the Storm

1. Plot the storm centre on the chart.
2. Construct a circle to equal the storm radius.
3. Construct tangential lines to the storm circle at approximately 40° from the forecast path.
4. Construct quadrant from the storm centre to equal 1 days movement of the storm (24 hrs x speed of storm). This is then known as the 'imminent danger area'.
5. By projecting the storms movement for an additional 24 hour period, the 'probable danger area' can be charted.

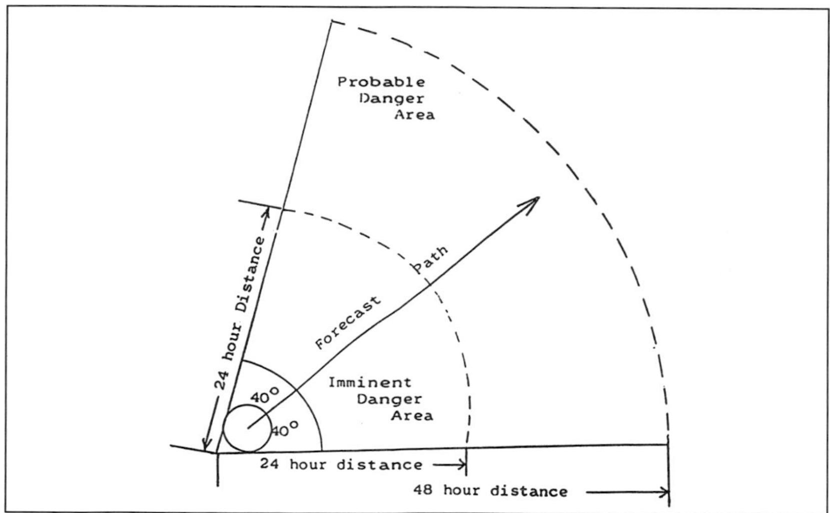

Diagram 8.9: Plotting the Storm

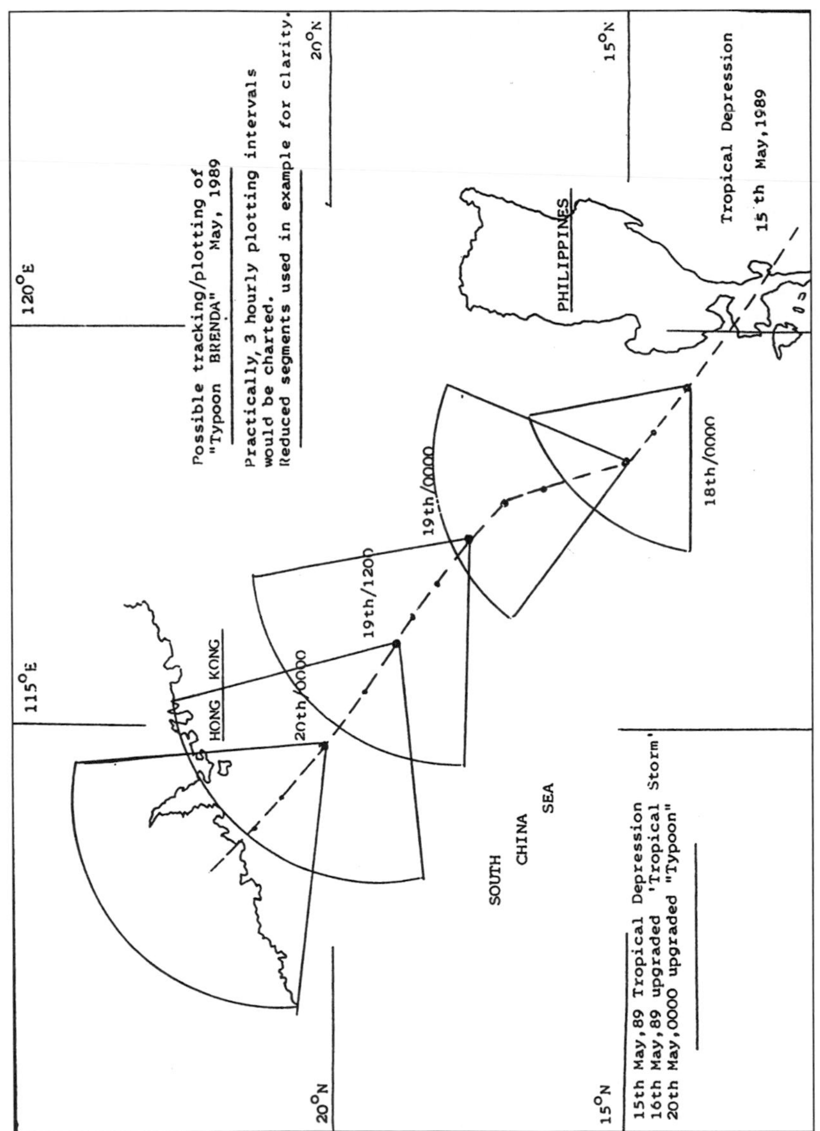

Diagram 8.10: Plotting Example Tropical Revolving Storm

8.2 TRS – Establishing Ships Location

The location of a vessel in the proximity of a tropical revolving storm is determined by observation of the 'true wind shift' and of any 'pressure change'.

Wind observation	N. Hemisphere	S. Hemisphere
Veering	Vessel located in Dangerous Semi-Circle	Vessel located in Navigable Semi-Circle
	If the pressure is falling vessel is in the advance quadrant	
Backing	V/1 located in Navigable Semi-Circle	V/1 located in Dangerous Semi-Circle
	If the pressure is falling vessel is in the advance quadrant	
Steady	If the pressure is falling the vessel is in the 'PATH' of the storm.	

8.3 TRS – Avoiding Action (Vessel at Sea)

8.3.1 Northern Hemisphere

Vessel in Dangerous Semi-Circle:

If the wind is observed to be veering the vessel must be confirmed as being in the 'dangerous semi-circle'. The Master should then make the best possible speed keeping the wind on the starboard bow between 1 and 4 points; alterations of course to starboard being made to keep the wind on this bow as it continues to veer.

Vessel in Navigable Semi-Circle:

If the wind is observed to be backing the vessel in the 'navigable semi-circle', the Master should make all possible speed with the wind on the starboard quarter; alterations of course to port being made to keep the wind on this quarter as it continues to back.

Vessel in the Path or Nearly in the Path:

When the wind is remaining steady or nearly steady, the Master should alter course to obtain the wind well on the starboard quarter and proceed towards the navigable semi-circle. Once within this semi-circle he should alter course to port to maintain the wind on this quarter.

8.3.2 Southern Hemisphere

Vessel in Dangerous Semi-Circle:

If the wind is backing the vessel must be confirmed as being in the 'dangerous semi-circle'. The Master should make the best possible speed keeping the wind on the port bow between 1 and 4 points. Alterations of course to port being made to keep the wind on this bow as it continues to back.

Vessel in Navigable Semi-Circle:

If the wind is observed to veer, the vessel is in the 'navigable semi-circle'. The Master should make all possible speed with the wind on the port quarter. Alterations of course to starboard being made to keep the wind on this quarter, as it continues to veer.

Vessel in the Path or Nearly in the Path:

When the wind is remaining steady or nearly steady, the Master should alter course to obtain the wind well on the port quarter and proceed towards the navigable semi-circle. Once within this semi-circle he should alter course to starboard to maintain the wind on this quarter.

Location	N. Hemisphere	S. Hemisphere
Dangerous Semi-Circle (A)	Put wind on the starboard bow and alter course to Starboard as the wind 'Veers'	Put the wind on the port bow and alter course to port as wind 'backs'
Dangerous Semi-Circle (C) Path (B)	Put wind on the starboard quarter and alter course to port as the wind 'backs'	Put the wind on the port quarter and alter course to starboard as the wind 'veers'

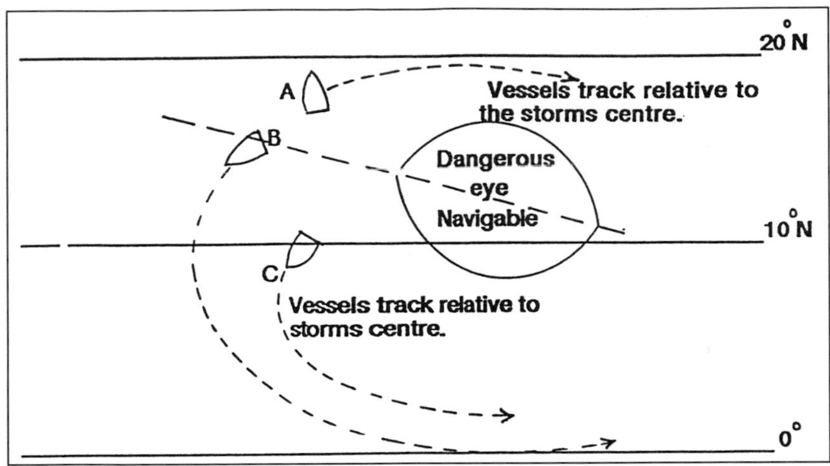

Diagram 8.11: Action of Vessel in TRS Vicinity

8.3.3 application of Buys Ballot's Laws for TRS

Example

A vessel in the southern hemisphere observes the wind in an approaching cyclone to blow from East North East (ENE). How is the probable centre of the storm estimated if the wind then changes to North North East (NNE)?

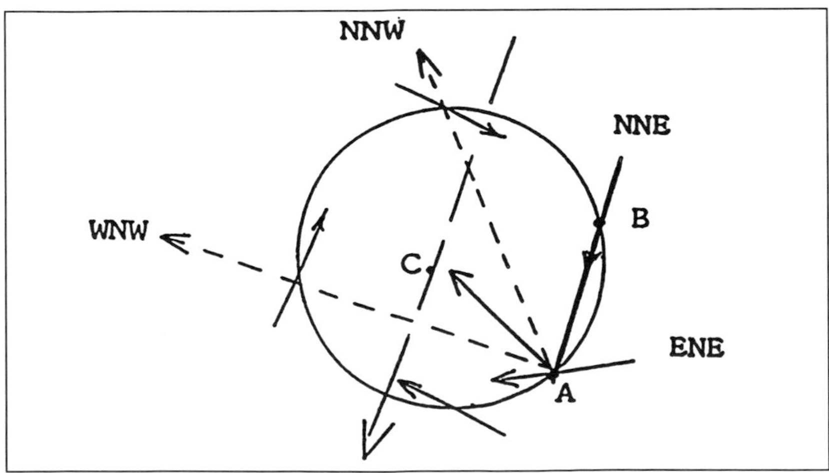

Diagram 8.12: Circle Represents Right Hand Wind Circulation in Southern Hemisphere.

'A' represents the position of the ship when the wind is ENE.

Face the wind – Take a bearing 8 compass points left = NNW.
Take a bearing 12 compass points left = WNW.

(Taking bearings LEFT because the vessel is in southern hemisphere).

Centre of storm bears between NNW and WNW (represented by AC).

'B' represents the position of the ship when the wind is NNE.

Construct AB

'AB' then represents the apparent track/path of the storm.

(Storm moving from B towards A).

NB. Ships range from the storm can be estimated by use of the wind force being experienced at the ships position.

8.3.4 regional information – Tropical Revolving Storms

Indian Ocean Storms

These generally originate about latitude 10° south, longitude 70° east and travel in a west south west direction towards Mauritius. They tend to haul more southerly as they proceed to a point of recurve at about latitude 20° south.

The position of the 'vertex' will vary considerably in both latitude and longitude. The season is from October to July, with December to April being the worst months.

A specific feature of storms in this region is the very large angle of indraught experienced by cyclones passing over Mauritius. This is sometimes so great that in some parts of the storm the wind may be observed to blow directly towards the storm centre.

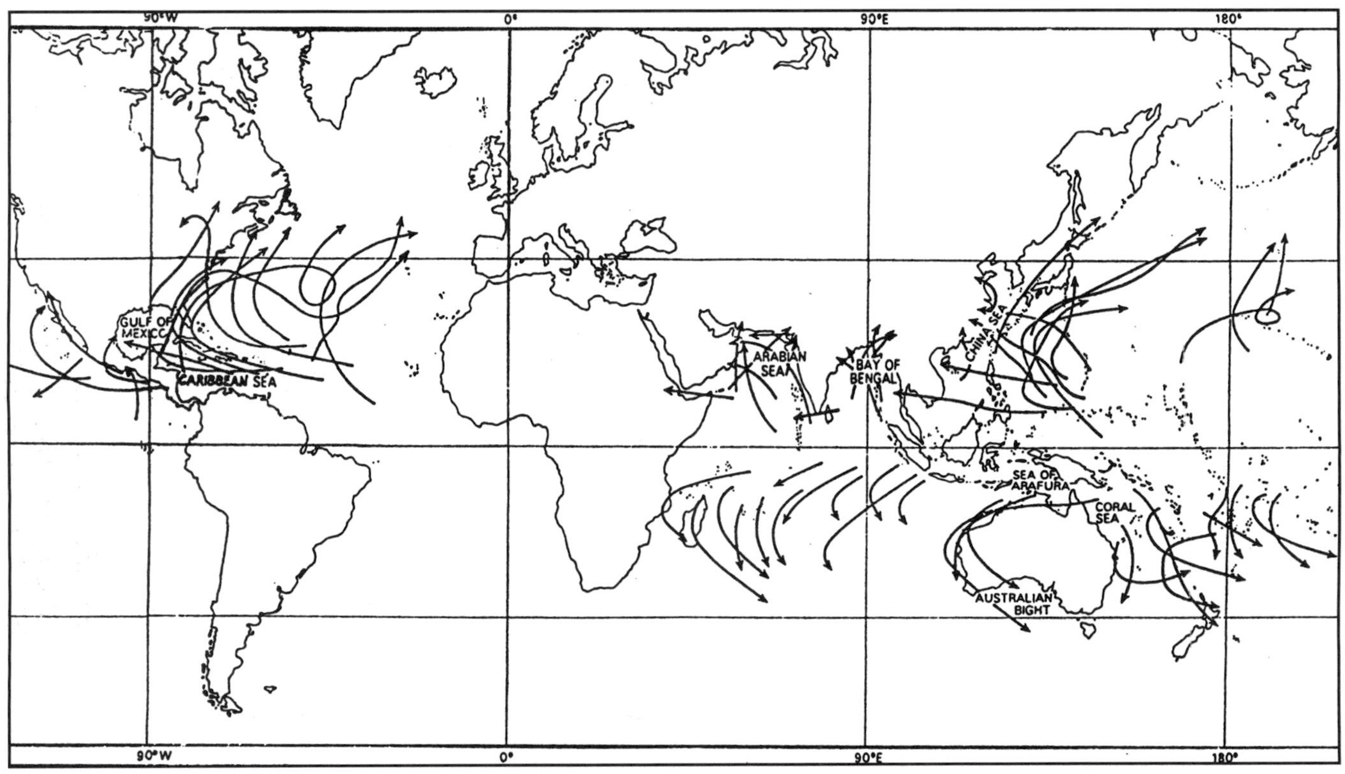

TRS – Movement Record

Diagram 8.13: Ships' Range From the Storm can be Estimated by use of the Wind Force Being Experienced at the Ship's Position.

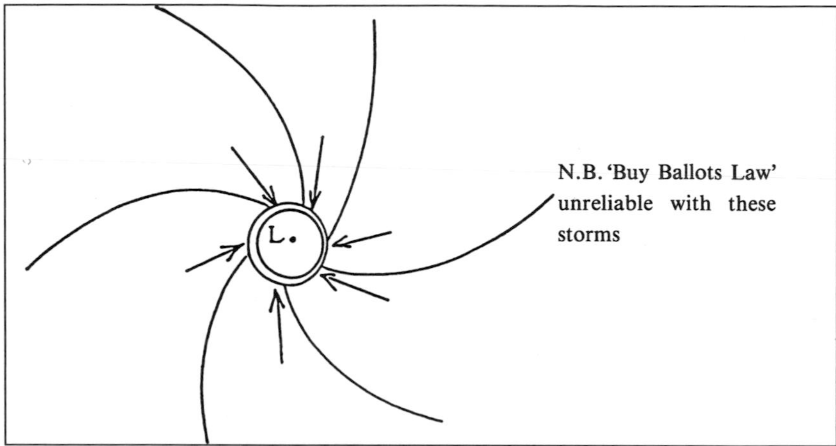
L.
N.B. 'Buy Ballots Law'
unreliable with these
storms

Diagram 8.14: The Unrealibility

The speed of a TRS in the Indian Ocean is between 50 to 200 nautical miles per day (2.5-8.0 kts). They are known to travel at their slowest at the beginning and end of the season.

Arabian Sea Storms

These generally originate near the Laccadive Islands or a little to the west or north of them. They tend to travel in a curved path towards the Arabian Coast from May/June, and towards the Indian coast in November. These periods often coinciding with the times of change of the monsoons, the storms usually bringing exceptionally heavy rainfall to the Bombay area.

Bay of Bengal

These storms may originate anywhere in the bay or may on occasions enter the bay from the Gulf of Thailand. They have a tendency to travel in a north easterly to north westerly direction before and after the monsoon seasons. The speed of travel varies but the general average is about 200 miles per day. Paths of storms are irregular because the general circulation is seasonal and interrupted by the monsoons, consequently the point of curvature cannot be reliably defined.

South Pacific Storms

These storms generally originate in the area north east of the Fiji Islands, travelling to the south west, and hauling more towards the pole as they proceed. The normal season for storms in this area is between November to April, with the worst months being January to

March. Once developed their speed averages about 200 miles per day and the point of recurve is often observed to be around latitude 20° south.

* 1986 April. Hurricane 'Martin' caused the worst flooding in Suva, Fiji, 10 people died and caused damage in excess of 26 million dollars.

China Sea, Taiwan, Japan and North Pacific

These storms usually originate to the north eastward of the Philippine Islands. They tend to travel in a west north westerly direction towards the Chinese mainland. Some recurve and move north easterly towards Japan. Experienced all year round, worst months July-October.

* 1985 Oct. Typhoon 'Brenda' was the first storm to affect South Korea in 20 years. 69 people were lost and 1,459 fishing boats were destroyed.

* 1977 July. Typhoon 'Thelma' destroyed Kao-Hsiung Harbour, Taiwan. Thirty persons died, and 32 ships were sunk. This was recorded as being the most destructive event since the second world war.

North Atlantic Hurricanes

These storms originate at about latitude north 10° and travel in a west north westerly direction. The general movement is towards the West Indies hauling northwards towards the pole as they proceed. Some have been known to sweep into the Gulf of Mexico, but usual behaviour is for them to recurve in about latitude 30° north. The tendency then is for them to move eastward of north and experience has shown that the southern ports of the USA and the eastern atlantic coasts of the USA, are frequently effected.

* 1983 August. Hurricane 'Alicia' developed over the Gulf of Mexico, and came ashore near Galveston, Texas. A storm surge of several metres high caused extensive coastal damage.

* 1988 September. Hurricane 'Gilbert' described as the most intense cyclone on record in the western hemisphere, devastated large areas of Jamaica. Greatest loss of life occurred in Mexico which it hit twice. Associated rains caused the Santa Catarina river to burst its banks with the loss of 200 lives.

Tornadoes and Waterspouts

It is appropriate at this time to discuss the navigation in and around a 'tornado', especially so when it is realised that they are a compact whirling storm. The diameter of them will vary between 50 to 1000 metres and their wind speed may reach as high as 450 knots. They are quite noticeable as a slim column, which is almost vertical, made up of dust, condensation and some debris, usually protruding from and attached to an area of cumulonimbus cloud. Tornadoes are often accompanied by thunder, lightening and/or hailstones.

Waterspouts are tornadoes which have passed over water. When sighted they appear as a column of water which joins the cloud to the sea surface. The column will be caused to bend as the upper and lower sections move at different speeds, eventually breaking to disintegrate.

Large shipping tend to give a wide berth to waterspouts as loose articles on deck would be swept clear with possible associated damage. However, small craft should be aware of the acute danger of navigating too close to them and alter their course away in ample time.

Generally speaking they move at about 15 knots in a mainly easterly direction and may only last for a short period (approximately up to 1 hour). Certain areas of the world are more susceptible than others, for example the United Kingdom experience on average 1 every 2 years, whereas the USA has around 150 per year.

Where a tornado effects the coastline, extensive damage is usually the end product. House roofs are torn away and trees often uprooted with its ferocity. Mariners are advised to alter the course away and avoid the immediate areas of waterspouts. Good 'house keeping' by having clean and clear decks, with all parcels of cargo well secured, will go a long way to eliminating serious damage in the event of a tornado affecting the ships position.

Tidal Bores

A body of water with a wall like front which may be seen to surge up rivers. Notable examples are encountered in Hangchow Bay, China and the River Severn in England. They are generated because river estuaries act as a funnel causing a rise in the height of water as it flows upstream. Maximum height approx. 8 metres, observed in the North Amazon River.

Speed of tidal bore will be related to its height and the water depth ahead of it. Where a river has an outflow current the velocity of the bore would be correspondingly reduced. Mariners should note that dangerous bores are well noted in sailing directions, and small vessels are advised to navigate with extreme caution in and around noted estuaries.

Tidal Waves *(Tsunamis)*

Tidal waves is a common misnomer for what should be correctly called 'Tsunamis'. They are caused by underwater landslides, earthquakes and volcanic eruptions. When encountered at sea their height rarely exceeds one metre, but their length is often between 50 to 250 miles. Consequently they do not tend to pose a hazard for ships. However, they do travel very fast. An example of the speed of travel was observed from an earthquake in the Aleutian Trench in the North Pacific in 1946. A 'Tsunamis' generated from the disturbance took 4 hours 34 minutes to reach Honolulu. The distance was 2000 nautical miles so the speed of travel was approximately 438 m.p.h. The results of this wave were such that 25 million dollars of damage was caused and 173 persons killed when the wave struck Honolulu.

International co-operation has now caused a 'Tsunamis warning service' to be established, based in Honolulu, and supported by the countries which border on the Pacific Ocean. In the case of an alert, mariners are strongly advised to head for open sea conditions and clear of shallows. Alerts being activated by seismographic equipment, but generally the intensity of the 'Tsunamis' cannot by reliably forecast. Anchorages, buoy moorings, or even tied up alongside cannot be considered as a reliable position. Dangerous encounters and collision with floating debris during the passing phase of a Tsunamis is a common hazard.

The most recent example of a major 'Tsunami' was recorded on 26th December, 2004 where an undersea earthquake of magnitude '9' on the Richter Scale devastated the Indian Ocean regions causing the loss of an estimated 300,000 persons.

After shocks assumed from this disaster were still experienced three months after the incident took place, with an earthquake of magnitude 8.7 being recorded for 75 seconds, approximately 120 miles offshore of the Sumatra coastline, in a position 800 miles North West of Jakarta. The after shock being virtually in the identical position of the original quake.

It is believed that any disturbance over a magnitude of 7.5 on the Richter Scale, could generate a Tsunami Wave. The disaster of December, 2004 caught many casualties on the foreshore, tourists and locals in and around beach areas. Shipping which was affected, was generally limited to those vessels anchored or positioned close inshore. Other vessels in open sea areas, faired much better with little damage reported. Survivors, however, were being picked up in various parts of the Indian Ocean weeks after the event, clinging to flotsam.

The worst affected areas from the Tsunami Wave, were on the coastlines of Sumatra, Sri Lanka, East coast of India, Maldive Islands and as far off as Somalia, approximately 4,000 miles from the epicentre.

Chapter Nine

S.A.R. NAVIGATION AND GMDSS

9.1 Introduction

With any search and rescue operation within the marine environment there are bound to be defined 'key players'. Without doubt the Master of a vessel engaged in a search mode will be a major influence on the success or failure of the operation. The Navigation Officer of either a search unit or an On Scene Co-ordinating vessel, will also carry a high responsibility from the time that any distress message is received.

Other major participants will be involved as and when location is achieved, bearing in mind that the term 'location' is not the same thing as 'recovery'. The coxswain of a rescue boat, or the 'aircrew' from a helicopter will become positive players at a later stage when recovering survivors.

In order to provide a comprehensive appreciation of all the activity which will concern itself in a successful rescue, certain elements of general seamanship have been introduced with the navigational aspects. The author makes no apology for this in the belief that the two topics overlap considerably.

9.2 Action on Receipt of Distress Message

- Immediate Action:
  1. The Master must acknowledge the distress message.
  2. Obtain radio bearing of distress transmitter (if possible).
  3. Establish plain language communication as soon as possible. (Obtain identity, position, course, speed and ETA).

4. Maintain continuous radio communication watch.
5. Maintain continuous radar watch (double watches).
6. Post extra look-outs at high vantage points.
7. Obtain target definition.

- Subsequent Action:
  1. Contact Rescue Co-ordination Centre (RCC) via coast radio.
  2. Order navigator to plot positions and establish a course to rendezvous and update ETA.
  3. Relay distress message on other frequencies if appropriate.
  4. Plot other vessels within the search vicinity together with their respective movements.
  5. Update distress information, i.e. weather at distress site, numbers of casualties, total number of persons at scene, number and type of survival craft and if any emergency location aids.
  6. Bridge team at alert status and manual steering engaged.

- Vessel Preparation:
  1. Prepare ship's hospital to receive casualties.
  2. Turn out rescue boat ready for immediate launch.
  3. Gear up rescue boat's crew (immersion suits and lifejackets).
  4. Rig, guest warp, accommodation ladder, scrambling nets and a derrick/crane if required.
  5. Test and trim searchlights.
  6. Check that line throwing apparatus is readily available.
  7. Test communications systems to rescue boat/bridge.
  8. Order 'stand by engines' but remain at maximum sea speed.

- Establish an on scene co-ordinator or on scene commander

  (If no specialised craft, eg, warship/military plane is available the most suitable merchant ship will assume this role).

9.2.1 DSC distress alerts

Digital Selective Calling (Automatic transmissions under GMDSS) are used from ship-to-shore to alert Rescue Co-ordination Centres (RCC's) either direct or via a Coast Radio Station (CRS) or through a Land Earth Station (LES). The alert is instigated by a Ship Earth Station (SES) or the use of an EPIRB, and/or terrestrial services using DSC assigned calling frequencies from ships or EPIRB's.

Ship-to-Ship distress alerts are employed to alert other vessels in the vicinity of a distressed vessel and are based on the use of DSC in the VHF and MF bands.

NB. Acknowledgement of a DSC Distress Alert is normally made by use of DSC by an RCC or Coast Radio Station only.

Ships which receive a DSC Distress Alert from another ship should defer acknowledgement of the signal for a short interval in order to give the Coast Radio Station time to acknowledge the alert transmission first.

In the event of no reply within five minutes from a CRS, the transmission must then still be acknowledged by Radio Telephone. If no reply from the distressed party, and the DSC is repeated it will be necessary to send a DSC acknowledgement on the same distress frequency on which the distress alert was received. The nearest Coast Radio Station should then be advised by any available means.

Ships receiving a DSC Distress Alert on VHF or MF are not permitted to relay the call by DSC under any circumstances (They may relay the signal by other means).

A vessel so receiving a DSC Distress Alert from another ship on any of the HF DSC frequencies must:

1. NOT ACKNOWLEDGE
2. Set watch on appropriate RT and Telex frequencies.
3. If the alert is not acknowledged by a CRS inside 5 minutes and no distress communications are heard between a Coast Radio Station and the ship in distress, then the receiving station must relay the distress ashore by any means to a Coast Radio Station.

9.2.2 the role of the On Scene Co-ordinator (OSC)

The main function of any vessel accepting the role of On Scene Co-ordinator will be that of communications. The selected vessel must effectively become a communications platform. To this end the duty could be carried out by a vessel some distance off the incident but clearly if acting On-Scene this would be more desirable.

The OSC is the direct link to the Coast Guard at the Marine Rescue Co-ordination Centre and the various other search units engaged in the operation. The type of communications that could be expected, would include:

Distress response acknowledgements.
Position reports of all active units. (Posreps)
Search-progress reports,(positive and negative)
Target definition and status.
Weather reports.
Advice on search pattern types.
Track space advice.
Search speed advice.
Datum position.
Endurance factors of search units.
Air search reports.
Ship reporting systems – general information AMVER, AUSREP etc.
Navigation warnings
Ships general particulars: type, facilities, ETA, endurance, capabilities.
Casualty information, debriefs from survivors, next of kin contacts.
Requests for medical advice or additional resources.

On Scene Co-ordination vessels would additionally maintain ship-to-ship communications and display the International Code Flags 'FR'. The Master of the OSC would advise on selective duties for respective search units and provide direction to develop the search area.

For on-scene operations any vessel inclusive of the OSC, would benefit from high quality plotting facilities. However, it would be beneficial if this amenity was also established within search units. All participating vessels, but especially the OSC should maintain detailed records of their own ships movements and activities while engaged in the SAR operation. Masters of OSC vessels need to be particularly aware of the emphasis that can expect to be placed on 'Log Books' and the timing of orders affecting the movement of search units and communications with shoreside authorities.

An SAR incident running log account, may prove extremely useful to Masters in the long term.

9.2.3 designating the OSC

With any SAR situation many variables could influence the selection of not only an OSC, but also the selection of individual search units, S/U's; the weather conditions and geography in relation to the position, to name but two. Where a choice for the OSC has to be made, and no military unit is available, that choice will probably be made taking account of the following factors:

1) Can the proposed vessel provide the necessary communication platform to carry out the task?
2) Has the vessel the manpower to conduct own ship routine and the additional emergency duties required by an OSC?
3) What is the position of the vessel from the DATUM.
4) Is the vessel equipped with the skills and equipment to carry through the duty?
5) Has the vessel the necessary endurance?
6) What is the experience of the Master?
7) Is the nature of the cargo hazardous or perishable?
8) What is the speed of the vessel?
9) What is the draught of the vessel (relevant for shoal water operations)?
10) Designation of OSC status requires the mutual agreement of the Master(s) where more than one ship is involved.

It should be borne in mind that the OSC is meant to co-ordinate search units and may not be the first vessel on scene, neither will it necessarily be involved in the actual recovery of persons from the sea. The function of the S/U's is to recover persons from the water and as such, they need recovery methods such as rescue boats.

Unless the OSC is jointly operating as a search unit, this vessel would not necessarily require the immediate first contact or aid requirements, as desired by search units. Neither does it have to be within the immediate area, although it is clearly an advantage to be as close as practical and certainly within R/T-VHF range.

NB. The warship is ideal because it has adequate manpower, excellent plotting facilities, often equipped with aircraft cover and no commercial pressure by way of perishable cargo. It is also self sufficient with ample endurance, speed and manoeuvring capability, together with medical and recovery methods if required. All these amenities, as well as probably the best communication links that any sea-going mobile is likely to possess.

9.2.4 the role of the Bridge Team

Duties of the Master

In any search and rescue operation the role of the Ship's Master has to be that of 'conning' the vessel. This in itself is a major consideration in view of the fact that many other operational units could be active in the area and the risk of collision is greatly increased. The proximity of navigational hazards is always present and the need for immediate and positive response is often not just desirable but necessary.

The management of the bridge team and the direct control of associated operations will fall to the Master's authority. This is especially so where junior officers lack experience and are seeking operational guidance. There will be a need for the Master to oversee all communications and become directly involved with any search pattern and the respective movements of the vessel. Shipboard facilities such as recovery methods, medical treatment of survivors and communications analysis will be essential in order to achieve a successful outcome.

Navigation Officer

The duties of the navigator will be tremendous in an SAR operation. He should be considered as the Master's right hand man. Not only will the 'search area' be required to be plotted, but also any alteration of course points required by the search pattern. In the case of the On-Scene Co-ordinator (OSC) all areas being searched by other units will also be required to be plotted to formulate an overall picture of the operational area.

It will be necessary for the navigator to note and record searched areas. He will also need to project ETA's as and when applicable and co-ordinate surface movements with possible aircraft activity. The ship's speed and fuel resources may also become a factor for consideration, depending on the size of vessel and general circumstances at the time.

The navigator will need to consider the possibility of sudden changes from recognised search patterns, in the light of updated information. Casualty sightings, poor visibility, and/or internal shipboard problems may make deviations from expected performance necessary. Rendezvous calculations with other units may also be expected.

Officer of the Watch

In addition to the navigator, the watch officer will be required to monitor the ship's performance, e.g., position, speed, course etc. A continuous radar watch, especially in active areas, must be considered essential and Masters should consider "doubling watches" to facilitate the search vessel's requirements.

Watchkeeping duties will be ongoing and encompass such special duties as:

The display of special signals, monitoring weather conditions, maintaining and updating communications, traffic avoidance, effective and constant lookout and conning the vessel in the absence of the Master. Consideration towards fellow watch-keepers, by way of meal reliefs and the avoidance of fatigue should also be assumed as part and parcel of the duty officer's tasks.

Radio/Communications Officer

With the introduction of GMDSS, many watch officers will assume the role of communications officer. Passenger vessels and warships will probably retain designated communication operators for some time to come. With this in mind Masters should establish and maintain regular communications with the Rescue Co-ordination Centre and/or other search units. To do this effectively continuous guarding of alarm and working frequencies will be required by Radio/communication officers.

Transmission/reception contents should include:

Updated weather reports, results of searched areas, position reports of ship, position reports of all sightings of wreckage/ survivors, updates of information received from survivors (following debrief), status reports relayed from other search units, operational changes (such as change of track space), changes in visibility inside search area, equipment or resource requirements, identity and homing signals, pollution reports and navigational hazards as appropriate.

With any operation of this nature the link from the Master to the Rescue Co-ordination Centre is vital for effective and reliable communications. It is essential that early communications are established and retained by the on scene commander and individual search units.

Engine Room

It may be disputed that the engine room is part of the bridge team. Mariners should remember that control of the vessel is only possible while you retain engine power. It is therefore prudent for Masters to encourage and develop involved links between the navigational bridge and the engine control room. The outdated thinking of 'oil and water' between deck and engine room, does not breed efficiency, they must be seen to mix, in the interest of the casualty.

Watch officers should therefore endeavour to keep the engine room informed of surface activities. Early warning on 'standbys' or 'engine movements' are appreciated whenever possible and response times can be improved. Teamwork will without doubt, complement a ship's overall performance.

9.2.4 developing the search area

Initially the Datum for the search area will need to be plotted. Where multiple search units are employed to search select areas, each area should be allocated geographic co-ordinates. This would reduce the possibility of overlap, time wasting and assist reporting to eliminate specific sea areas.

Once the search area(s) has been established and an appropriate pattern confirmed the **'Track Space'** for the unit or units so engaged must be established. This must be selected to provide adequate safe separation between searching units while at the same time taking into account the following:

a) the target size and definition.
b) the state of visibility on scene.
c) the sea state inside the designated search area.
d) the quality of the radar target likely to be presented.
e) height of eye of lookouts.
f) speed of vessel(s) engaged in search operations.
g) number of search units (S/U's) engaged.
h) time of available daylight remaining.
i) Masters experience.
j) recommendations from MRCC.
k) height above sea level (for aircraft)

Additional influencing factors:

- Night searches can be ongoing with effective searchlight coverage.
- Length of search period may be restricted by the endurance of the vessels engaged.
- Target may be able to make itself more prominent if it retains self help capability.
  (Assuming the target remains at surface level and doesn't sink.)

Pattern and respective track space should be selected with reference to the IAMSAR Volume III manual and with respect to the circumstances prevailing at the incident.

9.3 IAMSAR Search Patterns

Many different types of search patterns are available to SAR units and in conjunction with the On Scene Co-ordinator (OSC) an appropriate pattern to suit the conditions would be put into operation. Most of the following examples are suitable for either air or surface units, but in all cases the navigator of the search craft will play a 'key' role.

The majority of searches take place within defined limits, depending on the target's capability and endurance. Individual search units are usually designated a specific area and the navigator will need to plot these extreme boundaries before instigation of the pattern.

Obviously the type of pattern and track space employed should reflect the nature and size of target as well as taking into account the prevailing weather conditions, especially the state of visibility. Where more search units are employed the accuracy is generally increased and/or the area of coverage is increased.

The expanding square search pattern can be employed by either surface vessels or aircraft search units. Where more than one aircraft is involved, they would fly at different heights and on headings 45° off the original.

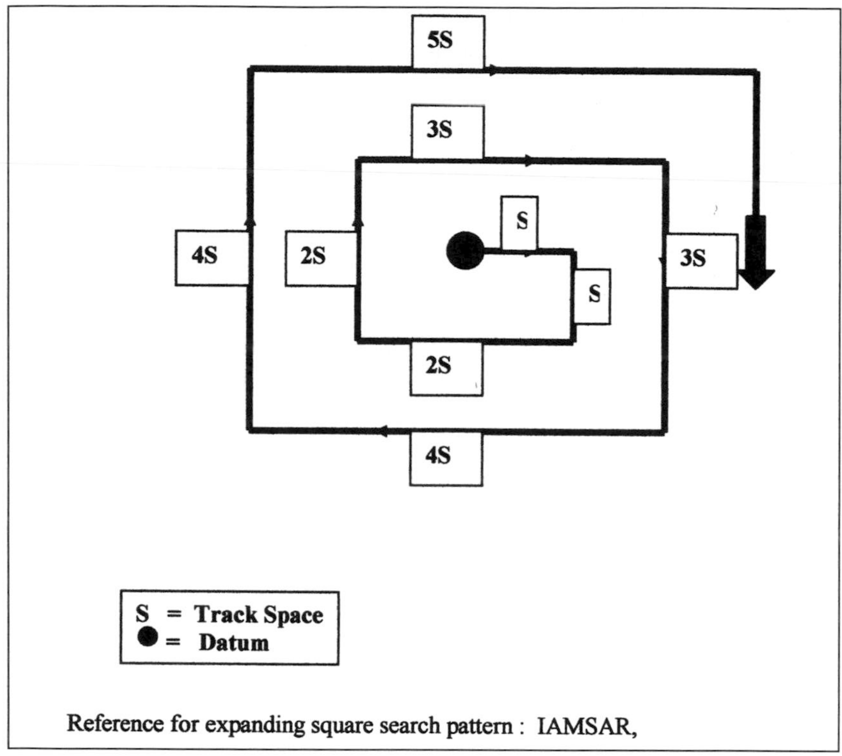

Diagram 9.1: Expanding Square Search Pattern – One Ship

The CSP begins at the probable location of the target and expands outward in concentric squares. Accurate navigation is required to monitor the ship's position towards course alteration points. (All course alterations being 90°)

The track spacing, which will vary depending on visibility and sea conditions, relative to the type of target.

The sector search pattern is employed when the position of the target is known with reasonable accuracy and the search is over a small area, as in 'man overboard', or where the casualty has been sighted and then lost.

A suitable marker i.e. smoke float or beacon is used as reference, and dropped at the most likely position of the target. All turns are 120° to starboard. This pattern gives a very high probability of detection close to datum and spreads the search over the probable area quickly.

Upon completion of the first search, re-orientate the pattern 30° to the right and re-search as shown by the dashed line.

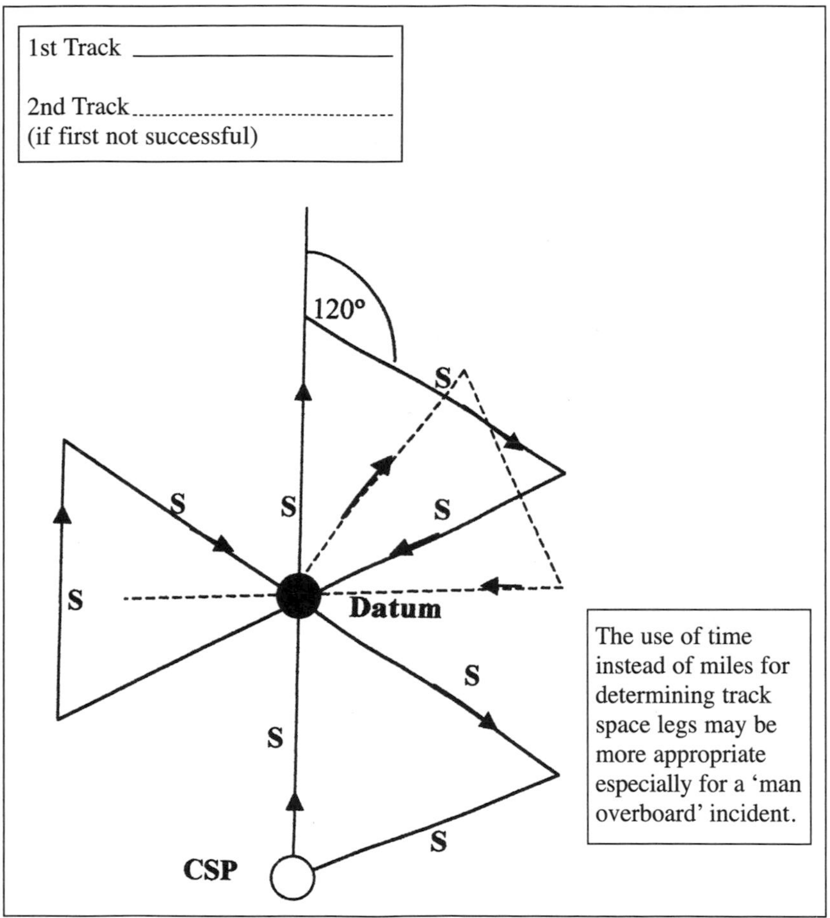
1st Track
2nd Track
(if first not successful)
120°
S
S
S
S
S
S
S
S
S
Datum
CSP
The use of time instead of miles for determining track space legs may be more appropriate especially for a 'man overboard' incident.

Diagram 9.2: Sector Search – One Ship

Where 'S' represents Track Space (Distance or time variable)
CSP represents Commencement of Search Pattern

9.3.1 parallel search pattern

Used when the search area is large or where only the approximate location is known and uniform coverage is necessary.

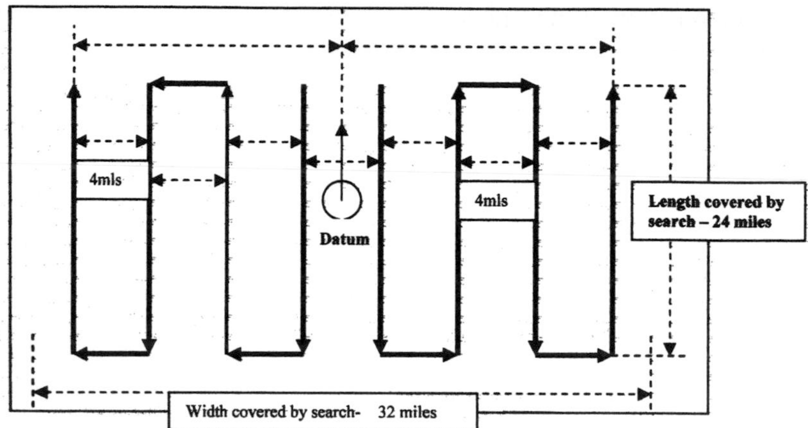

Diagram 9.3: Parallel Search – Two (2) Ships

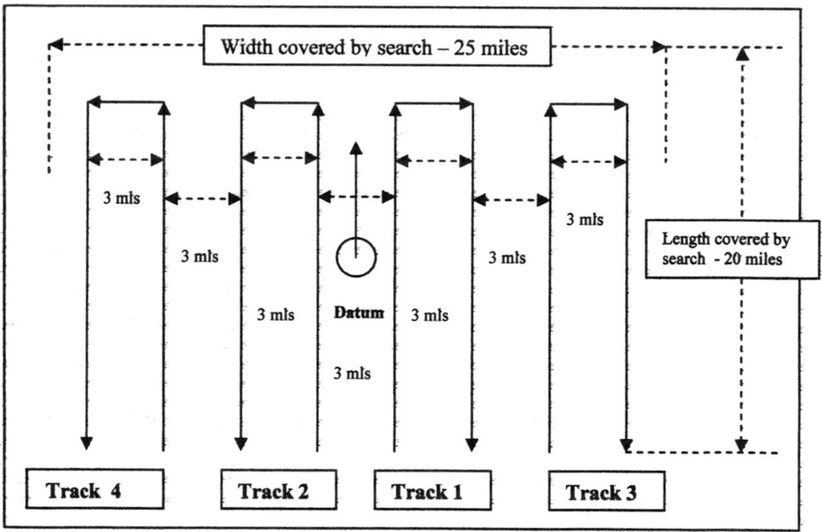

Diagram 9.4: Parallel Search – Four (4) Ships

*Arrow from Datum indicates the direction of drift.

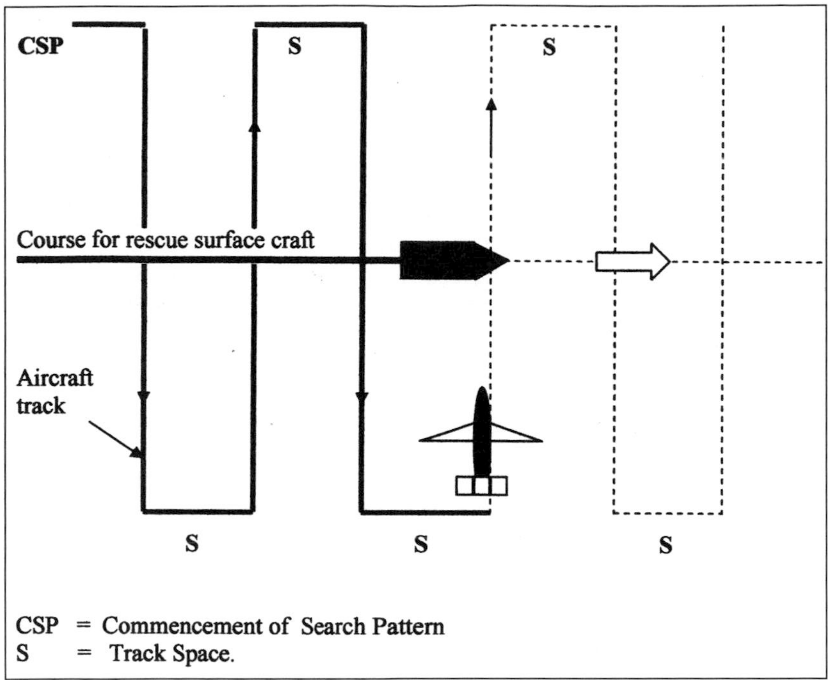

Diagram 9.5: Co-ordinated Creeping Line Search – One Ship and One Aircraft

The co-ordinated creeping line search combines the use of both aircraft and surface unit(s). The surface unit proceeds along the major axis of the search area while the air unit(s) plan their advance to match the ship's movement.

NB: Fixed wing aircraft (other than seaplanes) can only locate, effective communications can subsequently lead to recovery by the surface units.

Greater accuracy is achieved with increased unit numbers. Aircraft would tend to fly at a height which would permit visible detection. However, where more than one aircraft is employed a varied height for each above surface level would be in the interest of air collision avoidance.

9.3.2 search units

The ideal search vessel would be equipped to locate and recover casualties, and have on-board medical facilities available. To this end effective radar and suitable manpower to carry out extensive plotting operations must also be considered a distinct advantage. The unit would require the endurance to complete the task, hopefully without undue commercial pressure, as would be found with a ship carrying perishable cargo.

Unlike search aircraft that have extended range over and above surface vessels, the surface search craft would be able to recover survivors from the sea by means of Fast Rescue Craft (FRC). At the present time few, if any, fixed wing aircraft have the ability to recover after location has been achieved. They can locate but almost all SAR aircraft, once outside helicopter range, must work in a manner which incorporates surface recovery craft.

Whether search units are of a surface or air description, they all need effective communications prior to operating in the field. High sided transports pose difficulties for casualties and therefore vessels with a lower freeboard and good manoeuvrability are generally better suited to effect recovery operations once location has been achieved.

9.4 Distress Alert Procedures

9.4.1 distress – Master's responsibilities

On receipt of any distress signal the Master or Officer in charge is legally obliged to acknowledge and respond to that signal. In the event that the distress signal is not in the immediate area then it would be considered normal practice for a potential rescue vessel to wait a short interval to allow other vessels closer to the scene, to respond.

The obligation to render assistance to a vessel or aircraft in distress at sea must be considered with the highest priority. No communication can take precedence over a distress message and the Master of another vessel must respond. It should however be noted that a vessel may be relieved of this duty to assist a distressed vessel when:

1. The Master of a ship is unable to respond positively when he may himself be in distress, or the action would stand his own vessel in immediate danger, or
2. When circumstances make it unreasonable for him to respond, e.g. Vessel in China Sea receives distress signal from English Channel area.

Following receipt of a distress signal the 'alert machinery' is as follows:

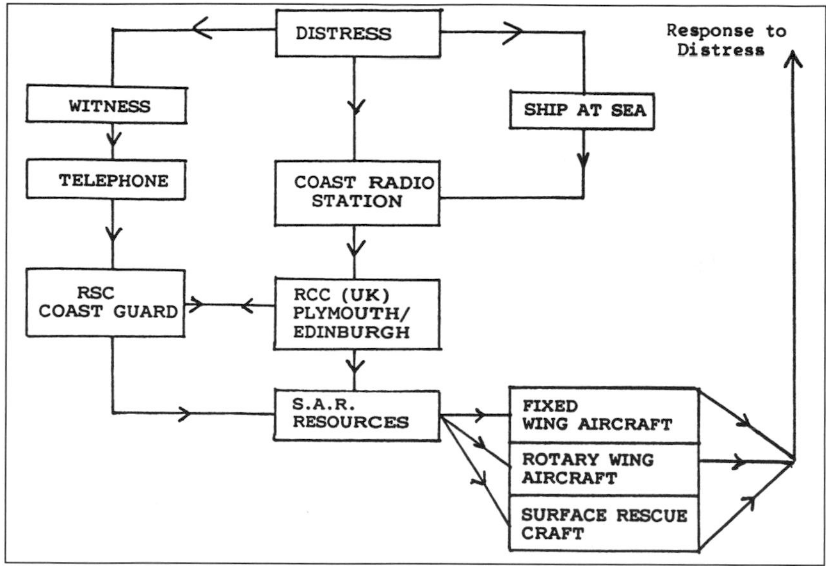

Diagram 9.6: Distress Alert System

9.4.2 fast rescue craft

Many of the current rescue authorities around the world operate fast rescue type craft of a semi-rigid inflatable type. Both the Royal National Lifeboat Institution and the U.K. Coast Guard have these craft available in the event of them being required.

The craft, depending on size and engine power, have speeds in excess of thirty knots. With this potential power and shallow draught, they have a fast response time, often into shallow and difficult areas. It is common practice for operators of such craft to leave their base at high speed and arrive very quickly at the scene of an incident. The return rate of speed will often be reduced to ease the comfort of casualties and will depend on the circumstances of the case in hand.

They are normally crewed by two or three men, again depending on the size of the craft. First coxswain, second coxswain and/or an observer/swimmer. Standard equipment would include; External lifelines, paddles, navigation lights, bellows, internal grablines and repair kit.

Additional equipment may include: First aid kit, radio, search-light compass, anchor and warp, boat hook, bilge pump and fire extinguisher.

These rescue craft are extremely manoeuvrable at high speed and generally perform better 'on the plane'. Transport in one can be exhilarating over short periods, but is equally exhaustive when operated over long periods of time.

9.4.3 rescue boats

Launch and recovery of rescue boats is achieved by three and four legged bridles. The operation can be carried out from vessels when stationary or making way at slow speed.

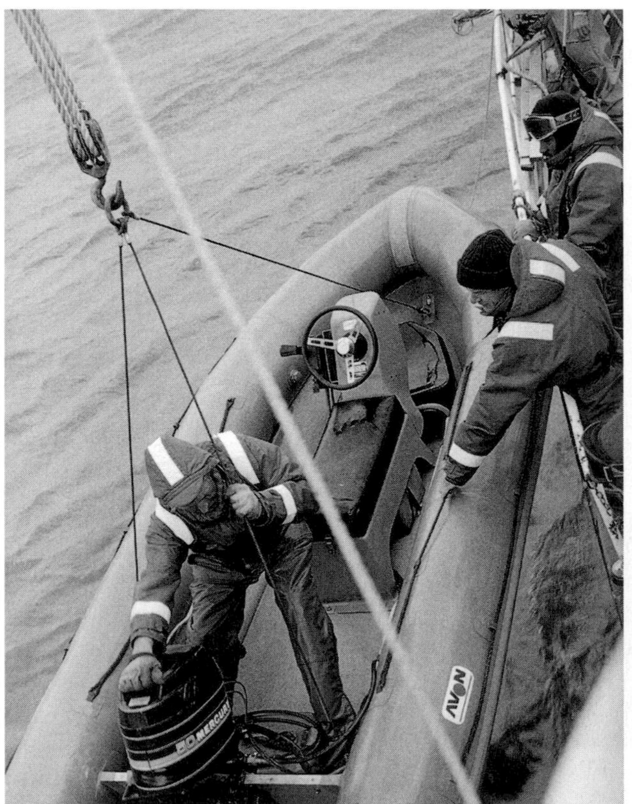

Pic. 30: FRC being recovered by means of a three legged wire bridle.

S.A.R. – Communications

2182 kHz	Designated S.A.R. aircraft. Compulsory R/T distress frequency.
500 kHz	Automatic distress frequency.
8364 kHz	Emergency long range distress frequency.
121.5 MHz	Aeronautical distress frequencies carried by all designated S.A.R. aircraft.
243 MHz	E.P.I.R.B.'s.
406 MHz	E.P.I.R.B., Satellite alert world coverage.
156.8 Hz (Ch. 16)	Desirable VHF.
3032 kHz	R/T for S.A.R. 'on scene' use.
5680 kHz	
123.1 MHz	Air and surface 'on scene' use.

Pic. 31: FRC seen operational in open sea conditions. The three man crew, shown with prominent radar reflector and inflatable capsize aid at the stern of the craft.

9.5 Global Maritime Distress and Safety System (GMDSS)

9.5.1 introduction

The Global Maritime Distress and Safety System has been developed by the International Maritime Organization. It has replaced the previous radio distress system and has been included in the amendments to the SOLAS 1974 convention. The GMDSS has involved considerable automation and has made use of the Inmarsat's satellites to provide reliable communications.

9.5.2 compliance with the system

1. All ships must comply with GMDSS by 1st February 1999.

9.5.3 types of vessels affected

The GMDSS requirements affect all passenger ships and all cargo ships of 300 grt. or over.

9.5.4 equipment carriage requirements

Ships will require specific items of equipment, based on the sea area in which the vessel operates. There are four designated sea-areas and these are defined in the tabulated carriage requirements.

At present two types of terminals are available:

Inmarsat-A offers the use of voice, data, facsimile and telex based communications.

Inmarsat-C this is smaller and offers text and data messaging at lower speeds.

Both terminals provide worldwide coverage with the exception of the extreme polar regions.

9.5.5 GMDSS functional requirements

The equipment provided has been identified by the IMO as being suitable to carry out the following operations:

- ship-to-shore distress alerting
- shore-to-ship distress alerting
- ship-to-ship distress alerting
- search and rescue co-ordination
- on scene communication
- transmission and receipt of locating signal

- transmission and receipt of maritime safety information
- general radio communications
- bridge-to-bridge communications

9.6 Termination of Distress Situation and/or Search Procedure

9.6.1 termination where incident is successful

Whether the search and rescue incident is successful or unsuccessful, a time will come when the operation will be terminated. In the case of a successful outcome, where all parties have been accounted for, then the On Scene Co-ordinator (OSC) should immediately inform all search facilities that the search incident is now terminated. The time of termination being recorded in the log books of affected units.

The OSC would also inform the SAR Mission Co-ordinator of the termination of operations within a final 'sitrep'. This communication would provide up-to-date information on any survivors recovered and their physical condition, together with relevant details on deceased persons, if known and the condition of any distressed craft and whether it poses a danger to navigation.

9.6.2 termination where incident is unsuccessful

It would be expected that the On Scene Co-ordinator would continue the search operation until all reasonable hope of recovering survivors has past. This time could be difficult to assess and would be agreed upon between the OSC and the Mission Co-ordinator (SMC).

Clearly when to terminate an operation will depend on a variety of factors, not least if survivors are known to be in open water, in a survival craft, in immersion suits or other waterproof clothing and the prevailing weather conditions at the time. Air and sea temperatures would certainly influence any decision as to when to terminate search operations. Additionally, the search may be affected by the search units endurance capacity, effectiveness in high sea conditions and whether daylight will be lost.

The probability that survivors can sustain themselves in the prevailing conditions becomes the deciding factor as to when agreement to terminate operations will be made. However, once the decision to terminate is made, the following procedure is suggested as a line of action:

1) Inform all search facilities and active units of the termination and provide an official termination log time.
2) All surface craft should be ordered to proceed on passage.
3) A message to all ships in, or passing through the search area, should be advised for transmission by the OSC/SMC.
4) OSC to inform the SMC that all operational units have been stood down. A final 'sitrep' to this effect would include any outcomes of the operation either favourable or adverse.

9.6.3 distress alert – completion

When a distress situation is resolved and radio traffic has ceased on the frequencies which have been used for distress traffic the RCC controlling the SAR operation shall cause a transmission to be made indicating distress traffic has finished.

This transmission will consist of:–

- the distress signal MAYDAY
- the call ALL STATIONS or CQ (Spoken as CHARLIE QUEBEC) three times.
- the words THIS IS (or DE spoken as DELTA ECHO)
- the call sign or other identification of the station sending the message.
- the time of handing in of the message.
- the name and call sign of the mobile station.
- may include details of the outcome of the incident.
- the words SEELONCE FEENEE.

FREQUENCIES FOR DISTRESS AND SAFETY COMMUNICATIONS FOR GLOBAL MARITIME DISTRESS AND SAFETY SYSTEM

TYPE OF COMMUNICATIONS		DISTRESS AND SAFETY FREQUENCIES	NOTES ON PARTICULAR FREQUENCIES
NAVTEX	NBDP	518kHz	
	NBDP	4209.5kHz	
	NBDP	490kHz	AFTER FULL IMPLEMENTATION OF GMDSS
R/T	MF/HF	2182kHz	ALSO GENERAL CALLING
		3023kHz	AERONAUTICAL SAR
		4125kHz	ALSO AERONAUTICAL SAR
		5680kHz	AERONAUTICAL SAR
		6521kHz	
		8291kHz	
		12290kHz	
		16420kHz	
	VHF	156.8MHz	ALSO GENERAL CALLING CH 16
		156.650MHz	INTERSHIP SAFETY CH 13
		156.3MHz	AERONAUTICAL SAR, CH 6 INTER-SHIP
DSC		2187.5kHz	
		4207.5kHz	
		6312kHz	
		8414.5kHz	
		12577kHz	
		16804.5kHz	
TELEX	NBDP	2174.5kHz	
		4177.5kHz	
		4210kHz	SAFETY ONLY
		6268kHz	
		6314kHz	
		8376.5kHz	
		8416.5kHZ	SAFETY ONLY
		12520kHz	
		12579kHz	SAFETY ONLY
		16695kHz	
		16806.5kHz	SAFETY ONLY
		19680.5kHz	SAFETY ONLY
		22376kHz	SAFETY ONLY
		26100.5kHz	SAFETY ONLY
EPIRB		121.5MHz	ALSO AERONAUTICAL EMERGENCY
		123.1MHz	AUXILIARY TO 121.5 FOR SAR (NOT EPIRB)
		406MHz	LOW POLAR ORBIT SATELLITE EPIRB
		1645.5 – 1646.5MHz	GEOSTATIONARY SATELLITE EPIRB
SATELLITE		1626.5 – 1645.5MHz	
RADAR		9200 – 9500MHZ	SART (SEARCH AND RESCUE RADAR TRANSPONDER)

9.7 Ship Carriage Requirements for GMDSS

All ships to which the amended 1974 SOLAS convention applies are required to carry the GMDSS radio equipment, depending on the sea areas in which they operate.

One of the basic principles on which the GMDSS carriage requirement is based is that a vessel has the capability of transmitting ship to shore distress alerts by at least two separate and independent means. The requirements are such that other means of communication are also required and these regulate the specific carriage requirements by ships in accordance with their respective sea area of operation.

Summary of requirements for GMDSS radio equipment are as follows:

a) Sea Area A1 ships will carry VHF equipment and either a satellite EPIRB or a VHF EPIRB.
b) Sea Area A2 ships will carry VHF and MF equipment and a satellite EPIRB.
c) Sea Area A3 ships will carry VHF, MF a satellite EPIRB and either HF or satellite communication equipment.
d) Sea Area A4 ships will carry VHF, MF and HF equipment and a satellite EPIRB.

Additionally, all ships will carry equipment for receiving MSI broadcasts.

The Solas Convention as amended 1988, stipulates a time scale when installations are expected to meet GMDSS requirements.

All ships constructed after 1st February 1992 to be fitted with radar transponder and two way VHF radio telephone apparatus for survival craft.

All ships to be fitted with a NAVTEX receiver and satellite EPIRB by 1st August 1993.

All ships constructed before 1st February 1992 to be fitted with radar transponder and two way VHF R/T apparatus for survival craft by 1st February 1995.

All ships constructed after 1st February 1995 to comply with appropriate regulations for GMDSS.

All ships to be fitted with at least one radar capable of operating in the 9 GHz band by 1st February 1995.

All ships to comply with GMDSS requirements by 1st February 1999.

Pic. 32: Example GMDSS shipboard communications terminal

Every ship which falls within GMDSS will be provided with minimum standards of equipment in order to carry out the functional requirements for specific sea areas of trading:

1. A VHF installation with a capability of transmitting and receiving DSC on channel 70 and radio telephony on channels 6, 13 and 16.
2. Equipment which allows a continuous DSC watch to be maintained on VHF channel 70.
3. Radar transponder (SART) operating in the 9 GHz band.
4. The capability to receive the International Navtex service broadcasts when operating in any area where NAVTEX is provided.
5. An onboard facility for the reception of Marine Safety Information (MSI) by the Inmarsat's Enhanced Group Call system (EGC) when engaged on voyages where NAVTEX coverage is not provided.

6. Satellite Emergency Position Indicating Radio Beacon (EPIRB) capable of being manually activated and with float free facility and automatic activation.

9.7.1 personnel

Designated GMDSS vessels will be required to carry personnel qualified in distress and safety radio communications procedures. These persons will be certificated personnel who satisfy the radio regulations and the administering authority.

During a distress incident these persons will be designated as having primary responsibility for radio communications.

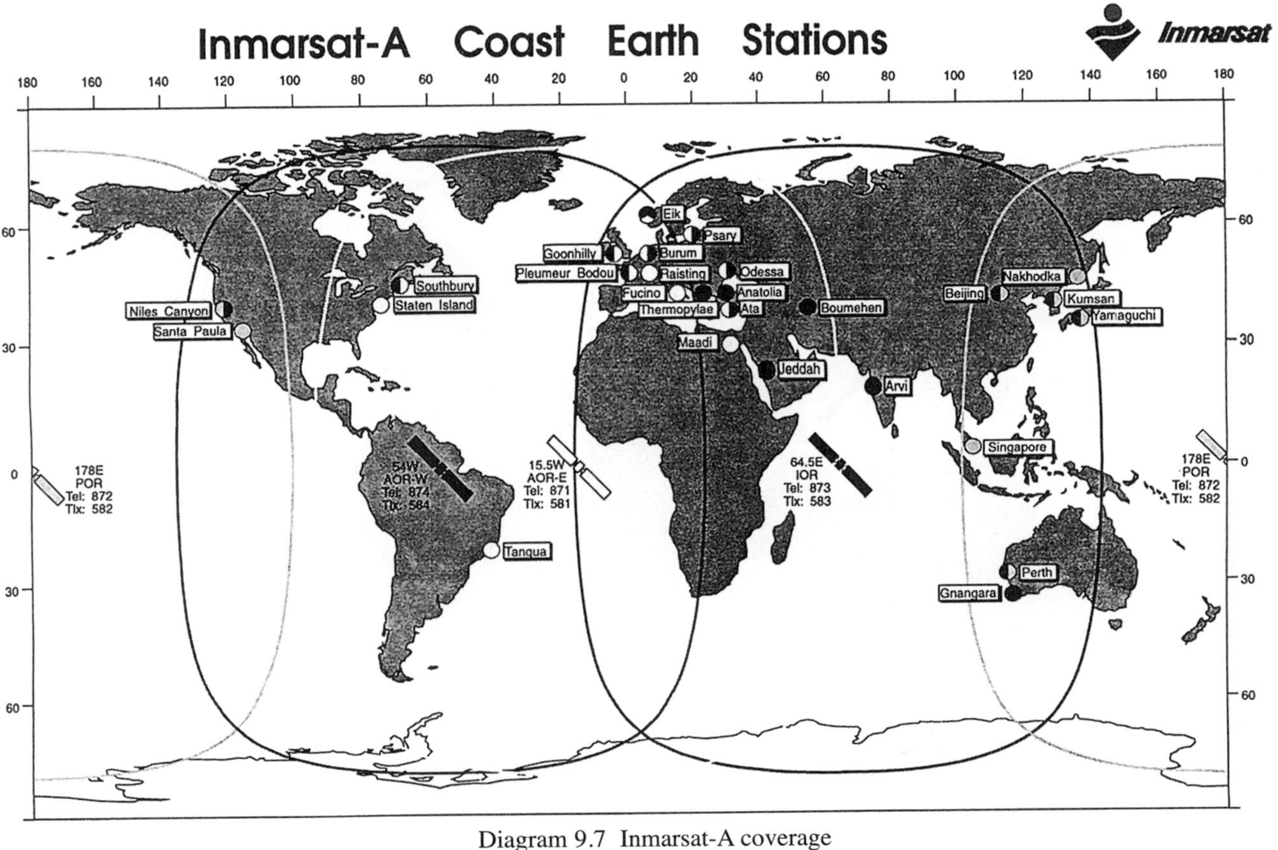

Diagram 9.7 Inmarsat-A coverage

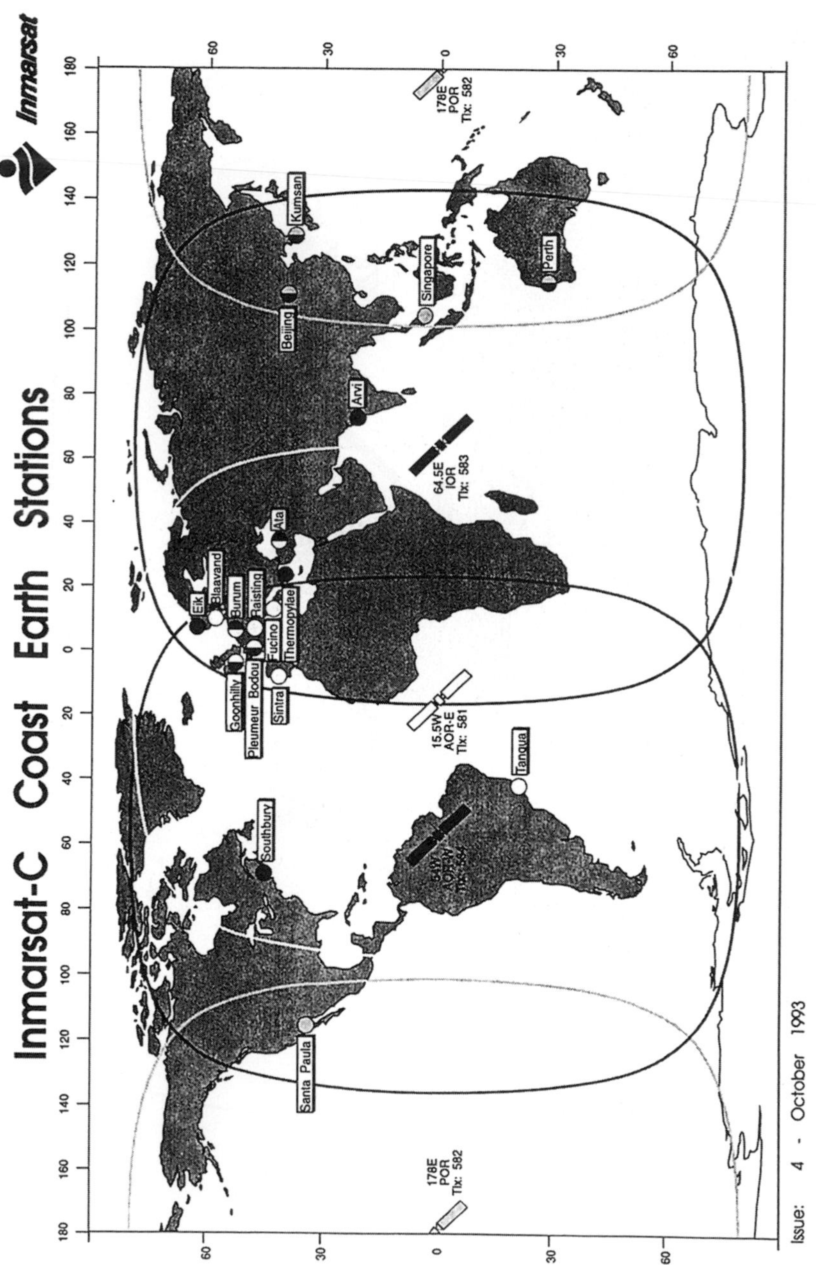

Diagram 9.8 Inmarsat-C coverage

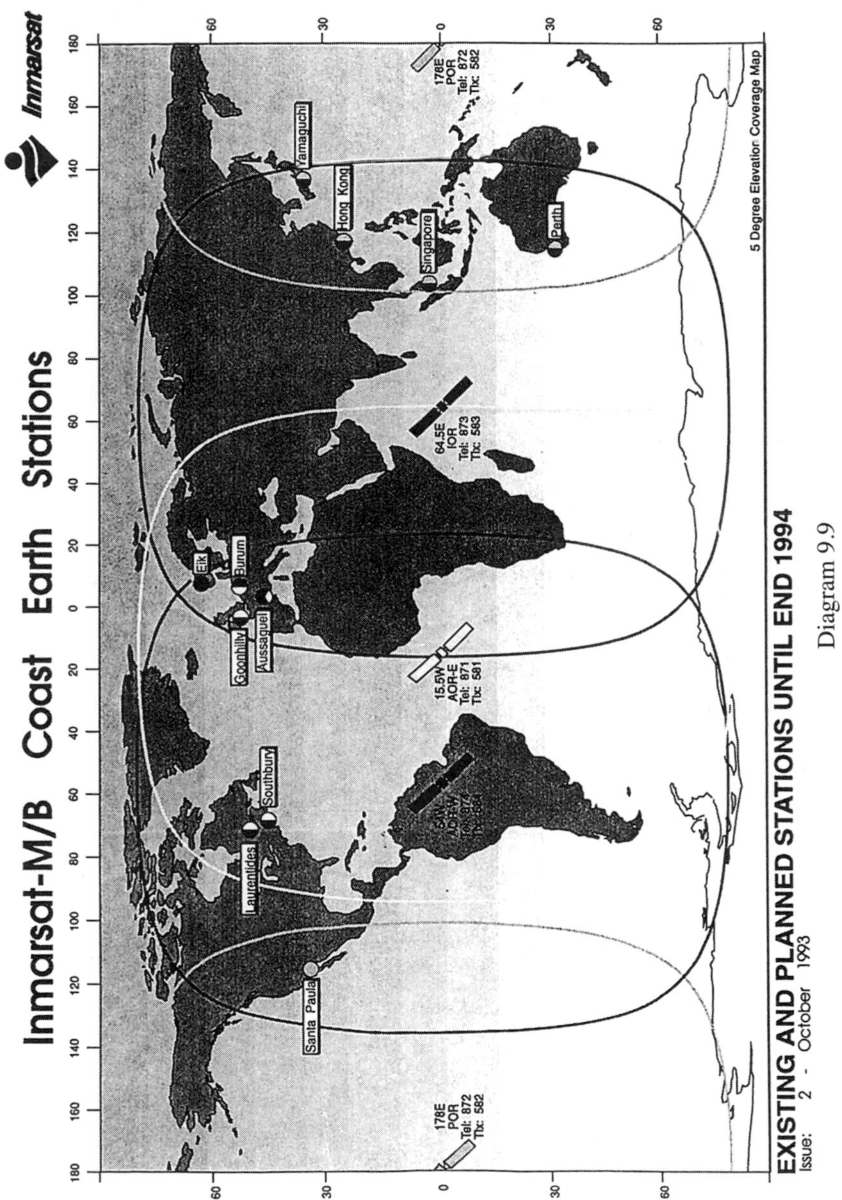
Inmarsat-M/B Coast Earth Stations
Inmarsat
Santa Paula
Laurentides
Southbury
Goonhilly
Aussaguel
Burum
Eik
Singapore
Hong Kong
Yamaguchi
Perth
178E
POR
Tel: 872
Tlx: 582
15.5W
AOR-E
Tel: 871
Tlx: 581
64.5E
IOR
Tel: 873
Tlx: 583
5 Degree Elevation Coverage Map
EXISTING AND PLANNED STATIONS UNTIL END 1994
Issue: 2 - October 1993

Diagram 9.9

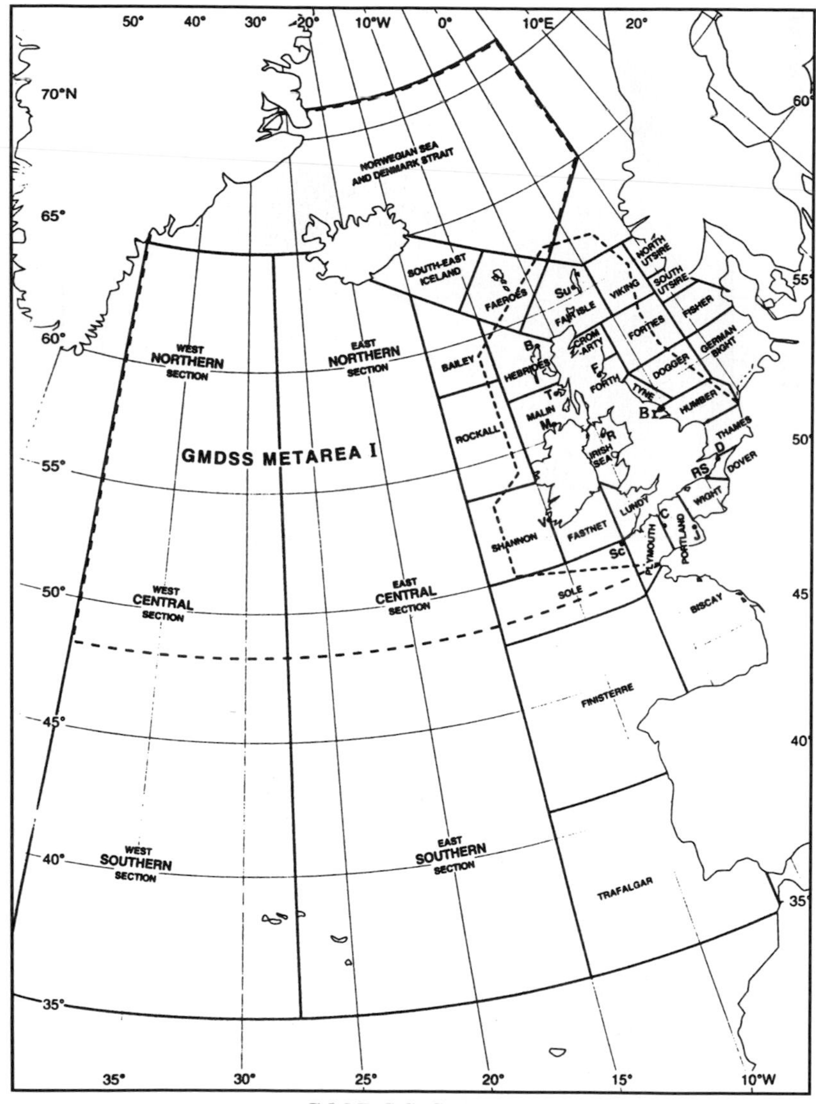

G.M.D.S.S. Sea Area
Diagram 9.10: Sea Areas and Associated Marine Communication Areas for G.M.D.S.S.

EMERGENCY POSITION INDICATING RADIO BEACONS
(E.P.I.R.B.'s)

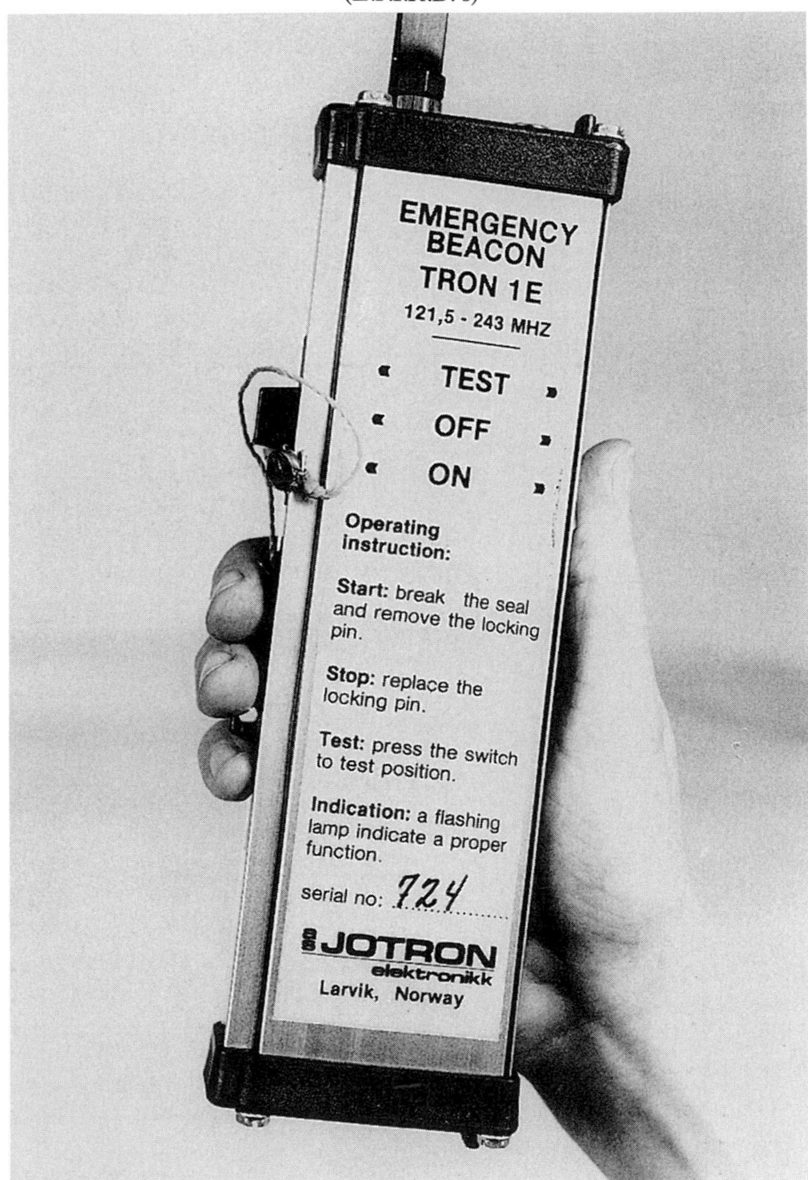

Pic. 33: TRON 1E Type EPIRB manufactured by Jotron Electronics AS operates on 121.5 and 243 MHz. Hand held and simple to activate. Battery operated and fitted with test facility

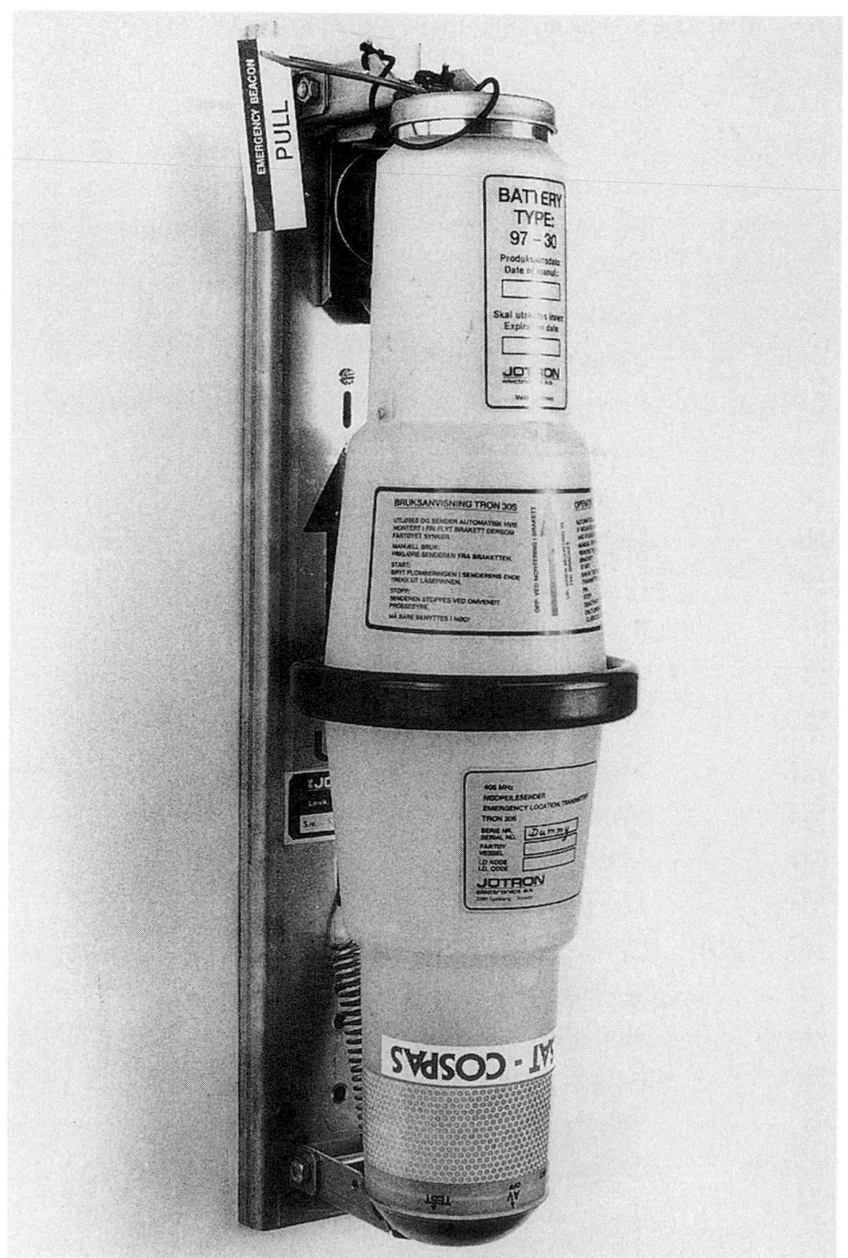

Pic. 34: Type EPIRB operates on 121.5, 243 and 406 HHz.
It provides global coverage, location capability in conjunction with SARSAT/COSPAS satellite systems. May be fitted with hydrostatic float free system.

9.8 Abbreviations Employed with GMDSS and SAR Operations

A/C	Aircraft
ACC	Area Control Centre
ACO	Aircraft Co-Ordinator
AES	Aeronautical Earth Station
AFN	Aeronautical Fixed Network
AFTN	Aeronautical Fixed Telecommunications Network
AIP	Aeronautical Information Publication
AIS (i)	Automatic Identification System
AIS (ii)	Aeronautical Information Services
AM	Amplitude Modulation
AMS	Aeronautical Mobile Service
AMS(R)S	Aeronautical Mobile Satellite (route) Service
AMSS	Aeronautical Mobile Satellite Service
AMVER	Automated Mutual Assistance Vessel Rescue
ANC	Air Navigation Commission
ARCC	Aeronautical Rescue Co-ordination Centre
ARSC	Aeronautical Rescue sub Centre
ATC	Air Traffic Control
ATN	Aeronautical Telecommunications Network
ATS	Air Traffic Services
CES	Coast earth Station
COSPAS	Space System for search of Vessels in Distress
CRS	Coast Radio Station
C/S	Call Sign
C/S	Creeping Line Search
CSC	Creeping Line Search Co-ordinated
CSP	Commence Search Point
CW	Continuous Wave
DF	Direction Finding
DMB	Datum Marker Buoy
DME	Distance Measuring Equipment

DR	Dead Reckoning
DSC	Digital Selective Calling
EGC	Enhanced Group Calling
ELT	Emergency Locator Transmitter
EPIRB	Emergency Position Indicating Radio Beacon
ETA	Estimated Time of Arrival
ETD	Estimated Time of Departure
ETV	Emergency Towing Vessel
FIC	Flight Information Centre
FIR	Flight Information Region
FM	Frequency Modulation
FRC	Fast Rescue Craft
F/V	Fishing Vessel
GES	Ground Earth Station
GHz	Giga Hertz
GLONASS	Global Orbiting Navigation Satellite System
GMDSS	Global Maritime Distress and Safety System
GNSS	Global Navigation Satellite System
GPS	Global Positioning System
GS	Ground Speed
gt (grt)	Gross Tonnage
HF	High Frequency
IAMSAR	International Aeronautical and Maritime Search and Rescue Manual
ICAO	International Civil Aviation Organisation
IFR	Instrument Flight Rules (Instrument Flying Rating)
ILS	Instrument Landing System
IMARSAT	International Mobile Satellite Organisation
IMC	Instrument Meteorological Conditions
IMO	International Maritime Organisation
INS	Inertia Navigation System
INTERCO	International Code of Signals
ITU	International Telecommunications Union

JASREP	Japanese Ship Reporting System
JRCC	Joint (aeronautical and maritime) Rescue Co-ordination Centre
kHz	kilohertz
KOSREP	Korean Ship Reporting System
LES	Land Earth Station
LKP	Last Known Position
LUT	Local User Terminal
m	metres
MCA	Maritime Coastguard Agency
MCC	Mission Control Centre
MF	Medium Frequency
MHz	Megahertz
MMSI	Maritime Mobile Service Identity
MRCC	Maritime Rescue Co-ordination Centre
MRSC	Maritime Rescue Sub-Centre
MSI	Maritime Safety Information
M/V	Merchant Vessel (Motor Vessel)
NAVTEX	Co-ordinated Broadcast and Automatic Reception of MSI on 518 kHz Using NBDP
NBDP	Narrow Band Direct Printing
NM	Nautical Mile
OSC	On Scene Co-ordinator
OSV	Offshore Supply Vessel
PIW	Person In Water
PLB	Personal Locator Beacon
POB	Persons Onboard
R	Search Radius
RCC	Rescue Co-ordination Centre
RF	Radio Frequency
RSC	Rescue Sub Centre
R/T	Radio Telephone
RTG	Radio Telegraphy

SAR	Search and Rescue
SARSAT	Search and Rescue Satellite – Aided Tracking
SART	Search and Rescue Transponder
SC	Search Co-ordinator
SCC	SAR Co-ordinating Committee
SDP	Search Data Provider
SES	Ship Earth Station
SITREP	Situation Report
SMC	SAR Mission Co-ordinator
SOLAS	International Convention for the Safety of Life at Sea
SPOC	SAR Point of Contact
SRR	Search and Rescue Region
SRU	Search and Rescue Unit
SS	Expanding Square Search
SU	Search Unit
T (i)	True Course
T (ii)	Search Time available
TAS	True Air Speed
TLX	Teletype
TS	Track Line Search
UHF	Ultra High Frequency
UIR	Upper Flight Information Region
USAR	Urban Search and Rescue
USCG	United States Coastguard
UTC	Co-ordinated Universal Time
V	SAR Facility Ground Speed
VFR	Visual Flight Rules
VHF	Very High Frequency
VMC	Visual Meteorological Conditions
VOR	VHF Omni Directional Radio Range
VS	Sector Search
WMO	World Meteorological Organisation

9.9 Ship Reporting Systems

Many areas of the world operate local ship reporting procedures, English Channel, River St. Lawrence Canada, to mention but two of the well known systems in current operation. These tend to be local operations for thc safety of navigation. Ship reporting systems like AMVER or AUSREP have a distinctive and different purpose. They are designed and operated to maximise efficiency in co-ordinating assistance from merchant vessels in the immediate vicinity or close to a distress incident.

Information supplied by vessels allows the system to select and determine the most suitably equipped and appropriately situated ship to render early assistance in the event of a marine emergency. Probably the most popular ship reporting systems are:

AMVER operated by U.S. Coast Guard/Atlantic Oceans/Pacific Oceans

AUSREP operated within the Australian SAR area

INSPIRES operates within the Indian SAR area

JASREP – Japanese Ship Reporting System has been established to co-ordinate SAR operations in and around the area of Japan. It operates between the mainland of Asia to a boundary position of Latitude 17° N, Longitude 165° E. and is a voluntary reporting system.

MADAGASCAR reporting service exists around the Madagascar area within latitudes 5° south to 30° south between the African Coast and longitude 60° east.

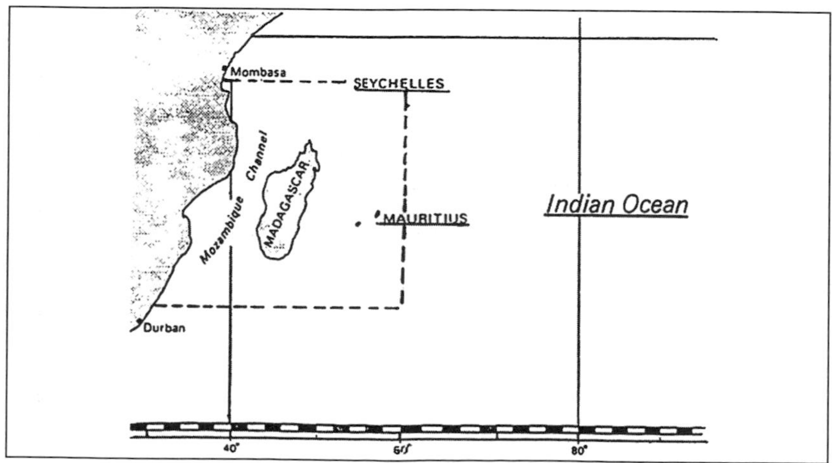

Diagram 9.11: The Madagascar Zone

9.10 AMVER and AUSREP Systems

Principle of any ship reporting system is to utilise the resources of the many merchant vessels which are at sea at any one time, following a maritime incident. These ships very often have the potential to make an early arrival at an emergency scene. The purpose of AMVER is to maximise the efficiency in co-ordinating assistance in order to save life and property.

AMVER – the Automated Mutual-Assistance Vessel Rescue System

Participating vessels transmit their positions and intended future movements via the AMVER radio station.
(Obtained from the AMVER User's Manual).

Message format can be obtained from the Admiralty List of Radio Signals.

Additional information may be obtained from:

Commander	Commander	Commandant
Atlantic Area	Pacific Coast Area	U.S. Coast Guard
U.S. Coastguard	U.S. Coastguard	Washington DC
Governors Island	Government Island	20593
New York,	Alameda	
N.Y. 10004-5099	California	
U.S.A.	94501-5100	

A.M.V.E.R.

The AMVER ship reporting system is operated by the United States Coastguard for the benefit of all vessels irrespective of nationality. Participating vessels over one thousand gross tons which are engaged on voyages of twenty-four hours or more contribute on a voluntary basis.

The operation is conducted worldwide through a radio station network via which vessels can despatch their reports free of charge (designated stations only).* The objectives are to co-ordinate mutual assistance for the purpose of distress or search and rescue activities.

AMVER centres are based in New York and San Francisco where automatic data processing is achieved. Initial ship's data regarding the vessel's size, speed, communications, equipment and facilities being

*UK stations now charge for AMVER communications

kept on confidential record. No information is passed on except that relevant to SAR operations.

MESSAGES

Transmissions normally take place during the normal communications schedule of the ship:

Sailing Plan:	They may be given days or even weeks prior to departure. It's content should include the ship's name and call sign. The time and port of departure, together with the port of destination, should also be included. A provisional ETA, with the proposed routing track, together with any special resources on board should also be stated.
Departure Report	Despatched as soon as possible after departure. It should include the ship's name, time of departure and the port from which the ship is sailing.
Position Report	Should be despatched within 24 hours after departure and within every 48 hours thereafter that. This report should include the ship's name, time and the position (latitude and longitude), together with the port of destination and ETA, at this port. Additional information may include speed, present course or other relevant comments.
Arrival Report	Despatched just prior to, or on arrival at, the port of destination. The report should include the ship's name and call sign, the relevant position and time.
Deviation Report	Used to report any changes to the sailing plan. Details of diversions, courses and speeds with revised ETA may be appropriate with deviation.

AUSREP – Ship Report System

Mandatory system for all Australian Ships when navigating inside the designated area and for all foreign ships, from arrival in their first Australian Port until their departure from the last Australian Port.

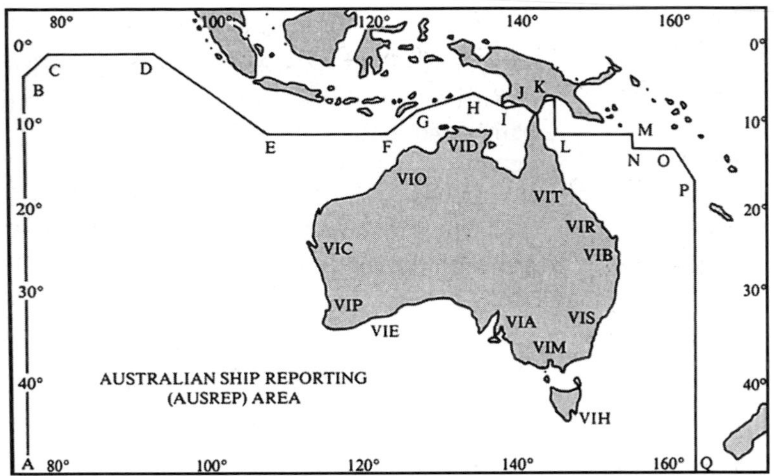

Diagram 9.12: The ship reporting system became mandatory in Australian waters on 1st April 1982. For the purpose of AUSREP, Australian waters cover nearly ten per cent of the earth's surface.

Ships despatch their messages through any Australian Coast Radio Station addressed "Cosurcen Canberra". Schedules and frequencies are listed in the Admiralty List of Radio Signals Vol. I (Part II).

The system is operated by the Australian Coastal Surveillance Centre (ACSC) based in Canberra and its principle objectives are:

1. To limit the time between the loss of a vessel and the initiation of search and rescue action in cases where no distress signal is despatched.
2. To limit the search area for rescue action.
3. To provide up-to-date information on shipping in the event of a search and rescue incident developing.

To this end all vessels navigating within the Ausrep area are requested to co-operate and respect the specific guidelines of the controlling centre.

AUSREP – Format of Reports

Sailing Plan (SP) Report

Despatched when entering the area or up to two hours after departure from port.

To include:

1. AUSREP SP
2. Ship's name.
3. Call sign.
4. Port of departure or, if entering Ausrep area, ship's position.
5. Date and time (GMT) of departure or of the time of position.
6. Port of destination.
7. Date and time of ETA (GMT). If leaving the area the ETA at the boundary limits.
8. Intended route.
9. Estimated speed of vessel.
10. A nominated daily reporting time (GMT).
11. Relevant remarks, e.g. intermediate port stops.

Position Report (PR)

Despatched daily at a nominated time.

To include:

1. AUSREP PR
2. Ship's name
3. Call sign
4. Position, course and speed
5. Date and time of ship's position given (GMT)
6. Remarks (i.e. any change in information previously passed in the sailing plan, or a change in the nominated reporting time, or revised routing information, any change in speed or destination etc.)

The last position report should also confirm ETA or, if leaving the area, then this should be indicated by adding "FINAL REPORT".

Arrival Report (AR)

Despatched once a vessel is within two hours steaming of the Pilot Station.

To include:

1. AUSREP AR
2. Ship's name
3. Call sign
4. Port of arrival
5. Date and time (GMT) of report

NB: If a report is six hours overdue, then the coast radio station will broadcast a priority signal within their traffic lists, requesting an IMMEDIATE RESPONSE.

Other vessels should report sightings and/or communications with the overdue vessel.

If the report is twenty one hours overdue, the signal will be upgraded to an 'URGENT SIGNAL'.

9.10.1 rendezvous problems

The need for navigators to establish a course to rendezvous with another target is not an every day occurrence at sea. However, any vessel could be called upon to contribute to an SAR operation and on that somewhat unusual occasion the need to be able to establish the course to steer and the closing speed to provide an ETA must be considered the navigators job.

For convenience the following examples have been illustrated on radar plotting sheets, and the reader should note that many of these problems could be equally resolved by calculation or alternative constructional methods.

Example 1

At 0800 hrs on the 16th July, your vessel receives a distress message from a vessel bearing 015° (T) distance 100 nautical miles. The vessel in distress has a cargo hold fire and is currently steering 050° (T) at twelve knots. Course and speed being adopted to suit the prevailing wind conditions.

If your own ship's maximum speed is 18 knots, what course must you steer to rendezvous with the target as soon as possible. What is your ETA at the rendezvous?

Method

1. Consider your own vessel stopped. (Centre of construction – see page 285). (Ref. "A") (Centre moved to facilitate plot scale)

2. Plot the target vessel bearing and distance (015° x 100'). (Ref. "B")

3. Use a convenient time period (e.g. 6 hours).

4. Lay off the movement of the target for this time period. (6 hrs at 12 kts = 72' on 050° T). (Ref. "BX")

5. Step back own ships movement (for the same time period), from 'X'. (Distance 6 hrs x 18 kts = 108'). (Ref. "XY")

6. Construct course to steer from own ships centre 'A' so that AC parallels XY (AC/XY).

7. Extend target ships movement 'BX' to intercept own ships movement at 'C'.

8. Obtain the direction of the course to steer (AC) = 037° (T).

9. Obtain the closing distance, represented by "BY" = 41 miles.

10. Obtain the combined effective speed
$$\frac{41'}{6\text{ hrs}} = 6.9\text{ kts.}$$

11. Obtain the time to rendezvous by:
$$\frac{\text{Total Distance}}{\text{Eff/speed}} = \frac{100}{6.9} = 14.19\text{ hours (14hrs 30')}$$

12. ETA from 0800 hrs = 2230 hrs.

Example 1

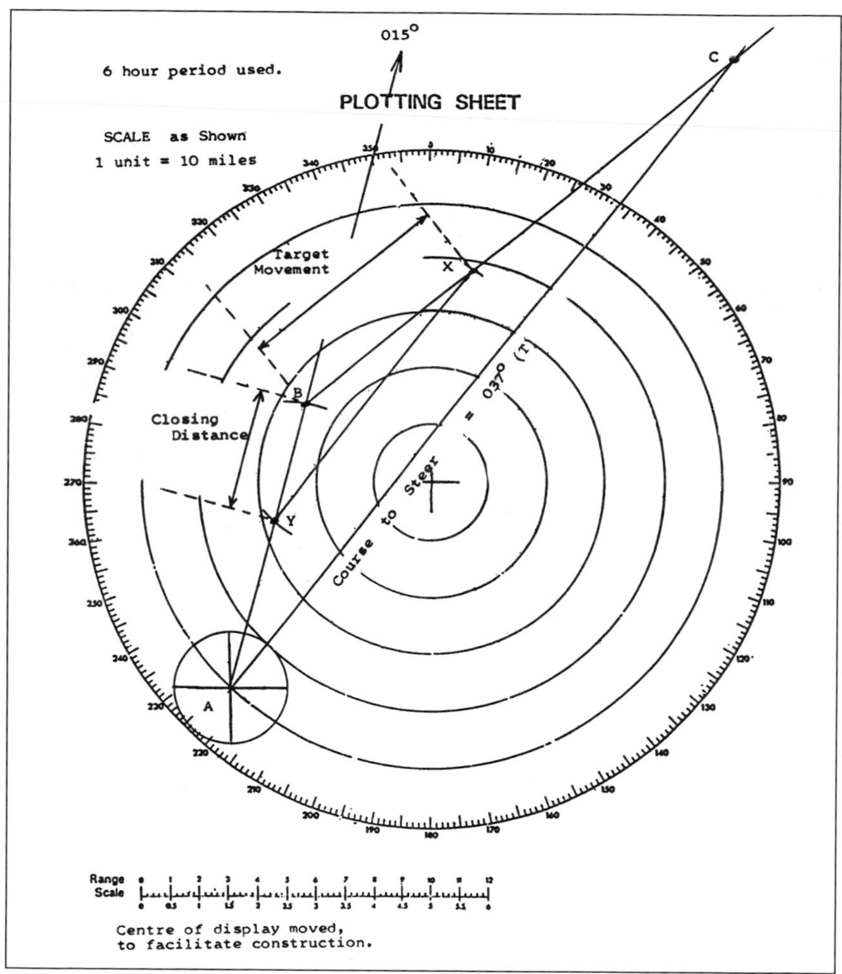

Diagram 9.13: Rendezvous – Example '1' Plot

Example 2

A medical emergency occurs aboard a target ship which bears 143° (T) at a distance of 175 nautical miles from you. The target ships course and speed are 280° (T) x 15 knots. Both vessels are effected by a current setting 200° (T) at 2 knots. What course must your vessel steer to make the rendezvous in the shortest possible time. What will be the ETA of the rendezvous if the time is now 0600 hours.

Method

1. Consider own vessel stopped at centre of construction. (Ref. "A")

2. Plot the target vessel (143° x 175'). (Ref. "B")

3. Use a convenient time period (e.g. 10 hours).

4. Lay off the targets movement for this time period. (10 hrs at 15 kts = 150' on 280° T). (Ref. "BX")

5. Step back own ships movement for the same time period, from 'X'. (Distance 10 hrs x 20 kts = 200 miles) (Ref. "XY") to cut targets bearing AR extended to intercept at 'Y'.

6. 'XY' represents course to steer to rendezvous = 176° (T).

7. 'BY' represents the closing distance = 278 miles.

8. Effective speed = $\frac{\text{Closing Distance}}{\text{Time Interval}} = \frac{278}{10}$ = 27.8 kts.

9. Time to rendezvous found by: $\frac{\text{Total Distance Apart}}{\text{Effective Speed}}$

$$= \frac{175}{27.8} = 6.3 \text{ hours (6 hrs 18')}$$

10. ETA of rendezvous = 1218 hrs same day

NB: The current in the question is effecting both vessels and can subsequently be ignored for the purpose of the construction.

Example 2

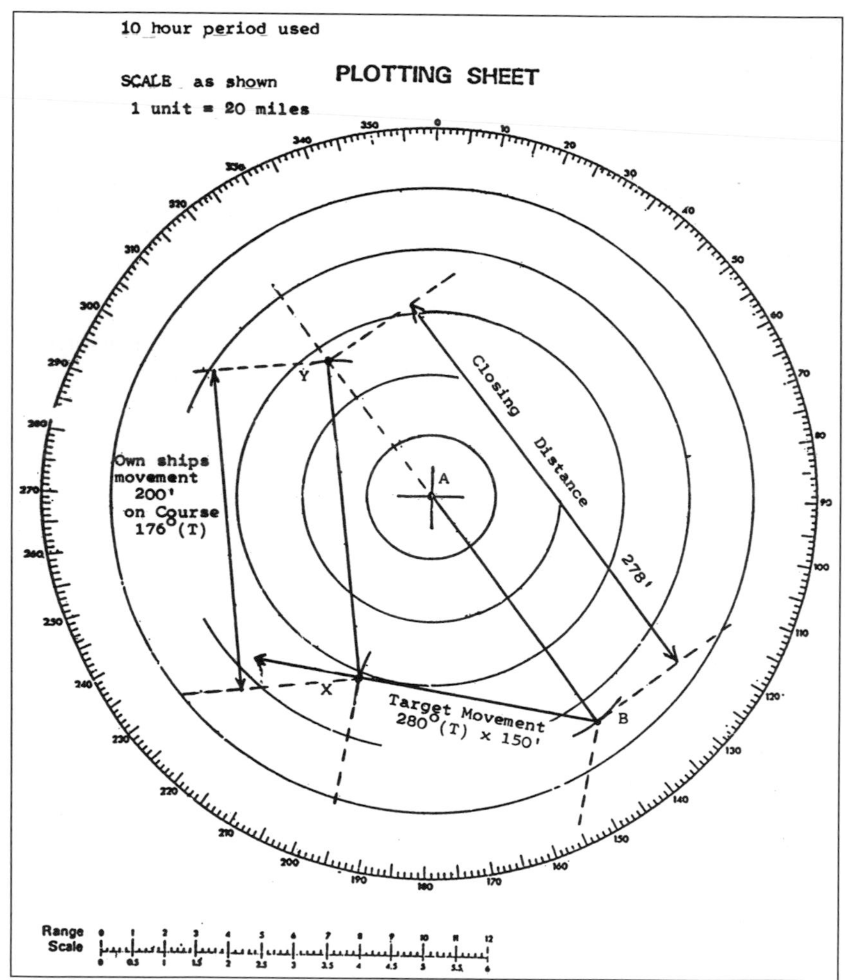

Diagram 9.14: Rendezvous – Example '2' Plot

Example 3

You are requested to rendezvous and stand-by another vessel which has been damaged by fire. The damaged vessel is heading for port on a course of 210° (T) at a speed of 6 knots. The radar bearing and range of this vessel from you is 115° (T) distance 16 miles.

Your orders are to take up station on the damaged vessel 1 mile off her starboard quarter on a bearing of 135° relative to this ships head. Own vessels maximum speed is 14 knots.

Obtain: a) the course to steer to rendezvous;
b) the time taken to reach the on station position;
c) the bearing at which you would expect to sight the vessel if the visibility is 5 miles.

Method

1. Assume own vessel stopped. (Centre of construction has been moved to facilitate page size). (Ref. "A")
2. Plot target position, bearing and distance (115° x 16.0'). (Ref. "B")
3. Establish rendezvous position (Ref. "R") (Plot relative bearing 135° from targets head equal to 345° (T) x 1.0').
4. Join own ship to rendezvous point. (Ref. track "AR")
5. Plot the targets movement from "R" (Course 210° x 6.0') (Using the rendezvous position as target). (Ref. "X")
6. Step back own ships movement from "X", to cut "AR" at "Y" (1 hour at 14.0 knots = 14 miles). (Ref. "XY")
7. 'XY' represents the course to steer to rendezvous = 137° (T).
8. Closing distance = Closing speed (1 hour construction used) = 13.7 kts.

9. Total distance to rendezvous position 'R' = 15.4 miles, therefore time to rendezvous =

$$\frac{\text{Total Dist}}{\text{Eff. Speed}} = \frac{15.4}{13.7} = 1.12 \text{ hours (1 hour 7')}$$

10. From target position 'B' step back a 5.0 mile range to cut and intercept track 'AR' at "S".

    Measure the bearing of when your vessel sights target vessel at 5.0' range = 123.5° (T).

Example 3

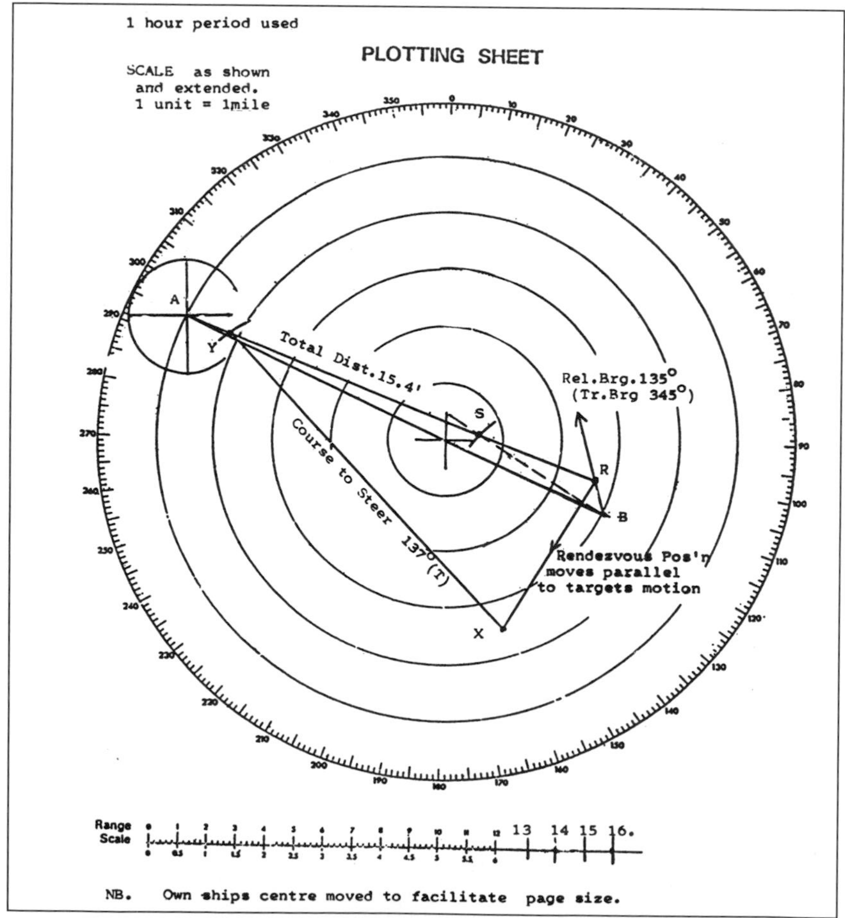

Diagram 9.15: Rendezvous – Example '3' Plot

Example 4

Your vessel is in a position latitude 38° 40'S, longitude 120° 49'E, at 1700 hrs GMT, when a distress message is received. Your maximum speed is 14 knots and you are required to rendezvous with the vessel in distress at position latitude 37° 48'S longitude 119° 33'E. Her course is WNW at 8.0 knots. Find the gyro course to steer to meet the rendezvous if your ships gyro compass has an error of 2° High. Allow 4° for leeway if a strong easterly wind is blowing.

Method

NB. It is necessary to obtain the bearing and distance of the target vessel prior to proceeding with the rendezvous resolution.

Own Ship	Lat.	38°	40' S	Long	120°	49' E
Distress	Lat.	37°	48' S	Long	119°	33' E
D.Lat.			52' N	D. Long	1°	16' W

Mean Lat. 38° 14' S. Dep. = 59.7' (By Traverse Table)
Bearing & Range of distress = 311° (T) x 79.2 miles (By Tr/Table)

1. Consider your own vessel stopped (Centre of construction has been moved to facilitate page size). (Ref. "A')

2. Plot the distress vessel (311° x 79.2'). (Ref. "B")

3. Use convenient time period (e.g. 10 hours).

4. Lay-off the movement of the distressed vessel. (Ref. "BX") (10 hrs at 8.0 kts = 80 miles on course (WNW) 292½° T.)

5. Step back own ships movement (for same period of 10 hrs) from 'X'. (Distance of 140 miles to intercept 'AB' at "Y")

6. 'XY' represents the course to steer to rendezvous = 301° (T).

7. Measure closing distance 'BY' = 62 miles.

8. Effective speed = $\dfrac{\text{Closing Distance}}{\text{10 hr time period}} = \dfrac{62}{10}$ = 6.2 knots.

9. Time to rendezvous = $\dfrac{\text{Tot. Distance}}{\text{Eff. Speed}} = \dfrac{79.2}{6.2}$

= 12.77 hrs. (12 hr. 46')

10. Answers:

Course to steer	= 301° T.	Original Time	1700GMT
(East Wind) Leeway	= + 4°	Time to R'vous	1246
Course to counter	= 305° T.	R'vous Time	0546
Gyro error	= 2° H.	Zone (E. Long)	0800
Gyro Course	= 307° G.	R'vous Zone Time	1346 ZT.
		The following day.	

Example 4

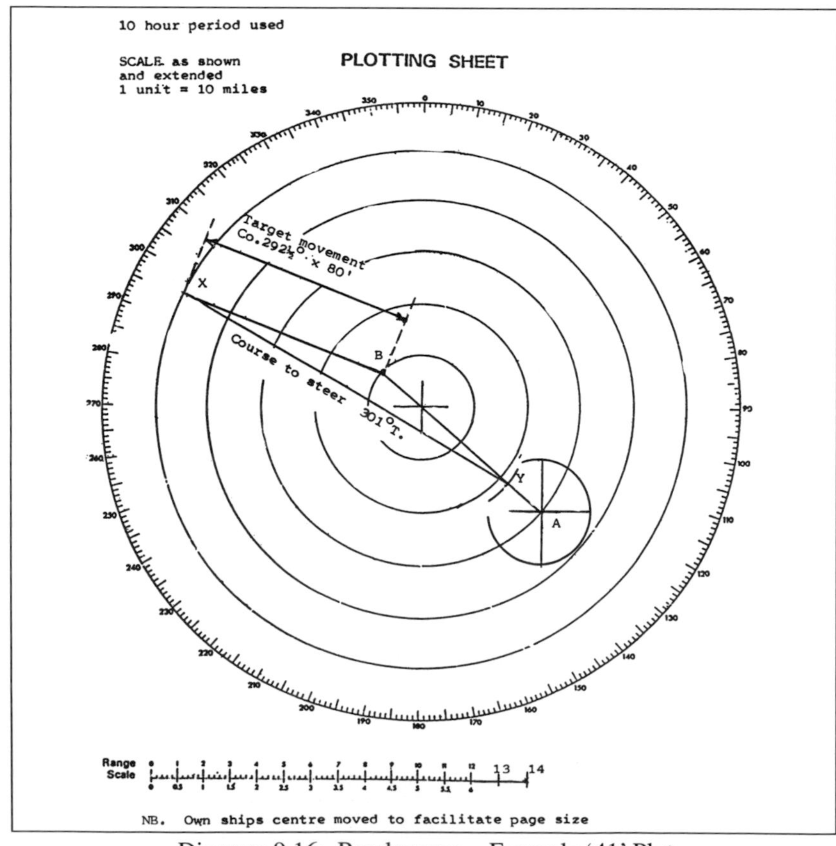

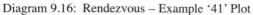

Diagram 9.16: Rendezvous – Example '41' Plot

Many problems, especially those in examinations, involve the use of current. They may also, through lack of information, require approximate positions to be established, prior to completing final answers. The following notations are meant as a guide to obtaining the final solution, where problems may be particularly testing.

1) If a current is given and a first approximate position is required, then the current should be ignored when working the first approximation. Accuracy is questionable anyway and the time factor for resolving the problem may be critical.

2) A current, if known, should be introduced at the second approximate position. This will provide a more accurate final rendezvous position.

3) To find the course to steer, by the other vessel, the current should be ignored.
i.e. Use the 'D. R.' of the rendezvous, to find course and distance of the other ship.

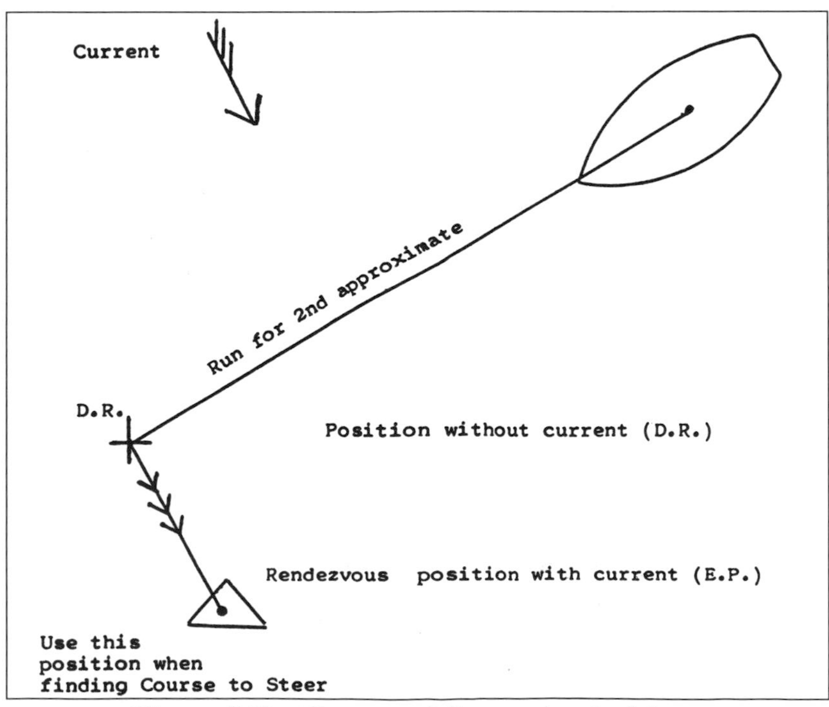

Diagram 9.17: Allowance of Current when Applying to 2nd Approximation Rendezvous Problems

Chapter Ten

MARINE HELICOPTER OPERATIONS

10.1 Routine Helicopter Engagement

When any vessel is to engage with an aircraft, whether it is for an emergency or a routine operation, the responsibility of the ship lies with the Master. The safe operation of the aircraft lies with the pilot and each rank should consider fully their obligations prior to commencing operations. It is normal practice for the ship's/company agents to arrange and contract the type of aircraft with the capabilities to carry out the engagement. It should be realised that helicopters engaged in marine operations should be twin engined and fitted with emergency flotation gear. In the case of a night engagement the aircraft would also require Instrument Flying Rating (IFR).

10.2 Master's Duties – Prior to Operation

The overall safety of the vessel should be of paramount concern throughout and to this end the Master would be expected to brief all operational personnel before rendezvous takes place.

The position of engagement should be plotted and the immediate area should be investigated. Adequate sea room, clear of obstructions and preferably with little or no traffic movements, is to be preferred.

An approach course towards the position should be appropriate to the general conditions. An approach speed in conjunction with this course should be proposed and the engine room informed accordingly.

Because of fuel limitations and the subsequent endurance of the aircraft, time is of the greatest importance to the pilot. Masters should therefore endeavour to assist in the conservation of fuel by steering towards the approaching aircraft whenever practical.

The Master's duties will include the 'con' of the vessel and time spent on the bridge before engagement will ensure all safety elements and respective checks can be made in plenty of time.

Manual steering will need to be employed and lookouts posted in ample time. Deck parties for helicopter reception will need to be deployed to carry out various equipment checks.

Special signals (ball-diamond-ball) will need to be made ready for display when the aircraft is sighted.

The Watch Officer should be maintaining the navigational watch throughout this operation.

The ship's position should be plotted with regularity and traffic avoidance should be an ongoing activity under the supervision of the Master.

Radar should be operational and all targets plotted to establish a clear area of operation.

Communications with the aircraft will probably occur before visual contact is established and relevant information should be prepared beforehand. A VHF listening watch from the onset would be required.

10.3 Helicopter to Ship Recognition

Helicopter pilots do not always find themselves engaged with a single ship operation and where more than one vessel is involved ship's Masters should endeavour to make their own ship more identifiable. This can be achieved in several ways and any or all might prove useful to gain the attention of the pilot and/or aircrew and make the vessel more prominent:

1. Provide the name and type of vessel designated. e.g. Container Ship.

2. Provide a confirmed rendezvous position in Latitude/Longitude or bearing and distance from a prominent landmark.

3. Display the ships call sign in International Code Flags.

4. Transmit a radio 'homing signal'.

5. Provide a description of the vessels colour scheme. e.g. Superstructure white, topside grey, boot topping red, upper decks green, emblem on funnel etc.,

6. Mark the deck operational area with an 'H' or 'Yellow Spot' as appropriate.

7. Make a volume of white smoke.

8. Display navigation signals Black Ball, Black Diamond, Black Ball as per the requirements of the COLREGS.

9. On sighting the helicopter provide a reverse bearing from the ship by radio.

10. Display wind sock indicator if available (Smoke or flags as alternative).

10.4 Air to Surface Communications in Routine Helicopter Activity

Pilots will expect an early radio contact which will identify the ship's name (or call sign). Confirmation of the rendezvous position, together with the vessel's course and speed and the ETA, would normally be passed between the two vehicles. Additional information with regard to the sea conditions, barometric pressure and wind direction at the site of engagement may be requested by the aircraft on approach. Clarification of the contact and engagement may also be sought. Such items as 'deck position' for either hoist or landing and details of relevant passenger/cargo being transferred, may also be required.

Pilots may request Masters to alter course or adjust speed for the actual period of engagement. The aircraft's approach, relative to the wind direction, could well dictate the need for a change of course by the vessel. It would be normal practice for the state of readiness of the vessel to be passed to the aircraft prior to the commencement of operations. Confirmation that the deck reception party was at a state of readiness and that fire parties were on stand-by would be expected.

NB: In the event of failure in radio communications, special light signals are prescribed as per the ICS '*Guide to Helicopter/Ship Operations*'.

Pic. 35: Pilotage delivery at sea onboard a tanker.

Pic. 36: Jayhawk helicopter HH-60 operated by the USCG as a medium range recovery aircraft.

Pic. 37: Routine landing procedure – RFA tanker.

10.5 Air Support

The use of helicopters in rescue operations has become an accepted norm. Their extensive use, together with commendable success, is possible only when incidents occur within their operational range. (Sea Kings are limited to 250 nautical miles radius without refuelling). Additional air support is possible, some helicopters can refuel while in flight (Jolly Green Giants) but additional back-up services are required in the way of tanker aircraft. Alternative support from the air could possibly be by dropping support material to a distress situation, e.g. life rafts, pumps, rations, communication equipment etc. However, it is pointed out that any operation which involves helicopters or other air support is extremely expensive and would not be called upon unless all other methods had either been exhaustively tried or the situation had deteriorated to such an extent that air support was the only viable response.

A typical air drop is shown, where a fixed wing aircraft drops a heli-raft to a would-be distress situation.

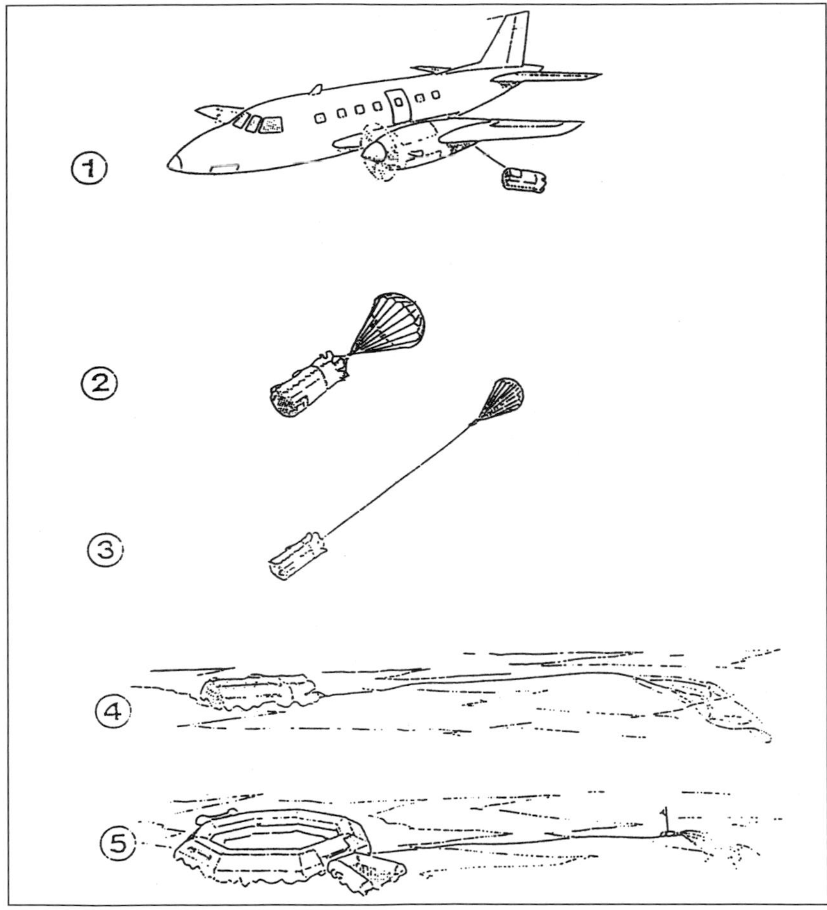

Diagram 10.1: The sequence of events when dropping liferaft from an aircraft.

1. The liferaft is packed, complete with survival pack into a special valise fitted with a static line and hook, the hook being attached to an anchor point inside the aircraft.
   When the raft is ejected from the door of the aircraft, the static line draws an activation pin from one end of the valise (Fig. 1).
2. The liferaft falls free, a spring vane parachute emerges and opens (Fig. 2).
3. The raft continues to fall in the same direction as the aircraft while a line is pulled from the valise against the drag of the parachute (Fig. 3).
4. The liferaft will strike the water first, to be followed by the 150 metres of line and then the chute (Fig. 4).
5. Once settled on the water, the raft will inflate automatically by the operation of a water activated unit.
   The parachute acts as a sea anchor with an attached float activated by a lifejacket operating head, a water activated light being secured to the float (Fig. 5).

1. Incident Report September, 1993.
   The RAF flew 3600 miles (round trip) from their base in the Falkland Islands to drop a 10 man liferaft and survival equipment from a Hercules transport, to Russian seaman adrift in the South Atlantic.

   The seamen had abandoned their vessel after cargo shifted in heavy seas. The position was nearly two thousand miles from Cape Town and 1750 miles east of the Falklands.

2. Jolly Green Giants – January, 1989.
   Two Sikorsky HH53C helicopters rescued 32 persons from the sinking bulk Carrier "*YARRAWONGA*" 750 miles west of Lands End. The operation required the aircraft to refuel while in flight, from hercules tanker transports.

Pic. 38: Air sea rescue operation. A Sea King Mk 2, helicopter carrying out winching procedure over the M.V. *Craigantlet*. (Reconstruction)

10.6 Air to Surface Hoist Operation

Pic. 39: A Royal Navy Sea King Helicopter engages in a hoist operation. Small deck area and rigging obstructions are of natural concern to aircrew members.

NB: Operational height of aircraft from the deck of the surface vessel and the existing weather conditions.

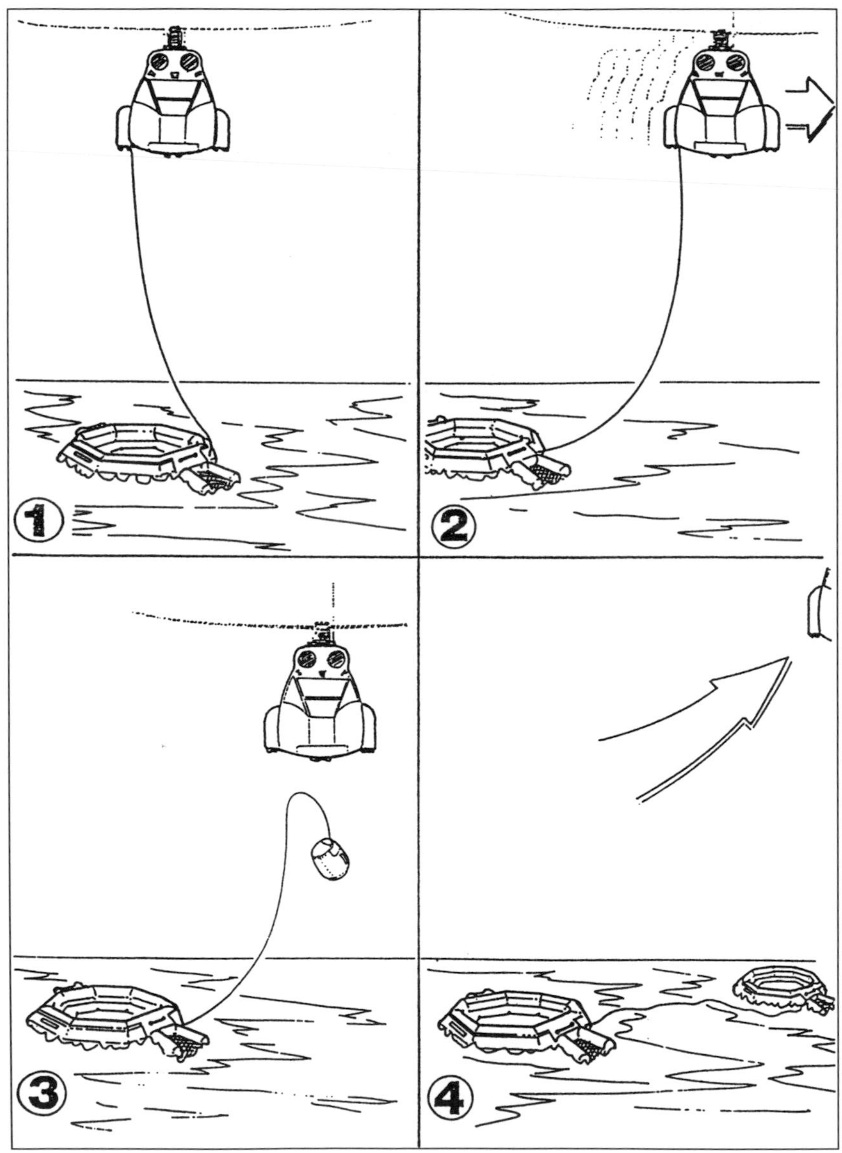

Diagram 10.2: Aviation liferafts being dropped to the surface by support aircraft.

UK SAR HELICOPTER COVERAGE AND MILITARY AIR COVER

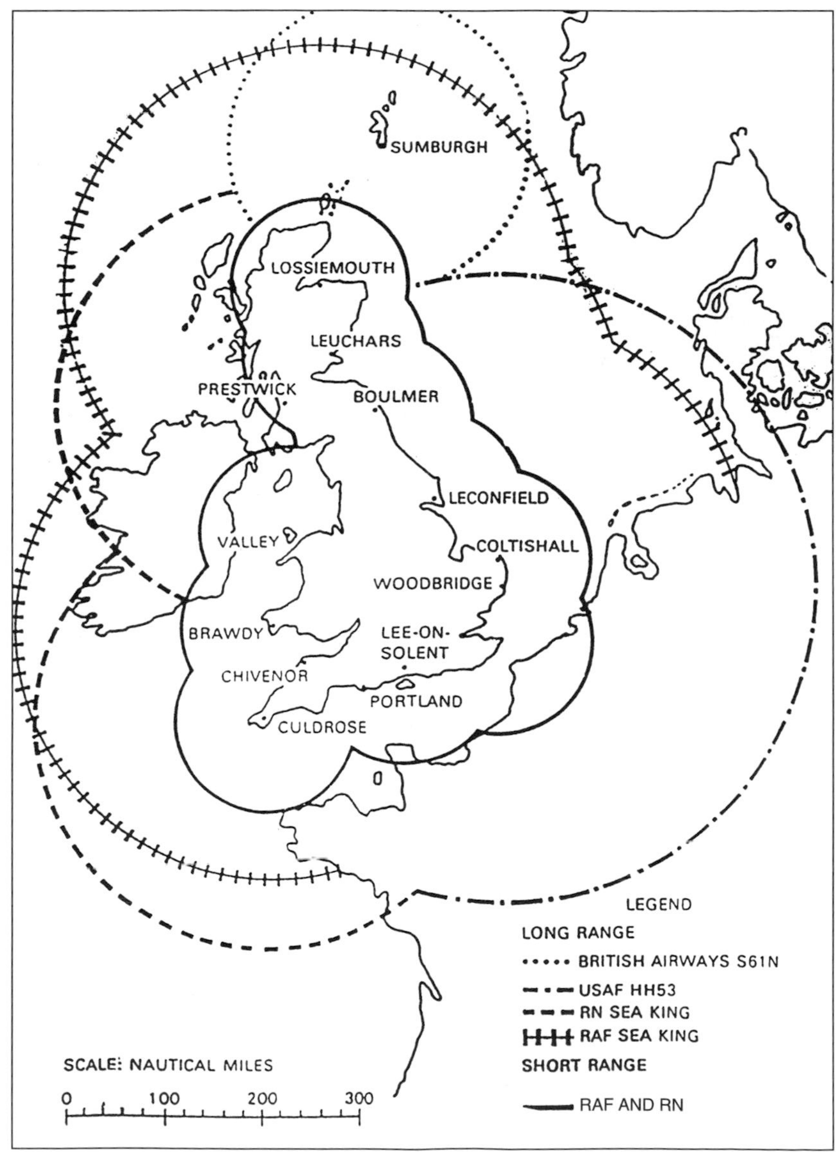

Diagram 10.3: Additional coverage by HM Coastguard S61N helicopters are available from Sumburgh, Lee on Solent and Portland.

Pic. 39: S61N, Sikorsky helicopter engaged in North Sea ferry operations from Aberdeen Heli-port, Scotland.

10.7 Helicopter Recovery

Marine rescues often involve helicopters either civil or military. In the event of a rotary winged aircraft being called in by the coastguard, mariners should be aware of basic format.

Most authorities operate on similar lines to the United Kingdom with generally only slight variations in procedure. In the majority of circumstances a member of the aircrew will descend from the aircraft prior to co-ordinating hoist operations. It is unlikely that the aircraft will attempt to touch the surface.

Landing on the surface would require an amphibious type aircraft and sea conditions would, by necessity, be ideal.

Would-be survivors must obey the instructions of the airman/ frogman. No possessions will be taken, the objective being to save life. Survivors should in no way hamper or try to assist the aircrew. If a passive attitude is adopted you would find that the hoist operation proceeds in a successful manner.

The rescue personnel are professionals and risk their own lives in rescue operations. Let them carry out their job with the minimum of aggravation. If you avoid panic and do what they tell you, your safety is virtually assured.

Single Hoist

This will occur by means of the lifting strop lowered from the winch of the aircraft. Place the strop over the head and under the armpits. Tighten up on the toggle clamp and ensure that the strop is comfortable across the back. Place your arms at the sides of the body after giving the thumbs up sign to the aircraft observer. (Some authorities require survivors to hold the clamp of the strop).

The airman will be recovered with the last survivor. When reaching the entrance to the aircraft, survivors in the strop should do nothing but wait for the instructions of the observer, follow his instructions and he will get you into the aircraft. In general, lifejackets will remain on throughout the period of operation.

Warning

In all hoist operations from helicopters a build-up of static electricity will occur prior to the wire being earthed. The pilot, who is in charge of the aircraft throughout, will earth this static charge by means of dipping into the sea or bouncing on the ship's deck, before commencing hoist procedures. Under no account should personnel attempt to touch the wire or strop before the static charge is removed.

Double Hoist

This will be the most common, where an aircrew member is hoisted with the survivor/casualty. Provided the survivor is conscious, a vertical lift will take place where the airman straddles the survivor. His legs, about the sides of the survivor, tend to act as a steadying influence during the hoist.

Again, attention is drawn to the fact that the person being rescued has little to do except assume a passive role. The airman will position the individual in the strop. When the hoist has attained the level of the access to the aircraft the aircrew will manoeuvre survivors from the wire into the aircraft. All the survivor has to do is follow the instructions of his/her rescuers.

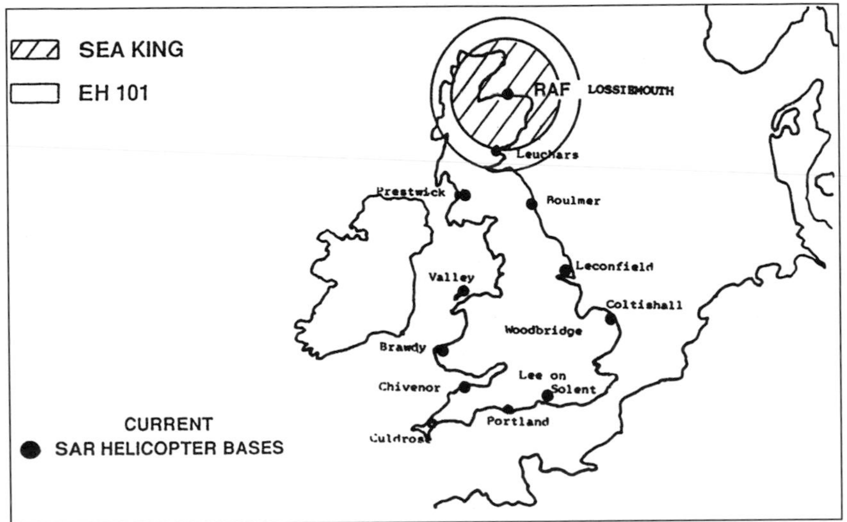

Diagram 10.4: *SAR Coverage 1 hour from call out* *Sea King/EH 101 – Merlin*

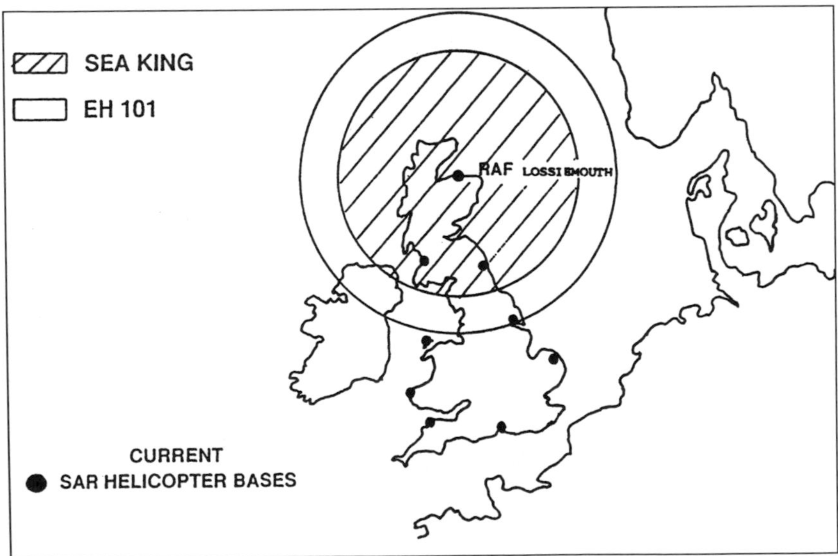

Diagram 10.5: *SAR Coverage 2 hours from call out* *Sea King/EH 101 – Merlin*

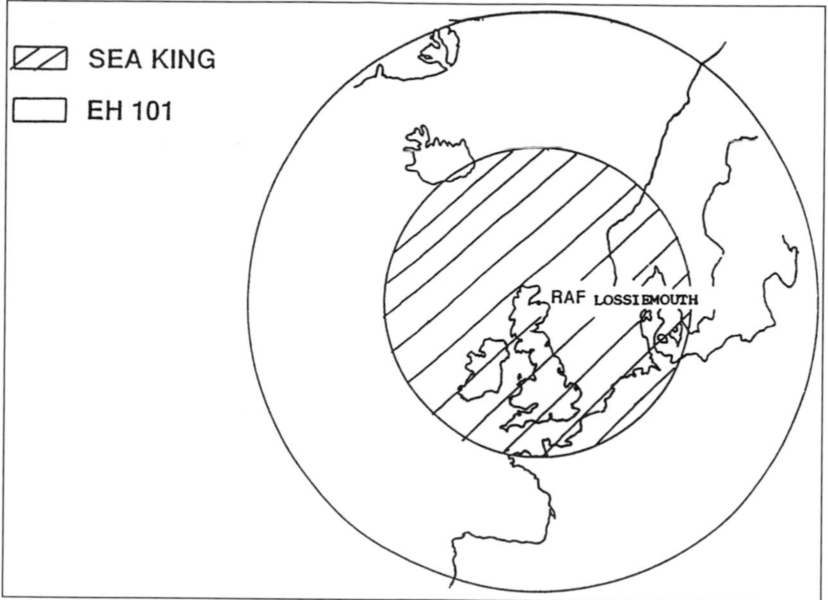

Diagram 10.6: *SAR Coverage (Fly through with maximum fuel)*
Sea King/EH 101 – Merlin

10.8 Helicopter Recognition

Pic. 41: RAF Sea King aircraft.
The winch is seen above the access doorway on the starboard side.

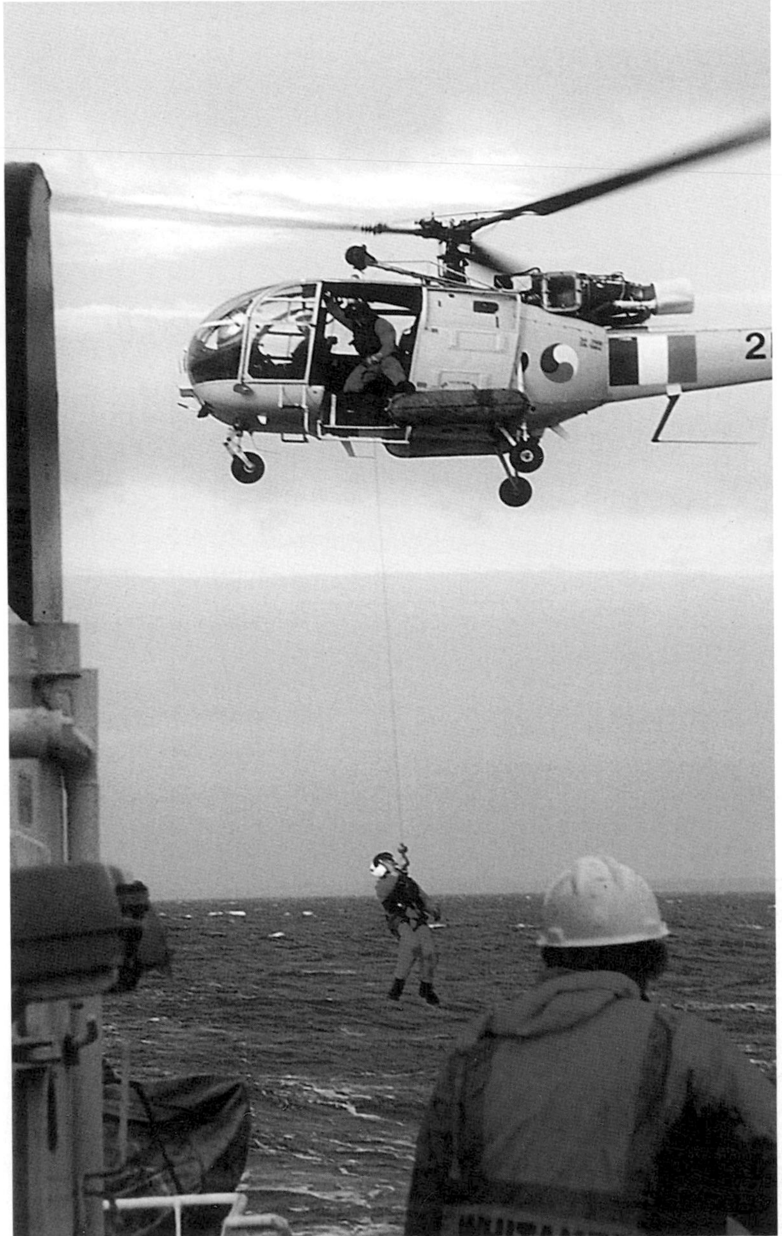

Pic. 42: An 'Alouette 3' helicopter fitted with floatation gear, engages in personnel transfer off the Falkland Islands, South Atlantic.

Helicopter Types and Operational Abilities

Type	Range nm. Operational	Payload (Human)	Speed kts	Remarks
Sea King	270	22	125	Range may be increased by reserve tanks
Puma	300	19	145	
S76	202	14	155 max	+ 30 minutes fuel reserve
Seahawk	200 est.	15 max	126	military
Sea Dragon/ Sea Stallion (Jolly Green Giants)	unlimited	55	150	Unlimited Rg with in flight re-fuelling
Dauphin 2 SA365	350	14	130	+ 30 minutes reserve fuel
Chinook	575	44	135	Tandem rotors
JayHawk	300	4 ≠ 6	146	USCG operation
Bell 214ST	250	20	145	Offshore/Transport
EH 101 Merlin	550	30	160	SAR for the 1990's

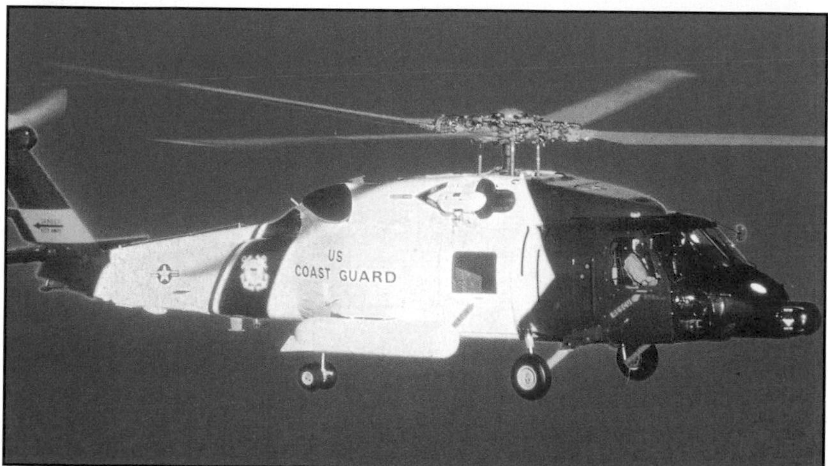

Pic. 43: Medium range recovery HH-60J Jayhawk helicopter in operations with the USCG.

10.9 Helicopter Evacuation Check-off List (MEDIVAC)

Patients Condition

Possible diagnosis, if known
Current condition of patient
Current medication patient is on and dosage taken
Pulse rate
Blood pressure
Past medical history, which may be significant
Any medication that patient may be allergic to
State: Is the patient ambulatory or incapacitated

Documentation (secured in waterproof cover)

Passport/Discharge 'A' documents for identification
Record of medication administered, quantity and time of administration
Shore-side contact address and telephone numbers if known

Weather Conditions

Sky condition (clear, overcast, broken)
Estimated cloud ceiling
Precipitation (rain, fog, drizzle, snow)
Wind direction and speed
Sea state condition

General Information

Ship's name and type of vessel
Vessels present position
Intended rendezvous position (Await confirmation)
Vessels course and speed
Departure port and next arrival port
ETA next arrival port

Chapter Eleven

OFFSHORE NAVIGATION

11.1 Navigation in and Through Offshore Development Areas

Any vessel passing close to or through areas of 'offshore activity' either for oil or gas resources, must expect to encounter particular navigational problems. The types of activities which tend to be continually ongoing are varied and could include any or all of the following:

Small boat activity, with or without divers, semi submersibles, anchor handling operations, either laying or recovering anchors. Helicopter movements to and from rigs and/or stand-by vessels. Mooring buoys, suspended well heads, towing movements or survey activity. 'No go' areas being prolific because of recommended safety clearance zones and rig movement causing concern with irregular position fixing duties.

When associated problems are also considered Masters and Navigators should take particular note that limitations on the use of anchors, because of undersea pipelines, manifolds etc. could be problematic in an emergency. Since the advent of 'slant drilling techniques' the radius of activity around an offshore installation could well be extended beyond what you may normally expect.

It is not unusual to encounter fairways for vessels to follow when proceeding through these regions (e.g. Gulf of Mexico). The fact that considerable volumes of small traffic may also be using the same fairways or even crossing them to attain a position on station at an installation is to be expected. Should these conditions prevail with poor visibility then obvious caution when proceeding must be a major concern. The type of problems Masters can expect to encounter in the vicinity of offshore installations are as follows:

11.2 Types of Offshore Structures and Hazards to Navigation

Production Platform

Slant drilling, small traffic, safety zones, toxics, helicopter operations, manifolds and undersea working, limitations on use of anchors, back scattering light.

Exploration Rigs (Non-permanent)

Position changing, chart unmarked, navigational corrections to chart are required, unspecified safety zones, anchor operations ongoing, mooring and marker buoys being widely deployed, towing activities are possible.

Seismic Survey Vessels

Restricted in ability to manoeuvre, possible diving operations or other undersea operations may require speed reductions by through vessels, marker or survey buoys on the surface, cables and other floating obstructions.

Wellheads

No anchoring because of submerged pipelines and undersea construction. Suspended well heads may or may not be charted. Some interference may be anticipated in use of the echo sounder. Tanker activity and mooring of tankers may be ongoing.

Jack-Up Installation

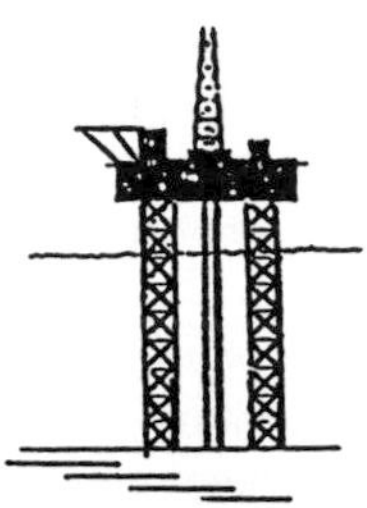

A typical example of an exploration structure. It is fitted with movable legs which are 'jacked-down' to the sea bed, once the rig has been towed onto site position. As the legs are turned down the floating barge section is raised above the surface level. It is usually found in operation in comparatively shallow depths 100-150 metres, the depth of operation being dictated by the length of the legs.

Fixed – Production Platform (Concrete Gravity)

First designed for gas recovery at depths of 30 to 50 metres. They are generally a very large structure often towering as much as 350 metres in height and now engaged in both oil and gas recovery.

Helicopter operations could be anticipated with considerable surface traffic in and around the installation. Tanker activity could be close by.

Protection safety zones must be expected and positions would normally expect to be charted.

Fixed – Production Platform (Steel Piled)

Large structure probably with under water manifolds in the proximity of the installation. Safety zones will be in operation and sub-sea vehicles could be operating in the area on manifold or pipeline inspections.

Seabed wellheads are a normal feature of production platforms and the use of anchors by through vessels may be restricted.

Floating – Semi-submersible (Production)

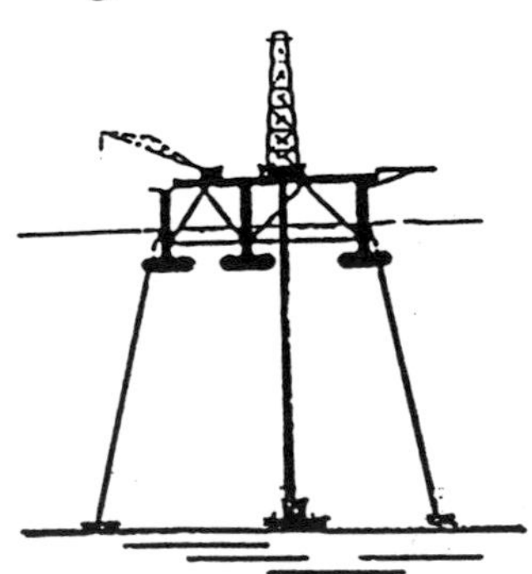

Self-propelled platform supported on submerged pontoons. These pontoons can be ballasted to raise or lower the rig. Submerged pontoons beneath the surface are less influenced by wave action. The vertical movement is reduced and this generally allows continuous working of the rig.

Operating depth about 400 metres, and the position is held by up to 8 anchors or by dynamic positioning. Marker buoys and surface traffic can be expected to be encountered around these rigs.

Floating-Drill Ship

Combine product production with product storage. The tanks of the drill ship being employed to hold prior to transfer into tankers. Use of a seabed 'riser' in both the Drill Ship, and the Semi-Submersible via well heads. A wide berth is recommended to all through traffic.

Guyed Tower

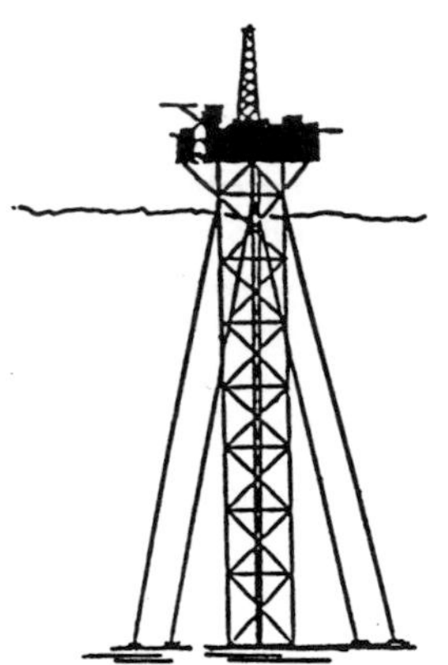

Lightweight and inherently buoyant steel tower which supports the platform, it's position being maintained by radial guy lines.

Drilling and production work can take place from these types of installations. Depth of operation is approximately 400 metres.

Alternative securing may be in the form of widespread guys to seabed 'Clumps' (weights) with associated anchors, 20 guy lines would not be considered exceptional. This type of structure provides the advantages of a fixed 'jacket' without the additional cost.

The Tension Leg Platform (TLP)

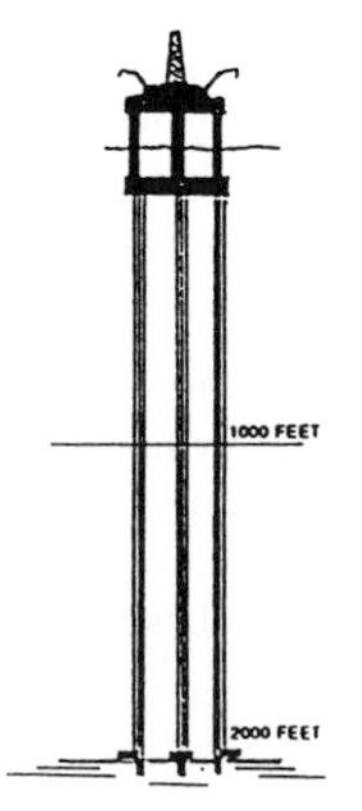

The tension leg platform is a tethered structure and can be encountered in depths between 120 and 1500 metres.

Oil process work is carried out and the operation is conducted by means of several sea-bed risers. Hydrocarbon products being pumped back down to an export pipeline. These rigs first came on line in the North Sea.

Position of the installation is held by excess buoyancy in the platform (15% – 25% of the structures displacement). This virtually eliminated roll and pitch motions on the rig.

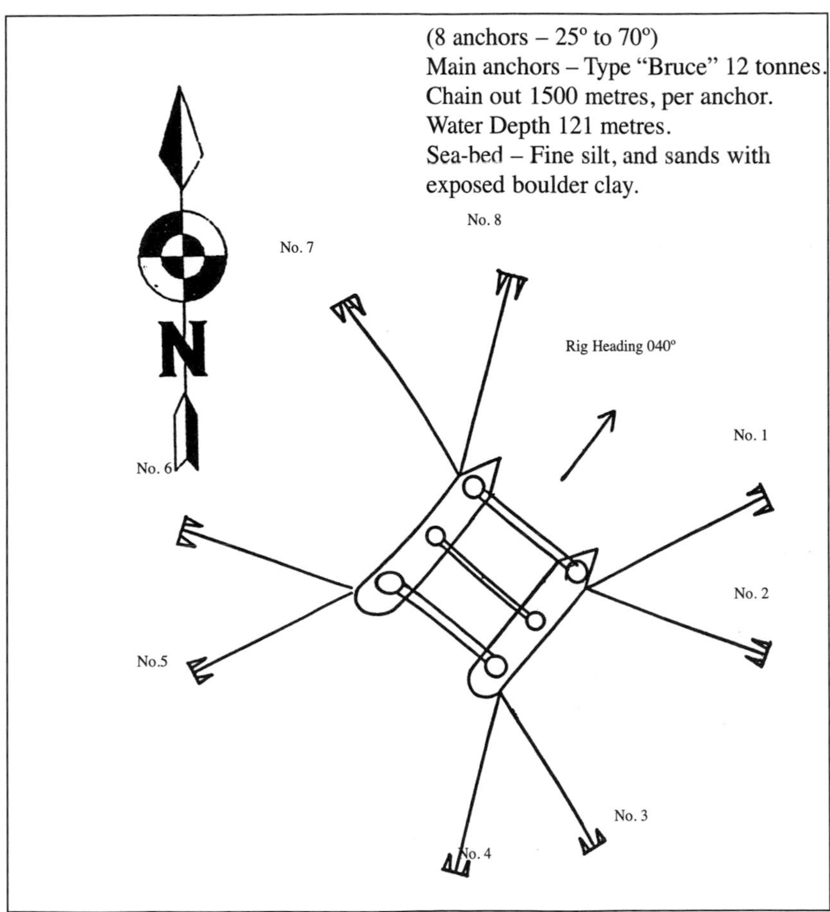

Diagram 11.1: Standard Mooring Array for Offshore Installation

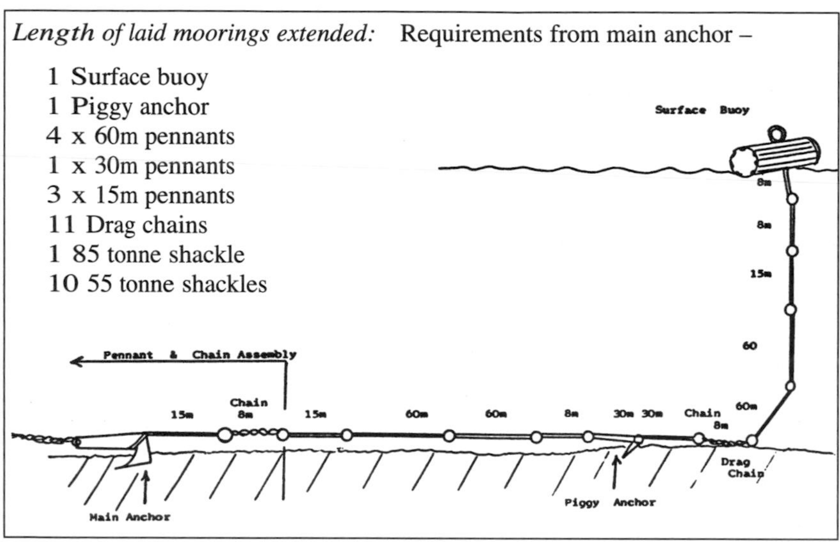

Diagram 11.2: Back-up (Piggy Anchor) Arrangement

11.3 Offshore Navigation

Passage plans often bring vessels into the confines of offshore operational areas. In the event of vessels passing through such an area the Master should advise the Navigation Officer with regard to certain obvious precautions when making up his passage plan for the Masters approval:

1. All the vessels proposed tracks should respect safety zones and fairways. (Ref. Mariners Handbook minimum safe recommended distances passing offshore installations 500m.)
2. Observe a safe practical speed when passing through the region to take account of special operations like towing or diving activities.
3. Update all charts with current navigation warnings, especially new dangers or 'rig moves' and respective positions.
4. Early warning of transfer from automatic steering to manual steering prior to entry into the area.
5. Highlight 'safety zones' around rigs, 'no go' areas, or areas of reduced soundings.
6. Emphasise monitoring points and radar conspicuous targets.
7. Use of appropriate publications and largest scale chart for the area.
8. Show focal points of heavy traffic density and where Master would be required to 'con' the vessel.

9. When allowing for contingency plans in the event of an emergency or for poor visibility, the use of anchors may not be a first option in offshore areas.
10. Early warning points for look-outs, use of engines, or for the purpose of doubling watches if required.

NB. At least two separate and distinct position fixing methods should be available to watch officers.

Navigation through fairways could be adversely effected by cross currents and both a primary and secondary position fixing method should be continuously available.

11.3.1 position fixing of offshore installations

The prudent navigator would investigate the positions of all installations, especially "fixed positions" like production platforms, and note the difference between these and moveable rigs such as exploration barges or drill rigs.

Information on production platforms being found in the following sources: Admiralty List of Lights, Sailing Directions, Annual Summary Notice to Mariners, Special Position Charts of a non navigational type. Navigation warnings regarding new developments.

Information on exploration rigs would be found in: Preliminary and Temporary Notices to Mariners (P's and T's), radio VHF warnings, Pilots and Port Authorities, local knowledge of company agents and from other shipping sources, also from the rig itself. All reports should be checked for variance.

11.3.2 recognition of offshore installations

The sheer size of an offshore structure, together with skyline silhouette, provides an easy target for the experienced mariners eye during the hours of daylight. However, during the hours of darkness the recognition may not be as simple without prior knowledge of the displayed navigational signals/lights.

Offshore installations should display red lights on each corner with an all round light (white), and these are associated with considerable background and working lights.

The red (corner) lights .... Range 2.0 miles
All round white light .... Range 15.0 miles

All these navigational lights are flashing 'U' in Morse code (· · –) at 15 second intervals.

11.3.3 in poor visibility

Installations are obliged to sound fog recognition signals as are other vessels on the high seas. Morse 'U' is sounded at 30 second intervals and must have an audible range of 2 nautical miles.

NB: In the event of failure of the all round white light, a back-up light of the same characteristics, but visible for 10 miles is automatically brought into operation.

Additionally:
Identification panels are carried so as to be visible from any direction. These panels will be either illuminated or on a retro-reflective background and will display the name of the rig or other designated identification mark. Normal display is by black letters on a yellow background.

Flare Boom

Many operational platforms will, through the nature of their operations, accrue unwanted gases and this is often burnt off via an extended flare boom. The burn-off is distinctive and clearly visible and vessels should not associate it with distress.

Radar Detection

All rigs and offshore installations usually provide an excellent radar target. However, where stand-by or supply boats are alongside these may not be clearly discernible from the installation itself. Additional small targets may also be prominent by way of marker buoys or moored lighters and close observation, especially when heavy levels of sea clutter are being experienced, is recommended.

11.4 Offshore Navigation – Summary of Miscellaneous Points

1. **Rig Positions** – Moveable drilling rigs and some fixed installations may have indicator buoys placed around the perimeter and extend towards the specified safety zone. These buoys may be frequently altered and rarely, if ever, will their positions be noted in navigation warnings.

NB: The position of the installation is specified in warnings but not necessarily all the relevant marker buoys.

2. **Development Sites** – New production jackets which are in the process of being constructed may not always project over and above the waterline. Approaching vessels may therefore experience little or no visual contact when navigating in close proximity to new developing positions.

3. **Large and Heavy Towing Operations** – Large offshore structures are often towed into position prior to establishing a permanent or semi-permanent position. Although normal anti collision regulations apply, watch officers should be aware of the need to provide a wide berth to these operations where appropriate.

   Several tugs could well be involved in towing moveable exploration rigs or similar structures. This could involve vessels having reduced sea room especially when navigating in or close to specified fairways. Early action to avoid approaching or creating a close quarters situation should be considered as a prudent action.

4. **The Use of Anchors** – In offshore regions anchors should be limited to emergency use only. Extensive pipelines, manifolds and undersea operations are well known features of offshore operations and the use of anchors should be in clear waters where there is an absence of obstruction.

5. **Tankers Off Loading/Loading** – The use of Single Buoy Moorings, (SBM's) is a main feature of many offshore regions. The movement of the tanker will be greatly influenced by tides/currents, an/or weather. Vessels engaged on regular trade through the region should subsequently provide a wide berth to such operations. In adverse weather conditions tankers may have to disengage, abruptly from the 'SBM' and due regard to passing distances of such operations should be considered in the light of prevailing weather conditions.

6. **Identification** – The majority of installations are well marked by name plates, navigational lights and/or specific markings. However, some unmanned structures may have limited markings

or no markings at all. Following bad weather or stormy conditions navigational marks may be damaged or destroyed and mariners may experience some difficulty in identification.

7. **Radar Use** – It is recommended that a continual radar watch is maintained in poor visibility and at night when on passage through an offshore region. This may mean that a 'double watch' rota is employed for a short period of transit through any high density areas.

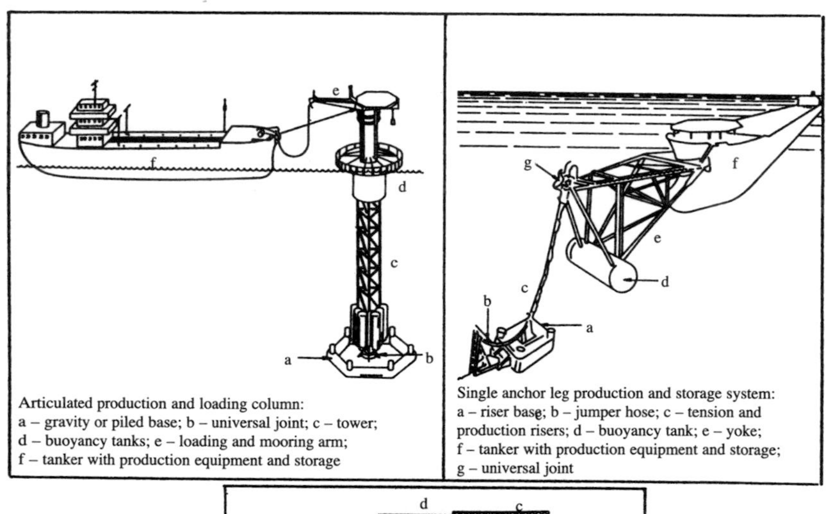

Articulated production and loading column:
a – gravity or piled base; b – universal joint; c – tower;
d – buoyancy tanks; e – loading and mooring arm;
f – tanker with production equipment and storage

Single anchor leg production and storage system:
a – riser base; b – jumper hose; c – tension and production risers; d – buoyancy tank; e – yoke;
f – tanker with production equipment and storage;
g – universal joint

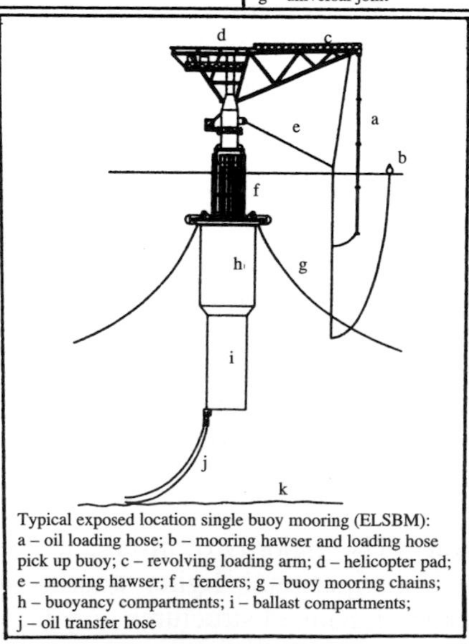

Typical exposed location single buoy mooring (ELSBM):
a – oil loading hose; b – mooring hawser and loading hose pick up buoy; c – revolving loading arm; d – helicopter pad;
e – mooring hawser; f – fenders; g – buoy mooring chains;
h – buoyancy compartments; i – ballast compartments;
j – oil transfer hose

Diagram 11.3: Offshore Mooring Operations

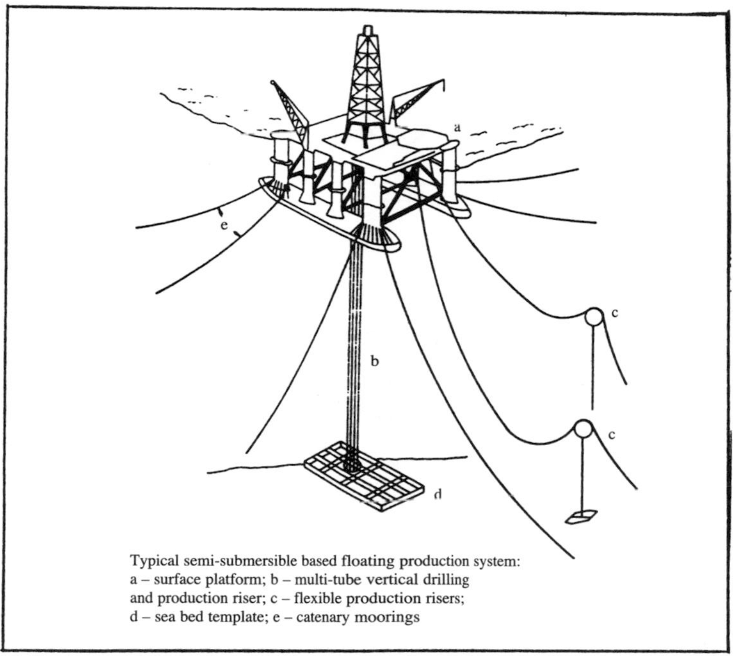

Typical semi-submersible based floating production system:
a – surface platform; b – multi-tube vertical drilling
and production riser; c – flexible production risers;
d – sea bed template; e – catenary moorings

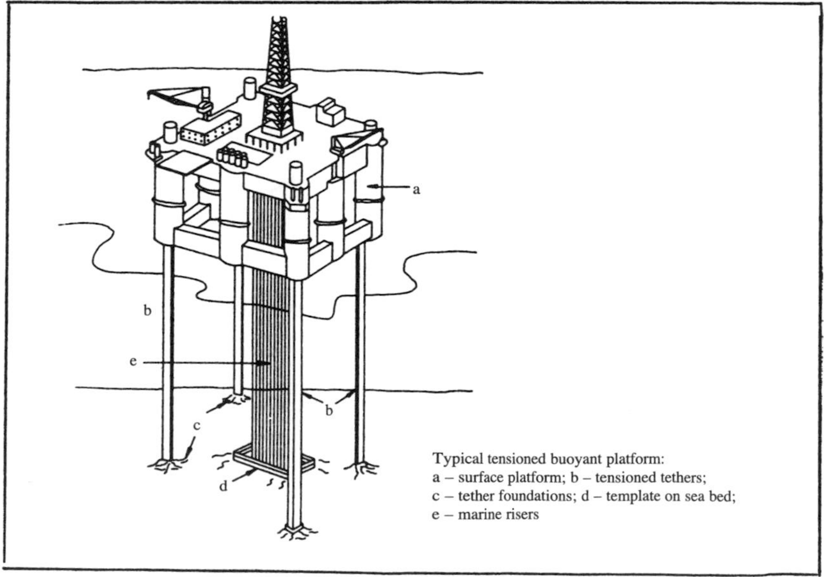

Typical tensioned buoyant platform:
a – surface platform; b – tensioned tethers;
c – tether foundations; d – template on sea bed;
e – marine risers

Diagrams 11.4 and 11.5: Offshore Example Structures and Areas of Navigational Hazards

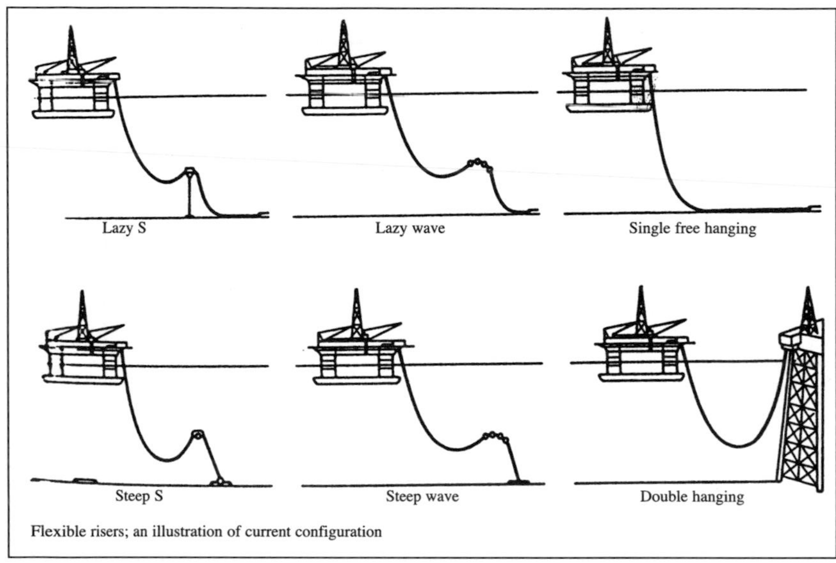

Flexible risers; an illustration of current configuration

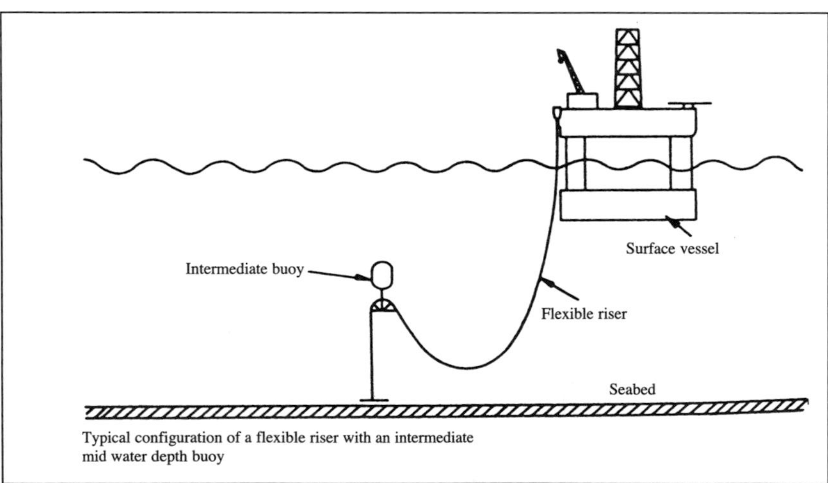

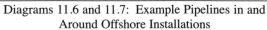

Typical configuration of a flexible riser with an intermediate mid water depth buoy

Diagrams 11.6 and 11.7: Example Pipelines in and Around Offshore Installations

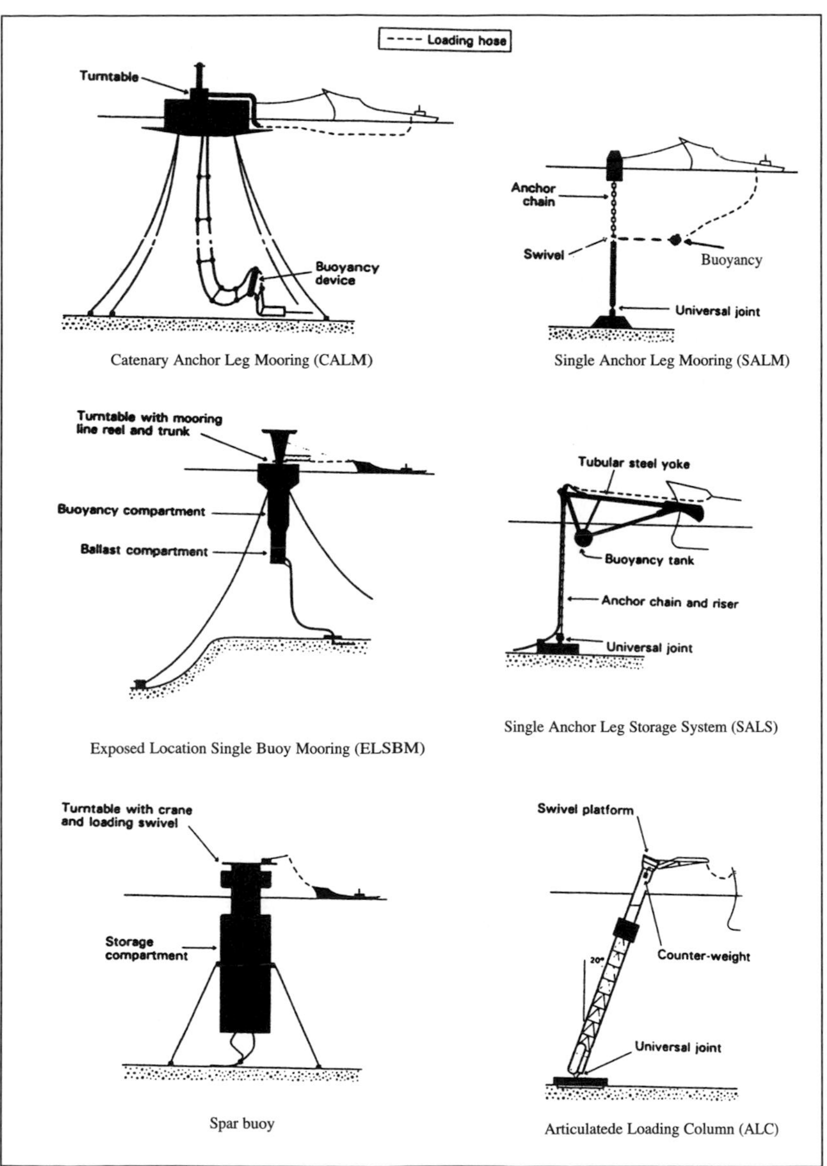

Diagram 11.8: Offshore Mooring Systems

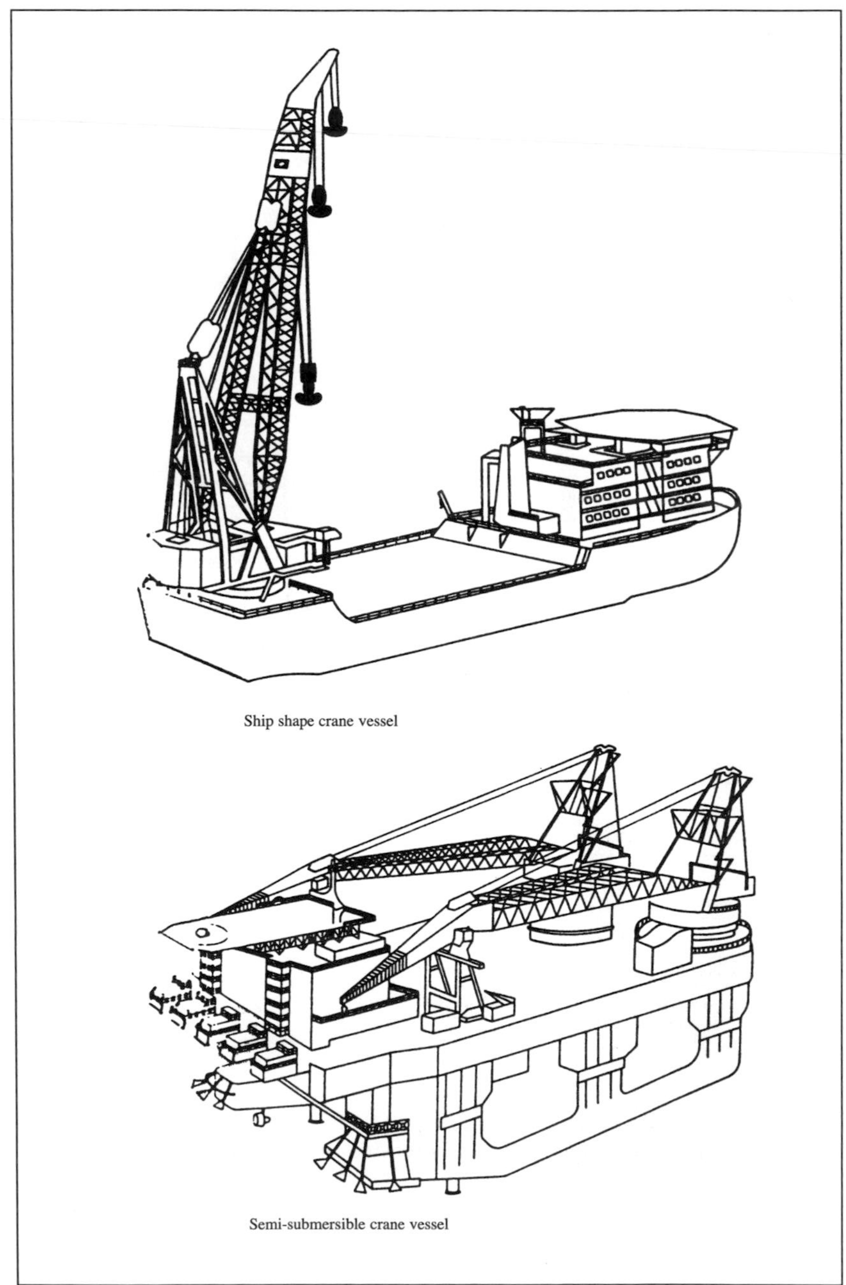

Ship shape crane vessel

Semi-submersible crane vessel

Diagram 11.9: Examples of Offshore Traffic

Pic. 44: Structures and Aspects of Offshore Installations.

Useful Sources of Offshore References and Information

When contemplating a passage through an offshore region, Masters and Navigators should seek out all relevant sources of information that may influence the required tracks. To this end reference to the following is highly recommended.

1. Navigational charts affecting the area in question.
2. Annual Summary of Notices to Mariners for current notices in force.
3. Routing Manual for guidance on recommended tracks.
4. Sailing directions regarding local knowledge, positions and fairways.
5. Local by-laws obtainable from the respective territorial authorities.
6. Weekly Notice to Mariners for current movements and updates.
7. Navigational warnings via coastal radio stations.
8. Relevant 'M' Notices:
   M1290.......... Safety Zones
9. Bridge Procedures for recommended safe practice.
10. Information from the installation itself. Position and movement.
11. Information (current) received from other outward/home-ward bound shipping.
12. Mariners Handbook for general background.
13. Pilots and Pilotage Authorities for buoy movements and positions.
14. Harbour Authorities for new navigational hazards and areas of new developments.
15. Operators charts (non-navigational) for limits of field operations.
16. Companies Agents for information current to arrival/ departure.
17. Admiralty List of Lights for positions and light characteristics.
18. Old 'Log Books' from previous voyages through the same region may also contain useful information.
19. Current or tidal stream atlas for local areas. Especially important for current stream directions crossing fairways.
20. Offshore Engineering – an introduction Angus Mather, Witherbys Publishing ISBN 1 85609 186 4.

DEPARTMENT OF TRANSPORT MERCHANT SHIPPING NOTICE NO. M.1290

OFFSHORE INSTALLATIONS – OBSERVANCE OF SAFETY ZONES

Notice to Shipowners, Masters, Officers and Seamen of Merchant Ships and Other Sea-going Vessels and to Owners, Skippers and Crews of Fishing Vessels

1. The attention of mariners is drawn to the 500 metre safety zones established around offshore oil and gas installations on the United Kingdom Continental Shelf. It is an offence, under Section 23(1) of the Petroleum Act 1987, to enter a safety zone except under the circumstances outlined in paragraph 5 below.

2. Safety zones exist not only to protect mariners by reducing the risk of collision but also to protect the lives and property of those working in the oil and gas industry, (divers and submersible vehicles are particularly vulnerable), and to reduce the risk of damage to the marine environment.

3. Under the Petroleum Act 1987 all oil and gas installations which project above the sea surface at any state of the tide are automatically protected by a safety zone.

4. Safety zones for subsea installations are established by Statutory Instrument in the form of Offshore Installations (Safety Zones) Orders, published by Her Majesty's Stationery Office. The existence of safety zones established by these Orders is promulgated by Admiralty Notices to Mariners, Radio Navigational Warnings and Fisheries Departments' fortnightly bulletins. Safety zones around subsea installations are invariably marked by light buoys on the surface laid as closely as practicable to the centre of the zone.

5. Safety zones can only be entered under the following conditions:

- (i) With the consent of the Secretary of State, or a person authorised by him;
- (ii) To lay, test, inspect, repair, alter, renew or remove a submarine cable or pipe-line;
- (iii) To provide services for an installation within the zone or to transport persons to or from it, or under authorisation of a government department to inspect it;
- (iv) For a general lighthouse authority vessel to perform duties relating to the safety of navigation;
- (v) To save life or property, owing to stress of weather or when in distress.

6. Entry into a safety zone by an unauthorised vessel makes the owner, master and others who have contributed to the offence liable on summary conviction to a fine not exceeding £2,000 at the present time, and on conviction on indictment, to imprisonment for a term not exceeding 2 years, or to a fine or to both.

7. Development areas are certain fields, marked on Admiralty Charts which are being developed or are currently producing oil or gas. Within these areas there are likely to be construction and maintenance vessels, including submarine craft, divers and obstructions possibly marked by buoys. Supply vessels and, in some cases, tankers, frequently manoeuvre within these fields. Mariners are strongly advised to keep outside such areas.

8. Vessels which are transitting or passing close to areas of offshore activity should navigate with care through or near these areas giving due consideration to safe speed and safe passing distances, taking into account the prevailing weather conditions and the presence of other vessels or dangers. A continuous listening watch should be maintained on VHF channel 16 when navigating in or near areas where offshore activities are taking place.

9. It is important for the safety of all those working in the hostile environment offshore that mariners respect the safety zones around offshore installations by keeping clear of them at all times. Mariners are advised always to assume the existence of a safety zone unless they have information to the contrary.

Department of Transport
Marine Directorate
London WC1V 6LP
September 1987

Dd 9610873 14,000 9/87 Ed (249751)

Chapter Twelve

TIDE CALCULATIONS

12.1 Introduction

All the following examples have been worked using the Admiralty Tide Tables. In the case of European Tides Volume 1, European Waters 1987 has been employed. In the case of Pacific Tides Volume 3. Pacific Ocean 1988 has been employed.

NB: Alternative methods of resolving tidal problems may be used and if these are required the reader is directed to examples found in the front of the Admiralty Tables.

Prior to working through the following examples marine students are advised to make themselves familiar with the terms and definitions on the following pages.

For practical use the mariner is advised that the predictions are given for average meteorological conditions. In the event that conditions differ from the average, variations in the tidal heights and times can be anticipated. Such changes can be caused by unusually high or low barometric pressure, strong winds causing 'storm surges', or 'negative surges'.

Attention is drawn to references in the Annual Summary of Notices to Mariners, specifically:

No's '1' & '15', regarding under keel clearance and allowance and negative surge warning services.

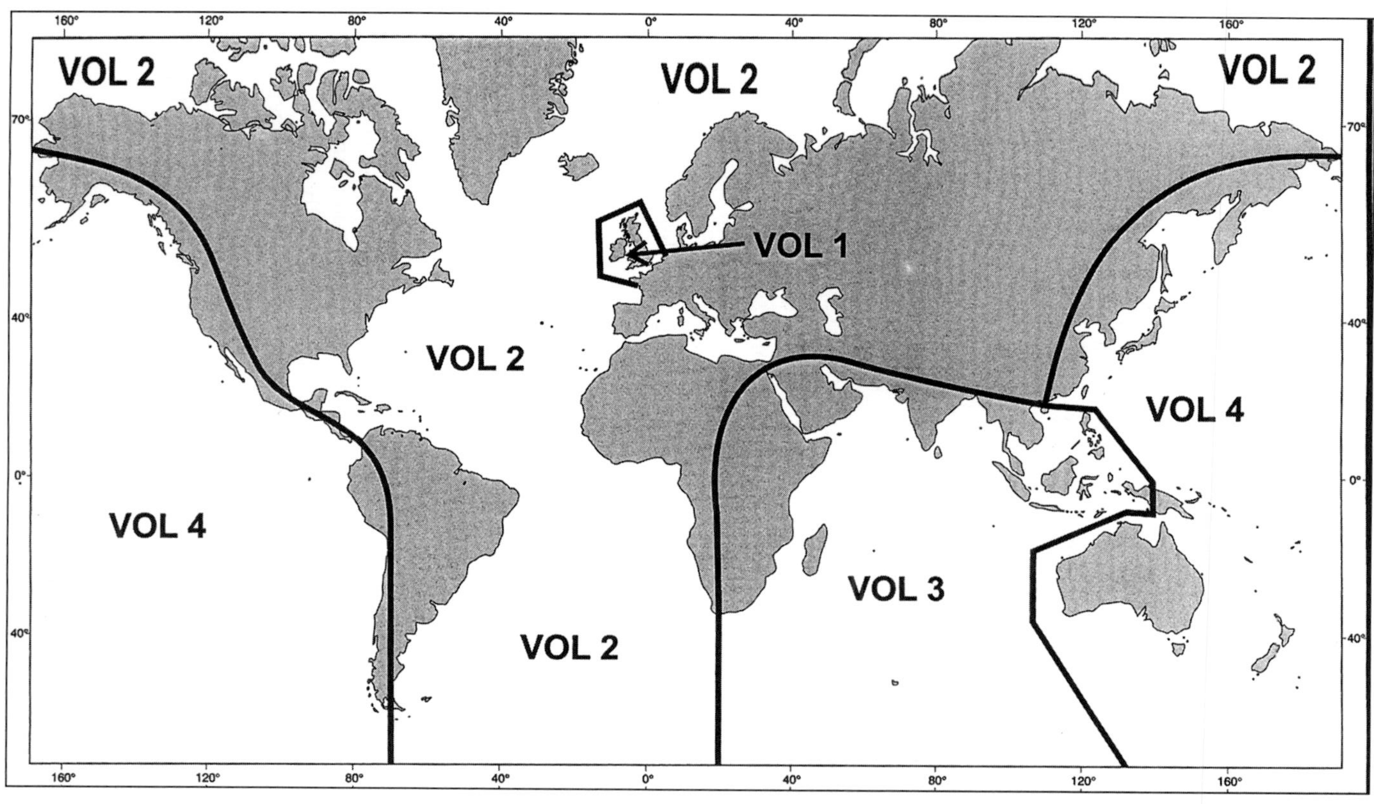

Diagram 12.1: Limits of Admiralty Tide Tables

Volume 1 – United Kingdom and Ireland (including European Channel Ports)
Volume 2 – Europe (excluding United Kingdom and Ireland), Mediterranean Sea and Atlantic Ocean
Volume 3 – Indian Ocean and South China Sea
Volume 4 – Pacific Ocean

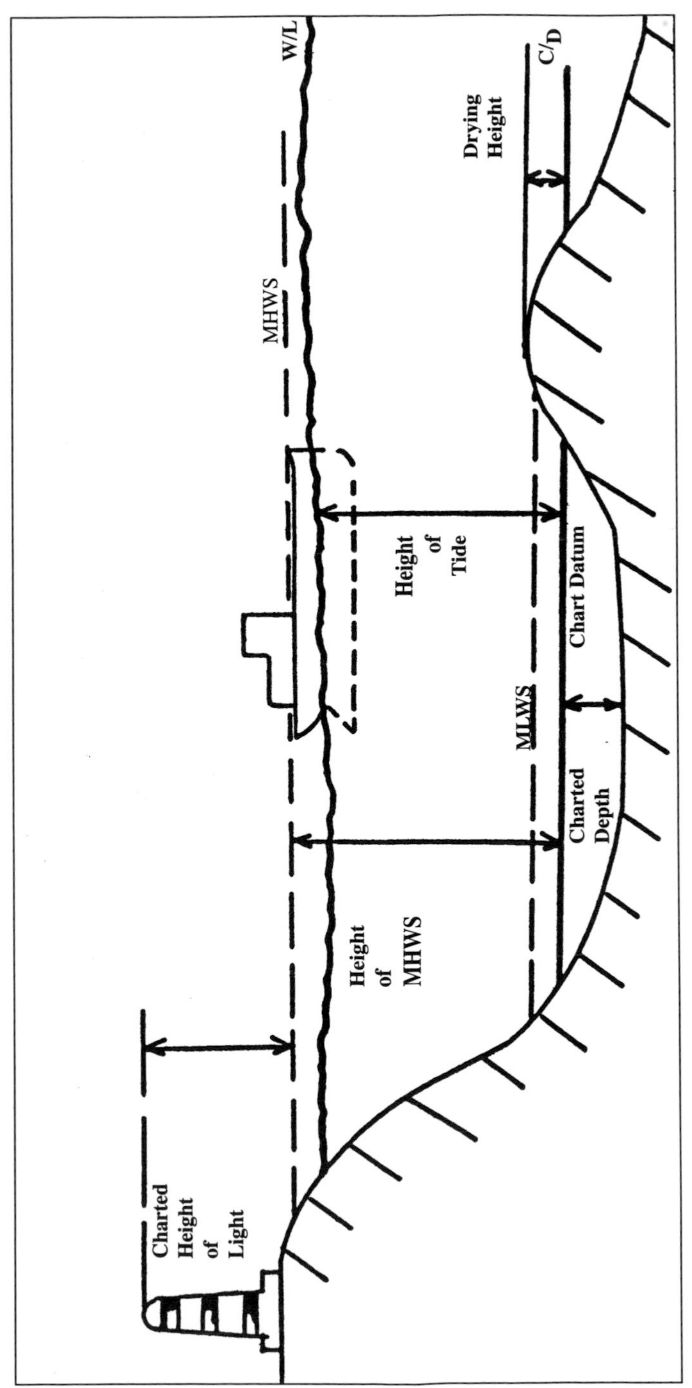

Diagram 12.2: Tidal Terminology

Tidal/Tides – Definitions

(a) *SPRING TIDE* is a tide occurring twice a month, of maximum range, when the sun and moon are in conjunction or opposition.

(b) *NEAP TIDE* is a tide occurring twice a month, of minimum range, when the moon is in quadrature.

(c) *HEIGHT OF TIDE* is the height of the water level, at any particular time, measured above chart datum, by taking the height of low water, and adding the rise of the tide.

(d) *M.H.W.S.* is the height of *Mean High Water Spring* Tides, taken as an average, throughout a year when the average maximum declination of the moon is 23½°, of two successive high waters in 24 hours when the range of tide is greatest.

(e) *M.L.W.S.* is the average height obtained by the two successive low waters during the same period.

(f) *M.H.W.N.* The height of *Mean High Water Neap* Tides, is the average of two successive high waters when the range of tide is least – same conditions as in (d).

(g) *M.L.W.M.* is the average height obtained from two successive low waters during the same period.

(h) *RANGES OF TIDES* are the differences in height between successive high waters and low waters or low waters and high waters.
NB: in most cases, the range of a tide will be slightly different to the tidal range before, and to the one after, as the time of spring or neap tides approaches.

(i) *SPRING RANGE* is the difference in height between M.H.W.S. and M.L.W.S. It is normally the greatest range experienced, occasionally exceeded when astronomical conditions cause L.A.T., and/or when meteorological conditions (wind) build up or reduce the water level.

(j) *NEAP RANGE* is the difference in height between M.H.W.N. and M.L.W.N. It is normally the smallest range experienced, under normal conditions.

(k) *CHART DATUM* is the standard depth, usually at the level of M.L.W.S. (or L.A.T. in some ports) from which to measure depths of shoals, or heights or rocks etc. which show above the water at low tide.

(l) *HEIGHT OF SHORE OBJECTS,* is charted above M.H.W.S. and to find correct height, add fall of tide below M.H.W.S.

12.2 Standard Port Tide Examples

Example 1.

Find the height of the tide off Liverpool at 1400 hrs on 20th May, 1987.

HW	1704	7.7m
LW	1112	2.0m
Range		5.7m Neaps

Extract from Table		
	MAY	
20th	0416	8.2
W	1112	2.0
	1704	7.7
	2342	2.7

Method: Plot heights of high and low water on graph.
Construct graph between these points.
Insert high water time in 'HW' box

Apply the required time 1400 hrs to the HW time and insert the hourly rates into the remaining boxes.

Construct a vertical to intercept the curve from that point of 1400 hrs.

From the point of intersection with the curve construct a horizontal to intersect the graph line.

Construct a vertical towards the height scale, and read height off scale.
= 4.6 metres

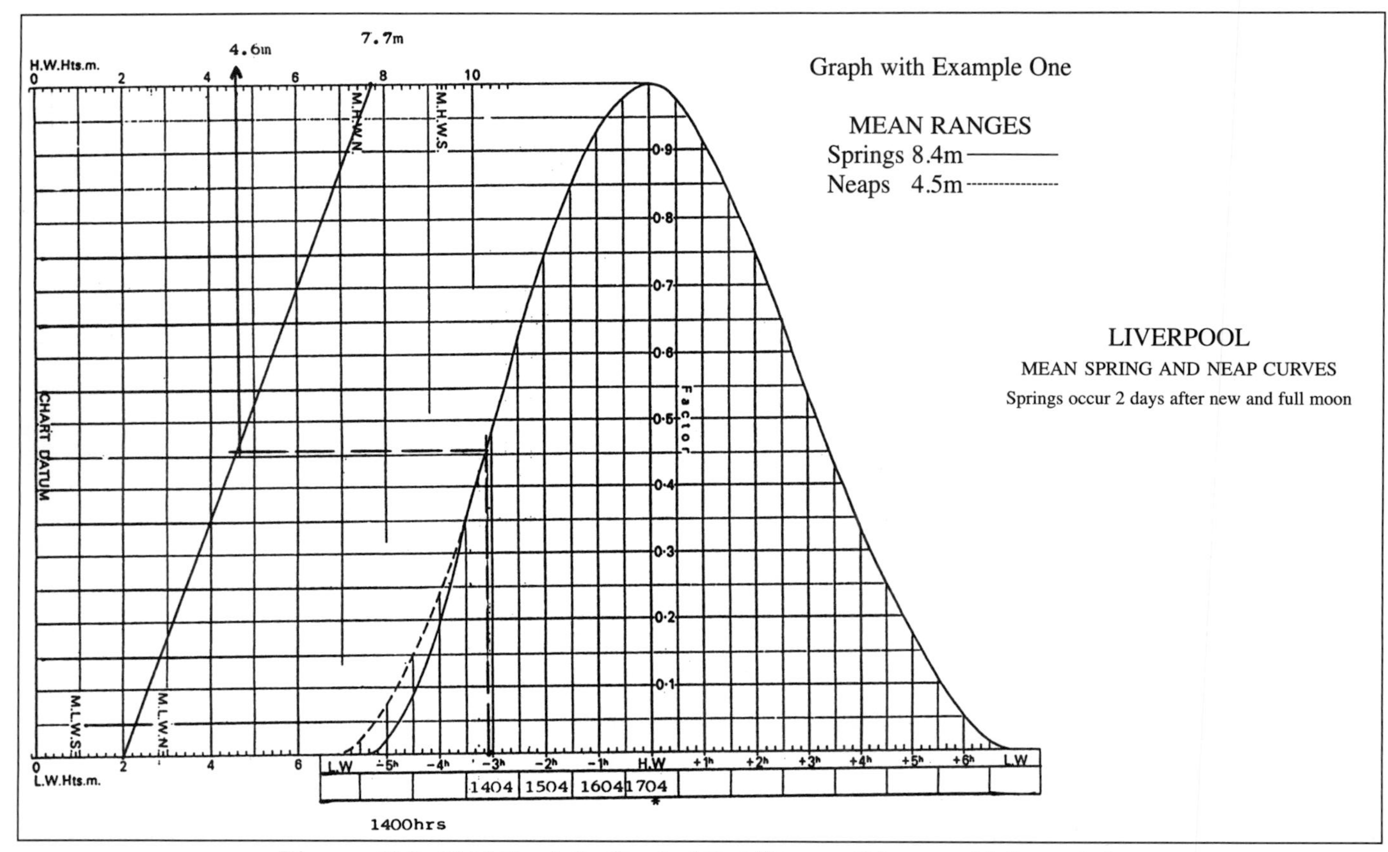

Diagram 12.3: Tidal Graph for Standard Port 'Liverpool' for use with Example 1

Example 2.

A vessel with a draught of 9.4 metres anchors off Liverpool, at 1030 hrs on the 6th June, 1987. At what time, on the next rising tide would she be able to cross a bar which is charted as 5.0 metres, with a clearance of 0.5 metres beneath the keel.

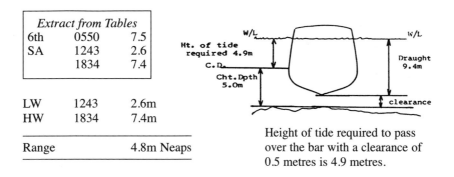

Extract from Tables		
6th	0550	7.5
SA	1243	2.6
	1834	7.4

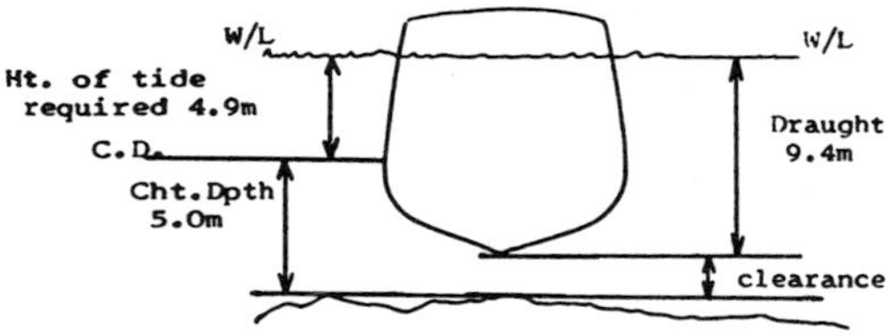

LW	1243	2.6m
HW	1834	7.4m
Range		4.8m Neaps

Height of tide required to pass over the bar with a clearance of 0.5 metres is 4.9 metres.

Method: Note rising tide between 1243 to 1834 hrs.
Plot heights of high & low waters on graph.
Construct graph line between these points.
Insert high water time in 'HW' box.

Establish 4.9 metre height required on upper scale.
Construct a vertical from this point to intersect graph line.

From this intersection construct a horizontal to meet the rising curve.

From this point construct a vertical to intersect with the lower time scale
= 1534 hrs (for a ht of tide = 4.9m)

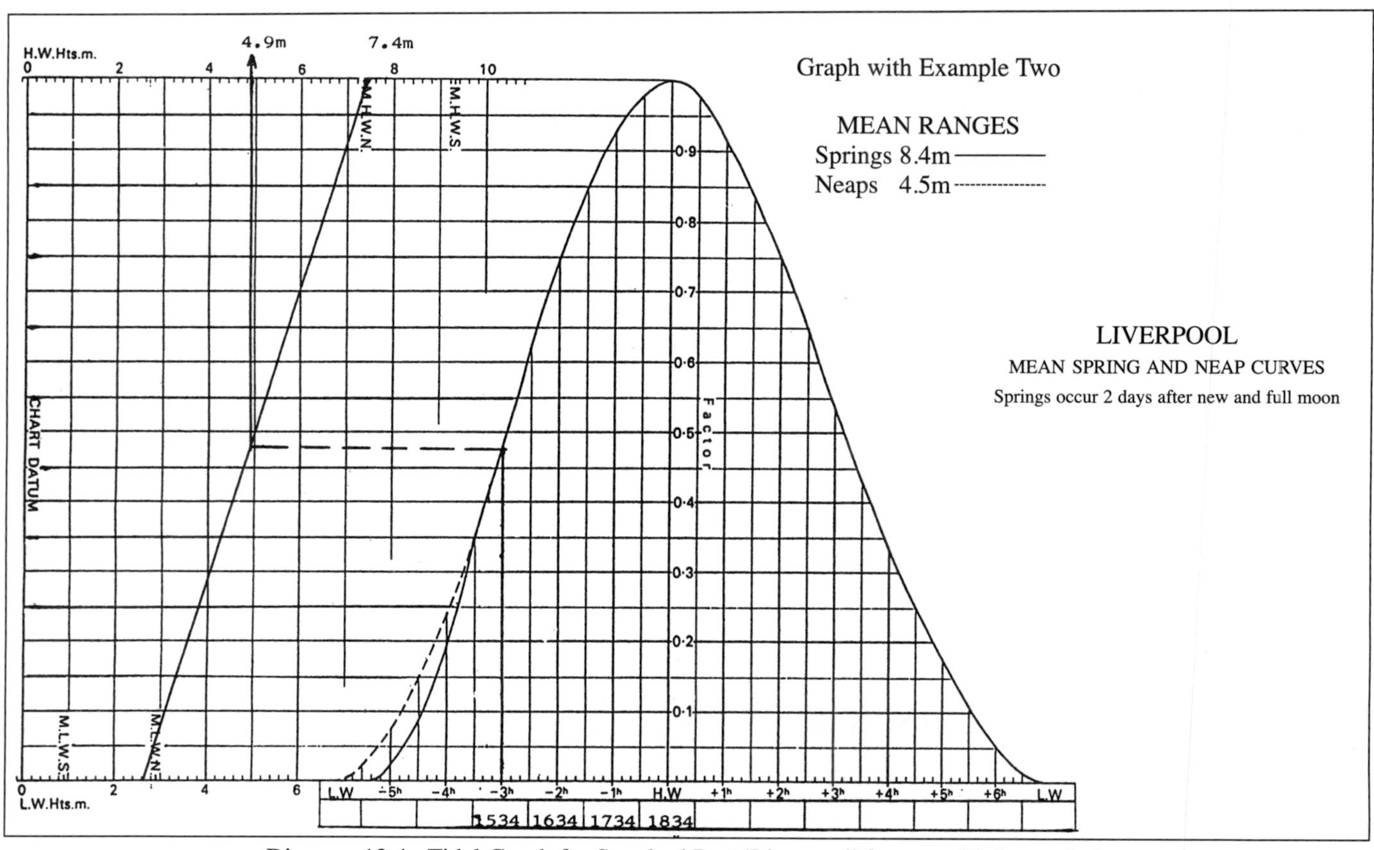

Diagram 12.4: Tidal Graph for Standard Port 'Liverpool' for use with Example 2

Example 3. Secondary Port

Calculate the underkeel clearance of a vessel whose draught is 4.5 metres at Portpatrick at 1130 GMT on 3rd March 87. When the charted depth is 3 metres.

Times	**LW**	**HW**
L'pool Pred	0751	1326
Pt. Pat Diff	– 0034	+0020
Pt. Pat Pred	0717	1346

Heights	LW	HW
L'pool	0.7	9.7
L'pool S/C	0.1	0.1
L'pool Pred	0.8	9.8
Pt. Pat Diff	– 0.53	– 5.79
	0.27	4.01
Pt. Pat S/C	0.0	0.0
Pt. Pat Pred	0.27	4.01

From graph height of tide at 1130 = 2.8 m.
therefore underkeel clearance = 1.3m.

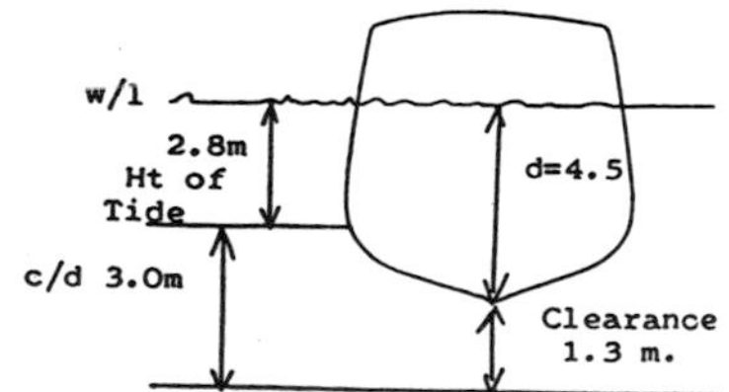

HW

1200	+ 0018	1200
1800	+ 0026	1326
6hrs	8'	1hr 26'
360'	8'	86

$\frac{8}{360}$ x 86 = 1.91 = 2'

0018 + 2' = 0020

LW

0200	0000	0200
0800	– 0035	0751
6hrs	35'	5hr 51'
360'	35'	351'

$\frac{35}{360}$ x 351 = 34'

0000 + 34 = – 0034

HW

9.3	– 5.5	9.3
7.4	– 4.4	9.8
1.9	1.1	0.5

$\frac{1.1}{1.9}$ x 0.5 = 0.29

– (5.5 + 0.29) = – 5.79

LW

2.9	– 2.0	0.9
0.9	– 0.6	0.8
2.0	1.4	0.1

$\frac{1.4}{2.0}$ x 0.1 = 0.07

– (0.6 + 0.07) = – 0.53

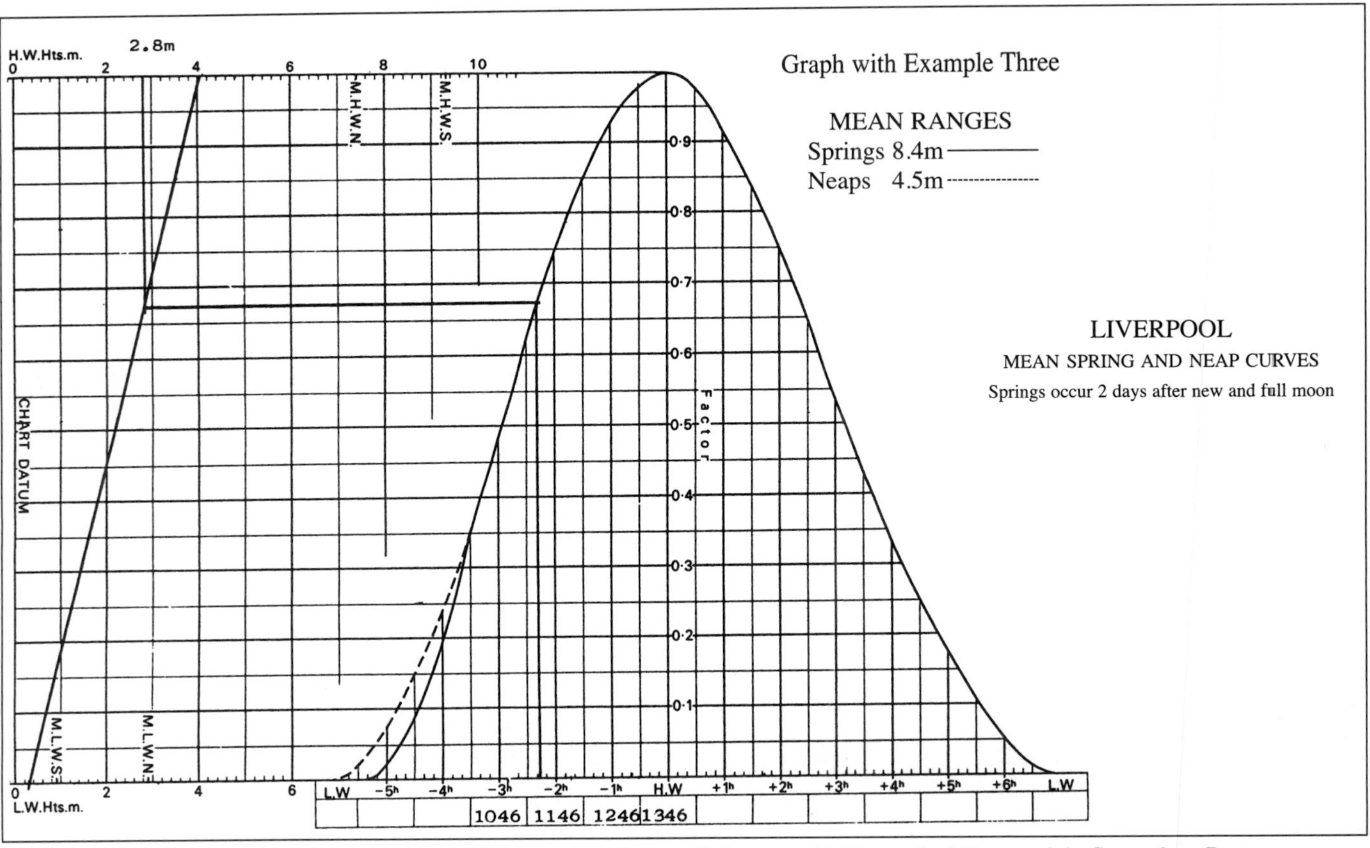

Diagram 12.5: Tidal Graph for Standard Port 'Liverpool' for use with Example 3 Portpatrick, Secondary Port

Example 4. Secondary Port

Find the height of a light at Portpatrick charted as 37 metres, at 2130 hrs on 21st June, 1987.

Times	**HW**	**LW**
L'pool Pred	1948	0227
Pt. Pat Diff	+ 0024	– 0003
Pt. Pat Pred	2012	0224

Heights	HW	LW
L'pool	7.8	2.4
L'pool S/C	0.0	0.0
L'pool Pred	7.8	2.4
Pt. Pat Diff	– 4.7	– 1.65
	3.1	0.75
Pt. Pat S/C	0.0	0.0
Pt. Pat Pred	3.1	0.75

From graph height of tide at 2130 hrs = 2.8 metres

M.H.W.S. L'pool	9.3 m.
Pt. Pat Diff.	– 5.5 m.
Pt. Pat M.H.W.S.	3.8 m.
Cht. Ht. of light	37.0 m.
Ht above Cht. Dat.	40.8 m.
Ht of tide	2.8 m.
Ht. of light	38.0 m.

Working

HW

0000	+ 0018	2400
1800	+ 0026	1948
6hrs	8'	4hr 12'
360'	8'	252'

$\frac{8}{360}$ x 252 = 5.6 (approx 6')

0018 + 6' = 24'

LW

0200	0000	0200
0800	– 0035	0227
6hrs	35'	27'
360'	35'	27'

$\frac{35}{360}$ x 27 = 2.62 (approx 3')

0000 + 3' = – 0003

HW

9.3	– 5.5	9.3
7.4	– 4.4	7.8
1.9	1.1	1.5

$\frac{1.1}{1.9}$ x 1.5 = 0.8

– (5.5 – 0.8) = – 4.7

LW

2.9	– 2.0	2.9
0.9	– 0.6	2.4
2.0	1.4	0.5

$\frac{1.4}{2.0}$ x 0.5 = 0.35

– (2.0 – 0.35) = – 1.65

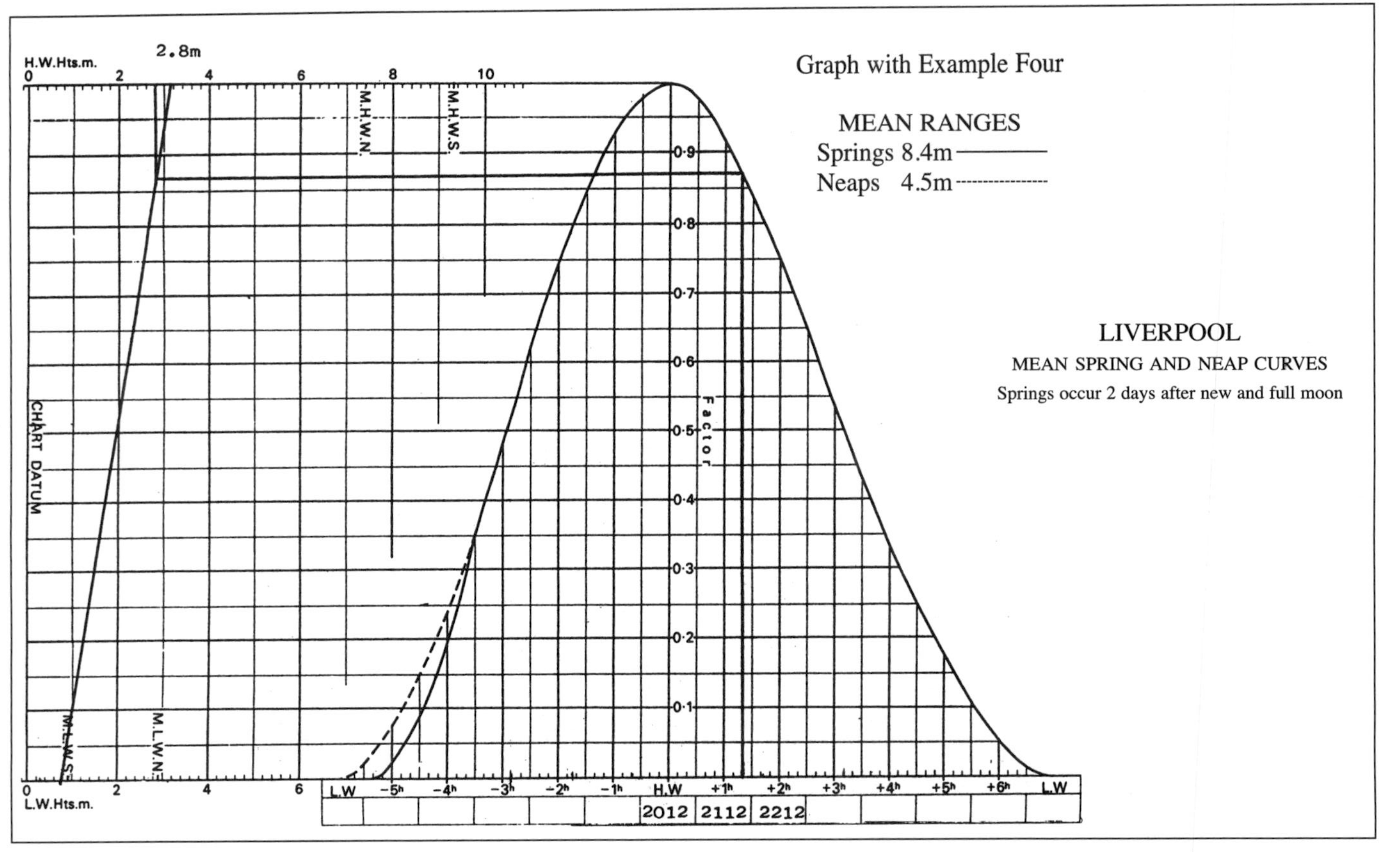

Diagram 12.6: Tidal Graph for Standard Port 'Liverpool' for use with Example 4 Portpatrick, Secondary Port

ENGLAND, WEST COAST – LIVERPOOL

LAT 53'25'N LONG 3'00'W

TIME ZONE GMT — TIMES AND HEIGHTS OF HIGH AND LOW WATERS — YEAR 1987

JANUARY

Day	TIME	M	Day	TIME	M
1 TH	0614 1150 1845	1.0 9.7 0.8	16 F	0614 1204 1848	1.9 8.9 1.7
2 F	0018 0703 1239 1935	9.5 1.0 9.7 0.7	17 SA	0022 0648 1236 1921	8.7 1.8 8.9 1.6
3 SA	0109 0749 1328 2025	9.3 1.1 9.6 0.8	18 SU	0056 0721 1310 1957	8.7 1.7 8.9 1.6
4 SU	0157 0836 1416 2112	9.1 1.4 9.4 1.0	19 M	0130 0758 1342 2032	8.6 1.8 8.8 1.7
5 M	0246 0924 1504 2159	8.7 1.7 9.1 1.4	20 TU	0202 0833 1418 2107	8.5 1.9 8.7 1.8
6 TU	0334 1012 1553 2248	8.3 2.1 8.6 1.9	21 W	0242 0911 1454 2145	8.3 2.1 8.5 2.1
7 W	0426 1105 1647 2342	7.9 2.6 8.2 2.4	22 TH	0322 0952 1539 2228	8.1 2.4 8.3 2.3
8 TH	0525 1205 1749	7.5 2.9 7.8	23 F	0413 1042 1633 2325	7.9 2.7 8.1 2.6
9 F	0042 0632 1314 1857	2.7 7.3 3.1 7.6	24 SA	0516 1149 1743	7.7 2.8 7.8
10 SA	0147 0741 1422 2005	2.9 7.4 3.0 7.6	25 SU	0042 0634 1312 1906	2.7 7.7 2.8 7.8
11 SU	0249 0842 1524 2104	2.8 7.6 2.8 7.8	26 M	0205 0751 1436 2025	2.6 7.9 2.5 8.1
12 M	0342 0932 1614 2153	2.6 8.0 2.5 8.0	27 TU	0318 0900 1549 2132	2.2 8.4 2.0 8.5
13 TU	0426 1016 1659 2237	2.4 8.3 2.2 8.3	28 W	0421 1000 1652 2231	1.7 8.9 1.4 9.0
14 W	0505 1055 1737 2313	2.2 8.6 2.0 8.5	29 TH ●	0518 1054 1750 2323	1.3 9.4 0.8 9.3
15 TH	0540 1130 1814 2349	2.0 8.7 1.8 8.6	30 F	0608 1143 1839	0.9 9.7 0.4
			31 SA	0011 0655 1229 1926	9.7 0.7 9.9 0.3

FEBRUARY

Day	TIME	M	Day	TIME	M
1 SU	0055 0737 1312 2008	9.5 0.7 9.9 0.4	16 M	0035 0707 1249 1938	9.0 1.2 9.2 1.1
2 M	0137 0818 1354 2047	9.3 0.9 9.7 0.7	17 TU	0107 0740 1320 2009	9.0 1.2 9.2 1.2
3 TU	0216 0856 1433 2124	9.0 1.3 9.3 1.2	18 W	0140 0813 1352 2040	8.9 1.4 9.1 1.4
4 W	0256 0934 1514 2202	8.5 1.8 8.8 1.9	19 TH	0213 0846 1427 2112	8.8 1.6 8.9 1.7
5 TH	0336 1014 1557 2242	8.0 2.4 8.2 2.5	20 F	0251 0922 1507 2150	8.5 2.0 8.6 2.2
6 F	0423 1102 1651 2333	7.5 3.0 7.5 3.1	21 SA	0336 1009 1559 2244	8.1 2.4 8.1 2.6
7 SA	0523 1211 1801	7.1 3.4 7.0	22 SU	0438 1113 1712	7.7 2.8 7.6
8 SU	0046 0649 1340 1930	3.4 6.9 3.5 6.9	23 M	0004 0604 1248 1852	3.0 7.4 2.9 7.4
9 M	0211 0813 1500 2047	3.4 7.1 3.2 7.2	24 TU	0148 0737 1427 2022	2.9 7.6 2.6 7.8
10 TU	0319 0915 1600 2141	3.1 7.6 2.7 7.7	25 W	0310 0854 1546 2132	2.4 8.2 1.9 8.4
11 W	0410 1002 1647 2223	2.7 8.1 2.3 8.1	26 TH	0416 0955 1649 2227	1.8 8.9 1.2 9.0
12 TH	0451 1040 1725 2259	2.3 8.5 1.9 8.5	27 F	0509 1044 1742 2313	1.2 9.4 0.6 9.4
13 F	0527 1113 1800 2332	1.9 8.8 1.5 8.7	28 SA ●	0556 1129 1825 2354	0.8 9.8 0.2 9.6
14 SA	0600 1147 1832	1.6 9.0 1.3			
15 SU	0004 0634 1218 1904	8.9 1.4 9.2 1.1			

MARCH

Day	TIME	M	Day	TIME	M
1 SU	0638 1210 1906	0.5 10.0 0.1	16 M	0611 1151 1841	1.1 9.3 0.8
2 M	0034 0716 1249 1941	9.6 0.5 9.9 0.3	17 TU	0008 0645 1222 1913	9.3 0.9 9.5 0.8
3 TU	0110 0751 1326 2015	9.4 0.7 9.7 0.7	18 W	0041 0719 1255 1945	9.3 0.9 9.5 0.9
4 W	0144 0825 1401 2046	9.1 1.1 9.3 1.3	19 TH	0113 0752 1328 2016	9.3 1.1 9.3 1.2
5 TH	0218 0856 1436 2115	8.7 1.7 8.7 1.9	20 F	0148 0826 1405 2049	9.0 1.4 9.0 1.6
6 F	0251 0929 1514 2146	8.2 2.3 8.1 2.6	21 SA	0227 0904 1449 2128	8.7 1.8 8.6 2.2
7 SA	0331 1007 1602 2226	7.6 2.9 7.4 3.3	22 SU	0315 1952 1543 2224	8.2 2.3 7.9 2.8
8 SU	0426 1106 1709 2336	7.0 3.5 6.7 3.8	23 M	0421 1102 1706 2351	7.6 2.8 7.3 3.2
9 M	0550 1252 1853	6.6 3.7 6.5	24 TU	0554 1245 1852	7.3 2.9 7.3
10 TU	0310 0740 1430 2025	3.8 6.8 3.4 6.9	25 W	0141 0730 1425 2020	3.0 7.6 2.4 7.8
11 W	0253 0850 1534 2119	3.4 7.2 2.8 7.5	26 TH	0303 0843 1539 2122	2.4 8.3 1.6 8.4
12 TH	0348 0936 1620 2159	2.8 7.9 2.2 8.1	27 F	0403 0939 1635 2212	1.7 8.9 1.0 8.9
13 F	0428 1013 1659 2234	2.3 8.4 1.7 8.5	28 SA	0452 1026 1722 2252	1.1 9.4 0.6 9.3
14 SA	0504 1047 1733 2305	1.8 8.8 1.3 8.8	29 SU ●	0536 1108 1801 2330	0.8 9.7 0.4 9.4
15 SU ○	0537 1119 1807 2337	1.4 9.1 1.0 9.1	30 M	0614 1146 1838	0.6 9.8 0.4
			31 TU	0007 0649 1222 1910	9.4 0.6 9.7 0.6

APRIL

Day	TIME	M	Day	TIME	M
1 W	0039 0721 1256 1940	9.3 0.8 9.4 1.0	16 TH	0014 0657 1231 1921	9.5 0.8 9.5 0.9
2 TH	0112 0754 1330 2008	9.0 1.2 9.0 1.5	17 F	0050 0734 1310 1957	9.4 1.0 9.3 1.2
3 F	0142 0823 1404 2034	8.7 1.7 8.5 2.0	18 SA	0131 0813 1352 2034	9.1 1.3 8.9 1.7
4 SA	0215 0854 1440 2103	8.3 2.3 8.0 2.6	19 SU	0215 0857 1443 2119	8.8 1.7 8.2 2.3
5 SU	0253 0931 1524 2141	7.7 2.8 7.3 3.2	20 M	0310 0953 1546 2221	8.2 2.2 7.8 2.8
6 M	0342 1023 1628 2241	7.2 3.4 6.7 3.8	21 TU	0420 1111 1712 2353	7.8 2.5 7.4 3.1
7 TU	0459 1158 1807	6.7 3.6 6.5	22 W	0547 1245 1845	7.6 2.5 7.5
8 W	0032 0646 1341 1942	4.0 6.7 3.4 6.8	23 TH	0127 0712 1408 2002	2.8 7.9 2.0 7.9
9 TH	0206 0805 1449 2039	3.5 7.2 2.8 7.4	24 F	0240 0820 1515 2100	2.3 8.4 1.5 8.4
10 F	0305 0856 1538 2121	2.9 7.8 2.2 8.0	25 SA	0339 0914 1609 2146	1.7 8.8 1.1 8.8
11 SA	0350 0935 1620 2156	2.3 8.3 1.7 8.5	26 SU	0427 1000 1654 2227	1.3 9.2 0.9 9.0
12 SU	0430 1010 1658 2230	1.8 8.8 1.3 8.9	27 M	0508 1041 1732 2304	1.1 9.3 0.8 9.2
13 M	0506 1044 1734 2304	1.3 9.1 1.0 9.2	28 TU ●	0546 1119 1805 2227	1.0 9.4 0.9 9.2
14 T ○	0544 1119 1811 2339	1.0 9.4 0.8 9.4	29 W	0621 1154 1836	1.0 9.3 1.1
15 W	0621 1154 1846	0.8 9.5 0.7	30 TH	0011 1655 1229 1907	9.1 1.2 9.0 1.4

ENGLAND, WEST COAST – LIVERPOOL

LAT 53°25′N LONG 3°00′W

TIME ZONE GMT — TIMES AND HEIGHTS OF HIGH AND LOW WATERS — YEAR 1987

MAY

Day	TIME	M	Day	TIME	M
1 F	0042	8.9	16 SA	0035	9.4
	0727	1.5		0724	0.9
	1303	8.7		1259	9.2
	1935	1.8		1944	1.3
2 SA	0114	8.6	17 SU	0121	9.2
	0759	1.8		0809	1.1
	1337	8.3		1349	8.9
	2004	2.2		2029	1.7
3 SU	0148	8.3	18 M	0212	8.9
	0830	2.3		0901	1.5
	1415	7.9		1444	8.4
	2034	2.6		2121	2.1
4 M	0226	7.9	19 TU	0310	8.5
	0908	2.7		1002	1.8
	1458	7.4		1549	8.0
	2115	3.1		2224	2.5
5 TU	0314	7.4	20 W	0416	8.2
	0959	3.0		1112	2.0
	1556	7.0		1704	7.7
	2210	3.5		2342	2.7
6 W	0419	7.0	21 TH	0529	8.1
	1112	3.3		1227	2.0
	1713	6.8		1819	7.7
	2332	3.7			
7 TH	0542	6.9	22 F	0057	2.6
	1238	3.1		0641	8.1
	1836	6.9		1337	1.9
				1928	7.9
8 F	0100	3.5	23 SA	0206	2.3
	0659	7.2		0747	8.3
	1347	2.7		1440	1.7
	1941	7.4		2026	8.2
9 S	0208	3.0	24 SU	0304	2.0
	0758	7.7		0843	8.6
	1444	2.3		1534	1.5
	2030	7.9		2115	8.5
10 SU	0300	2.4	25 M	0355	1.7
	0844	8.2		0931	8.7
	1534	1.8		1620	1.5
	2112	8.4		2157	8.7
11 M	0348	1.9	26 TU	0440	1.6
	0927	8.6		1014	8.8
	1619	1.4		1659	1.5
	2152	8.8		2236	8.5
12 TU	0433	1.5	27 W ●	0519	1.5
	1007	9.0		1054	8.8
	1701	1.1		1734	1.5
	2230	9.2		2313	8.8
13 W	0515	1.2	28 TH	0557	1.5
	1048	9.3		1132	8.8
	1742	0.9		1807	1.6
	2311	9.4		2347	8.8
14 TH	0558	0.9	29 F	0632	1.6
	1130	9.4		1207	8.7
	1822	0.9		1839	1.7
	2351	9.5			
15 F	0641	0.9	30 SA	0021	8.7
	1214	9.4		0707	1.7
	1903	1.0		1243	8.5
				1910	1.9
			31 SU	0055	8.6
				0740	1.9
				1319	8.3
				1941	2.2

JUNE

Day	TIME	M	Day	TIME	M
1 M	0131	8.4	16 TU	0208	9.2
	0816	2.1		0903	1.0
	1357	8.0		1440	8.7
	2016	2.5		2118	1.7
2 TU	0209	8.1	17 W	0301	9.0
	0854	2.4		0957	1.3
	1439	7.7		1536	8.4
	2058	2.7		2213	2.0
3 W	0253	7.8	18 H	0357	8.7
	0941	2.6		1054	1.5
	1527	7.4		1637	8.0
	2146	3.0		2313	2.3
4 TH	0345	7.6	19 F	0458	8.4
	0035	2.7		1153	1.8
	1624	7.2		1740	7.8
	2245	3.2			
5 FR	0445	7.4	20 SA	0018	2.4
	1137	2.8		0601	8.2
	1729	7.2		1255	2.0
	2354	3.2		1846	7.7
6 SA	0550	7.5	21 SU	0123	2.5
	1243	2.6		0707	8.1
	1834	7.4		1358	2.1
				1948	7.9
7 SU	0104	2.9	22 M	0227	2.4
	0653	7.7		0808	8.1
	1347	2.4		1456	2.2
	1933	7.8		2044	8.0
8 M	0208	2.6	23 TU	0324	2.3
	0751	8.1		0903	8.2
	1446	2.0		1548	2.1
	2026	8.2		2132	8.2
9 T	0305	2.2	24 W	0414	2.1
	0844	8.4		0952	8.3
	1539	1.7		1631	2.1
	2115	8.7		2216	8.4
10 W	0359	1.8	25 TH	0501	2.0
	0935	8.8		1035	8.4
	1630	1.4		1711	2.0
	2202	9.0		2255	8.6
11 TH ○	0449	1.4	26 F ●	0542	1.9
	1024	9.1		1116	8.4
	1718	1.2		1746	2.0
	2249	9.3		2333	8.7
12 F	0540	1.1	27 SA	0619	1.8
	1113	9.3		1154	8.5
	1804	1.1		1819	1.9
	2337	9.4			
13 SA	0629	0.9	28 SU	0008	8.7
	1204	9.3		0655	1.8
	1850	1.1		1229	8.4
				1853	2.0
14 SU	0025	9.5	29 M	0043	8.7
	1720	0.8		0728	1.8
	1255	9.2		1304	8.4
	1938	1.2		1927	2.0
15 M	0116	9.4	30 TU	0117	8.6
	0811	0.8		0804	1.8
	1347	9.0		1341	8.3
	2026	1.4		2002	2.1

JULY

Day	TIME	M	Day	TIME	M
1 W	0154	8.4	16 TH	0242	9.4
	0840	1.9		0936	0.9
	1418	8.1		1510	8.6
	2040	2.3		2148	1.6
2 TH	0230	8.3	17 F	0329	9.0
	0918	2.1		1021	1.4
	1457	7.9		1559	8.2
	2122	2.5		2237	2.1
3 F	0311	8.1	18 SA	0419	8.5
	1000	2.3		1111	1.9
	1541	7.7		1652	7.8
	2207	2.7		2332	2.5
4 SA	0356	7.9	19 SU	0516	8.0
	1048	2.4		1207	2.4
	1631	7.6		1756	7.5
	2301	2.8			
5 SU	0449	7.8	20 M	0036	2.8
	1144	2.6		0622	7.6
	1732	7.6		1312	2.8
				1907	7.4
6 M	0004	2.9	21 TU	0151	2.9
	0554	7.8		0735	7.5
	1252	2.6		1420	2.8
	1839	7.7		2016	7.5
7 TU	0116	2.8	22 W	0300	2.8
	0703	7.9		0843	7.6
	1402	2.4		1522	2.7
	1945	8.0		2114	7.9
8 W	0227	2.5	23 TH	0400	2.5
	0811	8.1		0939	7.9
	1507	2.1		1613	2.5
	2047	8.4		2203	8.2
9 TH	0332	2.0	24 F	0449	2.2
	0914	8.5		1026	8.1
	1606	1.7		1655	2.3
	2143	8.8		2244	8.5
10 F	0433	1.6	25 SA ●	0532	2.0
	1012	8.9		1105	8.4
	1701	1.4		1733	2.1
	2237	9.2		2320	8.7
11 SA ○	0530	1.1	26 SU	0608	1.8
	1105	9.2		1140	8.5
	1753	1.1		1807	1.9
	2329	9.5		2354	8.8
12 SU	0624	0.8	27 M	0642	1.6
	1157	9.3		1214	8.6
	1843	1.0		1839	1.8
13 M	0018	9.7	28 TU	0028	8.9
	0716	0.5		0713	1.5
	1248	9.4		1246	8.7
	1931	0.9		1912	1.7
14 TU	0107	9.7	29 W	0100	8.9
	0805	0.4		0745	1.5
	1337	9.3		1319	8.6
	2018	1.0		1945	1.7
15 W	0155	9.6	30 TH	0131	8.8
	0851	0.6		0818	1.5
	1423	9.0		1351	8.5
	2103	1.3		2010	1.8
			31 FR	0204	8.7
				0851	1.7
				1425	8.4
				2054	2.0

AUGUST

Day	TIME	M	Day	TIME	M
1 SA	0236	8.5	16 SU	0338	8.4
	0925	2.0		1023	2.2
	1501	8.2		1602	7.8
	2143	2.3		2244	2.7
2 SU	0314	8.3	17 M	0428	7.8
	1004	2.3		1112	2.9
	1545	7.9		1701	7.3
	2217	2.6		2350	3.2
3 M	0402	8.0	18 TU	0537	7.2
	1052	2.6		1222	3.4
	1640	7.7		1822	7.0
	2315	2.9			
4 TU	0505	7.7	19 W	0119	3.4
	1200	2.8		0709	7.0
	1754	7.5		1349	3.5
				1954	7.2
5 W	0034	3.0	20 TH	0244	3.2
	0628	7.6		0830	7.2
	1327	2.8		1504	3.2
	1917	7.7		2100	7.6
6 TH	0202	2.7	21 F	0348	2.7
	0752	7.8		0928	7.7
	1446	2.5		1559	2.8
	2030	8.1		2148	8.1
7 F	0318	2.2	22 SA	0244	2.2
	0905	8.2		1012	8.1
	1553	2.0		1641	2.3
	2134	8.7		2227	8.6
8 SA	0426	1.6	23 SU	0515	1.8
	1006	8.8		1047	8.5
	1651	1.5		1716	2.0
	2228 6.8	9.3		2301	8.9
9 SU ○	0525	1.0	24 M ●	0549	1.6
	1059	9.2		1120	8.7
	1744	1.0		1749	1.7
	2319	9.7		2333	9.1
10 M	0617	0.5	25 TU	0619	1.4
	1147	9.5		1151	8.9
	1832	0.7		1819	1.5
11 TU	0005	10.0	26 W	0004	9.2
	0703	0.2		0650	1.2
	1232	9.6		1221	9.0
	1916	0.6		2227	1.4
12 W	0049	10.1	27 TH	0034	9.2
	0747	0.2		0721	1.2
	1316	9.5		1250	9.0
	1957	0.7		1923	1.4
13 TH	0131	9.9	28 F	0103	9.2
	0827	0.4		0751	1.3
	1357	9.2		1321	8.9
	2037	1.0		1955	1.5
14 F	0213	9.6	29 SA	0133	9.0
	0905	0.9		0822	1.5
	1436	8.8		1352	8.7
	2115	1.5		2027	1.8
15 SA	0254	9.1	30 SU	0204	8.8
	0942	1.5		0853	1.9
	1517	8.3		1426	8.5
	2156	2.1		2101	2.2
			31 M	0240	8.5
				0927	2.3
				1508	8.2
				2143	2.6

ENGLAND, WEST COAST – LIVERPOOL

LAT 53'25'N LONG 3'00'W

TIME ZONE GMT — TIMES AND HEIGHTS OF HIGH AND LOW WATERS — YEAR 1987

SEPTEMBER

Day	TIME	M	Day	TIME	M
1 TU	0328 1013 1603 2242	8.1 2.8 7.7 3.0	16 W	0455 1126 1736	6.9 3.8 6.8
2 W	0433 1125 1723	7.6 3.2 7.4	17 TH	0046 0641 1319 1926	3.7 6.6 3.9 7.0
3 TH	0011 0611 1307 1902	3.1 7.3 3.2 7.5	18 F	0220 0812 1442 2034	3.3 7.1 3.5 7.5
4 F	0151 0748 1436 2022	2.8 7.6 2.7 8.1	19 SA	0322 0905 1534 2121	2.8 7.6 2.9 8.1
5 SA	0314 0903 1545 2125	2.1 8.2 2.1 8.8	20 SU	0407 0946 1614 2159	2.2 8.2 2.4 8.6
6 SU	0419 0959 1641 2216	1.4 8.9 1.4 9.4	21 M	0444 1020 1648 2233	1.8 8.6 2.0 8.9
7 M ○	0513 1047 1729 2302	0.7 9.4 0.9 9.9	22 TU	0518 1051 1720 2304	1.4 8.9 1.6 9.2
8 TU	0600 1129 1812 2344	0.3 9.6 0.6 10.1	23 W ●	0550 1120 1753 2333	1.2 9.1 1.4 9.3
9 W	0642 1210 1853	0.1 9.7 0.5	24 TH	0621 1150 1825	1.1 9.2 1.2
10 TH	0025 0755 1324 2006	9.9 0.6 9.3 1.0	25 F	0003 0652 1219 1857	9.4 1.1 9.2 1.3
11 F	0103 0842 1524 2104	2.8 7.6 2.8 7.8	26 SA	0034 0723 1252 1931	9.4 1.2 9.2 1.4
12 SA	0141 0829 1359 2042	9.5 1.2 8.9 1.6	27 SU	0104 0754 1324 2004	9.2 1.5 9.0 1.7
13 SU	0218 0901 1434 2118	8.9 1.8 8.4 2.2	28 M	0140 0825 1401 2040	8.9 1.9 8.7 2.1
14 M	0257 0935 1517 2200	8.3 2.6 7.8 2.9	29 TU	0219 0901 1446 2127	8.5 2.4 8.3 2.5
15 TU	0346 1016 1610 2304	7.5 3.3 7.2 3.5	30 W	0311 0952 1545 2231	8.0 2.9 7.8 3.0

OCTOBER

Day	TIME	M	Day	TIME	M
1 TH	0426 1111 1713	7.4 3.4 7.4	16 F	0001 0558 1227 1834	3.7 6.6 4.1 6.9
2 F	0007 0611 1259 1850	3.1 7.2 3.3 7.6	17 SA	0133 0728 1355 1949	3.4 6.9 3.7 7.4
3 SA	0147 0744 1425 2009	2.6 7.7 2.7 8.3	18 SU	0236 0826 1451 2040	2.9 7.5 3.1 7.9
4 SU	0303 0851 1529 2108	1.9 8.4 2.0 9.0	19 M	0324 0907 1534 2119	2.3 8.1 2.5 8.4
5 M	0403 0942 1621 2156	1.2 9.0 1.4 9.5	20 TU	0403 0942 1612 2155	1.9 8.5 2.1 8.8
6 TU	0452 1026 1706 2240	0.7 9.4 1.0 9.9	21 W	0440 1014 1647 2227	1.5 8.9 1.7 9.1
7 W ○	0534 1105 1747 2319	0.5 9.5 0.7 10.0	22 TH ●	0515 1045 1722 2259	1.3 9.1 1.4 9.3
8 TH	0612 1143 1825 2358	0.4 9.6 0.7 9.9	23 F	0549 1118 1758 2332	1.1 9.3 1.3 9.4
9 F	0648 1218 1902	0.6 9.5 0.9	24 SA	0624 1151 1835	1.1 9.4 1.3
10 SA	0035 0721 1252 1937	9.7 1.0 9.2 1.3	25 SU	0007 657 1227 1937	9.4 1.3 9.4 1.4
11 SU	0110 0752 1326 2011	9.2 1.5 8.9 1.8	26 M	0045 0731 1304 1949	9.2 1.5 9.2 1.6
12 M	0147 0822 1401 2046	8.7 2.1 8.4 2.4	27 TU	0124 0808 1347 2032	8.9 1.9 8.8 2.0
13 T	0225 0853 1440 2125	8.1 2.8 7.9 3.0	28 W	0212 0850 1437 2125	8.5 2.4 8.4 2.4
14 W	0311 0931 1531 2224	7.4 3.4 7.3 3.5	29 TH	0311 0948 1543 2235	7.9 2.9 7.9 2.7
15 TH	0417 1033 1649	6.8 3.9 6.9	30 F	0430 1109 1706	7.5 3.2 7.7
			31 SA	0005 0603 1245 1832	2.7 7.4 3.1 7.9

NOVEMBER

Day	TIME	M	Day	TIME	M
1 SU	0128 0724 1401 1944	2.3 7.8 2.6 8.4	16 M	0131 0724 1348 1940	3.0 7.3 3.3 7.7
2 M	0239 0826 1503 2042	1.8 8.4 2.0 8.9	17 TU	0226 0813 1442 2027	2.6 7.8 2.8 8.1
3 TU	0335 0917 1555 2131	1.3 8.8 1.6 9.3	18 W	0314 0856 1527 2110	2.1 8.2 2.3 8.5
4 W	0423 0959 1640 2214	1.0 9.1 1.3 9.5	19 TH	0357 0934 1610 2148	1.8 8.7 1.9 8.9
5 TH ○	0505 1038 1720 2254	0.9 9.3 1.1 9.6	20 F	0438 1012 1652 2227	1.5 9.0 1.6 9.2
6 F	0543 1116 1800 2333	1.0 9.4 1.1 9.5	21 SA ●	0519 1049 1734 2308	1.3 9.3 1.4 9.3
7 SA	0617 1151 1836	1.2 9.3 1.3	22 SU	0558 1129 1817 2349	1.3 9.4 1.3 9.4
8 SU	0010 0649 1225 1913	9.3 1.5 9.1 1.6	23 M	0638 1210 1859	1.3 9.4 1.3
9 M	0046 1721 1300 1948	8.9 1.9 8.8 2.0	24 TU	0034 0719 1255 1944	9.2 1.5 9.3 1.4
10 TU	0123 0751 1335 2023	8.5 2.3 8.5 2.4	25 W	0120 0801 1342 2034	9.0 1.8 9.0 1.7
11 W	0201 0823 1415 2103	8.0 2.8 8.1 2.9	26 TH	0213 0850 1437 2129	8.6 2.2 8.7 1.9
12 TH	0246 0901 1501 2153	7.5 3.2 7.6 3.2	27 F	0312 0948 1539 2235	8.2 2.5 8.4 2.1
13 F	0342 0953 1604 2304	7.1 3.7 7.2 3.4	28 SA	0421 1058 1648 2346	7.9 2.8 8.2 2.2
14 SA	0455 11112 1723	6.8 3.9 7.1	29 SU	0536 1214 1800	7.7 2.8 8.2
15 SU	0025 0617 1242 1839	3.3 6.9 3.7 7.3	30 M	0056 0649 1326 1909	2.1 7.9 2.5 8.4

DECEMBER

Day	TIME	M	Day	TIME	M
1 TU	0202 0752 1429 2009	1.9 8.1 2.2 8.6	16 W	0121 0707 1341 1927	2.8 7.5 3.1 7.8
2 W	0301 0846 1525 2103	1.7 8.4 2.0 8.8	17 TH	0222 0804 1442 2023	2.5 7.9 2.7 8.1
3 TH	0352 0934 1614 2150	1.6 8.7 1.8 8.9	18 F	0317 0854 1536 2114	2.2 8.3 2.2 8.5
4 F	0437 1016 1659 2234	1.6 8.9 1.6 9.0	19 SA	0407 0942 1627 2203	1.8 8.8 1.8 8.9
5 SA ○	0516 1055 1740 2315	1.6 9.0 1.6 9.0	20 SU ●	0454 1028 1716 2251	1.6 9.1 1.5 9.1
6 F	0551 1133 1819 2353	1.7 9.0 1.7 8.8	21 M	0540 1115 1805 2340	1.4 9.4 1.2 9.3
7 M	0625 1208 1856	1.8 8.9 1.8	22 TU	0627 1201 1855	1.2 9.5 1.0
8 TU	0031 0657 1243 1933	8.7 2.0 8.8 2.0	23 W	0029 0713 1250 1945	9.3 1.3 9.6 1.0
9 W	0106 0730 1320 2008	8.4 2.2 8.6 2.2	24 TH	0119 0759 1340 2034	9.2 1.4 9.5 1.0
10 TH	0144 0804 1357 2044	8.2 2.5 8.3 2.5	25 F	0209 0847 1430 2125	8.9 1.6 9.3 1.2
11 F	0223 0840 1439 2125	7.9 2.8 8.0 2.7	26 SA	0303 0938 1524 2217	8.6 1.9 9.0 1.5
12 SA	0308 0925 1525 2214	7.6 3.1 7.7 2.9	27 SU	0357 1033 1619 2313	8.3 2.2 8.7 1.8
13 SU	0400 1019 1619 2312	7.3 3.3 7.5 3.0	28 M	0458 1134 1720	7.9 2.5 8.4
14 M	0459 1122 1720	7.2 3.4 7.4	29 TU	0015 1603 1241 1827	2.1 7.7 2.6 8.1
15 TU	0017 1604 1234 1825	3.0 7.2 3.3 7.5	30 W	0120 0712 1351 1935	2.3 7.7 2.6 8.0
			31 TH	0226 0816 1458 2039	2.4 7.9 2.5 8.1

KALIMANTAN, WEST AND SOUTH COASTS, JAVA SEA

No.	PLACE	Lat. N.	Long. E.	TIME DIFFERENCES HHW (Zone –0800)	TIME DIFFERENCES LLW (Zone –0800)	HEIGHT DIFFERENCES (IN METRES) MHHW	MLHW	MHLW	MLLW	M.L. Z_0 m.	
4848	AIR MUSI (OUTER BAR)	see page 6				3.1	Δ	Λ	0.9		
5193	Pulau Temaju	0 30	108 50	–0220	–0117	–1.9	Δ	Δ	–0.5	0.80	
5194	Pontianak Outer Bar (Kleine Kapoeas) I	0 05	109 08	–0119	–0100	–1.7	Δ	Δ	–0.4	0.90	
		S.	E.								
5195	Pontianak	0 01	109 20	–0021	+0002	–1.9	Δ	Δ	–0.4	0.80	
5196	Tanjong Saleh	0 05	109 10	–0055	–0020	–2.1	Δ	Δ	–0.4	0.80	
5147	MIRI	see page 33				1.6	Δ	Δ	0.5		
5200	Sukadana	1 14	109 57	–1145	–1105	+0.4	Δ	Δ	0.0	1.19	*t*
5201	Sungai Pawan	1 46	109 54	–1140	–1135	+0.2	Δ	Δ	0.0	1.10	*t*
	JAVA SEA										
5204	Tanjung Kuala Jelai	2 59	110 44	*p*	*p*	–0.9	Δ	Δ	–0.2	0.50	
	Sungai Kota Waringin										
5205	Kuala Sapu I	2 54	111 26	*p*	–*p*	–0.2	Δ	Δ	+0.1	1.00	
5207	Sungai Aru Tobal	3 10	111 48	*p*	–*p*	–0.4	Δ	Δ	–0.2	0.70	
5208	Kuala Pembuang	3 25	112 34	*p*	–*p*	+0.3	Δ	Δ	+0.3	1.30	
5214	SUNGAI BARITO	see page 39				2.2	1.5	1.2	0.3		
5209	Sampit Baai I	3 00	113 03	*p*	*p*	+0.1	+0.1	0.0	+0.2	1.40	
	Sungai Mendawai										
5210	Pegatan	3 17	113 21	+0019	+0035	0.0	–0.1	0.0	+0.2	1.30	*t*
	Sungai Kahajan										
5211	Tanjong Damaran	3 19	114 05	+0006	+0017	+0.1	+0.2	+0.3	+0.2	1.50	*t*
5212	Pangkoh	3 05	114 10	+0124	+0156	–0.1	+0.2	+0.2	+0.4	1.50	*t*
	Sungai Barito										
5214	OUTER BAR	3 34	114 29	STANDARD PORT			See Table V			1.30	
5215	Banjermasin	3 20	114 36	+0116	+0117	–0.3	0.0	+0.2	+0.2	1.30	
5216	Sungai Tabanio	3 45	114 36	+0119	+0114	–0.4	0.0	+0.2	+0.3	1.30	
						MHWS	MHWN	MLWN	MLWS		
5228	BALIK PAPAN	see page 42		MHW	MLW	2.6	1.5	1.3	0.2		
	Selat Laut										
5219	Kampong Baru	3 25	116 01	*p*	*p*	–0.3	0.0	0.0	+0.3	1.40	
	SELAT MAKASAR										
5221	Teluk Klumpang	3 01	116 13	*p*	*p*	–0.2	0.0	0.0	+0.2	1.40	
5223	Tanjong Pamukan	2 34	116 29	+0004	+0003	–0.1	+0.1	–0.1	+0.1	1.40	

SEASONAL CHANGES IN MEAN LEVEL

No.	Jan. 1	Feb. 1	Mar. 1	Apr. 1	May 1	June 1	July 1	Aug. 1	Sep. 1	Oct. 1	Nov. 1	Dec. 1	Jan. 1
4718	+0.1	0.0	0.0	0.0	0.0	0.0	–0.1	–0.1	–0.1	0.0	+0.1	+0.1	+0.1
4848	+0.1	+0.2	+0.2	+0.1	0.0	–0.1	–0.1	–0.2	–0.2	–0.1	0.0	0.0	+0.1
4912	+0.2	+0.2	+0.1	0.0	–0.1	–0.1	–0.1	–0.1	–0.1	0.0	+0.1	+0.2	+0.2
5147	+0.1	0.0	–0.1	–0.1	–0.1	0.0	0.0	0.0	0.0	0.0	+0.1	+0.1	+0.1
5167-5169	+0.1	0.0	0.0	0.0	0.0	–0.1	–0.1	–0.1	0.0	0.0	+0.1	+0.1	+0.2
5170, 5171	+0.2	+0.1	0.0	0.0	–0.1	–0.1	–0.1	–0.1	–0.1	0.0	+0.1	+0.1	+0.2
5172-5196	+0.1	0.0	0.0	0.0	0.0	–0.1	–0.1	–0.1	0.0	0.0	+0.1	+0.1	+0.1
5200-5214	+0.1	+0.1	+0.1	+0.1	0.0	0.0	–0.1	–0.1	–0.1	–0.1	0.0	0.0	+0.1
5215	+0.2	+0.2	+0.1	0.0	0.0	0.0	–0.1	–0.2	–0.2	–0.1	0.0	+0.1	+0.2
5216-5222	+0.1	+0.1	+0.1	+0.1	0.0	0.0	–0.1	–0.2	–0.2	–0.1	0.0	+0.1	+0.1
5228	+0.2	+0.2	+0.2	+0.2	+0.1	0.0	–0.2	–0.3	–0.3	–0.	0.0	+0.1	+0.2
6938	+0.2	+0.1	0.0	0.0	0.0	–0.1	–0.2	–0.2	–0.1	0.0	+0.2	+0.2	+0.2
6996	0.0	–0.1	–0.1	–0.1	0.0	0.0	0.0	0.0	0.0	+0.1	+0.1	+0.1	0.0

SCOTLAND, WEST COAST

No.	PLACE	Lat. N.	Long. W.	TIME DIFFERENCES High Water (Zone G.M.T.)		Low Water		HEIGHT DIFFERENCES (IN METRES) MHWS	MHWN	MLWN	MLWS	M.L. Z_0 m.	
404	GREENOCK	(see page 86)		0000 and 1200	0600 and 1800	0000 and 1200	0600 and 1800	3.4	2.9	1.0	0.4		
	Firth of Clyde												
391	Southend, Kintyre	55 19	5 38	−0020	−0040	−0040	+0035	−1.3	−1.2	−0.5	−0.2	1.17	
392	Sanda Island	55 17	5 35	−0040	−0040	⊙	⊙	−1.0	−0.9	⊙	⊙	⊙	
393	Campbeltown	55 25	5 36	+0010	−0040	+0005	+0020	−0.5	−0.3	+0.1	+0.2	1.82	
393a	Loch Ranza	55 43	5 18	−0015	−0040	−0005	−0010	−0.4	−0.3	−0.1	0.0	1.71	
	Loch Fyne												
394	East Loch Tarbert	55 52	5 24	+0005	+0005	−0020	+0015	0.0	0.0	+0.1	−0.1	1.92	
395	Inverary	56 14	5 04	+0011	+0011	+0034	+0034	−0.1	+0.1	−0.5	−0.2	⊙	
	Kyles of Bute												
396	Rubha Bodach	55 55	5 09	−0020	−0010	−0007	−0007	−0.2	−0.1	+0.2	+0.2	1.78	
396a	Tighnabruich	55 55	5 13	+0007	−0010	−0015	−0015	0.0	+0.2	+0.4	+0.5	2.08	
	Firth of Clyde (cont.)												
398	Millport	55 45	4 56	−0005	−0025	−0025	−0005	0.0	−0.1	0.0	+0.1	1.94	
399	Rothesay Bay	55 51	5 03	−0020	−0015	−0010	−0002	+0.2	+0.2	+0.2	+0.2	1.90	
399a	Wemyss Bay	56 53	4 53	−0005	−0005	−0005	−0005	0.0	0.0	+0.1	+0.1	⊙	
	Loch Long												
399b	Coulport	56 03	4 53	−0005	−0005	−0005	−0005	0.0	0.0	−0.1	−0.1	1.82	
399c	Lochgoihead	56 10	5 54	+0015	0000	−0005	−0005	−0.2	−0.3	−0.3	−0.3	1.71	
401	Arrochar	56 12	4 45	−0005	−0005	−0005	−0005	0.0	0.0	−0.1	−0.1	⊙	
	Gare *Loch*												
402	Rosneath (Rhu Pier)	56 01	4 46	−0005	−0005	−0005	−0005	0.0	−0.1	0.0	0.0	2.02	
402a	Shandon	56 03	5 49	−0005	−0005	−0005	−0005	0.0	0.0	0.0	−0.1	⊙	
402b	Garelochhead	56 05	4 50	0000	0000	0000	0000	0.0	0.0	0.0	−0.1	⊙	
	River Clyde												
403	Helensburgh	56 00	4 44	0000	0000	0000	0000	0.0	0.0	0.0	0.0	⊙	
403	GREENOCK	55 57	4 46	STANDARD PORT				See Table V				2.00	
405	Port Glasgow	55 56	4 41	+0015	+0005	+0010	+0020	+0.2	+0.1	0.0	0.0	⊙	
406	Bowling	55 56	4 29	+0020	+0010	+0030	+0055	+0.6	+0.5	+0.3	+0.1	⊙	
406a	Renfrew	55 53	4 23	+0025	+0015	+0035	+0100	+0.9	+0.8	+0.5	+0.2	⊙	
407	Glasgow	55 51	4 17	+0025	+0015	+0035	+0105	+1.3	+1.2	+0.6	+0.4	2.77	
	Firth of Clyde (cont.)												
408	Brodick Bay	55 35	5 08	0000	0000	+0005	+0005	−0.2	−0.2	0.0	0.0	1.86	
409	Lamlash	55 32	5 07	−0016	−0036	−0024	−0004	−0.2	−0.2	⊙	⊙	⊙	
410	Ardrossan	55 38	4 49	−0020	−0010	−0010	−0010	−0.2	−0.2	+0.1	+0.1	1.86	
411	Irvine	55 36	4 41	−0020	−0020	−0030	−0010	−0.3	−0.3	−0.1	0.0	⊙	
412	Troon	55 33	4 49	−0025	−0025	−0020	−0020	−0.2	−0.2	0.0	0.0	1.91	
413	Ayr	55 28	4 41	−0025	−0025	−0030	−0015	−0.4	−0.3	+0.1	+0.1	⊙	
414	Girvan	55 15	4 49	−0025	−0040	−0035	−0010	−0.3	−0.3	−0.1	0.0	1.82	
	Loch Ryan												
4142	Stranraer	54 55	5 03	−0020	−0020	−0017	−0017	−0.4	−0.4	−0.4	−0.2	⊙	
452	LIVERPOOL	(see page 90)		0000 and 1200	0600 and 1800	0200 and 1400	0800 and 2000	9.3	7.4	2.9	0.9		
415	Portpatrick	54 50	5 07	+0018	+0026	0000	−0035	−5.5	−4.4	−2.0	−0.6	2.08	
	Wigtown Bay												
420	Drummore	54 41	4 53	+0030	+0040	+0015	+0020	−3.4	−2.5	−0.9	−0.3	3.32	
420a	Port William	54 43	4 40	+0030	+0030	+0025	0000	−2.9	−2.2	−0.8	⊙	⊙	
421	Isle of Whithorn	54 42	4 22	+0020	+0025	+0025	+0005	−2.4	−2.0	−0.8	−0.2	3.74	
422	Garlicstown	54 47	4 21	+0025	+0035	+0030	+0005	−2.3	−1.7	−0.5	⊙	⊙	
	Wigtown Bay												
422a	Kirkcudbright Bay	54 48	4 04	+0015	+0015	+0010	0000	−1.8	−1.5	−0.5	−0.1	⊙	
424	Hestan Islet	54 50	3 48	+0025	+0025	+0020	+0025	−1.0	−1.1	−0.5	0.0	4.21	
425	Southerness Point	54 52	3 36	+0030	+0030	+0030	+0010	−0.7	−0.7	⊙	⊙	⊙	
426	Annan Waterfoot	54 58	3 16	+0050	+0105	+0220	+0310	−2.2	−2.6	−2.7	↕	⊙	☆
430	Torduff Point	54 58	3 09	+0105	+0140	+0520	+0410	−4.1	−4.9	↕	↕	⊙	☆
431	Redkirk	54 59	3 06	+0110	+0215	+0715	+0445	−5.5	−6.2	↕	↕	⊙	☆

⊙ No data.
§ Dries out except for river water.
↕ The tide does not normally fall below Chart Datum.
☆ See notes on page 344.
c For intermediate heights, use harmonic constants (see Part III) and N.P. 159.
x M.L. inferred.

ENGLAND, WEST COAST, ISLE OF MAN, WALES

No.	PLACE	Lat. N.	Long. W.	TIME DIFFERENCES High Water (Zone G.M.T.)		Low Water		HEIGHT DIFFERENCES (IN METRES) MHWS	MHWN	MLWN	MLWS	M.L. Z_0 m.	
452	LIVERPOOL.	(see page 90)		0000 and 1200	0600 and 1800	0200 and 1400	0700 and 1900	9.3	7.4	2.9	0.9		
	England												
	Solway *Firth*												
432	Silloth	54 52	3 24	+0010	+0040	+0045	+0055	–0.1	–0.3	–0.6	–0.1	⊙	
433	Maryport	54 43	3 30	+0017	–+0032	+0020	+0005	–0.7	–0.8	–0.4	0.0	⊙	
434	Workington	54 39	3 34	+0020	+0020	+0020	+0010	–1.1	–1.0	–0.1	+0.3	4.42	
435	Whitehaven	54 33	3 36	+0005	+0015	–+0010	+0005	–1.3	–1.1	–0.5	+0.1	4.53	
436	Tarn Point	54 17	3 25	+0005	+0005	+0010	0000	–1.0	–1.0	–0.4	0.0	⊙	
437	Duddon Bar	54 09	3 20	+0003	+0003	+0008	+0002	–0.8	–0.8	–0.3	0.0	⊙	
	Morecambe Bay												
440	Barrow (Ramsden Dock)	54 06	3 12	+0015	+0015	+0020	+0020	–0.2	–0.3	–0.1	+0.1	4.97	
440a	Haws Point	54 03	3 10	+0010	+0010	+0010	+0010	–0.1	–0.3	–0.1	+0.1	4.89	
440b	Ulverston	54 11	3 04	+0020	+0040	⊙	⊙	0.0	–0.1	⊙	⊙	⊙	
440c	Arnside	54 12	2 51	+0100	+0135	⊙	⊙	+0.5	+0.2	⊙	⊙	⊙	
440d	Morecambe	54 04	2 52	+0005	+0010	+0030	+0015	+0.2	0.0	0.0	+0.2	⊙	
441	Heysham	54 02	2 55	+0005	+0005	+0015	0000	+0.1	0.0	0.0	+0.2	5.10	
	River Lune												
442	Glasson Dock	54 00	2 51	+0020	+0030	+0220	+0240	–2.7	–3.0	⊙	⊙	⊙	☆
4428	Lancaster	54 03	2 49	+0110	+0030	⊙	⊙	–5.0	–4.9	§	§	⊙	
	River Wyre												
443	Wyre Lighthouse	53 57	3 02	–0010	–0010	+0005	0000	–0.1	–0.1	⊙	⊙	⊙	
444	Fleetwood	53 56	3 00	0000	0000	+0005	–0000	–0.1	–0.1	+0.1	+0.3	4.98	
445	Blackpool	53 49	3 04	–0015	–0005	–0005	–0015	–0.4	–0.4	–0.1	+0.1	⊙	
	River Ribble												
446	Preston	53 46	2 45	+0010	+0010	+0335	+0310	–4.0	–4.1	–2.8	–0.8	⊙	☆
	Liverpool Bay												
447	Southport	53 39	3 01	–0020	–0010	⊙	⊙	–0.3	–0.1	⊙	⊙	⊙	
448	Formby	53 32	3 07	–0015	–0010	–0020	–0020	–0.1	–0.1	0.0	+0.1	5.15	
450	Rick Channel	53 27	3 07	–0030	–0030	–0030	–0030	–0.2	0.0	–0.2	0.0	⊙	
	River Mersey												
452	LIVERPOOL	53 25	3 00	STANDARD PORT					See Table V			5.14	
453	Eastham	53 19	2 57	+0003	+0006	+0015	+0030	+0.4	+0.3	–0.1	–0.1	5.3	*x*
455	Hale Head	53 19	2 48	+0030	+0025	⊙	⊙	–2.4	–2.5	⊙	⊙	⊙	
456	Widnes	53 21	2 44	+0040	+0045	+0400	+0455	4.2	–4.4	–2.5	–0.3	⊙	
456a	Fiddler's Ferry	53 22	2 39	+0100	+0115	+0540	+0450	–5.9	–6.3	–2.4	–0.4	⊙	
	River Dee												
461	Hilbre Island	53 23	3 13	–0015	–0012	–0010	–0015	–0.3	–0.2	+0.2	+0.4	1.86	
462	Mostyn Quay	53 19	3 16	–0020	–0015	–0020	–0020	–0.8	–0.7	⊙	⊙	⊙	
463	Connah's Quay	53 13	3 03	0000	+0015	+0355	+0340	–4.6	–4.4	§	§	⊙	☆
464	Chester	53 12	2 54	+0105	+0105	+0500	–+0500	–5.3	–5.4	§	§	⊙	☆
	Isle of Man												
466	Peel	54 14	4 42	–0021	+0010	0000	–0010	–4.0	–3.2	–1.4	–0.4	2.90	
467	Ramsey	54 19	4 22	–0003	+0012	0000	–0015	–2.1	–1.7	–0.3	+0.1	4.05	
468	Douglas	54 09	4 28	–0004	–0004	–0022	–0032	–2.4	–2.0	–0.5	–0.1	3.78	
468a	Port St. Mary	54 04	4 44	+0005	+0015	–0010	–0030	–3.4	–2.7	–1.2	–0.3	3.21	
469	Calf Sound	54 04	4 48	+0005	+0005	–0015	–0025	–3.2	–2.6	–0.9	–0.3	⊙	
469a	Port Erin	54 05	4 46	–0005	+0015	–0010	–0050	–4.1	–3.2	–1.3	–0.4	2.73	
	Wales												
470	Colwyn Bay	53 18	3 43	–0035	–0025	⊙	⊙	–1.5	–1.3	⊙	⊙	⊙	
471	Llandudno	53 20	3 50	–0035	–0025	–0025	–0035	–1.9	–1.5	–0.5	–0.2	4.03	
478	HOLYHEAD	(see page 94)		0000 and 1200	0600 and 1800	0500 and 1700	1100 and 2300	5.7	4.5	2.0	0.7		
471a	Conwy	53 17	3 50	+0020	–+0020	⊙	+0050	+2.1	+1.6	+0.3	⊙	⊙	
	Menai Strait												
472	Beaumaris	53 16	4 05	+0025	+0010	+0055	+0035	+2.0	+1.6	+0.5	+0.1	4.22	
473	Menai Bridge	53 13	4 09	+0030	+0010	+0100	+0035	+1.7	+1.4	+0.3	0.0	4.05	
474	Port Dinorwic	53 11	3 13	–0015	–0025	+0030	0000	0.0	0.0	0.0	+0.1	3.38	

SEASONAL CHANGES IN MEAN LEVEL

No.	Jan. 1	Feb. 1	Mar. 1	Apr. 1	May 1	June 1	July 1	Aug. 1	Sep. 1	Oct. 1	Nov. 1	Dec. 1	Jan. 1
391-398	+0.1	0.0	–0.1	–0.1	–0.1	–0.1	0.0	0.0	0.0	0.0	+0.1	+0.1	+0.1
399-407	+0.2	+0.1	0.0	–0.1	–0.1	–0.1	–0.1	–0.1	0.0	0.0	+0.1	+0.2	+0.2
408-4142	+0.1	0.0	–0.1	–0.1	–0.1	–0.1	0.0	0.0	0.0	0.0	+0.1	+0.1	+0.1
415-444	0.0	0.0	0.0	–0.1	–0.1	–0.1	0.0	0.0	0.0	0.0	+0.1	+0.1	0.0
445-464	0.0	0.0	–0.1	–0.1	0.0	0.0	0.0	0.0	0.0	0.0	+0.1	+0.1	0.0
466-478	+0.1	0.0	0.0	–0.1	–0.1	–0.1	0.0	0.0	0.0	0.0	+0.1	+0.1	+0.1

12.3 Co-tidal/Co-range Charts

The purpose of these charts is to obtain the times and heights of high water in offshore areas and between secondary ports. The use of the charts will be enhanced if the mariner is aware of the following definitions:

Co-Tidal Lines These are lines joining places which all have the same Mean High Water Interval (MHWI).

Co-Range Lines These are lines which join places having the same Mean Spring Range (MSR).

M.H.W.I. Is the interval between the moons meridian passage at Greenwich and the next high water time at a particular place.

NB: A comparison between the MHW Intervals is a direct comparison between the Mean High Water Times.

M.S.R. Is the range between Mean High Water Springs and Mean Low Water Springs.

Examples in the use of Co-range/Co-tidal charts:

Co-Tidal Chart Exercise (All examples use 1987 ATT)

Example 1.

Find the time and the height of high water at a position:

Latitude 53° 10' N, Longitude 01° 50' E, during the morning of 10th October, 1987.

Standard Port *IMMINGHAM*

Extract from Tables: –		
	October	
10	0127	1.0
SA	0724	7.5
	1349	1.2
	1951	7.0

Predictions:–
HW = 0724 ht. = 7.5 m.

	MHWI	MSR
Required Position	6hr 10'	3.0
Immingham	5hr 36'	6.4
Time Difference	0hr 34'	Ht. Ratio = $\frac{3.0}{6.4}$

HW Immingham = 0724
Time Difference = 34'
Required HW Time = 0758 hrs

Height 7.5 m.

$$\text{Required Ht.} = 7.5 \times \frac{3.0}{6.4}$$

$$= 3.52 \text{ m.}$$

Method:

1. Plot the required position on the chart.
2. Obtain the nearest Standard Port.
3. Take the predictions from the Admiralty Tide Tables for high water height and time.
4. Extract MHWI and MSR values from the chart for the required position.
5. Calculate the time difference between the Standard Port and the actual position.
6. Apply the time difference to time of HW, of the port, to give HW at the required position.
7. Obtain the height ratio (from MSR values) and multiply against Standard Ports height of HW to give HW at position.

Example 2.

Find the height and time of high water in a position:

Latitude 58° 00' N, Longitude 01° 00' E, on the 8th May, 1987.

Standard Port *ABERDEEN*

Extract from Tables: –

	0312	1.9
8	0907	3.2
F	1548	1.3
	2209	3.3

Predictions:–
HW = 2209 ht. = 3.3 m.

	MHWI	MSR
Required Position	1222	1.4
Aberdeen *(1225 + 0056)	= 1321	3.7
Time Difference	59'	Ht. Ratio = $\frac{1.4}{3.7}$

HW Aberdeen	=	2209
Time Difference	=	– 59'
Required HW Time	=	2110 hrs

Height 3.3 m.

Required Ht. = $3.3 \times \frac{1.4}{3.7}$

= 1.25 m.

---

*The line of MHWI which is marked 0^h is also 12h 25' referred to the previous moons transit. Therefore when the required position and standard port lie on opposite sides of this line it is necessary to apply the figure 12H 25' to one or other of the MHWI's to ensure that the differences obtained refer to the same moon's transit.

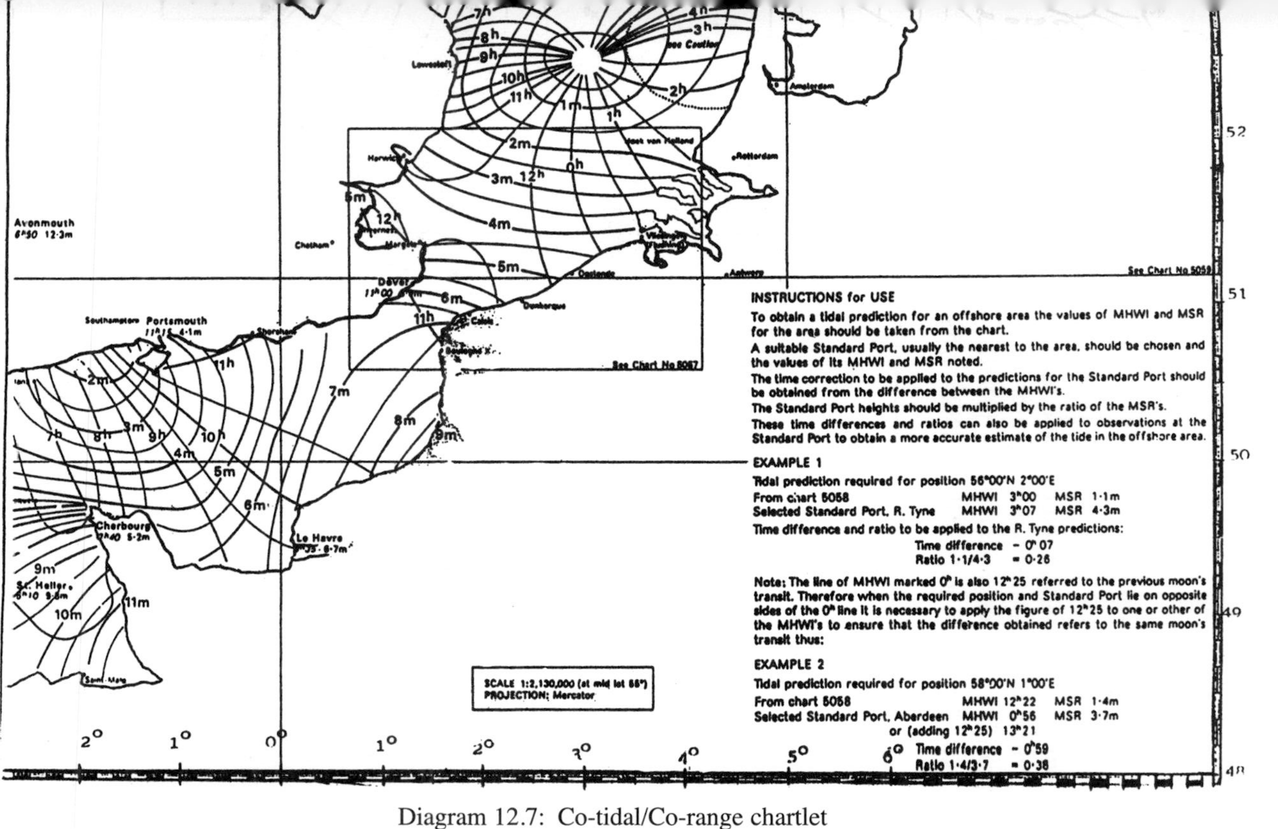

Diagram 12.7: Co-tidal/Co-range chartlet

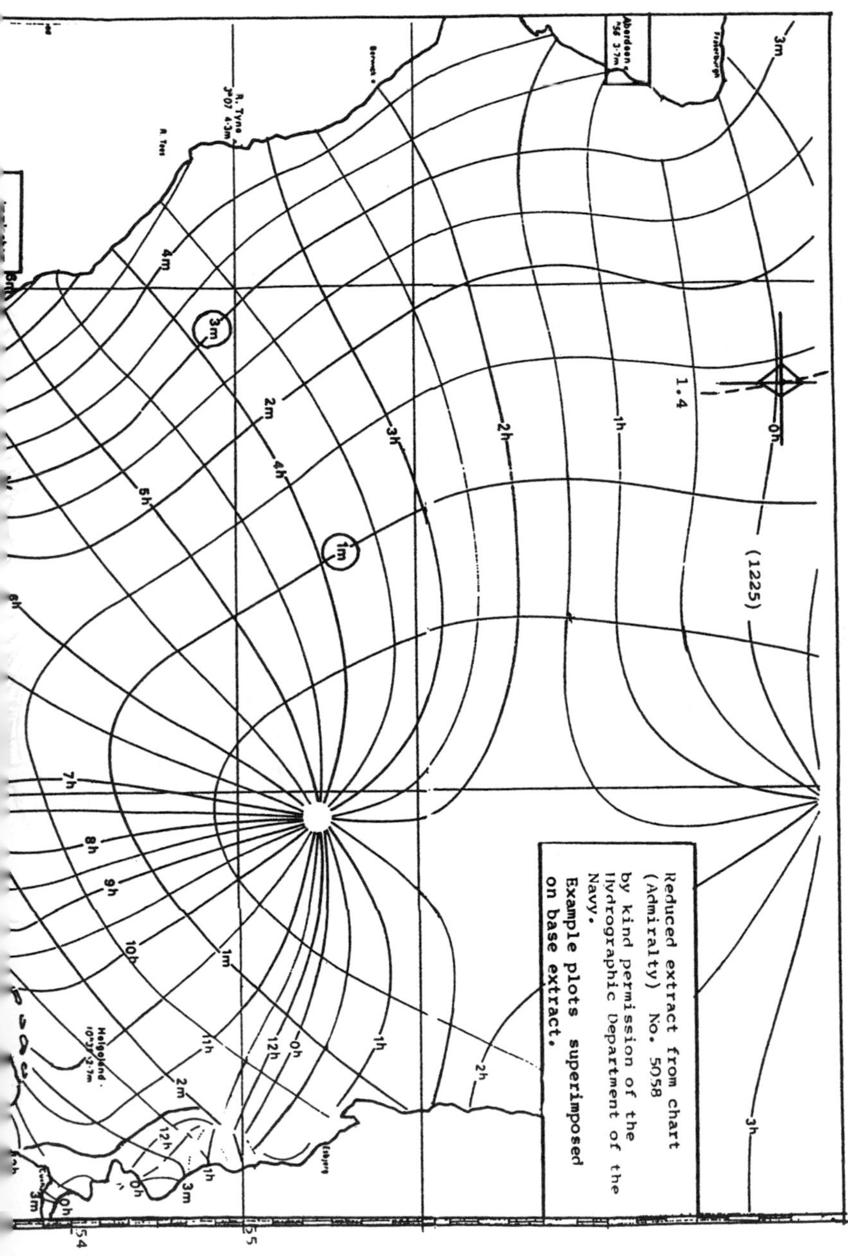

Reduced extract from chart (Admiralty) No. 5058 by kind permission of the Hydrographic Department of the Navy.
Example plots superimposed on base extract.

12.4 Pacific Tidal Calculations

All the following examples have been worked using the Admiralty Tide Tables Vol. 3 for1988, covering the Pacific Ocean. The mariner should be aware of certain differences in terminology employed and methods used when working Pacific Tides as compared with European Tides.

Main differences include:

1) In some Ports

   MHWS may be represented as Mean High High Water (MHHW)
   MHWN may be represented as Mean Low High Water (MLHW)
   MLWN may be represented as Mean High Low Water (MHLW)
   MHWS may be represented as Mean Low Low Water (MLLW)

2) Only one tidal curve is used for all ports.
   (As opposed to each Standard European Port having its own curve).

3) Not all ports have two high waters/two low waters per day.

4) If the duration of rise or fall is less than 5 hours or greater than 7 hours, then the tidal curve cannot be used.
   i.e. Times and heights between predicted HW and LW cannot be found using the curve.
   When using the curve: Three curves are available for the durations 5, 6, and 7 hours. Use the appropriate curve or interpolate between curves.

5) When dealing with Secondary Ports, the 'seasonal change' is employed in the same way as for European Ports.

6) Height differences may require Interpolation/extrapolation in a similar manner as employed with European Ports.

7) Time differences do not require interpolation. Use MHW or MLW differences where zone time changes if any are included.

Pacific Tides

Example 1.

Find the times and heights of high water and low water at Tebon (5187) on the 25th May, 1988.

Times	HW	LW
Cua Cam	2124	1019
Cua Cam	+ 56	÷ 56
Tebon Times	2220	1115

Heights		
Cua Cam	1.9	1.6
Cua Cam Sea Corr'n	0	0
Cua Cam	– 1.15	– 0.96
Tebon	0.75	0.64
Tebon Sea Corr'n	0	0
Tebon Heights	0.75 m	0.64 m

Method: To obtain times

a) Look up port name in geographical index and obtain respective number. (e.g. Tebon = 5187).
b) By inspection of Standard Port List obtain the page number of the port being used. (e.g. Tebon used in conjunction with the Standard Port – Cua Cam).
c) Inspect tables for Cua Cam and extract relevant HW and LW data for the respective date, i.e. heights and times.
d) Apply the time differences between Standard/Secondary Port as specified. (ref. Pg 359 Cua Cam/Tebon = + 56' HW/LW). Tebon times for HW and LW are 2220 and 1115 respectively

To obtain heights

e) Apply seasonal correction to HW and LW values obtained for Cua Cam.
f) Obtain and apply height differences between Standard/ Secondary Ports:

Obtain range at Cua Cam:–

(i) (HW-LW) 2.9 – 0.9 = 2.0
(ii) (HW and Pred. HW) 2.9 – 1.9 = 1.0
(iii) (LW and Pred. LW) 0.9 – 1.6 = – 0.7

Interpolate Ht. Difference x Tebon Range (– 0.5 – 1.8) = 1.3

$$HW\ Diff - 1.8 - \left(\frac{1.0}{2.0} \times 1.3\right) \quad LW\ Diff - 0.5 + \left(-\frac{0.7}{2.0} \times 1.3\right)$$

$$= -\ 1.15 \qquad\qquad + -\ 0.96$$

g) Obtain Tebon values without seasonal correction.
h) Apply Sea/Corr'n to obtain Tebon values 0.75m and 0.64m for HW & LW respectively.

SARAWAK, TUDJUH GROUP, KALIMANTAN, WEST COAST

No.	PLACE	Lat. N.	Long. E.	TIME DIFFERENCES HHW	(Zone – 0800) LLW	HEIGHT DIFFERENCES (IN METRES) MHHW	MLHW	MHLW	MLLW	M.L. Z_0 m.	
4848	SUNGAI SARAWAK (PULAU LAKEI)	see page 6		MHW	LLW	4.8	4.4	2.1	1.2		
	Batang Sadong										
5167	Kuala Sadong	1 33	110 46	+0020	+0105	+0.2	+0.4	–0.2	–0.2	3.20	*d*
5168	Sungai Ensengie	1 25	110 39	+0050	+0235	+0.8	+1.0	–0.2	–0.2	3.54	☆*d*
5169	Simunjan	1 24	110 45	+0115	+03205	+1.0	+1.1	–0.4	–0.2	3.54	☆*d*
	Sungai Sarawak										
5170	Pending ....S	1 33	110 23	+0023	+0018	+0.4	+0.5	+0.2	+0.1	3.42	
5171	Kuching ....MS	1 34	110 21	+0100	+0100	–0.1	0.0	+0.1	0.0	3.13	☆
5171a	Batu Kitang	1 27	110 17	+0234	+0300	–2.1	–2.0	–1.0	–0.6	1.75	☆
5172	PULAU LAKEI...........................	1 45	110 30	STANDARD PORT			See Table V			3.10	☆
5173	Santubong............................S	1 43	110 19	+0005	+0007	–0.5	–0.3	0.0	–0.1	2.90	☆
5174	Pulau Satang...........................	1 47	110 10	–0001	–0001	–0.9	–0.7	–0.2	–0.3	2.58	☆
	Sungai Lundu										
5174a	Kuala Lundu...........................S	1 42	109 55	+0019	+0023	–0.8	–0.5	+0.1	+0.1	2.43	☆
5174b	Pasar Lundu............................	1 40	109 51	+0052	+0106	–1.0	–0.7	–0.1	0.0	2.66	☆
5175	Sematan...............................	1 48	109 47	+0005	–0005	–0.8	–0.7	–0.1	–0.2	2.66	☆
5176	Telok Serabang	2 00	109 40	–0005	–0007	–1.1	–0.8	–0.2	–0.2	2.53	☆
4902	TRENGGANU	see page 15		HHW	LLW	1.7	1.0	1.0	0.4		
	Tudjuh Kepulauan			(Zone – 0700)							
	Anambas Kepulauan										
5177	Selat Peninting	3 14	106 15	–0045	–0009	–0.1	Δ	Δ	+0.1	1.0	*x*
5177a	Impul Passage..........................	3 44	105 40	–0052	–0032	–0.2	Δ	Δ	0.0	1.0	*tx*
	Natuna Kepulauan										
5178	Pulau Laut	4 45	108 00	*p*	*p*	–0.7	Δ	Δ	–0.1	0.7	*x*
5179	Sedanau...............................	3 48	108 02	*p*	*p*	–0.3	+0.2	+0.2	0.0	1.0	*x*
6938	MUI VUNG TAU	see page 159				3.5	3.3	2.2	0.9		
5180	Subi Kecil.............................	3 03	108 51	–00524	–0022	–1.5	–1.4	–0.9	–1.4	1.4	*x*
						MHWS	MHWN	MLWN	MLWS		
4718	SINGAPORE	see page 3		MHW	MLW	2.7	2.0	1.1	0.5		
5181	Pulau Serasan..........................	2 30	109 00	–0833	–0825	–0.4	–0.2	–0.1	0.0	1.4	*tx*
5182	South Haycock	2 16	108 54	–0826	–0825	–1.3	–0.9	–0.6	–0.3	0.8	*tx*
						MHHW	MLHW	MHLW	MLLW		
4848	AIR MUSI (OUTER BAR)	see page 6		HHW	LLW	3.1	Δ	Δ	0.9		
	Tambelan Kepulauan										
5185	Tambelan Bay	0 59	107 34	–0349	–0311	–2.2	Δ	Δ	–0.5	0.6	*x*
6996	CUA CAM	see page 165				2.9	Δ	Δ	0.9		
	Badas Kepulauan										
5187	Tebon	0 35	107 06	+0056	+0056	–1.8	Δ	Δ	–0.5	0.7	*x*
5172	SUNGAI SARAWAK (PULAU LAKEI)	see page 36		MHW	LLW	4.8	4.4	2.1	1.2		
	Kalimantan			(Zone – 0800)							
5189	Tanjong Datu	2 05	109 39	+0011	+0008	–1.9	–1.7	–0.9	–0.5	1.9	*x*
						MHWS	MLWN	MHWN	MLWS		
4718	SINGAPORE	see page 3		MHW	MLW	2.7	2.0	1.1	0.5		
5190	Sungai Paloh	1 46	109 16	–0733	–0731	–0.5	–0.3	–0.2	0.0	1.30	
5191	Pemangkat I	1 11	108 59	*p*	*p*	–1.8	–1.2	–0.7	–0.2	0.60	

Δ Tide is usually diurnal.
☆ See notes on page 388.
M Tides predicted in Malaysian Tide Tables.
S Tides predicted in Sarawak Tide Tables.
I Tides predicted in Indonesian Tide Tables.
p For predictions use harmonic constants (Part III) and N.P.159.
t Time differences approximate.
x M.L. inferred.

Extract from Pacific tide tables.

Example 2.

To what draught can a vessel load in Hong Kong Harbour in order to pass over a 4.0 metre shoal with 1.5 metre under keel clearance at 1830 hrs ZT, on 25th January, 1988.

Extract from Tables: –		
	0107	1.9
25th	0740	0.8
M	1503	1.7
	2015	1.1

HW	1503	1.7
LW	2015	1.1
Duration	5h. 12'	

Required time	1830
HW time	1503
Interval	3h 27'

(Therefore use 5-6 hr graph)

Height of tide at 1830 hrs from graph	= 1.25 metres
Depth to shoal (Charted)	= 4.0 metres
Total depth	= 5.25 metres
Clearance required	= 1.5 metres
Draught	= 3.75 metres

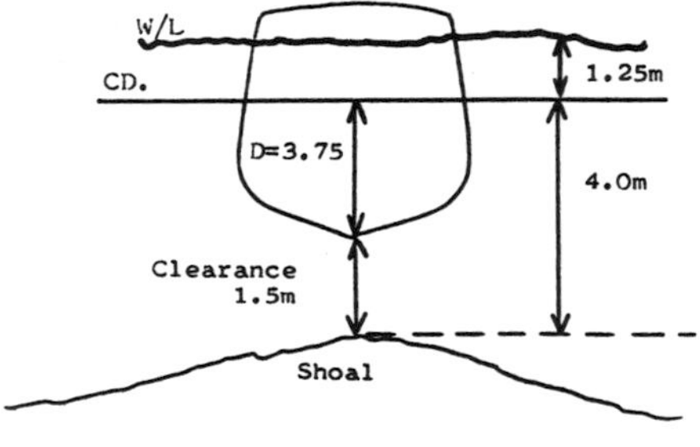

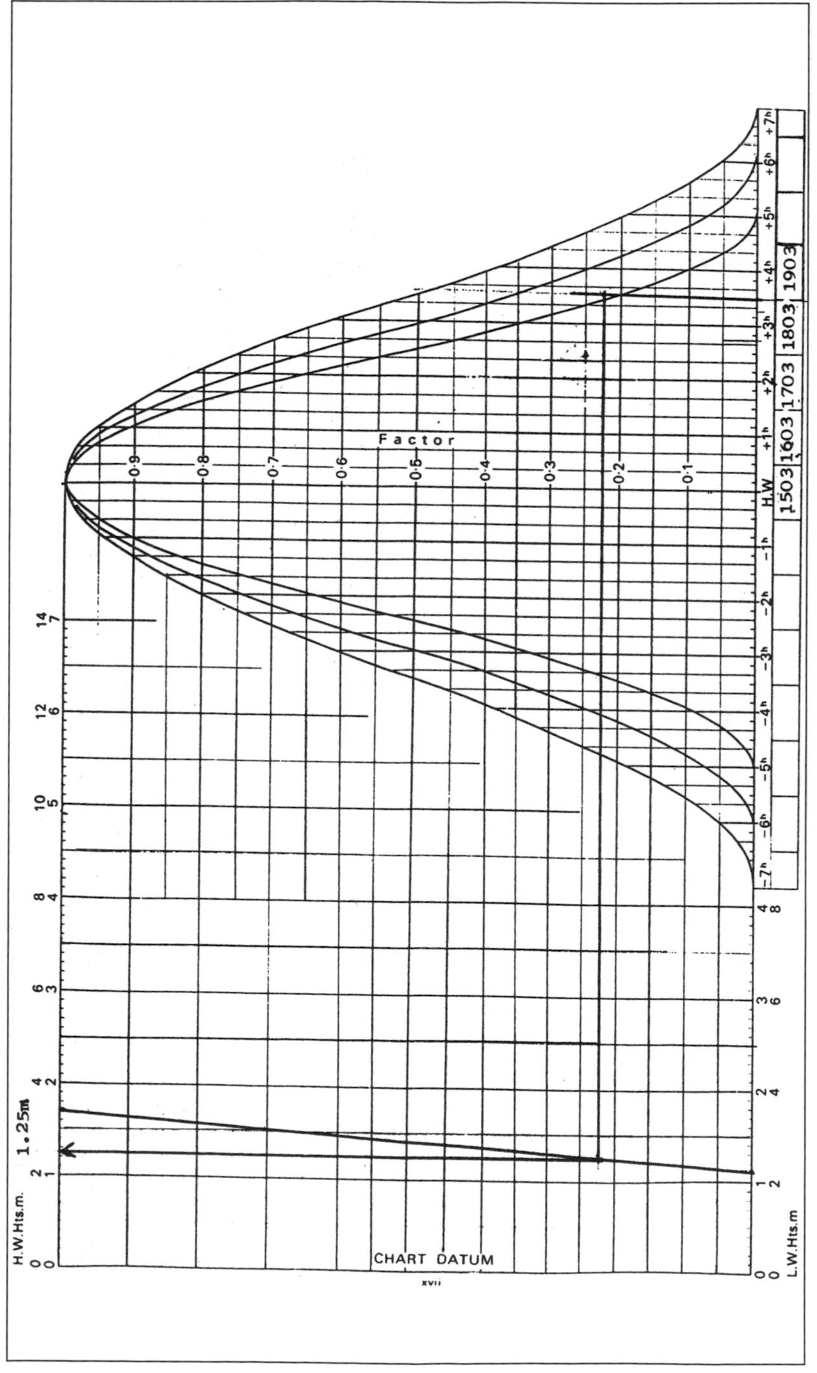

Diagram 12.8: For finding the height of the tide at times between high and low water

12.5 Pacific Tidal Stream Examples

(All examples used are based on Admiralty Tide Tables Vol. 3, Pacific Ocean 1988)

---

1) (i) State what the times of 'slack water' will be at San Francisco entrance (Golden Gate) on 23rd May, 1988.

(ii) State also the maximum directions and rates of tidal stream and the times that they occur?

Extract from tables:
Positive (+) Direction 065 Negative (–) Direction 245

	Slack	Maximum	Rate
	0127	0345	1.1
23	0621	0932	– 2.8
M	1341	1653	2.4
	2006	2234	– 1.8

(i) Slack Water times: 0127, 0621, 1341 and 2006

(ii)

0345	065°	at 1.1 knots
0932	245°	at 2.8 knots
1653	065°	at 2.4 knots
2234	245°	at 1.8 knots

Method:

Inspect the tables and locate Part 1A-Tidal stream predictions

a) Extract the relevant page number for the required port from the index list of ports.
b) Turn to the respective port and date required.
c) Extract times of slack water from table for the date.
d) Extract times for the maximum tidal stream for the date required.
e) Extract the rates for the obtained maximum times.
f) Compare the positive and negative values with the directions given in the table.

USA – SAN FRANCISCO BAY ENTRANCE (GOLDEN GATE)

LAT 37°49'N LONG 122°29'W

TIDAL STREAM PREDICTIONS (RATES IN KNOTS)

TIME ZONE +0800 | POSITIVE (+) DIRECTION 065 NEGATIVE (–) DIRECTION 245 | YEAR 1987

APRIL

Day	Slack Time	Maximum Time	Rate
1 F	0032	0320	–3.7
	1656	0948	3.3
	1253	1535	–3.5
	1907	2156	3.1
2 SA	0056	0350	–4.0
	0729	1023	3.3
	1335	1612	–3.3
○	1933	2223	2.9
3 SU	0119	0425	–4.3
	0804	1059	3.3
	1418	1647	–2.9
	1958	2254	2.7
4 M	0143	0502	–4.4
	0841	1141	3.2
	1504	1728	–2.5
	2024	2329	2.4
5 TU	0210	0543	–4.3
	0923	1226	3.0
	1556	1813	–2.1
	2055		
6 W		0008	2.1
	0242	0629	–4.2
	1013	1317	2.8
	1658	1904	–1.7
	2135		
7 TH		0055	1.8
	0323	0720	–4.0
	1115	1421	2.5
	1809	2004	–1.3
	2232		
8 F		0152	1.5
	0417	0819	–3.9
	1226	1537	2.6
	1923	2113	–1.2
9 SA	0004	0304	1.3
	1532	0926	–3.8
	1339	1653	2.8
	2028	2224	–1.3
10 SU	0147	0423	1.5
	0700	1036	–3.9
	1444	1800	3.2
	2120	2336	–1.8
11 M	0301	0540	2.0
	0822	1139	–4.1
	1540	1851	3.6
	2203		
12 TU		0036	–2.6
	0400	0647	2.7
	0934	1241	–4.3
	1629	1934	3.9
	2241		
13 W		0125	–3.4
	0452	0744	3.4
	1038	1336	–4.3
	1714	2014	4.0
	2316		
14 TH		0207	–4.2
	0540	0837	3.9
	1137	1427	–4.2
	1757	2052	4.0
	2351		
15 F		0249	–4.9
	0626	0926	4.3
	1234	1514	–3.9
	1837	2128	3.9
16 SA	0025	0331	–5.3
	0712	1015	4.5
	1328	1557	–3.5
●	1917	2208	3.6
17 SU	0100	0411	–5.4
	0758	1059	4.4
	1421	1643	–3.0
	1956	2247	3.2
18 M	0135	0454	–5.3
	0846	1148	4.1
	1515	1729	–2.5
	2037	2328	2.7
19 TU	0213	0537	–5.0
	0936	1239	3.6
	1611	1815	–2.0
	2122		
20 W		0011	2.2
	0253	0626	–4.5
	1031	1338	3.1
	1711	1908	–1.5
	2216		
21 TH		0102	1.7
	0341	0717	–3.9
	1133	1441	2.7
	1816	2007	–1.1
	2329		
22 F		0206	1.3
	0439	0812	–3.4
	1239	1603	2.5
	1922	2119	–1.0
23 SA	0055	0317	1.1
	0552	0916	–3.1
	1345	1712	2.5
	2021	2317	–1.1
24 SU	0213	0446	1.2
	0710	1029	–2.9
	1443	1806	2.6
	2108		
25 M		0020	–1.6
	0314	0559	1.5
	0821	1139	–2.9
	1533	1851	2.8
	2146		
26 TU		0055	–2.1
	0403	0654	2.0
	0925	1231	–2.9
	1616	1926	2.9
	2219		
27 W		0116	–2.6
	0445	0739	2.4
	1021	1312	–3.0
	1654	1955	2.9
	2248		
28 TH		0145	–3.2
	0524	0818	2.8
	1112	1355	–3.0
	1727	2024	2.9
	2316		
29 F		0213	–3.8
	0600	0853	3.2
	1159	1433	–2.9
	1759	2050	2.9
	2343		
30 SA		0246	–4.2
	0635	0931	3.5
	1244	1510	–2.8
	1829	2119	2.8

MAY

Day	Slack Time	Maximum Time	Rate
1 SU	0009	0322	–4.6
	0710	1009	3.6
	1329	1549	–2.7
○	1858	2151	2.7
2 M	0036	0359	–4.8
	0746	1047	3.7
	1414	1628	–2.4
	1927	2225	2.6
3 TU	0105	0438	–4.9
	0825	1129	3.6
	1503	1713	–2.2
	1959	2302	2.4
4 W	0138	0521	–4.9
	0910	1214	3.5
	1555	1801	–1.9
	2037	2347	2.1
5 TH	0217	0608	–4.8
	1000	1306	3.3
	1653	1850	–1.6
	2125		
6 F		0038	1.8
	0304	0701	–4.5
	1058	1406	3.1
	1755	1949	–1.5
	2234		
7 SA		0138	1.6
	0404	0759	–4.2
	1201	1511	3.1
	1856	2054	–1.5
8 SU	0009	0249	1.5
	0520	0902	–3.9
	1306	1620	3.1
	1950	2203	–1.8
9 M	0139	0412	1.7
	0649	1007	–3.7
	1407	1717	3.3
	2037	2312	–2.5
10 TU	0250	0529	2.1
	0814	1116	–3.5
	1503	1812	3.4
	2119		
11 W		0010	–3.2
	0350	0640	2.8
	0930	1218	–3.4
	1555	1857	3.5
	2158		
12 TH		0058	–4.0
	0442	0739	3.4
	1038	1319	–3.2
	1643	1939	3.5
	2236		
13 F		0144	–4.7
	0530	0833	4.0
	1138	1411	–3.1
	1727	2021	3.4
	2313		
14 SA		0227	–5.2
	0616	0920	4.3
	1234	1502	–2.9
	1811	2102	3.3
	2350		
15 SU		0308	–5.5
	0701	1005	4.4
	1327	1543	–2.6
●	1852	2143	3.1
16 M	0028	0351	–5.5
	0746	1052	4.3
	1417	1629	–2.3
	1933	2221	2.8
17 TU	0106	0432	–5.3
	0831	1135	4.0
	1506	1711	–2.0
	2015	2301	2.5
18 W	0145	0515	–5.0
	0918	1224	3.7
	1556	1756	–1.8
	2059	2347	2.1
19 TH	0227	0601	–4.6
	1007	1312	3.3
	1647	1845	–1.5
	2150		
20 F		0036	1.7
	0312	0645	–4.1
	1058	1407	2.9
	1740	1934	–1.3
	2254		
21 SA		0133	1.4
	0403	0738	–3.6
	1152	1504	2.6
	1833	2032	–1.3
22 SU	0010	0234	1.2
	0506	0831	–3.2
	1247	1559	2.5
	1922	2136	–1.4
23 M	0127	0345	1.1
	0621	0932	–2.8
	1341	1653	2.4
	2006	2234	–1.8
24 TU	0234	0504	1.3
	0738	1032	–2.5
	1431	1742	2.4
	2045	2330	–2.3
25 W	0329	0609	1.7
	0851	1129	–2.3
	1518	1821	2.4
	2120		
26 TH		0017	–2.9
	0415	0707	2.2
	0956	1224	–2.2
	1600	1857	2.5
	2154		
27 F		0100	–3.5
	0457	0752	2.7
	1054	1315	–2.2
	1641	1936	2.5
	2226		
28 SA		0135	–4.0
	0536	0837	3.1
	1147	1403	–2.2
	1718	2009	2.5
	2258		
29 SU		0216	–4.5
	0614	0915	3.5
	1236	1446	–2.2
	1755	2044	2.6
	2331		
30 M		0256	–4.9
	0653	0953	3.8
	1323	1531	–2.2
	1830	2125	2.6
31 TU	0005	0336	–5.2
	0733	1037	3.9
	1409	1614	–2.1
○	1907	2206	2.6

JUNE

Day	Slack Time	Maximum Time	Rate
1 W	0043	0421	–5.4
	0815	1120	4.0
	1457	1659	–2.1
	1946	2248	2.5
2 TH	0124	0506	–5.4
	0900	1206	4.0
	1546	1748	–2.0
	2032	2335	2.4
3 F	0209	0554	–5.3
	0949	1255	3.8
	1636	1839	–2.0
	2129		
4 SA		0028	2.2
	0301	0645	–5.0
	1040	1346	3.7
	1726	1933	–2.0
	2239		
5 SU		0127	2.0
	0403	0740	–4.5
	1133	1441	3.5
	1816	2031	–2.2
6 M	0000	0235	1.9
	0517	0837	–3.9
	1229	1538	3.3
	1903	2133	–2.6
7 TU	0120	0355	2.0
	0642	0941	–3.3
	1326	1635	3.2
	1948	2235	–3.1
8 W	0231	0515	2.3
	0807	1048	–2.8
	1423	1727	3.0
	2032	2337	–3.7
9 TH	0334	0630	2.8
	0927	1156	–2.4
	1519	1821	2.9
	2116		
10 F		0031	–4.3
	0429	0733	3.4
	1038	1302	–2.2
	1613	1912	2.9
	2159		
11 SA		0122	–4.8
	0520	0828	3.8
	1140	1401	–2.1
	1704	1955	2.8
	2243		
12 SU		0208	–5.1
	0608	0921	4.1
	1235	1454	–2.0
	1752	2043	2.8
	2326		
13 M		0252	–5.3
	0653	1005	4.1
	1324	1537	–2.0
	1837	2124	2.7
14 TU	0008	0335	–5.3
	0737	1048	4.1
	1409	1618	–1.9
●	1919	2207	2.6
15 W	0049	0418	–5.2
	0819	1129	3.9
	1452	1659	–1.9
	2000	2248	2.4
16 TH	0130	0457	–4.9
	0901	1207	3.7
	1534	1735	–1.8
	2042	2330	2.2
17 F	0210	0538	–4.6
	0942	1248	3.4
	1616	1819	–1.9
	2128		
18 SA		0013	2.0
	0252	0620	–4.3
	1023	1327	3.1
	1657	1901	–1.8
	2220		
19 SU		0058	1.8
	0338	0705	–3.8
	1104	1409	2.9
	1737	1949	–1.9
	2321		
20 M		0154	1.5
	0431	0752	–3.3
	1145	1448	2.6
	1817	2038	–2.0
21 TU	0030	0254	1.4
	0536	0844	–2.7
	1228	1533	2.4
	1856	2129	–2.3
22 W	0139	0402	1.4
	0653	0939	–2.2
	1314	1620	2.2
	1935	2222	–2.6
23 TH	0242	0516	1.6
	0813	1036	–1.8
	1404	1709	2.1
	2014	2318	–3.1
24 F	0336	0625	2.0
	0929	1139	–1.6
	1457	1758	2.0
	2055		
25 SA		0010	–3.6
	0425	0725	2.5
	1035	1238	–1.5
	1550	1847	2.1
	2136		
26 SU		0058	–4.1
	0510	0814	3.0
	1133	1336	–1.6
	1639	1934	2.2
	2218		
27 M		0147	–4.6
	0554	0902	3.4
	1224	1425	–1.7
	1726	2018	2.4
	2302		
28 TU		0233	–5.1
	0637	0945	3.8
	1312	1512	–1.9
	1809	2105	2.6
	2346		
29 W		0318	–5.5
	0720	1026	4.1
	1357	1559	–2.1
○	1853	2150	2.8
30 TH	0031	0407	–5.7
	1803	1109	4.3
	1440	1646	–2.3
	1939	2239	2.9

Extract from Pacific tide tables.

Chapter Thirteen

SOURCES OF NAVIGATIONAL INFORMATION CHARTS AND PUBLICATIONS

13.1 The Navigational Chart

If the history of charts is investigated the origins will probably lie in and around the 1st Century A.D. and for todays mariners to even remotely consider using a chart of this period for navigation would be quite unthinkable. The experienced mariner has come to realise that no chart is infallible and for one or more of several reasons an element of caution should always be exercised. Absolute reliability because of age of survey or imperfect survey immediately come to mind as reasons for exercising caution when employing any navigational aid.

The first Admiralty chart was published in 1801, and since then technical innovation has improved accuracy and detail to give the maritime world a comparatively high standard of navigational chart. The date of survey of each chart is therefore a major consideration when placing reliability and accuracy on the content. Examples of this are easy to see if soundings are considered which were charted by means of the hand lead line, as compared with today where electronics can be more precisely employed.

Reliability of charts (Reasons for caution in their use)

1) Date of survey – Methods of early survey are not as efficient as modern techniques.
2) Survey detail – May be incomplete or incorporate mistakes from old survey methods.

3)	Topographical alterations	–	Changes in topography are ongoing and will continue to occur subsequent to survey.
4)	Magnetic variation	–	Will continue to change with the passing of time.
5)	Nature of sea bottom	–	In many areas of the world the nature of the sea bed is unstable, very often due to volcanic action and soundings may not be a true representation.
6)	Scale of chart	–	Although the largest scale of chart is always recommended for use, this scale may impose restrictions and limitations on information displayed. Caution advised with small scales.
7)	Corrections and updates	–	The time in obtaining corrective information and applying revisions to the chart can mean vessels could encounter new uncharted dangers.

13.1.1 information contained in the chart

Admiralty Chart Agents – These are world-wide and keep fully corrected stocks of charts capable of meeting day to day requirements. Addresses of chart agents can be found in the Annual Summary of Admiralty Notices to Mariners and also in the catalogue of Admiralty Charts. This catalogue also provides a total listing of all Admiralty and some Australian/New Zealand charts together with respective prices.

Each chart will have the following notations and titles:

Title of chart	–	Usually placed on a land mass area so as not to effect navigation. The title generally describes the geographic extremities of the charted area.
The Number of the chart	–	Shown at the bottom right hand corner and the top left hand corner (inverted). Also found on the label on the back of the chart.

The date of publication	–	Shown in the bottom margin, in the middle of the chart. The notation will also carry the place where publication takes place e.g. (Published at Taunton 28th May 1976).
Dates of new editions	–	New edition dates are shown to the right of the date of publication. (All previous corrections and previous copies of the chart are cancelled).
Dimensions of the chart	–	Shown in millimetres is displayed in the margin at the bottom right hand corner.
Date of printing	–	This is shown on the reverse on the label of the chart.
The units used for depth	–	Stated in bold letters under the title of the chart. e.g. (DEPTHS in METRES)
The scale of the chart	–	This is carried under the stipulated units of depth, close to the region of the title.
Date of Survey	–	This is a notation form, under the title block, naming the survey authorities.
Heights (for charted objects)	–	A notation under the title block which stipulates the units for which heights have been calibrated (e.g. metres). Also a reference from which heights are measured above. e.g. (MHWS).
Tidal Information (extensive)	–	Information relevant to various ports on the chart is printed in tabular form and placed in a suitable position on the chart.
Tidal Stream Information	–	Indicated by tidal diamonds or by tidal stream arrows when information suitable for the tabular format is not available.

Additional cautions and notations in respective positions may highlight anomalies in tidal predictions and possible depths which could affect under keel clearance.

When ordering or describing a particular chart:

1) Stipulate the chart number.
2) State the title of the chart.
3) State the date of publication.
4) State the date of printing.
5) State the date of last new edition. (if any)
6) Provide the number or date of the last small correction (if known).

13.1.2 updating charts and publications

Admiralty Notices to Mariners

Prior to any voyage it is the Masters responsibility to ensure that all charts and relevant publications are on board the vessel and that they are corrected to date, corrections being obtained from the weekly editions of notices to mariners. These are consecutively numbered from the beginning of each year providing fifty-two (52) issues.

Each weekly notice is comprised of six sections:–

I Index to Section II together with explanatory notes.

II Notices for the correction of charts. These include all notices affecting navigational charts and are listed consecutively from the onset of the year. The section also includes temporary (T) and preliminary (P) notices relevant to the week. The last weekly notice of each month will also list the temporary and preliminary notices which are remaining current.

Any new editions of charts published, together with new publications issued are listed in this section. Typical examples of publications include: Sailing directions or light lists etc. Latest editions of publications are listed at the end of March, June, September and December.

III Navigational warnings are reprinted in this section. All warnings which are in force are included in the first weekly notice of each year. Additionally, all long-range warnings issued during the week are included in this section and listed on a monthly basis.

Lists of NAVAREA, HYDROLANT, and HYDROPAC messages.

IV All corrections affecting Admiralty sailing directions which are published that week. A cumulative list of those corrections in force is also published on a monthly basis.

V All corrections required for the Admiralty list of lights and fog signals. (Mariners are advised that these corrections may not be coincident with any chart correcting information.)

VI Corrections to the Admiralty list of radio signals, are contained in this last section.

Cumulative List of Admiralty Notices to Mariners

For the purpose of checking and up-dating charts a list of the serial numbers of permanent notices is published.These notices will have been issued in the previous 2 years and will affect Admiralty Charts together with Australian and New Zealand Charts which have been re-published within the Admiralty series.

Annual Summary of Admiralty Notices to Mariners

This is published at the beginning of each year and contains the regular and important notices which cover the same topic or subject annually. It also contains all the temporary and preliminary notices affecting sailing directions which are in force at the end of the previous year.

The annual summary covers many diverse subjects from information on tidal surges to actions of the Master in the event of collision. Distress procedures and marine operations with aircraft and military are detailed features. The work of the Coast Guard, and the Royal National Lifeboat Institution are included together with virtually any navigational safety advice. e.g. offshore wind farms – positions and safety zones.

13.1.3 chart corrections

The main source of corrective material for Admiralty Charts is generally obtained from the issue of the weekly notices to mariners as issued by the Hydrographic Department of the Navy. (Canadian Charts – Canadian Notice to Mariners) (United States Charts – U.S. Weekly Notices are published by the U.S. Defence Mapping Agency) also U.S. Coast Guard local notice to mariners.

Charts stocked and supplied by the Hydrographic Department are not corrected for temporary or preliminary notices, and mariners are advised that these should be applied to affected areas in pencil, by the mariner, as appropriate. Weekly notices provide confirmation of temporary or preliminary notices in effect and a list of the notices in force is also included in the annual summary of notices to mariners.

The Hydrographic Department also publish a chart correction log. This contains a summary of correction sheets for the corrections that affect each chart folio. The charts being listed in numerical order with the relevant notices listed. Australian and New Zealand charts contained in Admiralty folios are also indicated together with new charts and new editions listed.

13.1.4 block corrections

Weekly notices often include areas of charts, which have been reproduced for affixing to the chart in the form of a corrected portion. These areas are known as 'blocks'. The purpose of the block may be twofold, not only to indicate new information but also to obliterate or delete items previously shown. Some distortion can be expected when adjoining the block to the chart and this can be minimised by pasting the charted area, as opposed to pasting the cut out block. (The paste can cause excessive distortion to the small area of the block).

Block examples are shown overleaf.

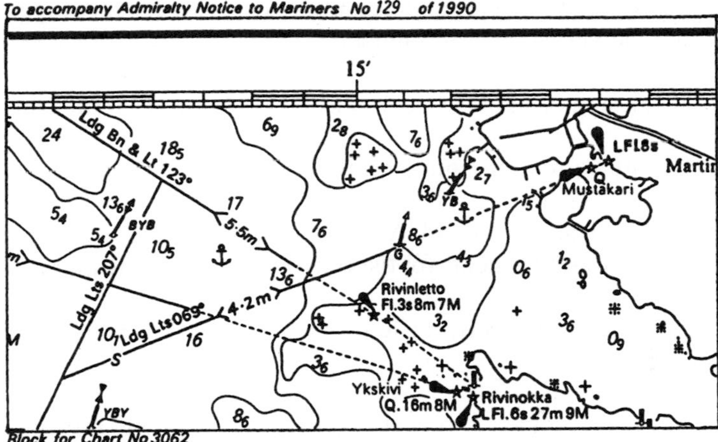

129. BALTIC SEA – Gulf of Bothnia – Finland, west coast – Approaches to Oulu – Martinniemi – leading lights and buoyage amended.
The accompanying block shows changes to leading lights and buoyage in the approach to Martinniemi (65° 12' 7N, 25° 17' .5E).

Overlay Correction Tracings

A more modern method of chart correction which is now used extensively by all chart depots and agents. Precise corrections can be transferred from a tracing directly onto the chart by the mariner.

Chart Correction Procedures

The correction of charts is usually delegated to the ship's 'Navigation Officer' and this duty would be carried out under an adopted procedure dictated by the company and/or the Master.

1. All charts must be corrected under a "Chart Management System".
2. Working charts to be corrected first and the previous last corrections noted by its consecutive number.
3. The correction being made, must be identified in the bottom left hand corner of the chart by its number and date.
4. No erasures or the use of snow paint is allowed on the chart.

5. All new charts, new editions, must be ordered and logged on board the vessel prior to sailing.

6. Any missing or damaged charts must be reported to the Master.

7. All chart corrections must be recorded in the Chart Correction Log.
(The publication NP 133A may be obtained from appointed Admiralty Chart Agents for the purpose of recording corrections).

8. Chart corrections to be made in accord with the Weekly Notices to Mariners.

9. Where block corrections are to be made, these are to be applied so as not to cause distortion. i.e. paste the chart, not the cut out block correction.

10. All corrections (other than T's and P's), must be made in ink.

11. Temporary (T's) and Preliminary (P's) to be made in pencil.

12. The 'Cumulative List' to be consulted for current notices when making corrections.

13. All navigation warnings, from whatever source, relevant to the chart should be noted on the chart.

14. Chart 'Folio's' should be maintained in respect of the recommendations as per the Mariners Handbook. (NP 100, Chapter 1).

13.1.5 corrections to ship's official publications

It is normal practice that one of the ship's Officers will be designated the duty of correcting and maintaining the ships official publications.

1. All annual publications must be ordered well in advance for the next year.
(e.g. Nautical Almanac, Tide Tables, etc.)

2. All new editions must be ordered as per instructions in Weekly Notices to Mariners.

3. All supplements must be ordered and replaced as appropriate.

4. The 'Communications Officer' is designated to correct the Admiralty List of Radio Signals (ALRS).

5. The Third Officer is designated to correct the Admiralty List of Lights.

6. All publications must be logged on board by the Navigation Officer, prior to the vessel sailing.

7. A log account of all corrections is to be maintained.

8. Those publications that require to be endorsed, following correction, must be endorsed by the person making the correction.

9. Official publications must be retained on the Navigation Bridge.

10. All corrections to be entered in ink as appropriate.

List of Statutory Publications required to be Carried by Merchant Ships (in accord with the Merchant Shipping (Carriage of Nautical Publications) Regulations 1998) Effective for UK Registered ships and other vessels while in UK waters.

Vessels must carry a complete set of Navigational Charts and Publications considered necessary for the intended voyage. Specifically the required publications are:–

1. The Mariners Handbook.

2. Merchant Shipping Notices, (MSN's) (MGN's, and MIN's)

3. Lists of Radio Signals.

4. Lists of Lights.

5. Sailing Directions.

6. Nautical Almanac.

7. Navigational Tables.

8. Tide Tables

9. Tidal Stream Atlases.

10. Weekly Notices to Mariners.

11. International Code of Signals

12. Operating and maintenance instructions for navigational aids carried.

13. A Code of Safe Working Practice

14. Annual Summary of Notices to Mariners.

It is pointed out that the above publications are the statutory requirement and a well found ship would generally carry a selection of additional desirable publications inclusive of:

Ocean Passages of the World, Admiralty Distance Tables, A copy of the Regulations for the Prevention of Collision at Sea, IAMSAR manuals, Bridge Procedures Guide, Guide to Port Entry, ICS Guide to Helicopter Operations at Sea, Chart Abbreviations 5011, Ship Masters Medical Guide, A Ships (IMO) Routing Manual, IMDG Code.

Together with stability information and relevant ships plans.

13.1.6 compiling and maintaining charts

Sources of Information: In order to provide not only a safe but efficient service, the hydrographic departments of the various authorities around the world correct and update the navigational charts supplied. These corrections are obtained by information from original surveys and from re-surveys. In the case of the United Kingdom the Royal Navy operate survey vessels for this particular task.

Other governments carry out similar activities and an exchange of information is possible through the 'International Hydro-graphic Bureau' in Monaco. This has now become known as the International Hydrographic Organisation (IHO).

Information is also gleaned from port and harbour authorities and independent surveying organisations regarding plans and surveys of local areas. Especially important in the case of expansion of port and harbour facilities. Breakwaters being extended, new buildings and/or specific landmarks being constructed, etc.

Additional information is also obtained from a variety of persons within the marine environment via the use of 'Hydrographic Notes'. These note formats are contained in blank form within the Weekly Notices to Mariners (Form Ref H. 102 Admiralty Notices). Instructions of forwarding information are included in the Weekly Notice.

H. 102 (October, 1985)

HYDROGRAPHIC NOTE

(for instructions, see overleaf)

Date ....

Ref. No. ....

Name of ship of sender ....

Address: ....

....

....

General locality ....

Subject ....

Approx. Position Lat. .... Long. ....

British Admiralty Charts affected ....

Latest Notice to Mariners held ....

Publications affected (Edition No., date of latest supplement, page and Light list No. etc.)

....

Details:–

NAVIGATION FOR MASTERS

(To accompany Form H. 102)

Name of ship or sender: ....

Address: .... Ref. No. ....

.... Date ....

....

1. NAME OF SHIP	
2. GENERAL REPAIRS Principal activities and trade. Latest population figures and date. Number of ships or tonnage handled per year. Maximum size of vessel handled. Copy of Port Handbook if available.	
3. ANCHORAGES Designation, depths, holding ground shelter afforded.	
4. PILOTAGE Authority for requests. Embarkation position. Regulations.	
5. DIRECTIONS Entry and berthing information. Tidal Streams. Navigational aids.	
6. TUGS Number available and max. hp.	
7. WHARVES Names, numbers or positions. Lengths. Depths alongside. Heights above Chart Datum. Facilities available. 8. CARGO HANDLING Containers, lighters, Ro-Ro etc.	

9. CRANES Brief details and max. capacity.	
10. REPAIRS Hull, machinery and underwater. Ship and boat yards. Docking or slipping facilities. Give size of vessels handled or dimensions. Hard and ramps. Divers.	
11. RESCUE AND DISTRESS Salvage, lifeboat, Coastguard, etc.	
12. SUPPLIES Fuel with type and quantities available. Fresh water with rate of supply. Provisions.	
13. SERVICES Medical. De-ratting. Consuls. Ships chandlery, compass adjustment, tank cleaning, hull painting.	
14. COMMUNICATIONS Road, rail and air services available. Nearest airport or airfield. Port, radio and information service with frequencies and hours of operating.	
15. PORT AUTHORITY Designation, address and telephone number.	
16. SMALL CRAFT FACILITIES Information and facilities for small craft (eg yachts) visiting the port. Yacht Clubs, berths, etc.	
17. VIEWS Photographs (where permitted) or the approaches, leading marks, the entrance to the harbour, etc. Picture postcards may also be useful.	

13.2 The World-Wide Navigational Warning System (WWNWS)

In the interests of continued safe navigation practice, the Inter-national Hydrographic Service (IHO) and the International Marine Organization (IMO) have jointly established a global Navigational Hazard Warning System. The service is provided in the English language by radio and may also be promulgated by Notices to Mariners where appropriate.

There are three types of warnings:

(i) Navarea warnings.
(ii) Coastal warnings.
(iii) Local warnings.

NAVAREA WARNINGS – These cover the whole world, which for the purpose of distribution is divided into sixteen (16) geographic areas. The long-range warnings are issued by an Area Co-Ordinator on frequencies as listed in the Admiralty List of Radio Signals.

COASTAL WARNINGS – These are issued from the country or origin and effect a specific coastal region, in the area of the hazard.

LOCAL WARNINGS – These may supplement coastal warnings and provide detailed information which often relates directly to inshore waters. As such, they may not affect ocean-going vessels to the same extent as vessels working inshore. The warnings often originate from coastguards, and may be transmitted in the national language only.

Content of Warnings

The navigational warnings will advise mariners of such changes as:

Newly discovered wrecks, changes to navigational aids, on-going search and rescue operations, cable laying activity or other underwater work, anti-pollution operations, or where natural hazards are present.

Communication and Transmission of Warnings

One of the main methods, and certainly the greatest expanding method of transmissions is by the use of the NAVTEX service. This is currently being developed in other areas of the world and it must be anticipated that this system will dominate in the future.

The United States also issues long range warnings in the form of "HYDROLANT's" or "HYDROPAC's" and information concerning current warnings can be located in the U.S. Weekly Notices to Mariners.

(Additional reading, Rcf. Not. 13 Annual Summary)

Changes to Merchant Shipping Notices

Recent changes with regard to Merchant Shipping Notices have been made by the Marine Safety Agency:

As from 1997, **Merchant Shipping Notices will be known as MSN's** and will convey mandatory information which must be complied with under UK legislation.

In addition:

Marine Guidance Notes **(MGNs)** will also be issued with regard to specific topics.
e.g. SOLAS, MARPOL, etc.

also:

Marine Information Notes (MINs) will be issued concerning administration detail aimed at training establishments, equipment manufacturers etc.

These will be published with a self-cancellation date.

Each of the above will carry a suffix:–

(M) effective for Merchant Ships

(F) effective for Fishing Vessels

(M + F) effective for both Merchant Ships and Fishing Vessels

Chapter Fourteen

ELECTRONIC NAVIGATIONAL SYSTEMS

14.1 Introduction

The experienced navigator will tell you the days of the sextant are numbered, the day of software is here. And so it is, but not for everybody ... immediately. This age is already seeing giant steps forward with digital plotting systems, Electronic Chart Display and Information Systems (ECDIS), GPS, Integrated Bridge Systems with visual reality and continuous alarm monitoring. The day has indeed arrived, where the navigator is required to know his way around the Computer Keyboard.

There is a need, for marine students to move with the times and achieve proficiency with the VDU, the terminal, the integrated bridge system and to be aware of the data base contents and how to acquire necessary data – quickly and efficiently.

The Master of the ship should not feel left out in this IT explosion. The young men of our future will seek guidance from senior officers. It is imperative, in the authors opinion, that both junior and senior officers learn from each other. Some day soon that junior will be a ship's Master amongst new bridge systems and he may welcome and need the energies of that bright young man just out from the world of College Simulators.

Pic. 45 Apelco 7000 LCD Chartplotter.

Pic.46 Integrated Bridge System – Open space and clear view, lending to a 'One Man Bridge Operation'.
Nucleus Integrated Navigation System (NINAS)
Central Docking Mode Display Unit, communications, helm and telegraph.
Primary and Secondary automatic plotting radars either side. Ninas Workstation, GPS receiver and Electronic Chart Display Unit.

14.2 The Integrated Navigation System

The reality of a one man bridge operation has become an acceptable format. What was once an ideal dream has been turned into a reliable aid to safer navigation. Any errors which occur have a tendency to be human from lack of experience with the equipment being employed, rather than mechanical.

The provision of a centralised navigation monitoring operation can and does ease the workload of the experienced user. Considerable data from numerous sources can be amassed to provide a total picture for the watch officer when the vessel is either at sea in open water conditions, entering port in a docking or unberthing mode, or coastal on passage from one port to another.

Monitoring points would include sensors to deliver the following type of information:

Ships Speed (Velocity sensor) – typical log read-out to provide speed over the ground and speed through the water. This has long been an input feature of modern radars. Displayed in knots.

Ships heading sensor – usual feedback from a Master Gyro Compass. Guarded by off-course alarm system providing both visual and audible watchkeeper alarms.

Rudder Angle sensor – analogue display on a Navigation VDU display. Additional to rudder angle indication at the position of the helmsman.

Auto Pilot – incorporated for vessel control and/or information source for display of current status of vessel.

Rate of Turn sensor – particularly relevant for the larger vessel with large turning circle. Analogue display to Navigation VDU.

Depth sensor – echo sounder feedback. Digital display on a VDU set in Navigation mode.

Position continuous monitoring from either a GPS or DGPS. Position update on demand, with latitude and longitude on VDU display.

14.3 Sensor Inputs and Interfaces

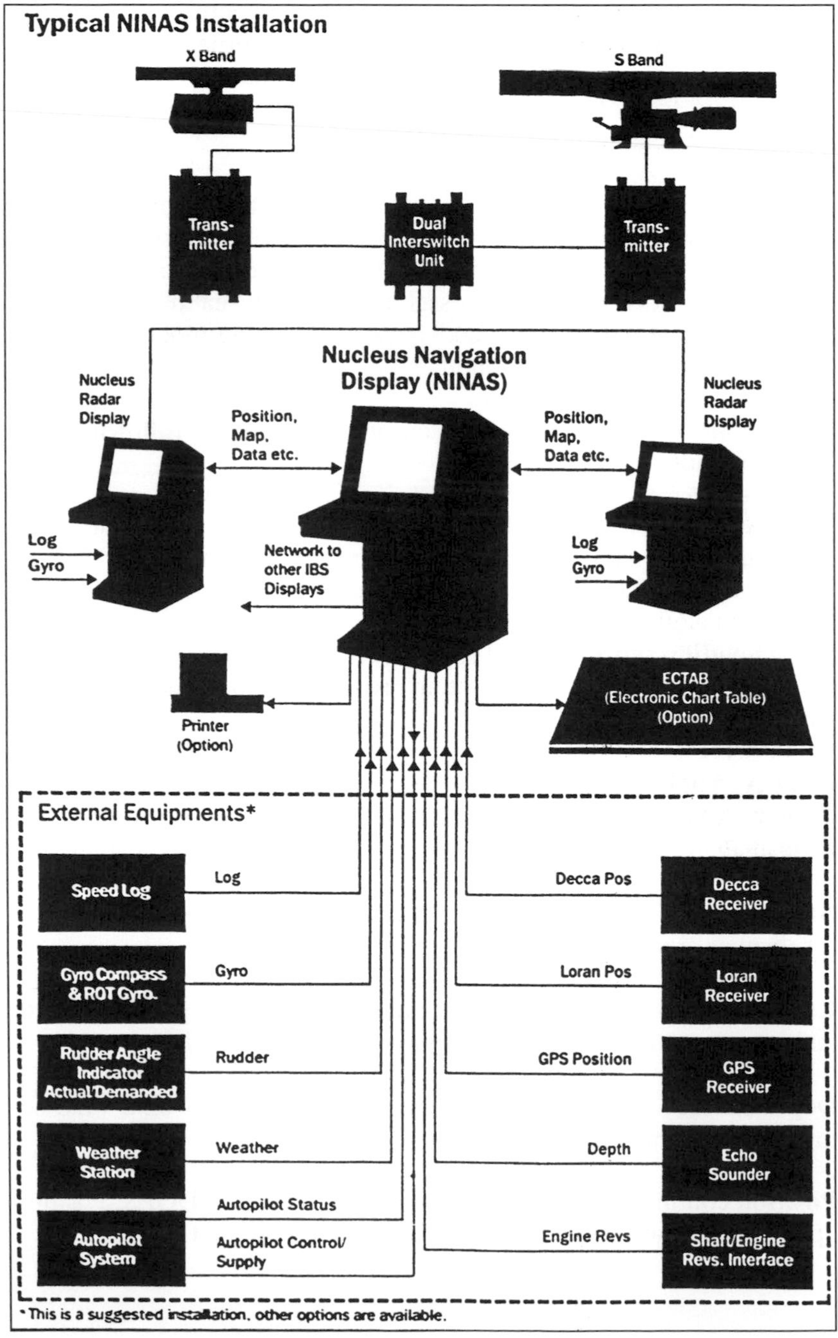

Diagram 14.1: Typical NINAS Installation

Position check displays Some systems have limited range and coverage. Alarm monitoring where secondary system positions do not coincide with primary satellite position fixing system.

Automatic track sensor to allow track analysis and auto correction or manual override. Interfaced with electronic chart system.

ARPA interfaced with both Navigation VDU and Electronic Chart Display. Anti collision data on +20 targets can be acquired and introduced visually onto the charted display. Passage data with parallel index lines waypoint input and guard zones are recognised features. Four colour, presentation with ample scope for a selection of identification symbols.

Additional inputs from:

Radio Direction Finder.
Roll sensors.
Pitch sensors.
Bow thrust performance.
Rate of approach stern radars.
CPP pitch angle.
Anemometer.
Sea temperature.
Barometric pressure sensor.
Cargo sensors.
Engine performance parameters.

A fully integrated system would also incorporate a Navigators Electronic Note Pad. This would provide satellite information on demand for numerous navigational aspects e.g:

Port information, weather details, navigation warnings, navigation records, Company and Masters standing orders, voyage calculations, magnetic variation, together with system alarm details and any required stored data from ships personnel.

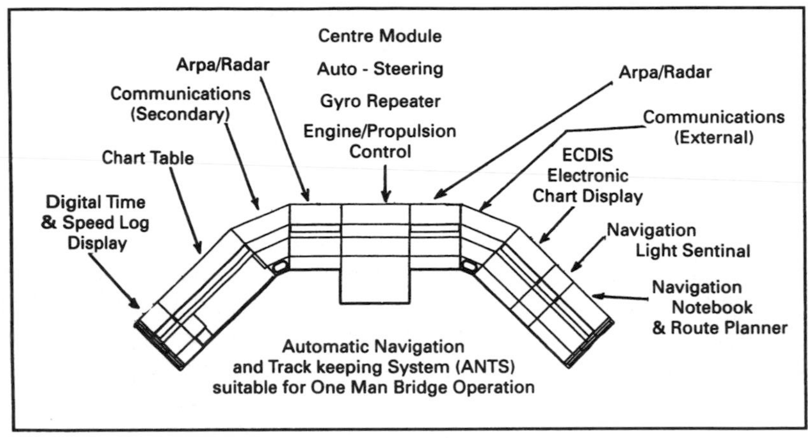

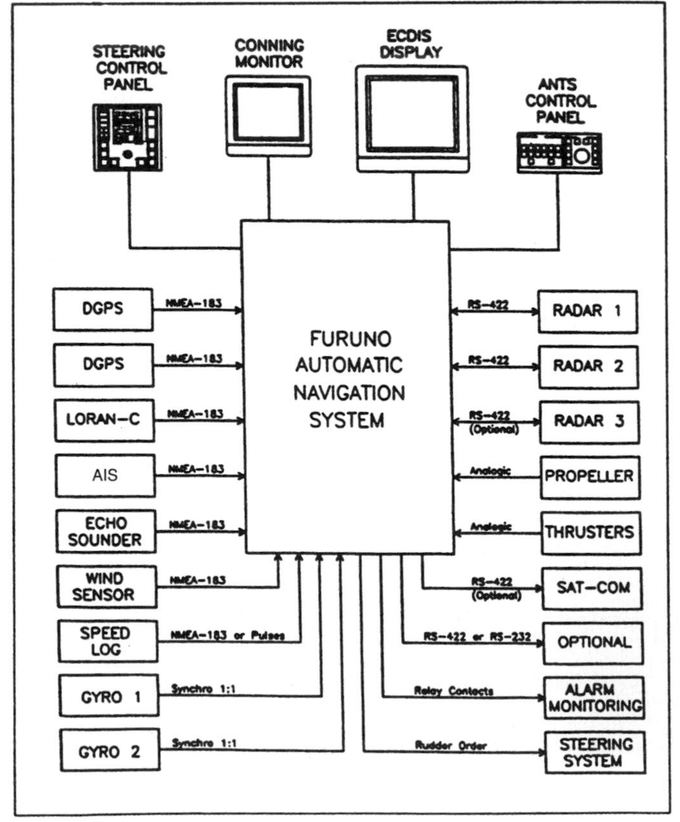

Diagrams 14.2 and 14.3: Integrated (Modular design) Bridge System's

Additional Facilities

Multi-language option.
Zoom +/– viewing.
CD data storage.
Route/Passage library.
Day/Night alternative displays.
Shock absorbant unit

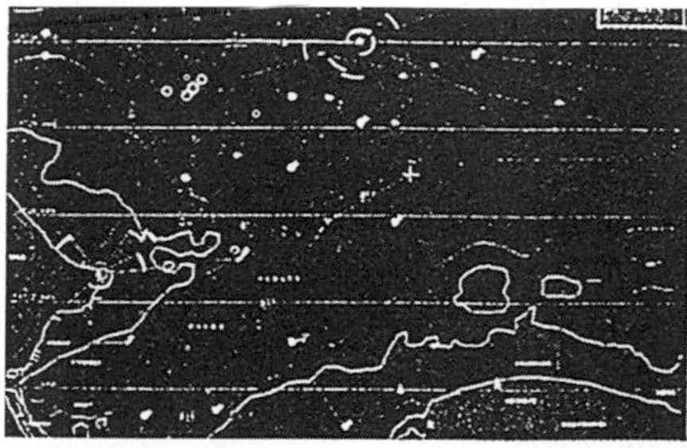

Pic. 47 Navigation aids, night display

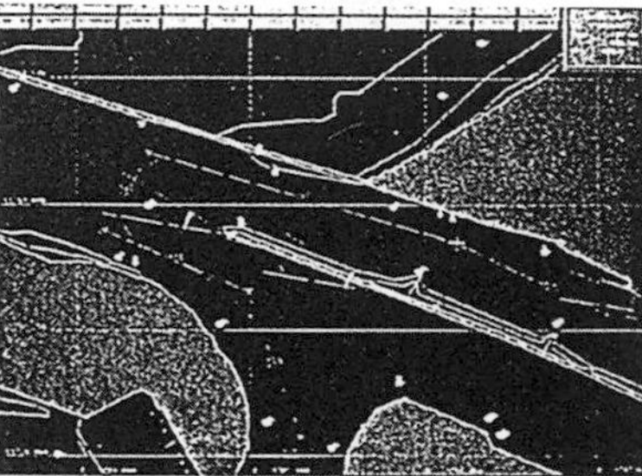

Route planning, night display

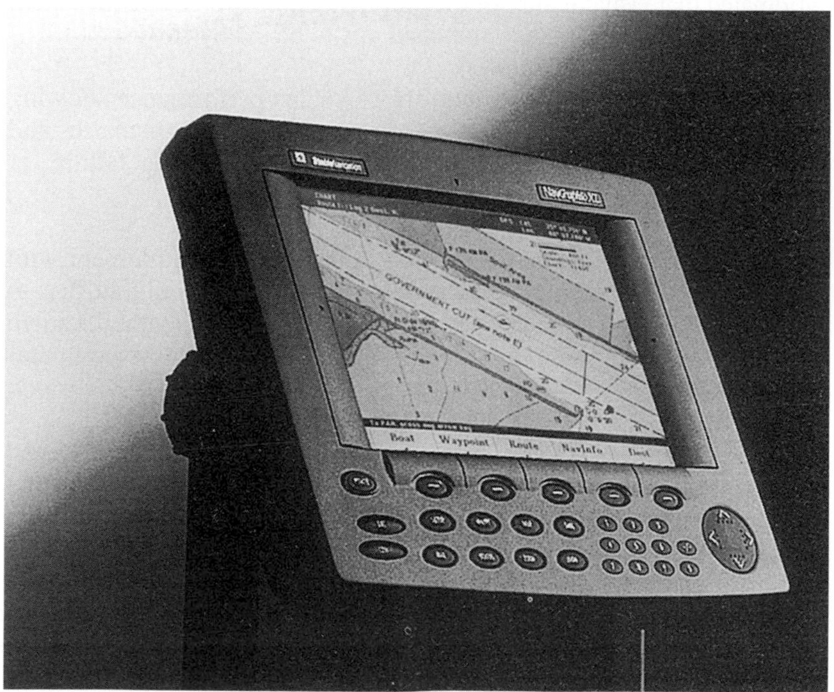

Pic. 48 Electronic Chart Display.

14.4 Electronic Chart Display and Information Systems (ECDIS)

The development of an acceptable Electronic Chart Display System is currently on going and at the time of publication the officially produced data is likely to become available soon. This is not to say that Electronic Chart Systems (ECS) are not already in use. The fact that they do not all meet the performance standard that has been developed by IMO and the International Hydrographic Organisation is a reality. For vessels which are covered by the SOLAS regulations an ECS system cannot at this time replace the use of paper charts. (Additional Reference Notice No. 25 Annual Summary Notices to Mariners).

Clearly a major requirement for any future system must possess an equally efficient correction service to provide continuous reliability. The ECDIS is being developed to provide increased safety over and above that of the paper chart. Interfaced with DGPS/GPS it is anticipated that visual reality of the ships position will be a requirement for the eventual performance standard yet to be set by IMO.

It will allow the Navigator to monitor the ships performance showing intended and actual tracks of the vessel, monitored by eight alarms and seven indicators to warn the navigator of equipment failure or potentially hazardous navigational situations.

The Navigating Officer may not be to concerned at this moment with the methods being employed to develop ECDIS it should suffice to know that the graphic image is being produced from a method known as raster-scan. This can then display the final image on the computer screen.

In the past paper charts have always had limitations, fixed scales and limited data in some cases, depending on survey dates and methods of survey. It is expected that with input and development on digital data from other Hydrographic Offices most of these limitations can be eliminated and allow the navigator to be free of chart boundaries. The quality of the data may well be restricted to that of earlier paper charts but the alternative could be to carry out extensive re-surveys and this would clearly not be a practical proposition in the time available to meet current needs.

Ship's Masters have always held the navigational charts of the UK and associated Hydrographic Offices in high esteem. The concern for quality control in the production of any system is therefore essential for credibility to be maintained. To this end all data supplied is derived from authorised paper charts or from compilations intended for paper chart production.

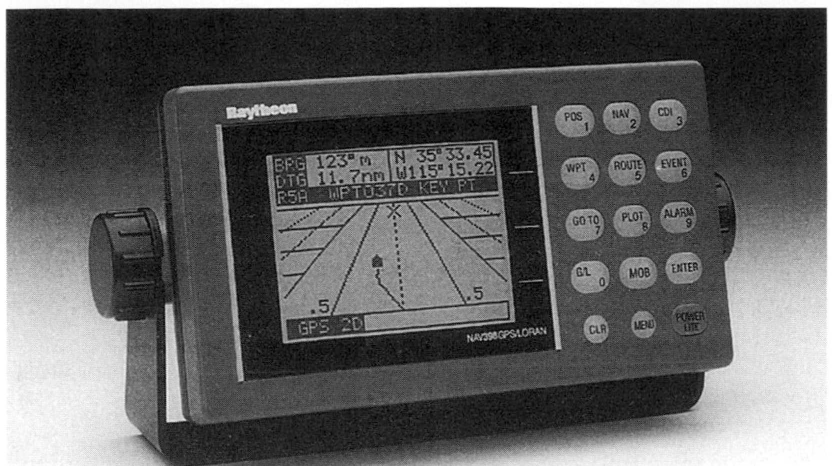

Pic. 49 Raytheon Marine Company
Nav 398 GPS/Loran.

Development of ECDIS is moving towards a graphic display of a continuous rolling chart which will display the ships position in real time. The system will be expected to provide the professional mariner with a "Traffic Overview" which should effectively reduce the watch officers workload and so reduce stress. Radar information being transferred to the sea-chart display would provide a real time picture of the traffic situation.

A passage planning feature via a variable number of 'way points' would permit a route to be planned in detail taking into account all navigational aids, beacons, lights, traffic separation schemes etc. This would be possible because the system would not only be a visual chart display, but also a data/information system. This would relate to such items as wrecks, lighthouses, light sectors, national boundaries, recognised routing systems or anything thought relevant to the overall passage plan. It should relieve the need to resort to books and tables as all the information could be called up and displayed. The user being allowed to add, remove or store relevant information which could be recalled to the display on request. This feature would allow updates to be inserted whenever required.

Pic. 50 GPS navigation centre desktop or bulkhead mounted.

The monitoring principle of passage planning would be achieved by an Automatic Navigation and Track System (ANTS). This would provide close and continuous monitoring of not only the vessels actual position but also of water depth. An 'anti-grounding' alarm system being incorporated through an echo sounder interface.

Additional sensors would activate respective alarms for the vessel being off course by standard interface to Gyro, Magnetic or Fluxgate compass. Similarly an off track situation would be sensed by position reference sensors i.e. GPS, DGPS or, Loran C.

14.4.1 variable features

The provisional IMO Performance Standards for ECDIS have so far influenced the development of the system and the mariner can expect to experience most if not all of the following features with Integrated Bridge Capability:

1) Built in world chart. Chart card library which allows the Navigator to access any of the charted areas.

2) Liquid Crystal Display (LCD) screen. Auto scroll, zoom and pan functions. Main menu and flexible windows type display. Easily viewable under any conditions of daylight or darkness.

3) Own ship movement. Course Over Ground (COG), Speed Over Ground (SOG). Leg and total distance display/record, with range bearing and time to next waypoint.

4) Chart features include full screen chart view with selectable navaids, geographic names, traffic lanes, restricted areas etc., Data window inset for own ships Lat/Long, SOG/COG, Range and Bearings etc.

5) Route and Track detail. Automatic plotting of intended course and automatic tracking of past course. Reverse route function and position error correction.

(Various manufacturers include a variable number of waypoints, 500-1000 would not be unusual. Also track length up to 2500 nautical miles and memory capability for 20 independent routes would reflect an expected standard).

Pic. 51 Electronic Chart Display Monitor can be free standing or incorporated into an integrated bridge system.

6) Alarm systems for arrival, cross track error, anchor drift and Man Overboard would be additional to Anti-Grounding alarm, off-course or position error. Any loss of fixed data, power failure or equipment malfunction would also be alarm protected.

7) Language of operation menus, English, French, Italian, German or Spanish.

8) Additional features may include event markers with different symbols/different colour codes. Local and GMT timings, selectable depth scales metres/feet/fathoms with digital readouts. Variable tracking intervals by either time or distance, heading vector, magnetic variation display and extensive memory.

14.4.2 the advantages of ECDIS

1. Electronic Navigation Charts (ENC's) are vector charts which do not wear out and the cost of replacing and renewal is removed.

2. Once on board the vessel the ship is no longer dependant on external chart suppliers to provide paper charts.

3. No storage problems, as with paper charts.

4. Time and labour saving in chart correction methods. Automatic chart correction service included in approval.

5. Full navigation information is available at a single control position.

6. Real time display of current position is continually available, without the distraction of separate plotting applications.

7. Simplifies watch handover procedures, being controlled at a single consol.

8. Easy way point and passage planning applications with automatic hazard alarms and distance calculations.

9. Scroll ahead facility to enable checking of route hazards on advance tracks.

10. Workload and fatigue is reduced by trained watchkeepers.

11. No need to change charts when in busy waters. ENC's being seamless and as such without borders.

12. Reduced risk of human error with adequately trained operators.

The Admiralty Raster Charts (ARC's) are exact reproductions of Admiralty Charts as issued by the UK Hydrographic Office. (The Australian equivalent is the Seafarer Charts). Raster charts are permitted for use by the ECDIS Performance Standards (A817) as in the form of Raster Chart Display System (RCDS) but in this mode there are limitations. (Additional reference Chapter V, SOLAS).

14.4.3 safety and redundancy of integrated systems

The integrated navigation systems of today raise the obvious question of 'What if ... an essential component or system fails?

To counter this, built in redundancy is part of each system and all the essential units are doubly represented. Design is such that in the event of failure of one function, this is isolated to avoid leading to the failure of other functions.

When classified for 'One Man Bridge Operation' (OMBO) it is usual to find 2 radars, 2 gyro compasses, 2 GPS position fixing systems, 2 power sources and two ECDIS compliant units. Each element being capable of operating independently and/or within the integrated system. In some cases the Classification Societies require automatic change-over in case of failure, or a manual selection as with autopilots, to provide an additional option.

Many shipboard operations are now conducted under a label of 'Bridge Control' with a One Man Bridge (OMB) concept. To ensure that such a routine is viable the Integrated bridge is designed to take account of:–

1. Ergonomics.
2. Automation of Navigation.
3. Monitoring.
4. Safety and redundancy.
5. System support and maintenance.

Correct layout and unit position, is usually determined between the ship owner and the classification regulations. Det Norske Veritas,

(DNV) being the first Society to define how an 'Integrated System' should look and subsequently providing a specific designation DNV-W1, to signify 'One Man Bridge' operational capability.

Such designation takes full account of ergonomics within the design, instrumentation, documentation and training.

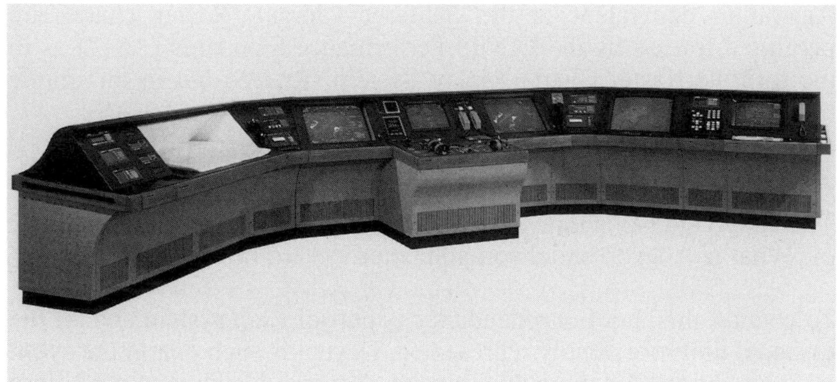

Pic. 52 Integrated bridge design to suit control, communications and navigational instrumentation

14.4.4 Summary

Use of Electronic Navigation Charts at this moment in time would seem to reflect the future of navigation. However, current limitations exist in general operations and redundancy packages by way of hardware and software must be in place for full ECDIS approval. RCDS operations, must still carry an appropriate chart folio of up-to-date paper charts.

The Electronic chart is already active with the integrated bridge and can be interfaced with virtually all other bridge operations. There remains an obvious need for operators to familiarise themselves with the equipment to avoid human error. Simulated training can expect to be a beneficial by product of this major development.

14.5 Compass Systems (modernisation)

The old sea dog of yesterday will tell today's high tech mariner, that the compass was the most important instrument on board the vessel. This particular author would still agree with that old sea dog .... but the compass has changed somewhat from the faithful magnetic compass of the sailing ship days. The modern vessel would expect to be equipped with one and probably two 'Digital Gyro's' together with numerous repeaters to associated instruments. It could well have a Transmitting Magnetic Compass (TMC) or 'Flux Gate' compass, which both tend to leave the somewhat old fashioned magnetic compass in the shade.

NB. When a power failure occurs and the gyros go off-line, that old fashioned magnetic compass could well be reassuring to even the most modern of mariners. Although a modern compass may not desynchronise because of loss of power, interruption or change over.

Carriage requirements still legally require that all vessels are equipped with a standard magnetic compass (Reference Chapter V, SOLAS.)

14.6 Modern Gyro Arrangements

The navigation requirements of modern shipping demand the highest standards of monitoring the ships head. Several systems are commercially available which employ either a single or double unit operation. Twin gyro compasses satisfy redundancy needs for classification regulations.

Standard equipment will usually take the form of a gyroscopic compass unit being directly linked to a control element. Operating on a Direct Current (DC) power supply of 24 volts. The controller will interact with the operators input parameters to the Gyro Unit (and/or to a TMC unit, if fitted). A connection unit from the control element will allow numerous repeaters to function by way of:

> Bridge wing repeaters, course printer, Rate of Turn (RoT) Indicator, Overhead full view compass card (analogue or digital display),Interfaced to Radar/ECDIS operational units and with various alarm outputs.

The modern day gyro compass will provide accurate heading with a built in test facility. It will also probably have self adjusting digital transmission to all repeater outputs, removing the need for manual adjustment to these units. Compass errors could be reduced by inclusion of a static and dynamic speed error correction making the unit suitable for vessels operating at high speeds (up to 70 knots). A high rate of follow-up of 75°/second, not being unusual. Standard construction would resist shock and vibration and the unit would reflect compliance with IEC 945 and IMO Resolution A 424 (XI).

TMC Unit

Where a Transmitting Magnetic Compass unit is engaged, values of variation and deviation can be set. Subsequently all output users could be switched over to the magnetic compass sensor and the corrected magnetic compass course could be digitally displayed and alarm protected.

Fibre Optic Gyroscope

This is a solid state, fully electronic gyro compass suitable for all marine applications including High Speed Craft. The unit which is strapped down to the vessel eliminates the use of a gimbal system and provides heading information, roll and pitch, together with rate of turn about three axis.

The fundamental principal of the fibre-optic gyro is the invariance of the speed of light. (The Litton Marine model, employs what is known as the 'Sagnac Effect').

A fibre optic coil being used as a sensitive rate sensor which is capable of measuring the speed of rotation of the earth. A combination of three such coils (Gyroscopes) together with two electronic level sensors are able to determine the direction of true north.

The three rate of turn signals with information from the level sensors compute the direction of the earths rotation from which the geographical north can be derived. The unit has a short settling time, thirty (30) minutes and provides high dynamic accuracy without course and speed error.

The unit is without moving parts, very reliable and maintenance free. In the event of a malfunction a secondary redundancy unit can be exchanged. Various outputs inclusive of repeaters to radars, auto pilots, can be interfaced with displays in digital and analogue variants.

Main features include:

- Solid state technology with no moving parts.
- Short settling time.
- Meets IMO recommendations.
- Compact unit of low weight.
- All repeaters self-aligning.
- Built in test function.
- Low power consumption.

- High dynamic accuracy.
- No maintenance.
- Allowance for second gyro compass input.
- Allowance for magnetic compass input.
- Automatic emergency power change over.
- LCD display.
- Alarm monitored.

NB. The 'Sagnac Effect' is based on two light waves travelling in opposite directions around a circular light path, resulting in a phase shift. This phase difference being directly calibrated to rotation rate.

Auto-Pilots, Steering Systems and Compass Heading Relations

The ships compass delivers the heading data and this information is directly applied to the ships steering system. The heading being interpreted either by the helmsman in the case of manual steering or by the Auto-Pilot when in a closed loop, automatic control system.

Steering Applications

Most steering systems aboard commercial shipping are incorporated with an Automatic Steering Unit, which includes Follow Up, Non-follow up, Remote and Automatic modes of steering. (In addition to manual control).

Follow Up (FU) Mode

When the position of the wheel is changed the rudder will begin to move and continue moving until it reaches the ordered position as indicated by the helm. If the helm is returned to midships or any other position the rudder will immediately 'follow up' and respond to the new command, taking up a new position.

Non-Follow Up (NFU) Mode

Where the non-follow up tiller steering is employed, the rudder moves in the desired direction from activation of the tiller. The position of the rudder being verified by means of the Rudder Indicator. If the tiller is returned to the midships position the rudder remains in the present position and does not follow the tiller movement back to the midships position. The rudder will only be caused to move from the present position with further activation when a new Port or Starboard command is received.

Remote Mode

Bridge wing stations very often contain pilotage controls. To effect one of these 'Remote Stations' the Auto-Pilot remains in Auto until one of the remote stations is selected by an ACCEPT control. Once this is activated the Auto-Pilot goes into a 'Stand -By' mode and will be so indicated on the main display. Should it be necessary to switch between remote stations activating the ACCEPT control switch activates the required station. Most systems incorporate a tiller NFU controller within each remote station.

Automatic Mode

This mode provides automatic heading control taking account of dynamic parameters such as speed and the head movement. This is achieved by adapting the steering control output to provide a course with minimal rudder motion. Individual functions for weather and sea conditions are selected inputs from the auto-pilot.

Auto Pilots

The use of the automatic pilot is not meant to replace the helmsman when the vessel is navigating in restricted waters, under pilotage or during specific manoeuvres. Ideally, it is meant to operate above certain speeds, namely 5 knots +, below this speed it may have a tendency to wander. It is interfaced with the Gyro compass so in the event of Gyro failure the auto-pilot would wander with the gyro heading. An essential element of the unit is therefore the 'Off Course Alarm', usually set to activate at 5° or 10° from the desired heading.

NB. The alarm is not linked to Gyro failure and would subsequently NOT be activated in the event that the gyro compass failed. The gyro compass may be fitted separately with a gyro failure alarm system.

Auto Pilot Controls

Most auto-pilot units use similar controls and include the following:

Permanent Helm – A control which is employed only if there is a constant influence affecting the ships heading. i.e. strong beam sea, or continuous cross wind.

Then a permanent counter, of say up to 5° may be set in opposition to the affecting element.

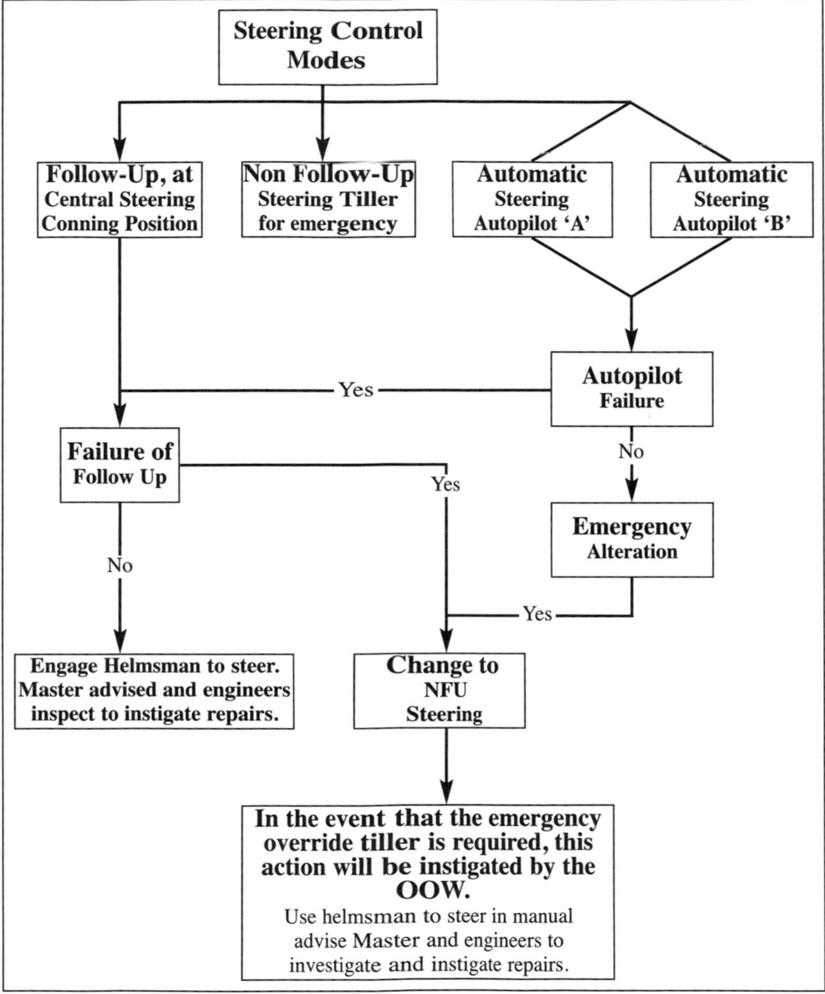

Diagram 14.4: Steering Procedures

Rudder Control – This control determines the amount of degrees of rudder to apply, for every degree the ships head falls away from her course.

Counter Rudder – This control provides the amount of counter rudder which will be applied once the vessel has started swinging back towards the correct desired heading.

Weather Control – A control which is meant to counteract the effects of weather and sea conditions. Especially useful if the vessel is tending to 'yaw' excessively.

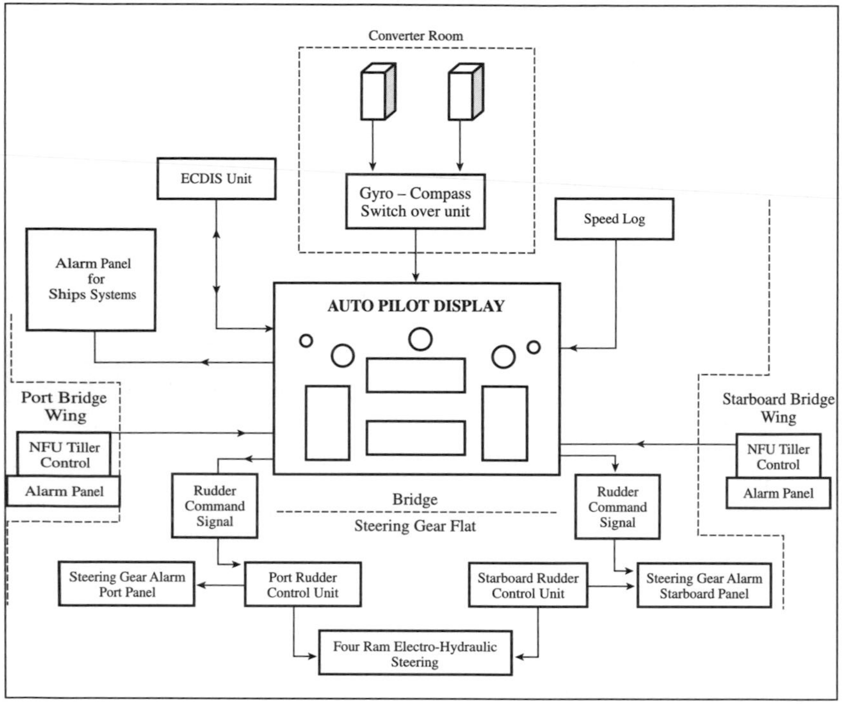

Diagram 14.5: Steering and Automatic Pilot Stations

APPENDIX

EXTRACT FROM THE MERCHANT SHIPPING (AUTOMATIC PILOT AND TESTING OF STEERING GEAR) REGULATIONS 1981 (SI 1981 NO. 571)

Use of the Automatic Pilot – Regulation 4

1. The master shall ensure that an automatic pilot, where fitted, shall not be used in areas of high traffic density, in conditions of restricted visibility nor in any other hazardous navigational situation unless it is possible to establish manual control of the ship's steering within 30 seconds.

2. Before entering any area of high traffic density, and whenever visibility is likely to become restricted or some other hazardous navigational situation is likely to arise, the master shall arrange, where practicable, for the officer of the watch to have available without delay the services of a qualified helmsman who shall be ready at all times to take over the manual steering.

3. The changeover from automatic to manual steering and vice versa shall be made by, or under the supervision of, the officer of the watch, or, if there is no such officer, the master.

4. The master shall ensure that the manual steering gear is tested (a) after continuous use of the automatic pilot for 24 hours and (b) before entering any areas where navigation demands special caution.

14.7 Radar

Marine radars have advanced considerably since the early development years following world war two, when merchant vessels first started to acquire radar as an aid to navigation. The word RADAR being an abbreviation from Radio Direction And Range.

The equipment itself has proved invaluable as an anti-collision aid for vessels navigating in conditions of poor visibility. Additionally, it has also been employed as another position fixing method for short range, coastal operations.

The idea of reflecting electro-magnetic waves from a target could well be traced back to the years of Thomas Edison (1885). What became clear in the practical application was, that radar energy could identify the position of the target but could not determine the course and speed of that target. In the case of marine radar the course and speed of the target had to be determined by a systematic plotting operation by the observer.

Pic. 53 Control consol, set into integrated bridge units.

This plotting procedure is still widely practised today either manually or in the case of the more updated technological equipment, with Automatic Radar Plotting Aids (ARPA). The navigator should note that all the ARPA will do is carry out a series of calculations automatically, and clearly a lot quicker than the human observer could do. It will not make anti-collision manoeuvres.

All plotting activities, in conjunction with radar equipment will have inherent errors, and it should be realised that even the sophisticated ARPA's as with other instruments, have a delay factor before displaying the obtainable data. (Albeit a small delay).

14.7.1 radar plotting errors

a) Errors in range of targets.
b) Errors in bearings of targets.
c) Incorrect estimation of own vessels data.
d) Errors in timing of the plotting interval.
e) Incorrect interpretation of target data.

a) Range Errors
Errors in obtaining a defined range of a target will depend on several factors, not least the quality of the equipment being used and the skill of the observer. The observer should employ the fixed range rings when possible and interpolate between them with the "Variable Range Marker" (VRM). The near edge of the echo should be employed as the point to establish range.

The brilliance control should be applied to the range rings to establish a fine hard line to provide the cleanest range possible. If the equipment is new, then an anticipated error of up to 2.5% of the range scale in use can be expected. Should the equipment have been in service some years the percentage error could be as much as 5% of the range scale.

If the target is slow moving the accuracy of the plot is more likely to be less accurate than one with a target moving quickly.

Regular checking of the VRM against the fixed range rings is to be recommended especially if the VRM is being continually employed to define the range of the target.

b) Errors in Bearings
The type of display employed could well reflect considerably on the accuracy of any bearing obtained. For example:

If a display is stabilised then a greater accuracy in the obtained bearing is achieved compared to a relative motion display, which may show up to +/–2°. If a head-up, unstabilised display is being used then the ships head must be noted at the instant the bearing is taken. This lends to the involvement of human error if on manual steering at the time or an inaccuracy risk if the vessel is experiencing unsettled bow movement.

As the bearing, in most displays, is normally obtained from the screen centre (not applicable to off-centre displays) then the initial setting up and ensuring that the heading marker and the centring is correct is essential for accuracy in bearings.

c) Use of own vessels data – incorrectly
Accurate plotting exercises can only be realised if a correct input of the observers own vessel's course and speed can be assured. Errors in own vessels course and speed will result in large errors in the course and speed of the target estimates.

The observer should maintain a continual check on own ships performance and the plotting interval should be increased to reduce the margin of error that could be affected in nearest approach of target.

d) Irregular timing of Plotting Interval
Where manual plotting is engaged the plotting interval becomes subject to human error. Lack of concentration by the observer or unexpected interruptions could render the plot unreliable.

Increasing the number of plots and reducing the time interval between the plots tends to lend to improved accuracy and reliability of the targets performance. Any plot needs to be completed in a systematic manner to allow correct analysis.

e) Incorrect interpretation of the targets data
A plot can be unreliable for numerous reasons, but if the correct principles have been applied then the observer could expect to obtain acceptable information on the target. Levels of accuracy being adequate for practical anti-collision manoeuvres.

The observer should realise that radar is still an aid to navigation. Plotting activity must be carried out in a systematic manner with increased plotting intervals. The target will require close monitoring which could incur human failings. To minimise this and provide greater reliability 'Clear Weather' plotting should be encouraged by masters just as much as 'Foul Weather' plotting. Daytime and visual comparison with plotted information should be encouraged as a means of on-board training.

14.7.2 radar plot analysis

Once the systematic plot is established the observer is faced with the task of obtaining the maximum information from the construction namely:

1) Course and Speed of the target.
2) Distance and Time target will pass ahead/astern of own ship.
3) CPA and TCPA.
4) Aspect of target.
5) Relative bearing of target.

The decision to act, or not, on this information must then be taken. Such a decision should take account of all the options available; i.e. Stop Engines, Reduce Speed, Increase Speed, Alter Course to Port/Starboard, or operate astern propulsion.

Whatever manoeuvre is chosen it must be legal and take into account the Regulations for the Prevention of Collision at Sea (COLREGS).

Any action taken must be safe and substantial to:

a) produce an adequate CPA
b) provide clear indication to an external observer, the degree of change.

Consideration should be directed to 'Why' the action was taken, and what will the new consequences of that action be. It should also be seen not to bring the vessel into a new close quarters situation with either the same or another target.

NB. Mariners may raise an eyebrow at the option to increase speed, mentioned above. This should not be taken out of context and the author would clarify that an increase in speed can be just as effective in collision avoidance as a decrease in speed. However, it is not being advocated that observing vessels should be quick to increase speed. This option, which is all that it is, must be accompanied by long range scanning to ascertain what the vessel is moving towards.

An increase in speed provides less time to assess an oncoming situation and must, by its very nature, not be a readily

acceptable manoeuvre to the cautious Master. Circumstances may however, make it a prudent action. e.g. A target vessel closing from directly astern.

The Basic Radar Plot – Head-Up Presentation

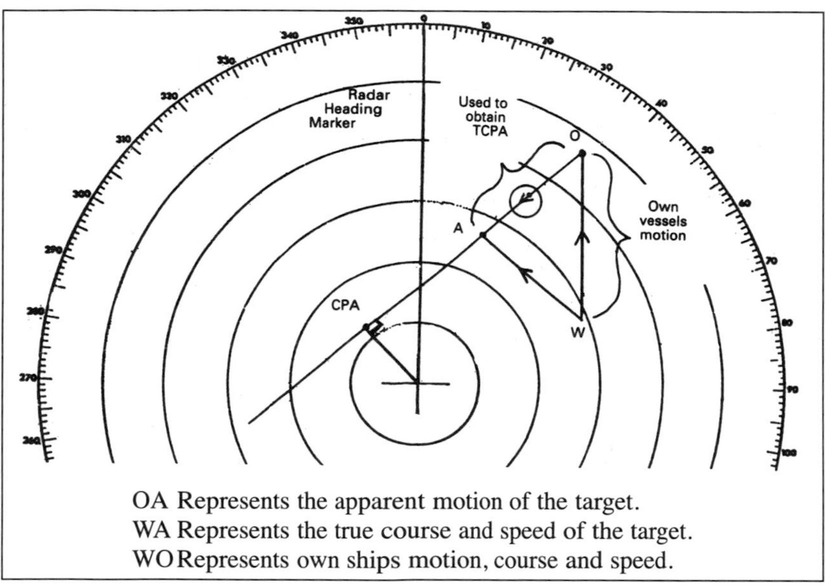

OA Represents the apparent motion of the target.
WA Represents the true course and speed of the target.
WO Represents own ships motion, course and speed.

Diagram 14.6: Plotting Sheet

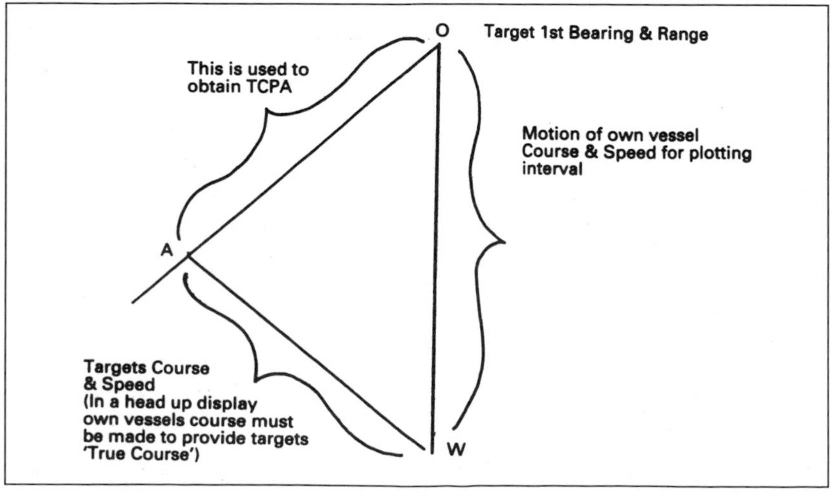

Diagram 14.7: Expanded detail of the basic 'AOW' triangle.

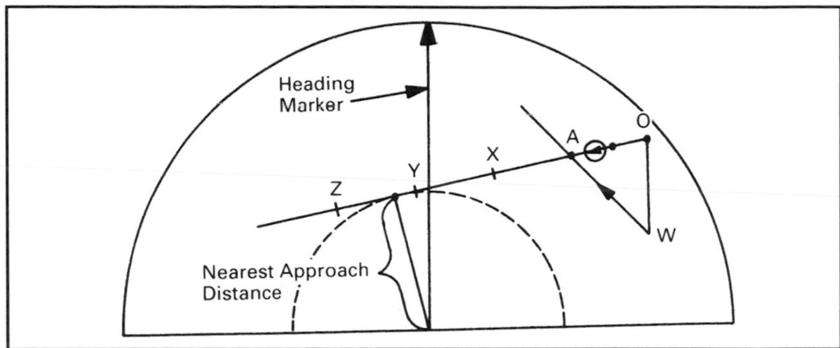

Assume target is observed at 0800 hrs 'O'
" 0810 " 'A'
" 0820 " 'X'
" 0830 " 'Y'
Time of Nearest Approach (just after point 'Y')
= *0833 hrs approx.*

Diagram 14.8: Radar Plotting – Nearest Approach

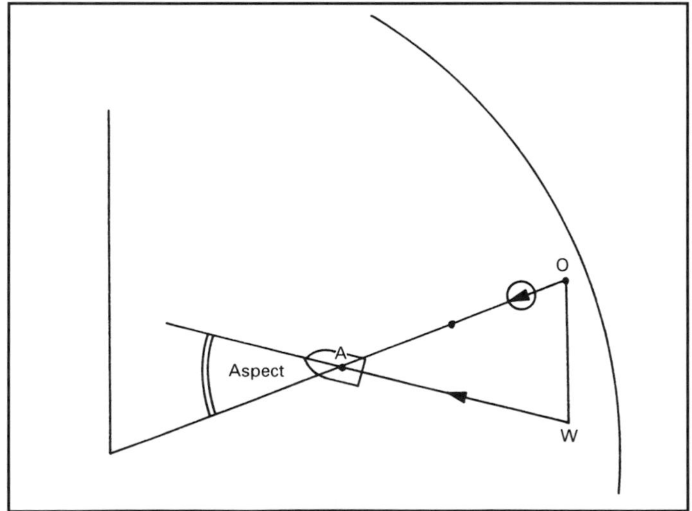

Definition
The Aspect is defined as the relative bearing of own vessel as taken from the target.
or
That angle contained between the ships head of the target and the bearing of the target.

Diagram 14.9: Radar Plotting – Aspect

Reduction of Speed – Course maintained following initial plot which indicates a collision situation.

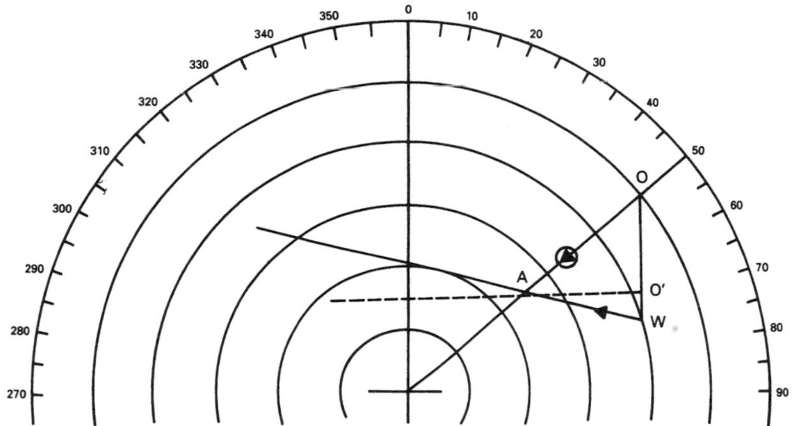

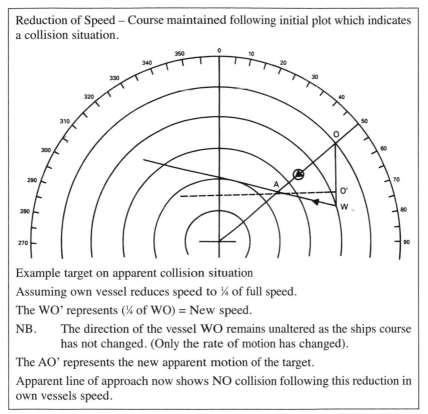

Example target on apparent collision situation

Assuming own vessel reduces speed to ¼ of full speed.

The WO' represents (¼ of WO) = New speed.

NB. The direction of the vessel WO remains unaltered as the ships course has not changed. (Only the rate of motion has changed).

The AO' represents the new apparent motion of the target.

Apparent line of approach now shows NO collision following this reduction in own vessels speed.

Diagram 14.10: Radar Plotting – Avoiding Action by Own Vessel

Alteration of Course by 90° to Starboard – Speed maintained following initial plot which indicates a collision situation.

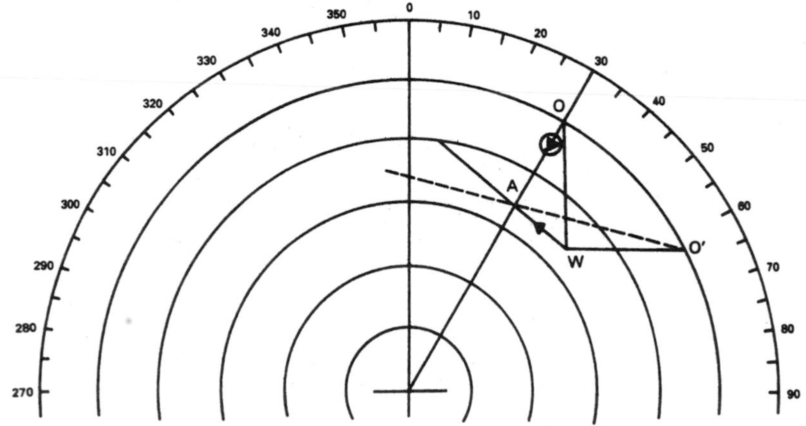

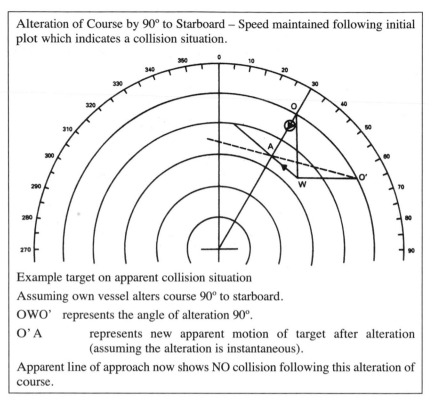

Example target on apparent collision situation

Assuming own vessel alters course 90° to starboard.

OWO' represents the angle of alteration 90°.

O' A represents new apparent motion of target after alteration (assuming the alteration is instantaneous).

Apparent line of approach now shows NO collision following this alteration of course.

Diagram 14.11: Radar Plotting – Avoiding Action by Own Vessel

14.7.3 radar – presentation methods

1. Ships Head Up unstabilised. (Relative Motion)
2. North Up, stabilised. (Relative Motion)
3. North Up, stabilised off-centre. (Relative Motion)
4. Sea Stabilised. (True Motion)
5. Ground Stabilised. (Ground Stabilised)

---

1) Relative Motion – Ships Head Up – Unstabilised.

Main Advantages – Relative bearings provide a quick indication of the targets bearing in relation to own ships head. Also a direct comparison with a visual contact.

Main disadvantages – The observer must ascertain the ships heading from the helmsman when actually taking the bearing. Echo paints will blur on the screen when altering course or if own ship is steering badly.

Relative movement of an echo is difficult to determine due to the movement of own ships head.

2) Relative Motion – North Up stabilised

Main Advantages – This presentation allows direct comparison with the chart. Movement of own ships head does not cause blur or smear of targets on screen. Course changes do not cause picture rotation, which could produce a confusing image. The accuracy of the bearing is good and the CPA can be easily obtained. Observation of the relative movement of the echo can be continued as long as the after glow remains.

Disadvantage – subject to gyro compass performing correctly. Any defect in Master Gyro would directly effect radar picture.

3) Relative Motion – North Up stabilised, off-centre

Main Advantages – With the increased range visible on screen an earlier warning of approaching targets can be obtained. It is better for parallel index usage, and no centring error is involved.

Disadvantages – Less warning from beam or astern targets with the increase in the ahead range. Must have an Electronic Bearing Indicator (EBI) because the mechanical bearing cursor cannot be employed with off-centre display.

NB. Off-Centre Displays

The majority of marine radar units offer an off-centre presentation in addition to the own ship, fixed centre presentation. This additional facility allows the point of origin to be shifted to the lower part of the screen and provides the distinct advantage of looking ahead over a greater range. The alternative would require the observer to select a longer range operation which would only offer reduced target definition.

If the off-centre operation is required it would mean that the timebase would have to produce a longer scan than that required by the range in use. For example if the 6 mile range is employed then the timebase is effected to nominally sweep the trace from the centre to the screen edge in 75 microseconds, and then return back. However, if operating in off-centre mode the displayed range from own vessel could be nearly twice the selected range of 6 miles and the timebase would need to be extended to take this into account.

The off-centre is a feature of 'True Motion' presentation.

4) True Motion Sea Stabilised

Main advantages – This presentation indicates the course of all ships through the water, and set and drift can be clearly identified by observing the movement of a stationary echo.

Any alteration of the targets course or speed is displayed immediately while if own ship alters course echoes remain unaffected. Centring error is eliminated and an increased range ahead is achieved to provide earlier warning of approaching echoes.

Disadvantages – Resetting of the centre spot is required, which could occur at an awkward time and break continuity. Own ships data could cause false movement to be screened, e.g. Compass error, or incorrect speed input.

5) True Motion ground Stabilised

Main advantages – Has many of the advantages of the Sea Stabilised but indicates course and speed over the ground not through the water. This is useful in pilotage waters. Also separation of stationary and moving echoes can be an asset.

Disadvantages – As above this presentation has all similar disadvantages as a Sea Stabilised presentation with the exception that course and speed of own ship through water is not indicated and tide controls require frequent adjustment to allow for change in tides.

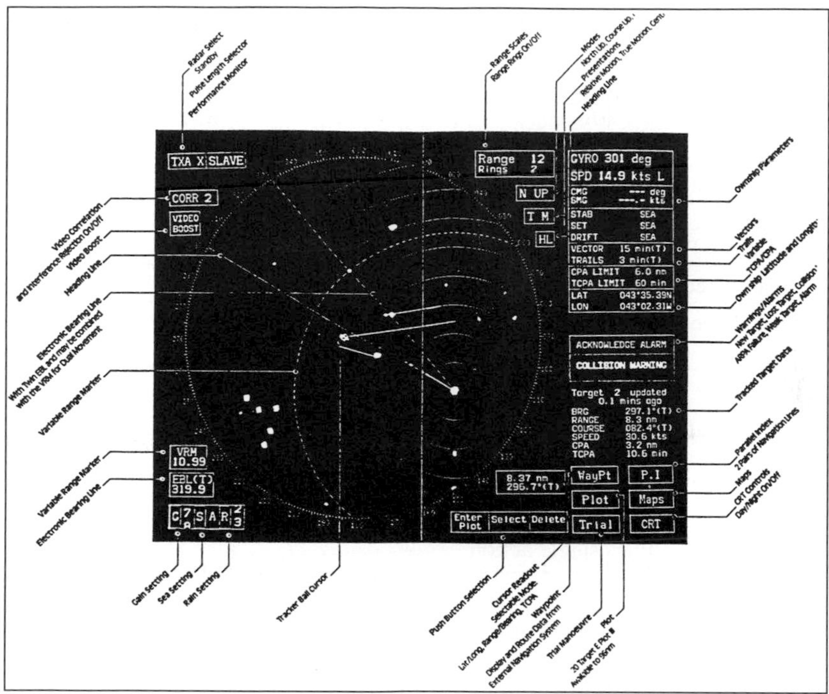

Diagram 14.12: RADAR – Modern Marine Display

14.7.4 example

The following is a completed radar plot which has been compiled aboard a vessel which is steering 315° (T) at a speed of 12 knots in reduced visibility.

Find the single alteration of course or reduction of speed which would be effective at 0924 hours, that would achieve a CPA of 2.0 miles.

Describe and justify the action taken, bearing in mind that other target vessels may take action at the same time.

(With any plotting related question full acknowledgement to the content of all the Regulations for the Prevention of Collision at Sea should be taken into account).

14.7.5 methodology

Draw up a list of all the possible options that your own vessel could take and by the process of elimination resolve the options to obtain the legal, and practical action that would be possible in the presented plots:

Option to Vessel	Viability of Option Application	Reject or Approve
Alt. Course Starboard	Illegal – altering towards a vessel abaft the Starboard beam	X
Alt. Course Port.	Illegal – targets are forward of the beam	X
Increase Speed	Dangerous with targets crossing ahead	X
Reduce Speed	Possible action is legal and could answer the question criteria	√
Go Astern	Not practical and would not be readily apparent	X
Stop	Dangerous – would bring targets into close quarters	X
Combination of Speed/Course action	Denied by wording of question requiring a single action	X

a) Enter the ships heading and fore and aft line extended.

b) Insert the required range circle of the desired CPA (i.e. 2nm range).

c) Insert beam bearing extended.

d) Project all target plots to the time of taking action, namely to where the targets will be at 0924.

e) Insert desired line of approach of the worst scenario target from the 0924 position to a position tangential to the range circle.

f) Step back this direct line of approach into the original OAW triangle to obtain reduction of speed.

g) Use the obtained reduction of speed on the remaining targets to ensure that the question criteria is met and that the reduction in speed answers the question.

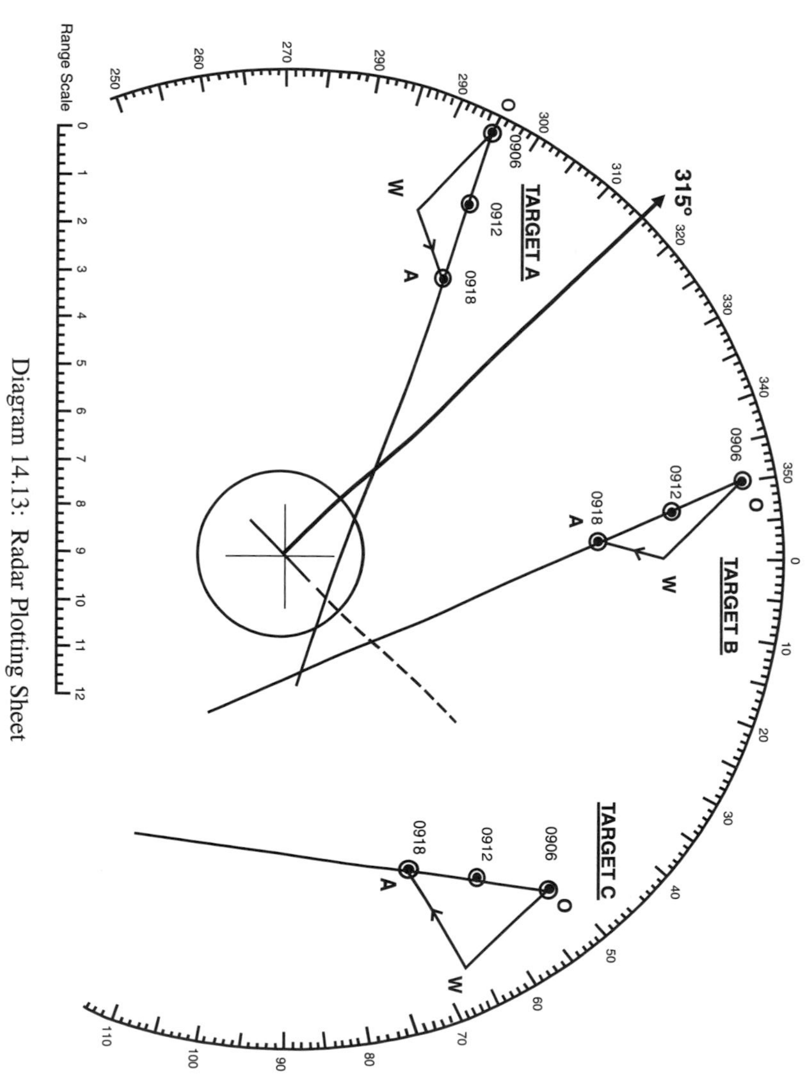

Diagram 14.13: Radar Plotting Sheet

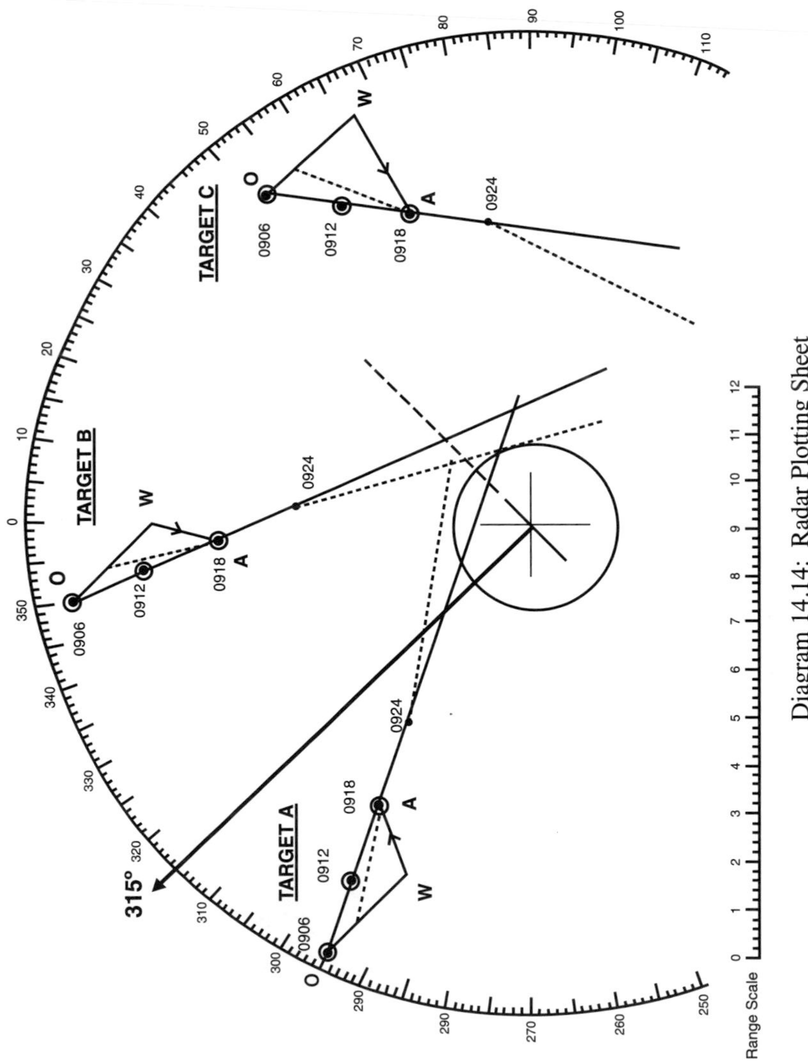

Diagram 14.14: Radar Plotting Sheet

14.7.6 justification of action

Following the reduction in speed:

Target 'A' will cross ahead of own vessel at an increased range, which satisfies the question criteria.
Target 'B' will pass down own ships starboard side at a CPA of 2nms, which satisfies the question criteria.
Target 'C' will pass astern of own vessel at an approximate CPA of 3.5nms, which satisfies the question criteria.

The reduction of speed to approximately ¾ full speed of twelve knots, an effective reduction of only 3 knots would not be readily apparent to other observing vessels.

Although the action is legal and does not contradict the Regulations for the Prevention of Collision at Sea. The action also satisfies the example question criteria.

Other alternative actions would either be illegal in the circumstances, or alternatively not resolve the situation nor answer the question asked.

The action does not bring the vessel into a close quarters situation with any other target, it is legal and effectively keeps all targets at a CPA of 2nms or more. The action is considered acceptable when ascertaining the mariners ability to interpret and analyse a radar plotting situation.

Action taken was only carried out once maximum information was available on all three respective targets. Action was not taken on scanty information, but with maximum information from three AOW triangles used for systematic plotting procedures.

14.8 Global Positioning Systems (GPS)

The GPS system has been developed by the United States military and is now widely available for all commercial and private use. The U.S. Defence Department have retained a reservation to scramble the GPS signal for example in times of hostile activity and this is known as 'Selective Availability' (SA).

The theoretical accuracy under SA conditions, for civilian use, is limited to plus or minus 100 metres. However experiences during the Gulf War when SA was switched off provided accuracy estimated at +/– 05 metres. The long term outcome for SA, has to date not been disclosed.

The GPS-NAVSTAR system operates with 24 satellites in three orbital planes, 10900 nautical miles above the earth, in a 12 hour period. This results in between six and eleven satellites being accessible to the receiver, anywhere in the world. Positional accuracy being less than 100 metres for 95% of the time.

(Note comparison D-GPS accuracy page 423).

14.8.1 the position fix

The navigator would establish his/her position by receiving very high frequency signals from the selected satellites. Operational frequencies of 1227 MHz, and 1575 MHz are emitted from the orbital satellites and although weak when they reach the earths surface, they are virtually free from other electrical/radio interference.

The position is achieved provided that the receiver has at least three satellites in view. The distance from the user to each of the selected satellites is measured and these three ranges provide a three dimensional position. The three ranges being obtained by measuring the time of propagation.

All receivers display the position in Latitude and Longitude and can be plotted directly onto the navigational chart.

Navigators will however, have experienced some charts bearing a notation that the Satellite position may need an applied correction prior to setting on the chart. Generally the correction is small but not always so.

(NB. Currently the Hydrographic Office is conducting a survey on the subject of GPS Position Shift and charted difference 2005/6)

The satellites are so spaced in orbit that at any time a minimum of six satellites are available to users anywhere in the world. Each satellite continuously transmits position and time data which allows the user to obtain an accurate fix at any time of the day, anywhere in the world and in all weather conditions.

The receiver clock error (Rx.) being applied to the respective satellite ranges to provide a definitive fix of the vessels position.

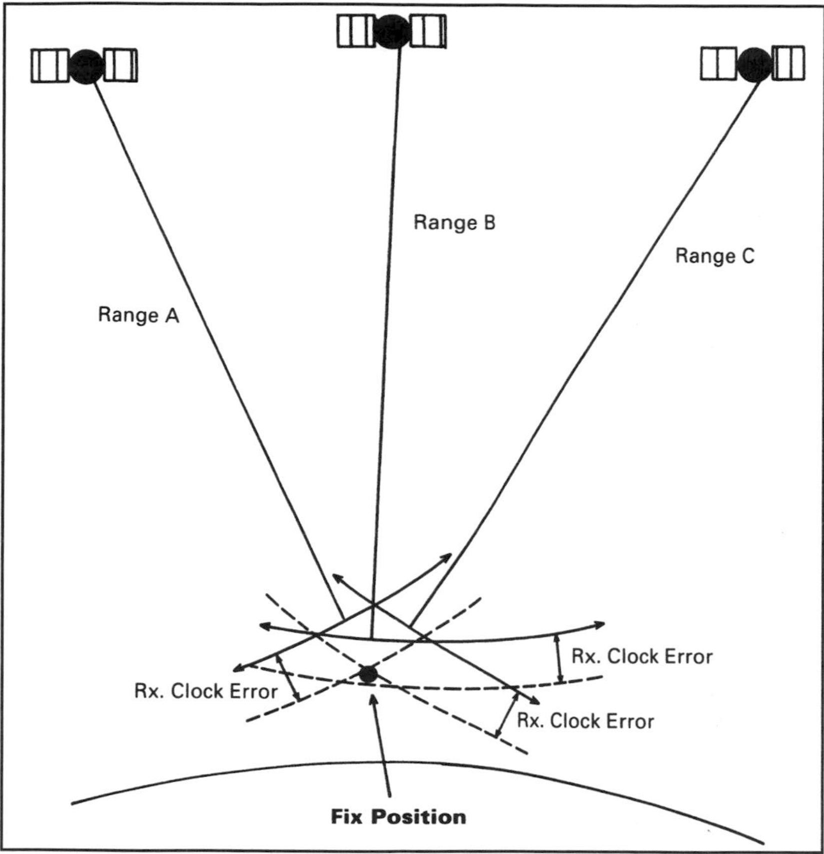

Diagram 14.15: The GPS Position Fix

The geometry of the position fix can be seen from the two position circles. When two satellites are employed all positions on the circles are the same range from the respective satellites. As these satellites are continually moving the crossing angles of the position circles are always changing. If a third satellite is involved with a subsequent third position circle, then the positional error is reduced.

The resulting accuracy of the position becomes dependent on what is known as Horizontal Dilution of Precision (HDOP). Which is assumed to be a single value. This value is subsequently multiplied by the range measurement from the satellite in determining position error.

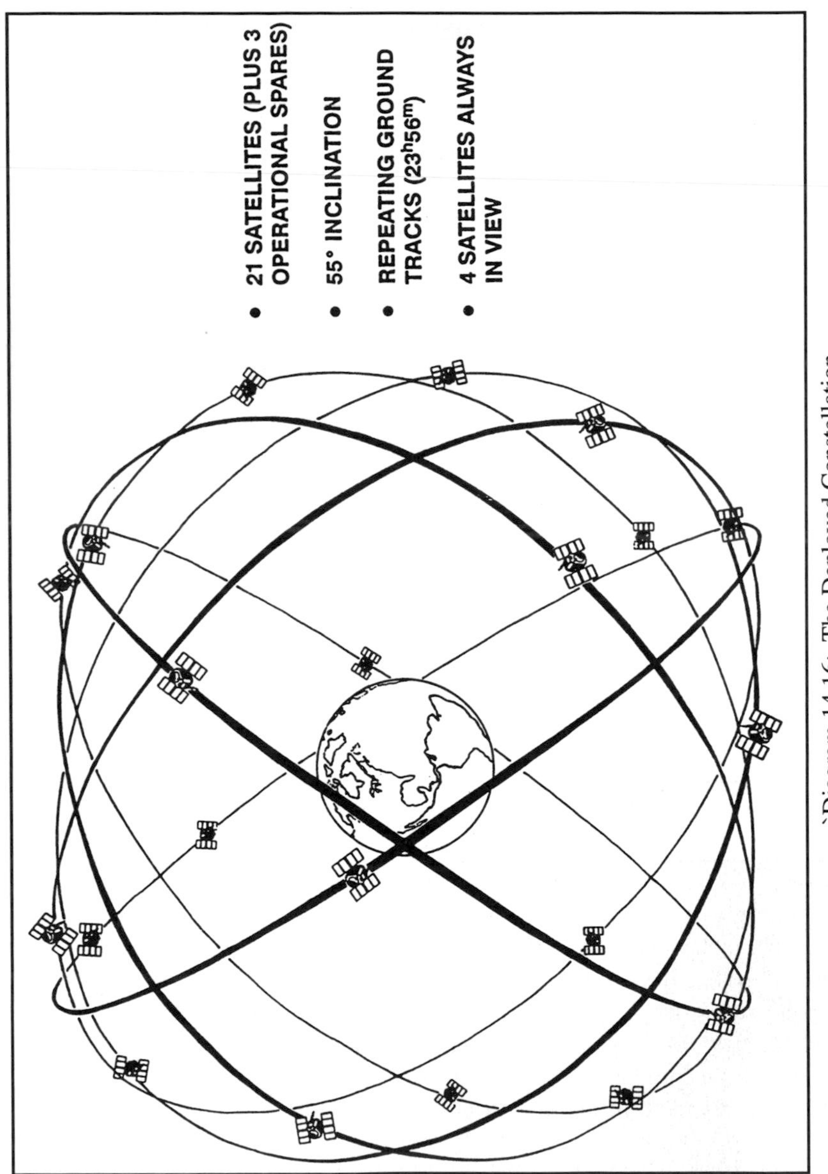

• 21 SATELLITES (PLUS 3 OPERATIONAL SPARES)
• 55° INCLINATION
• REPEATING GROUND TRACKS (23h56m)
• 4 SATELLITES ALWAYS IN VIEW

`Diagram 14.16: The Deployed Constellation

If the range measurement is considered it will be realised that this depends on measuring the time of propagation from the satellite to the navigator. This must assume that the receiving clock is synchronised with the satellite clock. The reality is that errors in range will be incurred by delays when transmission passes through the troposphere and the ionosphere and the result is known as a pseudo-range. (False Range)

The mariners GPS receiver will provide accuracy of approximately 100 metres by engaging the pseudo-range for three satellites and the corrected receiver clock errors.

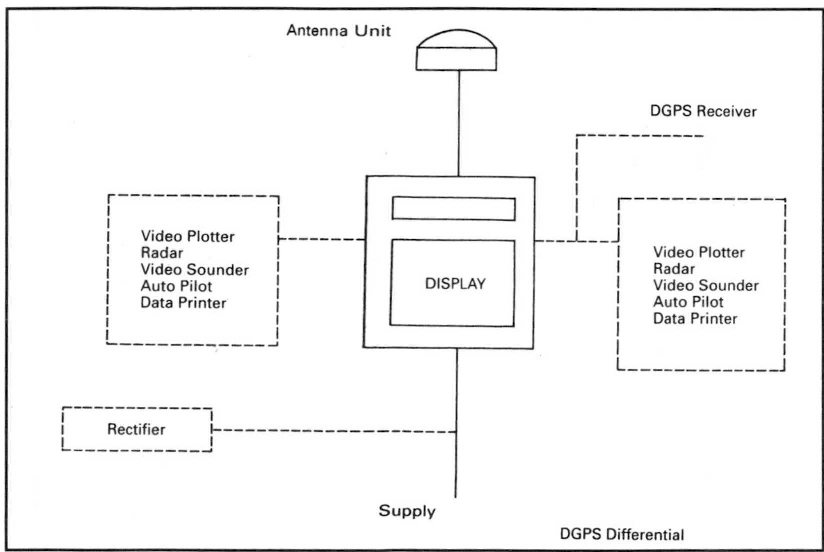

Diagram 14.17: GPS Navigation System

Pic. 54 Raytheon Marine Company
Nav 298 GPS/Loran.

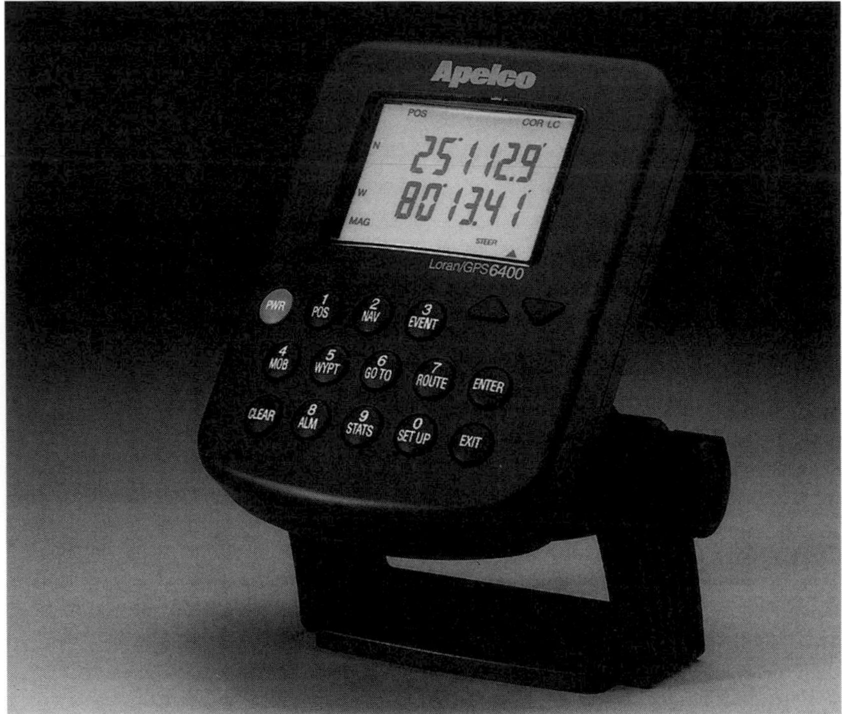

Pic. 55 Apelco 6400 Loran/GPS

The accuracy of the GPS fix equates to a multiple of the error in the range measurement and the HDOP. Many GPS receivers have pre-set limits which exclude satellites having large HDOP values. Clearly the smaller the value of the HDOP the better the accuracy of the fix.

NB. Some manufacturers allow the navigator to input designated limits of HDOP and will display status of each satellite.

The accuracy of any positional fix will be dependent on the type of errors incurred. Range measurements are based on not only the satellite clock which is monitored by the control segment of the system, but also on the assumption that the position of the transmitting satellite is itself in the correct position.

Fluctuations in the satellite clock and the satellite position can produce an overall error of up to 20 metres approx. inclusive of refractive errors.

Improved accuracy is obtainable when the satellites are near to right angles to one another.

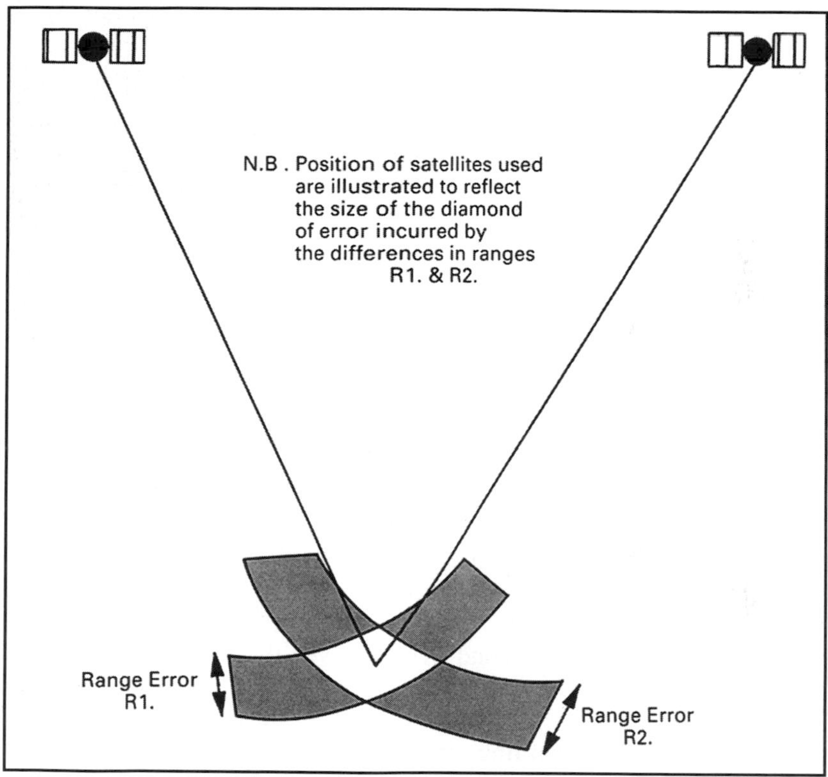

Diagram 14.18: The GPS Position Fix
The Horizontal Dilution of Precision

14.8.2 measurement accuracy

Practically, the positional accuracy will depend on the position of the satellites being used because of the intersecting angles of the position lines (Ranges) from the transmitters.

14.8.3 GPS system errors

Although the errors involved are small and quoted accuracy of 100 metres is the anticipated norm, in practice accuracy of under 65 metres is not unusual. The main errors are known as:

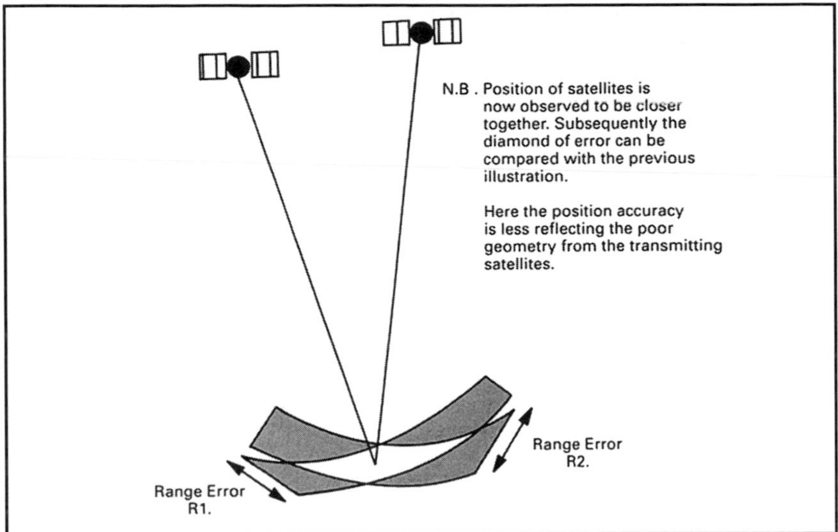

Diagram 14.19: Comparison of diamond of error with satellite positional change.

Satellite Clock Error

Each satellite is equipped with a highly accurate atomic clock with a known or predictable variation from GPS time. These satellites are monitored from a ground support and although may deviate approximately to a milli-second over a seven day period they can be corrected. However, the time error could induce range errors which are difficult to decipher from the satellites small orbital altitude changes that could occur. The resulting error should not normally exceed +/– 2 metres.

Multi-path Error

This error is one which is caused by reception of data from the Space Vehicle (SV) from more than one source. An example of this may be observed from a reflecting surface close to the antenna. This is a variable error because the siting of each receiver and aerial unit is local to a specific vessel. Insured error values would not be expected to be above 5 metres.

Chart Datum Error

The GPS system is based on a chart datum which is a derivative of the World Geodetic System 1984 (WGS 84). British Admiralty Charts, European Charts and other areas of the world generally employ a local datum. Consequently navigators must apply a correction to GPS fixes before transferring to the chart.

New Charts and New Editions published since 1981 carry a notation usually near the title, when applicable to the fact:

The amount of shift between satellite derived positions and chart positions. Namely a difference to be added to Latitude Longitude.

Clearly this could be a laborious task to a navigator on the coast and most GPS receivers have a selection of datums available to suit the charted area. A choice of the respective datum allows the correction to positions to be made automatically by the receiver.

NB. Electronic chart systems may be set to one datum when the operator could well be switching to another chart with another datum. Care is needed to maintain plotting accuracy.

Refraction Errors

These are variable and are incurred as the signals from the satellites pass through the ionosphere and the troposphere. The user would not expect accuracy to be impaired by more than 20 metres from refractive errors.

Mariners have always been trained with safety as the priority and with sophisticated instruments it would be all too easy to become complacent. Manufacturers of GPS systems warn that adverse weather conditions could affect overall performance specifically – heavy rain, snow and thunder storms.

It is also worth noting that a well known, world-wide shipping company retains an active policy of insisting all Deck Officers take weekly sights. There was an occasion when a junior Third Mate placed the ships position 200 miles away from the GPS position. After receiving the ridicule from his more senior colleagues it was found that the GPS was suffering a malfunction. Much to the relief of the junior third mate.

It should be remembered that all instruments suffer from a delay factor which may be greater or lesser, depending on the data being acquired. The mariners eyes do not have the same problem and visual fixing together with an effective lookout can often be healthily reassuring.

14.9 Differential GPS (DGPS)

At the time of publication the DGPS system is the most accurate of navigation systems available to commercial users. By over-coming the effects of "Selective Availability" (S/A) and the other errors incurred in GPS systems positional accuracy of approximately five (5) metres can be achieved.

14.9.1 principle of operation

DGPS cannot operate without the current GPS signal. A stationary GPS receiver is positioned precisely in a known position to measure the difference between the true position and that position ascertained by the stationary receiver. The difference between the two positions (the error) is then transmitted by radio to the mobile DGPS receivers.

The DGPS user will use this differential error information on the GPS system to correct for positional accuracy.

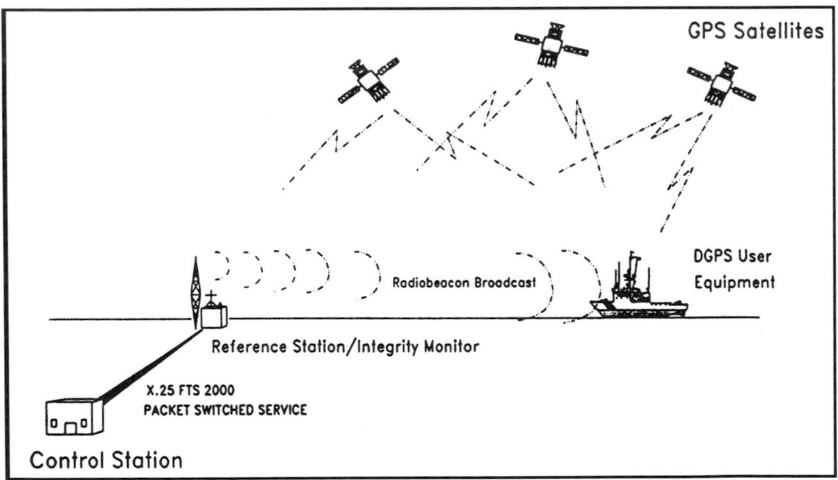

Diagram 14.20: DGPS Elements

14.9.2 use of DGPS

Although the coverage areas of DGPS are at the present time limited, many additional radio transmitting beacons are planned for the future. Expansion areas include Europe and the Mediterranean, Alaska, the Great Lakes, Caribbean, New Zealand, Australia and Hawaii. Extensive coverage already exists around Scandinavia, the Baltic Sea, Iceland and the United Kingdom, as well as Canada and USA, although the UK operates a pay/charge system.

Additional receiver equipment is required by the user in order to collect the navigational signals from all the satellites in view, plus the differential corrections from the DGPS station in the reception of DGPS signals, and most manufacturers have an add on unit to allow for this. The latest GPS receivers are inclusive of DGPS capability.

The DGPS system is essentially two receivers tuned to process information not only from the GPS satellites but also from a fixed land based station. As the position of the land base is known, any error in fixing position can be quantified and transmitted to user operators. Clearly any standard GPS errors can be eliminated to provide enhanced accuracy of plus/minus 5m.

Pic. 56 DGPS Beacon Receiver PBR 1000.

14.10 Use of the Echo Sounder

The echo sounder is probably the most reassuring of all navigation instruments. It provides the Master with virtually continuous indication of the vessels underkeel clearance. Echo sounders are generally designed to operate and record depths assuming a velocity of sound in water of 1500 metres per second.

NB. The velocity of sound in water in actual fact can vary from approximately 1445 to 1535 metres per second and may be influenced at the same place by temperature and salinity at any one time.

However, this should not affect the accuracy of the instrument by more than 5% away from the true values.

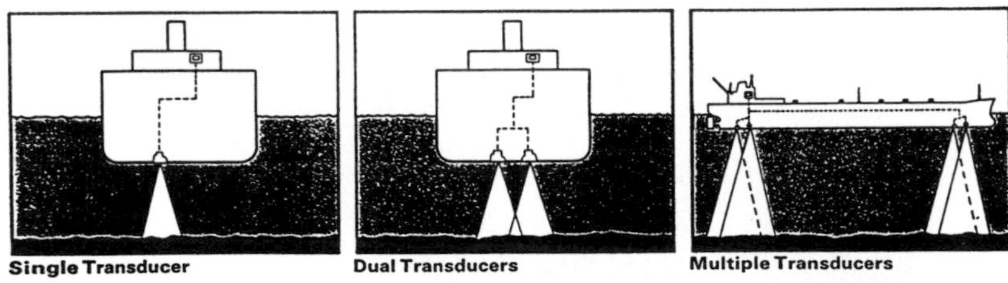

Diagram 14.21: Transducer positioning.

Echo sounding equipment must comply with the IMO performance standards and the specifications issued by the Marine Safety Agency. Transducers should be situated clear of hull projections and openings in order to provide satisfactory performance.

Some larger, high tonnage vessels may be fitted with multiple transducers and the position of these should be known. This is especially important when navigating in areas of limited depth when heel or trim could directly influence the measured depth under the keel.

Echo sounder graphic display is normally sited on the bridge but the modern concept is to interface depth recorders into an integrated navigation display unit providing digital read out as well as a graphical print-out.

14.10.1 echo sounding – principle of operation

The echo sounding principle operates on the basis of measuring pulses of sound energy transmitted from the bottom of the vessel, and reflected back upwards from the sea bed. The depth under the vessel is a proportional measurement of the time interval from the moment of transmission to reception.

Assume the velocity of sound in water is = 1500 metre/second.

Let the time interval between transmission and reception = t seconds.

Let the distance to the sea bed and back be represented by 2s metres.
but:

distance = Speed x Time

$$2s = 1500 \times t$$

$$s = \frac{1500}{2} \times t$$

where s represents the depth of water under the transmitter.

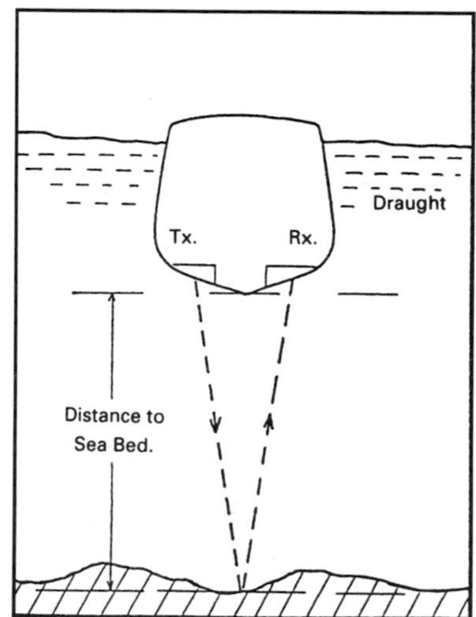

Diagram 14.22: Principle of Operation

14.10.2 operational accuracy

It is essential that the navigator ensures that the pen arm is referenced at the zero mark of the scale intended for use. If this is not correctly set, then an additional error known as 'Transmission Line Error' could be incurred.

The actual calculation of depth is based on the propagation of sound through water as being 1500 metres per second. However, this value will vary around the world due to salinity, temperature values and pressure changes. The mariner is reminded that the 1500 m/sec. is an international standard and provides an acceptable degree of accuracy for most commercial shipping requirements. Where it may become necessary to apply a correction then Admiralty Tables (NP 139) can supply fine corrections.

Should a vessel be fitted with separate Tx/Rx Transducers mariners should note that a pythagorean error could effect the observed depth. This would be more accentuated in shallow waters where the slant distance is measured, not the vertical distance under the keel.

When operating in greater depths the pythagorean error is minimal and can usually be ignored.

14.10.3 echo sounder – operational details

The installation of an echo sounder, must comply with the performance standards set by IMO and the performance specifications of the Marine Safety Agency. Equipment would be such as to be capable of operation over at least two separate ranges in order to provide a measurement from 2 metres to 400 metres. Operational frequencies vary but normally function well between 30-50 kHz. Audible noise from the ship itself is generally below 30 kHz and so minimal interference occurs with the sounders efficiency.

Effects of Squat

Most vessels record the actual depth of water under the transducer. If a vessel is known to experience squat (possibly in excess of 2.0 metres) the recorded depth will still reflect the depth under the transducer, irrespective of the value of squat.

Clearly, deep draughted vessels or those concerned with underkeel clearance may require actual depths fore and aft and as such should consider the fitting of additional transducers to indicate the depth being encountered from stem to stern.

Chart Comparison – Indicated Depth

Mariners are reminded that most sounders provide the depth under the transducer, not the actual charted depth. Before making a comparison with the chart account should be taken of the ships draught and any height of tide at the time of sounding

The siting of the transducer could also be relevant. A fixed correction may be applicable if the transducer was not situated at the lowest level of the keel. Similarly, an excessive trim in way of the transducer could also influence accuracy relating to overall underkeel clearance (UKC).

Echo Sounding – False Echoes

All echo sounding equipment is liable to incur false readings for one reason or another. Mariners can expect changing conditions to affect the values of obtained depths or even obtain double or multiple echoes.

False Bottom Echoes

A false reading may occur from a correctly adjusted sounder if a returning echo is received after the stylus has completed one or more revolutions and the next pulse is transmitted.

Sounding machines have a variety of scales, and if for example one revolution of the stylus corresponds to say 300 metres, an actual depth of say 40 metres could be recorded as '40', or '340' or even '640' metres.

Double Echoes

A double echo is caused by the transmitted pulse being reflected from the sea bottom and then being reflected a second time from the water surface, before being returned the second time from the sea bed into the receiver.

The second echo is never as strong as the first 'True' echo and it could be faded if the sensitivity control was to be reduced.

Multiple Echoes

Usually occur in depths greater than 100 metres. The transmitted pulse being reflected several times from the sea bed to either the sea surface or the ships hull. This may cause several echoes to be recorded and an adjustment of the sensitivity control could provide a more positive trace on the true depth.

Additional False Echoes may be caused by the following:

a) Layers of water of differing densities cause different speeds of propagation of sound.
b) Submarine fresh water springs.
c) Shoals of fish.
d) Kelp or seaweed.
e) Electrical faults or manufactured noise levels too high.
f) Turbulence in the water from cross currents or eddies.
g) The deep scattering layer set at about 300 to 450 metres below the surface. This layer tends to move closer to the surface at night and consists of plankton and fish.
h) Excessive aeration.

14.10.4 measurement of speed/distance

Marine Speed Logs

A necessity for continuous ship monitoring has always required the navigator to be aware of his vessels speed, both through the water and effectively over the ground. Accurate navigation has also employed relevant distance over the ground or through a set period of time.

It is then little wonder that speed logs have entered the world of microprocessors and moved with the times. The seemingly romantic days of the 'dutchmans log', or the 'rotator log' have been surpassed with a vengence.

There are many manufactured examples available to the mariner, the majority of which carry all or most of the following:

1. Clearly arranged transflective Liquid Crystal Display (LCD).

2. User friendly with simple calibration and coded set-up procedures.

3. Storage facility for operational data, in the event of power failure.

4. Electromagnetic measuring principle providing a high level of sensitivity.

5. No moving parts in a sensing element, which can be easily replaced without dry docking.

6. Main and repeater display units with alternative; console, bulkhead or bracket mountings.

7. Resettable daily and voyage mileage counters.

8. Enhanced accuracy by programmable storage of water temperature and salinity values.

9. Digital and analogue speed output/display.

10. Integrated stop watch facility.

11. Built in test facility.

12. Highly accurate speed indication of vessels movement through the water, even at low speeds.

13. Microprocessor technology providing exceptional reliability.

14. Compatible for ARPA requirements and meeting IMO and safety resolutions.

Speed Logs

Many examples of speed logs are multifunctional by way of providing not only speed but distance parameters. Depth alarms may also be an incorporated feature. Most manufacturers have risen to the needs of the end user and designed specific logs for particular types of vessels, namely:

All types of vessels employed in deep water (Speed range from –5 to +25 knots) – Blade sensor.

High speed vessels e.g. Hydrofoils (Speed range from –5 to +80 knots) – Flush sensor.

Shallow water operators (Speed range from –5 to +35 knots) – Flush sensor.

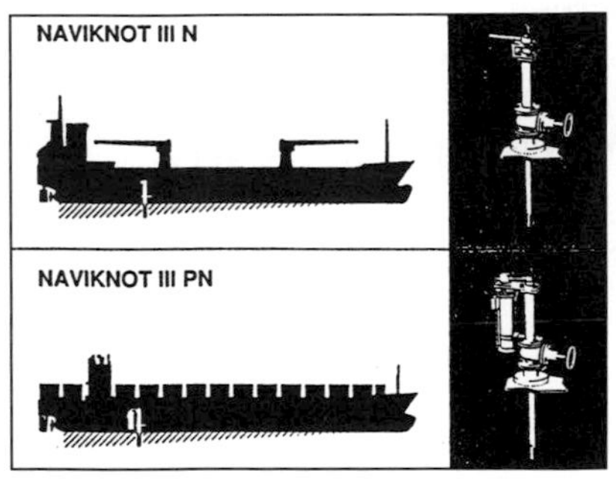

Commercial vessels fitted with 'Blade Sensors'.

Usually engaged in deep water type IIIN, manually deployed type IIIPN, pneumatically deployed.

Display units are positioned on the bridge with any control unit.

Senior position to suit most convenience.

Diagram 14.23 Speed Log Deployment

Speed Logs – Example

One of the most common speed log systems is the Electro Magnetic Speed Log, manufactured by C.Plath. The 'Naviknot III', flush fitting speed sensor has the capability of measuring speed over a range from -5 to +80 knots. The fitting is suitable for steel and aluminium hull designs of any mono, or multi-hull vessel inclusive of Surface Effect Ships (SES) and the Small Waterplane Area Twin Hull Ships (SWATHS).

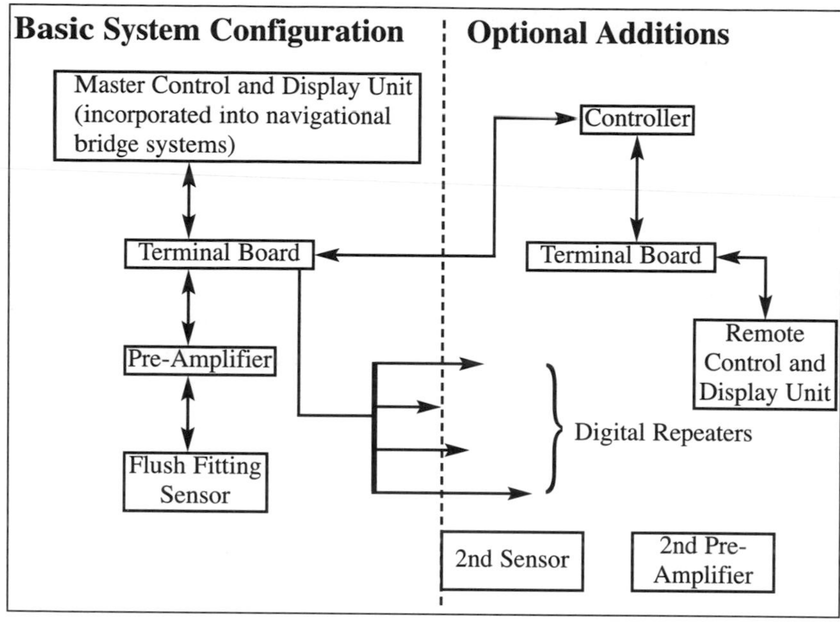

Diagram 14.24: Speed Log Configuration

14.10.5 speed log features

1. Liquid Crystal Display (LCD) screen.
2. Complies with IMO Resolution A-478 (XII) .
3. Satisfies IMO requirements for ARPA
4. Measurement accuracy fulfils IMO Resolution A.824(19)
5. Built-in test facility.
6. High accuracy even at low speeds.
7. No moving parts in the sensor.
8. Single system has the capability to drive a maximum of twenty (20) remote control and display units.
9. Re-settable daily mile counters.
10. Total mile counter.
11. Micro-processor technology provides exceptional reliability.
12. Operational data remains stored in the event of a power failure.
13. Digital output and user friendly.
14. Sensors can be replaced without dry-docking.
15. Integrated stopwatch facility.
16. Water depth alarm facility.

17. Facility for water temperature and salinity values to be stored.
18. Electromagnetic and Doppler sensors.
19. Each system can be operable with two sensors.
20. Satisfies specifications of Classification Society, Germanischer Lloyd.

Accuracy:

1. Speed relative to the water flow at the location of the sensor < +/_ 0.1 knot

2. Distance travelled, based on the measured speed < +/_ 0.1 %

Model Variants for:

Vessel types.
Manual deployment.
Speed variations (inclusive of High Speed Craft).
External fitment as opposed to internal.
Naviknot III FNF (Flush Fitted Sensor) for external hulls in either steel or aluminium.
Speed range from –5 to 35 knots.

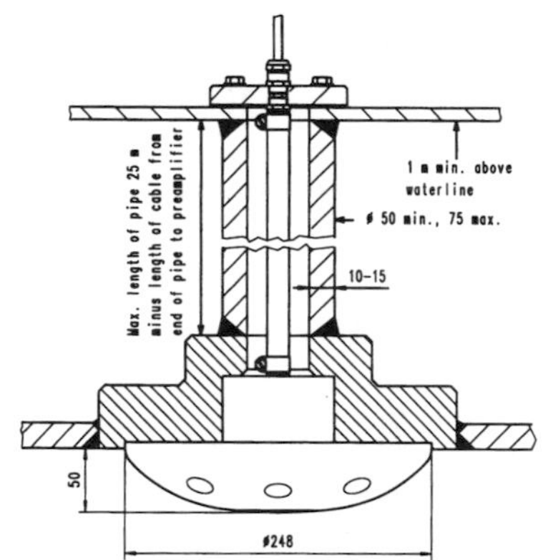

Diagram 14.25 Flush Fitting Speed Log

14.11 Automatic Identification System (AIS)

In 1997 the draft performance standards for a universal shipborne Automatic Identification System (AIS) were finalised. Working parties were subsequently set up by IALA and the ITU to establish the technical characteristics for an operational system and these were adopted by the IMO Maritime Safety Committee at its 69th session in 1998. Proposed amendments to Chapter V of the SOLAS convention were made in 1999 and a schedule for fitting AIS to new and existing ships was set.

The current identification of target ships at sea from radar is a problem. It is not possible to establish what echo is which ship or determine with complete certainty whether a collision situation exists or not. Where VTS is involved a similar lack of target information makes the task of monitoring traffic that much more difficult without positive information.

One of the prime functions of the AIS operation permits positive identification of targets and allows continuous tracking of vessels over lengthy voyages. If this is considered against continuous radar coverage an increased number of tracking stations would have to be established and this would be extremely costly to set up, operate and maintain.

The proposed AIS programme is:

AIS transponders are to be fitted on all ships over 300gt constructed after 01/07/02 and also on ships built before 2002 as follows:

1. Passenger Ships not later than 01/07/03.
2. Tankers not later than first survey after 01/07/03.
3. Other ships > 5000 gt not later than 01/07/04.
4. Other ships >10,000 gt < 5000 gt not later than 01/07/05.
5. Other ships > 3000 gt < 10,000 gt not later than 01/07/06.
6. Other ships > 300 gt < 3000 gt not later than 01/07/07.

Ships not on international voyages constructed before 01/07/02 not later than 01/07/08.

14.11.1 transponder information

Each transponder will:

1. Provide the ships: Identity, Type, Position, Speed and Navigational status.
2. Receive similar data from other ships.
3. Monitor and track ships
4. Exchange data with shore bases.

14.11.2 AIS unit components

Each transponder is expected to contain four modular units:–

GPS	**VHF Tx/Rx**
Controller	**Power Unit**

The ITU specify that the receiver is dual frequency.

NB. At the time of writing it is not yet known whether a separate GPS system will be a requirement or whether the ships existing positioning system will be sufficient.

The units are expected to function automatically with little or no human operator intervention. The Controller assembles all positional data and message format for transmission and reception respectively over the various modes of operation.

14.11.3 message format

The IMO has specified three standard message types:

1. **Static Message** – Contains the ships IMO number, call sign and name, together with dimensions of ships length and beam, type of ship and the location of the position fixing antenna aboard the vessel.

2. **Dynamic Message** – Contains the ships position with indicated accuracy and integrity status, time of report, course over the ground, speed over the ground, heading, rate of turn, navigational status and optionally, angles of heel, pitch and roll.

3. **Voyage Related Messages** – Contain, ships draught, types of hazardous cargo carried, destination and ETA (at Masters discretion) and optionally the route plan in way-point format.

14.11.4 operational AIS

The AIS will be compatible with Radar, ARPA, and ECDIS for the multi facets for which the system is designed for, namely:

Identification of targets

Each message will contain the MMSI number to effect identification from a data base. It is probable that whichever onboard system is in use, be it Radar, ARPA or ECDIS an information window will open to display a complete ships' data profile.

Targets acquired in a similar manner from a VTS shore base, would detail target information in much the same way to a VTS operator.

Tracking

Targets will have the capability of being tracked themselves by other ships or a VTS operation and at the same time have the ability to track other ships themselves. This would effectively be achieved by frequently received AIS position reports from the intended target. The ITU has specified the update intervals for dynamic reports as noted in the following tables.

AIS Update Intervals of Message

Message Type	Interval Time/Period
Static Information	Every 6 minutes and on request
Dynamic Information	Depends on Speed/Course Alteration (see following table)
Voyage Related Information	Every 6 minutes, when data has been amended and on request.
Safety Related Messages	As required.

AIS Dynamic Information – Update Intervals

Ship Dynamics	Reporting Interval
Ship at Anchor	3 minutes
Ship at 0 - 14 knots	12 seconds
Ship at 0 - 14 knots and changing course	4 seconds
Ship at 14 -23 knots	6 seconds
Ship at 14-23 knots and changing course	2 seconds
Ship at over 23 knots	3 seconds
Ship at over 23 knots and changing course	2 seconds

14.11.5 additional navigation/motion data

The AIS position reports already include notation for 'rate of turn' and 'ships heading'. Such information is relevant for anti-collision because it allows the determination of 'aspect' which to date has not been acquired accurately or confirmed without a visual contact or manual plot. This information could also be enhanced by a key code to specify the navigational status of the vessel, whether she is : at anchor, underway, NUC, or restricted.

Such detailed information on any target could determine the responsibility between 'Give Way' vessels and 'Stand On' vessels when in a 'Rule of the Road' collision scenario.

14.11.6 traffic movement – related messages

The benefits of monitoring traffic movement and providing continuous updated information to vessels in transit through narrow or congested waters is of potential benefit to pilots and ships Masters alike. Canals, rivers, narrow fairways, or shoal regions could all have tight monitoring systems linked directly to the VTS work station. All traffic related signals and text messages can be displayed on board and in the VTS controlled environment, without causing disruption to the normal functions of the AIS.

14.11.7 additional uses

Interested parties in addition to VTS operations, such as Coastguards, SAR personnel, Ship Reporting systems and pilotage services, all have everything to gain from an effective operational AIS.

14.11.8 summary

The AIS will at last identify the radar echo to the mariner. Since radar was developed over 50 years ago and electronic detection of targets became possible, all that has been available is the knowledge of the changing position of the target. This mandatory system will provide an essential profile on respective targets allowing all participants access to all target information and anti-collision analysis. What it will not do is change actual weather conditions or install transponders on the smaller fishing boat or yacht under 300 gt. Neither will AIS replace radar and remove the need for good seamanship.

Its benefits will clearly become readily acceptable to the next generation geared to a high technology future. Though the need to keep pace with innovation, and train with new equipment will become the essential by-product for our personnel both ashore and afloat.

14.12 Voyage Data Recorders (VDR)

(Black Box -Recorder)
It is now a requirement that all passenger ships and vessels over 3000 gt, which are built after July 2002 must be fitted with a Voyage Data Recording unit (VDR).

The Maritime Safety Committee (MSC) has also agreed that VDR's are to be fitted to all existing Ro-Ro Passenger vessels and High Speed Craft already in operation. The new regulations agreed by IMO, have caused a feasibility study to be commissioned in 2004 into the mandatory carriage of VDR's on existing 'Cargo Ships'.

The principle of marine 'Black Boxes' has evolved because of the transport relationship with the aviation industry, which has had black box technology on all passenger aircraft for many years. The monitoring of all principal elements within the mode of transport has shown itself indispensable in resolving aircraft accidents and subsequently improving long term industrial safety. The question would now tend to be why has the marine industry taken so long to introduce what many would now consider as a basic monitoring device?

The revised Chapter V, of SOLAS, will make carriage mandatory for certain types of vessels. IMO has made recommendations on the data that VDR's are expected to record and includes the following:

a) date and time,
b) ship's position and speed,
c) course/heading,
d) bridge audio – One or more microphones situated on the navigation bridge to record conversations near the conning position and at relevant operational stations like; Radars, chart tables, communication consoles etc,
e) main alarms and P/A systems,
f) engine orders and responses,
g) rudder orders and responses,
h) echo sounder recordings,
i) status of watertight and fire doors,
j) status on hull openings,
k) acceleration and hull stress levels. (Only required where a vessel is fitted with response monitoring equipment).

The information should be stored 24 hours a day over a 7 day week period. It should be contained in a crash proof box, painted orange and fitted with an acoustic device to aid recovery after an accident. The system will be a fully automatic, memory unit which will be 'tamper free' and always monitoring, even when the vessel is tied up alongside. VDR's are expected to provide continuous operation for at least two hours following a power failure and are also alarm protected in the event of malfunction of any of the VDR's elements.

14.13 Radio Direction Finders (DF)

14.13.1 introduction

Although Direction Finding equipment on board vessels is no longer considered an essential element of the ships navigation equipment, some ships have still retained the DF on board. Despite its demise, it must still be considered useful in the event of a distress situation provided personnel have the ability to use it. To this end the author makes no apology for retaining the topic within this text.

a) for obtaining Radio Bearings of marine and selected aero beacons, and
b) for taking Radio Bearings of vessels in distress.

The distinct advantage of the system is that it is unaffected by restricted visibility conditions and may be employed when the observing station is out of sight of the transmitting station or casualty.

14.13.2 principal of operation

The early direction finders operated on the basis of radio waves being transmitted from a shore station. The lines of force committed from the transmitting aerial were then received by a rotating loop aerial established on the vessel.

It is widely accepted that when magnetic lines of force pass through a coil, a voltage will be induced. This principle is directly used by the insertion of windings into the loop aerial, effectively turning the aerial into a large coil.

As the transmitted lines of force increase and decrease an alternating voltage is established in the coil. The actual voltage in the loop will then be greater when the loop aerial is turned towards the transmitter. Clearly the directional aerial could be related to the vessels compass in order to provide the required bearing of the transmitter.

14.13.3 reference to: Admiralty List of radio signals.

Marine radio beacons and sample aero beacons can be identified by the navigator on inspection of Volume 2 of the Admiralty List of Radio Signals, respective to the area of operation.

Information available in the list regarding radio beacons would include such items as: Call sign, range, operational frequency, transmission schedules and position of station.

14.14 Operational Errors Experienced with Direction Finders

14.14.1 coast effect

Radio Beacons are nearly always located in coastal regions and subsequently electromagnetic waves are influenced as they pass over land masses and then over the sea surface (or *vice versa*). This apparent refraction causes:

a) a small error when the bearing is being taken from the ship and
b) a much larger error when the bearing is being taken from a shore side station.

During the period of daylight the ionosphere is ionized by sunlight. However at night the ionized layers are reduced and sky wave may interfere with ground wave transmission over relatively short ranges.

Although the ground wave will generally not be affected, the sky wave, after reflection, could well cause an incorrect bearing to be obtained by the receiving aerial. The sky wave cutting the loop aerial causing polarization to change and an E.M.F. will be noted.

The observer should be alert for the symptoms of night effect which can render bearings unreliable:

(a) a slurred zero by a constantly changing sky wave.
(Geographic area may contain mountain ranges or steep coastlines between transmission and reception stations)
(b) cross bearings of different beacons are producing a 'cocked hat.'
(c) signal 'fading' may be experienced.

Night effect may last some time and where it becomes necessary to take radio bearings navigators are advised to take numerous bearings over a short period, with a view to averaging. In any event where night effect is established any result must be treated as being less than reliable.

DIRECTION FINDER EQUIPMENT

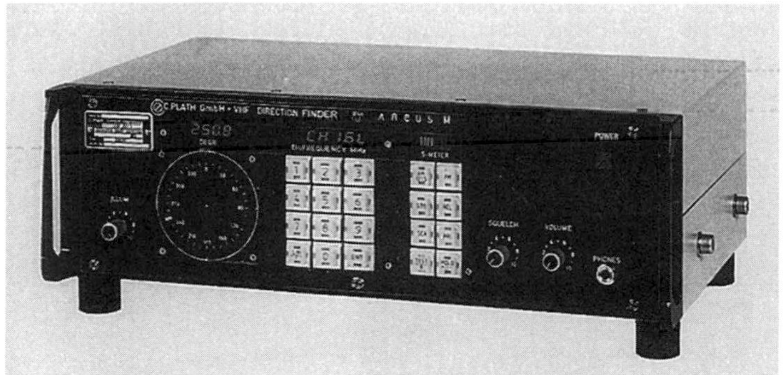

Pic. 57 VHF Marine Radio Direction Finder Unit. Manufactured by C. Plath GmbH

DIRECTION FINDER – aerial equipment

Pic. 58 Crossed Loop Bellini-Tosi type aerial, with integrated sense antenna. Operation 100 kHz and 4 MHz.

14.15 Visual Cathode Ray Tube (CRT) Display of D.F.

The loops of a Bellini Tosi aerial are connected to the deflector plates of a C.R.T. The direction of the original transmission is then reproduced as a line on the tube face towards the direction of the transmitting station.

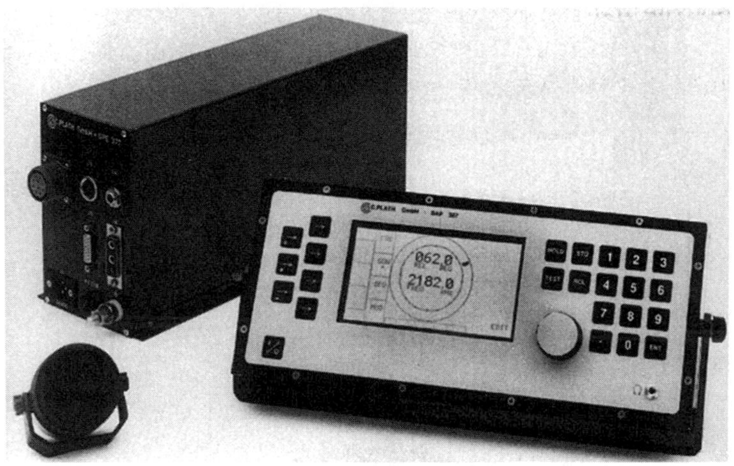

Pic. 59 Radio Direction Finder and Homing Device

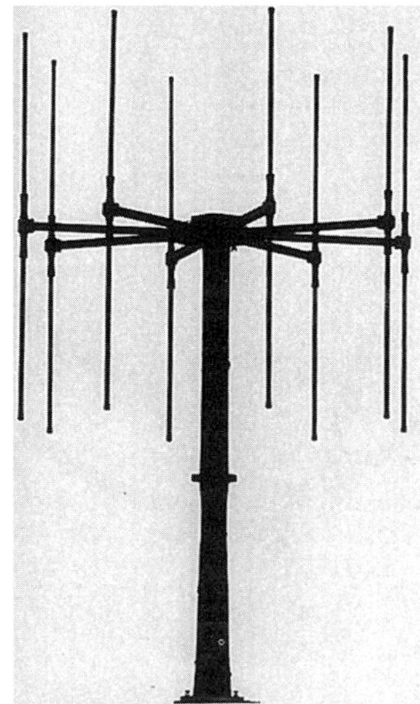

Pic. 60 Typical VHF – DF antenna
operation 20 – 180 MHz

Correction of Radio (Great Circle) Bearing to Mercatorial Bearing

NB. The navigator will require to lay the obtained DF bearings onto a Mercator Chart and will subsequently be required to apply the half convergency correction.

**Example: A vessel in an Estimated Position of Lat. 50° 30' N Long. 30° 00' W observes a Radio Bearing of 130° from transmitting beacon in position Lat. 55° 20' N Long. 05° 50' W.
The ships head at the time of taking the bearing is 310°.
Find the correct Mercatorial Bearing to lay off on the chart.**

Bearing Observed	130°	Relative.
Quadrantal Correction	3¼°	(obtained from calibration curve)
Corrected Radio Brg.	126¾°	Relative
Ships Head	310°	True
	436¾°	
	360°	
G.C. Bearing	76¾°	
Half convergency Corr'n	+9¾°	Correction is always allowed towards the equator
Mercatorial Bearing	086½°	True

Bearings on the chart must always be laid off FROM the radio station.

NB. Half Convergency Correction is obtained by reference to Nautical Tables, e.g. Norries or Burtons.

Table of Mean Latitude against Difference of Longitude of the ship and radio station.

14.16 The Electronic Log Book

The age of the electronic log book is upon us and it would seem that the days of the conventional, paper deck and engine room log books are numbered. Current designs of electronic logs have seemingly been based on the page format of the historical paper log book and the information recorded can be similarly aligned. The benefits of using this format in an electronic log will be seen as being user friendly and must be expected to reduce copious amounts of paper work.

The system would allow information to be downloaded to shore-based authorities.

The log-book will no doubt develop as a digital communication link, direct to maritime authorities and possibly reduce the need for official boardings. Log entries and reports being transmitted over great distances via the use of the internet highway.

The extension of the log book could also be seen in the use of the Oil Record Book, maintenance reports, communication log extracts, onboard management decisions, night order records, etc.

Screen displays would indicate date and time of entries, the person making the entry and detailed incident reports. Position inputs and navigational data, being interfaced with the ships monitoring aids and incorporated as and when desired. Keyboard and LCD display would expect to complete the hardware.

14.7 Dynamic Positioning (DP)

Dynamic Positioning is an entire system necessary to enable a vessel to automatically hold station and heading, without resorting to the use of anchors or moorings. The types of vessels so equipped are usually specialised craft such as:

Diving Support Vessels (DSV), Supply Vessels for the Offshore Industry, Cable Laying or Survey Ships and Heavy Lift Vessels. Other examples can be found amongst Drilling Ships, Fire-fighting Vessels, Dredgers, Offshore Loading Tankers, Flotel Accommodation Units, and Semi Submersibles.

In order for DP to be effective the vessel will be equipped with thrust units capable of producing transverse thrust and/or azimuth thrusters which can provide thrust in any direction. In simplified form, these thrust units are brought into operation to control the six freedoms of movement of the vessel.

Control is achieved 'automatically' but the DP system will incorporate a manual "Joystick" controller. Combined use of both Automatic and manual functions can be employed to suit the needs of the vessel.

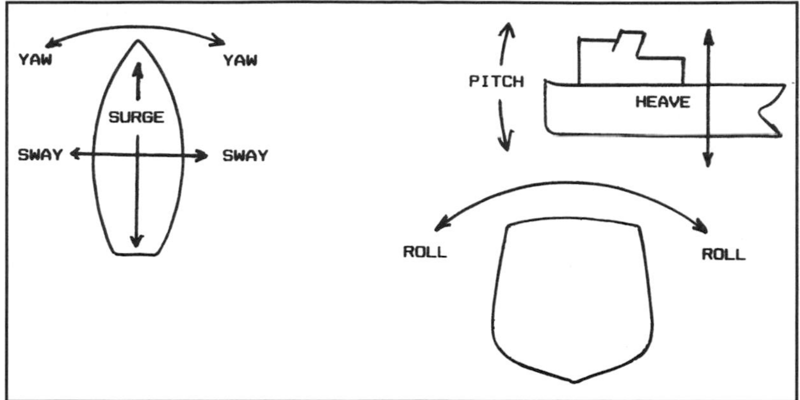

Diagram 14.26: The ship's degrees of freedom.

Example: Auto control of the vessels surge movement combined with manual control of Yaw and Sway.

Station Holding with a DP system can be achieved by several methods of Position Reference Techniques. However, probably the most widely used are:

(i) Taut Wire Position Reference System.
(ii) Hydroacoustic Position Reference System.
(iii) Artemis Microwave Position Reference System.

(i) Taut Wire (PRS)
In this system a weight of approximately 0.5 tonne is lowered to the sea bed on an extended ships boom. The wire is turned to a constant tension which is set to about 0.25 tonne tension.

The length of the wire paid out, together with the angle to the vertical in both the longitudinal and the transverse planes, is monitored by sensors at the lead sheave and winch. The position of the vessel being defined from the data being relayed back from the sensors into the D.P. System.

(ii) Hydroacoustic (PRS)
This system employs a transducer on the bottom of the ship and transponders which are positioned on the sea bed. The vessel transmits acoustic signals towards the transponders. The received signal is re-transmitted back to the ship (similar to echo sounding), the range and direction from the transponder can then be determined.

The ships position, being defined in relation to the transponder, is relayed into the D.P. system.

(iii) Artemis Microwave (PRS)
With this system a radio link is established between two transceivers. One being mounted in a fixed position usually on an installation, while the other is mounted as a mobile on the vessel.

A microwave link joins the two via antennae and the signal passing between the two can be interpreted to provide range and bearing which can then be passed to the D.P. system.

14.7.1 principles of dynamic positioning

onboard units

D.P.Console situated on the Bridge.
Computer Bank – May be duplicated in certain vessel types.
Off station sensors and alarm systems.
Gyroscopic compass.
Power Supply – Usually Diesel-Electric or direct drive diesel. Plus the D.P. systems own Uninterruptable Power Supply.
Vertical Referenced Sensors. (Monitoring of Roll and Pitch).

A D.P. Operator would also provide a manual override in the event of a 'drift off' or 'drift on' situation occurring.

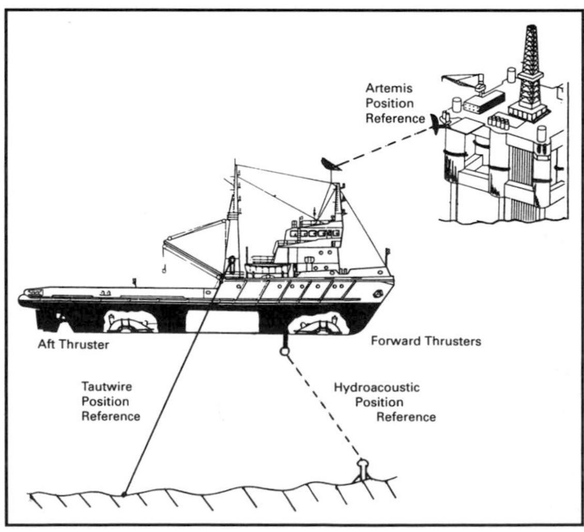

Diagram 14.27: Dynamic Positioning, sit up.

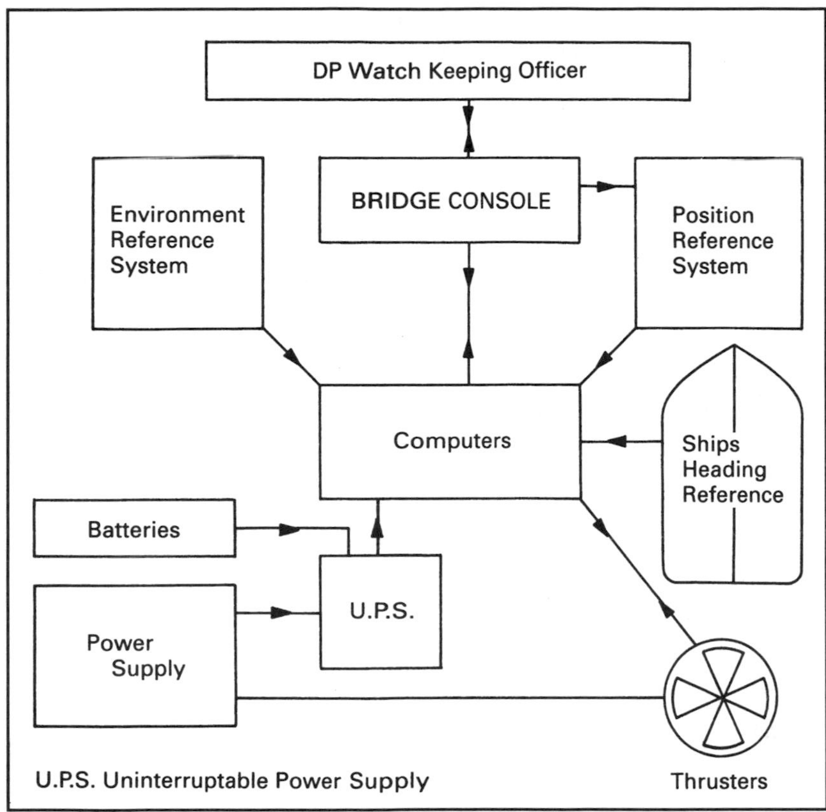

Diagram 14.28: DP Operation.

14.17.2 dynamic positioning – watchkeeping duties

The Watch Officers duties aboard a DP vessel will vary considerably depending on the function and operation of the vessel. For example the needs of the Diving Support Vessel (DSV) would differ to the needs of a platform supply vessel.

A general requirement for DP watchkeeping is for two officers to be on the bridge. One being a designated DPO, while the other would attend to all other watch keeping duties. When accepting the watch the DPO would ascertain the relevant status of:

1) The vessels position.
2) Work in progress – by external divers, diving bell, ROV.
3) Operational data on position reference systems in use, or on stand-by.

4) Internal and external communication channels.
5) Weather forecasts and meteorological information.
6) Power supply management and alarm system.
7) DP performance and alarm parameters.

It is usual practice to maintain a DP status 'chalkboard' which provides details regarding active generators, thruster status, and indicates Position Reference elements engaged. It provides, at a glance, an immediate appraisal of the DP operation and remains a powerful, visual overview for the DPO.

Additional documentation, by way of log books and DP performance records, would also be maintained. DSV's often work with "footprint" diagrams providing DP capability and/or diving station information charts.

Specialised operations are normally conducted in conjunction with associated check-lists pertinent to the task. Reference to Masters Standing Orders covering DP operations would also form the basis for recognised safe working practice.

14.17.3 Masters standing orders for DPO's

(These may include the following examples:)

a) the DP watch should not be relieved during an ongoing manoeuvre.
b) minimum three Position References (PR) must be employed when engaged in diving operations.
c) minimum two PR's employed when navigating under 100 metres to a surface construction.
d) respective check-lists to be completed before commencing operations. e.g. Diving.
e) vessel to be established and steady for 30 minutes prior to commencing activity.
f) capability graph and all alarm systems checked and set.
g) escape/contingency plan to be established prior to station holding.
h) call Master at any time if concerned or in doubt.

DEPARTMENT OF TRANSPORT MERCHANT SHIPPING NOTICE No. **M.1221**

DYNAMICALLY POSITIONED VESSELS AND THE DANGERS TO DIVERS OPERATING FROM SUCH VESSELS

Notice to Shipowners, Masters and Officers of Merchant Ships and Fishing Vessels

This Notice supersedes Notice No. M.895

1. The attention of mariners is drawn to the special limitations imposed on Dynamically Positioned Vessels by the nature of their work and the need for them to operate in sea conditions as favourable as possible. Further, these vessels when operating in the diving support mode are required to hold position most accurately often very close to the legs of platforms. In the event of movement of the vessel, which may be due, for example, to the wash of a passing ship, risk of serious injury to the divers and/or damage to the vessel or platform could occur.

2. In view of these considerations, mariners are requested to give as wide a berth as possible to vessels displaying the signals required by Rule 27 paragraphs (b) and (d) as applicable of the International Regulations for Preventing Collisions at Sea 1972, as amended. It they are unable to pass at least ½ mile-clear, they should reduce speed when navigating near such vessels. To assist in identification Dynamically Positioned Diving Support Vessels should, when engaged in diving operations, also use the single letter "A" of the International Code of Signals using any method of signalling which may be appropriate.

3. It is also recommended that a Dynamically Positioned Vessel should, before commencing diving operations, ascertain that no other vessel is operating in its immediate vicinity. The vessel should also broadcast on the appropriate frequencies a navigation warning to all ships indicating the nature of its operation and such broadcast should be repeated at intervals whilst the operation is in progress. Additionally the vessel should ensure that the broadcasts are acknowledged by the appropriate coastal radio station who will rebroadcast them in their routine schedules.

4. Attention is also drawn to the provision of Rule 36 of the Regulations referred to in paragraph 2 above which enables a vessel to make signals to attract the attention of another vessel to alert her to a danger which may exist.

14.18 Communications – NAVTEX

With the GMDSS requirements established the majority of Merchant Vessels will be required to have a NAVTEX receiver and printer. The international service is expected to be developed world-wide for promulgation of navigation, meteorological, and safety messages.

The dedicated equipment operates on 518 kHz and has an integral role within the GMDSS and the World Wide Navigation Warning System (WWNWS). Areas of operation are established by the position of transmitters but the expected range of reception is expected to be within 200 nautical miles.

Message priority is listed as being:

(i) Vital
(ii) Important
(iii) Routine

Certain messages may be rejected by the ship when they are not applicable. However, some messages cannot be rejected on the grounds of safety, namely:

Navigational Warnings, Meteorological Warnings and Search and Rescue messages. (Codes A, B, D and L).

Categories of messages are as follows:

A. Coastal Navigation Warnings.
B. Meteorological Warnings.
C. Ice Reports.
D. Search and Rescue Alerts.
E. Meteorological Forecasts.
F. Pilot Message
G. AIS.
H. LORAN Message.
I. Spare.
J. SATNAV.
K. Other electronic navigational aid – system message.
L. Navarea warnings – inclusive of rig listings.
M. – Y. No category has yet been allocated.
Z. No message on hand.

Navtex receivers can be either desk mounted or bulkhead mounted and must be fitted with a self testing ability. A Navtex handbook is issued with the equipment for use by the operator.

The user may elect to receive messages from a single transmitter appropriate to the vessels area or from several transmitters when the geographic position allows. The power of transmitters being such as to avoid undue interference from each other. However, it is normal practice to programme the receiver to print-out messages from the nearest transmitter to the ships position.

14.18.1 message format

Each message will commence with a 'header code' followed by four characters to indicate:

a) The origin, the type and the number of the message. (Message numbers run from 01 to 99, and then repeated).
b) Certain messages are dated and timed after the header code. e.g. Weather transmissions.
c) All messages conclude with the group NNNN.

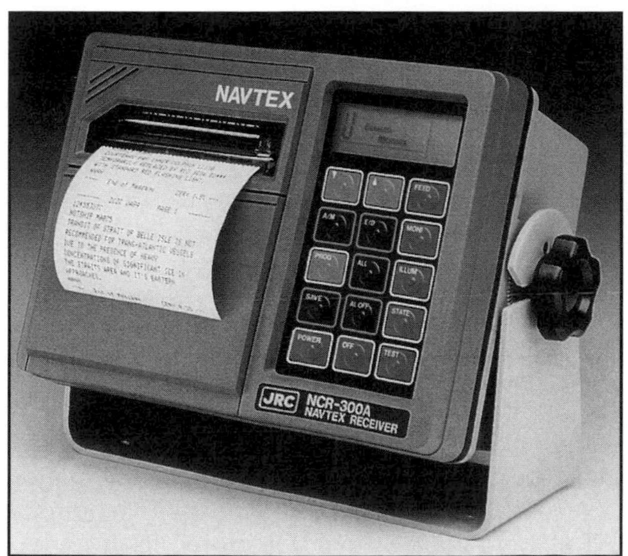

Pic. 61 The NCR-300A NAVTEX Receiver receives and prints out navigation and weather warnings, and search-and-rescue alerts. It delivers information up to 400 miles offshore.

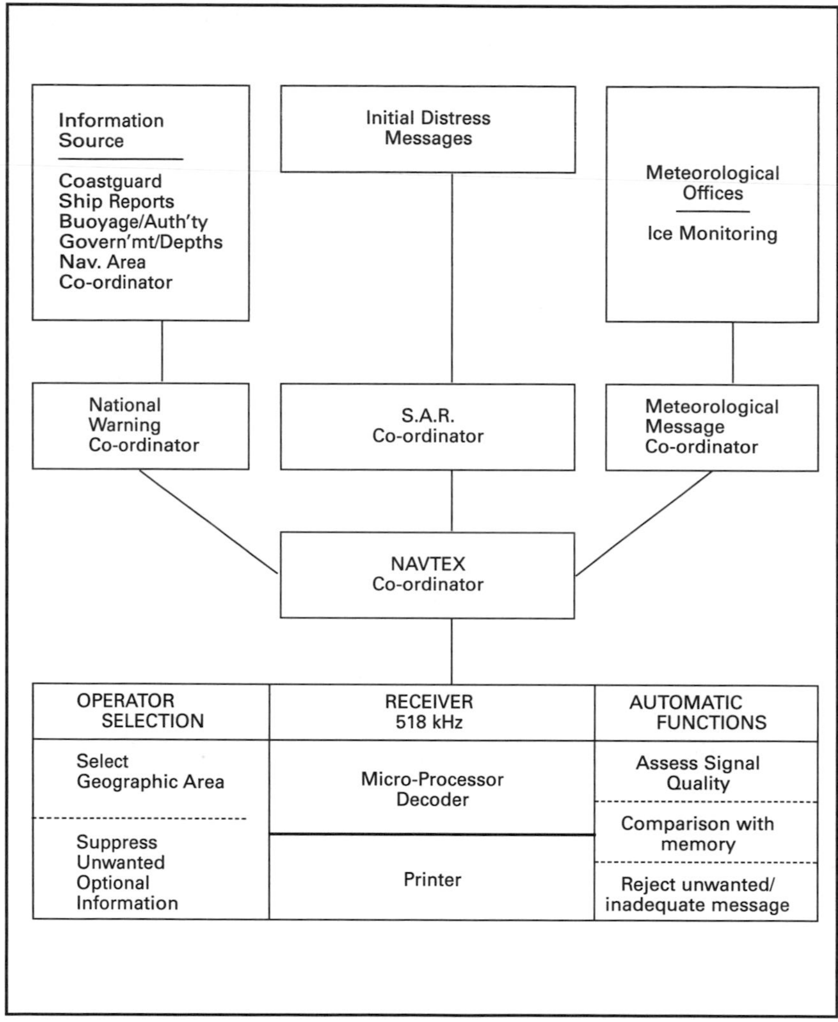

Diagram 14.29: Communications Provision

With the development of GMDSS and its implementation in 1999 the need for automated mobile transmit and receiving stations aboard merchant vessels has become a necessary requirement. The INMARSAT C, Ship-Earth Station has proved itself useful for ships trading outside of Navtex areas (GMDSS Sea Area A3). The equipment has the capability to receive Navigation Warnings, Weather Data, Distress Communications together with urgency and safety information.

The facility is inclusive of a "Store and Forward" Telex relay. It is compatible with on board instrumentation, e.g. GPS. It is economical and easy to operate and can provide Enhanced Group Calling (EGC).

Communications are not in 'real time' with this system and are conducted through a shore based Satellite Coast Earth Station (CES). The term S.E.S. is now more commonly known as a Mobile Earth Station (MES) and refers to all mobile units.

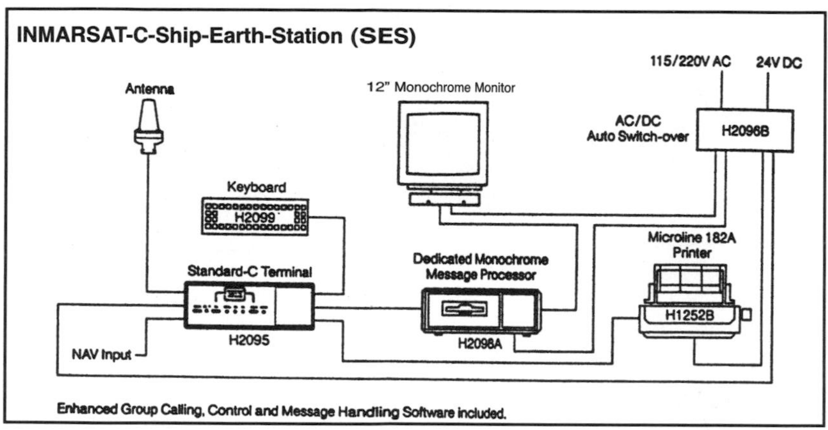

Diagram 14.30: Communication terminal – transceiver and Computer/Message handling system.

14.19 GMDSS – Communication Equipment Example

A compact communication terminal which comprises of a transceiver and a computer/message handling system. This particular model manufactured by 'Philips Navigation A/S', complies with both the Inmarsat and the GMDSS specifications.

The unit offers telex, position and data reporting service, mobile to shore fax, EGC message reception with automatic geographic area selection, Access codes and GMDSS facilities.

Additional features include reception storage of 128 Kbyte together with a dedicated distress button, which is well protected against inadvertent use. GPS and printer interface.

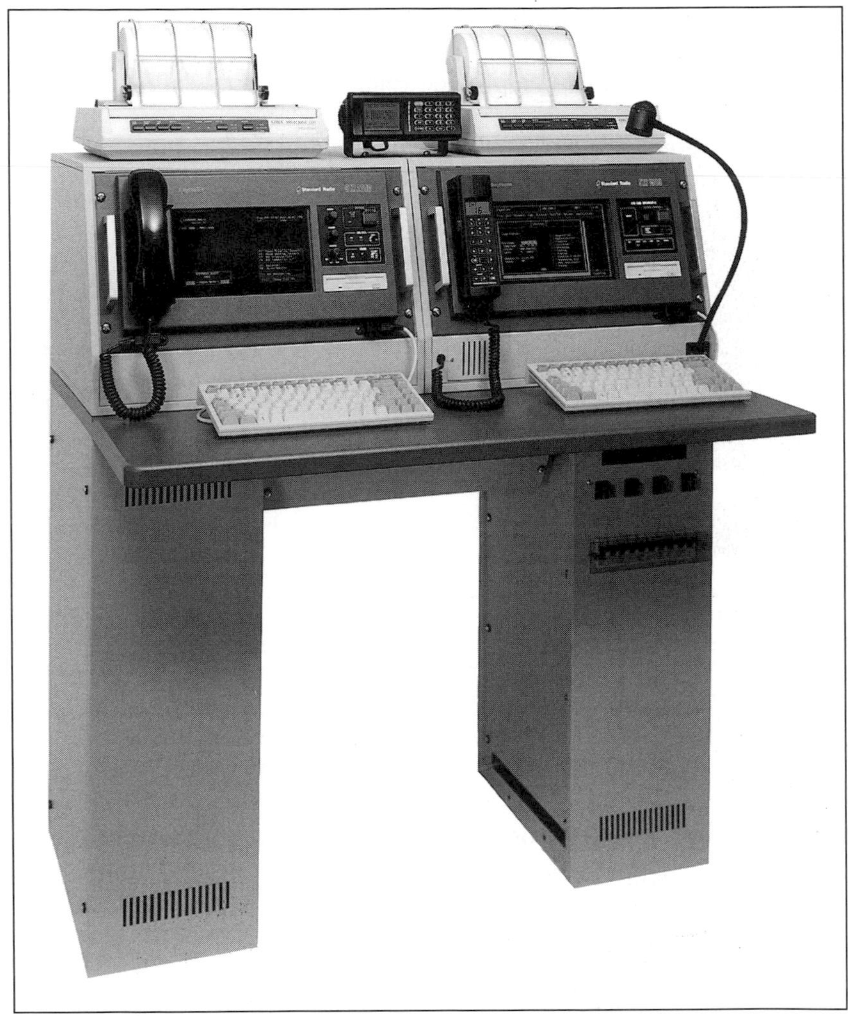

Pic. 62 Communications Terminal-transceiver and Computer/Message Handling system.

Raytheon VHF

Pic. 63 GMDSS communications – Example VHF for use in marine ship-to-ship, ship-to-shore communications.

Husun 70

Pic. 64 Full coverage of international channels, dual watch Channel 16, and fitted with priority override. Handset operation and provision is made for remote loudspeaker.

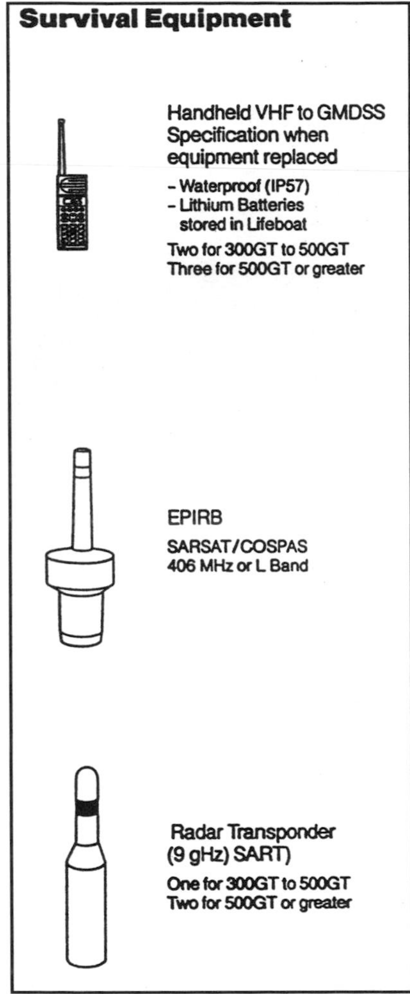

Survival Equipment
Handheld VHF to GMDSS Specification when equipment replaced
- Waterproof (IP57)
- Lithium Batteries stored in Lifeboat
Two for 300GT to 500GT
Three for 500GT or greater
EPIRB
SARSAT/COSPAS
406 MHz or L Band
Radar Transponder
(9 gHz) SART)
One for 300GT to 500GT
Two for 500GT or greater

Diagram 14.31: Emergency – Electronic Aids.

Solas Convention as amended 1991 requires every passenger vessel and on every cargo vessel over 500 tons gross to be equipped with at least three two-way radios, for use with survival craft.

Fixed installations may be an alternative if fitted into survival craft.

Regulation 7, of the SOLAS convention as amended in 1991. The requirement for vessels engaged in sea areas: A1, A2 and A3, are such that they must have the capability of transmitting a ship-to-shore distress alert by a 406 MHz EPIRB through the polar orbiting satellite (COSPAS-SARSAT)

Or if the vessel is engaged on voyages only within INMARSAT areas, then through the INMARSAT geo-stationary satellite.

EPIRBS may be fitted with remote activation.

Radar transponders operating in the 9GHz band are required to be carried on either side of the vessel for both a passenger ship and a cargo vessel of 500 tons gross or more.

Alternative stowage may be in survival craft, or be readily transferred to survival craft.
(Exception the 6 man liferaft positioned forward or aft)

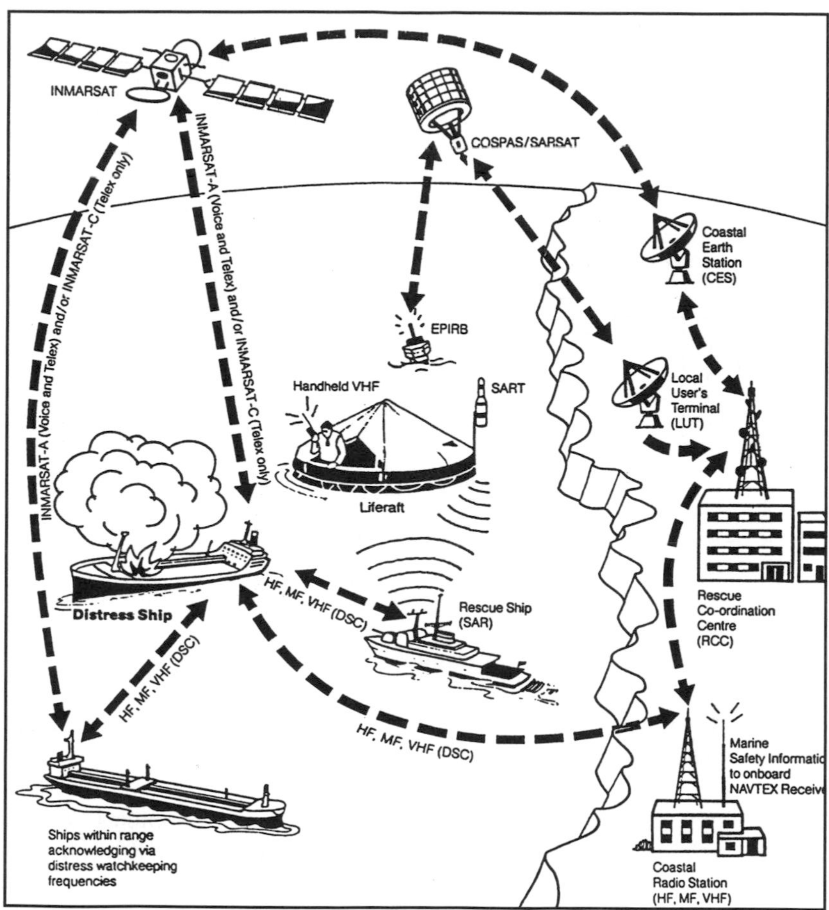

GMDSS: Concept (Areas A1, A2, A3)

Diagram 14.32: Emergency Communication Link

Distress Response

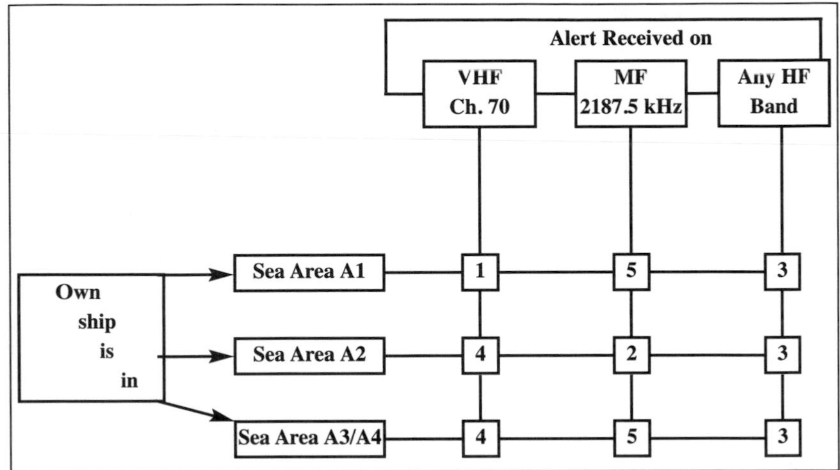

Diagram 14.33: Radio Reaction to Distress

1. a) tune to RT Channel 16 and listen for distress communication.
   b) acknowledge receipt of the alert using RT on channel 16 and carry out distress communication.
   c) if the alert is not responded to by a shore station, acknowledge by DSC on Channel 70 and relay the alert ashore by any means.

2. a) tune to 2182 kHz and listen for distress communication.
   b) acknowledge receipt of the alert using RT on 2182 kHz and carry out distress communication.
   c) if the alert is not responded to by a shore station, acknowledge by DSC on 2187.5 kHz and relay the alert ashore by any means.

3. a) tune to RT distress frequency in the band on which the distress alert is received.
   b) do NOT acknowledge either by RT or DSC.
   c) wait at least 3 minutes for a shore station to send DSC acknowledgement.
   d) if no shore station acknowledgement or RT distress communication is heard relay the alert ashore by any means.
   e) if within VHF or MF range of the distress position try to establish RT contact on Channel 16 or on 2182 kHz.

4. a) tune to RT VHF Channel 16 and listen for distress.
   b) acknowledge receipt of the alert using RT Channel 16 and carry out distress communications.

c) if the alert continues, relay it ashore by any means.
d) acknowledge the alert by DSC on Channel 70.

5. a) tune to RT 2182 kHz and listen for distress communication.
b) acknowledge receipt of the alert using RT 2182 kHz and carry out distress communications.
c) if the alert continues relay it ashore by any means.
d) acknowledge the alert by DSC on 2187.5 kHz.

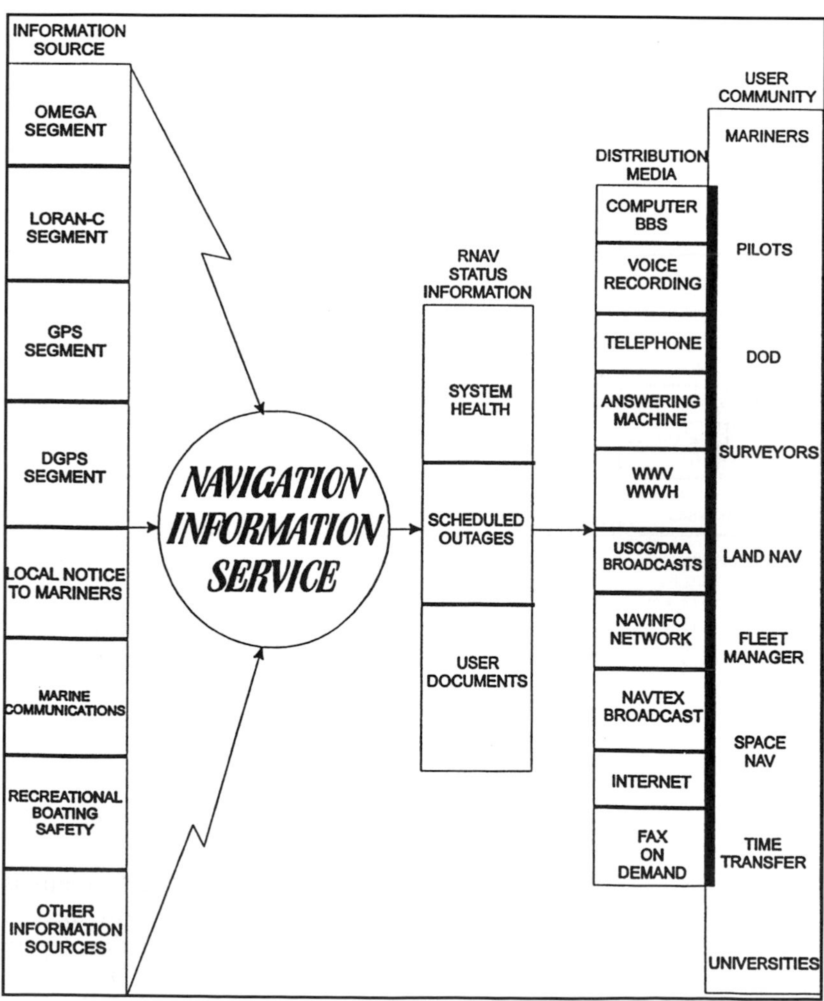

Diagram 14.34: US Coast Guard – Navigation Information Service (NIS) for use by the Civilian Community with GPS/DGPS

14.20 The NIS Quick Reference OAB Distribution

The Navigation Information Service provides the Operational Advisory Broadcasts through the following services:

SERVICE	AVAILABILITY	INFO TYPE	CONTACT NUMBER
NIS WATCHSTANDER	24 hours a day	USER INQUIRIES	PHONE (703) 313-5900 FAX (703) 313-5920
NIS COMPUTER BULLETIN BOARD SERVICE	24 hours a day	STATUS FORE/HIST/OUTAGES NGS DATA OMEGA/FRPMISC INFO	BBS (703) 313-5910 (300-28800 bps) - or - SprintNet (X25) 31103501132800
Internet	24 hours a day	STATUS FORE/HIST/OUTAGES/ NGS DATA/OMEGA/FRP AND MISC INFO	http://www.navcen.uscg.mil gopher//gopher.navcen.uscg.mil
Fax on Demand	24 hours a day	STATUS FORE/HIST/OUTAGES/ NGS DATA/OMEGA/FRP AND MISC INFO	(703) 313-5931/5932
NIS VOICE TAPE RECORDING	24 hours a day	STATUS FORECASTS HISTORIC	(703) 313-5906 - OMEGA (703) 313-5907 - GPS
WWV	Minutes 14 & 15	STATUS FORECASTS	2.5 5 10 15 and 20 MHz
WWVH	Minutes 43 & 44	STATUS FORECASTS	2.5 5 10 and 15 MHz
USCG MIB	When broadcasted	STATUS FORECASTS	VHF Radio marine band
DMA BROADCAST WARNINGS	When broadcasted Outages	STATUS FORECASTS	
DMA WEEKLY NOTICE TO MARINERS	Published & mailed weekly	STATUS FORECAST OUTAGES	(301) 227-3126
DMA NAVINFONET AUTOMATED TO MARINERS SYSTEM	24 hours a day	STATUS FORECASTS HISTORIC ALMANACS	(301) 227-3351 300 BAUD (301) 227-5925 1200 BAUD (301) 227-4360 2400 BAUD
NAVTEX DATA BROADCAST	6 TIMES DAILY	STATUS FORECAST OUTAGES	518 KHZ

SOLAS Chapter V (Implemented under UK Legislation by the Merchant Shipping (Safety of Navigation Regulations 2002))

Masters should be aware that from July 2002, many topics directly related to the safe navigation of the vessel have been incorporated into Chapter V of SOLAS.

As a result of this revision, many Guidance (MGN's) Notices have been withdrawn, with associated relevant texts being included in the context of Chapter V.

The SOLAS Chapter V, and its annexes provides respective information on the following topics:

Navigational warnings.
Meteorological scrviccs and warnings.
The Ice Patrol Service.
Search and Rescue services.
Life saving signals.
Hydrographic services.
Ships routing.
Ship reporting systems.
Vessel Traffic Services (VTS)
Establishment and operation of aids to navigation.
Ships manning.
Principles related to Bridge Design, the design and arrangement of Navigational Systems, equipment and bridge procedures.
Maintenance of equipment.
Electromagnetic compatibility
Approval surveys and performance standards of navigational systems, equipment and voyage data recorders.
Carriage requirements for shipborne navigational systems and equipment.
Voyage data recorders.
International Code of Signals.
Navigation Bridge visibility.
Pilot transfer arrangements.
Use of heading and/or track controlling systems.
Operation of main source of electrical power and steering gear.
Steering gear testing and drills.
Nautical Charts and publications.
Records of navigational activities.
Life saving signals to be used by ships, aircraft or persons in distress.
Operational limitations.
Danger messages.
Information required in danger messages.
Distress messages: obligations and procedures.
Safe navigation and avoidance of dangerous situations.
Misuse of distress signals.

NAVIGATION SELF-EXAMINER

Charts and Publications

Q1. List in general terms the reliability of navigational charts.

Ans. No chart is completely reliable because:

(a) incomplete surveys or alterations in topography.
(b) date and methods of survey not being as dependable because the measuring instruments previously employed were not as accurate e.g. lead and line compared with electronics.
(c) alterations occur subsequent to the time of survey. Sea bottom may also be unstable and not present a correct representation as per old surveys.
(d) paper charts may have some distortion when being printed, due to various causes.
(e) magnetic variation will change with the passing of time.
(f) the use of small scale charts requires extreme caution and mariners are continually advised to use the largest scale chart available.

Q2. For what aspects of navigation would you expect to use a gnomonic chart?

Ans. The gnomonic chart is used for:

(a) Great circle sailing.
(b) Polar navigation in high latitudes.
(c) For the large scale plans of harbour approaches.

Q3. When referring to charts, what is a 'new edition'?

Ans. When a chart is completely or partly revised it will be dated and marked as 'new edition', set to the right of the date of publication.

All previous copies of the chart are cancelled.

Q4. What is a 'new chart'?

Ans. A chart which is published for the first time.

The date of publication being inserted outside the bottom margin in the middle of the chart.

Q5. When correcting charts by applying a 'block' correction what would you paste, the block or the chart and why?

Ans. The area of the chart where the block is to be affixed is pasted. The block should be pencilled around when in position and the pencil area of the chart pasted.

If the block was pasted the moisture in the paste would cause excessive distortion to the block and cause inaccuracy when fixing. Also the chart paper would be expected to be of stronger texture than that used for the blocks, as cut from notices to mariners.

Q6. Who issues and publishes the 'weekly notices' to mariners?

Ans. The Hydrographic Department of the navy.

Q7. What is a 'new danger' and how is it marked for identification by the mariner?

Ans. A new danger is the term used to describe newly discovered hazards which have not yet been indicated in nautical publications. They include naturally occurring obstructions such as sandbanks and rocks or man made dangers such as wrecks.

New dangers are marked in accordance with the IALA buoyage system and will have at least one of the marks duplicated.

The duplicate mark will be identical to its partner in all respects and may carry a 'RACON' providing a signal of Morse 'D'. The signal length being of 1 nautical mile on the radar display.

The duplicate mark may be removed when the appropriate authority is satisfied that information concerning the new danger has been sufficiently promulgated.

Q8. When transferring positions from one chart to another, how would the Master instruct a Junior Officer to ensure that the operation was carried out correctly?

Ans. Transfer the position by use of 'bearing and distance', from a fixed point which is common to both charts. The new position should be checked against the old position by means of latitude and longitude.

NB. The scale of charts may differ.

Always obtain an additional fix of the ship's position as soon after the transfer as time permits.

If magnetic compass bearings are being used ensure that the magnetic variation on one chart is not different to that of the next chart.

Always transfer to the largest scale chart available.

Q9. What information on the chart may be used to assess the possibility of lesser depth occurring between the charted depths.

Ans. Carry out a detailed chart inspection to include all and any notations inset into:

(a) the borders of the chart.
(b) under the title blocks of the chart.
(c) the source data block – for dates of surveys.
(d) special navigation notes on land or sea areas.

Tidal stream information, as charted, is referred to the high water at a particular port. Greater distances from the port of reference could reflect greater unreliability on the information being used.

Some charts will carry special reference to tidal levels and charted data.

I would also take into account Annual Notices to Mariners Nos. 1 and 15 which refer to tidal surges and the warning service.

Mariners should also remember that topography changes with time. The last date of survey would provide the navigator with a relative standard of reliability of the charted information.

Q10. What would you use a 'co-tidal/co-range' chart for?

Ans. The chart is used to find the times and heights of high water in offshore areas and at places which lie between secondary ports.

Ice

Q11. Describe the sources of information which are available to the Master, regarding the latest 'ice situation' in the North Atlantic?

Ans. Ice reports – available from the ice patrol and distributed by the U.S. Naval Oceanographic Office.

Navtex – ice reports via various transmitters, e.g. Norwegian Sea and Icelandic areas by Norway.

Designated Ice Officer available at the Meteorological Office, Bracknell, ENGLAND.

Ice Charts – as supplied by Admiralty Hydrographic Department of the Canadian Hydrographic Service.

Radio – advisory warning reports from Halifax, Nova Scotia. Ref: to Admiralty List of Radio Signals.

Reports from other shipping which is outward bound from respective ice affected regions.

General reference should be made to relevant publications such as:

Mariners Handbook, Ocean Passages of the World, Admiralty Sailing Directions and Weekly Notices to Mariners.

Q12. What instructions should the Master give to the officer of the watch, when participating with other vessels in an ice convoy?

Ans. He should be informed of the ship's position within the convoy and the position in relation to that of the ice breaker or command vessel.

A specified distance must be maintained between own vessel and the vessel ahead. The greatest benefit being at about 150 metres from the ice breaker, however, this distance must be such as to allow the vessel to stop without collision if so ordered.

The OOW may receive orders to operate astern propulsion at any time while in convoy and if so ordered should do so immediately. Full use of engines and all navigation equipment should be readily available at all times, together with full communication systems, including international code flags. Ships details of speed, length, draught and tonnage should be passed to the command vessel at the onset.

Q13. State the navigational problems that you would expect to encounter when navigating in cold climates, inside ice regions, with respect to the use of:

Beacons and sectored lights for position fixing purpose?

Ans. Where ice conditions are prevalent, windows of lights may be covered by frost or ice which will greatly reduce sighting and visible range of the light. The lantern glass may also be subject to moisture build-up with temperature changes that could further diffuse the lights rays. Snow build-up, especially in extreme conditions could cause complete obscurity of the light for navigation purposes.

Any of the above could well create uncertainty where sector lights are employed. The width of sectors being directly affected by increased levels of frost or ice build up in and around the lamp. The width of sectors in coloured lights could well appear more or less white. The greatest effect is on weak or green lights. White lights tend to extend their sector width in such conditions.

Q14. Where would you expect to obtain ice information for navigation in the Baltic Sea?

Ans. General reference should be made to all official publications which provide ice information and additionally to:

Baltic Pilot Vol 1	Publication No. 18
Baltic Pilot Vol 2	Publication No. 19
Baltic Pilot Vol 3	Publication No. 20
Mariners Handbook	Publication No. 100
ALRS	Publication No. 283

Relevant charts of the area and the use of the weekly notices to mariners should be consulted for 'T' and 'P' notices.

Weather reports and facsimile charts from the Meteorological Office, Bracknell.

Both the Finnish and Swedish Ice Services operate ice-breakers and local information can be obtained from these and Kiel harbour radio.

Q15. What physical indications would the mariner observe when entering an area where ice conditions might prevail?

Ans. The sea temperature would be set about 1° C. Sea birds and wildlife may be sighted far from land. Ice fragments may be sighted on the surface. Ships position being associated with a known ice region or close to a cold iceberg bearing current.

Tropical Revolving Storm

Q16. A vessel is along side in harbour, when a tropical revolving storm is forecast. The projected path of the storm would put the vessel in the dangerous semi-circle as the storm passes over.

What options are open to the Master of the vessel?

Ans. The Master should consider 'letting go' his moorings in plenty of time and moving into open water to ride out the storm at sea. The decision should be taken early and should leave the vessel 'hove to' clear of harbour roads. The possibility of obtaining the lee of an island clear of the dangerous semi-circle, is more likely if the decision to clear the harbour is made earlier rather than later.

If the vessel intends to remain in port, then additional moorings should be stretched. The ships side should be well fended and the gangway hoisted clear of the quayside.

The progress of the storm should be monitored and its position plotted on the chart. Weather forecasts should be kept updated. In all cases the ship should be secured against heavy weather and all cargo work halted. Engines should be readily available.

Q17. What geographical conditions are most favourable for the formation of a tropical revolving storm?

Ans. A tropical revolving storm would normally form and develop in an area where there is a large continent with a large expanse of sea area to the eastward, in which there are many small islands and coastlines which run north/south, e.g. Gulf of Mexico, East Coast of Africa.

Formation would take place between 5°-10° latitudes, north or south of the Equator when the sea temperature is high in the region of +27° C. It would not form or develop in the South Atlantic Ocean.

Q18. Why do tropical revolving storms not form and develop in the South Atlantic Ocean.*

Ans. The waters of the South Atlantic are comparatively cool at surface level. A possible reason for this is that the equatorial trough, (the doldrums) does not penetrate into the South Atlantic, which could account for cool surface water. Tropical revolving storms form over regions of the highest sea surface

* NB A TRS was recorded in the South Atlantic in 2004. Such a rarity can generally be discounted.

temperatures. Large supplies of water vapour being accumulated by air passing over the warmer sea surface. The South Atlantic cooler surface waters do not lend themselves to conditions which allow TRS formation.

Weak cyclonic circulations are also unknown in this region and TRS would require cyclonic circulation, (tropical depression) as an essential condition for its development.

Routing

Q19. Which areas would you consider that climatological routing to be appropriate and satisfactory?

Ans. North Atlantic, predominantly westbound.
South Atlantic and North Pacific (winter months).

Q20. Describe the types of vessels that would use the various types of prescribed routes?

Ans. Ice free route – vessels without or only partly ice strengthened (Ice Classification A1).

All weather route – passenger vessels, or roll-on roll-off ferries.

Deep Water Route – vessels constrained by their draught, e.g. deep laden tankers.

Climatic route – all ships, especially container vessels.

Q21. What benefits are gained by the owner/charterer when the shoreside 'ROUTING' service is employed for the ship?

Ans The owners or charterers will obtain post-voyage information for management and accounting purposes, and additionally:

(a) round the clock accurate monitoring of the vessels progress.
(b) comparisons between actual and alternative routes. (These demonstrate the benefits of the service).
(c) comparisons of the actual speeds achieved against charter speeds, after making appropriate allowance for weather and currents.
(d) documented information regarding the weather related performance of the vessel throughout the whole voyage.

(e) routed vessels may attract more favourable insurance premiums.

Q22. State what factors the Master would consider when selecting an optimum ocean passage?

Ans. Pre-statement: Any route selected should not stand the vessel into danger and the prime consideration should be the safe navigation throughout the voyage.

(a) shortest distance may not always be the most acceptable because of ice and prevailing bad weather. Least time over a short distance does not always follow and the Master would need to consider the overall weather pattern for all areas of the proposed route. Seasonal changes may affect final choice.
(b) depending on the nature of the cargo, consideration towards limiting damage, especially to sensitive cargoes, must be a major factor.
(c) charter party clauses may stipulate that the voyage is conducted at a 'constant speed'. In order to achieve this 'Shoreside Routing Services' may well influence the Masters final choice of route.
(d) whichever route is selected the Master would take into account the capabilities of his own vessel. Any special features, such as ice strengthening, or being a low powered vessel, could effect the safe passage of the ship.
(e) reference to Ocean Passages (NP 136) and consideration to recommendations from this publication would also be considered prudent by any Master selecting an ocean passage route.
(f) loadlines may also influence the selected route.

Q23. When acting as Master, what instructions and precautions would you take if your vessel was approaching the Grand Banks off Newfoundland during the month of March?

Ans. The region of the Grand Banks at this time of year is notorious for icebergs, growlers, pack ice and fog. Gales are known to be frequent and severe. It is also an area well used by deep sea traffic (European to North American Trades) and extensively by fishing boats. More recently offshore exploration has commenced for the recovery of oil, gas and minerals.

As Master of the vessel I would alert all watch officers to the known hazards prior to entering the region. I would stress the need for extreme vigilance when conducting their watch. To ensure this I would draw up standing orders for the actions of the OOW when:

(a) encountering poor visibility.
(b) if ice is expected or sighted near the ships course.
(c) or if heavy weather is being experienced.

I would also communicate with the coast radio station and obtain the regular reports from the International Ice Patrol. I would expect the OOW to plot all known ice positions on the navigational chart.

Weather reports would be monitored at regular intervals and instructions would remain with the OOW to call the Master in the event of any changes being experienced in the prevailing weather.

In the event of poor visibility being encountered in this region I would 'double watches' and maintain a continual radar watch by a second watch-keeper.

Once entering the region, the Master would proceed at a safe speed relevant to the prevailing conditions. In any case, main engines would be on a stand-by status as soon as the vessels position is observed to be approaching the known ice limits.

Additionally I would expect all watch officers to advise look-out personnel of the dangers of the region and that they would be expected to report all ice sightings, together with all traffic movements. Manual steering would be employed when entering and passing through this region.

Q24. Consider a vessel which is expected to sail from San Francisco to Yokohama in January, the Master is considering three alternative routes:

'A' Direct great circle.
'B' A rhumb line which remains within the summer load line at latitude 35° 00' N.
'C' A route north of the Aleutian Islands.

What factors would the Master take into consideration when deciding the most appropriate passage?

Ans:

FACTOR	ROUTE 'A'	ROUTE 'B'	ROUTE 'C'
Distance	4440 miles	4772 miles	4505 miles
Currents	Variable	Adverse 1 kn.	Part Favourable 1 kn.
Winds	Gales (contrary)	Occ. Gales (cont)	Gales (favourable)
Icebergs	Not likely	No	Possible
Loadline	Winter	Summer	Winter
Steaming Time	Medium	Greatest	Least
Possible Damage	Greatest	Least	Medium

The overall safety of the vessel throughout would influence the final decision, together with the nature of the cargo and the economics of each route.

NB. The prudent Master would also consult such publications as Ocean Passages of the World, The North Pacific Pilot (vol. 23) and the Sailing Directions and Planning Guide for the North Pacific Ocean (publication 152 of the Defence Mapping Agency of the USA).

With regard to the 'C' route the Bering Sea is north of the usual storm path. Vessels westbound would therefore benefit from favourable winds and following seas, the vessel being situated in the favourable semi-circle.

Vessels would not expect to encounter opposing currents and the route would therefore be acceptable to low powered ships.

IAMSAR

Q25. Whilst proceeding towards a marine distress situation, where casualties are known to be in the water, discuss what preparations you would make aboard your vessel.

Ans. Depending on the general circumstances and the available equipment on board my vessel the following actions would be considered:

(a) plot the rendezvous position, datum point, (last known position) of casualty, together with any search pattern limits.
(b) establish communications with Rescue Co-ordination Centre (RCC) and pass own position, ETA and other relevant details to co-ordinator.
(c) obtain current weather report.
(d) maintain my own vessel on operational status, radar watch, manual steering and lookouts posted, when nearing the area of distress.
(e) prepare hospital to treat for hypothermia and shock.
(f) turn out rescue boat ready for immediate launch, stand-by emergency boat crews and rig guest warp.
(g) assess potential navigational hazards for own ship.
(h) update target information and revise ETA to the rescue co-ordination centre.
(i) keep engine room informed regarding manoeuvring speed.
(j) plot prevailing currents and estimate drift on target.
(k) continually monitor the vessels progress and note all activities in the log book.
(l) note charted positions for purpose of deviation.
(m) brief operational personnel prior to engagement, e.g. Boats coxswain, medical staff, officer of the watch.

Q26. If a vessel is to engage in a helicopter winching operation from the deck of the vessel, where should the Master effect the relative wind direction?

Ans. Depending on the availability of deck space, if the operation is to take place:–

(a) Aft Deck – Wind 30° Port Bow.
(b) Midships – Wind 30° Port Bow or Beam wind.
(c) Forward – Wind 30° Starboard Quarter.

Q27. A vessel is requisitioned to engage in an IAMSAR search, what would the duties of the navigation officer?

Ans. The navigator would need to plot the search area limits together with the datum point. The adopted search pattern together with all course alteration points would be charted. A track space and the position of the CSP (commence search pattern) would be designated, and an appropriate speed established.

Q28. What type of messages are transmitted by vessels which are participants of the AMVER organisation?

Ans. (a) a sailing plan before departure.
(b) a departure report, as soon as possible after departure.
(c) a position report at the first 24 hours then 48 hours after.
(d) an arrival report on reaching destination.
(e) deviation report when the vessel diverts from the sailing plan.

Pilotage

Q29. Summarise the navigational precautions and preparations for a vessel engaging with a smaller craft?

Ans. Establish and brief the 'bridge team' i.e. lookouts, helmsman, OOW, pilot, radar operator, communications officer and engine room.

Assess the approach plan with regard to navigational dangers, currents and tidal effects and underkeel clearance. Advance early warning and instructions to engine room with regard to manoeuvring.

Exhibit correct signals and monitor all communications. Carry out specific instrument and propulsion checks prior to engagement. Obtain local weather information. Manoeuvre to create a lee for small boats coming along-side. Establish visual contact and retain it throughout the operation. Record and maintain log books and make full use of relevant navigational publications.

NB. Avoid interaction with smaller craft.

Q30. If your vessel was approaching a 'pilot station', and did not require the services of the marine pilot, what actions would the Master take on the bridge?

Ans. Reduce speed on approach towards the pilot roads. Brief lookout personnel to watch for small boats or pilot cutters. Enter the speed reduction in the log book relative to the ships position. Contact the pilot station (or boat) and inform them of your name, course, speed and intentions.

Q31. When undertaking a long river passage what information would the Master give to the pilot when he boards?

Ans. (a) draught of the vessel.
(b) present position, course and detail of compass errors.
(c) engine status and speeds at respective revolutions.
(d) type of propeller and position of thruster units – if any.
(e) type of machinery and number of propellers.
(f) ships details regarding length and breadth. Whether the vessel is fitted with bulbous bow or not. State of readiness of anchors.
(g) list of VHF guarded channels.
(h) radar status – head up, stabilised, true motion etc.
(i) radar range.
(j) port from which the ship has last departed.
(k) port from which the ship is bound and the nature of cargo.
(l) any defects or deficiencies regarding navigational equipment.

Additionally the Master would introduce himself by name and much of the above information would be indicated to the pilot by means of a display pilot information board.

Miscellaneous

Q32. Describe a good location for the magnetic compass?

Ans. It should be positioned on the fore and aft centre line of the vessel (exceptions: aircraft carriers etc.) with adequate height to provide an all round view.

It should be housed in a binnacle at or near the steering position and far enough away from the navigational instruments so as not to be affected by electrical effects. (Ref. Annex 20 Section 5 of SOLAS Chapter V.)

Q33. When would you expect to carry out a 'compass-swing'?

Ans. (a) with a new ship, after completion of ship trials. A new vessel would also carry out a swing prior to a maiden voyage, during that voyage and at the end of the voyage.

(b) when large structural alterations have occurred to the superstructure or to the hull.
(c) following a collision or stranding when major repairs become necessary. If bridge electrical apparatus is installed which could influence the magnetic effect in close proximity to the compass position.
(d) following a long lay-up period and the vessel being brought back into active service.
(e) in the event of a large fire on board or if the vessel is struck by lightning.

Q34. When checking the compass by means of the AMPLITUDE method state the correct position of the sun when carrying out the observation.

State also why this method of observation is considered unreliable when navigating in high latitudes?

Ans. When observing the amplitude by the sun, the lower limb should be half a diameter above the visible horizon.

NB. The visible horizon does not coincide with the celestial horizon because of the combined effects of refraction, parallax and dip.

In high latitudes the rate that the body is changing its azimuth is comparatively large. Consequently a small change in altitude results in a large change in azimuth.

These conditions would make the accuracy of the observation unreliable, unless the observer could be precise regarding the time that the body's centre was on the observers visible horizon. (A correction is required)

Q35. When using radar as a navigation aid, discuss the difference between 'blind' and 'shadow' sectors?

Ans. Blind and shadow sectors can be caused by obstructions on land, by other vessels or more commonly, obstructions aboard your own vessel.

i.e. Masts, samson posts, and cross trees.

Both types of sectors can be experienced in either the horizontal or vertical. With regard to target detection the radar beam is completely cut off in a blind sector, whereas the shadow sector allows reduced target definition at a shorter range than normal.

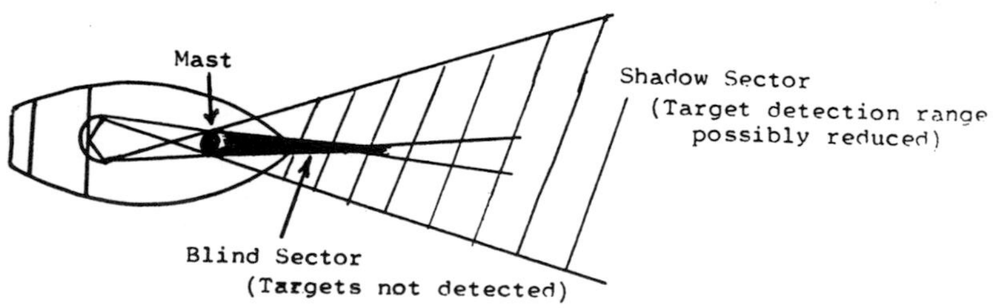

Q36. State what factors would affect the amount of 'squat' a vessel could expect to experience and list also what signs might be observed by the OOW, if a vessel was being affected by shallow water effects.

Ans. Factors affecting 'SQUAT'

a)	speed of vessel	The value of squat is directly related to speed^2
b)	draught/depth of water (Ratio)	High ratio equates to a greater rate of squat.
c)	high engine revolutions	High revs, will increase stern trim.
d)	position of the longitudinal centre of buoyancy (LCB)	Determines the trimming effect.
e)	type of bow fitted.	Affects wavemaking and pressure distribution.
f)	length/breadth ratio	Short-tubby ships squat more.
g)	block coefficient (C^b)	A vessel with a large C^b will experience greater squat.
h)	breadth/channel width	High ratio will cause greater squat.

i) Trim	Greater squat is experienced with a bow trim than a stern trim.

Signs that a vessel is experiencing 'squat'.

Speed and R.P.M. will decrease and vibration may occur. The steering is usually affected and the vessel becomes sluggish to manoeuvre.

Waves from the ships movement increase in amplitude and the wake left by the vessel may change colour and become mud-stained.

Suggested immediate action – reduce speed.

Q37. State the factors that the Master would take into consideration when determining the manning and composition of watches on a vessel about to make a passage through the English Channel via the Dover Strait?

Ans. The Master should take account of the number of watch keeping personnel on board the vessel and the roles that respective ranks can perform.

i.e. Watch officers, helmsman, lookouts, communications, pilot, etc.

He should consider the abilities and the endurance of personnel and remember that fatigue could effect efficiency.

The weather, especially the state of visibility, would influence directly decisions to engage double watches especially when a continuous radar watch may be required. Continual monitoring of weather forecasts must be considered essential and to this end the use of key personnel should be prudent to match critical stages of the passage plan.

e.g. Dover Strait area.

The degree of experience that watch officers and crew have of the ships systems and of the area could influence which personnel are assigned to specific areas of the passage.

Early planning and anticipated focal points of high traffic density should be compatible with the use of the most experienced watch personnel. High traffic density would also dictate when the Master MUST be in attendance on the bridge.

The need for rest and meal reliefs should be considered and the Master should ensure that these times, as well as watch hand-overs, are conducted in a correct manner.

With any busy waterway the navigation and safety of the vessel is paramount and Masters should take into account that position fixing and communications may lead to distraction of that most essential element of keeping a proper and effective lookout. The watch officer alone, especially one with limited experience, may find reassurance with the addition of another pair of 'eyes on the bridge'.

If traffic or weather dictates the need to double watches the Master should not hesitate in instigating this option.

Q38. What line of action would the Master probably take when called to the bridge by a junior watch officer who reports a mine clearance vessel ahead on the vessels track?

Ans. The Master would probably order the vessel stopped, or the speed reduced, to allow time to establish communications with the warship. Communications are established by VHF radio following station identification or by flashlight morse (Aldis Lamp), if radio silence prevails.

Confirmation would be obtained regarding:

a) is the warship engaged in exercise, or
b) is the warship engaged on actual mine clearance.

The Master would also request information regarding any clear navigable water areas, as well as any areas defined that are known to be obstructed by mines.

An alteration of course towards clear waters would be made following recommendations by the warship. Any alteration being such as to give the mine clearance vessel a wide berth and should not bring the vessel within 1000 metres of the warship.

Obstructed areas would be plotted on the chart, especially important for vessels which are intending a return passage through the same area.

NB: If would be normal practice for navigational warnings to be issued when mine clearance operations are either expected or known to be ongoing. Subsequent checks should therefore be made with local coast radio stations.

Following the many recent conflicts around the world mariners are advised that hostile areas where mines may have been laid may still be active possibly due to indiscriminate mine laying during the times of conflict. Extreme caution should be exercised where the geography and the history of the location reflect this possibility.

Q39. On your approach to a port, you sight a vessel which has run aground.

What action would the Master be expected to make with regard to the safe navigation of his vessel?

Ans. A probable line of action would be for the vessel to be immediately stopped and all way taken off. This would allow time to make a full chart assessment and allow the positions of both the vessel aground and your own vessel to be plotted on the chart.

The echo sounder may well be operational, but if not then a prudent Master would require this instrument switched on and ongoing soundings recorded.

Although the vessel aground is not in distress, useful communications could be established in order to obtain the existing draught of the vessel and the time that she grounded.

(Time of grounding would allow the state of tide to be determined).

Alternative routing may have to be investigated in order for your own vessel to navigate clear of the obstructing vessel and any shallow waters. Alternative tracks would be observed from a comprehensive chart assessment, made earlier.

Masters should at all times be aware of their own draught and be concerned regarding underkeel clearance. State of tide should be investigated and any approaches to ports and harbours should be made with adequate underkeel clearance.

The use of a contingency, such as going to an anchorage and obtaining the services of a pilot, would of course be additional considerations that may be thought appropriate under the circumstances.

NB: Vessels aground may draw attention to their plight and exhibit relevant signals, such as:

'L' You should stop your vessel instantly.

or

'U' You are running into danger.

Q40. Your vessel is scheduled to carry out a routine helicopter land on/take off operation. What line of action would the Master expect to take in order to establish a safe navigational situation for the conduct of the operation.

Ans. The Master should meet with all heads of departments and other interested parties regarding the detailed conduct of the operation.

NB: Additional personnel could well include the watch officer, and the deck landing officer.

A chart assessment of the intended area of engagement should be made to ensure that the safe navigation of the vessel is maintained throughout:

a) Adequate sea room is available in alternative directions.

(Actual course being determined by the wind direction/ pilots requirements).

b) that the area of engagement is clear of navigational obstructions and shallows, and that the area is not going to obstruct other traffic operations, e.g. Cross traffic separation schemes.

c) underkeel clearance is adequate to allow time to complete the operation.

d) that state of machinery is on 'stand by' and that manoeuvring speed is maintained.

Relevant times of stand-by to be advised.

e) communications officer to be in contact with:
   i) The aircraft as soon as possible.
   ii) The deck landing officer.
   iii) Internal stations, e.g. engine room.

f) deck preparations to be completed on route to include: Wind direction indicator, and navigation signals for 'restricted in ability to manoeuvre' to be made ready.

Deck area cleared and obstructions by way of rigging removed.

Contingency – rescue boat turned out.

g) weather report monitored.

h) time of manual steering to be engaged, pre-determined. Also when lookouts would be placed and deck fire party placed on stand by.

MARINE SAFETY – ANNEX TO VOLUME

The International Regulations for the Prevention of Collisions at Sea

Table of Contents of the International Regulations

INTERNATIONAL REGULATIONS FOR PREVENTING COLLISIONS AT SEA, 1972

(as amended by resolutions A464(XII), A626(15), A678(16), A736(18) and A910(22))

PART A - GENERAL

Rule 1
Applications

(a) These Rules shall apply to all vessels upon the high seas and in all waters connected therewith navigable by seagoing vessels.

(b) Nothing in these Rules shall interfere with the operation of special rules made by an appropriate authority for roadsteads, harbours, rivers, lakes or inland waterways connected with the high seas and navigable by seagoing vessels. Such special rules shall conform as closely as possible to these Rules.

(c) Nothing in these Rules shall interfere with the operation of any special rules made by the Government of any State with respect to additional station or signal lights, shapes or whistle signals for ships of war and vessels proceeding under convoy, or with respect to additional station or signal lights or shapes for fishing vessels engaged in fishing as a fleet. These additional station or signal lights, shapes or whistle signals shall, so far as possible, be such that they cannot be mistaken for any light, shape or signal authorised elsewhere under these Rules.

(d) Traffic separation schemes may be adopted by the Organization for the purpose of these Rules.

(e) Whenever the Government concerned shall have determined that a vessel of any special construction or purpose cannot comply with the provisions of any of these Rules with respect to the number, position, range or arc of visibility of lights or shapes, as well as to the disposition and characteristics of sound-signalling appliances, such vessel shall comply with such other provisions in regard to the number, position, range or arc of visibility of lights or shapes, as well as to the disposition and characteristics of sound-signalling appliances, as her Government shall have determined to be the closest possible compliance with these Rules in respect of that vessel.

Rule 2
Responsibility

(a) Nothing in these Rules shall exonerate any vessel, or the owner, master or crew thereof, from the consequences of any neglect to comply with these Rules or of the neglect of any precaution which may be required by the ordinary practice of seamen, or by the special circumstances of the case.

(b) In construing and complying with these Rules due regard shall be had to all dangers of navigation and collision and to any special circumstances, including the limitations of the vessels involved, which may make a departure from these Rules necessary to avoid immediate danger.

Rule 3
General definitions

For the purpose of these Rules, except where the context otherwise requires:

(a) The word "vessel" includes every description of water craft, including non-displacement craft, WIG craft and seaplanes, used or capable of being used as a means of transportation on water,

(b) The term "power-driven vessel" means any vessel propelled by machinery.

(c) The term "sailing vessel" means any vessel under sail provided that propelling machinery, if fitted, is not being used.

(d) The term "vessel engaged in fishing" means any vessel fishing with nets, lines, trawls or other fishing apparatus which restrict manoeuvrability, but does not include a vessel fishing with trolling lines or other fishing apparatus which do not restrict manoeuvrability.

(e) The word "seaplane" includes any aircraft designed to manoeuvre on the water.

(f) The term "vessel not under command" means a vessel which through some exceptional circumstance is unable to manoeuvre as required by these Rules and is therefore unable to keep out of the way of another vessel.

(g) The term "vessel restricted in her ability to manoeuvre" means a vessel which from the nature of her work is restricted in the ability to manoeuvre as required by these Rules and is therefore unable to keep out of the way of another vessel. The term "vessels restricted in their ability to manoeuvre" shall include but not be limited to:

(i) a vessel engaged in laying, servicing or picking up a navigation mark, submarine cable or pipeline;

(ii) a vessel engaged in dredging, surveying or underwater operations;

(iii) a vessel engaged in replenishment or transferring persons, provisions or cargo while underway;

(iv) a vessel engaged in the launching or recovery of aircraft;

(v) a vessel engaged in mine clearance operations;

(vi) a vessel engaged in a towing operation such as severely restricts the towing vessel and her tow in their ability to deviate from their course.

(h) The term "vessel constrained by her draught" means a power-driven vessel which, because of her draught in relation to the available depth and width of navigable water, is severely restricted in her ability to deviate from the course she is following.

(i) The word "underway" means that a vessel is not at anchor, or made fast to the shore, or aground.

(j) The words "length" and "breadth" of a vessel mean her length overall and greatest breadth.

(k) Vessels shall be deemed to be in sight of one another only when one can be observed visually from the other.

(l) The term "restricted visibility" means any condition in which visibility is restricted by fog, mist, falling snow, heavy rainstorms, sandstorms or any other similar causes.

(m) The term "wing-in ground (WIG) craft" means a multimodal craft which, in its main operational mode, flies in close proximity to the surface by utilizing surface-effect action.

PART B - STEERING AND SAILING RULES

Section 1 - Conduct of vessels in any condition of visibility

Rule 4
Application

Rules in this Section apply in any condition of visibility.

Rule 5
Look-out

Every vessel shall at all times maintain a proper look-out by sight and hearing as well as by all available means appropriate in the prevailing circumstances and conditions so as to make a full appraisal of the situation and of the risk of collision.

Rule 6
Safe speed

Every vessel shall at all times proceed at a safe speed so that she can take proper and effective action to avoid collision and be stopped within a distance appropriate to the prevailing circumstances and conditions.

In determining a safe speed the following factors shall be among those taken into account:

(a) By all vessels:

- (i) the state of visibility;
- (ii) the traffic density including concentrations of fishing vessels or any other vessels;
- (iii) the manoeuvrability of the vessel with special reference to stopping distance and turning ability in the prevailing conditions;
- (iv) at night the presence of background light such as from shore lights or from back scatter of her own lights;
- (v) the state of wind, sea and current, and the proximity of navigational hazards;
- (vi) the draught in relation to the available depth of water.

(b) Additionally, by vessels with operational radar:

- (i) the characteristics, efficiency and limitations of the radar equipment;
- (ii) any constraints imposed by the radar range scale in use;
- (iii) the effect on radar detection of the sea state, weather and other sources of interference;
- (iv) the possibility that small vessels, ice and other floating objects may not be detected by radar at an adequate range.
- (v) the number, location and movement of vessels detected by radar;
- (vi) the more exact assessment of the visibility that may be possible when radar is used to determine the range of vessels or other objects in the vicinity.

Rule 7
Risk of collision

(a) Every vessel shall use all available means appropriate to the prevailing circumstances and conditions to determine if risk of collision exists. If there is any doubt such risk shall be deemed to exist.

(b) Proper use shall be made of the radar equipment if fitted and operational, including long-range scanning to obtain early warning of risk of collision and radar plotting or equivalent systematic observation of detected objects.

(c) Assumption shall not be made on the basis of scanty information, especially scanty radar information.

(d) In determining if risk of collision exists the following considerations shall be among those taken into account:

(i) such risk shall be deemed to exist if the compass bearing of an approaching vessel does not appreciably change;

(ii) such risk may sometimes exist even when an appreciable bearing change is evident, particularly when approaching a very large vessel or a tow or when approaching a vessel at close range.

Rule 8
Action to avoid collision

(a) Any action to avoid collision shall be taken in accordance with the rules of this Part and, if the circumstances of the case admit, be positive, made in ample time and with due regard to the observance of good seamanship.

(b) Any alteration of course and/or speed to avoid collision shall, if the circumstances of the case admit, be large enough to be readily apparent to another vessel observing visually or by radar; a succession of small alterations of course and/or speed should be avoided.

(c) If there is sufficient sea-room, alteration of course alone may be the most effective action to avoid a close-quarters situation provided that it is made in good time, is substantial and does not result in another close-quarters situation.

(d) Action taken to avoid collision with another vessel shall be such as to result in passing at a safe distance. The effectiveness of the action shall be carefully checked until the other vessel is finally past and clear.

(e) If necessary to avoid collision or allow more time to assess the situation, a vessel shall slacken her speed or take all way off by stopping or reversing her means of propulsion.

(f) (i) A vessel which, by any of these Rules, is required not to impede the passage or safe passage of another vessel shall, when required by the circumstances of the case, take early action to allow sufficient sea-room for the safe passage of the other vessel.

(ii) A vessel required not to impede the passage or safe passage of another vessel is not relieved of this obligation if approaching the other vessel so as to involve risk of collision and shall, when taking action, have full regard to the action which may be required by the Rules of this Part.

(iii) A vessel the passage of which is not to be impeded remains fully obliged to comply with the Rules of this Part when the two vessels are approaching one another so as to involve risk of collision.

Rule 9
Narrow channels

(a) A vessel proceeding along the course of a narrow channel or fairway shall keep as near to the outer limit of the channel or fairway which lies on her starboard side as is safe and practicable.

(b) A vessel of less than 20 metres in length or a sailing vessel shall not impede the passage of a vessel which can safely navigate only within a narrow channel or fairway.

(c) A vessel engaged in fishing shall not impede the passage of any other vessel navigating within a narrow channel or fairway.

(d) A vessel shall not cross a narrow channel or fairway if such crossing impedes the passage of a vessel which can safely navigate only within such channel or fairway. The latter vessel may use the sound signal prescribed in Rule 34(d) if in doubt as to the intention of the crossing vessel.

(e) (i) In a narrow channel or fairway when overtaking can take place only if the vessel to be overtaken has to take action to permit safe passing, the vessel intending to overtake shall indicate her intention by sounding the appropriate signal prescribed in the Rule 34(c)(i). The vessel to be overtaken shall, if in agreement, sound the appropriate signal prescribed in Rule 34(c)(ii) and take steps to permit safe passing. If in doubt she may sound the signals prescribed in Rule 34(d).

(ii) This Rule does not relieve the overtaking vessel of her obligation under Rule 13.

(f) A vessel nearing a bend or an area of a narrow channel or fairway where other vessels may be obscured by an intervening obstruction shall navigate with particular alertness and caution and shall sound the appropriate signal prescribed in Rule 34(e).

Rule 10

Traffic separation schemes

(a) This Rule applies to traffic separation schemes adopted by the Organization and does not relieve any vessel of her obligation under any other Rule.

(b) A vessel using a traffic separation scheme shall:

(i) proceed in the appropriate traffic lane in the general direction of traffic flow for that lane;

(ii) so far as practicable keep clear of a traffic separation line or separation zone;

(iii) normally join or leave a traffic lane at the termination of the lane, but when joining or leaving from either side shall do so at as small an angle to the general direction of traffic flow as practicable.

(c) A vessel shall, so far as practicable, avoid crossing traffic lanes but if obliged to do so shall cross on a heading as near as practicable at right angles to the general direction of traffic flow.

(d) (i) A vessel shall not use an inshore traffic zone when she can safely use the appropriate traffic lane within the adjacent traffic separation scheme. However, vessels of less than 20 metres in length, sailing vessels and vessels engaged in fishing may use the inshore traffic zone;

(ii) Notwithstanding sub-paragraph d(i), a vessel may use an inshore traffic zone when en route to or from a port, offshore installation or structure, pilot station or any other place situated within the inshore traffic zone, or to avoid immediate danger;

(e) A vessel other than a crossing vessel or a vessel joining or leaving a lane shall not normally enter a separation zone or cross a separation line except:

(i) in cases of emergency to avoid immediate danger;

(ii) to engage in fishing within a separation zone.

(f) A vessel navigating in areas near the terminations of traffic separation schemes shall do so with particular caution.

(g) The vessel shall, so far as is practicable avoid anchoring in a traffic separation scheme or in areas near its terminations.

(h) A vessel not using a traffic separation scheme shall avoid it by as wide a margin as possible.

(i) A vessel engaged in fishing shall not impede the passage of any vessel following a traffic lane.

(j) A vessel of less than 20 metres in length or a sailing vessel shall not impede the safe passage of a power-driven vessel following a traffic lane.

(k) A vessel restricted in her ability to manoeuvre when engaged in an operation for the maintenance of safety of navigation in a traffic separation scheme is exempted from complying with this Rule to the extent necessary to carry out the operation.

(l) A vessel restricted in her ability to manoeuvre when engaged in an operation for the laying, servicing or picking up of a submarine cable, within a traffic separation scheme, is exempted from complying with this Rule to the extent necessary to carry out the operation.

Section II - Conduct of vessels in sight of one another

Rule 11
Application

Rules in this Section apply to vessels in sight of one another.

Rule 12
Sailing Vessels

(a) When two sailing vessels are approaching one another, so as to involve risk of collision, one of them shall keep out of the way of the other as follows:

(i) when each has the wind on a different side, the vessel which has the wind on the port side shall keep out of the way of the other;

(ii) when both have the wind on the same side, the vessel which is to windward shall keep out of the way of the vessel which is to leeward;

(iii) if a vessel with the wind on the port side sees a vessel to windward and cannot determine with certainty whether the other vessel has the wind on the port or on the starboard side, she shall keep out of the way of the other.

(b) For the purposes of this Rule the windward side shall be deemed to be the side opposite to that on which the mainsail is carried or, in the case of a square-rigged vessel, the side opposite to that on which the largest fore- and -aft sail is carried.

Rule 13
Overtaking

(a) Notwithstanding anything contained in the Rules of Part B, Section I and II, any vessel overtaking any other shall keep out of the way of the vessel being overtaken.

(b) A vessel shall be deemed to be overtaking when coming up with another vessel from a direction more than 22.5 degrees abaft her beam, that is, in such a position with reference to the vessel she is overtaking, that at night she would be able to see only the sternlight of that vessel but neither of her sidelights.

(c) When a vessel is in any doubt as to whether she is overtaking another, she shall assume that this is the case and act accordingly.

(d) Any subsequent alteration of the bearing between the two vessels shall not make the overtaking vessel a crossing vessel within the meaning of these Rules or relieve her of the duty of keeping clear of the overtaken vessel until she is finally past and clear.

Rule 14
Head-on situation

(a) When two power-driven vessels are meeting on reciprocal or nearly reciprocal courses so as to involve risk of collision each shall alter her course to starboard so that each shall pass on the port side of the other.

(b) Such a situation shall be deemed to exist when a vessel sees the other ahead or nearly ahead and by night she would see the mast headlights of the other in a line or nearly in a line and/or both sidelights and by day she observes the corresponding aspect of the other vessel.

(c) When a vessel in in any doubt as to whether such a situation exists she shall assume that it does exist and act accordingly.

Rule 15
Crossing situation

When two power-driven vessels are crossing so as to involve risk of collision, the vessel which has the other on her own starboard side shall keep out of the way and shall, if the circumstances of the case admit, avoid crossing ahead of the other vessel.

Rule 16
Action by give-way vessel

Every vessel which is directed to keep out of the way of another vessel shall, so far as possible, take early and substantial action to keep well clear.

Rule 17
Action by stand-on vessel

(a) (i) Where one or two vessels is to keep out of the way the other shall keep her course and speed.

(ii) The latter vessel may however take action to avoid collision by her manoeuvre alone, as soon as it becomes apparent to her that the vessel required to keep out of the way is not taking appropriate action in compliance with these Rules.

(b) When, from any cause, the vessel required to keep her course and speed finds herself so close that collision cannot be avoided by the action of the give-way vessel alone, she shall take such action as will best aid to avoid collision.

(c) A power-driven vessel which takes action in a crossing situation in accordance with sub-paragraph (a)(ii) of this Rule to avoid collision with another power-driven vessel shall, if the circumstances of the case admit, not alter course to port for a vessel on her own port side.

(d) This Rule does not relieve the give-way vessel of her obligation to keep out of the way.

Rule 18
Responsibilities between vessels

Except where Rules 9, 10 and 13 otherwise require:

(a) A power-driven vessel underway shall keep out of the way of:

(i) a vessel not under command;

(ii) a vessel restricted in her ability to manoeuvre;

(iii) a vessel engaged in fishing;

(iv) a sailing vessel.

(b) A sailing vessel underway shall keep out of the way of:

(i) a vessel not under command;

(ii) a vessel restricted in her ability to manoeuvre.

(c) A vessel engaged in fishing when underway shall, so far as possible, keep out of the way of:

(i) a vessel not under command;

(ii) a vessel restricted in her ability to manoeuvre.

(d) (i) Any vessel other than a vessel not under command or a vessel restricted in her ability to manoeuvre shall, if the circumstances of the case admit, avoid impeding the safe passage of a vessel constrained by her draught, exhibiting the signals in Rule 28.

(ii) A vessel constrained by her draught shall navigate with particular caution having full regard to her special condition.

(e) A seaplane on the water shall, in general, keep well clear of all vessels and avoid impeding their navigation. In circumstances, however, where risk of collision exists, she shall comply with the Rules of this Part.

(f) (i) A WIG craft when taking-off, landing and in flight near the surface shall keep well clear of all other vessels and avoid impeding their navigation;

(ii) a WIG craft operating on the water surface shall comply with the Rules of this Part as a power-driven vessel.

Section III - Conduct of vessels in restricted visibility

Rule 19
Conduct of vessels in restricted visibility

(a) This Rule applies to vessels not in sight of one another when navigating in or near an area of restricted visibility.

(b) Every vessel shall proceed at a safe speed adapted to the prevailing circumstances and conditions of restricted visibility. A power-driven vessel shall have her engines ready for immediate manoeuvre.

(c) Every vessel shall have due regard to the prevailing circumstances and conditions of restricted visibility when complying with the Rules of Section I of this Part.

(d) A vessel which detects by radar alone the presence of another vessel shall determine if a close-quarters situation is developing and/or risk of collision exists. If so, she shall take avoiding action in ample time, provided that when such action consists of an alteration of course, so far as possible, the following shall be avoided:

(i) an alteration of course to port for a vessel forward of the beam, other than for a vessel being overtaken;

(ii) an alteration of course towards a vessel abeam or abaft the beam.

(e) Except where it has been determined that a risk of collision does not exist, every vessel which hears apparently forward of her beam the fog signal of another vessel, or which cannot avoid a close-quarters situation with another vessel forward of her beam, shall reduce her speed to the minimum at which she can be kept on her course. She shall if necessary take all her way off and in any event navigate with extreme caution until danger of collision is over.

PART C - LIGHTS AND SHAPES

Rule 20
Application

(a) Rules in this Part shall be complied with in all weathers.

(b) The Rules concerning lights shall be complied with from sunset to sunrise and during such times no other lights shall be exhibited, except such lights as cannot be mistaken for the lights specified in these Rules or do not impair their visibility or distinctive character, or interfere with the keeping of a proper look-out.

(c) The lights prescribed by these Rules shall, if carried, also be exhibited from sunrise to sunset in restricted visibility and may be exhibited in all other circumstances when it is deemed necessary.

(d) The Rules concerning shapes shall be complied with by day.

(e) The lights and shapes specified in these Rules shall comply with the provisions of Annex I to these Regulations.

Rule 21
Definitions

(a) "Masthead light" means a white light placed over the fore and aft centreline of the vessel showing an unbroken light over an arc of the horizon of 225 degrees and so fixed as to show the light from right ahead to 22.5 degrees abaft the beam on either side of the vessel.

(b) "Sidelights" means a green light on the starboard side and a red light on the port side each showing an unbroken light over an arc of the horizon of 112.5 degrees and so fixed as to show the light from right ahead to 22.5 degrees abaft the beam on its respective side. In a vessel of less than 20 metres in length the sidelights may be combined in one lantern carried on the fore and aft centreline of the vessel.

(c) "Sternlight" means a white light placed as nearly as practicable at the stern showing an unbroken light over an arc of the horizon of 135 degrees and so fixed as to show the light 67.5 degrees from right aft on each side of the vessel.

(d) "Towing light" means a yellow light having the same characteristics as the "sternlight" defined in paragraph (c) of this Rule.

(e) "All-round light" means a light showing an unbroken light over an arc of the horizon of 360 degrees.

(f) "Flashing light" means a light flashing at regular intervals at a frequency of 120 flashes or more per minute.

Rule 22
Visibility of lights

The lights prescribed in these Rules shall have an intensity as specified in Section 8 of Annex I to these Regulations so as to be visible at the following minimum ranges:

(a) In vessels of 50 metres or more in length:

- a masthead light, 6 miles;
- a sidelight, 3 miles;
- a sternlight, 3 miles;
- a towing light, 3 miles;
- a white, red, green or yellow all-round light, 3 miles.

(b) In vessels of 12 metres or more in length but less than 50 metres in length:

- a masthead light, 5 miles; except that where the length of the vessel is less than 20 metres, 3 miles;
- a sidelight, 2 miles;
- a sternlight, 2 miles;
- a towing light, 2 miles;
- a white, red, green or yellow all-round light, 2 miles.

c) In vessels of less than12 metres in length:

- a masthead light, 2 miles;
- a sidelight, 1 mile;
- a sternlight, 2 miles;
- a towing light, 2 miles;
- a white, red, green or yellow all-round light, 2 miles.

(d) In inconspicuous partly submerged vessels or objects being towed:

- a white all round light, 3 miles.

Rule 23
Power-driven vessels underway

(a) A power-driven vessel underway shall exhibit:

(i) a masthead light forward;

(ii) a second masthead light abaft of and higher than the forward one; except that a vessel of less than 50 metres in length shall not be obliged to exhibit such light but may do so;

(iii) sidelights;

(iv) a sternlight;

(b) An air-cushion vessel when operating in the non-displacement mode shall, in addition to the lights prescribed in paragraph (a) of this Rule, exhibit an all-round flashing yellow light.

(c) A wig craft only when taking-off, landing and in flight near the surface shall, in addition to the lights prescribed in paragraph (a) of this rule, exhibit a high intensity all-round flashing red light.

(d) (i) A power-driven vessel of less than 12 metres in length may in lieu of the lights prescribed in paragraph (a) of this Rule, exhibit an all-round white light and sidelights;

(ii) a power-driven vessel of less than 7 metres in length whose maximum speed does not exceed 7 knots may in lieu of the lights prescribed in paragraph (a) of this Rule, exhibit an all-round white light and shall, if practicable, also exhibit sidelights;

(iii) the masthead light or all-round white light on a power-driven vessel of less than 12 metres in length may be displaced from the fore and aft centreline of the vessel if centreline fitting is not practicable, provided that the sidelights are combined in one lantern which shall be carried on the fore and aft centreline of the vessel or located as nearly as practicable in the same fore and aft line as the masthead light or the all-round white light.

Rule 24
Towing and pushing

(a) A power-driven vessel when towing shall exhibit:

(i) instead of the light prescribed in Rule 23(a)(i) or (a)(ii), two masthead lights in a vertical line. When the length of the tow, measuring from the stern of the towing vessel to the after end of the tow exceeds 200 metres, three such lights in a vertical line;

(ii) sidelights;

(iii) a sternlight;

(iv) a towing light in a vertical line above the sternlight;

(v) when the length of the tow exceeds 200 metres, a diamond shape where it can best be seen.

(b) When a pushing vessel and a vessel being pushed ahead are rigidly connected in a composite unit they shall be regarded as a power-driven vessel and exhibit the lights prescribed in Rule 23.

(c) A power-driven vessel when pushing ahead or towing alongside, except in the case of a composite unit, shall exhibit:

(i) instead of the light prescribed in Rule 23(a)(i) or (a)(ii), two masthead lights in a vertical line;

(ii) sidelights;

(iii) a sternlight;

(d) A power-driven vessel to which paragraph (a) or (c) of this Rule applies shall also comply with Rule 23(a)(ii).

(e) A vessel or object being towed, other than those mentioned in paragraph (g) of this Rule, shall exhibit:

(i) sidelights;

(ii) a sternlight;

(iii) when the length of the tow exceeds 200 metres, a diamond shape where it can best be seen.

(f) Provided that any number of vessels being towed alongside or pushed in a group shall be lighted as one vessel.

(i) a vessel being pushed ahead, not being part of a composite unit, shall exhibit at the forward end sidelights;

(ii) a vessel being towed alongside shall exhibit a sternlight and at the forward end, sidelights.

(g) An inconspicuous, partly submerged vessel or object, or combination of such vessels or objects being towed, shall exhibit:

(i) if it is less than 25 metres in breadth, one all-round white light at or near the forward end and one at or near the after end except that dracones need not exhibit a light at or near the forward end;

(ii) if it is 25 metres or more in breadth, two additional all-round white lights at or near the extremities of the breadth;

(iii) if it exceeds 100 metres in length, additional all-round white lights between the lights prescribed in sub-paragraphs (i) and (ii) so that the distance between the lights shall not exceed 100 metres.

(iv) a diamond shape at or near the aftermost extremity of the last vessel or object being towed and if the length of the tow exceeds 200 metres an additional diamond shape where it can best be seen and located as far forward as is practicable.

(h) Where from any sufficient cause it is impracticable for a vessel or object being towed to exhibit the lights or shapes prescribed in paragraph (e) or (g) of this Rule, all possible measures shall be taken to light the vessel or object towed or at least to indicate the presence of such vessel or object.

(i) Where from any sufficient cause it is impracticable for a vessel not normally engaged in towing operations to display the lights prescribed in paragraph 9a) or (c) of this Rule, such vessel shall not be required to exhibit those lights when engaged in towing another vessel in distress or otherwise in need of assistance. All possible measures shall be taken to indicate the nature of the relationship between the towing vessel and the vessel being towed as authorized by Rule 36, in particular by illuminating the towline.

Rule 25

Sailing vessels underway and vessels under oars

(a) A sailing vessel underway shall exhibit:

(i) sidelights;

(ii) a sternlight;

(b) In a sailing vessel of less than 20 metres in length the lights prescribed in paragraph (a) of this Rule may be combined in one lantern carried at or near the top of the mast where it can best be seen.

(c) A sailing vessel underway may, in addition to the lights prescribed in paragraph (a) of this Rule, exhibit at or near the top of the mast, where they can best be seen, two all-round lights in a vertical line, the upper being red and the lower green, but these lights shall not be exhibited in conjunction with the combined lantern permitted by paragraph (b) of this Rule.

(d) (i) A sailing vessel of less than 7 metres in length shall, if practicable, exhibit the lights prescribed in paragraph (a) or (b) of this Rule, but if she does not, she shall have ready at hand an electric torch or lighted lantern showing a white light which shall be exhibited in sufficient time to prevent collision.

(ii) A vessel under oars may exhibit the lights prescribed in this Rule for sailing vessels, but if she does not, she shall have ready at hand an electric torch or lighted lantern showing a white light which shall be exhibited in sufficient time to prevent collision.

(e) A vessel proceeding under sail when also being propelled by machinery shall exhibit forward where it can best be seen a conical shape, apex downwards.

Rule 26

Fishing Vessels

(a) A vessel engaged in fishing, whether underway or at anchor, shall exhibit only the lights and shapes prescribed in this Rule.

(b) A vessel when engaged in trawling, by which is meant the dragging through the water of a dredge net or other apparatus used as a fishing appliance, shall exhibit:

(i) two all-round lights in a vertical line, the upper being green and the lower white, or a shape consisting of two cones with their apexes together in a vertical line one above the other;

(ii) a masthead light abaft of and higher than the all-round green light; a vessel of less than 50 metres in length shall not be obliged to exhibit such a light but may do so;

(iii) when making way through the water, in addition to the lights prescribed in this paragraph, sidelights and a sternlight.

(c) A vessel engaged in fishing, other than trawling, shall exhibit:

(i) two all-round lights in a vertical line, the upper being red and the lower white, or a shape consisting of two cones with apexes together in a vertical line one above the other;

(ii) when there is outlying gear extending more than 150 metres horizontally from the vessel, an all-round white light or a cone apex upwards in the direction of the gear;

(iii) when making way through the water, in addition to the lights prescribed in this paragraph, sidelights and a sternlight.

(d) The additional signals described in Annex II to these Regulations apply to a vessel engaged in fishing in close proximity to other vessels engaged in fishing.

(e) A vessel when not engaged in fishing shall not exhibit the lights or shapes prescribed in this Rule, but only those prescribed for a vessel of her length.

Rule 27

Vessels not under command or restricted in their ability to manoeuvre

(a) A vessel not under command shall exhibit:

(i) two all-round red lights in a vertical line where they can best be see;n

(ii) two balls or similar shapes in a vertical line where they can best be seen;

(iii) when making way through the water, in addition to the lights prescribed in this paragraph, sidelights and a sternlight.

(b) A vessel restricted in her ability to manoeuvre, except a vessel engaged in mine-clearance operations, shall exhibit:

(i) three all-round lights in a vertical line where they can best be seen. The highest and lowest of these lights shall be red and the middle light shall be white;

(ii) three shapes in a vertical line where they can best be seen. The highest and lowest of these shall be balls and the middle one a diamond;

(iii) when making way through water, a masthead light or lights, sidelights and a sternlight, in addition to the lights prescribed in sub-paragraph (i);

(iv) when at anchor, in addition to the lights or shapes prescribed in sub-paragraphs (i) and (ii), the light, lights or shape prescribed in Rule 30.

(c) A power-driven vessel engaged in a towing operation such as severely restricts the towing vessel and her tow in their ability to deviate from their course shall, in addition to the lights or shapes prescribed in Rule 24(a), exhibit the lights or shapes prescribed in sub-paragraphs (b)(i) and (ii) of this Rule.

(d) A vessel engaged in dredging or underwater operations, when restricted in her ability to manoeuvre, shall exhibit the lights and shapes prescribed in sub-paragraphs (b)(i), (ii) and (iii) of this Rule and shall in addition, when an obstruction exists, exhibit:

(i) two all-round red lights or two balls in a vertical line to indicate the side on which the obstruction exists;

(ii) two all-round green lights or two diamonds in a vertical line to indicate the side on which another vessel may pass;

(iii) when at anchor, the lights or shapes prescribed in this paragraph instead of the lights or shape prescribed in Rule 30.

(e) When ever the size of a vessel engaged in diving operations makes it impracticable to exhibit all lights and shapes prescribed in paragraph (d) of this Rule, the following shall be exhibited:

(i) three all-round lights in a vertical line where they can best be seen. The highest and lowest of these lights shall be red and the middle light shall be white;

(ii) a rigid replica of the International Code flag "A" not less than 1 metre in height. Measures shall be taken to ensure its all-round visibility.

(f) A vessel engaged in mine-clearance operations shall in addition to the lights prescribed for a power-driven vessel in Rule 23 or to the lights or shape prescribed for a vessel at anchor in Rule 30 as appropriate, exhibit three all-round green lights or three balls. One of these lights or shapes shall be exhibited near the foremast head and one at each end of the fore yard. These lights or shapes indicate that it is dangerous for another vessel to approach within 1000 metres of the mine clearance vessel.

(g) Vessels of less than 12 metres in length, except those engaged in diving operations, shall not be required to exhibit the lights and shapes prescribed in this Rule.

(h) The signals prescribed in this Rule are not signals of vessels in distress and requiring assistance. Such signals are contained in Annex IV to these Regulations.

Rule 28
Vessels constrained by their draught

A vessel constrained by her draught may, in addition to the lights prescribed for power-driven vessels in Rule 23, exhibit where they can best be seen three all-round red lights in a vertical line, or a cylinder.

Rule 29
Pilot vessels

(a) a vessel engaged on pilotage duty shall exhibit:

(i) at or near the masthead, two all-round lights in a vertical line, the upper being white and the lower red;

(ii) when underway, in addition, sidelights and a sternlight;

(iii) when at anchor, in addition to the lights prescribed in sub-paragraph (i), the light, lights or shape prescribed in Rule 30 for vessels at anchor.

(b) A pilot vessel when not engaged on pilotage duty shall exhibit the lights or shapes prescribed for a similar vessel of her length.

Rule 30
Anchored vessels and vessels aground

(a) A vessel at anchor shall exhibit where it can best be seen:

(i) in the fore part, an all-round white light or one ball;

(ii) at or near the stern and at a lower level than the light prescribed in sub-paragraph (i), an all-round white light.

(b) A vessel of less than 50 metres in length may exhibit an all-round white light where it can best be seen instead of the lights prescribed in paragraph (a) of this Rule.

(c) A vessel at anchor may, and a vessel of 100 metres and more in length shall, also use the available working or equivalent lights to illuminate her decks.

(d) A vessel aground shall exhibit the lights prescribed in paragraph (a) or (b) of this Rule and in addition, where they can best be seen:

(i) two all-round red lights in a vertical line;

(ii) three balls in a vertical line.

(e) A vessel of less than 7 metres in length, when at anchor, not in or near a narrow channel, fairway or anchorage, or where other vessels normally navigate, shall not be required to exhibit the lights or shape prescribed in paragraphs (a) and (b) of this Rule.

(f) A vessel of less than 12 metres in length, when aground, shall not be required to exhibit the lights or shapes prescribed in sub-paragraphs (d) (i) and (ii) of this Rule.

Rule 31
Seaplanes and WIG craft

Where it is impracticable for a seaplane or a WIG craft to exhibit lights and shapes of the characteristics or in the positions prescribed in the Rules of this Part she shall exhibit lights and shapes as closely similar in characteristics and position as is possible.

PART D – SOUND AND LIGHT SIGNALS

Rule 32
Definitions

(a) The word "whistle" means any sound signalling appliance capable of producing the prescribed blasts and which complies with the specifications in Annex III to these Regulations.

(b) The term "short blast" means a blast of about one second's duration.

(c) The term "prolonged blast" means a blast of from four to six seconds' duration.

Rule 33
Equipment for Sound Signals

(a) A vessel of 12 metres or more in length shall be provided with a whistle, a vessel of 20 metres or more in length shall be provided with a bell in addition to a whistle, and a vessel of 100 metres or more in length shall, in addition, be provided with a gong, the tone and sound of which cannot be confused with that of the bell.

(b) A vessel of less than 12 metres in length shall not be obliged to carry the sound signalling appliances prescribed in paragraph (a) of this Rule but if she does not, she shall be provided with some other means of making an efficient sound signal.

Rule 34
Manoeuvring and warning signals

(a) When vessels are in sight of one another, a power-driven vessel underway, when manoeuvring as authorized or required by these Rules, shall indicate that manoeuvre by the following signals on her whistle:

- one short blast to mean "I am altering my course to starboard";
- two short blasts to mean "I am altering my course to port";
- three short blasts to mean "I am operating astern propulsion".

(b) Any vessel may supplement the whistle signals prescribed in paragraph (a) of this Rule by light signals, repeated as appropriate, whilst the manoeuvre is being carried out:

(i) these light signals shall have the following significance

- one flash to mean "I am altering my course to starboard";
- two flashes to mean "I am altering my course to port";
- three flashes to mean "I am operating astern propulsion".

(ii) the duration of each flash shall be about one second, the interval between flashes shall be about one second, and the interval between successive signals shall be not less than ten seconds;

(iii) the light used for this signal shall, if fitted, be an all-round white light, visible at a minimum range of 5 miles, and shall comply with the provisions of Annex I to these Regulations.

(c) When in sight of one another in a narrow channel or fairway:

(i) a vessel intending to overtake another shall in compliance with Rule 9(e)(i) indicate her intention by the following signals on her whistle:

- two prolonged blasts followed by one short blast to mean "I intend to overtake you on your starboard side".
- two prolonged blasts followed by two short blasts to mean "I intend to overtake you on your port side".

(ii) the vessel about to be overtaken when acting in accordance with Rule 9(e)(i) shall indicate her agreement by the following signal on her whistle:

- one prolonged, one short, one prolonged and one short blast, in that order.

(d) When vessels in sight of one another are approaching each other and from any cause either vessel fails to understand the intentions or actions of the other, or is in doubt whether sufficient action is being taken by the other to avoid collision, the vessel in doubt shall immediately indicate such doubt by giving at least five short and rapid blasts on the whistle. Such signal may be supplemented by a light signal of at least five short and rapid flashes.

(e) A vessel nearing a bend or an area of a channel or fairway where other vessels may be obscured by an intervening obstruction shall sound one prolonged blast. Such signal shall be answered with a prolonged blast by any approaching vessel that may be within hearing around the bend or behind the intervening obstruction.

Rule 35
Sound signals in restricted visibility

In or near an area of restricted visibility, whether by day or night, the signals prescribed in this rule shall be used as follows:

(a) A vessel of 12 metres or more but less than 20 metres in length shall not be obliged to give the bell signals prescribed in paragraphs (g) and (h) of this Rule. However, if she does not, she shall make some other efficient sound signal at intervals of not more than 2 minutes.

(b) A power-driven vessel making way through the water shall sound at intervals of not more than 2 minutes one prolonged blast.

(c) A power-driven vessel underway but stopped and making no way through the water should sound at intervals of not more than 2 minutes two prolonged blasts in succession with an interval of about 2 seconds between them.

(d) A vessel not under command, a vessel restricted in her ability to manoeuvre, a vessel constrained by her draught, a sailing vessel, a vessel engaged in fishing and a vessel engaged in towing or pushing another vessel shall, instead of the signals prescribed in paragraphs (a) or (b) of this Rule, sound at intervals of not more than 2 minutes three blasts in succession, namely one prolonged followed by two short blasts.

(e) A vessel engaged in fishing, when at anchor, and a vessel restricted in her ability to manoeuvre when carrying out her work at anchor, shall instead of the signals prescribed in paragraph (g) of this Rule sound the signal prescribed in paragraph (c) of this Rule.

(f) A vessel towed or if more than one vessel is towed the last vessel of the tow, if manned, shall at intervals of not more than 2 minutes sound four blasts in succession, namely one prolonged followed by three short blasts. When practicable, this signal shall be made immediately after the signal made by the towing vessel.

(g When a pushing vessel and a vessel being pushed ahead are rigidly connected in a composite unit they shall be regarded as a power-driven vessel and shall give the signals prescribed in paragraphs (a) or (b) of this Rule.

(h) A vessel at anchor shall at intervals of not more than one minute ring the bell rapidly for about 5 seconds. In a vessel of 100 metres or more in length the bell shall be sounded in the forepart of the vessel and immediately after the ringing of the bell the gong shall be sounded rapidly for about 5 seconds in the after part of the vessel. A vessel at anchor may in addition sound three blasts in succession, namely one short, one prolonged and one short blast, to give warning of her position and of the possibility of collision to an approaching vessel.

(i) A vessel aground shall give the bell signal and if required the gong signal prescribed in paragraph (g) of this Rule and shall, in addition, give three separate and distinct strokes on the bell immediately before and after the rapid ringing of the bell. A vessel aground may in addition sound an appropriate whistle signal.

(j) A vessel of less than 12 metres in length shall not be obliged to give the above-mentioned signals but, if she does not, shall make some other efficient sound signal at intervals or not more than 2 minutes.

(k) A pilot vessel when engaged on pilotage duty may in additional to the signals prescribed in paragraphs (a), (b) or (g) of this Rule sound an identity signal consisting of four short blasts.

Rule 36
Signals to attract attention

If necessary to attract the attention of another vessel any vessel may make light or sound signals that cannot be mistaken for any signal authorised elsewhere in these Rules, or may direct the beam of her searchlight in the direction of the danger, in such a way as not to embarrass any vessel. Any light to attract the attention of another vessel shall be such that it cannot be mistaken for any aid to navigation. For the purpose of this Rule the use of high intensity intermittent or revolving lights, such as strobe lights, shall be avoided.

Rule 37
Distress signals

When a vessel is in distress and requires assistance she shall use or exhibit the signals described in Annex IV to these Regulations.

PART E – EXEMPTIONS

Rule 38
Exemptions

Any vessel (or class of vessels) provided that she complies with the requirements of the International Regulations for Preventing Collisions at Sea, 1960 (a), the keel of which is laid or which is at a corresponding stage of construction before the entry into force of these Regulations may be exempted from compliance therewith as follows:

(a) The installation of lights with ranges prescribed in Rule 22, until 4 years after the date of entry into force of these Regulations.

(b) The installation of lights with colour specifications as prescribed in Section 7 of Annex I to these Regulations, until 4 years after the date of entry into force of these Regulations.

(c) The repositioning of lights as a result of conversion from Imperial to metric units and rounding off measurement figures, permanent exemption.

(d) (i) The repositioning of masthead lights on vessels of less than 150 metres in length, resulting from the prescriptions of Section 3(a) of Annex I to these Regulations, permanent exemption.

(ii) The repositioning of masthead lights on vessels of less than 150 metres in length, resulting from the prescriptions of Section 3(a) of Annex I to these Regulations, until 9 years after the date of entry into force of these Regulations.

(e) The repositioning of masthead lights resulting from the prescriptions of Section 2(b) of Annex I to these Regulations, until 9 years after the date of entry into force of these Regulations.

(f) The repositioning of sidelights resulting from the prescriptions of Sections 2(g) and 3(b) of Annex I to these Regulations, until 9 years after the date of entry into force of these Regulations.

(g) The requirements for sound signal appliances prescribed in Annex III to these Regulations, until 9 years after the date of entry into force of these Regulations.

(a) See Cmnd. 2956 and Schedule 1 to the Collision Regulations (Ships and Seaplanes on the Water) and Signals of Distress (Ships) Order 1965 (S.I. 1965/1525).

(h) The repositioning of all-round lights resulting from the prescription of Section 9(b) of Annex I to these Regulations, permanent exemption.

ANNEX I
Positioning and technical details of lights and shapes

1 *Definition*

The term "height above the hull" means height above the uppermost continuous deck. This height shall be measured from the position vertically beneath the location of the light.

2 *Vertical positioning and spacing of lights*

(a) On a power-driven vessel of 20 metres or more in length the masthead lights shall be placed as follows:

(i) the forward masthead light, or if only one masthead light is carried, then that light, at a height above the hull of not less than 6 metres, and, if the breadth of the vessel exceeds 6 metres, then at a height above the hull not less than such breadth, so however, that the light need not be placed at a greater height above the hull than 12 metres.

(ii) when two masthead lights are carried the after one shall be at least 4.5 metres vertically higher than the forward one.

(b) The vertical separation of masthead lights of power-driven vessels shall be such that in all normal conditions of trim the after light will be seen over and separate from the forward light at a distance of 1,000 metres from the stern when viewed from sea-level.

(c) The masthead light of a power-driven vessel of 12 metres but less than 20 metres in length shall be placed at a height above the gunwale of not less than 2.5 metres.

(d) A power-driven vessel of less than 12 metres in length may carry the uppermost light at a height of less than 2.5 metres above the gunwale. When however a masthead light is carried in addition to sidelights and a sternlight or the all-round light prescribed in Rule 23(c)(i) is carried in addition to sidelights, then such masthead light or all-round light shall be carried at least 1 metre higher than the sidelights.

(e) One of the two or three masthead lights prescribed for a power-driven vessel when engaged in towing or pushing another vessel shall be placed in the same position as either the forward masthead light or the after masthead light; provided that, if carried on the aftermast, the lowest after masthead light shall be at least 4.5 metres vertically higher than the forward masthead light.

(f) (i) The masthead light or lights prescribed in Rule 23(a) shall be so placed as to be above and clear of all other lights and obstructions except as described in sub-paragraph (ii).

(ii) When it is impracticable to carry the all-round lights prescribed by Rule 27(b)(i) or Rule 28 below the masthead lights, they may be carried above the after masthead light(s) or vertically in between the forward masthead light(s) and the after masthead light(s) provided that in the latter case the requirement of Section 3(c) of this Annex shall be complied with.

(g) The sidelights of a power-driven vessel shall be placed at a height above the hull not greater than three-quarters of that of the forward masthead light. They shall not be so low as to be interfered with by deck lights.

(h) The sidelights, if in a combined lantern and carried on a power-driven vessel of less than 20 metres in length, shall be placed not less than 1 metre below the masthead light.

(i) When the Rules prescribe two or three lights to be carried in a vertical line, they shall be spaced as follows:

(i) on a vessel of 20 metres in length or more such lights shall be spaced not less than 2 metres apart, and the lowest of these lights shall, except where a towing light is required, be placed at a height of not less than 4 metres above the hull;

(ii) on a vessel of less than 20 metres in length such lights shall be spaced not less than 1 metre apart and the lowest of these lights shall, except where a towing light is required, be placed at a height of less than 2 metres above the gunwale;

(iii) when three lights are carried they shall be equally spaced.

(j) The lower of the two all-round lights prescribed for a vessel when engaged in fishing shall be at a height above the sidelights not less than twice the distance between the two vertical lights.

(k) The forward anchor light prescribed in Rule 30(a)(i), when two are carried, shall not be less than 4.5 metres above the after one. On a vessel of 50 metres or more in length this forward anchor light shall be placed at a height of not less than 6 metres above the hull.

3 *Horizontal positioning and spacing of lights*

(a) When two masthead lights are prescribed for a power-driven vessel, the horizontal distance between them shall not be less than one-half of the length of the vessel but need not be more than 100 metres. The forward light shall be placed not more than one-quarter of the length of the vessel from the stem.

(b) On a power-driven vessel of 20 metres or more in length the sidelights shall not be placed in front of the forward masthead lights. They shall be placed at or near the side of the vessel.

(c) When the lights prescribed in Rule 27(b)(i) or Rule 28 are placed vertically between the forward masthead light(s) and the after masthead light(s) these all-round lights shall be placed at a horizontal distance of not less than 2 metres from the fore and aft centreline of the vessel in the athwartship direction.

(d) When only one masthead light is prescribed for a power-driven vessel, this light shall be exhibited forward of amidships, except that a vessel of less than 20 metres in length need not exhibit this light forward of amidships but shall exhibit it as far forward as is practicable.

4 *Details of location of direction-indicating lights for fishing vessels, dredgers and vessels engaged in underwater operations*

(a) The light indicating the direction of the outlying gear from a vessel engaged in fishing as prescribed in Rule 26(c)(ii) shall be placed at an horizontal distance of not less than 2 metres and not more than 6 metres away from the two all-round red and white lights. This light shall be placed not higher than the all-round white light prescribed in Rule 26(c)(i) and not lower than the sidelights.

(b) The lights and shapes on a vessel engaged in dredging or underwater operations to indicate the obstructed side and/or the side on which it is safe to pass, as prescribed in Rule 27(d)(i) and (ii), shall be placed at the maximum practical horizontal distance, but in no case less than 2 metres, from the lights or shapes prescribed in Rule 27(B)(i) and (ii). In no case shall the upper of these lights or shapes be at a greater height than the lower of the three lights or shapes prescribed in Rule 27(b) (i) and (ii).

5 *Screens for sidelights*

The sidelights of vessels of 20 metres or more in length shall be fitted with inboard screens painted matt black, and meeting the requirements of Section 9 of this Annex. On vessels of less than 20 metres in length the sidelights, if necessary to meet the requirements of Section 9 of this Annex, shall be fitted with inboard matt black screens. With a combined lantern, using a single vertical filament and a very narrow division between the green and red sections, external screens need not be fitted.

6 *Shapes*

(a) Shapes shall be black and of the following sizes:

(i) a ball shall have a diameter of not less than 0.6 metres;

(ii) a cone shall have a base diameter of not less than 0.6 metres and a height equal to its diameter;

(iii) a cylinder shall have a diameter of at least 0.6 metres and a height of twice its diameter.

(iv) a diamond shape shall consist of two cones as defined in (ii) above having a common base.

(b) The vertical distance between shapes shall be at least 1.5 metres.

(c) In a vessel of less than 20 metres in length shapes of lesser dimensions but commensurate with the size of the vessel may be used and the distance apart may be correspondingly reduced.

7 *Colour specification of lights*

The chromaticity of all navigation lights shall conform to the following standards, which lie within the boundaries of the area of the diagram specified for each colour by the International Commission on Illumination (CIE).

The boundaries of the area for each colour are given by indicating the corner co-ordinates, which are as follows:

(i) White

x	0.525	0.525	0.452	0.310	0.310	0.443
y	0.382	0.440	0.440	0.348	0.283	0.382

(ii) Green

x	0.028	0.009	0.300	0.203
y	0.385	0.723	0.511	0.356

(iii) Red

x	0.680	0.660	0.735	0.721
y	0.320	0.320	0.265	0.259

(iv) Yellow

x	0.612	0.618	0.575	0.575
y	0.382	0.382	0.425	0.406

8 *Intensity of lights*

(a) The minimum luminous intensity of lights shall be calculated by using

$$I = 3.43 \times 10^{6} \times T \times D^{2} \times K^{-D}$$

where I is luminous intensity in candelas under service conditions,

T is threshold factor 2×10^{-7} lux,

D is range of visibility (luminous range) of the light in nautical miles,

K is atmospheric transmissivity.

For prescribed lights the value of K shall be 0.8, corresponding to a meteorological visibility of approximately 13 nautical miles.

(b) A selection of figures derived from the formula is given in the following table:

Range of visibility (luminous range) of light in nautical miles D	Luminous intensity of light in candelas for K = 0.8 I
1	0.9
2	4.3
3	12
4	27
5	52
6	94

Note: The maximum luminous intensity of navigation lights should be limited to avoid undue glare. This shall not be achieved by a variable control of the luminous intensity.

9 *Horizontal sectors*

(a) (i) In the forward direction, sidelights as fitted on the vessel shall show the minimum required intensities. The intensities shall decrease to reach practical cut-off between 1 degree and 3 degrees outside the prescribed sectors.

(ii) For sternlights and masthead lights at 22.5 degrees abaft the beam for sidelights, the minimum required intensities shall be maintained over the arc of the horizon up to 5 degrees within the limits of the sectors prescribed in Rule 21. From 5 degrees within the prescribed sectors the intensity may decrease by 50 per cent up to the prescribed limits: it shall decrease steadily to reach practical cut-off at not more than 5 degrees outside the prescribed areas.

(b) (i) All-round lights shall be so located as not to be obscured by masts, topmasts or structures within angular sectors of more than 6 degrees, except anchor lights prescribed in Rule 30, which need not be placed at an impracticable height above the hull.

(ii) If it is impracticable to comply with paragraph (b)(i) of this section by exhibiting only one all-round light, two all-round lights shall be used suitably positioned or screened so that they appear, as far as practicable, as one light at a distance of one mile.

10 *Vertical sectors*

(a) The vertical sectors of electric lights as fitted, with the exception of lights on sailing vessels underway shall ensure that:

(i) at least the required minimum intensity is maintained at all angles from 5 degrees above to 5 degrees below the horizontal;

(ii) at least 60 per cent of the required minimum intensity is maintained from 7.5 degrees above to 7.5 degrees below the horizontal;

(b) In the case of sailing vessels underway the vertical sectors of electric lights as fitted shall ensure that:

(i) at least the required minimum intensity is maintained at all angles from 5 degrees above to 5 degrees below the horizontal;

(ii) at least 50 per cent of the required minimum intensity is maintained from 25 degrees above to 25 degrees below the horizontal;

(c) In the case of lights other than electric these specifications shall be met as closely as possible.

11 *Intensity of non-electric lights*

Non-electric lights shall so far as practicable comply with the minimum intensities, as specified in the table given in Section 8 of this Annex.

12 *Manoeuvring light*

Notwithstanding the provisions of paragraph 2(f) of this Annex the manoeuvring light described in Rule 34(b) shall be placed in the same fore and aft vertical plane as the masthead light or lights and, where practicable, at a minimum height of 2 metres vertically above the forward masthead light, provided that it shall be carried not less than 2 metres vertically above or below the after masthead light. On a vessel where only one masthead light is carried the manoeuvring light, if fitted, shall be carried where it can best be seen, not less then 2 metres vertically apart from the masthead light.

13 *High-speed craft*

(a) The masthead light of high-speed craft may be placed at a height related to the breadth of the craft lower than that prescribed in paragraph 2(a)(i) of this Annex, provided that the base angle of the isosceles triangle formed by the sidelights and masthead light, when seen in end elevation, is not less than 27°.

(b) On high-speed craft of 50 metres or more in length, the vertical separation between fore mast and main mast light of 4.5 metres required by paragraph 2(a)(ii) of this Annex may be modified provided that such distance shall not be less than the value determined by the following formula

$$y = \frac{(a + 17\psi)C}{1000} + 2$$

where: y is the height of the main mast light above the foremast light in metres;

a is the height of the foremast light above the water surface in service condition in metres;

ψ is the trim in service condition in degrees;

C is the horizontal separation of masthead lights in metres.

14 *Approval*

The construction of lights and shapes and the installation of lights on board the vessel shall be to the satisfaction of the appropriate authority of the State whose flag the vessel is entitled to fly.

ANNEX II
Additional signals for fishing vessels fishing in close proximity

1 *General*

The lights mentioned herein shall, if exhibited in pursuant of Rule 26(d), be placed where they can best be seen. They shall be at least 0.9 metres apart but at a lower level than lights prescribed in Rule 26(b)(i) and (c)(i). The light shall be visible all round the horizon at a distance of at least 1 mile but at a lesser distance than the lights prescribed by these Rules for fishing vessels.

2 *Signals for trawlers*

(a) Vessels of 20 metres or more in length when engaged in trawling, whether using demersal or pelagic gear, shall exhibit:

(i) when shooting their nets, two white lights in a vertical line;

(ii) when hauling their nets, one white light over one red light in a vertical line;

(iii) when the net has come fast upon an obstruction, two red lights in a vertical line.

(b) Each vessel of 20 metres or more in length engaged in pair trawling shall exhibit:

(i) by night, a searchlight directed forward and in the direction of the other vessel of the pair;

(ii) when shooting or hauling their nets or when the nets have come fast upon an obstruction, the lights prescribed in 2(a) above.

(c) A vessel of less than 20 metres in length engaged in trawling, whether using demersal or pelagic gear or engaged in pair trawling, may exhibit the lights prescribed in paragraphs (a) or (b) of this Section, as appropriate.

3 ***Signals for purse seiners***

Vessels engaged in fishing with purse seine gear may exhibit two yellow lights in a vertical line. These lights shall flash alternately every second and with equal light and occultation duration. These lights may be exhibited only when the vessel is hampered by its fishing gear.

ANNEX III
Technical details of sound signal appliances

1 ***Whistles***

(a) ***Frequencies and range of audibility***

The fundamental frequency of the signal shall lie within the range 70-700 Hz. The range of audibility of the signal from a whistle shall be determined by those frequencies, which may include the fundamental and/or one or more higher frequencies, which lie within the range 180-700 Hz (+/–1 per cent) for a vessel of 20 metres or more in length, or 180-2100 Hz (+/–1 per cent) for a vessel of less than 20 metres in length and which provide the sound pressure levels specified in paragraph 1(c) below.

(b) ***Limits of fundamental frequencies***

To ensure a wide variety of whistle characteristics, the fundamental frequency of a whistle shall be between the following limits:

(i) 70-200 Hz, for a vessel 200 metres or more in length;

(ii) 130-350 Hz, for a vessel less than 75 metres but less than 200 metres in length;

(iii) 250-700 Hz, for a vessel less than 75 metres in length.

(c) ***Sound signal intensity and range of audibility***

A whistle fitted in a vessel shall be provided, in the direction of maximum intensity of the whistle and at a distance of 1 metre from it, a sound pressure level in at least one 1/3-octave band within the range of frequencies 180-700 Hz (+/–1 per cent) for a vessel of 20 metres or more in length, or 180-2100 Hz (+/–1 per cent) for a vessel of less than 20 metres in length, of not less than the appropriate figure given in the table below.

Length of vessel in metres	1/3rd-octave band level at 1 metre in dB referred to 2 x 10^{-5} N/m^2	Audibility range in nautical miles
200 or more	143	2
75 but less than 200	138	1.5
20 but less than 75	130	1
Less than 20	120[1] 115[2] 111[3]	0.5

[1]When the measured frequencies lie within the range 180-450 Hz.
[2]When the measured frequencies lie within the range 450-800 Hz.
[3]When the measured frequencies lie within the range 800-2100 Hz.

The range of audibility in the table above is for information and is approximately the range at which a whistle may be heard on its forward axis with 90 per cent probability in conditions of still air on board a vessel having average background noise level at the listening posts (taken to be 68 dB in the octave band centred on 250 Hz and 63 dB in the octave band centred on 500 Hz).

In practice the range at which a whistle may be heard is extremely variable and depends critically on weather conditions; the values given can be regarded as typical but under conditions of strong wind of high ambient noise level at the listening post the range may be much reduced.

(d) ***Directional Properties***

The sound pressure level of a directional whistle shall not be more than 4 dB below the prescribed sound pressure level on the axis at any direction in the horizontal plane within ±45 degrees of the axis. The sound pressure level at any other direction in the horizontal plane shall be not more than 10 dB below the prescribed sound pressure level on the axis, so that the range in any direction will be at least half the range on the forward axis. The sound pressure level shall be measured in that 1/3rd-octave band which determines the audibility range.

(e) ***Positioning of whistles***

When a directional whistle is to be used as the only whistle on a vessel, it shall be installed with its maximum intensity directed straight ahead.

A whistle shall be placed as high as practicable on a vessel, in order to reduce interception of the emitted sound by obstructions and also to minimize hearing damage risk to personnel. The sound pressure level of the vessel's own signal at listening posts shall not exceed 110 dB (A) and so far as practicable should not exceed 100 dB (A).

(f) ***Fitting of more than one whistle***

If whistles are fitted at a distance apart of more than 100 metres, it shall be so arranged that they are not sounded simultaneously.

(g) ***Combined whistle systems***

If due to the presence of obstructions the sound field of a single whistle or one of the whistles referred to in paragraph 1(f) above is likely to have a zone of greatly reduced signal level, it is recommended that a combined whistle system be fitted so as to overcome the reduction. For the purposes of the Rules a combined whistle system is to be regarded as a single whistle. The whistles of a combined system shall be located at a distance apart of not more than 100 metres and arranged to be sounded simultaneously. The frequency of any one whistle shall differ from those of the others by at least 10 Hz.

2 ***Bell or gong***

(a) ***Intensity of signal***

A bell or gong, or other device having similar sound characteristics shall produce a sound pressure level of not less than 100 dB at a distance of 1 metre from it.

(b) ***Construction***

Bells and gongs shall be made of corrosion-resistant material and designed to give a clear tone. The diameter of the mouth of the bell shall be not less than 300 mm for vessels of 20 metres or more in length. Where practicable, a power-driven bell striker is recommended to ensure constant force but manual operation shall be possible. The mass of the striker shall be not less than 3 per cent of the mass of the bell.

3 ***Approval***

The construction of sound signal appliances, their performance and their installation on board the vessel shall be to the satisfaction of the appropriate authority of the State whose flag the vessel is entitled to fly.

ANNEX IV
Distress signals

1 The following signals, used or exhibited either together or separately, indicate distress and need of assistance:

(a) a gun or other explosive signal fired at intervals of about a minute;

(b) a continuous sounding with any fog-signalling apparatus;

(c) rockets or shells, throwing red stars fired one at a time at short intervals;

(d) a signal made by radiotelegraphy or by any other signalling method consisting of the group ...---...(SOS) in the Morse Code;

(e) a signal sent by radiotelephony consisting of the spoken word "Mayday";

(f) the International Code Signal of distress indicated by N.C.;

(g) a signal consisting of a square flag having above or below it a ball or anything resembling a ball;

(h) flames on the vessel (as from a burning tar barrel, oil barrel, etc.);

(i) a rocket parachute flare or a hand flare showing a red light;

(j) a smoke signal giving off orange-coloured smoke;

(k) slowly and repeatedly raising and lowering arms outstretched to each side;

(l) the radiotelegraph alarm signal;

(m) the radiotelephone alarm signal;

(n) signals transmitted by emergency position-indicating radio beacons;

(o) approved signals transmitted by radiocommunication systems, including survival craft radar transponders.

2 The use or exhibition of any of the foregoing signals except for the purpose of indicating disstress and need of assistance and the use of other signals which may be confused with any of the above signals is prohibited.

3 Attention is drawn to the relevant sections of the International Code of Signals, the Merchant Ship Search and Rescue Manual and the following signals:

(a) a piece of orange-coloured canvas with either a black square and circle or other appropriate symbol (for identification from the air);

(b) a dye marker.

Geographic Index

Index

D